GLEIM® | Aviation

ELEVENTH
EDITION

PILOT HANDBOOK

A COMPREHENSIVE TEXT AND REFERENCE FOR ALL PILOTS

by

Irvin N. Gleim, Ph.D., CFII and Garrett W. Gleim, CFII

Gleim Publications, Inc.
PO Box 12848
University Station
Gainesville, Florida 32604

(800) 87-GLEIM or (800) 874-5346
(352) 375-0772

www.GleimAviation.com
aviationteam@gleim.com

For updates to the fourth printing of the eleventh edition
of *Pilot Handbook*

Go To: www.GleimAviation.com/updates

Or: Email update@gleim.com with **PH 11-4** in the
subject line. You will receive our current update
as a reply.

Updates are available until the next edition is published.

ISSN: 1092-1141
ISBN: 978-1-61854-061-4

This edition is copyright © 2016 by Gleim Publications, Inc. Portions of this manuscript are taken from
previous editions copyright ©1982-2015 by Gleim Publications, Inc.

First Printing: August 2016
Second Printing: October 2017
Third Printing: January 2019
Fourth Printing: March 2020

ALL RIGHTS RESERVED. No part of this material may be reproduced in any form whatsoever without
express written permission from Gleim Publications, Inc. Reward is offered for information exposing
violators. Contact copyright@gleim.com.

If you purchased this book without a cover, you should be aware that it is probably stolen property.
Old editions of our books are reported as "unsold and destroyed" to us and neither the author nor the
publisher has received any payment for this "stripped book." Please report the sale of books without
covers by calling (800) 874-5346.

Environmental Statement -- This book is printed on recyclable paper sourced
from suppliers certified using sustainable forestry management processes and is
produced either TCF (Totally Chlorine-Free) or ECF (Elementally Chlorine-Free).

Let Us Know!

Please send any corrections and suggestions for subsequent editions to the authors, c/o Gleim
Publications, Inc. Please submit corrections and suggestions at www.GleimAviation.com/Questions.

Also, please bring this book to the attention of flight instructors, ground instructors, fixed base
operators, and others interested in flying. Wide distribution of this series of books and increased
interest in flying depend on your assistance and good word. Thank you.

If necessary, we will develop an update for *Pilot Handbook*. Visit our website or email update@gleim.com
as described above for the latest updates. Updates for this edition will be available until the next edition is
published. To continue providing our customers with first-rate service, we request that technical questions
about our materials be submitted at www.GleimAviation.com/Questions. We will give each question
thorough consideration and a prompt response. Questions concerning orders, prices, shipments, or
payments will be handled via telephone by our competent and courteous customer service staff.

ABOUT THE AUTHORS

Irvin N. Gleim earned his private pilot certificate in 1965 from the Institute of Aviation at the University of Illinois, where he subsequently received his Ph.D. He is a commercial pilot and flight instructor (instrument) with multi-engine and seaplane ratings and is a member of the Aircraft Owners and Pilots Association, American Bonanza Society, Civil Air Patrol, Experimental Aircraft Association, National Association of Flight Instructors, and Seaplane Pilots Association. He is the author of flight maneuvers and practical test prep books for the sport, private, instrument, commercial, and flight instructor certificates/ratings and the author of study guides for the remote, sport, private/recreational, instrument, commercial, flight/ground instructor, fundamentals of instructing, airline transport pilot, and flight engineer FAA knowledge tests. Three additional pilot training books are *Pilot Handbook*, *Aviation Weather and Weather Services*, and *FAR/AIM*.

Dr. Gleim has also written articles for professional accounting and business law journals and is the author of widely used review manuals for the CIA (Certified Internal Auditor) exam, the CMA (Certified Management Accountant) exam, the CPA (Certified Public Accountant) exam, and the EA (IRS Enrolled Agent) exam. He is Professor Emeritus, Fisher School of Accounting, University of Florida, and is a CFM, CIA, CMA, and CPA.

Garrett W. Gleim earned his private pilot certificate in 1997 in a Piper Super Cub. He is a commercial pilot (single- and multi-engine), ground instructor (advanced and instrument), and flight instructor (instrument and multi-engine), and he is a member of the Aircraft Owners and Pilots Association, the National Association of Flight Instructors, and the Society of Aviation and Flight Educators. He is the author of study guides for the remote, sport, private/recreational, instrument, commercial, flight/ground instructor, fundamentals of instructing, and airline transport pilot FAA knowledge tests. He received a Bachelor of Science in Economics from The Wharton School, University of Pennsylvania. Mr. Gleim is also a CPA.

REVIEWERS AND CONTRIBUTORS

Paul Duty, CFII, MEI, AGI, Remote Pilot, is a graduate of Embry-Riddle Aeronautical University with a Master of Business Administration-Aviation degree. He is our aviation product manager and the Gleim Part 141 Chief Ground Instructor. Mr. Duty is an active flight instructor, commercial pilot, and remote pilot. He researched changes, wrote and edited additions, and incorporated revisions into the text.

Char Marissa Hajdaj, CFII, ATP, Glider, ASES, LTA, Remote Pilot, has over 17 years of aviation experience with a background in flight instruction and as a corporate pilot. As one of our aviation editors, she researched changes, wrote and edited additions, and incorporated revisions into the text.

Ryan Jeff, AGI, CSEL, CMEL, Remote Pilot, graduated summa cum laude from Embry-Riddle Aeronautical University with a degree in Aeronautics and a minor in Applied Meteorology. He researched changes, wrote and edited additions, and incorporated revisions into the text.

W. Rhett Lawton, CFI, CFII, MEI, ATP, Type Rating DA-50, B.S., Brigham Young University, M.B.A., Henderson State University, is one of our aviation editors. Mr. Lawton researched changes, wrote and edited additions, and incorporated revisions into the text.

Erik T. Vrooman, Commercial Pilot, A&P Mechanic, is a graduate of the maintenance program at Embry-Riddle Aeronautical University. In addition to working with Gleim, he is on staff with the College of Missionary Aviation. Mr. Vrooman researched material and incorporated revisions into the text.

Karl Winters, CFII, AGI, IGI, Remote Pilot, is a graduate of Purdue University, a flight instructor in the School of Aeronautics at Liberty University, and the Gleim Part 141 Assistant Chief Ground Instructor. As one of our aviation editors, he researched material and incorporated revisions into the text.

The CFIs who have worked with us throughout the years to develop and improve our pilot training materials.

The many FAA and NWS employees who helped, in person or by telephone, primarily in Gainesville, Orlando, Oklahoma City, and Washington, DC.

The many pilots who have provided comments and suggestions during the past several decades.

A PERSONAL THANKS

This manual would not have been possible without the extraordinary effort and dedication of Jacob Bennett, Julie Cutlip, Ethan Good, Blaine Hatton, Kelsey Hughes, Fernanda Martinez, Bree Rodriguez, Teresa Soard, Justin Stephenson, Joanne Strong, Elmer Tucker, Candace Van Doren, and Ryan Van Tress, who typed the entire manuscript and all revisions and drafted and laid out the diagrams, illustrations, and cover for this book.

The authors also appreciate the production and editorial assistance of Levi Bradford, Steven Critelli, Sirene Dagher, Melody Dalton, Michaela Giampaolo, Jim Harvin, Jessica Hatker, Kristen Hennen, Sonora Hospital-Medina, Belea Keeney, Katie Larson, Diana León, Michael Lupi, Bernadyn Nettles, Bryce Owen, Jake Pettifor, Shane Rapp, Drew Sheppard, and Alyssa Thomas.

Finally, we appreciate the encouragement, support, and tolerance of our families throughout this project.

ACKNOWLEDGMENT

TABLE OF CONTENTS

PREFACE

The primary purpose of *Pilot Handbook* is to consolidate and organize all FAA material relevant to all pilots in one easy-to-use book. This includes the Federal Aviation Regulations, the *Pilot's Handbook of Aeronautical Knowledge*, *Airplane Flying Handbook*, *Aviation Weather*, *Aviation Weather Services*, and many other FAA books, pamphlets, circulars, etc.

Most books create additional work for the user. In contrast, this book facilitates your effort. It is easy to use. The outline/illustration format, type styles, and spacing are designed to improve readability. Concepts are often presented as phrases rather than as complete sentences.

Pilot Handbook focuses on airplane flight training, rather than balloon, glider, or helicopter training. We are confident this handbook will be useful to all pilots. It will help keep you current and be an invaluable study aid to prepare for your flight (biennial) reviews.

Pilot Handbook is an integral component of both our sport pilot ground and flight training syllabus, which can be used under Part 61, and our private pilot ground and flight training syllabus, which can be used under either Part 61 or Part 141. If you do NOT have copies of the following books to help you prepare for the FAA knowledge test and the FAA practical test, call us at (800) 874-5346 or visit us online at www.GleimAviation.com:

Sport Pilot FAA Knowledge Test Prep
Sport Pilot Flight Maneuvers and Practical Test Prep
Sport Pilot Syllabus

Private Pilot FAA Knowledge Test Prep
Private Pilot Flight Maneuvers and Practical Test Prep
Private Pilot Syllabus

We wish you the very best as you complete your pilot certification, in subsequent flying, and in obtaining additional ratings and certificates.

All other pilots: Refer to the appropriate study units and subunits as you prepare for FAA pilot knowledge tests and FAA practical tests for advanced ratings and certificates. Study Appendix A as you prepare for your flight review. Study Appendix B before your instrument proficiency check. Finally, use this book as a reference handbook.

We encourage your suggestions, comments, and corrections for future editions. Please contact us at www.GleimAviation.com/Questions. Thank you.

Enjoy Flying Safely!
Irvin N. Gleim
Garrett W. Gleim
March 2020

INTRODUCTION AND
OVERVIEW OF CERTIFICATES AND RATINGS

Learning to fly and advanced flight training are fun. The purpose of this introduction is to encourage you to pursue flight training and also to encourage you to stimulate others to pursue flight training.

The primary scope of this book is to provide the knowledge needed to pass the FAA's sport and private pilot knowledge (written) tests and practical (flight) tests. To make studying easier, we have divided the relevant topics into 11 study units. Dividing the book in this manner has produced a number of large study units, especially the first four; however, the usefulness of this book for general reference is not diminished. This book is cross-referenced in the Gleim sport and private flight training books, as well as the instrument, commercial, and flight instructor flight training books.

Pilot Handbook provides information that is fundamental to all pilot and flight instructor certificates and/or ratings. While *Pilot Handbook* will be your primary text/reference book, there are topics that are appropriate to a specific certificate or rating that are not included. For example, pilots working toward the instrument rating will find information on the various IFR aeronautical charts described in the Gleim *Instrument Pilot Flight Maneuvers and Practical Test Prep* and *Instrument Pilot FAA Knowledge Test Prep* books. Commercial applicants will find information on high-altitude operations and operating high-performance airplanes in *Commercial Pilot Flight Maneuvers and Practical Test Prep*.

As you begin studying a study unit of this book, you should focus on the length of the study unit, the number of subunits, and how much you should attempt to cover in each sitting or study session. The length of the study units is not relevant to the use of the book for reference (i.e., after you have studied it initially).

INTRODUCTORY FLIGHTS FOR NON-PILOTS

Most people believe they are expected to experience flying as passengers, rather than as pilots. In contrast, when you see a "cool" automobile, you usually project yourself into the driver's seat and imagine yourself driving. We want you and others to do the same with airplanes. Imagine yourself In the left seat as the pilot. Try it – it's fun! Imagine yourself flying the airplane as the pilot when you see an airplane. Next, stop dreaming and start flying! If you are already a pilot, use this scenario with your friends to recruit them to become pilots, too.

You or your friends can learn more about being a pilot in the Gleim *Learn to Fly* booklet. It provides ideal advanced preparation for an introductory flight. It discusses airplanes and explains how they fly. It also introduces you to some basic flight maneuvers. You should read the booklet before your introductory flight to learn what's involved in flying an airplane. It will give you competence and confidence and make the flight more enjoyable. Determine the availability of introductory flight lessons at local airports. Make the availability of introductory flights known to friends with a potential interest in flight training.

Visit and encourage other interested parties to visit our website at www.GleimAviation.com for more information on learning how to fly. Gleim cooperates with and supports all aspects of the flight training industry. Organizations that recruit people to aviation and flight training in particular receive emphasis. Here are some great introductory offers made available by these organizations:

1. The Experimental Aircraft Association (EAA) offers the Young Eagles Program for want-to-be pilots ages 8 through 17. Call 1-877-806-8902 or visit the website at www.youngeagles.org to find out about their free flights.

2. AOPA hosts a "Learn to Fly" informational web page that contains information for those still dreaming about flying, those who are ready to begin, and those who are already making the journey. The goal of this program is to encourage people to experience their dreams of flying. To learn more about "Learn to Fly," visit www.aopa.org/learntofly.

3. The Civil Air Patrol (CAP) offers the Cadet Orientation Flight Program to introduce cadets to flying. It is designed to stimulate the cadet's interest in and knowledge of aviation. For more information about the CAP cadet program nearest you, visit www.gocivilairpatrol.com.

It's fun to fly! Spread the word to friends and colleagues.

ADVANCED FLIGHT TRAINING

The natural progression is sport or private certificate, instrument rating, commercial certificate, and flight instructor certificate. It is fun to progress through this sequence, which can lead to an exciting and rewarding pilot career. The requirements for each of these certificates/ratings are summarized beginning below and on the following pages.

FAA REQUIREMENTS TO OBTAIN A SPORT PILOT CERTIFICATE

1. Be at least 17 years of age (16 years of age to operate a glider or balloon).

2. Be able to read, speak, write, and understand the English language (certificates with operating limitations may be available for medically related deficiencies).

3. Possess a valid state driver's license or, if required, an FAA medical certificate.

   a. The sport pilot rule states that if an individual's most recent application for an FAA medical certificate has been denied, suspended, or revoked, that person may not use a driver's license as a medical certificate until the denial is cleared from the record.

   b. Additionally, 14 CFR 61.53 requires every pilot, from sport pilot to airline transport pilot, to be able to truthfully state before each flight that he or she is medically fit to operate the aircraft in a safe manner. As pilots, it is our responsibility to ensure that our current medical health in no way jeopardizes the safety of a flight.

   c. Your state driver's license is valid as long as you comply with the laws of your state.

      1) Most states require you to stop driving and notify the state department of motor vehicles if you have a significant change in your health. The more common medical issues that require suspension of driving privileges are

         a) Vision changes
         b) Loss of consciousness
         c) Impairment of judgment
         d) Loss of motor function
         e) Seizures or blackouts

      2) If your license is suspended or revoked due to traffic violations or alcohol/drug-related convictions, you cannot use your state driver's license to establish medical fitness; you would have to possess a third-class medical certificate.

4. Obtain an FAA student pilot certificate. A student pilot certificate can be accepted by an aviation safety inspector (ASI), a designated pilot examiner (DPE), a CFI, or an ACR.

    a. Your CFI or FBO will be able to recommend the most convenient way of obtaining a student pilot certificate.

    b. Additionally, you may contact your regional FAA Flight Standards District Office (FSDO) for assistance locating ASIs and DPEs in your area and ask for their contact information. To find the phone numbers of your regional FAA FSDO, visit the FAA's FSDO website at www.faa.gov/about/office_org/field_offices/fsdo.

    c. Contact the ASI, DPE, CFI, or ACR and schedule an appointment to obtain a student pilot certificate for sport pilot training. Bring the following documents and records to the appointment:

        1) A completed and signed FAA Form 8710-1, *Airman Certificate and/or Rating Application,* (or FAA Form 8710-11 for Sport Pilot only) via Integrated Airman Certification and Rating Application (IACRA), the web-based certification/rating application portal; the web address is http://iacra.faa.gov. Applicants also have the option to apply for a student pilot certificate in paper format on the FAA Form 8710-1 (or FAA Form 8710-11 for Sport Pilot only).

        2) An acceptable form of photo identification, e.g., a valid driver's license.

5. Receive and log ground training from an authorized instructor or complete a home-study course, such as studying this book, *Sport Pilot FAA Knowledge Test Prep,* and *Sport Pilot Flight Maneuvers and Practical Test Prep* or using our Online Ground School, to learn

    a. Applicable Federal Aviation Regulations that relate to sport pilot privileges, limitations, and flight operations.

    b. Accident reporting requirements of the National Transportation Safety Board.

    c. Use of the applicable portions of the *Aeronautical Information Manual* and FAA ACs (advisory circulars).

    d. Use of aeronautical charts for VFR navigation using pilotage, dead reckoning, and navigation systems.

    e. Recognition of critical weather situations from the ground and in flight, windshear avoidance, and the procurement and use of aeronautical weather reports and forecasts.

    f. Safe and efficient operation of aircraft, including collision avoidance, and recognition and avoidance of wake turbulence.

    g. Effects of density altitude on takeoff and climb performance.

    h. Weight and balance computations.

    i. Principles of aerodynamics, powerplants, and aircraft systems.

    j. Stall awareness, spin entry, spins, and spin recovery techniques, as applicable.

    k. Aeronautical decision making and risk management.

    l. Preflight action that includes

        1) How to obtain information on runway lengths at airports of intended use, data on takeoff and landing distances, weather reports and forecasts, and fuel requirements.

        2) How to plan for alternatives if the flight cannot be completed or delays are encountered.

6. Pass a knowledge test with a score of 70% or better.

    a. All FAA tests are administered at FAA-designated computer testing centers.

    b. The sport pilot knowledge test has a 2-hour time limit and consists of 40 multiple-choice questions selected from the questions in the FAA's sport pilot knowledge test bank.

    c. The FAA's published sport pilot questions, along with other similar questions, are reproduced in the Gleim *Sport Pilot FAA Knowledge Test Prep* book, as well as in FAA Test Prep Online and Gleim Online Ground School, with complete explanations.

7. Receive flight instruction and demonstrate skill (14 CFR 61.311).

    a. Obtain a logbook sign-off by your CFI on the following areas of operations:

        1) Preflight preparation
        2) Preflight procedures
        3) Airport, seaplane base, and gliderport operations, as applicable
        4) Takeoffs (or launches), landings, and go-arounds
        5) Performance maneuvers and, for gliders, performance speeds
        6) Ground reference maneuvers (not applicable to gliders or balloons)
        7) Soaring techniques (applicable only to gliders)
        8) Navigation
        9) Slow flight and stalls (as appropriate)
        10) Emergency operations
        11) Postflight procedures

8. Accumulate flight experience (14 CFR 61.313) according to the table below.

If you are applying for a sport pilot certificate with...	Then you must log at least...	Which must include at least...
(a) Airplane category and single-engine land or sea class privileges,	(1) 20 hours of flight time, including at least 15 hours of flight training from an authorized instructor in a single-engine airplane and at least 5 hours of solo flight training in the areas of operation listed in Sec. 61.311, and basic instrument maneuvers under simulated instrument conditions as indicated in Sec. 61.93(e)(12),	(i) 2 hours of cross-country flight training, (ii) 10 takeoffs and landings to a full stop (with each landing involving a flight in the traffic pattern) at an airport; (iii) One solo cross-country flight of at least 75 nautical miles total distance, with a full-stop landing at a minimum of two points and one segment of the flight consisting of a straight-line distance of at least 25 nautical miles between the takeoff and landing locations, and (iv) 2 hours of flight training with an authorized instructor on those areas of operation specified in Sec. 61.311 in preparation for the practical test within the preceding 2 calendar months from the month of the test.

9. Successfully complete a practical (flight) test, which will be given as a final exam by an FAA inspector or designated pilot examiner. The practical test will be conducted as specified in the FAA's Sport Pilot Practical Test Standards (FAA-S-8081-29).

    a. FAA inspectors are FAA employees and do not charge for their services.

    b. FAA-designated pilot examiners are proficient, experienced flight instructors and pilots who are authorized by the FAA to conduct practical tests. They do charge a fee.

    c. The FAA's Sport Pilot Practical Test Standards–Airplane are outlined and reprinted in the Gleim *Sport Pilot Flight Maneuvers and Practical Test Prep* book.

FAA REQUIREMENTS TO OBTAIN A PRIVATE PILOT CERTIFICATE

1. Be at least 17 years of age (16 years of age to operate a glider or balloon).

2. Be able to read, speak, write, and understand the English language (certificates with operating limitations may be available for medically related deficiencies).

3. Obtain at least a third-class FAA medical certificate (see the sample below).

    a. You must undergo a routine medical examination, which may be administered only by FAA-designated doctors called aviation medical examiners (AME).

    1) For operations requiring a private, recreational, or student pilot certificate, a first-, second-, or third-class medical certificate expires at the end of the last day of the month either

        a) 5 years (60 months) after the date of examination shown on the certificate, if you have not reached your 40th birthday on or before the date of examination or

        b) 2 years (24 months) after the date of examination shown on the certificate, if you have reached your 40th birthday on or before the date of examination.

    b. Even if you have a physical handicap, medical certificates can be issued in many cases. Operating limitations may be imposed depending upon the nature of the disability.

    c. Your certificated flight instructor (CFI) or fixed-base operator (FBO) will be able to recommend an AME.

    1) An FBO is an airport business that gives flight lessons, sells aviation fuel, repairs airplanes, etc.

    2) Also, the FAA publishes a directory that lists all authorized AMEs by name and address. You can access the directory at www.faa.gov/pilots/amelocator.

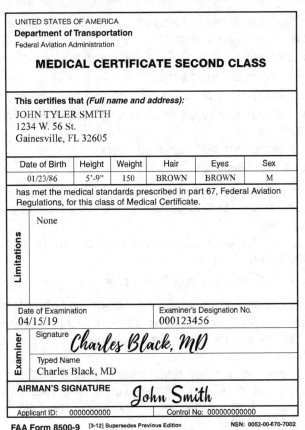

    d. If you have ever held a valid FAA medical certificate, you may be eligible for BasicMed, which is discussed in Study Unit 4.

4.   Obtain a student pilot certificate.

    a.   You must be at least 16 years of age (14 years of age to operate a glider or balloon) and be able to read, speak, write, and understand the English language to be eligible to receive a student pilot certificate.

    b.   To apply, you will meet in person with a flight instructor, FAA inspector at a local Flight Standards District Office, designated pilot examiner, or airman certificate representative from an approved Part 141 flight school. An application will be processed and sent to the FAA and TSA for review.

    c.   Upon approval, your student pilot certificate will be mailed to you.

        1)   This process may take 10-21 days.

5.   Receive and log ground training from an authorized instructor or complete a home-study course, such as studying this book, *Private Pilot and Recreational Pilot FAA Knowledge Test Prep*, and *Private Pilot Flight Maneuvers and Practical Test Prep* or using our Online Ground School, to learn

    a.   Applicable Federal Aviation Regulations that relate to private pilot privileges, limitations, and flight operations.

    b.   Accident reporting requirements of the National Transportation Safety Board.

    c.   Use of the applicable portions of the *Aeronautical Information Manual* and FAA ACs (advisory circulars).

    d.   Use of aeronautical charts for VFR navigation using pilotage, dead reckoning, and navigation systems.

    e.   Radio communication procedures.

    f.   Recognition of critical weather situations from the ground and in flight, windshear avoidance, and the procurement and use of aeronautical weather reports and forecasts.

    g.   Safe and efficient operation of aircraft, including collision avoidance, and recognition and avoidance of wake turbulence.

    h.   Effects of density altitude on takeoff and climb performance.

    i.   Weight and balance computations.

    j.   Principles of aerodynamics, powerplants, and aircraft systems.

    k.   Stall awareness, spin entry, spins, and spin recovery techniques for the airplane category ratings.

    l.   Aeronautical decision making and judgment.

    m.   Preflight action that includes

        1)   How to obtain information on runway lengths at airports of intended use, data on takeoff and landing distances, weather reports and forecasts, and fuel requirements.

        2)   How to plan for alternatives if the flight cannot be completed or delays are encountered.

6.   Pass a knowledge test with a score of 70% or better.

    a.   All FAA tests are administered at FAA-designated computer testing centers.

    b.   The private pilot knowledge test has a 2.5-hour time limit and consists of 60 multiple-choice questions selected from the airplane-related questions in the FAA's private pilot test bank.

    c.   The FAA's published airplane-related questions, along with other sample questions, are reproduced in the Gleim *Private Pilot and Recreational Pilot FAA Knowledge Test Prep* book, as well as in FAA Test Prep Online and Gleim Online Ground School, with complete explanations.

7. Accumulate flight experience (14 CFR 61.109). Receive a total of 40 hr. of flight instruction and solo flight time, including

    a. 20 hr. of flight training from an authorized flight instructor, including at least

        1) 3 hr. of cross-country, i.e., to other airports

        2) 3 hr. at night, including

            a) One cross-country flight of over 100 NM total distance

            b) 10 takeoffs and 10 landings to a full stop at an airport

        3) 3 hr. of instrument flight training in an airplane

        4) 3 hr. in airplanes in preparation for the private pilot practical test within 60 days prior to that test

    b. 10 hr. of solo flight time in an airplane, including at least

        1) 5 hr. of cross-country flights

        2) One solo cross-country flight of at least 150 NM total distance, with full-stop landings at a minimum of three points and with one segment of the flight consisting of a straight-line distance of more than 50 NM between the takeoff and landing locations

        3) Three solo takeoffs and landings to a full stop at an airport with an operating control tower

8. Receive flight instruction and demonstrate skill (14 CFR 61.107).

    a. Obtain a logbook sign-off by your CFI on the following areas of operations:

        1) Preflight preparation

        2) Preflight procedures

        3) Airport and seaplane base operations

        4) Takeoffs, landings, and go-arounds

        5) Performance maneuvers

        6) Ground reference maneuvers

        7) Navigation

        8) Slow flight and stalls

        9) Basic instrument maneuvers

        10) Emergency operations

        11) Night operations

        12) Postflight procedures

        13) Multi-engine operations (for only multi-engine airplanes)

    b. Alternatively, enroll in an FAA-certificated pilot school that has an approved private pilot certification course (airplane).

        1) These are known as Part 141 schools or Part 142 training centers because they are authorized by Part 141 or Part 142 of the Federal Aviation Regulations.

            a) All other regulations concerning the certification of pilots are found in Part 61 of the Federal Aviation Regulations.

9. Successfully complete a practical (flight) test, which will be given as a final exam by an FAA inspector or designated pilot examiner; it will be conducted as specified in the FAA's Private Pilot Airman Certification Standards (FAA-S-ACS-6).

    a. FAA inspectors are FAA employees and do not charge for their services.

    b. FAA-designated pilot examiners are proficient, experienced flight instructors and pilots who are authorized by the FAA to conduct practical tests. They do charge a fee.

    c. The FAA's Private Pilot Airman Certification Standards are outlined and explained in the Gleim *Private Pilot Flight Maneuvers and Practical Test Prep* book.

    d. The complete Airman Certification Standards and a detailed oral exam guide are available in the Gleim *Airman Certification Standards and Oral Exam Guide* book.

FAA REQUIREMENTS TO OBTAIN AN INSTRUMENT RATING

1. Hold at least a current private pilot certificate or be concurrently applying for a private certificate appropriate to the instrument rating sought.

2. Be able to read, speak, write, and understand the English language (certificates with operating limitations may be available for medically related deficiencies).

3. Hold a current FAA medical certificate.

    a. You must undergo a routine medical examination, which may be administered only by FAA-designated doctors called aviation medical examiners (AME).

    b. Even if you have a physical handicap, medical certificates can be issued in many cases. Operating limitations may be imposed depending upon the nature of the disability.

    c. Your certificated flight instructor-instrument (CFII) or fixed-base operator (FBO) will be able to recommend an AME.

        1) CFII is a flight instructor who has an instrument rating on his or her flight instructor certificate and is authorized to provide instruction for the instrument rating.

        2) An FBO is an airport business that gives flight lessons, sells aviation fuel, repairs airplanes, etc.

        3) Alternatively, you can go to the FAA website (www.faa.gov) and enter "AME" in the search box on the home page.

4. Receive and log ground training or complete a home-study course, such as using this book, *Instrument Pilot FAA Knowledge Test Prep*, *Instrument Pilot Flight Maneuvers and Practical Test Prep*, and *Aviation Weather and Weather Services* or using our Online Ground School, to learn

    a. Federal Aviation Regulations that apply to flight operations under IFR

    b. Appropriate information that applies to flight operations under IFR in the *Aeronautical Information Manual*

    c. Air traffic control system and procedures for instrument flight operations

    d. IFR navigation and approaches by use of navigation systems

    e. Use of IFR en route and instrument approach procedure charts

    f. Procurement and use of aviation weather reports and forecasts and the elements of forecasting weather trends based on that information and personal observation of weather conditions

    g. Safe and efficient operation of aircraft under instrument flight rules and conditions

    h. Recognition of critical weather situations and windshear avoidance

    i. Aeronautical decision making and judgment

    j. Crew resource management, including crew communication and coordination

5. Pass the FAA instrument rating knowledge test with a score of 70% or better.

    a. All FAA tests are administered at FAA-designated computer testing centers.

    b. The instrument rating test has a 2.5-hour time limit and consists of 60 multiple-choice questions selected from the airplane-related questions in the FAA's instrument rating test bank.

    c. The FAA's published airplane-related questions, along with other sample questions, are reproduced in the Gleim *Instrument Pilot FAA Knowledge Test Prep* book, as well as in FAA Test Prep Online and Gleim Online Ground School, with complete explanations.

6. Accumulate flight experience (14 CFR 61.65).

    a. 50 hr. of cross-country flight time as pilot in command, of which at least 10 hr. must be in airplanes

        1) The 50 hr. includes solo cross-country time as a student pilot, which is logged as pilot-in-command time.

        2) Each cross-country must have a landing at an airport that was at least a straight-line distance of more than 50 NM from the original departure point.

    b. A total of 40 hr. of actual or simulated instrument time in the areas of operations listed in 7. below, including

        1) 15 hr. of instrument flight training from a CFII

        2) 3 hr. of instrument training from a CFII in preparation for the practical test within the 2 calendar months preceding the practical test

        3) Cross-country flight procedures that include at least one cross-country flight in an airplane that is performed under IFR and consists of

            a) A distance of at least 250 NM along airways or ATC-directed routing

            b) An instrument approach at each airport

            c) Three different kinds of approaches with the use of navigation systems

    c. If the instrument training was provided by an authorized instructor, a maximum of 20 hr. permitted in an approved flight simulator or flight training device

7. Demonstrate flight proficiency (14 CFR 61.65). You must receive and log training, and obtain a logbook sign-off (endorsement) from your CFII on the following areas of operations:

    a. Preflight preparation

    b. Preflight procedures

    c. Air traffic control clearances and procedures

    d. Flight by reference to instruments

    e. Navigation systems

    f. Instrument approach procedures

    g. Emergency operations

    h. Postflight procedures

8. Alternatively, enroll in an FAA-certificated pilot school or training center that has an approved instrument rating course (airplane).

    a. These are known as Part 141 schools or Part 142 training centers because they are authorized by Part 141 or Part 142 of the Federal Aviation Regulations.

        1) All other regulations concerning the certification of pilots are found in Part 61 of the Federal Aviation Regulations.

9. Successfully complete a practical test, which will be given as a final exam by an FAA inspector or designated pilot examiner. The practical test will be conducted as specified in the FAA's Instrument Rating Airman Certification Standards (FAA-S-ACS-8).

    a. FAA inspectors are FAA employees and do not charge for their services.

    b. FAA-designated pilot examiners are proficient, experienced flight instructors and pilots who are authorized by the FAA to conduct flight tests. They do charge a fee.

    c. The FAA's Instrument Rating Airman Certification Standards are outlined and explained in the Gleim *Instrument Pilot Flight Maneuvers and Practical Test Prep* book.

    d. The complete Airman Certification Standards and a detailed oral exam guide are available in the Gleim Airman Certification Standards and Oral Exam Guide book.

FAA REQUIREMENTS TO OBTAIN A COMMERCIAL PILOT CERTIFICATE

1. Be at least 18 years of age and hold at least a private pilot certificate.

2. Be able to read, speak, write, and understand the English language. (Certificates with operating limitations may be available for medically related deficiencies.)

3. Hold at least a current third-class FAA medical certificate. Later, if your flying requires a commercial pilot certificate, you must hold a second-class medical certificate.

    a. You must undergo a routine medical examination which may only be administered by FAA-designated doctors called aviation medical examiners (AMEs).

        1) For operations requiring a commercial pilot certificate, a second-class medical certificate expires at the end of the last day of the 12th month following the date of examination shown on the certificate.

        2) For operations requiring a private or recreational pilot certificate, any class of medical certificate expires at the end of the last day of the month either

            a) 5 years (60 months) after the date of examination shown on the certificate, if you have not reached your 40th birthday on or before the date of examination or

            b) 2 years (24 months) after the date of examination shown on the certificate, if you have reached your 40th birthday on or before the date of examination

    b. Even if you have a physical handicap, medical certificates can be issued in many cases. Operating limitations may be imposed depending upon the nature of the disability.

    c. Your certificated flight instructor (CFI) or fixed-base operator (FBO) will be able to recommend an AME.

4. Receive and log ground training from an instructor or complete a home-study course, such as studying this book, *Commercial Pilot FAA Knowledge Test Prep*, and *Commercial Pilot Flight Maneuvers and Practical Test Prep* or using our Online Ground School, to learn

    a. Applicable Federal Aviation Regulations that relate to commercial pilot privileges, limitations, and flight operations

    b. Accident reporting requirements of the National Transportation Safety Board

    c. Basic aerodynamics and the principles of flight

    d. Meteorology to include recognition of critical weather situations, windshear recognition and avoidance, and the use of aeronautical weather reports and forecasts

    e. Safe and efficient operation of aircraft

    f. Weight and balance computations

    g. Use of performance charts

    h. Significance and effects of exceeding aircraft performance limitations

    i. Use of aeronautical charts and a magnetic compass for pilotage and dead reckoning

    j. Use of air navigation facilities

    k. Aeronautical decision making and judgment

    l. Principles and functions of aircraft systems

    m. Maneuvers, procedures, and emergency operations appropriate to the aircraft

    n. Night and high-altitude operations

    o. Procedures for operating within the National Airspace System

5.   Pass a pilot knowledge test with a score of 70% or better.

    a.   All FAA pilot knowledge tests are administered at FAA-designated computer testing centers.

    b.   The commercial pilot test has a 3-hour time limit and consists of 100 multiple-choice questions selected from the FAA's commercial pilot knowledge test bank.

    c.   The FAA's published airplane-related questions, along with other sample questions, are reproduced in the Gleim *Commercial Pilot FAA Knowledge Test Prep* book, as well as in FAA Test Prep Online and Gleim Online Ground School, with complete explanations.

6.   Accumulate flight experience (14 CFR 61.129). You must log at least 250 hr. of flight time as a pilot that consists of at least

    a.   100 hr. in powered aircraft, of which 50 hr. must be in airplanes

    b.   100 hr. as pilot in command flight time, which includes at least

        1)   50 hr. in airplanes
        2)   50 hr. in cross-country flight of which at least 10 hr. must be in airplanes

    c.   20 hr. of training in the areas of operation required for a single-engine or multi-engine rating that includes at least

        1)   10 hr. of instrument training of which at least 5 hr. must be in a single-engine or multi-engine airplane, as appropriate

        2)   10 hr. of training in an airplane that has a retractable landing gear, flaps, and controllable pitch propeller, or is turbine-powered

            a)   For a multi-engine rating, the airplane must be a multi-engine airplane and meet the other requirements.

        3)   One cross-country flight of at least 2 hr. in a single-engine or multi-engine airplane (as appropriate) in day-VFR conditions, consisting of a total straight-line distance of more than 100 NM from the original point of departure

        4)   One cross-country flight of at least 2 hr. in a single-engine or multi-engine airplane (as appropriate) in night-VFR conditions, consisting of a straight-line distance of more than 100 NM from the original point of departure

        5)   3 hr. in a single-engine or multi-engine airplane (as appropriate) in preparation for the practical test within the 2 calendar months preceding the test

    d.   10 hr. of solo flight (sole occupant of the airplane) in a single-engine airplane, or 10 hr. of flight time performing the duties of pilot in command in a multi-engine airplane with an authorized instructor, training in the areas of operations required for a single-engine or multi-engine rating (as appropriate), which includes at least

        1)   One cross-country flight of not less than 300 NM total distance, with landings at a minimum of three points, one of which is a straight-line distance of at least 250 NM from the original departure point

            a)   In Hawaii, the longest segment need have only a straight-line distance of at least 150 NM.

        2)   5 hr. in night-VFR conditions with 10 takeoffs and 10 landings (with each landing involving a flight in the traffic pattern) at an airport with an operating control tower

    e.   The 250 hr. of flight time as a pilot may include 50 hr. in an approved flight simulator or training device that is representative of a single-engine or multi-engine airplane (as appropriate).

7.   Hold an instrument rating. As a commercial pilot you are presumed to have an instrument rating. If not, your commercial certificate will be endorsed with a prohibition against carrying passengers for hire on flights beyond 50 NM, or at night.

8. Demonstrate flight proficiency (14 CFR 61.127). You must receive and log ground and flight training from an authorized instructor in the following areas of operations for an airplane category rating with a single-engine or multi-engine class rating.

   a. Preflight preparation
   b. Preflight procedures
   c. Airport and seaplane base operations
   d. Takeoffs, landings, and go-arounds
   e. Performance maneuvers
   f. Ground reference maneuvers (single-engine only)

      1) Multi-engine operations (multi-engine only)

   g. Navigation
   h. Slow flight and stalls
   i. Emergency operations
   j. High-altitude operations
   k. Postflight procedures

9. Alternatively, enroll in an FAA-certificated pilot school or training center that has an approved commercial pilot certification or test course (airplane).

   a. These are known as Part 141 schools or Part 142 training centers because they are authorized by Part 141 or Part 142 of the Federal Aviation Regulations.

      1) All other regulations concerning the certification of pilots are found in Part 61 of the Federal Aviation Regulations.

10. Successfully complete a practical (flight) test, which will be given as a final exam by an FAA inspector or designated pilot examiner. The flight test will be conducted as specified in the FAA's Commercial Pilot Airman Certification Standards (FAA-S-ACS-7).

   a. FAA inspectors are FAA employees and do not charge for their services.

   b. FAA-designated pilot examiners are proficient, experienced flight instructors and pilots who are authorized by the FAA to conduct practical tests. They do charge a fee.

   c. The FAA's Commercial Pilot Airman Certification Standards are outlined and explained in the Gleim *Commercial Pilot Flight Maneuvers and Practical Test Prep* book.

   d. The complete Airman Certification Standards and a detailed oral exam guide are available in the Gleim Airman Certification Standards and Oral Exam Guide book.

FAA REQUIREMENTS TO OBTAIN A FLIGHT INSTRUCTOR CERTIFICATE WITHOUT A SPORT PILOT RATING

1. Be at least 18 years of age.

2. Be able to read, speak, write, and understand the English language (certificates with operating limitations may be available for medically related deficiencies).

3. Hold a commercial or airline transport pilot (ATP) certificate with an aircraft rating appropriate to the flight instructor rating sought (e.g., airplane, glider).

   a. You must also hold an instrument rating to be a flight instructor in an airplane.

4. Use this book, *Flight/Ground Instructor FAA Knowledge Test Prep*, *Fundamentals of Instructing FAA Knowledge Test Prep*, *Flight Instructor Flight Maneuvers and Practical Test Prep*, *FAR/AIM*, and *Aviation Weather and Weather Services* to learn

   a. Fundamentals of instructing (FOI)

   b. All other subject areas in which ground training is required for recreational, private, and commercial pilot certificates and for an instrument rating

5. Pass both the FOI and the flight instructor knowledge tests with scores of 70% or better.

   a. All FAA knowledge tests are administered at FAA-designated computer testing centers.

   b. The FOI and flight instructor tests consist of 50 and 100 multiple-choice questions, with 1.5- and 2.5-hour time limits, respectively, selected from the FAA's flight and ground instructor knowledge test bank.

    c.   The FAA's published airplane-related questions, along with other sample questions, are reproduced in the Gleim *Flight/Ground Instructor FAA Knowledge Test Prep* book, as well as in FAA Test Prep Online and Gleim Online Ground School, with complete explanations.

    d.   You are not required to take the FOI knowledge test if you

        1)   Hold an FAA ground instructor certificate,

        2)   Hold a current teacher's certificate authorizing you to teach at an educational level of the 7th grade or higher, or

        3)   Are employed as a teacher at an accredited college or university.

6.   Demonstrate flight proficiency (14 CFR 61.187).

    a.   You must receive and log flight and ground training and obtain a logbook endorsement from an authorized instructor on the following areas of operations for an airplane category rating with a single-engine or multi-engine class rating.

        1)   Fundamentals of instructing
        2)   Technical subject areas
        3)   Preflight preparation
        4)   Preflight lesson on a maneuver to be performed in flight
        5)   Preflight procedures
        6)   Airport and seaplane base operations
        7)   Takeoffs, landings, and go-arounds
        8)   Fundamentals of flight
        9)   Performance maneuvers
        10) Ground reference maneuvers
        11) Slow flight, stalls, and spins (single-engine only)

            a)   Slow flight and stalls (multi-engine only)

        12) Basic instrument maneuvers
        13) Emergency operations
        14) Multi-engine operations (multi-engine only)
        15) Postflight procedures

    b.   A CFI who provides training to an initial applicant for a flight instructor certificate must have held a flight instructor certificate for at least 24 months and have given at least 200 hr. of flight training as a CFI.

    c.   You must also obtain a logbook endorsement by an appropriately certificated and rated flight instructor who has provided you with spin entry, spin, and spin recovery training in an airplane that is certificated for spins and has found you instructionally competent and proficient in those training areas, i.e., so you can teach spin recovery.

7.   Alternatively, enroll in an FAA-certificated pilot school that has an approved flight instructor certification course (airplane).

    a.   These are known as Part 141 schools or Part 142 training centers because they are authorized by Part 141 or Part 142 of the Federal Aviation Regulations.

        1)   All other regulations concerning the certification of pilots are found in Part 61 of the Federal Aviation Regulations.

    b.   The Part 141 course must consist of at least 40 hr. of ground instruction and 25 hr. of flight instructor training.

8.   Successfully complete a practical (flight) test, which will be given as a final exam by an FAA inspector or designated pilot examiner. The practical test will be conducted as specified in the FAA's Flight Instructor Practical Test Standards (FAA-S-8081-6D).

    a.   FAA inspectors are FAA employees and do not charge for their services.

    b.   FAA-designated pilot examiners are proficient, experienced flight instructors and pilots who are authorized by the FAA to conduct flight tests. They do charge a fee.

    c.   The FAA's Flight Instructor Practical Test Standards are outlined and reprinted in the Gleim *Flight Instructor Flight Maneuvers and Practical Test Prep* book.

FAA REQUIREMENTS TO OBTAIN A FLIGHT INSTRUCTOR CERTIFICATE WITH A SPORT PILOT RATING

1. Be at least 18 years of age.

2. Be able to read, speak, write, and understand the English language. If you cannot read, speak, write, and understand English for medical reasons, the FAA may place limits on your certificate as necessary for the safe operation of light-sport aircraft.

3. Hold at least a current and valid sport pilot certificate with category and class ratings or privileges, as applicable, that are appropriate to the flight instructor privileges sought.

   a. Have at least 150 hours of flight time as a pilot. That must include (for airplane certification)

      1) 100 hours of flight time as pilot in command, of which 50 hours are in a single-engine airplane.

      2) 25 hours of cross-country flight time, of which 10 hours are in a single-engine airplane.

      3) 15 hours of flight time as pilot in command in a single-engine airplane that is a light sport aircraft.

   b. Refer to 14 CFR 61.411 for time requirements of other categories of aircraft.

4. Use this book, *Flight/Ground Instructor FAA Knowledge Test Prep, Fundamentals of Instructing FAA Knowledge Test Prep, Flight Instructor Flight Maneuvers and Practical Test Prep, FAR/AIM,* and *Aviation Weather and Weather Services* to learn

   a. Fundamentals of instructing
   b. All other subject areas in which ground training is required for sport pilot certificates

5. Receive a logbook endorsement certifying that you are prepared for the knowledge tests from an authorized instructor who trained you or evaluated your home-study course on the aeronautical knowledge areas listed in 14 CFR 61.407.

6. Pass knowledge tests on

   a. The fundamentals of instructing

      1) Item 5.d. on page 13 explains when the FOI knowledge test is not required.

   b. The aeronautical knowledge areas for a sport pilot certificate applicable to the aircraft category and class for which flight instructor privileges are sought.

7. Receive a logbook endorsement from an authorized instructor who provided you with flight training on the areas of operation specified in 14 CFR 61.409 that apply to the category and class of aircraft privileges you seek. This endorsement certifies that you meet the applicable aeronautical knowledge and experience requirements and are prepared for the practical test.

   a. If you are seeking privileges to provide instruction in an airplane or glider, you must receive

      1) Flight training in those training areas in an airplane or glider, as appropriate, that is certified for spins, and

      2) A logbook endorsement from an authorized instructor indicating that you are competent and possess instructional proficiency in stall awareness, spin entry, spins, and spin recovery procedures.

8. Pass a practical test on the areas of operation specified in 14 CFR 61.409 that are appropriate to the category and class of aircraft privileges you seek, using an aircraft representative of that category and class of aircraft.

9.   Demonstrate flight proficiency in the areas below that are appropriate to the category and class of aircraft privileges you seek (14 CFR 61.409).

   a.   Technical subject areas
   b.   Preflight preparation
   c.   Preflight lesson on a maneuver to be performed in flight
   d.   Preflight procedures
   e.   Airport, seaplane base, and gliderport operations, as applicable
   f.   Takeoffs (or launches), landings, and go-arounds
   g.   Fundamentals of flight
   h.   Performance maneuvers and, for gliders, performance speeds
   i.   Ground reference maneuvers
   j.   Soaring techniques (for gliders)
   k.   Slow flight (not applicable to lighter-than-air, powered parachutes, and gyroplanes)
   l.   Spins (applicable to airplanes and gliders)
   m.   Emergency operations
   n.   Tumble entry and avoidance techniques (for weight-shift-control aircraft)
   o.   Postflight procedures

FAA REQUIREMENTS TO OBTAIN A GROUND INSTRUCTOR CERTIFICATE

1.   To be eligible for a ground instructor certificate, you must

   a.   Be at least 18 years of age.
   b.   Be able to read, write, speak, and understand the English language (certificates with operating limitations may be available for medically related deficiencies).
   c.   Exhibit practical and theoretical knowledge by passing the FOI and the appropriate ground instructor knowledge tests.

      1)   Item 5.d. on page 13 explains when the FOI knowledge test is not required.

2.   Ground instructor certificates cover three levels of certification:

   a.   Basic ground instructor (BGI) may provide

      1)   Ground training in the aeronautical knowledge areas required for a sport, recreational, or private pilot certificate
      2)   Ground training required for a sport, recreational, or private pilot flight review
      3)   A recommendation for the sport, recreational, or private pilot knowledge test

   b.   Advanced ground instructor (AGI) may provide

      1)   Ground training in the aeronautical knowledge areas required for any certificate issued under Part 61
      2)   Ground training required for any flight review
      3)   A recommendation for a knowledge test required for any certificate issued under Part 61
      4)   AGI privileges do not extend to those covered separately by the IGI certificate.

   c.   Instrument ground instructor (IGI) may provide

      1)   Ground training in the aeronautical knowledge areas required for an instrument rating to a pilot or instructor certificate
      2)   Ground training required for an instrument proficiency check
      3)   A recommendation for the instrument rating knowledge test for a pilot or instructor certificate

      NOTE: Gleim *Instrument Pilot FAA Knowledge Test Prep* covers the IGI knowledge test, which consists of 50 questions with a 2.5-hr. time limit.

3.   If you are not a CFI, the Federal Aviation Regulations require you to have a ground instructor certificate to teach ground school or to sign off applicants for the appropriate pilot knowledge test.

GLEIM ONLINE GROUND SCHOOL

1. The Gleim **Online Ground School (OGS)** course content is based on the Gleim Knowledge Test Prep books, FAA Test Prep Online, FAA publications, and Gleim reference books.

   a. Online Ground School courses are available for

1) Sport Pilot	6) Commercial Pilot
2) Private Pilot	7) Airline Transport Pilot (ATP)
3) CFI/CGI	8) Flight Engineer
4) Fundamentals of Instructing (FOI)	9) Canadian Certificate Conversion
5) Instrument Pilot	10) Military Competency

   b. OGS courses have the same study unit order as the Gleim FAA Knowledge Test books.

   c. Each course contains study outlines that automatically reference current FAA publications, the appropriate knowledge test questions, FAA figures, and Gleim answer explanations.

   d. OGS is always up to date.

   e. Users achieve very high knowledge test scores and a near-100% pass rate. In fact, we guarantee you will pass or we will refund your purchase price.

   f. **Gleim Online Ground School is the most flexible course available!** Access your OGS personal classroom from any computer with Internet access–24 hours a day, 7 days a week. Your virtual classroom is never closed!

   g. **Save time and study only the material you need to know!** The Gleim **Online Ground School** Certificate Selection will provide you with a customized study plan. You save time because unnecessary questions will be automatically eliminated.

   h. **We are truly interactive. We help you focus on any weaker areas.** Answer explanations for wrong choices help you learn from your mistakes.

Register for Gleim Online Ground School today:
www.GleimAviation.com/OGS

or

Demo Study Unit 1 for FREE at
www.GleimAviation.com/Demos

GLEIM FAA TEST PREP ONLINE

Computer testing is consistent with aviation's use of computers (e.g., Leidos Flight Service Online, flight simulators, computerized flight decks, etc.). All FAA knowledge tests are administered by computer.

Computer testing is natural after computer study, and computer-assisted instruction is a very efficient and effective method of study. Gleim **FAA Test Prep Online** is designed to prepare you for computer testing because our software simulates PSI. We make you comfortable with computer testing!

FAA Test Prep Online contains all of the questions in the Knowledge Test books, context-sensitive outline material, and on-screen charts and figures. It allows you to choose either Study Mode or Test Mode.

In Study Mode, the software provides you with an explanation of each answer you choose (correct or incorrect). You design each Study Session:

Topic(s) and/or FAA codes you wish to cover	Questions marked and/or missed from last session --
Number of questions	test, study, or both
Order of questions -- FAA, Gleim, or random	Questions marked and/or missed from all sessions --
Order of answers to each question --	test, study, or both
Gleim or random	Questions never seen, answered, or answered correctly

In Test Mode, the software emulates the operation of the FAA-approved PSI computer testing centers. When you finish your test, you can and should study the questions missed and access answer explanations. Thus, you have a complete understanding of how to take an FAA knowledge test and know exactly what to expect before you to go a computer testing center.

Gleim **FAA Test Prep Online** is an all-in-one program designed to help anyone with a computer, Internet access, and an interest in flying pass the FAA knowledge tests.

Study Sessions and Test Sessions

Study Sessions give you immediate feedback on why your answer selection for a particular question is correct or incorrect and allow you to access the context-sensitive outline material that helps to explain concepts related to the question. Choose from several different question sources: all questions available for that library; questions from a certain topic (Gleim study units and subunits); questions that you missed or marked in the last session you created; questions that you have never seen, answered, or answered correctly; questions from certain FAA learning statement codes; etc. You can mix up the questions by selecting to randomize the question and/or answer order so that you do not memorize answer letters.

You may then grade your study sessions and track your study progress using the performance analysis charts and graphs. The Performance Analysis information helps you to focus on areas where you need the most improvement, saving you time in the overall study process. You may then want to go back and study questions that you missed in a previous session, or you may want to create a Study Session of questions that you marked in the previous session. All of these options are made easy with **FAA Test Prep Online**'s Study Sessions.

After studying the outlines and questions in a Study Session, you can further test your skills with a Test Session. These sessions allow you to answer questions under actual testing conditions. In a Test Session, you will not know which questions you have answered correctly until the session is graded.

Recommended Study Program

1. Start with Study Unit 1 of the Knowledge Test you are studying for and proceed through study units in chronological order. Follow the three-step process below:

   a. First, carefully study the Gleim Outline.
   b. Second, create a Study Session of all questions in the study unit. Answer all questions in the Study Session and study the answer explanations.
   c. Third, create a Test Session of all questions in the study unit. Answer all questions in the Test Session.

2. After each Study Session and Test Session, create a new Study Session from questions answered incorrectly. This is of critical importance to allow you to learn from your mistakes.

Practice Test

Take an exam in the actual testing environment of the PSI testing centers. **FAA Test Prep Online** simulates the testing formats of these testing centers, making it easy for you to study questions under actual exam conditions. After studying with **FAA Test Prep Online**, you will know exactly what to expect when you go in to take your pilot knowledge test.

On-Screen Charts and Figures

One of the most convenient features of **FAA Test Prep Online** is the easily accessible on-screen charts and figures. Many of the questions refer to drawings, maps, charts, and other pictures that provide information to help answer the question. In **FAA Test Prep Online**, you can pull up any of these figures with the click of a button. You can increase or decrease the size of the images, and you may also use our drawing feature to calculate the true course between two given points (required only on the private pilot knowledge test).

Instructor Sign-Off Sheets

FAA Test Prep Online is capable of generating an instructor sign-off for FAA knowledge tests that require one. This sign-off has been approved by the FAA and can be presented at the computer testing center as authorization to take your test–you do NOT need an additional endorsement from your instructor.

In order to obtain the instructor sign-off sheet for your test, you must first answer all relevant questions in **FAA Test Prep Online** correctly. Then, select "Sign-Off Forms" under the "Tools" area on the Main Page. If you have answered all of the required questions, the instructor sign-off sheet will appear for you to print. If you have not yet answered all required questions, a list of the unanswered questions, along with their locations, will appear.

Order FAA Test Prep Online today:
(800) 874-5346 or www.GleimAviation.com
or
Demo Study Unit 1 for FREE at
www.GleimAviation.com/Demos

FREE UPDATES AND TECHNICAL SUPPORT

Gleim offers FREE technical support to all registered users of the current versions. Call (800) 874-5346, send an email to support@gleim.com, or fill out the technical support request form online (www.GleimAviation.com/contact). Additionally, Gleim FAA Test Prep Online is always up to date. The program is automatically updated when any changes (e.g., FAA question release) are made, so you can be confident that Gleim will prepare you for your knowledge test. For more information on our update service for books, turn to page ii.

STUDY UNIT ONE
AIRPLANES AND AERODYNAMICS

(56 pages of outline)

The purpose of this study unit is to introduce you to the parts of the airplane and to aerodynamics, i.e., the forces acting on the airplane in flight. As you study this and subsequent study units, write all new terms, definitions, etc., on a separate sheet of paper. At the end of each study session, review these new concepts to make sure you understand them.

1.1 DEFINITIONS

1. **Airfoils**

    a. **Airfoil** -- any surface designed to obtain a desired reaction force (i.e., lift) when in motion relative to the surrounding air. An airplane wing and a propeller blade are examples of an airfoil. The diagram below shows some common airfoils.

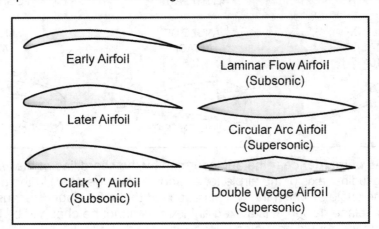

b.   **Camber** -- the curvature of the airfoil (e.g., the wing) from the leading edge to the trailing edge. In the diagram below, the curve on top of the airfoil is called the upper camber, and the curve on the bottom of the airfoil is called the lower camber.

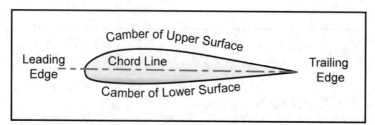

c.   **Chord line** -- an imaginary straight line drawn from the leading edge to the trailing edge of a cross section of an airfoil.

d.   **Leading edge** -- the edge of the airfoil that faces forward in flight and is normally rounded.

e.   **Trailing edge** -- the back edge of the airfoil that passes through the air last and is normally narrow and tapered.

2.   **Aerodynamics**

a.   **Angle of attack** -- the angle between the chord line of the wing and the relative wind (which is parallel to the flight path). The angle of attack is always based on the flight path, not the ground, as shown in the diagram below.

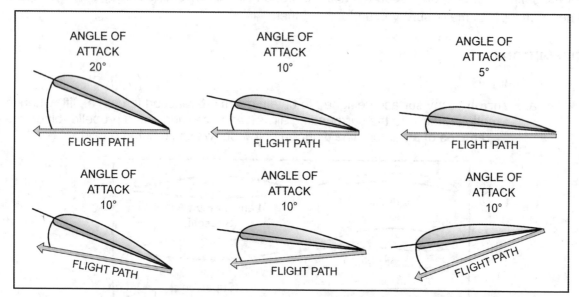

b.   **Angle of incidence** -- the angle formed by the chord line of the wing and the longitudinal axis of the airplane, as shown (exaggerated) in the diagram below. It is the angle at which the wing is attached to the fuselage. Because it is determined by airplane design, it is a fixed angle and cannot be changed by the pilot. Angle of incidence should not be confused with angle of attack.

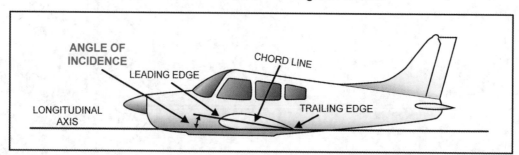

c.   **Attitude** -- the relationship of the airplane to the horizon, i.e., its pitch angle (nose up or down) and its bank angle (left or right). Attitude is measured in number of degrees of both pitch and bank.

d.   **Center of gravity** -- the point about which an airplane would balance if it were possible to suspend it at that point. It is the mass center of the aircraft or the theoretical point at which the entire weight of the aircraft is assumed to be concentrated.

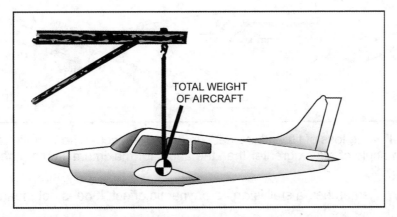

e.   **Center of pressure** -- the point along the chord line of a wing at which all the aerodynamic forces (including lift) are considered to be concentrated. For this reason, it is also called the **center of lift**.

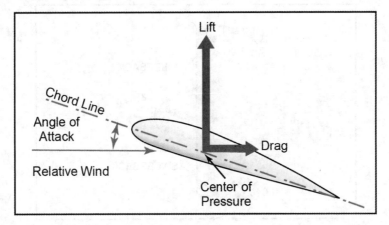

f.   **Dihedral** -- the angle at which the wings are slanted upward from the wing root to the wingtip.

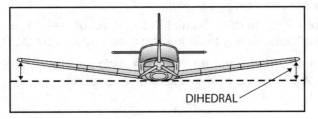

g. **Relative wind** -- the direction of the airflow produced by an object moving through the air. The relative wind for an airplane in flight flows parallel with and opposite to the direction of flight. Therefore, the actual flight path of the airplane, not the angle of the wing relative to the horizon, determines the direction of the relative wind, as shown below.

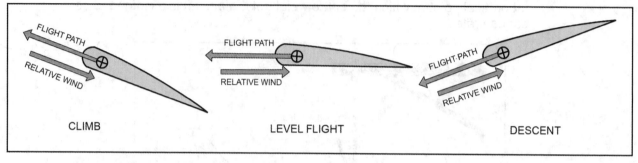

h. **Stall** -- the loss of lift and increase in drag that occur when an aircraft is flown at an angle of attack greater than the angle for maximum lift (i.e., the critical angle of attack).

    1) Remember, a stall is an aerodynamic effect. It does not mean the engine has stopped.

i. **Sweepback** -- the angle at which the wings are slanted rearward from the wing root to the wingtip.

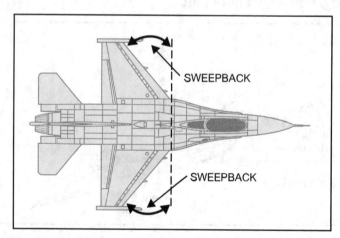

j. **Washout** -- wing design in which the wing is twisted so that the angle of incidence is less at the wingtip than at the wing root. This allows the ailerons to remain effective after the wing root begins to stall.

k. **Wing area** -- the entire surface of the wing (expressed in square feet), including control surfaces. It may include wing area covered by the fuselage.

    1) Control surfaces are the movable surfaces that control the attitude of the airplane, e.g., elevator, ailerons, and rudder.

l. **Wing planform** -- the shape or form of a wing as viewed from above. It may be long and tapered, short and rectangular, or various other shapes. The diagram below shows examples of various wing planforms.

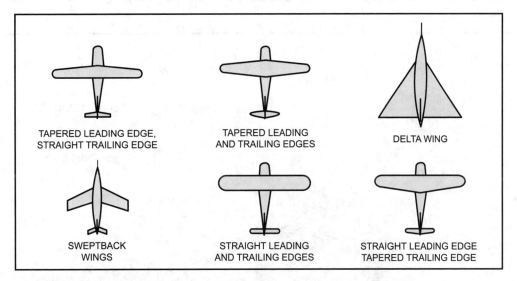

m. **Wingspan** -- the maximum distance from wingtip to wingtip.

3. **Speed and Velocity**

a. **Speed** -- the distance traveled in a given time.

b. **Vector** -- the graphic representation of a force. It is drawn as a straight line with the direction indicated by an arrow and the magnitude indicated by its length. When an object is being acted upon by two or more forces, the combined effect of these forces may be represented by a single vector called a resultant vector. The resultant vector may then be measured to determine the direction and magnitude of the combined forces, as shown below.

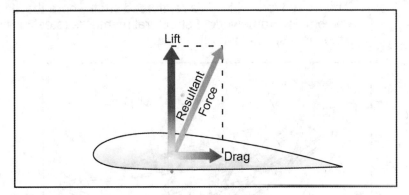

c. **Velocity** -- the speed or rate of movement in a certain direction. The term "velocity" is often incorrectly used to mean "speed."

d. **Acceleration** -- a change of velocity per unit of time. It means changing speed and/or changing direction, including starting from rest (positive acceleration), stopping (deceleration or negative acceleration), and turning. For example, an airplane flying in a circle at a constant speed is accelerating because its direction is changing, even though its speed is not.

1.2 THE AIRPLANE

1.   The diagram below illustrates the basic components of the airplane. The structural units of any conventional airplane include fuselage, wings, empennage (tail section), and landing gear.

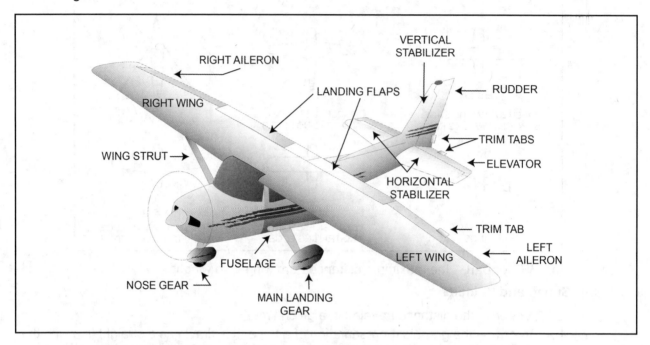

a.   The **fuselage** is the main component of the airplane. It serves as the common attachment point for the other major structural units of the airplane. It also houses the crew, passengers, cargo, instruments, and other essential equipment.

1)   There are several different types of fuselage structure, including

a)   The **truss** type, which is a reinforced shell where the skin is supported by a complex framework of structural members (steel or aluminum) that bear the main stress loads

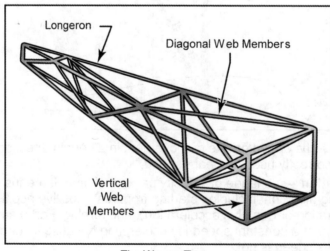

The Warren Truss.

b) The **monocoque** type fuselage, which has little or no internal bracing other than bulkheads, where the outer skin bears the main stress loads

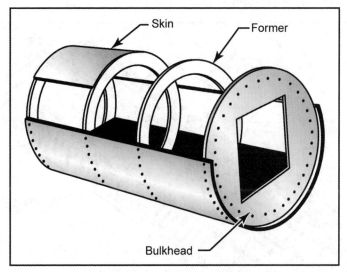

Monocoque fuselage design.

c) The **semi-monocoque** type fuselage, where the skin is reinforced by longerons or bulkheads that share the main stress loads

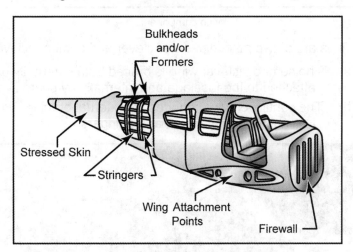

Semi-monocoque construction.

b.   **Wings** are airfoils attached to each side of the fuselage and are the main lifting surfaces supporting the airplane in flight. Numerous wing designs, shapes, and sizes are used by various manufacturers.

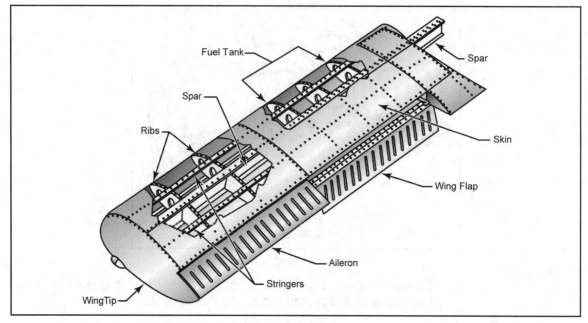

Wing components.

1)   Wings are of two main types–cantilever and semi-cantilever, as shown below.

a)   The semi-cantilever wing is braced both externally by means of wing struts attached to the fuselage and internally by spars and ribs.

b)   The cantilever wing requires no external bracing. The stress is carried by internal wing spars, ribs, and stringers.

Cantilever wing.   Semi-cantilever wing.

2)   Wings may be attached at the top, middle, or lower portion of the fuselage. These designs are called high, mid, and low wing, respectively.

a)   High wing vs. low wing. Airplanes with high wings (see the right image above) are more susceptible to the effects of wind while the airplane is on the ground. Airplanes with low wings (see the left image above) tend to allow better visibility above and around the plane while in flight and are less susceptible to the effects of wind while the airplane is on the ground. Airplanes with high wings provide better visibility of the ground when airborne, e.g., for sightseeing.

3) In most single-engine airplanes, the fuel tanks either are an integral part of the wing's structure or consist of flexible containers (or bladders) mounted inside the wing structure.

4) The wing has two movable surfaces known as **ailerons** and **wing flaps**.

  a) The ailerons are located outboard on the wings and move in opposite directions. If one is up, the other is down.

    i) The imbalance of lift caused by the movement of ailerons causes the airplane to bank.

  b) Flaps are located inboard on the wing and move together. They both extend downward, or retract upward, in unison.

    i) Flaps are not installed on all aircraft wings. Many classic fabric-covered aircraft were designed and built without wing flaps.

c. The **empennage** is commonly known as the tail section. It consists of fixed surfaces called the vertical stabilizer and the horizontal stabilizer as well as movable surfaces called the rudder and the elevator.

  1) The **vertical stabilizer** provides directional stability.
  2) The **horizontal stabilizer** provides longitudinal (pitch) stability.

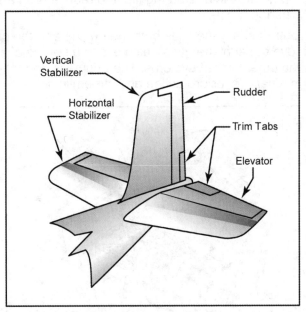

Empennage components.

d. The **landing gear** supports the airplane during the landing and on the ground. It consists of the main landing gear and either a nosewheel or a tailwheel.

  1) The main landing gear consists of two main wheels and struts. Each main strut is attached to the primary structure of the fuselage or the wing.

  2) Nosewheel (tricycle) airplanes have the third wheel in front of the main landing gear (i.e., under the nose). Tailwheel (conventional) airplanes have the third wheel under the tail.

    a) The nosewheel (or tailwheel) is designed to steer the airplane on the ground. It is not stressed for excessive impacts or loads. It is designed to carry only the weight of the forward (or rearward) portion of the airplane.

3)   The landing gear can also be classified as fixed or retractable, as shown below.

Fixed gear.   Retractable gear.

a)   Fixed gear means that the landing gear is always extended.

b)   Retractable gear means that the landing gear can be retracted into the wing or fuselage during flight to reduce drag and increase airplane performance.

e.   The **powerplant** usually includes both the engine and the propeller to provide the thrust to move the airplane. It can also act as a source of power for the electrical, vacuum, and other aircraft systems. The engine is normally covered by a cowling or enclosed in a nacelle for protection and streamlining.

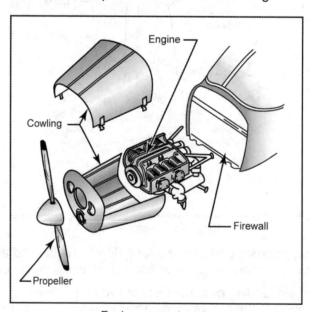

Engine compartment.

1.3 COMPOSITE CONSTRUCTION

1. The use of composite materials in aircraft construction can be dated to World War II when soft fiberglass insulation was used in B-29 fuselages. By 2005, over 35% of new aircraft were constructed of composite materials.

2. Composite materials are fiber-reinforced matrix systems.

    a. The matrix is the "glue" used to hold the fibers together and, when cured, gives the part its shape; however, the fibers carry most of the load. There are many different types of fibers and matrix systems.

    b. "Composite" is a broad term that may refer to materials such as fiberglass, carbon fiber cloth, Kevlar™ cloth, and mixtures of these.

3. Composites offer two primary advantages for construction: extremely smooth skins and the ability to easily form complex curved or streamlined structures that reduce drag.

    a. Additional advantages of composites include the following:

        1) Composites are generally lauded for being lightweight. (However, this is not always a characteristic because it depends on the structure.)

        2) Lack of corrosion leads to lower long-term maintenance costs.

        3) Composites perform well in a flexing environment and do not suffer from metal fatigue and crack growth as metals do.

Composite aircraft.

4. Composites are not without disadvantages.

    a. The most important disadvantage is the lack of visual proof of damage. Composites respond differently than other structural materials to impact, and there is often no obvious sign of damage.

        1) In a composite structure, a low-energy impact, such as a bump or a tool drop, may not leave any visible sign of the impact on the surface. Underneath the impact site there may be extensive delaminations, spreading in a cone-shaped area from the impact location.

        2) Any time you have reason to think there may have been an impact, even a minor one, it is best to have an inspector familiar with composites examine the structure to determine underlying damage.

    b. The potential for heat damage to the resin is another disadvantage of using composites. While "too hot" depends on the particular resin system chosen, many epoxies begin to weaken at temperatures over 150°F.

        1) White paint is often used on composites to minimize this issue. As a result, composite aircraft often have specific recommendations on allowable paint colors.

    c. Fluid spills are generally not a problem with modern composites using epoxy resin. However, if the fiberglass structure is made with some of the more inexpensive types of polyester resin, there can be a problem when using auto gas with ethanol blended into the mixture.

    d. Composite construction complicates lightning strike protection.

        1) Fine metal meshes such as copper or aluminum are typically bonded to the skin surfaces to conduct electricity away from components such as fuel tanks and avionics systems.

1.4 AXES OF ROTATION

1. The airplane has three axes of rotation around which it moves:

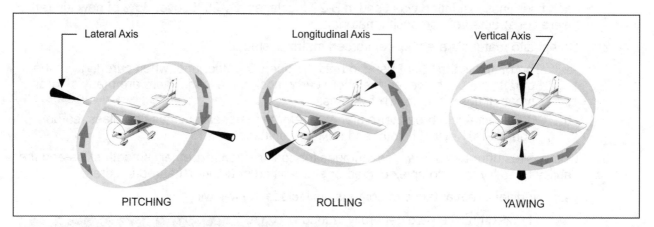

a. Lateral (pitch) axis -- an imaginary line from wingtip to wingtip

   1) Rotation about the lateral axis is called pitch and is controlled by the elevator. This rotation is referred to as longitudinal control or longitudinal stability. This may seem confusing, but consider that, as the airplane rotates about the lateral axis, the longitudinal axis (the front to rear axis) moves up and down.

   2) The rotation is similar to a seesaw. The bar holding the seesaw is the lateral axis, but the rotation is longitudinal.

b. Longitudinal (roll) axis -- an imaginary line from the nose to the tail

   1) Rotation about the longitudinal axis is called roll and is controlled by the ailerons. This rotation is referred to as lateral control or lateral stability. This may seem confusing, but consider that, as the airplane rotates about the longitudinal axis (i.e., rolls), the lateral axis (the line through the wingtips) moves up and down.

   2) The rotation is similar to a barbecue rotisserie in which the spit is the longitudinal axis but the rotation is lateral.

c. Vertical (yaw) axis -- an imaginary line extending vertically through the intersection of the lateral and longitudinal axes

   1) Rotation about the vertical axis is called yaw and is controlled by the rudder. This rotation is referred to as directional control or directional stability.

   2) The rotation is similar to a weathervane in which the post holding the vane is the vertical axis but the rotation is directional.

2. The airplane can rotate around one, two, or all three axes simultaneously. Think of these axes as imaginary axles around which the airplane turns, much as a wheel would turn around axles positioned in these same three directions.

   a. The three axes intersect at the airplane's center of gravity, and each is perpendicular to the other two.

1.5 FLIGHT CONTROLS AND CONTROL SURFACES

1. **Primary Flight Controls**

   a. The airplane's attitude (rotation about the three axes) is controlled by deflection of the primary flight controls. These are hinged, movable surfaces attached to the trailing edges of the wing and vertical and horizontal stabilizers. When deflected, these surfaces change the camber (curvature) and angle of attack of the wing or stabilizer and thus change its lift and drag characteristics.

      1) The pilot operates the flight controls through connecting linkage to the rudder pedals and the control yoke.

         a) The control yoke may be either a wheel or a stick.

   b. The **elevator** is attached to the rear of the horizontal stabilizer. The elevator is used to control pitch (rotation about the airplane's lateral axis) and is controlled by pushing or pulling the control yoke.

      1) You adjust the effective angle of attack of the entire horizontal stabilizer by raising or lowering the elevator.

         a) The airfoil made up by the horizontal stabilizer and elevator provide downforce on the tail. Downforce is lift that acts in a downward direction, opposite of the lifting force created by the main wing.

         b) You can think of the horizontal stabilizer and elevator as a wing that is mounted upside down, providing lift that acts downward, rather than upward.

      2) Applying back pressure on the control yoke (pulling the yoke toward you) raises the elevator. The raised elevator increases the horizontal stabilizer's negative angle of attack and consequently increases the downward tail force. This forces the tail down, increasing the airplane's pitch attitude and thus the angle of attack of the wings.

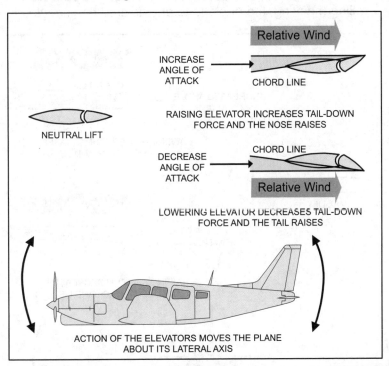

      3) Applying forward pressure to the control yoke (pushing it forward) lowers the elevator. The lowered elevator decreases the horizontal stabilizer's negative angle of attack and consequently decreases the downward force on the tail. The tail rises, decreasing the airplane's pitch attitude and thus the angle of attack of the wings.

4) Some airplanes have a movable horizontal surface called a **stabilator**, which combines the horizontal stabilizer and the elevator, such as on the Piper Warrior. When the control yoke is moved, the stabilator is moved to raise or lower its leading edge, thus changing its angle of attack and amount of lift.

   a) An **antiservo tab** is attached to the trailing edge of the stabilator and moves in the same direction as the trailing edge of the stabilator.

   b) The movement of the antiservo tab causes the tab to be deflected into the slipstream, providing a resistance to the movement of the stabilator that you can feel on the control yoke.

      i) Without this resistance, the control pressure from the stabilator would be so light that you would move the control yoke too far (overcontrol) for the desired result.

   c) The antiservo tab can also be used as a trim tab.

c. The **ailerons** (the French term for "little wings") are located on the rear of each wing near the wingtips. The ailerons are used to control roll (rotation about the longitudinal axis).

   1) The ailerons are interconnected in the control system to operate simultaneously in opposite directions from each other. As the aileron on one wing is deflected downward, the aileron on the opposite wing is deflected upward.

      a) Turning the control wheel or pushing the control stick to the right raises the aileron on the right wing and lowers the aileron on the left wing.

      b) Turning the control wheel or pushing the control stick to the left raises the aileron on the left wing and lowers the aileron on the right wing.

   2) When an aileron is lowered, the angle of attack on that wing is increased, which increases lift and drag. When an aileron is raised, the angle of attack is decreased, which decreases lift and drag. The operation of the ailerons permits rolling (banking) the airplane to any desired bank angle.

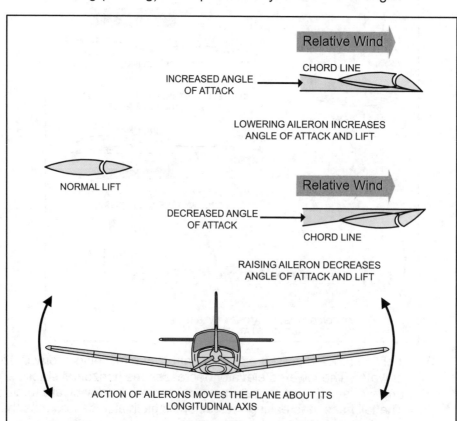

    3)   The airplane turns due to banking of the wings, which produces horizontal lift. With wings level, lift is perpendicular to the Earth. With wings banked, the lift has a horizontal component as well as a vertical component.

       a)   The horizontal component (the wings lifting sideways as well as up) counteracts the centrifugal force (inertia) pulling the airplane straight ahead.

  d.   The **rudder** is attached to the rear of the vertical stabilizer. Controlled by the rudder pedals, the rudder is used to control yaw (i.e., rotation about the airplane's vertical axis).

    1)   Pushing on the right pedal deflects the rudder to the right side and vice versa.

    2)   When the rudder is deflected to one side (left or right), it protrudes into the airflow, causing a horizontal force to be exerted in the opposite direction.

    3)   This pushes the tail in that direction and yaws the nose in the desired direction.

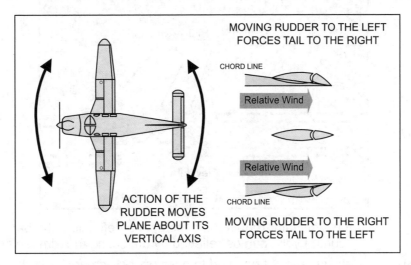

    4)   The primary purpose of the rudder in flight is to control yaw and help provide directional control of the airplane.

2.   **Secondary Flight Controls**

  a.   In addition to the primary flight controls, there is a group of secondary controls. These include trim devices of various types, wing flaps, leading edge devices, and spoilers.

  b.   **Trim devices** are commonly used to relieve you of the need to maintain continuous pressure on the primary controls. Thus, you can retrim at each power setting, airspeed, and/or flight attitude to neutralize control pressure.

    1)   These devices are small airfoils attached to, or recessed into, the trailing edge of the primary control surfaces (i.e., elevator, aileron, and/or rudder).

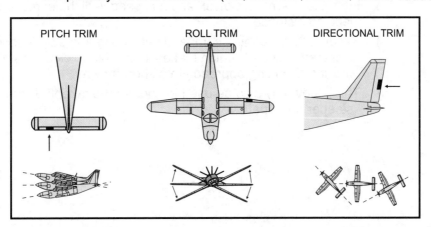

2) Trim tabs are moved in a direction opposite to the direction in which the primary control surface is deflected.

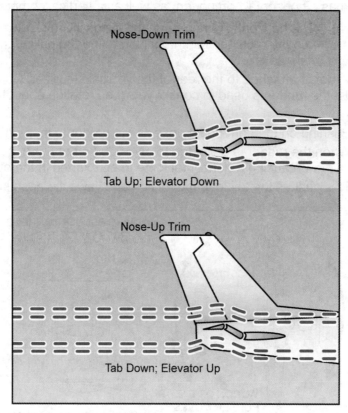

a) If the elevator requires a constant up deflection, the back pressure on the control yoke can be relieved by deflecting the trim tab down.

3) Trim tabs should not be used to position the primary control. Rather, control pressure should be used on the control yoke or rudder pedals to position the primary control; then the trim tab is adjusted to relieve the control pressure.

a) Most airplanes provide a trim control wheel or electric switch for adjustment of the trim devices. To apply a trim force, the trim wheel or switch must be moved in the desired direction.

b) The position in which the trim device is set can usually be determined by reference to a trim indicator in the cockpit.

c. **Wing flaps** are used on most airplanes to increase both lift and drag.

1) Flaps have three important functions:

a) First, they permit a slower landing speed, which decreases the required landing distance.

b) Second, they permit a comparatively steep angle of descent without an increase in speed, which makes it possible to clear obstacles safely when making a landing approach to a short runway.

c) Third, they may also be used to shorten the takeoff distance and provide a steeper climb path.

2) Types of wing flaps:

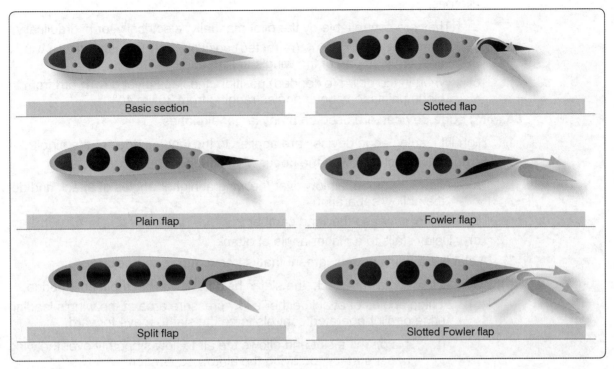

a) Plain flap -- a portion of the trailing edge of the wing on a hinged pivot

    i) Allows the flap to be moved downward, changing the chord line, angle of attack, and camber of the wing

b) Split flap -- a hinged portion of only the bottom surface of the wing

    i) Increases the angle of attack by changing the chord line
    ii) Creates the least change in pitching moment
    iii) Creates the greatest amount of drag

c) Slotted flap -- a portion of the trailing edge similar to a plain flap but with a gap between the trailing edge of the wing and the leading edge of the flap

    i) Permits air to pass through and delays the airflow separation along the top of the wing

d) Fowler flap

    i) Not only tilts downward but also slides rearward on tracks
    ii) Increases the angle of attack, wing camber, and wing area
    iii) Provides additional lift without significantly increasing drag
    iv) Provides the greatest amount of lift with the least amount of drag, which creates the greatest change in pitching moment

e) Slotted Fowler flap

    i) Similar in purpose to the Fowler flap
    ii) Adds energy to the airflow via the additional slots
    iii) The flap body continues further outward and downward, increasing airfoil camber
    iv) Provides an additional increase in lift coupled with an even greater increase in drag in comparison to the Fowler flap, with the corresponding flap position ideal for landing

       3)   Most wing flaps are hinged near the trailing edges of the wings, inboard of the ailerons.

           a)   They are controllable by the pilot manually, electrically, or hydraulically.

           b)   When they are in the up (retracted) position, they fit flush with the wings and serve as part of the wing's trailing edge.

           c)   When in the down (extended) position, the flaps pivot downward from the hinge points to various angles ranging from 30° to 40°.

  d.   **Leading edge devices** are used on many larger airplanes.

       1)   High-lift leading edge devices are applied to the leading edge of the airfoil.

       2)   Fixed slots direct airflow to the upper wing surface. Thus, fixed slots

           a)   Allow for smooth airflow over the wing at higher angles of attack and delay the airflow separation

           b)   Do not increase the wing camber

           c)   Delay stalls to a higher angle of attack

       3)   A slat Is a leading edge segment that is free to move on tracks.

           a)   At low angles of attack, the slat is held flush against the leading edge.

           b)   At high angles of attack, either a low pressure area at the wing's leading edge or pilot-operated controls force the slat to move forward.

               i)   This opens a slot and allows the air to flow smoothly over the wing's upper surface, delaying the airflow separation.

               ii)   Slats may increase wing camber and wing area.

  e.   **Spoilers**, found only on certain airplane designs and most gliders, are mounted on the upper surface of each wing. Their purpose is to "spoil" or disrupt the smooth flow of air over the wing, reducing the wing's lifting force. Using spoilers is a means of increasing the rate of descent without increasing the airplane's speed.

1.6 FORCES ACTING ON THE AIRPLANE IN FLIGHT

1.   Among the aerodynamic forces acting on an airplane during flight, four are considered to be basic because they act upon the airplane during all maneuvers. These basic forces in relation to straight-and-level, unaccelerated flight are

  a.   **Lift** -- the upward-acting force that opposes weight. Lift is produced by the dynamic effect of the air acting on the wing and acts perpendicular to the flight path through the wing's center of lift.

  b.   **Weight** -- the combined load of the airplane itself, the crew, the fuel, and the cargo or baggage. Weight pulls the airplane downward toward the center of the Earth because of the force of gravity. It opposes lift and acts vertically downward through the airplane's center of gravity.

  c.   **Thrust** -- the forward force produced by the engine/propeller. Thrust opposes or overcomes the force of drag. As a general rule, it is said to act parallel to the longitudinal axis.

  d.   **Drag** -- the rearward, retarding force that is caused by disruption of airflow by the wing, fuselage, and other protruding objects. Drag opposes thrust and acts rearward and parallel to the relative wind.

2. While in steady (unaccelerated) flight, the attitude, direction, and speed of the airplane will remain constant until one or more of the basic forces changes in magnitude.

    a. In steady flight, the opposing forces are in equilibrium.

        1) That is, the sum of all upward forces (not just lift) equals the sum of all downward forces (not just weight), and the sum of all forward forces (not just thrust) equals the sum of all rearward forces (not just drag).

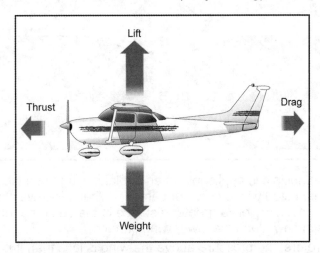

    b. When pressure is applied to one or more of the airplane controls, one or more of the basic forces changes in magnitude and becomes greater than the opposing force, causing the airplane to move in the direction of the applied force(s).

        1) EXAMPLE: If power is applied (increasing thrust) and altitude is maintained, the airplane will accelerate. As speed increases, drag increases until a point is reached at which drag again equals thrust. Then the airplane will continue in steady flight at a higher speed.

    c. Airplane designers make an effort to increase the performance of the airplane by increasing the efficiency of the desirable forces of lift and thrust while reducing, as much as possible, the undesirable forces of weight and drag.

3. **Lift**

    a. Lift is the force created by an airfoil when it is moved through the air. Although lift may be exerted to some extent by many external parts of the airplane, the four principal airfoils on an airplane are

        1) The wing
        2) The propeller
        3) The horizontal tail surfaces
        4) The vertical tail surfaces

b. **Bernoulli's Principle** states in part that "the internal pressure of a fluid (liquid or gas) decreases at points where the speed of the fluid increases." In other words, high speed flow is associated with low pressure, and low speed flow is associated with high pressure.

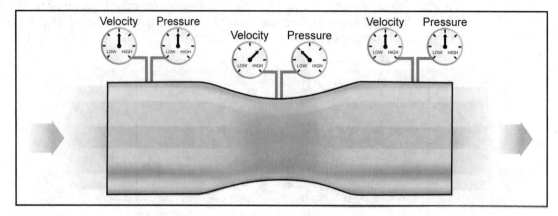

1) This principle is applicable to an airplane wing because it is designed and constructed with a curve or camber. When air flows along the upper wing surface, it travels a greater distance in the same period of time (i.e., faster) than the airflow along the lower wing surface.

2) Therefore, the pressure above the wing is less than it is below the wing. This generates a lift force over the upper curved surface of the wing.

c. **Newton's Third Law of Motion** states that "for every action, there is an equal and opposite reaction."

1) Due to the angle of incidence and/or the angle of attack, the lower surface of the wing deflects air downward (action force), which causes an upward force (reaction force).

d. Thus, both the development of low pressure above the wing and the reaction to the force and direction of air being deflected from the wing's lower surface contribute to the total lift, as shown below.

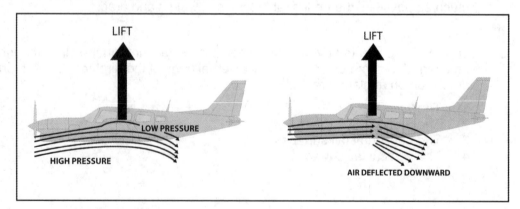

e. The amount of lift generated by the wing depends on several factors:

1) Speed of the wing through the air
2) Angle of attack
3) Planform of the wing
4) Wing area
5) Air density

f. Lift acts upward and perpendicular to the relative wind and the lateral axis. Although lift is generated over the entire wing, an imaginary point is established that represents the resultant (or sum) of all lift forces. This single point is the center of lift (CL), sometimes referred to as the center of pressure (CP).

4. **Weight**

    a.   Weight is the force caused by gravity accelerating the mass of the airplane toward Earth and is expressed in pounds.

        1)   Gravity is the downward force that tends to draw all bodies vertically toward the center of the Earth.

        2)   The airplane's center of gravity (CG) is the imaginary but determinable point on the airplane at which all weight is considered to be concentrated. It is the point of balance.

        3)   The CG is located along the longitudinal centerline of the airplane (imaginary line from the nose to the tail) and somewhere near, but forward of, the center of lift of the wing.

            a)   The location of the CG depends on the location and weight of the load (including cargo, fuel, passengers, etc.) placed in the airplane.

            b)   It is determined through weight and balance calculations made by the pilot prior to flight.

                i)   The exact location of the CG is important during flight because of its effect on airplane stability and performance.

    b.   Weight has a definite relationship with lift. This relationship is simple but important in understanding the aerodynamics of flying.

        1)   Lift is required to counteract the airplane's weight, which acts downward through the airplane's CG.

        2)   In straight-and-level, unaccelerated flight, when the lift force is equal to the weight force, the airplane is in a state of equilibrium and neither gains nor loses altitude.

            a)   If lift becomes less than weight, the airplane loses altitude.
            b)   If lift becomes greater than weight, the airplane gains altitude.

        3)   Thus, the more heavily the airplane is loaded, the greater the amount of lift that is required in flight.

5. **Thrust**

    a.   The propeller, acting as an airfoil, produces the thrust (forward force) that drives the airplane through the air. It receives its power directly from the engine and is designed to displace a large mass of air to the rear.

    b.   In order to maintain a constant airspeed, thrust and drag must remain equal.

        1)   If thrust is decreased while level flight is maintained and thrust remains less than drag, the airplane will slow down until its airspeed is insufficient to support it in the air.

        2)   If thrust is increased while level flight is maintained, the airplane will accelerate until thrust is again equal to drag.

6. **Drag**

    a.   Drag is the rearward-acting force resulting from the forward movement of the airplane through the air. Drag acts parallel to, and in the same direction as, the relative wind, as shown in the diagram. Every part of the airplane exposed to the air while the airplane is in motion produces some resistance and contributes to the total drag.

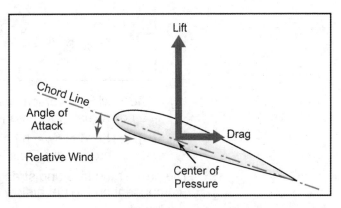

        1)   Total drag may be classified into two main types: induced drag and parasite drag.

b. **Induced drag** is the undesirable but unavoidable by-product of lift.

1) Whenever the wing is producing lift, the pressure on the lower surface of the wing is greater than that on the upper surface. As a result, the air tends to flow from the high-pressure area below the wingtip upward to the low-pressure area above the wing.

   a) In the vicinity of the wingtips, there is a tendency for these pressures to equalize, resulting in a lateral flow outward from the underside to the upper surface of the wing.

      i) This lateral flow imparts a rotational velocity to the air at the wingtips and trails behind the wings. Thus, flow about the wingtips will be in the form of two vortices trailing behind as the wings move forward. This is commonly referred to as **wingtip vortices**.

      ii) When viewed from behind the airplane, these vortices will circulate counterclockwise about the right wingtip (as shown below) and clockwise about the left wingtip.

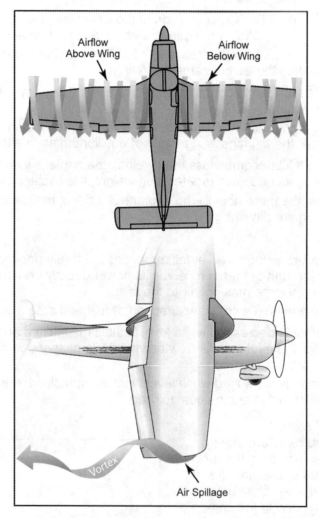

b) These wingtip vortices induce an upward flow of air beyond the wingtip and a downwash flow on and behind the wing's trailing edge.

      i) This downwash has nothing in common with the downwash to produce lift. This is the source of induced drag.

2) The greater the size and strength of the vortices and consequent downwash component on the net airflow over the wing, the greater the induced drag effect becomes.

3) This downwash over the top of the wing at the tip has the same effect as bending the lift vector rearward.

     a) Thus, the lift is slightly aft of perpendicular to the relative wind, creating a rearward lift component.

     b) This rearward component of lift is induced drag.

4) As the angle of attack increases, a greater negative pressure is created on the top of the wing, thus increasing induced drag.

     a) As airspeed decreases, angle of attack must increase to produce lift equal to the airplane's weight, causing an increase in induced drag.

     b) Induced drag varies inversely as the square of the airspeed.

         i) Reducing airspeed by half (e.g., from 120 kt. to 60 kt.) increases the induced drag by four times.

c. **Parasite drag** is the resistance of the air as the airplane passes through it.

1) Several factors affect parasite drag:

     a) The more streamlined an object, the less the parasite drag.

     b) The more dense the air moving past the airplane, the greater the parasite drag.

     c) The larger the size of the object in the airstream, the greater the parasite drag.

     d) As speed increases, the amount of parasite drag increases as the square of the velocity. If the speed is doubled, four times as much drag is produced.

2) Parasite drag can be further classified into form drag, skin friction, and interference drag.

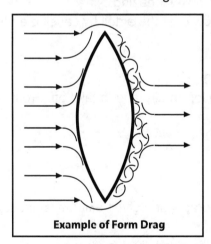 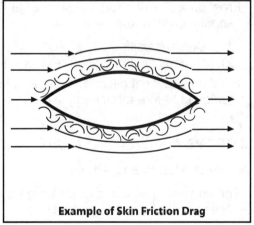

Example of Form Drag   **Example of Skin Friction Drag**

     a) **Form drag** is caused by the frontal area of the airplane components being exposed to the airstream.

         i) Streamlining an object will reduce form drag.

     b) **Skin friction** is the type of parasite drag that is most difficult to reduce. No surface is perfectly smooth; even machined surfaces, when inspected through magnification, have a ragged, uneven appearance.

         i) This rough surface will cause microscopic turbulent airflow over the surface, causing resistance to smooth airflow.

         ii) Skin friction can be minimized by applying a glossy, flat finish to surfaces; by eliminating protruding rivet heads, roughness, and other irregularities; and by keeping the airplane clean and waxed.

      c)   **Interference drag** is caused by interference of the airflow between adjacent parts of the airplane, such as the intersections of wings and tail sections with the fuselage. This drag combines the effects of form and skin friction drag.

         i)   Fairings are used to streamline these intersections and decrease interference drag.

   d.   The following graph shows the effect of speed on induced, parasite, and total drag.

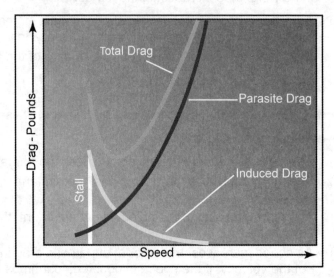

7.   **Frost**

   a.   Frost forms when the temperature of a collecting surface is at or below the dew point of the adjacent air and the dew point is below freezing.

   b.   Frost on wings disrupts the smooth airflow over the airfoil by causing early airflow separation from the wing. This

      1)   Decreases lift
      2)   Causes friction and increases drag

   c.   Frost may make it difficult or impossible for an airplane to take off. Frost should be removed before attempting takeoff.

1.7 DYNAMICS OF THE AIRPLANE IN FLIGHT

1.   **Lift, Angle of Attack, and Airspeed**

   a.   The amount of lift that a given wing generates at a given altitude is directly related to its angle of attack and airspeed.

      1)   As angle of attack or airspeed is increased, lift is increased.
      2)   We can express this relationship in the following equation:

$$L = \alpha \times V$$

      Where L is lift,
               α is angle of attack, and
               V is airspeed.

         a)   Note that this is not a precise equation. It merely serves to illustrate the relationship between these three elements.

    b.   As discussed earlier, when the airplane is in steady-state, unaccelerated flight, lift is equal to weight.

        1)   Because this makes lift a constant in steady-state flight, it can be seen that there is only one angle of attack for any given airspeed that will maintain the airplane in steady-state flight.

        2)   As airspeed increases, angle of attack must decrease, and vice versa.

        3)   A heavily loaded airplane must fly at a higher angle of attack for any given airspeed than the same airplane does when lightly loaded.

2.   **Drag, Angle of Attack, and Airspeed**

    a.   As airspeed decreases, angle of attack increases, causing an increase in induced drag.

        1)   However, parasite drag decreases as airspeed decreases.

    b.   The following graph illustrates the variations in parasite, induced, and total drag with airspeed for a typical airplane in steady, level flight.

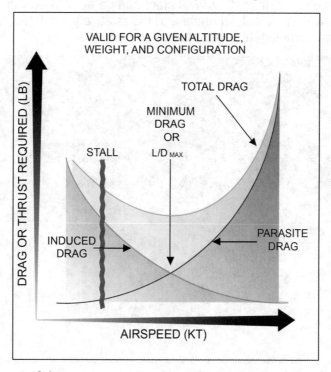

    c.   The amount of drag present at a given airspeed is equal to the amount of thrust required to maintain level flight at that airspeed and angle of attack.

        1)   If thrust is increased beyond that required for level flight, the airplane will climb unless it is retrimmed for a lower angle of attack and a higher airspeed.

        2)   If thrust is reduced, the airplane will descend.

    d.   Note on the drag vs. speed chart that the airspeed at which minimum drag occurs is the same airspeed at which the maximum lift/drag ratio (L/D_{MAX}) takes place.

        1)   At this point, the least amount of thrust is required for level flight.

        2)   Many important items of airplane performance are obtained in flight at L/D_{MAX}. These include

            a)   Maximum range and

            b)   Maximum power-off glide range. Thus, the airspeed for L/D_{MAX} is the airplane's best glide airspeed.

        3)   Flight below L/D_{MAX} produces more drag and requires more thrust to maintain level flight.

3. **Pitch, Power, and Performance**

    a. Adjusting the angle of attack varies the amounts of lift and drag produced by the wing.
    b. Adjusting the airplane's power varies the relationship of thrust to drag, allowing the airplane to change airspeed, altitude, or both.
    c. Thus, the pilot can achieve a desired performance from the airplane (in terms of airspeed and altitude) through a variety of pitch and power combinations.

        1) A climb may be initiated by raising the nose to increase the angle of attack, by increasing power, or by using both.
        2) A descent may be initiated by lowering the nose to reduce the angle of attack, by decreasing power, or by using both.
        3) To increase airspeed in level flight, power must be increased and angle of attack reduced to maintain level flight.
        4) To decrease airspeed in level flight, power must be reduced and angle of attack increased to maintain level flight.
        5) It is evident, then, that level flight can be performed with any angle of attack between the critical angle and the relatively small negative angles found sometimes at high speeds, as shown below.

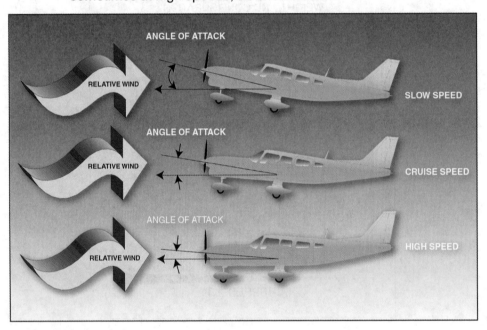

4. **Slow Flight**

    a. Slow flight is any airspeed from below normal cruise airspeed to the stall airspeed.
    b. When straight-and-level flight is maintained at a constant airspeed during slow flight, thrust is equal in magnitude to drag, and lift is equal in magnitude to weight, but some of these forces are separated into components.

        1) In slow flight, thrust no longer acts parallel and opposite to the flight path and drag, as shown on the next page. Note that thrust has two components:

            a) One acting perpendicular to the flight path in the direction of lift
            b) One acting along the flight path

        2) Because the actual thrust is inclined, its magnitude must be greater than drag if its component acting along the flight path is equal to drag.

            a) Note that the forces acting upward (wing lift and the component of thrust) equal the forces acting downward (weight and tail-down force).

        3) Wing loading (wing lift) is actually less during slow flight because the vertical component of thrust helps support the airplane.

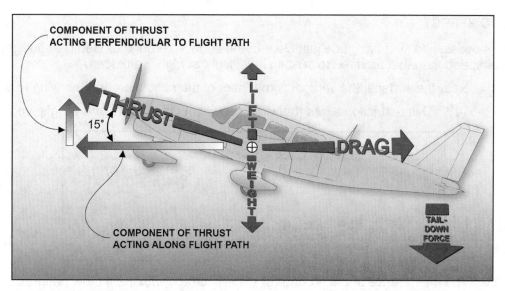

c. As the airspeed decreases from cruise to L/D$_{MAX}$, total drag and thrust decrease to maintain a constant altitude, as shown in the graph on page 43.

d. The speed at which minimum power is required also requires the lowest fuel flow to keep the airplane in steady, level flight. This speed is known as the speed for maximum endurance (V$_{ME}$).

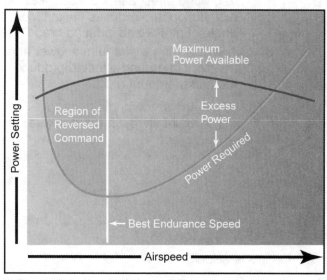

Power required curve.

1) Flight at speeds below V$_{ME}$ will require more power, not less, to maintain steady, level flight.

2) This is known as the **backside of the power curve** or **region of reversed command**.

   a) The region of reversed command means that more power (not less) is required to fly at slower airspeeds while maintaining a constant altitude.

3) When flying slower than V$_{ME}$, you should avoid the natural tendency to pull back on the control yoke in order to climb because increasing the angle of attack will increase drag and may cause the airplane to descend or stall (if the critical angle of attack is exceeded).

   a) You will gain altitude (climb) by increasing power and adjusting pitch to maintain the desired airspeed.

4) **Minimum controllable airspeed (MCA)** is the airspeed at which any further increase in angle of attack or load factor, or any further reduction in power (while maintaining a constant altitude), will result in a stall.

   a) Since you will be flying near the critical angle of attack, you cannot increase pitch (angle of attack) to gain altitude.

      i) To gain altitude, you need to increase power and lower the nose.

1.8 GROUND EFFECT

1.   It is possible to fly an airplane just clear of the surface (ground or water) at a slightly slower airspeed than that required to sustain level flight at higher altitudes.

    a.   Near the surface, the vertical component of the airflow around the wing is restricted.

        1)   This restriction alters the wing's upwash, downwash, and wingtip vortices.

    b.   The interference of the ground (or water) surface with the airflow patterns about the airplane in flight is called **ground effect**.

2.   The principal aerodynamic effects due to proximity of the ground are the changes in the aerodynamic characteristics of the wing.

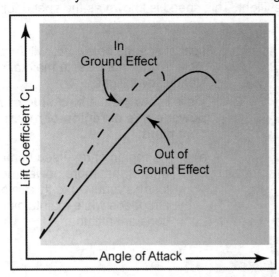

    a.   The reduction of the wingtip vortices due to ground effect alters the spanwise lift distribution and reduces the induced angle of attack and induced drag.

    b.   Thus, the wing will require a lower angle of attack in ground effect to produce the same amount of lift.

        1)   If the same angle of attack is maintained, lift will increase.

3.   Ground effect also will alter the thrust required versus velocity.

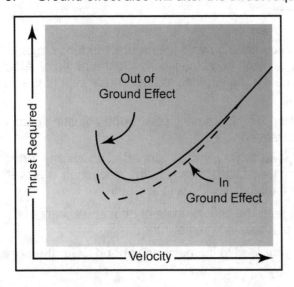

    a.   Because induced drag predominates at low airspeeds, the reduction of induced drag due to ground effect will cause the most significant reduction of thrust required at low airspeeds.

        1)   There is no effect on parasite drag.

4. In order for ground effect to be of significant magnitude, the wing must be quite close to the ground.

    a. The reduction of induced drag differs with the wing height above the ground.

        1) When the wing is at a height equal to its span, the reduction in induced drag is approximately 1.4%.

        2) When the wing is at a height equal to one-fourth its span, the reduction is approximately 23.5%.

        3) When the wing is at a height equal to one-tenth its span, the reduction is approximately 47.6%.

    b. Thus, a large reduction in induced drag will take place only when the wing is very close to the ground.

        1) Because of this, ground effect is usually recognized during the liftoff for takeoff or just prior to touchdown when landing and is more pronounced in low-wing airplanes.

5. An airplane leaving ground effect (i.e., taking off) will

    a. Require an increase in angle of attack to maintain the same amount of lift
    b. Experience an increase in induced drag and thrust required
    c. Experience a decrease in stability and a slight nose-up pitch

6. An airplane entering ground effect (i.e., landing) will encounter the opposite phenomena.

7. Ground effect permits airplanes to lift off the ground at airspeeds lower than adequate to continue a safe climb.

    a. You must make sure you have reached a safe airspeed before attempting to climb out during a takeoff.

    b. On landings, you must be aware of the airplane's tendency to float down the runway when ground effect is encountered at excessive airspeeds.

    c. In your training, you will learn how to use ground effect to its best advantage when departing from grass or other unpaved landing fields.

1.9 HOW AIRPLANES TURN

1. The lift produced by an airplane's wings is used to turn the airplane. When the wings are banked, the lift is separated into two components known as the vertical and horizontal components of lift.

    a. Until a force acts on the airplane, it tends to fly straight ahead due to inertia.

        1) Inertia describes the phenomenon that moving items continue to move in the same direction, i.e., straight flight.

    b. When the airplane begins to turn, inertia, or centrifugal force, pulls the airplane away from the turn, i.e., tends to make it fly straight ahead.

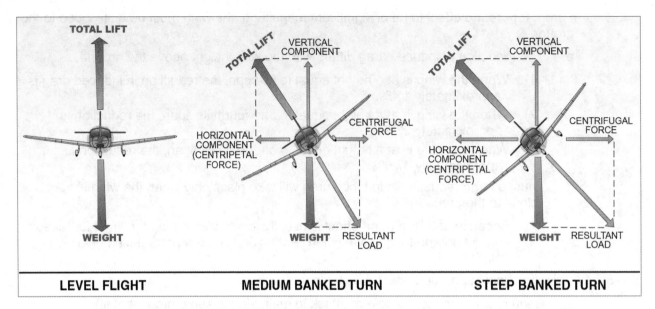

| LEVEL FLIGHT | MEDIUM BANKED TURN | STEEP BANKED TURN |

   c.   In a bank, the horizontal component of lift, or centripetal force, counteracts the centrifugal force.

       1)   Therefore, the greater the bank, the sharper the turn or the greater the rate of turn because more of the total lift goes into the horizontal component.

       2)   The horizontal component of lift is the force that pulls an airplane from a straight flight path to make it turn.

   d.   The rudder controls the yaw about the vertical axis.

       1)   When applying aileron to bank the airplane, the lowered aileron (on the rising wing) produces a greater lift and a greater drag than the raised aileron (on the lowering wing). This is commonly referred to as **adverse yaw**.

          a)   This increased aileron drag tends to yaw the airplane toward the rising wing (i.e., opposite the direction of turn) while the banking action is taking effect.

       2)   To counteract this adverse yaw, rudder pressure must be applied simultaneously with the ailerons in the desired direction of turn. This produces a coordinated turn.

       3)   For the purposes of this discussion, an airplane is in coordinated flight when it flies straight ahead through the relative wind, i.e., not sideways (about its vertical axis). In other words, the airplane is always turning at a rate appropriate to its angle of bank.

       4)   Once the airplane is at the desired bank, the pilot neutralizes the ailerons and the rudder.

2.   In a bank, the total lift consists of both horizontal lift (counteracting centrifugal force) and vertical lift (counteracting weight and gravity).

   a.   Therefore, given the same amount of total lift, there is less vertical lift in a bank than in straight-and-level flight.

   b.   Thus, to maintain altitude in a turn, you must increase back pressure on the control yoke (for a higher angle of attack to produce more lift) and/or increase power.

3.   The turn is stopped by decreasing the bank of the airplane to zero, i.e., rolling the wings to level.

1.10 TORQUE (LEFT-TURNING TENDENCY)

1.   Torque is a force or combination of forces that tends to produce a twisting or rotating motion of an airplane.

   a.   An airplane propeller spinning clockwise, as seen from the rear, produces forces that tend to twist or rotate the airplane in the opposite direction, thus turning the airplane to the left.

   b.   Airplanes are designed in such a manner that the torque effect is not noticeable to the pilot when the airplane is in straight-and-level flight at a cruise power setting.

   c.   The effect of torque increases in direct proportion to engine power and airplane attitude and inversely with airspeed.

   1)   If the power setting is high, the angle of attack high, and the airspeed slow, the effect of torque is greater.

   2)   Thus, during takeoffs and climbs, the effect of torque is most pronounced.

   a)   You must apply sufficient right rudder pressure to counteract the left-turning tendency and maintain a straight takeoff path.

   d.   Left-turning tendency (torque) is made up of four elements that cause or produce a twisting or rotating motion around at least one of the airplane's three axes.

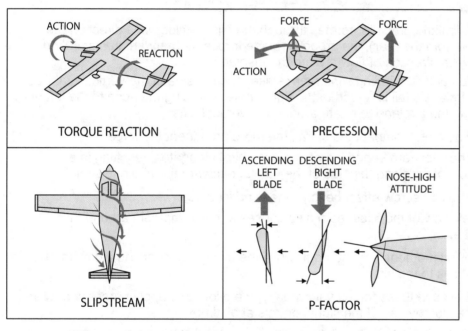

These four elements are

1)   Torque reaction from engine and propeller

2)   Corkscrewing effect of the slipstream

3)   Gyroscopic action (precession) of the propeller

4)   Asymmetrical loading of the propeller (P-factor)

2.   **Torque reaction.** This effect is based on Newton's Third Law of Motion, which states that for every action there is an equal and opposite reaction.

   a.   An airplane's propeller rotates in a clockwise direction (as seen from the rear). This produces a force that tends to roll the entire airplane counterclockwise (i.e., left) about its longitudinal axis.

   b.   This reaction can be understood by visualizing a rubber-band-powered model airplane.

   1)   Wind the rubber band in a manner that it will unwind and rotate the propeller in a clockwise direction (as viewed from the rear).

   2)   If the fuselage is released while the propeller is held, the fuselage will rotate in a counterclockwise direction (as viewed from the rear).

   3)   This effect of torque reaction is the same in a real propeller-driven airplane, except that, instead of the propeller being held by a hand, its rotation is resisted by air.

   c.   Torque reaction is stronger when power is significantly advanced while the airplane is flying at a very slow airspeed.

3. **Corkscrew (or spiraling slipstream) effect.** This effect is based on the reaction of the air to a rotating propeller blade.

    a.   The high-speed rotation of an airplane's propeller gives a corkscrew or spiraling rotation to the slipstream.

        1)   At high propeller speeds and low forward speeds (e.g., takeoffs, slow flight), this spiraling rotation is very compact and exerts a strong sideward force on the airplane's vertical stabilizer, as shown below.

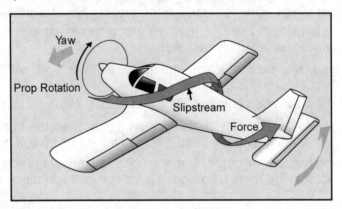

        2)   As the airplane propeller rotates through the air in a clockwise direction (as viewed from the rear), the propeller blade forces air rearward in a spiraling clockwise direction of flow around the fuselage.

        3)   A portion of this spiraling slipstream strikes the left side of the vertical stabilizer. The airplane's tail is forced to the right, thereby forcing the nose to the left and causing the airplane to rotate around the vertical axis.

           a)   The more compact the spiral, the more prominent the force.

    b.   As the airplane's forward speed increases, the spiral elongates, resulting in a straighter flow of air along the side of the fuselage toward the airplane's tail.

        1)   Thus, the corkscrew effect becomes less noticeable.

    c.   The corkscrew flow of the slipstream also causes a rolling moment around the longitudinal axis.

        1)   This rolling moment is to the right, while the rolling moment caused by torque reaction is to the left.

           a)   Because these forces vary greatly, the pilot must apply proper corrective action by use of the flight controls at all times.

4. **Gyroscopic action (precession).** This effect is based on one of the gyroscopic properties that apply to any object spinning in space (e.g., a rotating airplane propeller).

    a.   Before the gyroscopic effects of the propeller can be understood, it is necessary to understand the basic principle of a gyroscope.

        1)   All practical applications of the gyroscope are based upon two fundamental properties of gyroscopic action:

           a)   Rigidity in space
           b)   Precession (the one important for this discussion)

2) Precession is the resultant action or deflection of a spinning rotor when a deflecting force is applied to its rim.

   a) As can be seen in the figure below, when a force is applied, the resulting force takes effect 90° ahead of and in the direction of rotation.

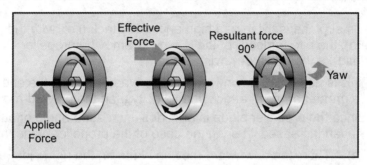

b. The rotating propeller of an airplane makes a very good gyroscope and thus has similar properties.

   1) Any time a force is applied to deflect the propeller out of its plane of rotation, the resulting force is 90° ahead of and in the direction of application.

      a) This causes a pitching moment, a yawing moment, or a combination of the two depending upon the point at which the force was applied.

c. This element has always been associated with, and considered more prominent in, tailwheel-type airplanes. It most often occurs when the tail is being raised during the takeoff roll as shown below.

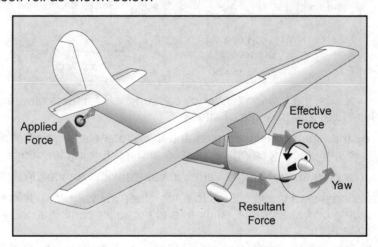

   1) This change in pitch attitude has the same effect as applying a force to the top of the propeller's plane of rotation.

   2) The resultant force acting 90° ahead causes a yawing moment to the left around the vertical axis.

   3) The magnitude of this moment depends on several variables, one of which is the abruptness with which the tail is raised (i.e., the amount of force applied).

d. When the nose is raised during the takeoff roll of a nosewheel-type airplane (i.e., rotation), the yawing moment will be to the right.

   1) The left-turning tendency that occurs when the nose is raised on a tricycle gear airplane is not primarily due to gyroscopic precession. It is more a combination of torque and P-factor when operating at high power settings.

e. As a result of gyroscopic action, any yawing around the vertical axis results in a pitching moment, and any pitching around the lateral axis results in a yawing moment.

   1) To correct for the effect of gyroscopic action, the pilot must use elevator and rudder properly to prevent unwanted pitching and yawing.

5. **Asymmetric propeller loading (P-factor).** The effects of P-factor, or asymmetric propeller loading, usually occur when the airplane is flown at a high angle of attack.

   a. Asymmetrical loading of the propeller simply means that the load on the upward-moving propeller blade is different from the load on the downward-moving propeller blade.

   b. When an airplane is flying at a high angle of attack (i.e., with the propeller axis inclined upward), the bite (or load) of the downward-moving propeller blade is greater than the bite (load) of the upward-moving blade.

      1) This is due to the downward-moving blade meeting the oncoming relative wind at a greater angle of attack and velocity than the upward-moving blade.

      2) Since the propeller blade is an airfoil, increased angle of attack and velocity mean increased lift or, in the case of the propeller blade, more thrust.

         a) Thus, the downward-moving blade on the right side (as viewed from the rear) has more thrust than the upward-moving blade, causing the airplane to yaw to the left.

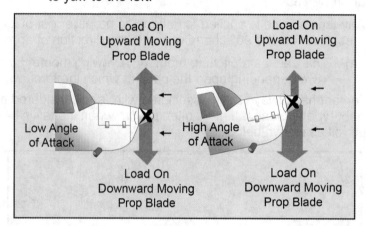

   c. At low speeds, the yawing tendency caused by P-factor is greater because the airplane is at a high angle of attack.

      1) As the airspeed is increased and the airplane's angle of attack is reduced, the asymmetrical loading decreases and the turning tendency is decreased.

6. Each of the four elements of torque varies in values with changes in flight situations.

   a. The relationship of these values to each other will vary with different airplanes depending on the airframe, engine, and propeller combinations as well as other design features.

   b. To maintain positive control of the airplane in all flight conditions, the pilot must apply the flight controls as necessary to compensate for these varying values.

7. It should be noted at this point that, although the rudder should never be used to turn the airplane, it is used to prevent the previously mentioned unwanted turning tendencies.

   a. Ailerons should never be used to counteract unwanted (adverse) yaw.

1.11 AIRPLANE STABILITY

1. Stability is the inherent ability of a body, after its equilibrium (i.e., steady flight) is disturbed, to return to its original position. In other words, a stable airplane will tend to return to the original condition of flight if disturbed by a force such as turbulent air.

   a. This means that a stable airplane is easier to fly.

   b. It does not mean that you can depend entirely on stability to return the airplane to the original condition. Even in the most stable airplanes, some conditions will require the use of airplane controls to return the airplane to the desired attitude. Less effort is needed to control the airplane, however, because of the inherent stability.

    c. The quality of an aircraft that permits it to be operated easily and to withstand the stresses imposed on it is the **maneuverability** of the aircraft.

    d. The capability of an aircraft to respond to the pilot's input, especially with regard to flight path and altitude, is its **controllability**.

    e. The two types of stability are static and dynamic. Within each of these are categories called positive, neutral, and negative stability.

        1) Because stability is desired around all three axes of an airplane, it can be classified as longitudinal, lateral, or vertical.

2. **Static stability** is the initial tendency that the airplane displays after its equilibrium is disturbed.

    a. Positive static stability is the initial tendency of the airplane to return to the original attitude, or equilibrium, after being disturbed.

        1) This tendency can be illustrated by a ball inside a bowl. If the ball is displaced from its normal resting place at the bottom of the bowl (i.e., its equilibrium), it will eventually return to its original position, as shown in the bottom left figure of the illustration below.

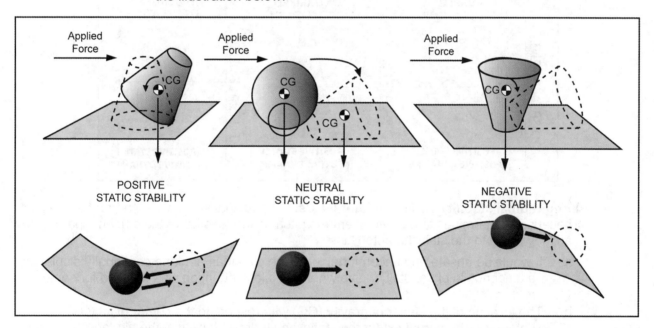

    b. Neutral static stability is the initial tendency of the airplane to remain in a new condition (attitude) after its equilibrium has been disturbed.

        1) This tendency can be illustrated by a ball on a flat, level surface. If the ball is displaced, it will come to rest at some new, neutral position and show no tendency to return to its original position, as shown in the bottom middle figure of the illustration above.

    c. Negative static stability is the initial tendency of the airplane to continue away from the original equilibrium (attitude) after being disturbed, as shown in the bottom right figure of the illustration above.

        1) This tendency can be illustrated by a ball on the top of an inverted bowl. Even the slightest displacement of the ball from its equilibrium will activate greater forces that will cause the ball to move in the direction of the applied force.

    d. Positive static stability is the most desirable characteristic because the airplane will initially attempt to return to its original trimmed attitude, as shown in the bottom left figure of the illustration above.

3.   **Dynamic stability** is the overall tendency that the airplane displays after its equilibrium is disturbed. It is determined by its oscillation tendency after the initial displacement.

   a.   Positive dynamic stability is the overall tendency of the airplane to return to its original attitude directly or through a series of decreasing oscillations (see the left figure in the illustration below).

   b.   Neutral dynamic stability is the overall tendency of the airplane to attempt to return to its original attitude, but the oscillations do not increase or decrease in magnitude as time passes (see the middle figure in the illustration below).

   c.   Negative dynamic stability is the overall tendency of the airplane to attempt to return to its original attitude, but the oscillations increase in magnitude as time progresses (see the right figure in the illustration below).

   d.   Thus, the most desirable combination of the types of stability is a combination of positive static stability with positive dynamic stability.

      1)   This combination will tend to return the airplane to its original attitude (or equilibrium).

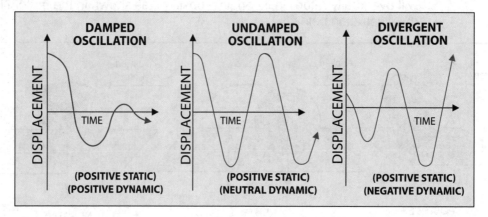

4.   **Longitudinal stability about the lateral axis.** Longitudinal stability is important to the pilot because it determines to a great extent the pitch characteristics of the airplane, particularly as they relate to the stall characteristics.

   a.   It would be unsafe and uncomfortable for the pilot if an airplane continually displayed a tendency to either stall or dive when the pilot's attention was diverted for some reason.

   b.   The location of the center of gravity (CG) with respect to the center of lift (CL) determines to a great extent the static longitudinal stability of the airplane.

      1)   Positive -- if center of lift is behind the center of gravity, as shown to the right

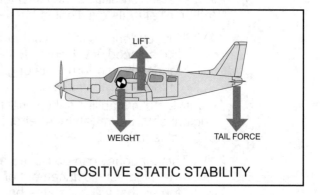

2) Negative -- if center of lift is in front of the center of gravity, as shown to the right

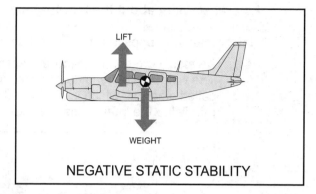

NEGATIVE STATIC STABILITY

3) Neutral -- if center of lift is at the center of gravity

c. Most airplanes are designed to have their CG located slightly forward of the CL to create a nose-down tendency so the airplane will have a natural tendency to pitch downward away from a stalling condition.

1) The nose-down tendency is offset by the position of the horizontal stabilizer, which is an inverted airfoil (camber on bottom) that produces a downward force. Additional downward force on the stabilizer is provided by the downwash from the propeller and the wings (except on T-tail airplanes).

a) If the airplane's speed decreases, the downwash on the tail is reduced, causing a decrease in the downward force on the horizontal stabilizer, thus causing the airplane's nose to pitch down.

i) As the airplane's speed increases in the nose-low attitude, the downward force on the horizontal stabilizer increases, causing the tail to be pushed downward and the nose to rise to a climbing attitude.

ii) If the airplane has positive dynamic stability, these oscillations will decrease until once again the downward force of the tail is equal to the nose-down tendency.

b) Increasing the airplane's speed has the opposite effect.

2) The further forward the CG is from the CL, the more longitudinal stability the airplane possesses.

a) The closer the CG is to the CL, the less stable the airplane.

3) Many airplanes have the line of thrust located lower than the CG. The propeller's thrust provides a nose-up pitching force to help overcome the inherent nose heaviness.

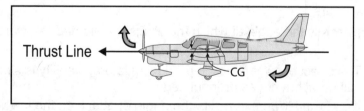

d. A common misconception about longitudinal stability is that an airplane is stable with respect to the horizon.

1) There is only one speed for each degree of angle of attack, and eventually the airplane will stabilize at the angle of attack and airspeed for which it is trimmed.

2) Thus, an airplane that is longitudinally stable will tend to return to its trimmed angle of attack after being disturbed from equilibrium.

5. **Lateral stability about the longitudinal axis.** Stability about the airplane's longitudinal axis, called lateral stability, helps to stabilize the lateral or rolling effect when one wing gets lower than the opposite wing. Four main design factors influence lateral stability.

   a. The most common procedure for producing lateral stability is known as wing **dihedral**. The wings on either side of the airplane join the fuselage to form a slight V or angle called dihedral, which is measured by the angle made by each wing above a line parallel to the lateral axis, as shown below.

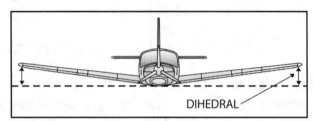

DIHEDRAL

   1) If a momentary gust of wind forces one wing of the airplane to rise and the other to lower, the airplane will roll into a bank.

      a) When an airplane is banked without turning, it tends to sideslip, or slide downward, toward the lowered wing.

      b) Because the wings have dihedral, the air strikes the low wing at a much greater angle of attack than the high wing.

      c) This increases lift on the low wing more than the high wing and tends to restore the wings to a level attitude, as shown below.

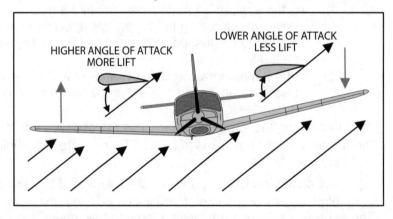

HIGHER ANGLE OF ATTACK
MORE LIFT

LOWER ANGLE OF ATTACK
LESS LIFT

   2) The effect of dihedral is to produce a rolling moment tending to return the airplane to a laterally balanced flight condition (i.e., wings level) when a sideslip occurs.

   b. **Sweepback** is the angle at which the wings are slanted rearward from the root to the tip.

      1) The effect of sweepback in producing lateral stability is similar to that of the dihedral but not as pronounced.

      2) If one wing lowers in a slip, the angle of attack on the low wing increases, producing greater lift. This results in a tendency for the lower wing to rise and return the airplane to level flight.

      3) Sweepback augments dihedral to achieve lateral stability.

      4) Another reason for sweepback is to place the center of lift farther rearward, which affects longitudinal stability more than it does lateral stability.

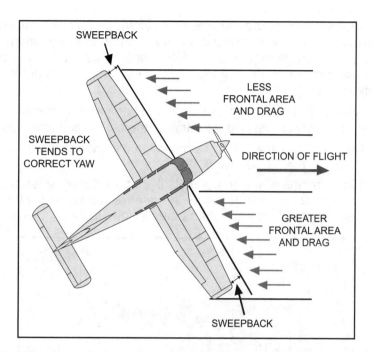

c.   During flight, the side area of the airplane's fuselage and vertical stabilizer react to the airflow in much the same manner as the keel of a ship.

   1)   This **keel effect** is the steadying influence on the airplane laterally about the longitudinal axis.

   2)   Such laterally stable airplanes are constructed so that the greater portion of the keel area is above and behind the center of gravity, as shown on the following page.

   3)   Thus, when the airplane slips to one side, the combination of the airplane's weight and the pressure of the airflow against the upper portion of the keel area (both acting about the CG) tends to roll and yaw the airplane back to wings-level flight.

d.   Weight distribution can be controlled to improve lateral stability.

   1)   Most airplanes have fuel tank(s) in each wing.

   2)   If the fuel is unequally distributed, the airplane will tend to roll toward the wing with more fuel.

   3)   This tendency can be corrected by starting the flight with equal fuel in each wing and, through proper fuel management, using fuel from both wings in equal amounts.

e.   Lateral stability or instability in turns.

   1)   Because of lateral stability, most airplanes will tend to recover from shallow banks automatically.

   2)   As the bank is increased to a medium banked turn, the wing on the outside of the turn travels faster than the wing on the inside of the turn. The increased speed increases the lift on the outside wing, which nearly cancels the stabilizing effect of lateral stability.

      a)   Thus, during a medium banked turn, an airplane tends to hold its bank constant and requires less control input on the part of the pilot.

   3)   During a steep banked turn, the increased lift on the outside wing becomes so great that it overcomes the airplane's lateral stability.

      a)   Thus, the pilot must apply slight aileron pressure opposite the turn to prevent overbanking.

6. **Directional stability about the vertical axis (yaw).** Directional stability is displayed around the vertical axis and depends to a great extent on the quality of lateral stability. If the longitudinal axis of an airplane tends to follow and parallel the flight path of the airplane through the air, whether in straight flight or curved flight, that airplane is considered to be directionally stable.

   a. Directional stability is accomplished by the vertical stabilizer or fin to the rear of the center of gravity on the upper portion of the tail section (see figure below).

      1) The surface of this fin acts similarly to a weathervane. It causes the airplane to turn into the relative wind.

      2) If the airplane is yawed out of its flight path during straight flight or turns, either by pilot action or turbulence, the relative wind exerts a force on one side of the vertical stabilizer and returns the airplane to its original direction of flight.

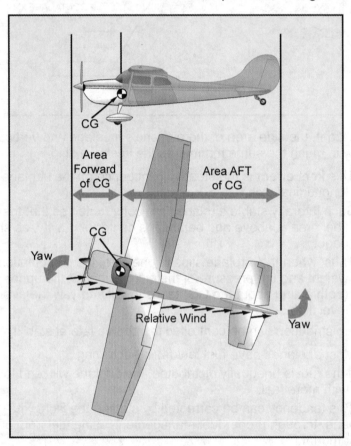

   b. Wing sweepback also aids in directional stability. If the airplane is rotated about the vertical axis, the airplane is forced sideways into the relative wind.

      1) Sweepback causes the leading wing to present more frontal area to the relative wind than the trailing wing.

      2) This increased frontal area creates more drag, which tends to force the airplane to return to its original direction of flight.

   c. The combined effects of the vertical stabilizer (fin) and sweepback can be compared with the feathers of an arrow. An arrow cannot travel through the air sideways at any appreciable rate of speed.

   d. Keel effect depends on the action of the relative wind on the side area of the airplane fuselage. In a slight slip, the fuselage provides a broad area upon which the relative wind will strike, forcing the fuselage to parallel the relative wind and thus helping to produce vertical or yaw stability.

7.   **Effects of lateral and directional stability.** While most airplanes are designed to be stable, the design factors that produce stability normally have some undesirable effects. The two most common are Dutch roll and spiral instability.

a.   **Dutch roll** is a combination rolling/yawing oscillation caused by wind gusts in turbulent air.

1)   When equilibrium is disturbed, the rolling motion precedes the yawing motion, and the rolling motion is more noticeable than the yawing motion.

2)   When the airplane rolls back toward level flight in response to dihedral effect, it rolls back too far and sideslips the other way.

a)   Thus, each oscillation overshoots the wings-level attitude because of the strong dihedral effect.

b)   If the Dutch roll is not decreased by the directional stability, it is considered objectionable.

3)   To counteract the Dutch roll tendency, the airplane may be designed to increase directional stability and decrease lateral stability.

a)   While suppressing the Dutch roll tendency, this design factor tends to cause spiral instability.

b.   **Spiral instability** exists when the directional stability of the airplane is very strong compared to the lateral stability.

1)   When equilibrium is disturbed and a sideslip is introduced, the strong directional stability tends to yaw the nose back into alignment with the relative wind, while the comparatively weak dihedral lags in restoring the lateral balance.

a)   Due to this yaw, the wing on the outside travels at a faster rate than the inside wing, thus increasing lift.

i)   This produces an overbanking tendency which, if not corrected by the pilot, will result in the bank angle becoming steeper and steeper.

b)   At the same time, the strong directional stability that yaws the airplane into the relative wind is actually forcing the nose to a lower pitch attitude.

c)   Thus, a slow downward spiral starts that, if not counteracted by the pilot, will gradually increase into a steep spiral dive.

2)   Normally, the rate of divergence in the spiral motion is so gradual that the pilot can control the tendency without any difficulty.

a)   Thus, if this rate of divergence is low, spiral instability is considered less objectionable than Dutch roll.

1.12 LOADS AND LOAD FACTORS

1.   Any force applied to deflect an airplane from a straight line produces a stress on its structure. The amount of this force is called load factor.

a.   **Load factor** is the ratio of the total load supported by the airplane's wings (i.e., lift) to the actual weight of the airplane and its contents:

$$\text{Load factor} = \frac{\text{Total load supported by the wings}}{\text{Total weight of the airplane}}$$

1)   EXAMPLE: An airplane has a gross weight of 2,000 lb. During flight, it is subjected to aerodynamic forces which increase the total load that the wing must support to 4,000 lb. The load factor is thus 2.0 (4,000 ÷ 2,000). The airplane wing is producing lift equal to twice the gross weight of the airplane.

b.   Another way of expressing load factor is the ratio of a given load to the pull of gravity, or "G." If the weight of the airplane is equal to 1G, and if a load of three times the actual weight of the airplane were imposed upon the wing due to curved flight, the load factor of 3 would be expressed as 3Gs.

    c.   In unaccelerated flight, the airplane is said to have a load factor of 1, i.e., the total lift that the wings are producing is equal to the gross weight of the airplane.

        1)   If the angle of attack of the wings is increased while airspeed remains constant, e.g., in a pull-up from a dive, the wings produce more lift and thus a higher load factor.

    d.   A positive load occurs when back pressure is applied to the elevator, causing centrifugal force to act in the same direction as weight.

        1)   A negative load occurs when forward pressure is applied to the elevator control, causing centrifugal force to act in a direction opposite to that of weight.

2.   **Load factors and airplane design.** To be certified by the FAA, the structural strength (maximum allowable load factor) of airplanes must conform with prescribed standards set forth by Federal Aviation Regulations. Airplanes are classified as to strength and operational use by means of the category system. Most general aviation trainer-type airplanes are classified in one or more of the following categories:

    a.   The normal category has a maximum limit load factor of 3.8 positive Gs and 1.52 negative Gs.

        1)   The limit load factor is the highest (both positive and negative) load factor that can be expected in normal operations under various situations. This load factor can be sustained without causing permanent deformation or structural damage to the airplane.

        2)   Permissible maneuvers include

            a)   Any maneuver incidental to normal flying

            b)   Stalls

            c)   Lazy eights, chandelles, and steep turns without angle of bank exceeding 60°

    b.   The utility category has a maximum limit load factor of 4.4 positive Gs and 1.76 negative Gs.

        1)   Permissible maneuvers include

            a)   All operations in the normal category

            b)   Spins (if approved for that airplane)

            c)   Lazy eights, chandelles, and steep turns with angle of bank exceeding 60°

    c.   The acrobatic category has a maximum limit load factor of 6.0 positive Gs and 3.0 negative Gs.

        1)   There are no restrictions except those shown to be necessary as a result of required flight tests.

    d.   This system indicates what operations can be performed in a given airplane without exceeding the load limit. You are cautioned to operate the airplane within the load limit for which the airplane is designed so as to enhance safety and still benefit from the intended use of the airplane.

    e.   An airplane's structure is designed to support a certain total load. It is vital that maximum gross weight limits as well as load factor limits be strictly observed.

3.   **Effect of turns on load factor.** A turn is made by banking the airplane so that horizontal lift from the wings pulls the airplane from its straight flight path. In a constant altitude coordinated turn, the resultant load is the result of two forces -- gravity and "centrifugal force," as shown on the next page. Remember, "centrifugal force" is a lay term for inertia as described by Newton's First Law.

    a.   In any airplane, if a constant altitude is maintained during the turn, the load factor for a given degree of bank is the same.

        1)   Regardless of airspeed and rate of turn, the total lift, and therefore the two components of lift shown on the next page, remain the same.

2) Because of this, there is no change in centrifugal force for any given bank, and thus the load factor remains constant.

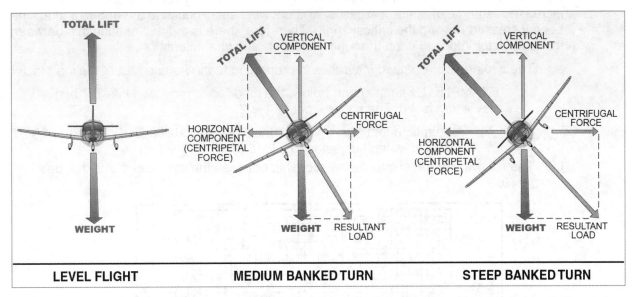

| LEVEL FLIGHT | MEDIUM BANKED TURN | STEEP BANKED TURN |

b. The load factor increases at a rapid rate after the angle of bank reaches 50°, as shown in the graph to the left below. The wing must produce lift equal to this load factor if altitude is to be maintained.

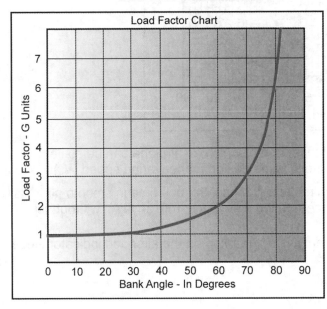

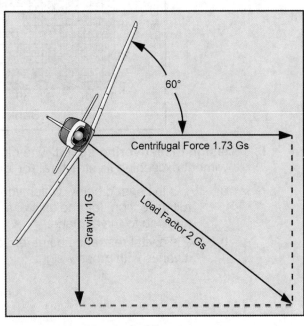

1) At an angle of bank of slightly more than 80°, the load factor exceeds 6.0, which is the limit load factor of an acrobatic airplane.

2) The approximate maximum bank angle for conventional light airplanes in a level coordinated turn is 60°, which produces a load factor of 2.0.

4. **Effect of load factor on stalling speed.** Any airplane, within the limits of its structure and the strength of the pilot, can be stalled at any airspeed. At a given airspeed, the load factor increases as angle of attack increases, and the wing stalls because the angle of attack has been increased beyond the critical angle. Therefore, there is a direct relationship between the load factor imposed upon the wing and its stalling characteristics.

    a. The airplane's stall speed increases in proportion to the square root of the load factor.

        1) EXAMPLE: Using the chart below, the load factor produced in a 75° banked, level turn is 4.0. The square root of 4 is 2.

            a) An airplane that has a normal unaccelerated stall speed of 45 kt. will stall at 90 kt. when subjected to a load of 4Gs.

    b. The following graph shows the relationship between the stall speed and the load factor.

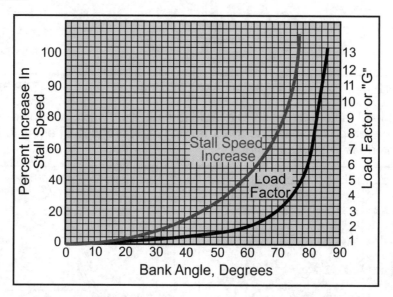

5. **Design maneuvering speed.** The maximum speed at which an airplane can be stalled without exceeding its structural (or load) limits is the design maneuvering speed (V_A).

    a. V_A is the speed below which you can move a flight control one time in smooth air to its full deflection, for one axis of airplane rotation only (pitch, roll, or yaw), without risk of damage to the airplane.

    b. V_A is a vital reference point for you, but it is not marked on the airspeed indicator since it varies with gross weight.

    c. V_A can be found in the FAA-approved Airplane Flight Manual (AFM) and/or Pilot's Operating Handbook (POH) for each airplane and/or on a placard within the cockpit.

        1)   Older general aviation airplanes may not have a published V_A in their AFM/POH. In this case, a general rule for determining the maneuvering speed is approximately 1.7 times the normal stalling speed.

            a)   Thus, an airplane that normally stalls at 35 kt. should never be stalled when the airspeed is above 60 kt. (35 kt. × 1.7 = 59.5 kt.).

        2)   If the AFM/POH specifies more than one V_A, you will notice that it decreases with weight.

            a)   A lighter airplane is subject to more rapid acceleration from turbulence and gusts than a heavier airplane.

            b)   A lighter airplane has a lower stalling speed than a heavier airplane, thus a lower V_A.

    d.   When operating below V_A, a damaging positive flight load cannot (theoretically) be produced. The airplane should stall before the load becomes excessive. Any combination of flight control usage, including full deflection of the controls or gust loads created by turbulence, should not create an excessive air load if the airplane is operated below V_A.

        1)   CAUTION: Certain adverse wind shears or gusts may cause excessive loads even at speeds below V_A.

        2)   Operating at or below design maneuvering speed does not provide structural protection against multiple full control inputs in one axis, or full control inputs in more than one axis at the same time.

        3)   Pilots should avoid full application of pitch, roll, or yaw controls to speeds below maneuvering speed, and avoid rapid and large alternating control inputs, as they may result in structural failures at any speed, including below V_A.

6.   **Effect of turbulence on load factor.** Turbulence in the form of vertical air currents can, under certain conditions, cause severe load stress on an airplane wing.

    a.   When an airplane flying at a high speed with a low angle of attack suddenly encounters a vertical current of air moving upward, the relative wind changes to an upward direction as it meets the airfoil. This increases the angle of attack of the wing.

    b.   All certificated airplanes are designed to withstand loads imposed by turbulence of considerable intensity. Nevertheless, gust load factors increase with increasing airspeed.

        1)   Therefore, it is wise in extremely rough air, as in thunderstorm or frontal conditions, to reduce the speed to below V_A.

        2)   As a general rule when severe turbulence is encountered, the airplane should be flown below V_A as shown in the AFM/POH and/or placard in the airplane. This speed is the one least likely to result in structural damage to the airplane (even if the control surfaces are fully deflected), yet it allows a sufficient margin of safety above stalling speed in turbulent air.

7. **V-G Diagram (Velocity versus G Loads)**

    a. The V-G diagram is a graphic representation of the operating limitations of a specific make and model of airplane under specified conditions (e.g., weight and configuration).

        1) Airplane manufacturers use numerous V-G diagrams when designing an airplane to define airspeed and load factor limits that specify that airplane's flight, or operating, envelope.

        2) Our discussion is based on the V-G diagram shown below.

            a) Airspeed (V) is shown on the horizontal axis with load factor (G) on the vertical axis.

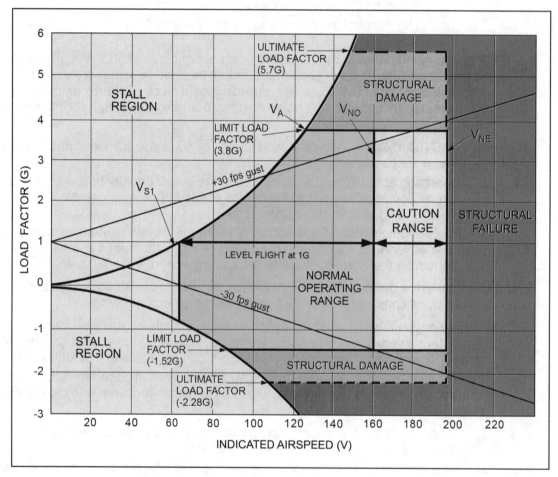

    b. The curved lines starting at 0 on the vertical axis represent the positive and negative lines of maximum lift capability.

        1) These lines indicate the maximum amount of lift the airplane can generate at a specified speed.

        2) The intersection of the maximum lift line and an airspeed line indicates the maximum load factor that can be placed on the airplane.

            a) At a given airspeed, the airplane will stall at any load factor greater than the maximum lift line.

c.   The lines at +3.8G and −1.52G represent the positive and negative limit load factors for this airplane, i.e., the limits for a normal category airplane.

1)   The lines at +5.7G and −2.28G are the ultimate load factors, i.e., the required safety factor of 1.5.

2)   Any load placed on the airplane between the limit load and ultimate load may cause permanent deformation of the airplane's primary structure (e.g., wings). A high rate of fatigue damage may be incurred, but the structure should not fail.

3)   A load placed on the airplane greater than the ultimate load factor will cause the airplane's primary structure to break.

d.   In smooth air and with wings level, the airplane is flying at 1G. The speed at which the airplane stalls at 1G is V_{S1}.

1) V_{S1} is marked on the airspeed indicator at the lower limit of the green arc.

2)   Any stall that occurs above 1G is an accelerated stall.

e. V_A is the airspeed that is at the intersection of the positive limit load factor and maximum lift lines.

1) V_A is design maneuvering speed, which is discussed beginning on page 62.

2)   Notice that, at speeds greater than V_A, the limit load factor will be exceeded before the airplane will stall.

f.   When an airplane is designed, certain airspeeds are established called designed airspeeds, such as the design maneuvering speed (V_A). Some important airspeed limitations are established from various design airspeeds and other factors.

1) V_{NO} is the maximum structural cruising speed, or maximum normal operating speed, and is shown on the airspeed indicator at the upper limit of the green arc.

a)   The airspeed range from V_{S1} to V_{NO} is the normal operating range.

b)   Flight above this airspeed should be conducted only in smooth air and with caution.

2) V_{NE} is the airplane's never-exceed speed and is marked by the red line on the airspeed indicator.

a)   If flight is attempted beyond V_{NE}, structural damage or failure may result from a variety of phenomena.

b)   The airspeed range from V_{NO} to V_{NE} is the caution range, i.e., the yellow arc on the airspeed indicator.

g.   The airplane design must also be concerned with the effect of vertical (up or down) wind gusts on the airplane.

1)   Vertical wind gusts will cause an increase in angle of attack and an increase in load factor, much in the same manner as if you abruptly pulled back or pushed forward on the control.

2)   This effect is why you should fly at a speed of V_A or less when you are flying in turbulent air.

h.   The airplane must be operated within the flight envelope to prevent the airplane's primary structure from being deformed or damaged. Thus, the airplane in flight is limited to a regime of airspeeds and load factors that do not exceed either of the following:

1)   The positive or negative limit load factors

2) V_{NE}

1.13 STALLS AND SPINS

1. **Stalls**

   a. A stall is a loss of lift and an increase in drag occurring when an aircraft is flown at an angle of attack greater than the angle for maximum lift. The angle of attack for maximum lift is also called the critical angle of attack.

      1) Thus, a stall occurs whenever the critical angle of attack is exceeded.

   b. To understand the stall phenomenon, some basic factors affecting aerodynamics and flight should be reviewed with particular emphasis on their relation to stall speeds. The stall speed is the speed at which the critical angle of attack is exceeded.

      1) When the angle of attack is increased to approximately 18° to 20° on most airfoils, the airstream can no longer follow the upper curvature of the wing because of the excessive change in direction. This is the critical angle of attack.

         a) As the critical angle of attack is approached, the airstream begins separating from the rear of the upper wing surface. As the angle of attack is further increased, the airstream is forced to flow straight back, away from the top surface of the wing and from the area of highest camber. See the figure below.

         b) This causes a swirling or burbling of the air as it attempts to follow the upper surface of the wing. When the critical angle of attack is reached, the turbulent airflow, which appeared near the trailing edge of the wing at lower angles of attack, quickly spreads forward over the entire upper wing surface.

         c) This results in a sudden increase in pressure on the upper wing surface and a considerable loss of lift. Due to both this loss of lift and the increase in form drag (a larger area of the wing and fuselage is exposed to the airstream), the remaining lift is insufficient to support the airplane and the wing stalls.

         d) To recover from a stall, the angle of attack must be decreased so that the airstream can once again flow smoothly over the wing surface.

            i)   Remember that the angle of attack is the angle between the chord line and the relative wind, not between the chord line and the horizon.

            ii) An airplane can be stalled in any attitude of flight with respect to the horizon, at any airspeed, and at any power setting, if the critical angle of attack is exceeded.

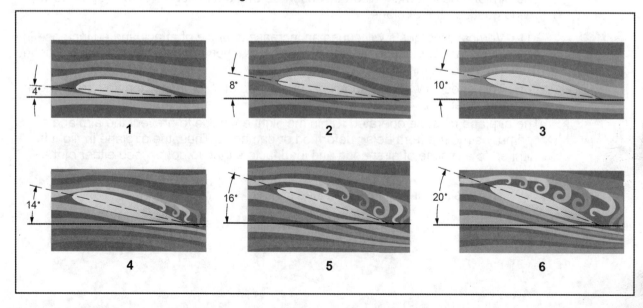

2) Most airplanes are designed so that the wings will stall progressively outward from the wing roots to the wingtips.

    a) The wings are designed with **washout**, i.e., the wingtips have less angle of incidence than the wing roots. The angle of incidence is the angle between the chord line of the wing and the longitudinal axis of the airplane.

    b) Thus, during flight, the tips of such wings have a smaller angle of attack than the wing roots.

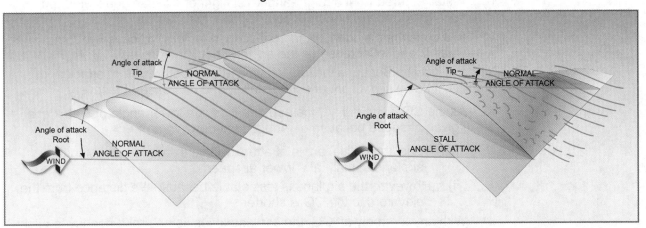

    c) A stall is caused by exceeding the critical angle of attack. Because the wing roots of an airplane will exceed the critical angle before the wingtips, the roots will stall first. The wings are designed in this manner so that control of the ailerons (which are located toward the tips of the wings) will be available at high angles of attack and give the airplane more stable stalling characteristics.

3) Configuration. Flaps, landing gear (if retractable), and other configuring devices can affect your airplane's stall speed. Flap extension will generally increase the lifting ability of the wings, thus reducing the stall speed.

    a) The effect can be seen by markings on the airspeed indicator, where the lower airspeed limit of the white arc (V_{S0}, power-off stall speed with gear and flaps in the landing configuration) is less than the lower airspeed limit of the green arc (V_{S1}, power-off stall speed with the flaps and gear up).

4)   Load factor. Your airplane's stall speed increases in proportion to the square root of the load factor.

    a)   Load factor is the ratio of the lifting force produced by the wings to the actual weight of the airplane and its contents, usually expressed in Gs.

        i)   EXAMPLE: An airplane with a normal unaccelerated stall speed of 45 kt. can be stalled at 90 kt. when subjected to a load factor of 4 Gs.

    b)   A stall entered from straight-and-level flight or from an unaccelerated straight climb will not produce additional load factors.

    c)   In a constant altitude turn, increased load factors will cause your airplane's stall speed to increase as the angle of bank increases.

5)   Center of gravity. Because the CG location affects both angle of attack and stability, it has a significant effect on stall speed and ease of recovery.

    a)   As the CG is moved aft, the airplane flies at a lower angle of attack at a given airspeed because of reduced tail-down force.

        i)   Thus, the critical angle of attack will be exceeded (causing the airplane to stall) at a lower airspeed.

        ii)   However, the airplane is less stable because the distance from the elevators to the CG is shorter.

    b)   With an extremely aft CG, the airplane loses its natural tendency to pitch nose down, making stall recovery more difficult.

        i)   If a spin is entered, the balance of forces on the airplane may result in a flat spin.

        ii)   Recovery from a flat spin may be impossible.

    c)   A forward CG location will often cause the critical angle of attack to be reached (and the airplane to stall) at a higher airspeed.

        i)   However, stall recovery is easier because the airplane has a greater tendency to pitch nose down, and the elevator is a greater distance from the CG.

6)   Weight. Although the distribution of weight has the most direct effect on stability, increased gross weight can also have an effect on an airplane's flight characteristics, regardless of the CG location.

    a)   The increased weight requires a higher angle of attack at a given airspeed to produce additional lift to support the weight.

    b)   Thus, the critical angle of attack will be exceeded (causing the airplane to stall) at a higher airspeed.

7)   Snow, ice, or frost on the wings. Even a small accumulation of snow, ice, or frost on your airplane can cause an increase in the stall speed.

    a)   Such accumulation changes the shape of the wing, disrupting the smooth airflow over the surface and thus increasing drag and decreasing lift.

    8) Turbulence can cause your airplane to stall at a significantly higher airspeed than in stable conditions.

        a) A vertical gust or wind shear can cause a sudden change in the relative wind and result in an abrupt increase in angle of attack.

            i) Even though a gust may not be maintained long enough for a stall to develop, the airplane may stall while you attempt to control the flight path, especially during an approach in gusty conditions.

        b) When flying in moderate to severe turbulence or strong crosswinds, you should maintain a higher than normal approach speed.

            i) In turbulent cruise flight, maintain an airspeed well above the indicated stall speed and below V_A (maneuvering speed).

c. Distractions

    1) Improper airspeed management resulting in stalls is most likely to occur when the pilot is distracted by one or more other tasks.

        a) Pilots at all skill levels must be aware of the increased risk of entering into an inadvertent stall/spin while performing tasks that are secondary to controlling the airplane.

    2) Some distractions include

        a) Locating a checklist

        b) Attempting a restart after an engine failure

        c) Flying a traffic pattern on a windy day

        d) Reading a chart

        e) Making fuel and/or distance calculations

        f) Attempting to retrieve items from the floor, back seat, or glove compartment

        g) Attempting to avoid an obstruction

d. Stall Recognition

    1) There are several ways to recognize that a stall is impending before it actually occurs. When one or more of these indicators are noted, initiation of a recovery should be instinctive.

        a) Vision is useful in detecting a stall condition by noting the attitude of the airplane and the airspeed approaching stall speed. This sense can be fully relied on only when the stall is the result of an intentional unusual attitude of the airplane.

        b) Hearing is also helpful in sensing a stall condition, because the tone level and intensity of sounds incidental to flight decrease as the airspeed decreases.

        c) Kinesthesia, or the mind's sensing of changes in direction of speed of motion, is probably the most important and the best indicator to the trained and experienced pilot. If this sensitivity is properly developed, it will warn of a decrease in speed or the beginning of a settling or "mushing" of the airplane.

d)   The feeling of control pressures is also very important. As speed is reduced, the "live" resistance to pressures on the controls becomes progressively less.

  i)   The airplane controls become less and less effective as you approach the critical angle of attack.

  ii)   In a complete stall, all controls can be moved with almost no resistance and with little immediate effect on the airplane.

   •   The rudder is least affected by the aerodynamics of a stall. In fact, the rudder can normally be used to maintain directional control throughout the stall and stall recovery.

   •   Attempting to use ailerons during a stall for directional control can deepen the stall and even lead to a spin. This is due to the increased angle of attack caused by the down aileron on an already stalled wing.

e)   Many airplanes are equipped with stall warning devices (e.g., a horn) to alert the pilot when the airflow over the wing(s) approaches a stall.

2)   It is vital that you maintain positive control of the airplane at all times.

  a)   Know your airplane.

   i)   Have an intimate familiarity with the pitch attitudes, power settings, and flap configurations appropriate to various phases of flight.

   ii)   Be aware of the sights and sounds of even the slightest changes of pitch, bank, and yaw.

  b)   Fly the airplane in trim. A trimmed airplane can (and should) be flown hands-off so that it remains stable while distractions are being handled.

e.   Stall Recovery

1)   First, the key factor in recovering from a stall is regaining positive control of your airplane by reducing the angle of attack.

  a)   Because the basic cause of a stall is always an excessive angle of attack, the cause must be eliminated by releasing the back elevator pressure that was necessary to attain that angle of attack or by moving the elevator control forward.

2)   Second, maximum allowable power should be promptly and smoothly applied to increase airspeed and to minimize the loss of altitude.

  a)   If carburetor heat is on, you need to turn it off.

3)   Third, straight-and-level flight should be established with coordinated use of the controls.

  a)   At this time, the wings should be leveled if they were previously banked.

  b)   Do not attempt to deflect the ailerons until the angle of attack has been reduced.

   i)   The adverse yaw caused by the downward aileron may place the airplane in uncoordinated flight, and if the airplane is still in a stalled condition, a spin could be induced.

2. **Spins**

    a. A spin is an aggravated stall that results in what is termed autorotation, in which the airplane follows a corkscrew path in a downward direction.

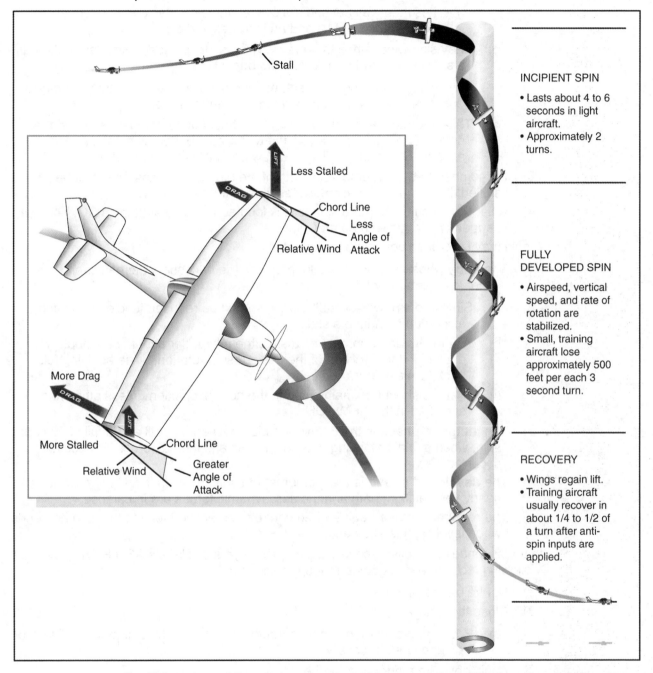

    1) If the nose of the airplane is allowed to yaw at the beginning of a stall, the wing will drop in the direction of the yaw.

        a) Unless rudder is applied to keep the nose from yawing, the airplane begins to slip toward the lowered wing.

        b) This causes the airplane to weathervane into the relative wind, i.e., toward the lowered wing, thus continuing the yaw.

2) At the same time, the airplane continues to roll toward the lowered wing.

    a) The lowered wing has an increasingly greater angle of attack due to the upward motion of the relative wind against its surfaces.

        i) It is then well beyond the critical angle of attack and suffers an extreme loss of lift and an increase in drag.

    b) The rising wing, since the relative wind is striking it at a smaller angle, has a smaller angle of attack than the opposite wing.

        i) The rising wing, in effect, becomes less stalled, and thus develops some lift, so that the airplane continues to roll.

    c) This autorotation, combined with the effects of centrifugal force and the different amounts of drag on the two wings, becomes a spin, and the airplane descends, rolling and yawing, until recovery is effected.

3) Remember that, in order to spin, both of the airplane's wings must first be stalled; then one wing becomes less stalled than the other.

4) A flat spin occurs when the spin axis is located near the airplane's CG. This can happen on aircraft with an aft CG.

b. A spin may be broken down into four phases:

1) The **entry phase** is when the pilot provides the necessary elements for the spin, either accidentally or intentionally.

    a) Similar to a power-off stall, power should be reduced to idle, then pitch increased to induce a stall.

    b) As the airplane approaches a stall, the full rudder should be smoothly applied in the direction of the desired spin rotation, while applying full back (up) elevator.

    c) Ailerons should be maintained in the neutral position unless otherwise specified in the AFM/POH.

2) The **incipient phase** is the transient period between a stall and a fully developed spin, when a final balancing of aerodynamic and inertial forces has not yet occurred.

3) The **developed phase** is that portion of the spin in which it is stabilized with a nearly vertical flight path and the aerodynamic forces are in balance.

4) The **recovery phase** begins when controls are applied to stop the spin and ends when level flight is attained.

c. In the absence of specific recovery techniques in your airplane's AFM/POH, the following technique is suggested for spin recovery:

1) Neutralize the ailerons.

2) Close the throttle.

    a) Power aggravates the spin characteristics and causes an abnormal loss of altitude in the recovery.

3) Apply opposite rudder to slow the rotation.

4) Apply positive forward elevator movement to break the stall.

    a) In some airplanes, opposite rudder and forward elevator may need to be held for some time before the spinning stops.

5) Neutralize the rudder as the spin rotation stops.

    a) Otherwise, excessive yaw can occur in the other direction, placing great strain on the airframe and potentially resulting in a secondary spin.

6) Return to level flight.

    a) Avoid excessive elevator back pressure, which could result in a secondary stall.

d.   It cannot be sufficiently stressed that the intentional spinning of an airplane for which spins are not specifically approved is prohibited and extremely dangerous.

1)   To be certified for spins in the normal and utility categories, an airplane must be recoverable from an incipient spin, not a fully developed spin (i.e., beyond one turn).

2)   The pilot of an airplane placarded against spins should assume that the airplane may become uncontrollable in a spin.

e.   Continued practice in stalls will help you develop a more instinctive and prompt reaction in recognizing an approaching spin.

1)   It is essential to learn to apply immediate corrective action any time it is apparent that the airplane is nearing spin conditions.

1.14 ANGLE OF ATTACK INDICATORS

1.   The FAA, along with the General Aviation Joint Steering Committee (GAJSC), is promoting the use of angle of attack (AOA) indicators as one of many safety initiatives aimed at reducing the general aviation accident rate.

a.   AOA indicators will specifically target loss of control (LOC) accidents.

b.   More than 25% of general aviation fatal accidents occur during the maneuvering phase of flight. Of those accidents, half involve stall/spin scenarios.

2.   AOA indicators improve pilot situational awareness by providing stall margin awareness.

a.   This is the margin that exists between the current AOA at which the airfoil is operating and the AOA at which the airfoil will stall (critical AOA).

b.   Speed by itself is not a reliable parameter to avoid a stall. An airplane can stall at any speed. AOA is a better parameter to use to avoid a stall because an airplane always stalls at the same critical AOA for a given aircraft configuration.

c.   The critical AOA does not change with weight, bank angle, temperature, density altitude, or center of gravity.

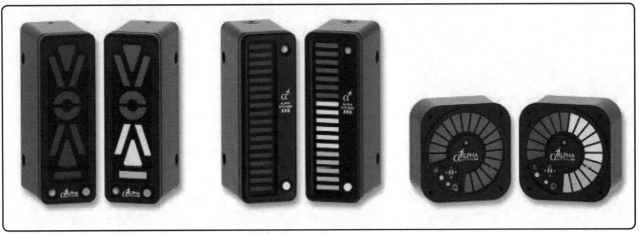

A Variety of AOA Indicators

d.   AOA indicators offer a visual representation of the energy management state of the airplane.

1)   The energy state of an airplane is the balance between airspeed, altitude, drag, and thrust and represents how efficiently the airfoil is operating.

2)   The more efficiently the airfoil operates, the larger the stall margin that is present.

e.   With this increased situational awareness pertaining to the energy condition of the airplane, pilots will have information needed to prevent a LOC scenario resulting from a stall or spin.

d.   It cannot be sufficiently stressed that the intentional spinning of an airplane for which spins are not specifically approved is prohibited and extremely dangerous.

   1)   To be certified for spins in the normal and utility categories, an airplane must be recoverable from an incipient spin, not a fully developed spin (i.e., beyond one turn).

   2)   The pilot of an airplane placarded against spins should assume that the airplane may become uncontrollable in a spin.

e.   Continued practice in stalls will help you develop a more instinctive and prompt reaction in recognizing an approaching spin.

   1)   It is essential to learn to apply immediate corrective action any time it is apparent that the airplane is nearing spin conditions.

1.14 ANGLE OF ATTACK INDICATORS

1.   The FAA, along with the General Aviation Joint Steering Committee (GAJSC), is promoting the use of angle of attack (AOA) indicators as one of many safety initiatives aimed at reducing the general aviation accident rate.

a.   AOA indicators will specifically target loss of control (LOC) accidents.

b.   More than 25% of general aviation fatal accidents occur during the maneuvering phase of flight. Of those accidents, half involve stall/spin scenarios.

2.   AOA indicators improve pilot situational awareness by providing stall margin awareness.

a.   This is the margin that exists between the current AOA at which the airfoil is operating and the AOA at which the airfoil will stall (critical AOA).

b.   Speed by itself is not a reliable parameter to avoid a stall. An airplane can stall at any speed. AOA is a better parameter to use to avoid a stall because an airplane always stalls at the same critical AOA for a given aircraft configuration.

c.   The critical AOA does not change with weight, bank angle, temperature, density altitude, or center of gravity.

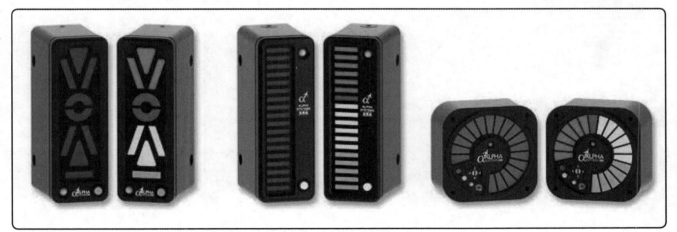

A Variety of AOA Indicators

d.   AOA indicators offer a visual representation of the energy management state of the airplane.

   1)   The energy state of an airplane is the balance between airspeed, altitude, drag, and thrust and represents how efficiently the airfoil is operating.

   2)   The more efficiently the airfoil operates, the larger the stall margin that is present.

e.   With this increased situational awareness pertaining to the energy condition of the airplane, pilots will have information needed to prevent a LOC scenario resulting from a stall or spin.

3. Limitations of AOA Devices

    a. Misunderstanding or misuse of the equipment can have disastrous results.

    b. Some items that may limit the effectiveness of an AOA indicator include

        1) Calibration techniques

        2) Probes or vanes not being heated

        3) The type of indicator itself

        4) Flap setting

        5) Wing contamination

    c. Pilots of general aviation airplanes equipped with AOA indicators should contact the manufacturer for specific limitations applicable to that installation.

    d. Pilots using AOA devices should have a comprehensive understanding of AOAs along with the specific operating characteristics and limitations of the AOA indicator installed in their aircraft.

END OF STUDY UNIT

STUDY UNIT TWO
AIRPLANE INSTRUMENTS, ENGINES, AND SYSTEMS

(60 pages of outline)

Study Unit 1, "Airplanes and Aerodynamics," explained the basic airframe and flight control surfaces. This study unit explains the airplane's systems. As you move upward to high-performance airplanes, you will probably pursue your commercial certificate. *Commercial Pilot Flight Maneuvers and Practical Test Prep* has a detailed discussion of operating high-performance airplanes.

2.1 PITOT-STATIC SYSTEM

1. The pitot-static system provides the source of atmospheric air pressure for operation of the

   a. Altimeter
   b. Vertical speed indicator
   c. Airspeed indicator

2. The two major parts of the pitot-static system are

   a. The pitot pressure chamber and lines
   b. The static pressure chamber and lines

3. The pitot pressure (also called the ram, impact, or total pressure) is taken from a pitot tube, which is normally mounted on or beneath the leading edge of the left wing (so it can be seen easily by the pilot, especially in icing conditions) and aligned with the relative wind.

   a. The pitot tube is mounted at a location that provides minimum disturbance or turbulence caused by the airflow around the airplane.
   b. The pitot line is connected only to the airspeed indicator.
   c. Some pitot tubes are equipped with an electric heating element to prevent ice from blocking the pitot tube.
   d. Pitot tubes also have a drain opening to remove water.

4.   The static pressure (pressure of the still air) is usually taken from the static line attached to a vent or vents mounted flush with the side of the fuselage.

    a.   In some airplanes, the static source is found on the back of the pitot tube.

    b.   The static pressure lines provide static air pressure to the altimeter, vertical speed indicator, and airspeed indicator.

5.   An alternate source for static pressure is provided in most airplanes in the event the static ports become clogged. This source is selected manually with a valve and usually is vented to the inside of the cockpit.

    a.   Because of the venturi effect of the flow of air around the cockpit, this alternate static pressure is usually lower than the pressure provided by the normal static air source.

        1)   Since the air flowing around the cockpit is accelerated, there is a lower pressure around the cockpit (similar to air flowing over a wing). The air pressure in the cockpit is then lower as well.

    b.   Because of this lower pressure, the following differences in the instrument indications usually occur when the alternate static source is used:

        1)   The altimeter may indicate a higher-than-actual altitude.

        2)   The vertical speed indicator will initially indicate a climb while in level flight, then return to a level indication.

        3)   The airspeed indicator will indicate a greater-than-actual airspeed.

6.   It is important that, during the visual inspection of your airplane, you check to ensure that none of the openings on the pitot tube and static vents are blocked.

    a.   If they are blocked, they should be cleared by a certificated maintenance technician.

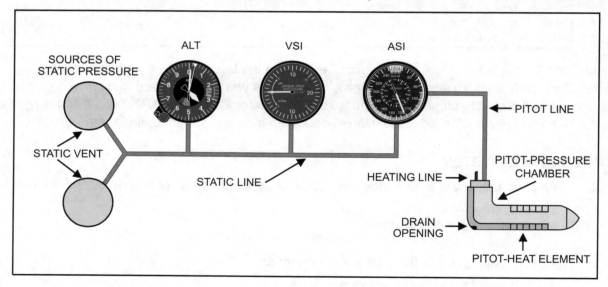

2.2 ALTIMETER

1. The altimeter (ALT) measures the height of the airplane above a given level. Since it is the only instrument that gives altitude information, the altimeter is one of the most important instruments in the airplane. Knowing the aircraft's altitude is vitally important to you for several reasons:

   a. You must be sure that the airplane is flying high enough to clear terrain or obstructions along the intended route.

   b. To reduce the possibility of a midair collision, you must maintain altitudes in accordance with air traffic rules.

   c. Altitudes are often selected to take advantage of favorable winds and weather conditions.

   d. You must know the altitude to calculate true airspeed.

2. **Principle of operation.** The pressure altimeter is simply an aneroid (mechanical) barometer that measures the pressure of the atmosphere at the altimeter's location to display an altitude indication in feet.

   a. The altimeter uses static pressure as its source of operation.

      1) Thus, altitude is determined in terms of air pressure.

   b. The basic component of the altimeter is the aneroid wafer.

      1) A stack of these wafers expands or contracts as atmospheric pressure changes and, through a shaft and gearing linkage, rotates the pointers on the dial of the altimeter.

   c. The presentation of altitude varies considerably among different types of altimeters. Some may have only one pointer (or hand), but most have three pointers.

      1) The altimeter below indicates an altitude of 14,500 ft.

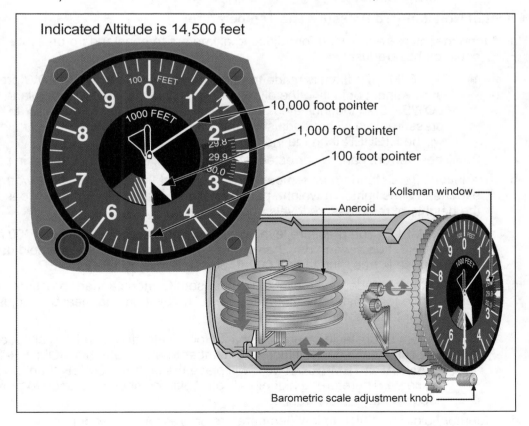

      2) Movement of the aneroid wafer element is transmitted through a gear train to the three pointers that sweep the calibrated dial to indicate the altitude.

         a) On the typical altimeter shown on the previous page, the shortest pointer indicates altitude in thousands of feet.

         b) The intermediate pointer indicates altitude in hundreds of feet. Note that the altimeter shown is subdivided into 20-ft. increments.

         c) The longest pointer indicates altitude in tens of thousands of feet.

  d. The altimeter is calibrated using the International Standard Atmosphere (ISA) table, which is a table of specific values (i.e., temperature, pressure, etc.) for each altitude. ISA values for temperature and pressure at sea level are 15°C (59°F) and 29.92 in. of mercury (Hg).

      1) Since actual atmospheric pressure continually changes, a means is provided to adjust the altimeter to compensate for nonstandard pressure.

         a) This adjustment is accomplished through a system by which the altimeter setting is set to a barometric scale located on the face of the altimeter.

         b) The area in which the altimeter setting is displayed is known as the Kollsman window.

      2) In the altimeter shown on the previous page, the altimeter setting knob is located on the lower-left corner of the instrument, and the barometric scale is located between the numerals 2 and 3.

         a) The altimeter on the previous page is set to 29.92 (in. of Hg), which is also 1,013.2 (hPa).

      3) The aneroid wafer in the altimeter expands to a definite size and causes the hands to indicate height above whatever pressure level is set into the altimeter setting window.

3. **Effect of Nonstandard Pressure and Temperature**

  a. If no means were provided for adjusting altimeters to nonstandard pressure, flight could be hazardous.

      1) EXAMPLE: If a flight is made from a HIGH pressure area to a LOW pressure area without adjusting the altimeter, the actual altitude of the airplane will be LOWER than the indicated altitude. If a flight is made from a LOW to a HIGH pressure area without adjusting the altimeter, the actual altitude of the airplane will be HIGHER than the indicated altitude.

      2) These errors can be corrected by setting the altimeter for changes in pressure.

  b. Variations from standard air temperature also affect the altimeter. On a warm day, the expanded air is lighter in weight, per unit volume, than on a cold day. Consequently, the heights of the pressure levels above the ground are raised.

      1) EXAMPLE: The pressure level at which the altimeter indicates 10,000 ft. will be HIGHER on a warm day than under standard conditions. On a cold day, the reverse is true, and the 10,000-ft. pressure level will be LOWER.

  c. The adjustment made by the pilot to compensate for nonstandard pressures does not compensate for nonstandard temperatures. The pilot has no means to adjust the altimeter for temperature.

      1) If terrain or obstacle clearance is a factor in selecting a cruising altitude, particularly at higher altitudes, remember to anticipate that COLDER-THAN-STANDARD TEMPERATURE will place the aircraft LOWER than the altimeter indicates. Therefore, a higher indicated altitude should be used to provide adequate terrain clearance.

  d. Memory aid: From high to low (temperature or pressure), look out below.

4. **Setting the altimeter.** To adjust the altimeter for variation in atmospheric pressure, adjust the pressure scale in the altimeter setting window (calibrated in inches of Hg) to correspond with the given altimeter setting.

    a. A flight service station (FSS) reporting the altimeter setting takes a measurement of its local atmospheric pressure hourly and corrects it to sea-level pressure. This altimeter setting is applicable only in the vicinity of the reporting station. Therefore, it is necessary to readjust the altimeter setting as the flight progresses.

    b. Federal Aviation Regulations (14 CFR) concerning altimeter settings

        1) The cruising altitude of an airplane below 18,000 ft. MSL shall be maintained by reference to an altimeter that is set to the current reported altimeter setting of a station located along the route of flight and within 100 NM of the airplane.

            a) If there is no such station, the current reported altimeter setting of an appropriate available station shall be used.

            b) In an airplane having no radio, the altimeter shall be set to the elevation of the departure airport or an appropriate altimeter setting available before departure.

        2) At or above 18,000 ft. MSL, the altimeter must be set to 29.92.

    c. Over high mountainous terrain, certain atmospheric conditions can cause the altimeter to indicate an altitude of 1,000 ft. or more HIGHER than the actual altitude.

        1) For this reason, a generous margin of altitude should be allowed.

        2) In addition, allow for possible downdrafts, which are particularly prevalent (and extremely dangerous) if high winds are encountered.

5. **Types of Altitude**

    a. **Absolute altitude** -- the vertical distance of the aircraft above the terrain. It is expressed as a number of feet AGL (above ground level).

    b. **True altitude** -- the vertical distance of the aircraft above sea level. It is expressed as a number of feet above MSL (mean sea level).

        1) Airport, terrain, and obstacle elevations found on aeronautical charts are given as true altitudes.

    c. **Indicated altitude** -- the altitude read directly from the altimeter after it is set to the local altimeter setting.

        1) While indicated altitude is referred to as the height above MSL (i.e., true altitude), it is only an approximate true altitude.

            a) Indicated altitude and true altitude are the same only when the atmospheric conditions and the ISA values are the same.

        2) Indicated altitude is used by all aircraft operating below 18,000 ft. MSL.

    d. **Pressure altitude** -- the altitude indicated on the altimeter when the altimeter setting window is adjusted to the ISA sea-level pressure of 29.92 in. of Hg.

        1) Pressure altitude is used when operating at or above 18,000 ft. MSL.

            a) Altitudes at and above 18,000 ft. MSL are called flight levels (FL).

                i) Delete the last two zeros to obtain the FL; i.e., 19,000 ft. MSL is FL 190.

        2) Pressure altitude is also used in airplane performance calculations.

e. **Density altitude** -- the pressure altitude corrected for nonstandard temperature variations.

   1) When the temperature is standard, pressure altitude and density altitude are the same.

   2) If the temperature is above standard, density altitude will be higher than pressure altitude. If the temperature is below standard, density altitude will be lower than pressure altitude.

   3) Knowledge of these factors is important because density altitude directly affects the airplane's performance.

2.3 VERTICAL SPEED INDICATOR

1. The vertical speed indicator (VSI) indicates whether the airplane is climbing, descending, or flying level. The rate of climb or descent is indicated in feet per minute (fpm). If properly calibrated, the indicator will register zero in level flight. In the figure below, the VSI indicates a climb at a rate of 1,000 fpm.

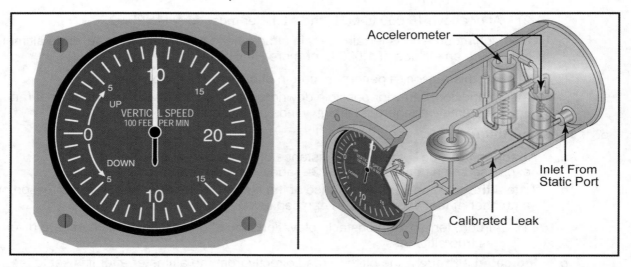

2. **Principle of operation.** Although the VSI operates solely from static pressure, it is a differential pressure instrument.

   a. The case of the instrument is airtight except for a restricted passage (also known as a calibrated leak) to the static line of the pitot-static system. The sealed case contains a diaphragm with connecting linkage and gearing to the indicator pointer. The diaphragm also receives air from the static line, but this is not a restricted passage.

   b. When the airplane is on the ground or in level flight, the pressures inside the diaphragm and the instrument case remain the same, and the pointer indicates zero.

   c. When the airplane climbs or descends, the pressure inside the diaphragm changes immediately. But the restricted passage causes the pressure of the rest of the case to remain higher or lower for a short time. This differential pressure causes the diaphragm to contract or expand. The movement of the diaphragm is indicated on the instrument needle as a climb or a descent.

2.4 AIRSPEED INDICATOR

1. The airspeed indicator indicates the speed at which the airplane is moving through the air.

   a. Airspeed must not be confused with groundspeed, which is the speed at which the airplane is moving across the ground.

2. **Principle of operation.** The airspeed indicator (ASI) is a differential air pressure instrument that measures the difference between the **total pressure** (measured from the pitot line) and static pressure. This difference is called **dynamic pressure**.

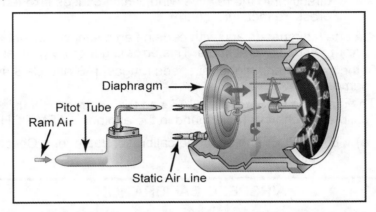

   a. To measure the dynamic pressure, the ASI is constructed as a sealed case in which a diaphragm is mounted.

      1) The pitot line (total pressure) is connected to one side of the diaphragm.
      2) The static line is connected to the other side of the diaphragm.

   b. As the airplane moves, total (or impact) pressure becomes greater than static pressure, causing the diaphragm to expand.

      1) Expansion or contraction of the diaphragm moves the indicator needle by means of gears and levers.

   c. The airspeed dial may be calibrated to convert dynamic pressure into units of knots (kt.), miles per hour (mph), or both.

   d. The ASI is calibrated to display an airspeed representative of a given dynamic pressure only at ISA sea-level values; thus, it does not reflect changes in density altitude.

3. **The Three Kinds of Airspeed Useful for Pilots**

   a. **Indicated airspeed (IAS)** is the direct instrument reading obtained from the ASI, uncorrected for variations in air density or installation and instrument errors.

      1) Your airplane's FAA-approved Airplane Flight Manual (AFM) and/or Pilot's Operating Handbook (POH) will list airspeed limitations and performance airspeeds based on IAS.
      2) The Federal Aviation Regulations and ATC will also use IAS for speed limitations.

b. **Calibrated airspeed (CAS)** is IAS corrected for installation and instrument errors.

1) Although manufacturers attempt to keep airspeed errors to a minimum, it is not possible to eliminate them along the entire airspeed operating range.

   a) Installation (position) error is caused by the static port(s) sensing erroneous static pressure. The slipstream flow causes disturbances at the static port(s) preventing true static pressure measurement.

   b) Also, at varying angles of attack, the pitot tube does not always point directly into the relative wind, which causes erroneous total (or impact) pressure measurement.

2) At certain airspeeds and with certain flap settings, the installation and instrument error may be several knots. This error is generally greatest at low airspeeds.

3) In the cruising and higher airspeed ranges, IAS and CAS are approximately the same.

4) To determine CAS, read the IAS and then correct it by using an airspeed calibration chart or table found in the airplane's AFM/POH.

   a) EXAMPLE: The airspeed calibration table for a Cessna 152 is shown below.

AIRSPEED CALIBRATION

CONDITIONS:
Power required for level flight or maximum rated RPM dive.

FLAPS UP

KIAS	40	50	60	70	80	90	100	110	120	130	140
KCAS	46	53	60	69	78	88	97	107	117	127	136

FLAPS 10°

KIAS	40	50	60	70	80	85	—	—	—	—	—
KCAS	44	52	61	70	80	84	—	—	—	—	—

FLAPS 30°

KIAS	40	50	60	70	80	85	—	—	—	—	—
KCAS	43	51	61	71	82	87	—	—	—	—	—

c. **True airspeed (TAS)** is CAS corrected for density altitude. TAS is the true speed of an airplane through the air.

1) Because air density decreases with an increase in altitude, the airplane must be flown faster at higher altitudes to cause the same dynamic pressure to be measured in the ASI.

   a) Therefore, for a given TAS, IAS decreases as altitude increases.

   b) For a given IAS, TAS increases with an altitude increase.

2) TAS can be determined by various methods.

   a) A flight computer can be used when CAS, outside air temperature (OAT), and pressure altitude are known.

   b) Some airspeed indicators (called true airspeed indicators) have this function built in. With an adjusting knob, pressure altitude is set opposite OAT in the window at the top of the instrument, as in the illustration below.

   i) The TAS is then read under the needle. On the airspeed indicator shown below, the IAS is 153 kt. (inner scale) or 168 mph (outer scale), and the TAS is approximately 198 mph.

   c) A cruise performance chart in the airplane's AFM/POH can be used to determine a planned, not actual, TAS.

   d) The following general rule may be used to approximate TAS: Add 2% to the IAS for each 1,000 ft. of altitude.

   i) EXAMPLE: Given IAS is 140 kt. and altitude is 6,000 ft., find TAS.

      Solution:

      2% × 6   = 12% (.12)
      140 × .12   = 16.8
      140 + 16.8   = 156.8 kt. (TAS)

4.   Most airplanes use a standard color code on airspeed indicators to highlight vital airspeed ranges.

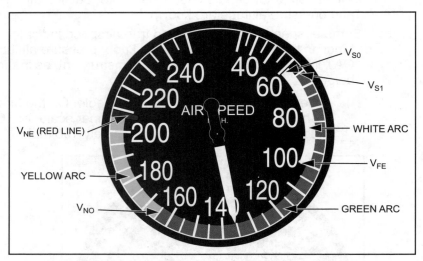

a.   The **white arc** represents the flap operating range.

   1)   The lower limit of the white arc is V_{S0}.

      a)   **V_{S0}** is the stalling speed or the minimum steady flight speed in the landing configuration.

      b)   In small airplanes, V_{S0} is the power-off stall speed in the landing configuration (i.e., flaps and landing gear down) at the maximum landing weight.

   2)   The upper limit of the white arc is V_{FE}.

      a)   **V_{FE}** is the maximum flap extended speed.

      b)   Operating with the flaps extended at higher airspeeds could result in severe strain or structural failure.

b.   The **green arc** represents the normal operating range.

   1)   The lower limit of the green arc is V_{S1}.

      a)   **V_{S1}** is the stalling speed or the minimum steady flight speed obtained in a specific configuration.

      b)   In small airplanes, V_{S1} is normally the power-off stall speed with the wing flaps and landing gear (if retractable) retracted at the maximum takeoff weight.

   2)   The upper limit of the green arc is V_{NO}.

      a)   **V_{NO}** is the maximum structural cruising speed.

      b)   You should not exceed V_{NO} except in smooth air and then only with caution.

c.   The **yellow arc** represents the caution range.

   1)   The lower limit of the yellow arc is V_{NO}, and the upper limit is V_{NE}.

   2)   You should fly at airspeeds within the yellow arc only in smooth air while using caution.

d.   The **red line** is V_{NE}.

   1)   **V_{NE}** is the never-exceed speed.

   2)   The never-exceed speed is the maximum speed at which the airplane can be operated safely and should never be exceeded intentionally.

   3)   Operating at airspeeds above V_{NE} could cause structural damage or failure.

5. **Other airspeed limitations.** Some other important airspeed limitations are not marked on the face of the airspeed indicator. These speeds are generally found on placards in view of the pilot and/or in the airplane's AFM/POH.

    a. **Design maneuvering speed (V_A)** is the speed below which you can move a flight control one time in smooth air to its full deflection, for one axis of airplane rotation only (pitch, roll, or yaw) without risk of damage to the airplane.

        1) It is the maximum speed at which an airplane may be stalled safely.

        2) Your airplane should be flown at or below this airspeed when rough air or severe turbulence is expected.

        3) V_A varies with the airplane's gross weight.

        4) Operating at or below design maneuvering speed does not provide structural protection against multiple full control inputs in one axis or full control inputs in more than one axis at the same time.

    b. **Landing gear operating speed (V_{LO})** is the maximum speed for extending or retracting the landing gear.

    c. **Best angle-of-climb speed (V_X)** is important when a short-field takeoff is required to clear an obstacle. It will allow the pilot to gain the most altitude in a given distance.

    d. **Best rate-of-climb speed (V_Y)** is the airspeed that will give the pilot the most altitude in a given period of time.

    e. **Best glide airspeed (V_{GLIDE})** is the airspeed that provides the best lift/drag (i.e., L/D_{MAX}) ratio angle of attack in a power-off glide. It will allow the airplane to glide the farthest.

    f. **Maximum continuous power speed (V_H)** is the maximum speed in level flight at maximum continuous power. For the sport pilot, an endorsement may be required depending on this speed.

6. The following list of performance speeds are for your review. These definitions, as well as the specific speeds for your airplane, need to be memorized. The letter V means velocity.

V_A	--	design maneuvering speed
V_{FE}	--	maximum flap extended speed
V_{GLIDE}	--	best glide speed
V_H	--	maximum continuous power speed
V_{LE}	--	maximum landing gear extended speed
V_{LO}	--	maximum landing gear operating speed
V_{NE}	--	never-exceed speed
V_{NO}	--	maximum structural cruising speed
V_R	--	rotation speed
V_{S0}	--	the power-off stalling speed or the minimum steady flight speed in the landing configuration (i.e., flaps and landing gear extended)
V_{S1}	--	the power-off stalling speed or the minimum steady flight speed obtained in a specified configuration (i.e., flaps and landing gear retracted)
V_X	--	speed for best angle of climb
V_Y	--	speed for best rate of climb

2.5 GYROSCOPIC FLIGHT INSTRUMENTS

1.   Several flight instruments contain gyroscopes that are used for their operation. These instruments are the turn indicator, the heading indicator, and the attitude indicator.

    a.   Gyroscopic instruments are operated by either a vacuum or an electrical system. In most light airplanes, the vacuum system powers the heading and attitude indicators, and the electrical system powers the turn indicator.

2.   **Vacuum system.** The vacuum or suction system spins the gyro by drawing a stream of air against the rotor vanes to spin the rotor at high speeds in essentially the same way as a water wheel or turbine operates. Normally, a vacuum pump is used to provide the vacuum required to spin the rotors. Some airplanes are equipped with a pressure pump that works in basically the same way except the air is pushed through the gyros rather than pulled through.

    a.   A typical vacuum system (illustrated below) consists of an engine-driven vacuum pump, a vacuum relief valve, an air filter, and tubing and manifolds necessary to complete the connections. A suction gauge on the airplane's instrument panel indicates the amount of vacuum in the system.

        1)   Some airplanes are equipped with a low-vacuum warning light to warn you of a possible low-vacuum condition. When the light is on, you should check the suction gauge and be prepared for erroneous readings on the vacuum-driven gyro instruments because the air flow is not spinning the gyros fast enough.

        2)   Some airplanes are also equipped with a standby vacuum system that is driven by the manifold induction system on the airplane engine.

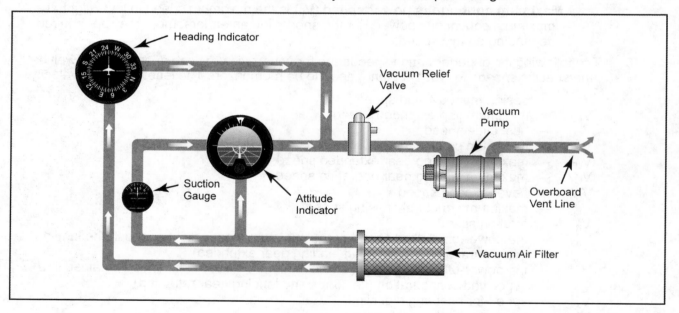

3. **Gyroscopic principles.** Any spinning object exhibits gyroscopic properties. A wheel designed and mounted to utilize these properties is called a gyroscope. The two fundamental properties of gyroscopic action are illustrated below: rigidity in space and precession.

    a. Rigidity in space can best be explained by applying Newton's First Law of Motion, which states: "A body at rest will remain at rest; or if in motion in a straight line, it will continue in a straight line unless acted upon by an outside force."

        1) An example of this law is the rotor of a universally (freely) mounted gyro. When the wheel is spinning, it exhibits the ability to remain in its original plane of rotation regardless of how the base is moved.

        2) The attitude indicator and the heading indicator use the gyroscopic property of rigidity for their operation. Therefore, their rotors must be universally mounted.

    b. Precession is the deflection of a spinning wheel when a deflective force is applied to its rim. The deflection is 90° ahead in the direction of rotation and in the direction of the applied force, as illustrated below.

        1) The rate at which the wheel precesses is directly proportional to the deflective force.

        2) The turn indicator uses the gyroscopic property of precession for its operation.

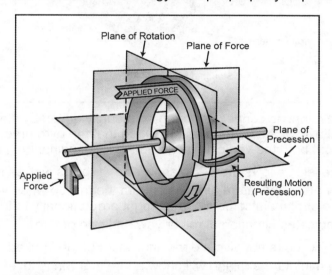

    c. Two important design characteristics of an instrument gyro are

        1) Great weight or high density for size
        2) Rotation at high speeds with low friction bearings

    d. The mountings of the gyro wheels are called "gimbals." They may be circular rings, rectangular frames, or a part of the instrument case itself (as in flight instruments).

2.6 TURN COORDINATOR

1. The turn coordinator (TC) is a type of turn indicator commonly used in airplanes to indicate rate and quality of turn and to serve as an emergency source of bank information if the attitude indicator fails.

    a. The TC is illustrated below.

    b. The TC is actually a combination of two instruments: a miniature airplane and an inclinometer (or ball).

        1) The miniature airplane is gyro-operated to show the rate of turn.

        2) The inclinometer reacts to gravity and/or centrifugal force to indicate the need for rudder to maintain coordinated flight.

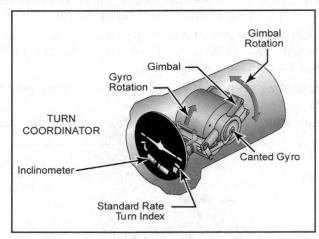

2. The miniature airplane is connected to a gyro (usually driven by electricity). Its design tilts the gimbal axis of the gyro up about 30° so that the gyro precesses in reaction to movement about both the vertical (yaw) and the longitudinal (roll) axes.

    a. This precession allows the TC to show rate of roll as well as rate of turn.

    b. Your view of the miniature airplane is from the tail, so when you roll to the right, the miniature airplane also banks to the right proportionally to the roll rate.

    c. The TC indicates direction of roll or yaw and rate of turn.

        1) The TC does not give a direct indication of the banked attitude of the airplane.

        2) The miniature airplane will show a turn in a wings-level yaw or during a turn while taxiing.

    d. For any given airspeed, a specific angle of bank is necessary to maintain a coordinated turn at a given rate. The faster the airspeed, the greater the angle of bank required to obtain a desired rate of turn.

    e. Standard-rate turn

        1) When the turn needle points to one of the small side marks, it indicates that the airplane is turning at a rate of 3° per sec.

        2) A rate of 3° per sec. is considered a standard-rate turn, and completing 360° of turn requires 2 min.

3.   The inclinometer of the TC consists of a sealed, curved glass tube containing kerosene and a ball which is free to move inside the tube. The fluid provides a dampening action, which ensures smooth and easy movement of the ball.

   a.   The tube is curved so that the ball tends to seek the lowest point, which is the center of the tube during coordinated flight. Two reference markers aid in determining when the ball is in the center.

   b.   During a coordinated turn, turning forces are balanced, causing the ball to remain centered in the tube. See the center TC in the diagram below.

   c.   If turning forces are unbalanced, i.e., if improper rudder is used, the ball moves away from the center of the tube in the direction of the excessive force.

      1)   In a skid, the rate of turn is too great for the angle of bank, and excessive centrifugal force moves the ball to the outside of the turn. See the left TC in the diagram below.

         a)   To achieve coordinated flight from a skid, you should increase the bank angle, reduce the rate of turn by reducing the rudder force to center the ball, or use a combination of both.

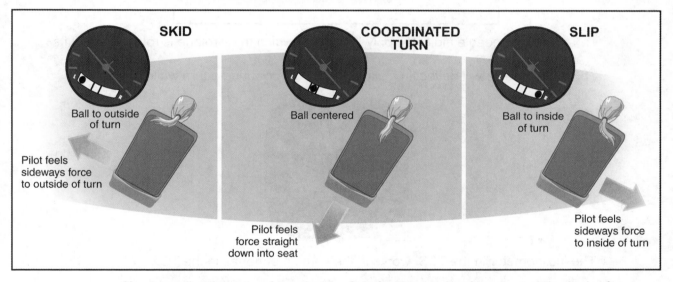

      2)   In a slip, the rate of turn is too slow for the angle of bank, and the lack of centrifugal force moves the ball to the inside of the turn. See the TC on the right in the diagram above.

         a)   To achieve coordinated flight from a slip, you should decrease the bank angle, increase the rate of turn by applying rudder pressure to center the ball, or use a combination of both.

      3)   Remember: In slips, you have used too little rudder (or opposite rudder). In skids, you have used too much rudder.

         a)   In all cases, apply rudder pressure on the side that the ball is exposed; i.e., step on the ball.

   d.   The ball then is a visual aid to determine coordinated use of the aileron and rudder control. During a turn, it indicates the quality of the turn, i.e., whether the airplane has the correct rate of turn for the angle of bank.

2.7 TURN-AND-SLIP INDICATOR

1. The turn-and-slip indicator (T&SI) is another type of turn indicator used in some older airplanes. The T&SI has a needle instead of a miniature airplane and indicates movement only around the vertical (yaw) axis, not the longitudinal (roll) axis.

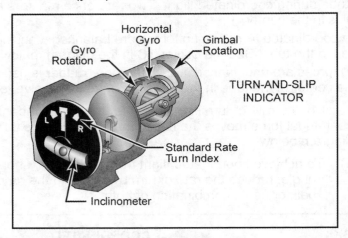

a. The turn needle indicates only the rate at which the airplane is rotating about its vertical axis.
b. The needle will deflect in a wings-level yaw or during a turn while taxiing.

2. The inclinometer in the T&SI works in the same manner as in the TC.

2.8 ATTITUDE INDICATOR

1. The attitude indicator (AI), with its miniature aircraft and horizon bar, depicts the attitude of the airplane.

   a. The relationship of the miniature airplane to the horizon bar is the same as the relationship of the real airplane to the actual horizon.

   b. The instrument gives an instantaneous indication of even the smallest changes in attitude.

   c. In most light airplanes, the AI is powered by the vacuum system.

2. The gyro in the attitude indicator is mounted on a horizontal plane and depends upon rigidity in space for its operation. The horizon bar is fixed to the gyro. It remains in a horizontal plane as the airplane is pitched or banked about its lateral or longitudinal axis. The dial (banking scale) indicates the bank angle.

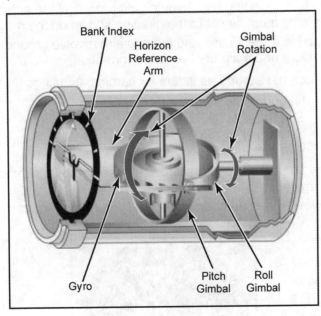

3. An adjustment knob is provided with which you may move the miniature airplane up or down to align it with the horizon bar to suit your line of vision. Normally, it is adjusted so that the wings overlap the horizon bar during straight-and-level cruising flight.

4. The AI is highly reliable and the most realistic flight instrument on the instrument panel. Its indications are very close approximations of the actual attitude of the airplane.

   a. It must be referred to often during flight into areas of restricted visibility or at any time when the actual horizon is not visible.

2.9 HEADING INDICATOR

1.   The heading indicator (HI) is a gyroscopic instrument commonly used in light airplanes as the primary source of heading information.

    a.   Errors in the magnetic compass are numerous, making straight flight and precision turns to headings difficult, particularly in turbulent air.

    b.   The HI is not affected by the forces that make the magnetic compass difficult to interpret.

    c.   In most light airplanes, the HI is powered by the vacuum system.

2.   Operation of the HI depends upon the gyroscopic principle of rigidity in space.

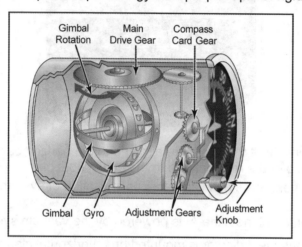

    a.   The rotor turns in a vertical plane. Fixed to the rotor is a compass card.

    b.   Since the rotor remains rigid in space, the points on the card hold the same position in space relative to the vertical plane.

    c.   Once the HI is operating (i.e., minutes after the airplane engine is started), the compass card must be set to the heading shown on the magnetic compass.

    d.   As both the instrument case and the airplane revolve around the vertical axis, the card provides clear and accurate heading information.

        1)   The compass card has letters for cardinal headings (N, E, S, W).

            a)   N represents heading 360° or 0°.
            b)   E represents 90°.
            c)   S represents 180°.
            d)   W represents 270°.

        2)   Each 30° interval of direction is represented by a number, the last zero of which is omitted.

        3)   Between these numbers, the card is graduated for each 5°.

3. Because of precession, caused chiefly by bearing friction or improper vacuum pressure, the HI may creep or drift from a heading to which it is set.

    a. Among other factors, the amount of drift depends largely upon the condition of the instrument. If the bearings are worn, dirty, or improperly lubricated, drift may be excessive.

    b. The HI should be compared to the magnetic compass every 15 min. for accuracy.

        1) This comparison can be done accurately only when the airplane is in straight, level, and unaccelerated flight.

4. The bank and pitch limits of the HI vary with the particular design and make of instrument.

    a. Some heading indicators found in light airplanes have limits of approximately 55° of pitch and 55° of bank.

        1) When either of these attitude limits is exceeded, the precessional force causes the instrument to tumble or spill, which causes the heading card to spin rapidly, and the instrument no longer gives the correct indication until reset.

        2) After spilling, the HI may be reset with the adjustment knob at the edge of the instrument.

    b. Other heading indicators are designed not to tumble.

2.10 MAGNETIC COMPASS

1. The magnetic compass (the only self-contained direction-seeking instrument in the airplane) is used primarily to set the heading indicator prior to flight and to verify its continued accuracy during flight. It contains two steel magnetized needles fastened to a float around the edge of which is mounted a compass card.

    a. The needles are parallel, with their north-seeking ends pointed in the same direction.

    b. One segment at a time of the floating compass card shows through the face of the instrument.

        1) The compass card has letters for cardinal headings (N, E, S, W).

        2) Each 30° interval of direction is represented by a number, the last zero of which is omitted. For example, 30° would appear as a 3 and 300° would appear as 30.

        3) Between these numbers, the card is graduated for each 5°.

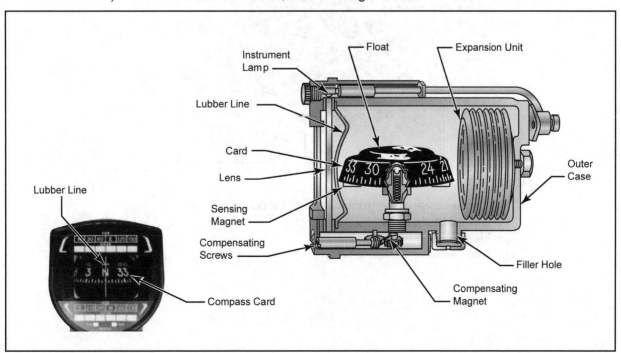

c. The float assembly, consisting of the magnetized needles, compass card, and float, is mounted on a pedestal and sealed in a chamber filled with white kerosene.

   1) This fluid decreases oscillations and lubricates the pivot point on the pedestal, and, due to buoyancy, part of the weight of the card is taken off the pivot that supports the card.

   2) The pedestal is the mount for the float assembly. The float assembly is balanced on the pivot, which allows free rotation of the card and allows it to tilt at an angle of up to 18°.

d. At the rear of the compass bowl, a diaphragm is installed to allow for any expansion or contraction of the liquid, thus preventing the formation of bubbles or possible bursting of the case.

e. A glass face is on one side of the compass, and mounted behind the glass is a lubber (reference) line by which compass indications are read.

2.11 COMPASS ERRORS

1. In order to use the magnetic compass effectively, a pilot must understand some basic properties of magnetism, their effect on the instrument, and the errors they produce.

   a. A magnet is a piece of metal that has the property of attracting another metal.

      1) The force of attraction is greatest at the poles (or points near each end of the magnet), and the least attraction is in the area halfway between the two poles.

   b. Lines of force flow from each end of these poles in all directions, bending around and flowing toward the other poles to form a magnetic field.

      1) Such a magnetic field surrounds the Earth, with the lines of force oriented approximately to the north and south magnetic poles.

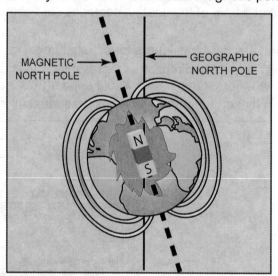

   c. Compass errors include

      1) Magnetic variation (technically not a compass error)
      2) Compass deviation
      3) Magnetic dip
      4) Compass card oscillation

2. **Magnetic variation** is the angular difference between true and magnetic north.

    a. Although the magnetic field of the Earth lies roughly north and south, the Earth's magnetic poles do not coincide with its geographic poles, which are used in the construction of aeronautical charts.

        1) At most places on the Earth's surface, the needles of a magnetic compass will not point to True North. They point to Magnetic North.
        2) Furthermore, local magnetic fields from mineral deposits and other conditions may distort the Earth's magnetic field and cause an additional error with reference to True North.

    b. Lines of equal magnetic variations are called isogonic lines and are plotted in degrees of east and west variation on aeronautical charts.

        1) A line connecting points of zero variation is called an **agonic line**.
        2) These lines are replotted periodically on aeronautical charts to correct any change that may have occurred as a result of the shifting of the poles or any changes caused by local magnetic disturbances.

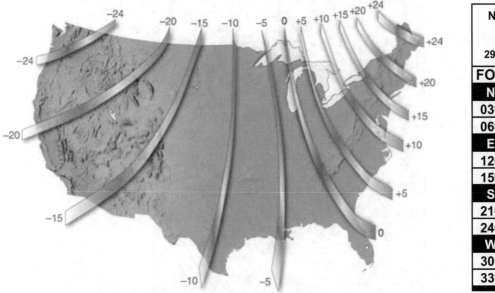

N201BZ	
DATE	
29 Aug '09	
FOR	STR
N	002
030	030
060	059
E	086
120	116
150	148
S	182
210	214
240	244
W	274
300	302
330	331

3. **Compass deviation** is the difference between the heading indicated by a magnetic compass in an airplane and the airplane's actual magnetic heading. The values for compass deviation are determined for every 30° of heading and are shown on a compass calibration card, such as the one shown above.

    a. The compass needles are affected not only by the Earth's magnetic field but also by magnetic fields generated when an airplane's electrical equipment is operated and by metal components in the airplane.

        1) These magnetic disturbances within the airplane (deviation) may deflect the needles slightly from alignment with Magnetic North.

    b. If an airplane changes heading, the compass' direction-sensitive, magnetized needles may continue to point in about the same direction while the airplane turns. As the airplane turns, metallic and electrical equipment in the airplane changes its position relative to the steel needles. As this happens, the equipment's influence on the compass needle changes, and compass deviation changes.

        1) Thus, deviation depends in part on the heading of the airplane and also on the electrical components in use.

c.   To reduce compass deviation error, each compass is checked and compensated periodically by adjustment.

1)   The errors remaining after "swinging" the compass are recorded on a compass correction card mounted in the airplane near the magnetic compass.

2)   To fly compass headings, you will need to refer to the compass correction card for corrected headings to steer.

4.   **Magnetic dip** is the tendency of the compass needles to point down as well as to the magnetic pole. The resultant error is known as dip error, greatest at the poles and zero at the magnetic equator.

a.   Note in the figure below how lines of force in the Earth's magnetic field are parallel to the Earth's surface at the magnetic equator and curve increasingly downward closer to the magnetic poles.

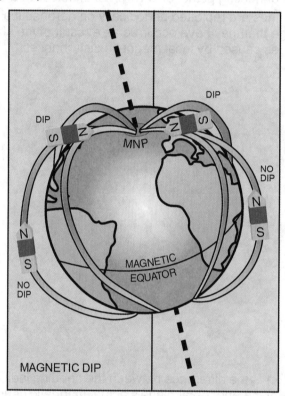

MAGNETIC DIP

1)   A magnetic needle will tend to assume the same direction and position as the line of force. Thus, the needle will be parallel with the Earth's surface at the magnetic equator but will point increasingly downward as it is moved closer to the magnetic pole.

b.   Since the compass card is designed to respond only to the horizontal plane of the Earth's magnetic field, it turns freely only in the horizontal plane. Any movement of the card from the horizontal results in dip errors.

c.   Discussion of these magnetic dip errors is limited to the Northern Hemisphere; the errors are reversed in the Southern Hemisphere.

1)   **Northerly and southerly turning error** is the most pronounced of the dip errors.

a)   Due to the mounting of the magnetic compass, when the airplane is banked, the card is also banked as a result of centrifugal force.

i)   While the card is in the banked attitude, the vertical component of the Earth's magnetic field causes the north-seeking ends of the compass to dip to the low side of the turn, giving an erroneous turn indication.

ii) This error is most apparent on headings of north and south.

b) If an airplane on a northerly heading turns east or west, the initial indication of the compass lags or indicates a turn in the opposite direction. This lag diminishes as the turn progresses toward east or west where there is no turning error.

c) If an airplane on a southerly heading turns toward the east or west, the initial indication of the compass needle will show a greater amount of turn than is actually made. This lead also diminishes as the turn progresses toward east or west.

d) If a turn is made to a northerly heading from any direction, the compass indication will lag behind the turn at northerly headings. Therefore, the rollout of the turn would be indicated before the desired heading is actually reached.

   i) Memory aid: **U**nder **S**hoot **N**orth

e) If a turn is made to a southerly heading from any direction, the compass indication will lead or be ahead of the turn at southerly headings. Therefore, the rollout would be indicated after the desired heading is actually passed.

   i) Memory aid: **O**ver **S**hoot **S**outh

f) The amount of lead or lag to be used when turning to northerly or southerly headings varies with, and is approximately equal to, the latitude of the locality over which the turn is being made.

   i) When turning to a heading of north, include the number of degrees of latitude in the lead for rollout, plus the lead normally used in recovery from turns.

   ii) When turning to a heading of south, maintain the turn until the compass passes south by the number of degrees of latitude, minus the normal roll-out lead.

g) When on an easterly or westerly heading, you will not notice an error while entering a turn to the north or south. The errors in d) and e) above become evident only after you are well into the turn.

2) **Acceleration error** is also due to the dip of the Earth's magnetic field.

   a) Due to the pendulous-type mounting, the aft end of the compass card is tilted upward when accelerating and downward when decelerating during changes of airspeed.

   i) This deflection of the compass card from the horizontal results in an error that is most apparent on headings of east and west only.

   b) When accelerating on either an east or a west heading, the error will cause the compass to indicate a turn toward north.

   c) When decelerating on either an east or a west heading, the error will cause the compass to indicate a turn toward south.

   d) Memory aid: **ANDS** means **A**cceleration -- **N**orth/**D**eceleration -- **S**outh.

5. **Compass card oscillation** error results from erratic movement of the compass card, which may be caused by turbulence or rough control technique.

   a. During oscillation, the compass is affected by all the factors previously discussed.

2.12 GLASS COCKPIT INSTRUMENTATION

1. It is now very common in general aviation airplanes to find glass cockpit instrumentation and automation of basic flight indications.

   a. All major aircraft manufacturers now have a full glass cockpit as standard or optional equipment.

   b. A **glass cockpit** is a system of electronic flight displays (EFDs) and associated components that display information, such as

      1) Aircraft flight attitude and direction
      2) Location via a moving map
      3) Pertinent engine information

   c. **Integrated avionics systems** take glass cockpits one step further by pairing them with communication and navigation radios, transponders, autopilots, weather and traffic display systems, and even cabin controls.

   d. These systems are designed to decrease pilot workload, enhance situational awareness, and increase the safety margin.

2. While all glass cockpit systems are slightly different, they almost always contain two central components.

   a. **Primary Flight Display (PFD)**

      1) The PFD usually consists of the 6 basic flight instruments (displayed electronically).

      2) Navigational instruction can also be displayed.

      3) Various insets of traffic, terrain, and moving map information can be selected.

      4) The image below describes how the basic flight instruments are represented on a PFD.

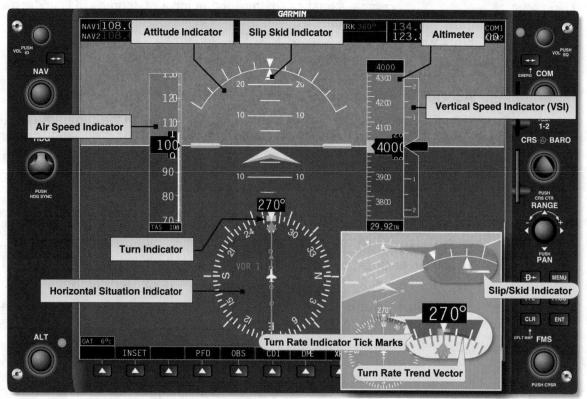

b. **Multi-Function Display (MFD)**

1) The MFD usually includes a large moving map (several map pages may be available) and engine instrumentation. With some installations, it is used as a backup for the PFD.

2) The MFD can usually interface with (display) weather radar, traffic avoidance systems, terrain warning systems, and various forms of navigational charts and/or instrument approach plates.

3) A typical MFD presentation is shown below.

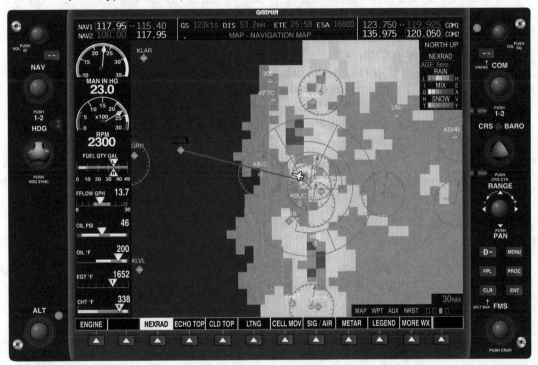

3. Glass cockpit systems get their display information from electronic sources instead of traditional pitot-static and vacuum systems. This increases the internal, error-monitoring capability of the units while making them more reliable and reducing maintenance.

a. An **Attitude and Heading Reference System (AHRS)** provides information typically given by gyroscopic instruments, such as

1) Attitude (pitch/bank) information
2) Heading
3) Rate of turn
4) Turn coordination

b. An **Air Data Computer (ADC)** provides information typically given by pitot-static instruments, such as

1) Airspeed
2) Altitude
3) Vertical speed

c. These devices are typically referred to as **Line Replaceable Units (LRUs)** because of their stand-alone nature and the ease with which they can be replaced.

4. Glass cockpit systems can reduce pilot workload and increase situational awareness.

a. Complete system knowledge is essential to be able to use it effectively.

1) Pilots with incomplete knowledge of advanced avionics systems will find that their workload is actually increased and their attention is shifted from flying the airplane.

2) This is fundamentally dangerous and must be avoided by thorough initial and recurrent systems training.

b.   The PFD presents all necessary flight information in one central location with trend displays, so the pilot is not only aware of what is happening with the airplane at any given time but also what will happen in the immediate future.

c.   The MFD provides the pilot with the "big picture," greatly increasing situational awareness.

1)   From the MFD you can monitor nearest airports, wind drift, terrain and landmarks, and weather and traffic information (if equipped).

5.   Glass cockpit systems increase safety through internal, automatic error-monitoring and alerting systems.

a.   A typical glass cockpit system will alert a pilot if any operational tolerance is exceeded in any system component.

b.   In the case of a PFD or MFD failure, information from both displays can be shown on a single screen, called **reversionary mode**.

c.   Troubleshooting a malfunctioning glass cockpit system is as easy as plugging a computer into the system, determining the error code, and replacing the malfunctioning unit.

1)   Failures in glass cockpit systems are very rare, but they do happen.

2)   Time between errors in glass cockpit systems are measured in thousands of hours rather than hundreds of hours for traditional instrumentation systems.

2.13 AIRPLANE ENGINES

1.   Since the engine develops the power to give the airplane its forward motion, thus enabling it to fly, you should have a basic knowledge of how an engine works and how to control its power.

a.   Knowledge of a few general principles of engine operation will help you obtain increased dependability and efficiency from the engine and, in many instances, will help you avoid engine failure.

b.   The airplane's AFM/POH should be consulted for specific operation and limitations of an airplane's engine.

2.   The engine is commonly referred to as the **powerplant**.

a.   Not only does the engine provide power to propel the airplane, but it powers the units which furnish electrical, hydraulic, and pneumatic energy for operation of electric motors, pumps, controls, lights, radios, instruments, retractable landing gear, and flaps.

1)   In many cases, the engine also provides heat for crewmembers' and passengers' comfort and for deicing equipment.

b.   In view of these varied functions, it is properly referred to as an engine or powerplant rather than as a motor.

3.   Most light training-type airplane engines are of the internal combustion, reciprocating type, which operate on the same principle as automobile engines.

a.   Internal combustion is the process by which a mixture of fuel and air is burned in a chamber from which the power can be taken directly.

b.   In a reciprocating engine, pressures from burning and expanding gases cause a piston to move up and down in an enclosed cylinder.

1)   This reciprocating motion of the piston is transferred through a connecting rod into rotary motion of a crankshaft that is attached directly or geared to a propeller.

4.   Reciprocating engines can be further classified by the manner in which the fuel is introduced into the cylinder.

    a.   In training-type airplanes, the usual method is by carburetion, a process of atomizing, vaporizing, and mixing fuel with air in a unit called a carburetor before the mixture enters the engine's cylinders.

        1)   The mixture of fuel and air is then drawn into each of the cylinders by the moving pistons or is forced under pressure into the cylinders by a turbocharger or supercharger.

    b.   The other method of supplying the combustible fuel is by fuel injection, whereby the fuel is injected under pressure by a pump directly into the cylinders (or just prior to the cylinders in some systems) where it vaporizes and mixes with air.

    c.   These methods are discussed in more detail in Subunit 2.16.

5.   The propeller, which uses the engine power to produce thrust, is discussed in Subunit 2.20.

6.   The basic parts of a reciprocating engine are the crankcase, cylinders, pistons, connecting rods, valves, spark plugs, and crankshaft, as shown below.

    a.   In the head or top of each cylinder are two valves and two spark plugs.

        1)   One of these valves opens and closes a passage leading from the carburetor (or induction manifold) and is called the intake valve.

        2)   The other opens and closes a passage leading to the outside (or exhaust manifold) and is called the exhaust valve.

    b.   Inside each cylinder is a movable piston that is attached to a crankshaft by means of a connecting rod.

        1)   When the rapidly expanding gases (resulting from the heat of combustion of the fuel/air mixture ignited by spark plugs) push the piston down within the cylinder, it causes the crankshaft to rotate.

        2)   At the same time, pistons in the other cylinders and attached to the same crankshaft are moved within their individual cylinders by the rotation of the crankshaft and go through exactly the same sequence or cycle.

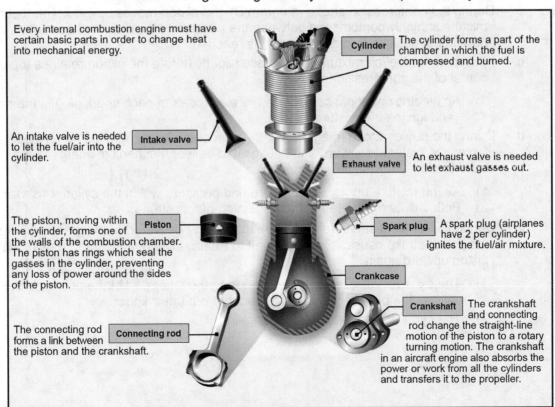

Every internal combustion engine must have certain basic parts in order to change heat into mechanical energy.

Cylinder — The cylinder forms a part of the chamber in which the fuel is compressed and burned.

An intake valve is needed to let the fuel/air into the cylinder. — **Intake valve**

Exhaust valve — An exhaust valve is needed to let exhaust gasses out.

The piston, moving within the cylinder, forms one of the walls of the combustion chamber. The piston has rings which seal the gasses in the cylinder, preventing any loss of power around the sides of the piston. — **Piston**

Spark plug — A spark plug (airplanes have 2 per cylinder) ignites the fuel/air mixture.

Crankcase

Crankshaft — The crankshaft and connecting rod change the straight-line motion of the piston to a rotary turning motion. The crankshaft in an aircraft engine also absorbs the power or work from all the cylinders and transfers it to the propeller.

The connecting rod forms a link between the piston and the crankshaft. — **Connecting rod**

2.14 HOW AN ENGINE OPERATES

1.   The series of operations or events through which each cylinder of a reciprocating engine must pass in order to operate continuously and deliver power is called an **engine cycle**.

   a.   For the engine to complete one cycle, the piston must complete four strokes, requiring two revolutions of the crankshaft.

   1)   The four strokes are the intake, compression, power, and exhaust.

   b.   Ignition of the fuel/air mixture at the end of the compression stroke adds a fifth event; thus, the engine cycle is known as the four-stroke, five-event cycle.

2.   The following describes one cycle of engine operation:

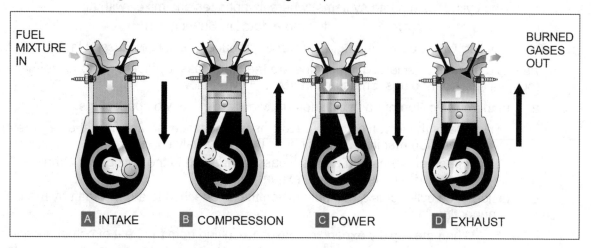

3.   a.   During the intake stroke (diagram A), the piston moves downward, the exhaust valve is closed, and the intake valve is open, drawing the fuel/air mixture into the cylinder.

   1)   When the piston approaches the lower limit of its downward stroke, the intake valve closes and traps the fuel/air mixture within the cylinder.

   b.   During the compression stroke (diagram B), the piston moves upward. The fuel/air mixture is highly compressed between the piston and the cylinder head when the uppermost position (top dead center) is reached.

   c.   Ignition of the fuel/air mixture takes place slightly before the piston reaches top dead center of the compression stroke.

   1)   An electric spark passes across the electrodes of each spark plug in the cylinder and ignites the mixture.

   d.   During the power stroke (diagram C), the gaseous mixture, expanding as it burns, forces the piston downward and causes it to deliver mechanical energy to the crankshaft.

   1)   As the mixture burns, temperature and pressure within the cylinder rise rapidly.
   2)   Both valves are closed at the beginning of this stroke.

   e.   During the exhaust stroke (diagram D), the energy delivered to the crankshaft during the power stroke causes the crankshaft to rotate on its bearings and thus move the piston upward again.

   1)   The exhaust valve, which opened during the latter part of the power stroke, allows the burned gases to be ejected from the cylinder.
   2)   The cycle is then ready to begin again.

3. Airplane engines normally have four or more cylinders. Each individual cylinder has its own four-stroke cycle, but all cylinders do not pass through the sequence of events simultaneously.

    a. While one cylinder is operating on the power stroke, others are passing through the compression, exhaust, or intake strokes.

        1) The strokes are accurately timed to occur in the correct sequence and at the right instant.

    b. This arrangement provides a steady flow of power.

4. In order to start the engine initially, the crankshaft must be rotated by an outside power source until the ignition and power events take place.

    a. This rotation is generally accomplished by an electric starter motor that is geared to the crankshaft.

2.15 IGNITION SYSTEM

1. The function of the ignition system is to provide an electrical spark to ignite the fuel/air mixture in the cylinders.

2. The ignition system of the engine is completely separate from the airplane's electrical system.

    a. The magneto-type ignition system is used on most reciprocating airplane engines.

3. A magneto is a self-contained, engine-driven unit that uses a rotating magnet inside a coil of wire to produce an electrical current. Additionally, the magneto has the systems necessary to increase the voltage of the electrical current to a sufficient level for the electrical current to arc across the gap of a spark plug and to distribute this electrical current to the proper spark plug at the proper time.

    a. The term "engine-driven" means that the magneto is geared to the crankshaft of the engine. Thus, the magnet will rotate only when the crankshaft is rotating.

    b. During engine start, the airplane's battery supplies power to the electric starter, which rotates the crankshaft, thus allowing the magnetos to produce the sparks for the ignition of the fuel in each cylinder.

    c. After the engine starts, the starter system is disengaged and the battery no longer contributes to the actual operation of the ignition system.

4. Airplane engines are equipped with a dual magneto ignition system, i.e., a left magneto and a right magneto.

    a. Each cylinder has two spark plugs. One magneto supplies the current to one set of plugs; the second magneto supplies the current to the other set of plugs.

b.   The ignition switch normally has five positions (from left to right): OFF, R, L, BOTH, and START.

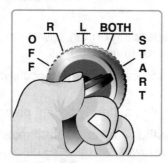

1)   The START position activates the electric starter to start the engine. You must hold the key in the START position until the engine starts. Then, after you release the key, a spring will automatically return the key to the BOTH position.

2)   In the BOTH position, both magnetos are supplying electrical current; thus, both spark plugs in each cylinder are firing.

3)   In the L (left magneto) or R (right magneto) position, only the selected magneto is supplying current; thus, only one of the spark plugs in each cylinder is firing.

4)   In the OFF position, the magnetos are grounded; i.e., the electrical current flows along a wire that is attached to the airplane structure. Grounding a magneto does not allow it to supply current to the spark plugs.

a)   If the ground is broken or disconnected, the magneto will supply current to the spark plugs even with the ignition switch OFF.

c.   The main advantages of the dual ignition system are

1)   Increased safety. If one magneto fails, the engine may be operated on the other magneto until landing.

2)   Improved engine performance. The use of two spark plugs in each cylinder allows for more complete and even combustion of the mixture because the fuel mixture will be ignited on each side of the combustion chamber and burn toward the center.

5.   It is important to leave the ignition switch on BOTH for flight and to turn it completely OFF after shutting down the engine.

a.   The entire purpose of the dual system is defeated when the switch is left on L or R, and the engine's performance is greatly affected.

b.   Even with the electrical master switch OFF, if the ignition switch is on either BOTH or L or R magnetos, the engine could fire if the propeller is moved from outside the airplane.

1)   Also, if the magneto switch ground wire is disconnected, the magneto is ON even when the ignition switch is in the OFF position.

6.   Even though most airplanes are equipped with electric starters, you should know the procedures and dangers involved in hand propping.

a.   It is recommended that a competent pilot, or a qualified person thoroughly familiar with the operation of all the controls, be seated at the controls in the cockpit and that the person turning the propeller be thoroughly familiar with this technique.

b. The traditional approach with the person "pulling through" the propeller in front of the propeller follows:

1) To start the plane, the propeller is rotated in the clockwise direction (as seen from the cockpit).

2) Never lean into the propeller as you pull it. You must not be in a position that would cause you to fall forward if your feet slip. You should have one foot forward and one foot back. As you pull down, you should shift your weight to your rear foot and back away.

3) You should not wrap your fingers around the propeller. You should have your fingers just over the trailing edge to prevent injury if the engine misfires (or backfires) and turns backward.

   a) Before pulling the propeller through slowly so the engine sucks gas into the cylinders, the person pulling the propeller should shout, "Brakes on, mag (magneto, i.e., ignition) off." The pilot inside the plane should confirm by repeating, "Brakes on, mag off." However, the person pulling the propeller should always assume the mag switch is on. That is, (s)he should always be in a safe position relative to the propeller and keep the area clear.

   b) Before moving the propeller, the pilot outside should check the brakes by pushing on the propeller blades near the spinner to see that the airplane cannot be pushed backward.

   c) After the propeller is pulled through a few times, it should be positioned with the left side (when facing the airplane from the front) at the 10 to 11 o'clock position. This position will facilitate spinning the propeller by pulling down against the engine's compression.

   d) When the person on the propeller is ready to attempt starting and the propeller (left blade when facing the nose of the plane) is at 10 to 11 o'clock, the person on the propeller should shout, "Brakes on, throttle cracked, mag on." The pilot in the plane should make the required adjustments and repeat, "Brakes on, throttle cracked, mag on."

      i) Note that some pilots prefer to use the term "contact" rather than "mag on."

   e) After checking to see that the brakes are on (by pushing the propeller blades close to the spinner), the person on the propeller should then spin the propeller as hard as possible by pulling down on the left blade. (S)he should stand on firm ground close enough to the propeller to be able to step away easily. As the propeller is pulled through, (s)he should step back from the propeller to avoid being hit as the engine starts.

4) If you are starting the engine by yourself, you should stand behind the propeller on the right side when facing the direction the airplane is facing. This position will permit you to place one foot in front of the right main tire in addition to having the brakes set full on or having the airplane tied down (both if possible). Note that this is an extremely dangerous procedure. USE EXTREME CARE.

   a) Some pilots also advocate this approach when there is a pilot in the cockpit at the controls.

2.16 INDUCTION SYSTEM

1.   In reciprocating aircraft engines, the induction system completes the process of taking in outside air, mixing it with fuel, and delivering this mixture to the cylinders.

   a.   The system includes the air scoops and ducts, the air filter, the carburetor or fuel injector system, the intake manifold, and (if installed) the turbo or superchargers.

   b.   Two types of induction systems are commonly used in reciprocating engines.

      1)   The **carburetor system** mixes the fuel and air in the carburetor before this mixture enters the intake manifold.

      2)   In a **fuel injection system**, the fuel is fed into injection pumps that force it under high pressure directly into (or just prior to) the cylinders where it mixes with air.

   c.   Traditional piston-powered airplane engines incorporate a throttle and mixture control device that is operated by the pilot in the cockpit to allow for reliable, efficient operation of the engine.

      1)   The **throttle** controls the amount of fuel/air mixture that goes into the engine. Generally, the more fuel/air mixture, the more power is developed by the engine.

         a)   The throttle is opened (i.e., more air being delivered to the fuel/air mixture) by a forward movement of the control and closed (i.e., less air being delivered to the fuel/air mixture) by a rearward movement of the control.

         b)   Engine power can be determined by the following instruments:

            i)   The **tachometer** indicates the speed at which the engine crankshaft is rotating. The dial is calibrated in revolutions per minute (RPM).

               •   In an airplane equipped with a fixed-pitch propeller, RPM is controlled by the throttle control.

               •   In an airplane equipped with a constant-speed propeller, RPM is controlled by the propeller control until the throttle is retarded to the point at which the propeller is against the high pitch stop; then RPM will decrease with further throttle reduction.

            ii)   The **manifold pressure (MP) gauge** is installed in airplanes with a turbocharger and/or a constant-speed propeller.

               •   This gauge indirectly indicates the power output of the engine by measuring the pressure of the air in the fuel/air induction manifold.

                  ▪   The higher the MP, the greater the power being developed by the engine.

               •   The dial is calibrated in inches of mercury (in. Hg).

    c)   Smooth, gentle throttle movements are necessary to prevent overly rapid
         cooling and heating of various engine parts.

         i)   Also, crankshaft counterbalances can be upset by rapid changes in
              throttle settings.

2)   The **mixture control** varies the amount of fuel being introduced to the fuel/
     air mixture, which is in turn being delivered to the cylinders. This control
     compensates for varying air densities as the airplane changes altitude.

     a)   Engines are designed to operate with maximum power at a set fuel/air ratio
          (approximately 1 part of fuel to 14 parts of air by weight). Because an
          airplane is constantly operating at varying altitudes that imply varying air
          densities, fuel flow must be varied to maintain the ratio of fuel to air that
          will produce optimal power.

          i)   If the fuel/air mixture is too rich, there is too much fuel in terms of the
               weight of the air.

               •   Excessive fuel consumption, rough engine operation, and
                   appreciable loss of power will occur.
               •   Also, a cooling effect causes below normal temperatures in the
                   cylinders, which results in spark plug fouling.

          ii) Conversely, operating with an excessively lean mixture (i.e., too
               little fuel in terms of the weight of the air) will result in rough engine
               operation, detonation, overheating, and a loss of power.

     b)   Carburetors are normally calibrated at sea-level pressure to meter the
          correct amount of fuel with the mixture control in a "full rich" position.
          Recall that, as altitude increases, air density decreases.

          i)   As altitude increases, the weight of air decreases, even though the
               volume of air entering the carburetor remains the same.

               •   To compensate, the mixture must be leaned (i.e., reduce the
                   amount of fuel) to maintain the proper fuel/air ratio.
               •   On older aircraft piston engines, such as Lycomings and
                   Continentals, the mixture control is operated manually.
               •   On newer aircraft piston engines, such as the Rotax 912
                   series, the mixture control is operated automatically.

    c)   Exhaust gas temperature (EGT) gauge

      i)   Many airplanes are equipped with an EGT.

- If used properly, this engine instrument can reduce fuel consumption by 10% because of its accuracy in indicating to the pilot the exact amount of fuel that should be metered to the engine.

      ii)   An EGT gauge measures, in degrees Celsius (or Fahrenheit), the temperature of the exhaust gases at the exhaust manifold.

- This temperature measurement varies with ratio of fuel to air entering the cylinders and thus can be used as a basis for regulating the fuel/air mixture.
- Regulating the fuel/air mixture on this basis is possible because the EGT sensor is very sensitive to temperature changes.

      iii)   Although the manufacturer's recommendation for leaning the mixture should be adhered to, the usual procedure for leaning the mixture on lower horsepower engines when an EGT gauge is available is:

- The mixture is leaned slowly while observing the increase in exhaust gas temperature on the EGT gauge.
- When the EGT reaches a peak, the mixture should be enriched until the EGT gauge indicates a decrease in temperature.
  - The recommended drop in the number of degrees can be found in the airplane's AFM/POH. The usual recommendation is approximately 25° to 75°.
  - Engines equipped with carburetors will run rough when leaned to peak EGT reading but will run smoothly after the mixture is enriched slightly.

    d)   A fuel-injected engine usually has a **fuel flow indicator** on the instrument panel. The mixture control is moved to set the manufacturer's recommended fuel flow.

    e)   In engines equipped with no instruments to help in leaning, a simplistic method is to lean the mixture until engine roughness develops and then to enrich the mixture slightly until the engine runs smoothly again.

2.   **Carburetor System**

    a.   The outside air enters the air intake in the front part of the engine cowling and passes through an air filter.

      1)   An alternate air source, located within the engine cowling, is available in the event the external air filter is obstructed by ice or other matter.

      2)   This source is selected by applying carburetor heat, which introduces heated, unfiltered air into the carburetor.

    b.   The air flows into the carburetor through the venturi (a narrow throat in the carburetor), which accelerates the air.

      1)   The increased speed of the air flow is accompanied by a decrease in pressure (Bernoulli's Principle), which draws the fuel from the main discharge nozzle into the airstream where it is mixed with the flowing air.

      2)   The fuel/air mixture is then drawn through the intake manifold and into the combustion chambers where it is ignited.

   c.   The "float-type carburetor" acquires its name from a float that rests on fuel within the float chamber. A needle attached to the float opens and closes an opening in the fuel lines.

        1)   By this means, the correct amount of fuel is metered into the carburetor, depending upon the position of the float, which is controlled by the level of fuel in the float chamber.

   d.   The throttle control varies the airflow by means of the throttle valve in the throat of the carburetor.

        1)   The accelerating pump is also connected to the throttle linkage.

           a)   This pump allows an extra amount of fuel to flow into the carburetor as the throttle is opened.

           b)   If the throttle is opened quickly, the airflow initially increases at a rate greater than the fuel flow, creating a lean mixture. The accelerator pump prevents this from occurring.

   e.   The idling system provides sufficient fuel to mix with the air to keep the engine idling at low RPM.

   f.   The economizer is connected to the mixture control linkage. Moving the mixture control back moves a small needle in the carburetor, which restricts the fuel flow through the main metering jet.

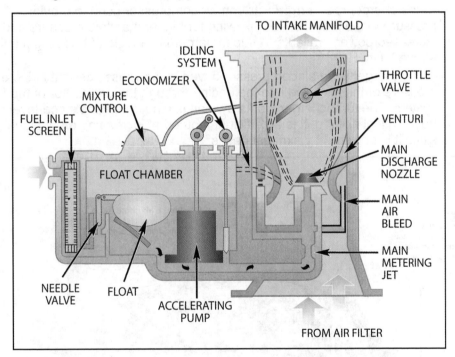

3. **Fuel Injection System**

   a.   The air intake for the fuel injection system is similar to that used in the carburetor system.

        1)   In many designs, the alternate air source is actuated automatically when the external air filter becomes obstructed.

           a)   The pilot may also manually activate the alternate air source.

        2)   The air passes to the cylinders where it is mixed with the fuel.

   b.   An engine-driven fuel pump provides pressurized fuel to the fuel injectors.

        1)   A specific amount of fuel is injected, based on mixture and throttle control settings.

        2)   The fuel is discharged into each cylinder's intake port where it mixes with the air.

    c.   Some of the advantages of fuel injection are

        1)   Less susceptibility to icing
        2)   Better fuel flow
        3)   Faster throttle response
        4)   Precise control of mixture
        5)   Better fuel distribution
        6)   Easier cold weather starts

    d.   Disadvantages of fuel injection are usually associated with

        1)   Difficulty in starting a hot engine

        2)   Vapor lock during ground operations on hot days

            a)   **Vapor lock** is a term used when fuel vaporizes (e.g., due to heat) and forms a vapor pocket in the fuel lines between the fuel tank and the induction system. These vapor pockets can result in a partial or complete block of the fuel flow.

        3)   Problems associated with restarting an engine that quits because of fuel starvation

4.   **Superchargers** and **turbochargers** are used to increase an engine's power output by compressing intake air to increase its density. This allows an airplane to fly at higher altitudes and with higher true airspeeds.

    a.   A supercharger is an **engine-driven** air compressor used to provide additional pressure to the induction air, allowing for higher manifold pressure and thus increased power available. A supercharger is capable of boosting manifold pressure above 30 in. Hg.

    b.   A turbocharger is an air compressor driven by **exhaust gases** that increase the pressure of the air going into the engine through the carburetor or the fuel injection system. The turbocharger works by maintaining an engine's sea-level horsepower up to critical altitude. It is an efficient method of increasing an airplane's performance since it is powered by exhaust gases.

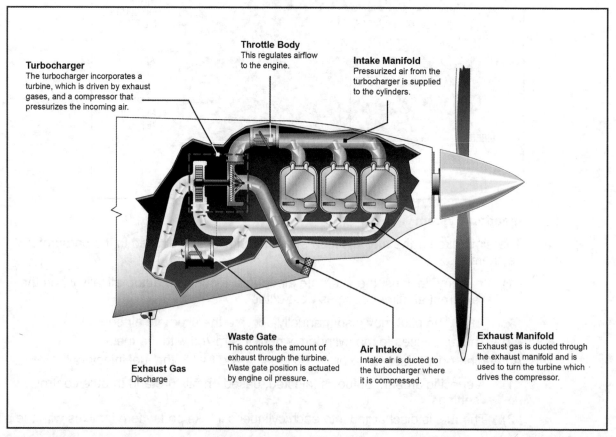

5. Reciprocating-engine icing conditions are a constant source of concern in airplane operations since they can result in loss of power and, if not eliminated, eventual engine malfunction or failure. This condition is known as **induction system icing**, which includes carburetor icing.

    a. Induction system icing may be characterized as impact, throttle, and fuel vaporization ice. Any one, or a combination of the three kinds of induction icing, can cause a serious loss of power by restricting the flow of the fuel/air mixture to the engine and by interference with the proper fuel/air ratio.

        1) **Impact ice** is formed by moisture-laden air (at temperatures below freezing) striking and freezing on elements of the induction system that are at temperatures of 0°C (32°F) or below. This type of icing affects an engine with fuel injection, as well as an engine that is carbureted.

            a) Under these conditions, ice may build up on such components as the air scoops, heat or alternate air valves, intake screens, and protrusions in the carburetor.

            b) Impact icing can be expected to build most rapidly when the ambient air temperature is about –4°C (25°F), when the supercooled moisture in the air is still in a semiliquid state.

        2) **Throttle ice** is usually formed at or near a partially closed throttle, typical of an off-idle or cruise power setting.

            a) Throttle icing occurs when water vapor in the air condenses and freezes because of the cooling restriction caused by the carburetor venturi and the throttle butterfly valve.

            b) This icing normally affects the carburetor-type engine but may also affect the fuel-injected engine.

        3) **Fuel vaporization icing** normally occurs in conjunction with throttle icing and is commonly called carburetor icing since it occurs predominately in float-type carburetors. It is not a problem in fuel injection systems because fuel is vaporized by other means.

            a) The vaporization of fuel, combined with the decreasing air pressure as it flows through the carburetor, causes a sudden cooling of the mixture.

            b) The temperature of the air passing through the carburetor may drop as much as 15°C (27°F) within a fraction of a second. Water vapor in the air is squeezed out by this cooling.

                i) If the temperature in the carburetor reaches 0°C (32°F) or below, the moisture will be deposited as frost or ice inside the carburetor passages.

                ii) Even a slight accumulation of ice will reduce power and may lead to complete engine failure, particularly when the throttle is partially or fully closed.

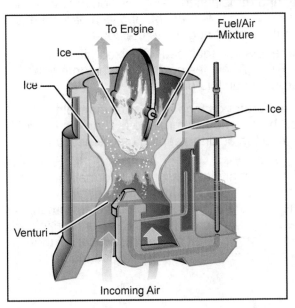

b. **Conditions conducive to carburetor icing.** On dry days, or when the temperature is well below freezing, there is generally not enough moisture in the air to cause trouble. But if the temperature is between –7°C (20°F) and 21°C (70°F), with visible moisture or high humidity, you should be constantly on the alert for carburetor ice.

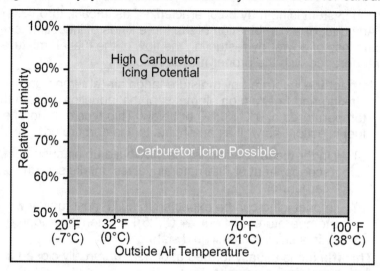

c. **Indications of carburetor icing.** For airplanes with fixed-pitch propellers, the first indication of carburetor icing is a loss of RPM. For airplanes with controllable pitch (constant-speed) propellers, the first indication is usually a drop in manifold pressure.

1) In both cases, a roughness in engine operation may develop later.

2) Airplanes with constant-speed propellers will not have a reduction in RPM since propeller pitch is automatically adjusted to compensate for the loss of power, thus maintaining constant RPM.

d. **Use of carburetor heat.** Carburetor heat is an anti-icing device that preheats the air before it reaches the carburetor. It can be used to melt any ice or snow entering the intake, to melt ice that forms in the carburetor passages (provided the accumulation is not too great), and to keep the fuel mixture above the freezing temperature to prevent formation of carburetor ice.

1) When conditions are conducive to carburetor icing during flight, periodic checks should be made to detect its presence. If icing is detected, FULL carburetor heat should be applied immediately and remain in the "on" position until you are certain that all the ice has been removed. If ice is present, applying partial heat or leaving heat on for an insufficient time might aggravate the condition.

2) When carburetor heat is first applied, airplanes equipped with fixed-pitch propellers will experience a drop in RPM. Airplanes equipped with controllable-pitch propellers will experience a drop in manifold pressure.

   a) If no carburetor ice is present, no further change in RPM or manifold pressure will occur until the carburetor heat is turned off. Then the RPM or manifold pressure will return to the original reading before heat was applied.

   b) If carburetor ice is present, RPM or manifold pressure will normally rise after the initial drop (often accompanied by intermittent engine roughness). This roughness is due to the ingestion of the water from the melted ice. When the carburetor heat is turned off, the RPM or manifold pressure will rise to a setting greater than that before application of the heat. The engine should also run more smoothly after the ice melts.

3) Whenever the throttle is closed during flight, the engine cools rapidly and vaporization of the fuel is less complete than when the engine is warm. In this condition, the engine is more susceptible to carburetor icing.

   a) If you suspect carburetor-icing conditions and anticipate closed-throttle operation, you should turn the carburetor heat to "full on" before closing the throttle and should leave it on during the closed-throttle operation. The heat will aid in vaporizing the fuel and preventing carburetor ice.

   b) Periodically, the throttle should be opened smoothly for a few seconds to keep the engine warm; otherwise, the carburetor heat may not provide enough heat to prevent icing.

4) Use of carburetor heat tends to reduce the power output of the engine and also to increase the operating temperature.

   a) Therefore, the heat should not be used when full power is required (as during takeoff) or during normal engine operation except to check for the presence or removal of carburetor ice.

   b) In extreme cases of carburetor icing, after the ice has been removed, it may be necessary to apply carburetor heat to prevent further ice formation.

   c) If carburetor ice still forms, apply FULL heat to remove it.

   NOTE: Partial use of the carburetor heat may raise the temperature of the induction air into the range that is likely for the formation of ice, thus increasing the risk of icing.

5) Check the engine manufacturer's recommendations for the correct use of carburetor heat.

e. **Carburetor air temperature gauge.** Some airplanes are equipped with this gauge that is useful in detecting potential icing conditions.

   1) Usually, the face of the gauge is calibrated in degrees Celsius. A yellow arc indicates the carburetor air temperatures at which icing may occur. This yellow arc ranges between –15°C and +5°C.

   2) If the air temperature and moisture content of the air are such that carburetor icing is improbable, the engine can be operated with the indicator in the yellow range with no adverse effects.

   3) However, if the atmospheric conditions are conducive to carburetor icing, the indicator must be kept outside the yellow arc by application of carburetor heat.

   4) Airplanes equipped with carburetor air temperature gauges are the only ones in which partial carburetor heat may be used.

f. **Outside air temperature (OAT) gauge.** Most airplanes are equipped with this gauge calibrated in degrees of both Celsius and Fahrenheit. The OAT gauge is useful for obtaining the outside or ambient air temperature for calculating true airspeed and also in detecting potential icing conditions.

2.17 FUEL SYSTEM

1. The fuel system stores fuel and transfers it to the airplane engine. Fuel systems are classified according to the way the fuel is moved to the engine from the fuel tanks: the "gravity feed" and the "fuel pump" systems.

   a. The **gravity feed system** uses the force of gravity to transfer fuel from the fuel tanks to the engine under sufficient pressure to meet the requirements of the engine.

      1) This system is common on high-wing airplanes with a carburetor-type engine in the lower horsepower range.

2)   An example of a gravity feed system is shown below.

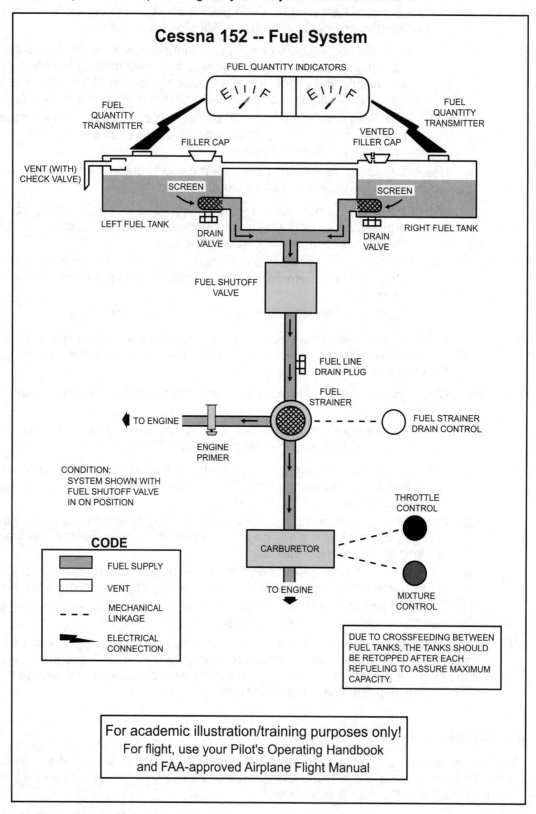

Cessna 152 -- Fuel System

b. The **fuel pump system** must be used in low-wing airplanes and airplanes with fuel-injected engines. Such a system generally has two fuel pumps.

1) The primary fuel pump is engine-driven (mechanical). It provides sufficient fuel pressure to the engine after start for all normal operations.

2) The auxiliary fuel pump (boost pump) is electrically driven and manually controlled by the pilot. It is used for engine start, for added safety during takeoff and landing, and for emergency situations in which the primary fuel pump has failed.

3) A **fuel pressure gauge**, which indicates the pressure in the fuel lines, is part of a fuel pump system. The normal operating pressure can be found in the airplane's AFM/POH or on the gauge by color coding.

4) An example of a fuel pump system is shown below.

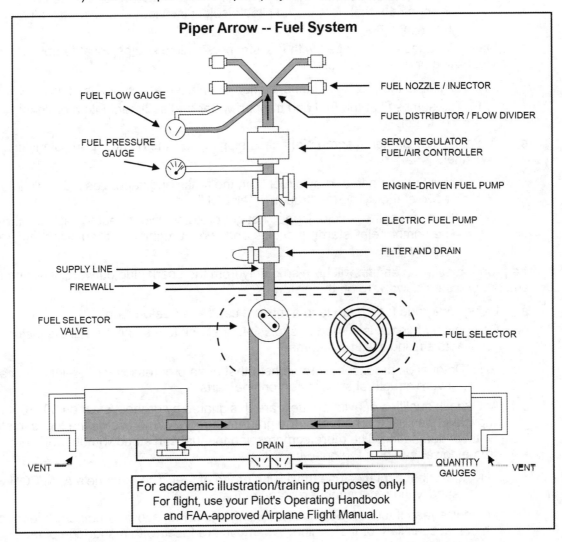

Piper Arrow -- Fuel System

FUEL FLOW GAUGE

FUEL PRESSURE GAUGE

SUPPLY LINE
FIREWALL

FUEL SELECTOR VALVE

VENT

FUEL NOZZLE / INJECTOR

FUEL DISTRIBUTOR / FLOW DIVIDER

SERVO REGULATOR FUEL/AIR CONTROLLER

ENGINE-DRIVEN FUEL PUMP

ELECTRIC FUEL PUMP

FILTER AND DRAIN

FUEL SELECTOR

DRAIN

QUANTITY GAUGES

VENT

For academic illustration/training purposes only!
For flight, use your Pilot's Operating Handbook
and FAA-approved Airplane Flight Manual.

2.   Most airplanes are designed to use space in the wings to mount fuel tanks. All tanks have filler openings covered by a cap.

   a.   Also included are lines connecting to the engine, a fuel gauge, strainers, and vents that permit air to replace the fuel consumed during flight.

   b.   Fuel overflow vents are provided to discharge fuel if it expands because of high temperatures.

   c.   Tanks have drain plugs or valves (sumps) at the bottom from which water and other sediment can be drained.

3.   Fuel lines transfer the fuel from the tanks to the engine.

   a.   Fuel lines pass through a selector assembly located in the cockpit.

   1)   The fuel selector assembly may be a simple on/off valve or a more complex arrangement that permits the pilot to select individual tanks or use all tanks at the same time.

   b.   Many airplanes are equipped with fuel strainers, called sumps, located between the fuel selector and the carburetor.

   1)   Similar to the fuel tank drains, sumps are placed at low points in the fuel lines.

   2)   The sumps filter the fuel and trapped water and sediment into a drainable container.

   c.   A manual fuel primer in some airplanes helps to start the engine, particularly in cold weather.

   1)   Activating the primer draws fuel from the tanks and vaporizes it directly into one or two of the cylinders through small fuel lines.

   2)   When an engine is cold, it does not generate sufficient heat to vaporize the fuel. The primer helps start the engine and keep it running until sufficient engine heat is generated.

4.   The proper fuel for an engine will burn smoothly from the spark plug outward, exerting a smooth pressure downward on the piston.

   a.   Using low-grade fuel or too lean a mixture can cause detonation.

   b.   Detonation or knock is a sudden explosion or shock to a small area of the piston top, similar to striking it with a hammer.

   1)   Detonation produces extreme heat that often progresses into preignition, causing severe structural stresses on engine parts.

   c.   Anti-knock qualities of aviation fuels are designated by grades, such as 80, 100LL (low lead), and 100. The higher the grade, the more compression the fuel can stand without detonating. The more compression the fuel can stand without detonation, the more power can be developed from it.

   1)   Most light airplanes use the 100LL grade of fuel. The airplane's AFM/POH will specify the recommended grade of fuel.

   d.   No engine manufacturer recommends using a fuel with a lower octane/grade rating than that specified for the engine. When you are faced with a shortage of the correct type of fuel, always use whatever alternate fuel grade is specified by the manufacturer or the next higher grade. Availability of different fuel grades at servicing facilities will be largely dependent on the classes of aircraft using the particular airport. The engine manufacturers have made information available concerning satisfactory alternate grade fuels for those that have been discontinued.

e. DO NOT USE AUTOMOTIVE FUEL unless the engine manufacturer recommends it or an appropriate supplemental type certificate (STC) has been obtained for an engine approving it for auto gas use.

f. Fuel color

1) Most fuel pumps or trucks are plainly marked indicating the type and grade of fuel. However, you should determine whether you are receiving the proper grade by the color of the fuel itself.

2) Dyes are added by the refinery for ready identification of the various grades of aviation gasoline:

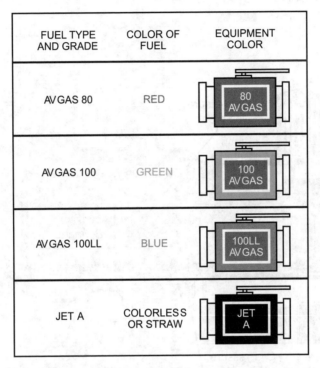

FUEL TYPE AND GRADE	COLOR OF FUEL	EQUIPMENT COLOR
AVGAS 80	RED	80 AVGAS
AVGAS 100	GREEN	100 AVGAS
AVGAS 100LL	BLUE	100LL AVGAS
JET A	COLORLESS OR STRAW	JET A

3) If accidentally mixed, any two of these fuels turn straw-colored.

5. During refueling, the flow of fuel through the hose and nozzle creates a fire hazard due to static electricity. Following some simple procedures can minimize the hazard.

a. A ground wire should be attached to the airplane before the cap is removed from the tank.

b. The refueling nozzle should be grounded to the airplane before and during refueling.

c. The fuel truck should also be grounded to the airplane and the ground.

2.18 OIL SYSTEM

1. The oil system provides a means of storing and circulating oil throughout the internal components of a reciprocating engine.

    a. Usually the oil is stored in a sump at the bottom of the engine crankcase.

        1) This is where the oil dipstick measures the amount of oil. Check the airplane's AFM/POH for the capacity and operating limits.

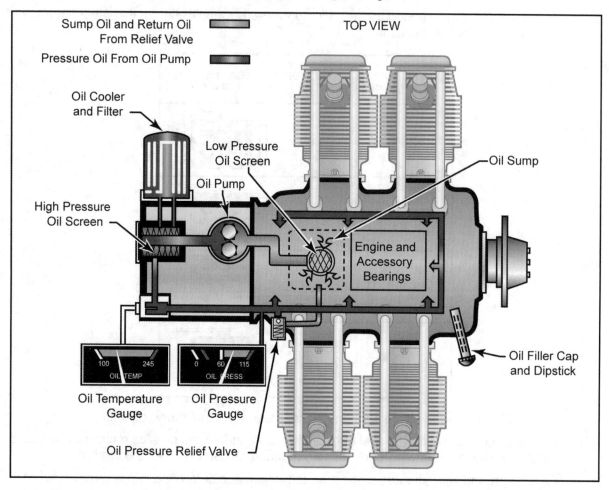

2. The four basic functions of engine oil are to

    a. Lubricate -- to maintain a film of lubricant on meeting surfaces between which relative motion occurs

    b. Seal -- as in the case of the oil seal between the cylinder walls and the piston and rings; also to prevent the passage of combustion gases past the pistons

    c. Clean -- by carrying off metal and carbon particles and other oil contaminants

    d. Cool -- by carrying heat away from hot engine parts and keeping their temperatures within acceptable limits. Cooling is most important. Always remember to maintain proper oil levels on long summer cross-country flights.

3. The wrong type of oil, or an insufficient oil supply, may interfere with any or all of the basic oil functions and cause serious engine damage. Use only oil that has been recommended by the engine manufacturer or its equivalent. Never use any oil additive that has not been recommended by the engine manufacturer and authorized by the FAA.

4. Each engine is equipped with an oil pressure gauge and an oil temperature gauge, which should be monitored to determine that the oil system is functioning properly.

    a. The **oil pressure gauge** indicates pounds of pressure per square inch (psi) and is color-coded with a green arc to indicate the normal operating range.

        1) At each end of the arc, some gauges have a red line to indicate high or low pressure.

        2) Low oil pressure can be the result of a mechanical problem or an inadequate amount of oil.

            a) Low oil pressure necessitates an immediate landing.

    b. The **oil temperature gauge** indicates the temperature of the oil and is color-coded in green to indicate the normal operating range.

        1) This gauge gives only an indirect and delayed indication of rising engine temperature.

        2) Many airplanes circulate the oil through an oil radiator for cooling.

5. Always make certain that the oil filler cap and the oil dipstick are secure after adding oil or checking the oil level. If these are left off or not properly secured, oil loss may occur. Remember, a proper oil supply and a properly functioning oil system are extremely important items for safe airplane operation. You cannot be too careful.

2.19 COOLING SYSTEM

1. The burning fuel within the cylinders produces intense heat, most of which is expelled through the exhaust. The remaining heat must be removed some other way to prevent the engine from overheating.

2. Most light airplane engines are air cooled. Cool air is forced (by the forward motion of the airplane in flight) into the engine compartment through openings in front of the engine cowl (the streamlined engine housing).

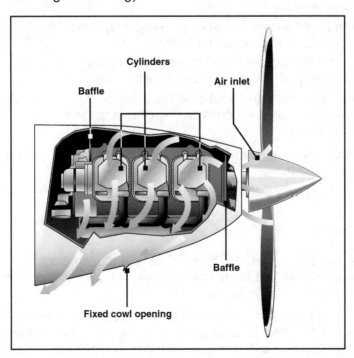

a. This ram air is routed by baffles over fins attached to the engine cylinders and other parts of the engine. As it passes through, this outside air absorbs the engine heat.

b. The hot air is expelled through one or two openings at the rear bottom of the engine cowling.

3.   Operating the engine at higher than its designed temperature can cause loss of power, excessive oil consumption, and detonation (untimed explosion of the burning fuel/air mixture). It will also lead to serious permanent damage, scoring the cylinder walls, damaging the pistons and rings, and burning and warping the valves. The pilot should monitor the engine instruments during flight to avoid excessive temperatures.

    a.   **Oil pressure gauge** -- indicates that the oil pump is working correctly to circulate the engine oil to all moving parts. Engine oil is very important both as a lubricant and for dissipating engine temperature.

    b.   **Oil temperature gauge** -- indicates the temperature of the oil. This gauge gives only an indirect and delayed indication of rising engine temperatures. However, it should be used to determine engine temperature if this is the only means available.

    c.   **Cylinder head temperature (CHT) gauge** -- an additional instrument in many airplanes that indicates a direct and immediate engine temperature change

    d.   Each of these instruments is usually color-coded with a green arc to indicate the normal operating range.

        1)   A red line indicates maximum or minimum allowable temperature or pressure.

        2)   Caution ranges may be indicated by a yellow arc, which may be below and/or above the green arc.

4.   To avoid or reduce excessive cylinder head temperatures, you can open the engine cowl flaps (if available), increase airspeed, enrich the mixture, or reduce power.

    a.   **Cowl flaps** are hinged covers that fit over the opening(s) through which the hot air is expelled. By adjusting the cowl flap opening, you can regulate the amount of airflow over the engine and thus the engine temperature during flight.

        1)   Restricting the flow of expelled hot air (closing the cowl flaps) will increase engine temperature.

        2)   If the engine temperature is high, the cowl flaps can be opened to permit a greater flow of air through the system, thereby decreasing the engine temperature.

        3)   The cowl flaps are usually opened during low-airspeed and high-power operations such as takeoffs and climbs.

        4)   During higher-speed and lower-power operations, such as cruising flight and descents, the cowl flaps are usually closed.

    b.   In airplanes not equipped with cowl flaps, the engine temperature can be controlled under normal operating conditions by changing the airspeed or the power output of the engine.

        1)   High engine temperatures can be decreased by increasing airspeed and/or reducing power.

    c.   A richer fuel-to-air mixture also helps an engine run cooler.

2.20 PROPELLERS

1.   A propeller is a rotating airfoil. It is thus subject to induced drag, stalls, and other aerodynamic principles that apply to any airfoil. The propeller provides the necessary thrust to move the airplane through the air.

    a.   The airplane propeller consists of two or more blades and a central hub to which the blades are attached. Each blade of an airplane propeller is essentially a rotating wing that produces forces that create the thrust to move the airplane through the air.

    b.   The power needed to rotate the propeller blades is furnished by the engine. The engine rotates the airfoils of the blades through the air at high speeds, and the propeller transforms the rotary power of the engine into forward thrust.

c.   A cross section of a typical propeller blade is shown below. This section or blade element is an airfoil comparable to a cross section of an airplane wing.

1)   One surface of the blade is cambered or curved, similar to the upper surface of an airplane wing, while the other surface is flat like the bottom surface of a wing.

2)   As with a wing, the leading edge is the thick edge of the blade that meets the air as the propeller rotates.

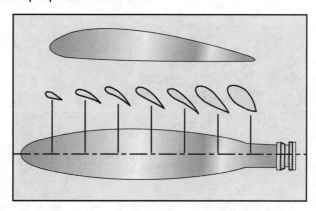

d.   To understand the action of a propeller, consider first its motion, which is both rotational and forward. As shown in the figure below, each section of a propeller blade moves downward and forward.

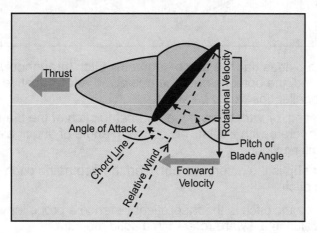

1)   The angle at which the air (relative wind) strikes the propeller blade is its angle of attack.

a)   The air deflection produced by this angle causes the dynamic pressure at the back side of the propeller blade to be greater than the atmospheric pressure, thus creating thrust.

b)   The shape of the blade also creates thrust because it is cambered like the airfoil shape of a wing.

i)   As the air flows past the propeller, the pressure on one side is less than that on the other.

ii)   As in a wing, this produces a reaction force in the direction of the lesser pressure.

•   The area of decreased pressure is in front of the propeller, and the force (thrust) is in a forward direction.

2)   Aerodynamically, thrust is the result of the propeller shape and the angle of attack of the blade.

e.   A propeller is twisted because the outer parts of the propeller blades, like all things that turn about a central point, travel faster than the portions near the hub (see below).

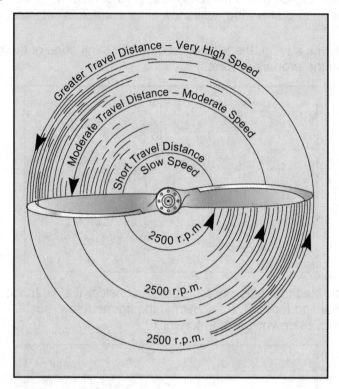

1)   If the blades had the same geometric pitch throughout their lengths, at cruise speed, the portions near the hub could have negative angles of attack while the propeller tips would be stalled.

2)   Twisting, or variations in the geometric pitch of the blades, permits the propeller to operate with a relatively constant angle of attack along its length when in cruising flight.

f.   **Propeller slip** is the difference between the geometric pitch of the propeller and its effective pitch.

1)   Geometric pitch is the theoretical distance a propeller would advance in one revolution if it were rotated in a solid medium.

   a)   Effective pitch is the actual distance a propeller moves forward through the air in one revolution.

2)   Geometric or theoretical pitch is based on no slippage, but actual or effective pitch includes propeller slippage in the air.

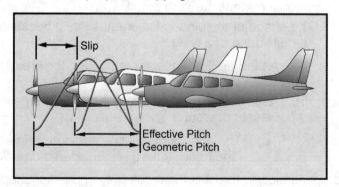

g. **Propeller efficiency** depends on the amount of slippage.

1) Since the efficiency of any machine is the ratio of the useful power output to the actual power output, propeller efficiency is the ratio of thrust horsepower to brake horsepower (i.e., the horsepower the engine is delivering to the crankshaft).

2) Propeller efficiency varies from 50% to 87%, depending on propeller slippage.

3) A propeller is most efficient, i.e., has the least amount of slippage, at angles of attack between 1° and 4°.

2. **Fixed-pitch propeller.** The pitch of this propeller is fixed by the manufacturer. It cannot be changed by the pilot.

a. The throttle controls the power output of the engine, which has a direct relationship to RPM.

1) The RPM is registered on the tachometer.

b. Fixed-pitch propellers are designed for best efficiency (i.e., ideal angle of attack) at one rotational and forward speed.

1) Any other combination of RPM and airspeed results in a less efficient angle of attack.

2) Each propeller is designed for a given airplane, engine combination, and flight condition.

c. A propeller may be designed to provide the maximum propeller efficiency for either takeoff, climb, cruise, or high-speed flight.

1) Any changes in these conditions result in lowering the efficiency of both the propeller and the engine.

3. **Controllable-pitch propellers.** The pitch of these propellers can be changed in flight by the pilot. These propellers vary from a simple two-position propeller to the constant-speed propeller, which allows any pitch angle between a minimum and maximum pitch setting. The following discussion refers to the constant-speed propeller:

a. An airplane equipped with a constant-speed propeller has two main power controls:

1) The throttle controls the power output of the engine (registered on the manifold pressure gauge).

a) The manifold pressure (MP) gauge is a simple barometer that measures the air pressure in the engine intake manifold in inches of mercury.

2) The propeller control regulates the engine RPM and, in turn, the propeller RPM.

a) The RPM is registered on the tachometer.

Manifold pressure gauge. Controlled by THROTTLE.

Tachometer. Controlled by PROP CONTROL.

b.   Constant-speed propeller systems consist of a governor unit which controls the pitch angle of the blades so the engine's speed (RPM) remains constant. The governor regulates the flow of oil into and out of the propeller hub to control the blade angle.

1)   The propeller governor can be controlled by the pilot so that any desired angle setting (within manifold pressure limits) and engine RPM can be obtained. By means of the propeller governor, the airplane's operational efficiency can be increased in various flight conditions.

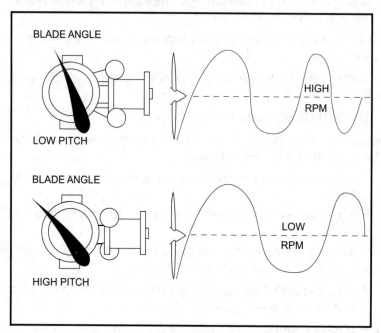

2)   Once the pilot has set the propeller to a given RPM, the propeller governor will automatically change the pitch to counteract any tendency for the engine to vary from this RPM.

a)   If MP or engine power is increased, the propeller governor automatically increases the pitch of the blade (i.e., more propeller drag) to maintain RPM.

c.   A controllable-pitch propeller permits the pilot to select the blade angle that will result in the most efficient performance for a particular flight condition.

1)   If the blade pitch is not increased as the airplane moves forward through the air, the angle of attack of the propeller is reduced.

a)   As the angle of attack is reduced, so is the thrust generated by the propeller.

b) The figure below shows how angle of attack is reduced when a propeller with a fixed pitch moves forward through the air.

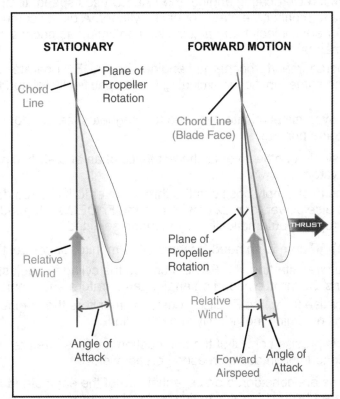

2) A low-pitch, high-RPM setting reduces propeller drag and allows maximum power for takeoff.

3) After airspeed is attained during cruising flight, the propeller pitch is changed to a higher angle or increased pitch. The blade takes a larger bite of air at a lower power setting, thus increasing the efficiency of the propeller, similar to the automatic shifting of gears from low to high in an automobile.

d. Any given RPM has a maximum MP that should not be exceeded.

1) If MP is excessive for a given RPM, pressure within the cylinders could be exceeded, thus placing undue stress on them.

2) If repeated too frequently, such stress could weaken the cylinder components and eventually cause engine failure.

3) Avoid high MP settings with low RPM.

4) Consult the airplane's AFM/POH, Section 5, for approved power settings.

2.21 FULL AUTHORITY DIGITAL ENGINE CONTROL (FADEC)

1. While common on turbine-powered aircraft for some time, FADEC systems are making their way into piston-powered general aviation airplanes as well.

a. Digital engine control systems use a computer to automate throttle, propeller, and/or mixture settings.

b. In a typical high-performance airplane, the pilot has separate controls for throttle, propeller RPM, and the fuel/air mixture setting.

1) A FADEC system combines these controls into two (or sometimes one) pilot control lever(s).

2) Based on the pilot's control input, the computer would balance throttle, propeller pitch, and even the fuel/air mixture for best performance.

2.   **FADEC Operation**

    a.   In a typical reciprocating engine, the FADEC uses speed, temperature, and pressure sensors to monitor the status of each cylinder. A digital computer calculates the ideal pulse for each injector and adjusts ignition timing as necessary to achieve optimal performance.

    b.   In a supercharged/turbocharged engine, the FADEC operates similarly and performs all of the same functions, excluding those specifically related to the spark ignition process.

    c.   FADEC systems eliminate the need for magnetos, carburetor heat, mixture controls, and engine priming.

        1)   A single throttle lever is characteristic of an aircraft equipped with a FADEC system.

        2)   The pilot simply positions the throttle lever to a desired detent such as start, idle, cruise power, or max power, and the FADEC system adjusts the engine and propeller automatically for the mode selected.

            a)   There is no need for the pilot to monitor or control the air/fuel mixture.

    d.   During aircraft starting, the FADEC primes the cylinders, adjusts the mixture, and positions the throttle based on engine temperature and ambient pressure.

    e.   During cruise flight, the FADEC constantly monitors the engine and adjusts fuel flow and ignition timing individually in each cylinder.

        1)   This precise control of the combustion process often results in decreased fuel consumption and increased horsepower.

3.   FADEC systems are considered an essential part of the engine and propeller control and may be powered by the aircraft's main electrical system.

    a.   In many aircraft, FADEC uses power from a separate generator connected to the engine. In either case, there must be a backup electrical source available because failure of a FADEC system could result in a complete loss of engine thrust.

        1)   FADEC systems usually do not have any form of manual override available. This places full control of the operating parameters of the engine with the computer.

    b.   To prevent loss of thrust, two separate and identical digital channels (each one capable of providing all engine and propeller functions without limitations) are incorporated for redundancy.

2.22 ELECTRICAL SYSTEM

1.   Electrical energy is required to operate the starter, navigation and communication radios, lights, and other airplane equipment.

    a.   Most light airplanes are equipped with a 12-volt battery and a 14-volt direct-current electrical system.

    b.   Some airplanes are equipped with a 24-volt battery and a 28-volt direct-current system to provide an electrical reserve capacity for more electrical equipment, including additional electrical energy for starting.

2.   A basic airplane electrical system consists of the following components:

    a.   Alternator or generator
    b.   Battery
    c.   Master switch or battery switch
    d.   Bus bar, fuses, and circuit breakers
    e.   Voltage regulator
    f.   Ammeter
    g.   Associated electrical wiring

3. Engine-driven generators or alternators supply electric current to the electrical system and also maintain a sufficient electrical charge in the battery (which is used primarily for starting).

    a. Electrical energy stored in a battery provides a source of electricity for starting the engine and a limited supply of electricity for use if the alternator or generator fails.

    b. The main disadvantage of a generator is that it may not produce a sufficient amount of electrical current at low engine RPM to operate the entire electrical system. Therefore, during operations at low engine RPM, the electrical needs must be drawn from the battery, which may quickly be depleted.

    c. Most airplanes are equipped with an alternator. It produces a sufficient amount of electrical current at low engine RPM by first producing alternating current, which is converted to direct current.

        1) Another advantage is that the electrical output of an alternator is more constant throughout the ranges of engine speed.

        2) Alternators are also lighter in weight, less expensive to maintain, and less prone to overloading during conditions of heavy electrical loads.

4. Some airplanes are equipped with receptacles to which ground power units (GPUs) can be connected to provide electrical energy for starting.

    a. GPUs are very useful, especially during cold weather starting.

    b. Do NOT start an engine using a GPU when the battery is dead. Electrical energy will be forced into the dead battery, causing the battery to overheat and possibly explode, resulting in damage to the airplane.

5. A **master switch** is installed to turn the electrical system on or off. Turning the master switch on provides electrical energy to all the electrical equipment circuits except the ignition system (which receives electricity from the magnetos).

    a. In addition, an alternator switch permits the pilot to exclude the alternator from the electrical system in the event of alternator failure. With the alternator switch off, the entire electrical load is placed on the battery.

        1) In such a case, all nonessential electrical equipment should be turned off to conserve the energy stored in the battery.

6. Although additional electrical equipment may be found in some airplanes, the following equipment commonly uses the electrical system:

    a. Starter motor
    b. Interior and exterior lighting
    c. Flaps
    d. Radio and navigation equipment
    e. Turn coordinator gyro
    f. Fuel gauges
    g. Stall warning system
    h. Pitot heat
    i. Clock
    j. Retractable landing gear

7.   A **bus bar** is used as a terminal in the airplane electrical system to connect the main electrical system to the equipment that uses the electricity. The bus bar simplifies the wiring system and provides a common point from which to distribute voltage throughout the system.

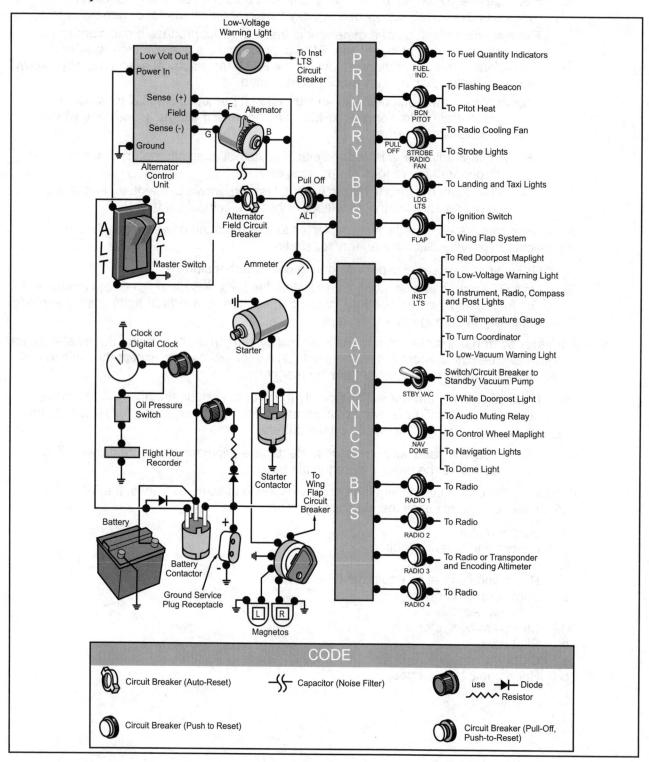

8.   Fuses or circuit breakers protect the circuits and equipment from electrical overload.

   a.   Spare fuses of the proper amperage limit should be carried in the airplane at all times to replace defective or blown fuses that are accessible to the pilot in flight.

   b.   Circuit breakers have the same function as a fuse but can be manually reset (rather than replaced) if an overload condition occurs in the electrical system.

   1)   They are usually manually reset by pushing them in when they "pop out."

   2)   If a circuit breaker pops out a second time after being reset, there is probably a short in that circuit. Accordingly, you should not continue to push the circuit breaker in. Fire may result.

   c.   Placards at the fuse or circuit breaker location identify the circuit by name and the amperage limit of the circuit.

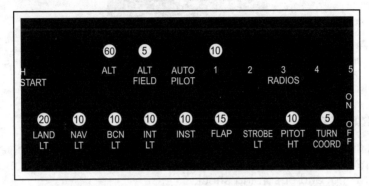

9.   An **ammeter** is an instrument used to monitor the performance of the airplane electrical system.

   a.   Not all airplanes are equipped with an ammeter. Some are simply equipped with a light that, when lit, indicates a discharge in the system as a generator/alternator malfunction.

   b.   An ammeter shows if the generator/alternator is producing an adequate supply of electrical power by measuring the amperes of electricity.

   1)   This instrument also indicates whether the battery is receiving an electrical charge.

   c.   Ammeters are either the center-zero or the left-zero type.

   1)   A center-zero ammeter shows charge to, or discharge from, the battery.

   a)   If the needle indicates a positive value, the battery is being charged.

   b)   If the needle indicates a negative value, the battery is being discharged. A discharge may occur during starting. At any other time, a negative value indicates an overload on the system or a defective alternator.

   i)   Most airplanes are equipped with an over-voltage relay, which trips the alternator off line if a safe voltage limit is exceeded. This condition is indicated by a negative value on the ammeter.

   •   To reset the alternator, turn the alternator master switch to the off position and then on again.

2) A left-zero ammeter (commonly known as a loadmeter) shows the amount of current coming from the alternator.

a) If the needle indicates zero and electrical equipment is being used, the alternator has failed, and current is being drawn from the battery.

3) After power is drawn from the battery for starting, the needle will indicate a noticeable positive charge value for a short time. Then it should stabilize to a lower positive charge value.

2.23 LANDING GEAR SYSTEM

1. The landing gear system supports the airplane during the takeoff run, landing, and taxiing, and when parked. The landing gear can be fixed or retractable and must be capable of steering, braking, and absorbing shock.

a. Most single-engine training airplanes are equipped with fixed landing gear.
b. Retractable gear is found on most high-performance airplanes.

2. **Retractable Landing Gear**

a. Retractable landing gear provides several benefits:

1) The primary benefit of retractable landing gear is the reduction in parasitic drag when the gear is retracted. Remember, as speed is doubled, drag is quadrupled.
2) The reduction in drag has a corresponding and related increase in airspeed. By having a clean airframe, more airspeed can be obtained with the same amount of horsepower.

b. Gear systems can be operated in a number of different ways. Some are electric, some are hydraulic, and some are hybrids called electro-hydraulic.

1) The electric system uses a reversible electric motor to power the system. Through a gear assembly, the electric motor turns a bellcrank, operating the push-pull cables and tubes that extend and retract the landing gear. As a backup, most electric systems have handcranks to lower the gear manually.
2) The hydraulic system uses an engine-driven hydraulic pump to force fluid under pressure through a series of valves, pipes, and actuators. The hydraulic pressure drives the gear up or down. For emergencies, a hand pump, compressed nitrogen, or a combination of both is used.
3) The electro-hydraulic system uses a reversible electric motor to drive the hydraulic pump. The gear selector switch is an electric switch that activates the electric motor and controls its direction. For emergency use, a hydraulic pressure dump switch is usually used. This switch releases the pressure, and the gear free-falls to the down and (sometimes) locked position.

    c.   Indicators are provided in the cockpit to indicate whether the gear is extended down and locked or retracted.

    d.   Many airplanes are equipped with gear warning devices that provide a visual or audible warning in case the pilot forgets to lower the landing gear prior to landing. These warning devices are activated in various manners.

        1)   Some have switches on the throttle that sense the reduction in power.

        2)   Others have sensors that are activated by external devices with the ability to sense slow airspeed.

        3)   On more advanced airplanes, radar altimeters cause the warning.

            a)   Radar altimeters determine height above the ground with radar rather than atmospheric pressure.

3.   The main landing gear assembly consists of two main wheels and struts. Each main strut is attached to the primary structure of the fuselage or the wing.

    a.   The landing gear shock-struts may be either self-contained hydraulic units or flexible spring-like structures.

        1)   These struts support the airplane on the ground and protect the airplane's structure by absorbing and dissipating the shock loads of landing and taxiing over rough surfaces.

        2)   Many airplanes are equipped with oleo or oleo-pneumatic struts, the basic parts of which are a piston and a cylinder.

            a)   The lower part of the cylinder is filled with hydraulic fluid, and the piston operates in this fluid.

            b)   The upper part is filled with air.

            c)   Several holes in the piston permit fluid to pass from one side of the piston to the other as the strut compresses and expands and forces the piston back and forth.

4.   The brakes and tires on your airplane are very important for safe operations. Check the airplane's AFM/POH for operation and recommended maintenance.

    a.   Brakes are used for slowing, stopping, or steering (at very slow speeds) the airplane. They must develop sufficient force to stop the airplane in a reasonable distance. They must

        1)   Hold the airplane stationary during engine run-ups

        2)   Permit steering of the airplane on the ground

    b.   The brakes are installed in each main landing wheel and are operated independently of each other.

        1)   Pressure is applied to the top portion of the left rudder pedal to control the left-hand brake.

        2)   Pressure is applied to the top portion of the right rudder pedal to control the right-hand brake.

    c.   Most small aircraft have an independent brake system powered by master cylinders, similar to those in your car.

       1) The system is composed of

          a) A reservoir

          b) Two master cylinders

          c) Mechanical linkage, which connects each master cylinder with its corresponding brake pedal

          d) Connecting fluid lines

          e) A brake assembly in each main landing gear wheel

    d.   Use the brakes in an efficient manner.

       1) Use a combination of power reduction, aerodynamic braking, and planning so as to use the least amount of braking action.

       2) Do not ride the brakes.

       3) Always taxi as though you have no brakes at all.

    e.   Ensure your tires are properly inflated and there is proper tread on the tires.

5.   A steerable nose gear permits you to control your airplane throughout all ground operations.

    a.   Most light airplanes are provided with steering capabilities through a simple mechanical linkage connected to the rudder pedals.

       1) Most common are push-pull rods to connect the pedals to fittings located on the pivotal portion of the nosewheel strut.

    b.   Larger airplanes may use a separate power source for more positive control during steering operations.

    c.   The nosewheel can vibrate and shimmy during taxiing, takeoff, or landing under certain situations.

       1) If shimmy becomes excessive, it can damage the nose gear or attaching structure.

       2) Most airplanes have a system with built-in features to prevent the shimmy.

    d.   On most tailwheel-type airplanes, directional control while taxiing is facilitated by the use of a steerable tailwheel, which operates along with the rudder.

       1) The steering mechanism remains engaged when the tailwheel is operated through an arc of 16° to 18° on each side of neutral and becomes full swiveling when turned to a greater angle.

       2) While taxiing, you should use the steerable tailwheel to make normal turns and keep your feet off the brake pedals to avoid unnecessary wear on the brakes.

2.24 ENVIRONMENTAL SYSTEM

1. Heating in most training airplanes is accomplished by an air intake in the nose of the airplane.

    a. The air is directed into a shroud, where it is heated by the engine exhaust.
    b. The heated air is then delivered through vents into the cabin or used for the defroster.

2. Cooling and ventilation are controlled by outlets.

    a. Some airplanes are equipped with an air conditioner for cooling.
    b. Outside air used for cooling and ventilation is normally supplied through air inlets that are located in the wings or elsewhere on the airplane.
    c. Learn how your airplane's system works by reading your AFM/POH.

3. Heat and defrost controls are located on the instrument panel or within easy reach.

    a. Most airplanes are equipped with outlets that can be controlled by each occupant of the airplane.
    b. Your AFM/POH will explain the operation of the controls.

2.25 DEICE AND ANTI-ICE SYSTEMS

1. **Airframe Ice-Protection Systems**

    a. Deicer boots are fabric-reinforced rubber sheets containing inflation tubes. They are normally cemented to the leading edges of the wings, vertical stabilizer, and horizontal stabilizer.

        1) During normal operation, vacuum pressure holds the boots in the deflated position.
        2) At the first sign of ice accumulation, the system is activated by the pilot. A pneumatic pump controlled by a timer inflates segments of the boots. This inflation breaks off the accumulated ice.

    b. The weeping wing system uses a special leading edge on the airplane's wings and stabilizers.

        1) The leading edge is laser drilled with very small holes.
        2) A deicing fluid is pumped out of these holes, causing any built-up ice to fall off. The remaining fluid deters further ice buildup.
        3) Ice protection is limited by the amount of fluid carried onboard the airplane.

    c. Thermal anti-icing uses heated air flowing through passages in the leading edge of wings, stabilizers, and engine cowlings to prevent the formation of ice.

        1) Heat source normally comes from combustion heaters in reciprocating-engine-powered airplanes and from engine bleed air in turbine-powered airplanes.

2. **Two Primary Methods Used in Propeller Ice Protection**

    a. Electric deicing

        1) The heating elements are enclosed in a rubber pad, which is normally cemented to the leading edge of the propeller blades near the hub.

    b. Fluid (normally isopropyl alcohol) anti-icing

        1) Normally the fluid is released from the slinger ring assembly out along the leading edge of the blades by centrifugal (i.e., outward) force.

3. Fuel system icing results from the presence of water in the fuel system, which may cause freezing of screen, strainers, and filters. When fuel enters the carburetor, the additional cooling may freeze the water.

   a. Normally, proper use of carburetor heat can warm the air sufficiently in the carburetor to prevent ice formation.

   b. Some airplanes are approved to use anti-icing fuel additives.

      1) Remember that an anti-icing additive is not a substitute for carburetor heat.

4. Pitot heat is an electrical system and may put a severe drain on the electrical system of some airplanes.

   a. Monitor your ammeter for the effect pitot heat has on your airplane's electrical system.

      1) Pitot heat should be used prior to encountering visible moisture near or below freezing temperatures, or in icing conditions.

5. Induction system (carburetor) ice-protection is probably the only ice protection system in your training airplane.

   a. Carburetor heat warms the air before it enters the carburetor.

      1) Used to remove and/or prevent ice formation

6. Icing conditions are to be avoided both in flight planning and in the air, unless your airplane is approved for flight into known icing conditions.

   a. Most training airplanes have placards that prohibit flight into known icing conditions.

7. Check your AFM/POH for the appropriate, if any, system in your airplane.

END OF STUDY UNIT

STUDY UNIT THREE
AIRPORTS, AIR TRAFFIC CONTROL, AND AIRSPACE

(74 pages of outline)

The purpose of this study unit is to describe airports in terms of the facilities you will use as a pilot. Relatedly, airport operations, air traffic control (ATC), radio communication procedures, and airspace classification are discussed.

3.1 RUNWAY AND TAXIWAY MARKINGS

1. **Airport pavement markings and signs** provide information that is useful to you during takeoff, landing, and taxiing.

    a. Uniformity in airport markings and signs from one airport to another enhances safety and improves efficiency.

    b. The FAA has established recommended standards for markings and signs that you should understand.

    c. Markings for runways are white.

        1) Heliport landing areas are also white except for hospital heliports, which use a red "H" on a white cross.

    d. Markings for taxiways, closed areas, hazardous areas, and holding positions (even if they are on a runway) are yellow.

2. **Runway Markings**

    a. A runway is marked in accordance with its present usage as a visual runway, nonprecision instrument runway, or precision instrument runway. You can use any of these runways for takeoff and landing.

        1) A **visual runway** is used for visual flight rules (VFR) operations. Its markings include

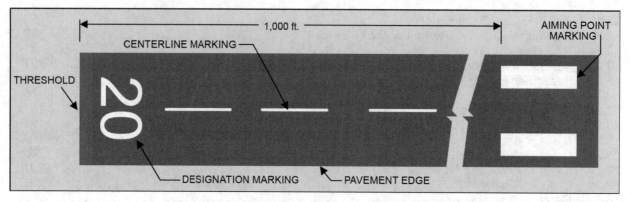

        a) **Designation marking.** Runway numbers and letters are determined from the approach direction. The runway number is the whole number nearest one-tenth the magnetic direction of the runway (e.g., a runway with a magnetic direction of 200° would be designated as runway 20). Letters differentiate between left (L), right (R), or center (C) parallel runways, if applicable.

            i)   For two parallel runways -- "L," "R"
            ii) For three parallel runways -- "L," "C," "R"

        b) **Centerline marking.** The runway centerline identifies the center of the runway and provides alignment guidance during takeoff and landing. The runway centerline is a dashed line.

        c) **Optional markings**

            i)   If the runway is used or intended to be used by international commercial transport, threshold markings are required.
            ii) If the runway is 4,000 ft. or longer and is used by jet aircraft, an aiming point marking is required.
            iii) Runway side stripes may be added if necessary.

2) A **nonprecision instrument runway** is served by a nonprecision instrument approach (i.e., no electronic glide slope), and its markings include

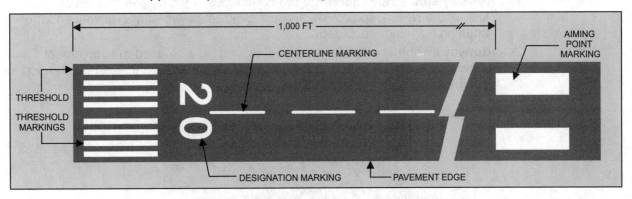

a) Designation marking

b) Centerline marking

c) **Threshold markings.** The runway threshold markings help you to identify the beginning of the runway that is available for landing. Threshold markings come in two configurations:

    i) Eight longitudinal stripes (four on each side of the centerline)

    ii) The number of stripes designated according to the width of the runway

d) **Aiming point marker.** The aiming point marker serves as a visual aiming point during landing. The aiming point markings are two broad white stripes located on each side of the runway centerline approximately 1,000 ft. from the landing threshold.

e) Optional markings -- runway side stripes

3) A **precision instrument runway** is served by a precision instrument approach, e.g., an instrument landing system (ILS). Its markings include

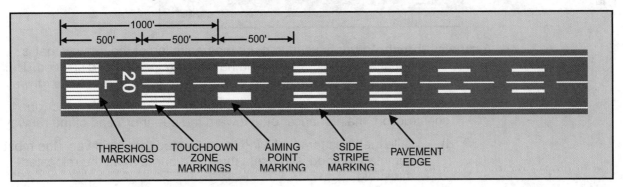

a) All the required markings for a nonprecision instrument runway.

b) **Touchdown zone marker.** The touchdown zone markings identify the touchdown zone for landing operations and are coded to provide distance information in 500-ft. increments.

    i) These markings consist of groups of one, two, and three rectangular bars arranged on each side of the centerline, as shown above.

b.   Additional runway markings

1)   **Runway side stripe markings** are continuous white stripes located on each side of the runway to provide a visual contrast between the runway and the abutting terrain or shoulders.

2)   **Runway shoulder markings** are yellow and may be used to supplement runway side stripes to identify the runway shoulder area that is not intended for use by aircraft, as shown below.

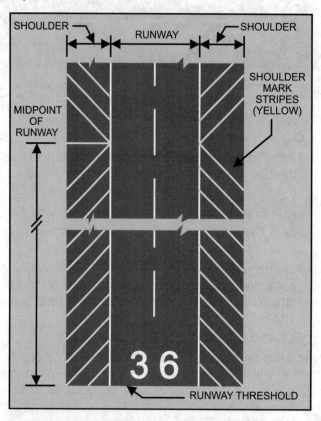

3)   A **runway threshold bar** is used to mark the beginning of the runway that is available for landing when the threshold has been relocated or displaced. The threshold bar is 10 ft. wide, white, and extends across the width of the runway.

a)   A **relocated threshold** is a threshold that is temporarily relocated (due to construction, maintenance, etc.) toward the departure end of the runway.

i)   While methods for identifying the relocated threshold vary, the most common method is to use a threshold bar to mark the relocated threshold.

b) A **displaced threshold** is a threshold that is not at the beginning of the paved runway.

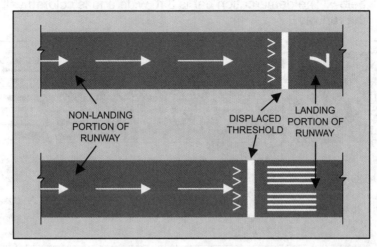

i) The paved area before the displaced runway threshold (marked by arrows) is available for taxiing, the takeoff of aircraft, and a landing rollout from the opposite direction, but not for landing in the direction of the runway in question.

ii) A threshold bar is located across the width of the runway at the displaced threshold.

iii) White arrows are located along the centerline in the area between the beginning of the runway and the displaced threshold.

iv) White arrowheads are located across the width of the runway just prior to the threshold bar.

4) **Chevrons** are used to show pavement areas (e.g., blast pads, stopways, etc.) aligned with the runway that are unusable for landing, takeoff, and taxiing. Chevrons are yellow.

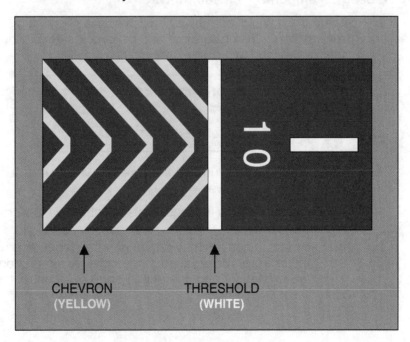

5)   A **demarcation bar** separates a runway that has a displaced threshold from a taxiway or an area marked by chevrons that precedes the runway, as shown below. The demarcation bar is 3 ft. wide and is colored yellow since it is not on the runway.

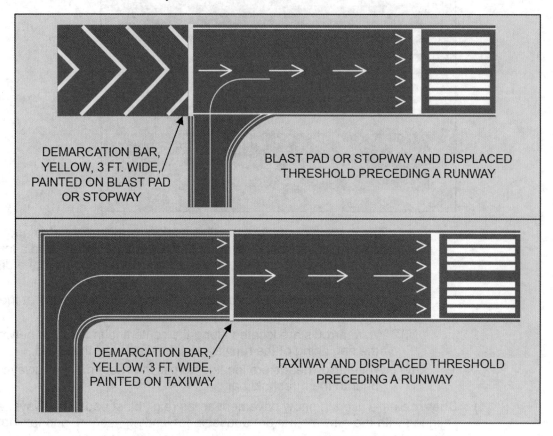

DEMARCATION BAR, YELLOW, 3 FT. WIDE, PAINTED ON BLAST PAD OR STOPWAY

BLAST PAD OR STOPWAY AND DISPLACED THRESHOLD PRECEDING A RUNWAY

DEMARCATION BAR, YELLOW, 3 FT. WIDE, PAINTED ON TAXIWAY

TAXIWAY AND DISPLACED THRESHOLD PRECEDING A RUNWAY

6)   **Closed or temporarily closed runway**

a)   A permanently closed runway has all runway lighting disconnected, all runway markings obliterated, and yellow crosses placed at each end of the runway and at 1,000-ft. intervals.

b)   A temporarily closed runway is marked by yellow crosses placed only at each end of the runway.

i)   An alternative is to place a raised lighted yellow cross at each end of the runway.

ii)   A visual indication may not be present depending on the reason for the closure, the duration of the closure, airport configuration, and the existence (and operating hours) of a control tower.

3.   **Taxiway Markings**

    a.   The **taxiway centerline** is a single continuous yellow line that provides a visual cue to permit taxiing along a designated path.

        1)   Ideally, your airplane should be kept centered over this line during taxiing to ensure wingtip clearance.

    b.   **Taxiway edge markings** are primarily used to define the edge of the taxiway when the taxiway edge does not correspond with the edge of the pavement. There are two types, depending on whether your airplane is permitted to cross the taxiway edge.

        1)   A continuous marking consists of a continuous double yellow line that should not be crossed.

        2)   A dashed marking consists of a broken double yellow line and indicates the edge of the taxiway where the adjoining pavement is also intended for use by aircraft, i.e., a parking ramp.

           a)   These dashed lines are 15 ft. long with 25-ft. gaps.

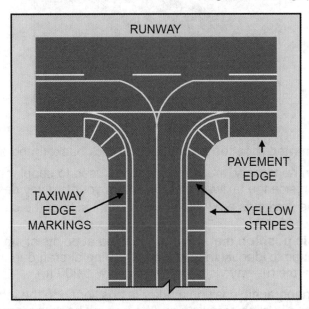

    c.   **Taxiway shoulder markings** indicate that the paved shoulders along the taxiway are unusable. Taxiway shoulder markings are yellow.

d. **Surface painted taxiway direction signs** have a yellow background with a black inscription and are provided when it is not possible to provide taxiway direction signs at intersections or when it is necessary to supplement such signs.

    1) These markings are located adjacent to the centerline with markings indicating turns to the left on the left side of the centerline and markings indicating turns to the right on the right side of the centerline.

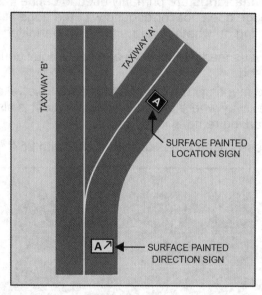

e. **Surface painted location signs** have a black background with a yellow inscription.

    1) When necessary, these markings are used to supplement location signs located alongside the taxiway and to confirm your taxiway designation.

    2) These markings are located on the right side of the centerline as shown in the figure above.

f. **Geographic position markings** are located at points along low visibility taxi routes and are used to identify the location of taxiing aircraft during low visibility operations (i.e., when the runway visual range is below 1,200 ft.).

    1) The geographic position marker is positioned to the left of the taxiway centerline in the direction of taxiing and has a pink background with a black number or a number and letter, as shown below.

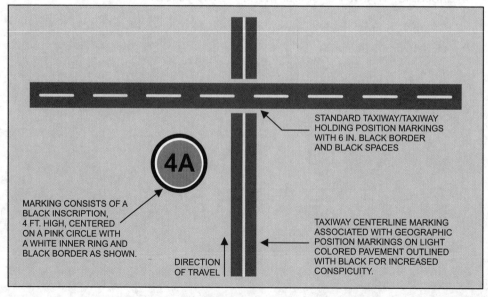

    2) The number corresponds to the consecutive position of the marking on the route.

g.   Closed or temporarily closed taxiway

1)   A permanently closed taxiway has all lighting disconnected and yellow crosses placed at each entrance of the taxiway and possibly at 1,000-ft. intervals.

2)   A temporarily closed taxiway is usually treated as a hazardous area that no part of the airplane may enter and is blocked with barricades.

a)   However, as an alternative, a yellow cross may be installed at each entrance to the taxiway.

4.   **Holding Position Markings**

a.   **Runway holding position markings** indicate where an aircraft is supposed to stop. They consist of four yellow lines, two solid and two dashed, extending across the width of the taxiway or runway. The solid lines are always on the side where the aircraft is to hold. Runway holding position markings are encountered at three locations.

1)   On taxiways, these markings identify the location where you are to stop when you do not have clearance to proceed onto the runway at a controlled airport or when you do not have adequate separation from other aircraft at an uncontrolled airport.

a)   When exiting the runway, you are not clear of the runway until all parts of your airplane have crossed the holding position marking.

2)   On a runway, these markings are installed only if the runway is used by ATC for "land, hold short" operations or taxiing.

a)   A sign with a white inscription on a red background is installed adjacent to these holding position markings.

b)   A land, hold short operation is one in which ATC instructions are "Cleared to land runway X; hold short of runway Y." If a pilot accepts this, (s)he must exit runway X or stop at the holding position prior to runway Y.

3)   Runway holding position markings are used at some airports when it is necessary to hold an aircraft on a taxiway located in the approach or departure area of a runway so that the aircraft does not interfere with the operation on the runway.

a)   This marking is collocated with the runway approach area holding sign.

b. **Holding position markings for ILS critical areas** consist of two yellow solid lines spaced 2 ft. apart connected by pairs of solid lines spaced 10 ft. apart extended across the width of the taxiway, as shown in the figure below.

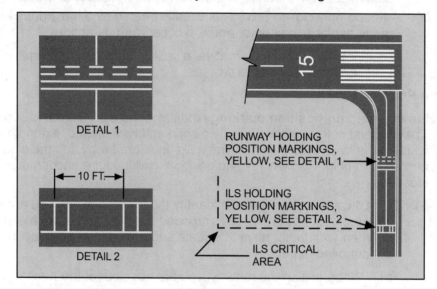

1) A sign with an inscription "ILS" in white on a red background is installed adjacent to these holding position markings.

2) When the ILS critical area is being protected, you must stop at the ILS holding position unless you have a clearance from ATC to proceed.

c. **Holding position markings for taxiway/taxiway intersections** consist of one dashed line extending across the width of the taxiway as shown below. They are installed on taxiways where ATC normally holds aircraft short of a taxiway intersection.

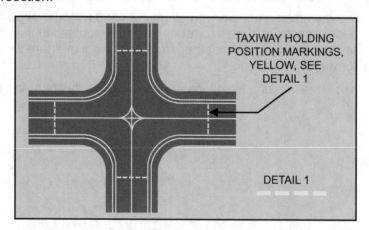

1) When the marking is not present and you are instructed by ATC "hold short of (taxiway)," you should stop at a point that provides adequate clearance from an aircraft on the intersecting taxiway.

d. **Surface painted holding position signs** have a red background with the intersecting runway's designation in white.

1) These markings may be used to supplement the runway holding position sign located alongside the taxiway.

2) This type of marking is normally used where the width of the holding position on the taxiway is greater than 200 ft.

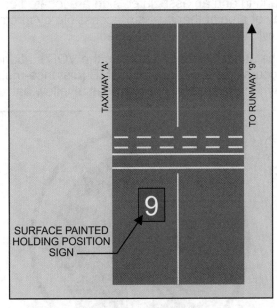

3) These markings are located on the left side of the centerline and prior to the holding position marking, as shown in the figure above.

5. **Other Markings**

a. **Vehicle roadway markings** are used to define a pathway for vehicle operations or crossing areas that are also intended for aircraft.

1) Vehicle roadway markings consist of a white solid line to delineate each edge of the roadway and a dashed line to separate lanes within the edges of the roadway.

a) An alternative to solid edge lines is the use of zipper markings (staggered lines).

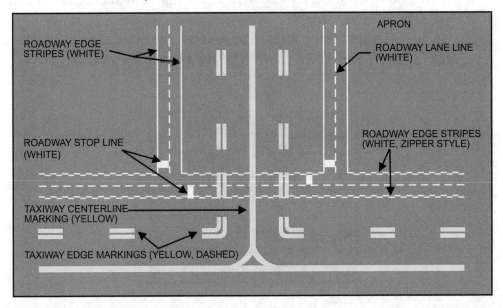

b. The **VOR receiver checkpoint marking** allows you to locate the position on the airport to perform a ground check of the VOR (VHF omnidirectional range) navigation instrument in your airplane, if equipped.

1) The VOR receiver checkpoint marking consists of a painted circle with an arrow in the middle; the arrow is aligned in the direction of the checkpoint direction to the VOR.

2) This marking and an associated sign are located on the airport ramp (apron) or taxiway at a point that is easily accessible by aircraft but where other airport traffic will not be unduly obstructed.

a) The associated sign contains the VOR station identifier and published course for the check and DME (distance-measuring equipment) data, when applicable. The sign has a yellow background with black inscription.

NOTES:
1. INTERIOR OF CIRCLE BLACK (CONCRETE SURFACES ONLY).
2. CIRCLE MAY BE BORDERED ON INSIDE AND OUTSIDE WITH 6 FT. BLACK BAND IF NECESSARY FOR CONTRAST.

c. **Non-movement area boundary markings** delineate the movement area, i.e., the area under air traffic control. These markings are yellow and are located on the boundary between the movement and non-movement areas.

1) The non-movement area boundary markings consist of two yellow lines, one solid and one dashed.

a) The solid line is located on the non-movement area side, while the dashed line is located on the movement area side.

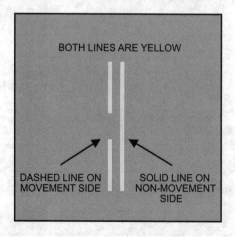

BOTH LINES ARE YELLOW

DASHED LINE ON MOVEMENT SIDE

SOLID LINE ON NON-MOVEMENT SIDE

d. **Helicopter landing area markings** are used to identify the landing and takeoff areas at public-use heliports and hospital heliports.

1) The letter "H" in the marking is oriented to align with the intended direction of approach.

2) A closed heliport will have a yellow cross over the "H."

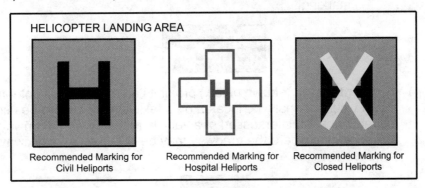

6. Airport signs are used on runways and taxiways to provide information. Six types of signs are installed on airports:

a. **Mandatory instruction signs** have white characters on a red background and are used to denote entrances to runways or critical areas and areas that airplanes are prohibited from entering.

1) A **runway holding position sign** is located at the holding position on taxiways that intersect a runway or on runways that intersect other runways.

a) A runway holding position sign on a taxiway will be installed adjacent to holding position markings on the taxiway pavement.

b) On a runway, if the runway is normally used by air traffic control for "land and hold short" operations or as a taxiway, holding position markings will be located only on the runway pavement adjacent to the sign. These may be referred to as runway signs or runway holding position signs.

c) The runway numbers on the sign are arranged to correspond to the respective runway threshold.

i) EXAMPLE: In the figure above, "15-33" indicates that the threshold for Runway 15 is to the left and the threshold for Runway 33 is to the right.

2) **Runway approach area holding position sign.** At some airports, it is necessary to hold an aircraft on a taxiway located in the approach or departure area for a runway so that the aircraft does not interfere with operations on that runway. In the figure below, the sign may protect the approach to Runway 15 and/or the departure for Runway 33.

15-APCH

3) **ILS critical area holding position sign.** At some airports, when the instrument landing system (ILS) is being used, it is necessary to hold an aircraft on a taxiway at a location other than the marked runway holding position.

   a)   In these situations, the holding position sign for these operations will have the inscription "ILS" and be located adjacent to an ILS holding position marking.

4) A **no entry sign** (shown below) prohibits an aircraft from entering an area. This sign would normally be located on a taxiway intended to be used in only one direction, at an intersection of a vehicle roadway with a runway or taxiway, or at a location where the roadway may be mistaken as a taxiway or other aircraft movement area.

b.   **Location signs** are used to identify either a taxiway or a runway on which the aircraft is located. Other location signs provide visual clues to pilots to assist them in determining when they have exited an area.

1) A **taxiway location sign** has yellow characters on a black background and a yellow border as shown below.

   a)   These signs are installed along taxiways either by themselves or in conjunction with direction signs or runway holding position signs.

2) A **runway location sign** is similar to the taxiway location sign except it will indicate on which runway the aircraft is located.

3) A **runway boundary sign** has a yellow background with a black inscription and a graphic depicting the pavement holding position marking, as shown below.

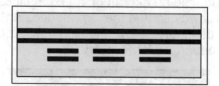

   a)   This sign, which faces the runway and is visible to the pilot exiting the runway, is located adjacent to the holding position marking on the pavement.

   b)   This sign is intended to provide pilots with another visual clue which they can use as a guide in deciding when they are "clear of the runway."

    4)   An **ILS critical area boundary sign** has a graphic depicting the ILS pavement holding position marking.

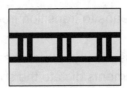

        a)   This sign is located adjacent to the pavement marking and is intended to assist pilots in deciding when they are "clear of the ILS critical area."

c.   **Direction signs** have black characters on a yellow background. The inscription identifies the designation(s) of the intersecting taxiway(s) leading out of the intersection that a pilot would normally be expected to turn onto or hold short of. Each designation is accompanied by an arrow indicating the direction of the turn.

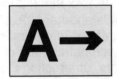

d.   **Destination signs** also have black characters on a yellow background indicating a destination on the airport. These signs always have an arrow showing the direction of the taxiing route to that destination.

    1)   Destinations commonly shown include runways, aprons (i.e., ramps), terminals, military areas (shown above), civil aviation areas, cargo areas, international areas, and fixed-base operators (FBOs).

e.   **Information signs** have black characters on a yellow background. They are used to provide the pilot with information on things such as areas that cannot be seen from the control tower, applicable radio frequencies, and noise abatement procedures.

f.   **Runway distance remaining signs** are located along one or both side(s) of the runway. These signs have white numbers on a black background.

    1)   The number on the sign indicates the distance (in thousands of feet) of runway remaining.

3.2 AIRPORT LIGHTING

1. **Approach Light Systems (ALS)**

    a. ALS provide the basic means to transition from instrument flight to visual flight for landing.

        1) Thus, ALS will be used only with precision and nonprecision instrument runways.

        2) Operational requirements dictate the sophistication and configuration of the ALS for a particular runway.

    b. ALS are a configuration of signal lights starting at the landing threshold and extending into the approach area for a distance of

        1) 2,400 ft. to 3,000 ft. for a precision instrument runway

        2) 1,400 ft. to 1,500 ft. for a nonprecision instrument runway

    c. Some ALS include sequenced flashing lights (SFL), which appear to you as a ball of light traveling toward the runway at a high speed.

    d. **LDIN** (lead-in light system) is another type of ALS. LDIN consists of one or more series of flashing lights installed at or near ground level that provide positive visual guidance along an approach path, either curving or straight, where special problems exist with hazardous terrain, obstructions, or noise abatement procedures.

    e. The following ALS are used with a precision instrument runway:

        1) **ALSF-1** -- approach light system with SFL in the ILS Category I configuration

        2) **ALSF-2** -- approach light system with SFL in the ILS Category II configuration

        3) **SSALR** -- simplified short approach light system with runway alignment indicator lights (RAIL)

            a) **RAIL** -- a type of ALS consisting of sequenced flashing lights installed only to supplement other light systems

        4) **MALSR** -- medium intensity approach light system with RAIL

            a) MALSR and SSALR have the same light configuration.

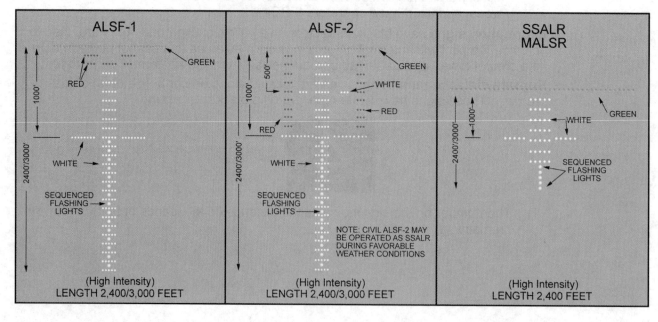

f.   The following ALS are used with a nonprecision instrument runway:

1) **SSALF** -- simplified short approach light system with SFL

2) **MALSF** -- medium-intensity approach light system with SFL

   a)   MALSF and SSALF have the same light configuration.

3) **ODALS** -- omnidirectional approach light system that consists of five lights located along the runway's extended centerline and two lights, one on each side of the runway's threshold

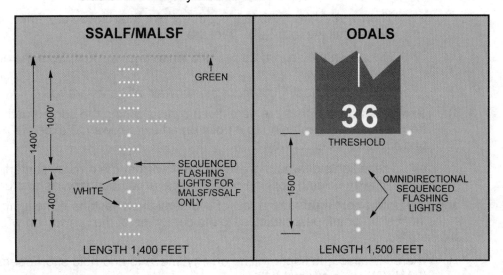

2.   **Runway Lights**

a.   **Runway edge lights** are used to outline the edges of the runway during periods of darkness or restricted visibility conditions.

1)   Runway edge lights are classified according to the intensity or brightness that they are capable of producing.

   a)   High-intensity runway lights (HIRL)

   b)   Medium-intensity runway lights (MIRL)

   c)   Low-intensity runway lights (LIRL)

2)   The HIRL and MIRL systems have variable intensity settings, and the LIRL system normally has one intensity setting.

3)   The runway edge lights are white, except that on instrument runways, yellow replaces white on the last 2,000 ft. or half the runway length, whichever is less, to form a caution zone for landings.

4)   Runway edge lights marking the ends of the runway (sometimes called runway end lights) show

   a)   Green to aircraft on approach, i.e., indicate the landing threshold

   b)   Red to aircraft taking off or on the landing rollout, i.e., indicate the end of the runway

5)   Runway edge lights help you identify runways as you approach the airport and also help you align your airplane on final approach.

b. **In-runway lighting** is installed on some precision approach runways to facilitate landing under adverse visibility conditions.

1) **Touchdown zone lighting (TDZL)** consists of two rows of flush white lights on either side of the centerline in the runway touchdown zone. The system starts 100 ft. from the landing threshold and extends to 3,000 ft. from the threshold or midpoint of the runway, whichever is less.

2) **Runway centerline lighting (RCLS)** consists of semi-flush centerline lights spaced at 50-ft. intervals along the runway centerline.

    a) When viewed from the landing threshold, the runway centerline lights are white until the last 3,000 ft. of the runway.

        i) Then they alternate red and white until 1,000 ft. from the end of the runway.

        ii) For the last 1,000 ft. of the runway, all lights are red.

3) **Taxiway lead-off lights** are semi-flush lights defining the curved path of travel from the runway centerline to a point on an exit taxiway to expedite movement of aircraft from the runway.

    a) These lights alternate green and yellow from the runway centerline to the runway holding position or ILS critical area boundary, as appropriate.

c. **Land and hold short lights** are a row of five semi-flush flashing white lights installed at the hold short point, perpendicular to the centerline of the runway on which they are installed.

1) Where installed, the lights will be on anytime land and hold short operations (LAHSO) are in effect.

    a) These lights will be off when LAHSO is not in effect.

3. **Taxiway Lights**

a. **Taxiway edge lights** are blue and outline the edges of taxiways during periods of darkness or restricted visibility conditions.

b. **Taxiway centerline lights** are green and used on some airports to mark the taxiway centerline during low visibility conditions.

c. **Clearance bar lights** consist of three in-pavement steady-burning yellow lights located at holding positions on taxiways to help you identify the holding position in low visibility conditions.

d. **Runway guard lights** are installed at taxiway/runway intersections and are primarily used to help you identify taxiway/runway intersections during low visibility conditions.

1) Runway guard lights consist of either a pair of elevated flashing yellow lights installed on either side of the taxiway or a row of in-pavement yellow lights installed across the entire taxiway at the runway holding position marking.

e. **Stop bar lights**, when installed, are used to confirm the ATC clearance to enter or cross the active runway in low visibility conditions.

1) Stop bars consist of a row of red, unidirectional, steady-burning in-pavement lights installed across the entire taxiway at the runway holding position and elevated steady-burning red lights on each side.

2) A controlled stop bar is operated in conjunction with the taxiway centerline lead-on lights, which extend from the stop bar toward the runway.

3) Following an ATC clearance to proceed, the stop bar is turned off and the lead-on lights are turned on. These lights are automatically reset by a sensor or timer.

a) You should never cross a red illuminated stop bar, even if an ATC clearance has been given to proceed onto or across the runway.

b) If, after you cross the stop bar, the lead-on lights are inadvertently extinguished, you should stop, hold your position, and contact ATC for further instructions.

4. **Runway End Identifier Lights (REIL)**

a. REILs are installed at many airports to provide rapid and positive identification of the approach end of a particular runway.

b. The REIL system consists of a pair of synchronized flashing lights located laterally on each side of the runway threshold.

1) The lights may be either omnidirectional or unidirectional facing the approach area.

c. The REIL system is effective for

1) Identification of a runway surrounded by a preponderance of other lighting
2) Identification of a runway which lacks contrast with surrounding terrain
3) Identification of a runway during reduced visibility

5. Control of lighting systems (approach, runway, taxiway) is managed by the control tower or by the Flight Service Station (FSS) where there is no operating control tower.

a. You may request that the lights be turned on or off.

b. Runway edge lights, in-runway lighting, approach lights, and some taxiway lights have intensity controls, which may be varied to meet your request.

c. Sequenced flashing lights may be turned on or off.

6. **Pilot control of lighting (PCL)** is available at many airports where there is no operating control tower or FSS.

a. All radio-controlled lighting systems operate on the same frequency, usually the common traffic advisory frequency (CTAF).

b. The control system consists of a three-step control responsive to seven, five, and/or three microphone clicks.

1) It is suggested that you always initially key the mike seven times to ensure that all controlled lights are at maximum available intensity.

2) You may lower the intensity (if applicable) by keying five or three times.

c. Due to the close proximity of airports using the same frequency, radio-controlled lighting receivers may be set at a low sensitivity requiring the airplane to be relatively close. The lights will usually be activated for 15 min.

d. The Chart Supplement contains descriptions of pilot-controlled lighting at all available airports and their frequencies.

7.   **Airport Rotating Beacons**

   a.   The primary purpose of these beacons is to identify the location of airports at night.
   b.   They usually flash 24 to 30 times per minute.
   c.   White and green alternating flashes indicate a lighted land airport for civil use.
   d.   Two whites and a green indicate a military airport.

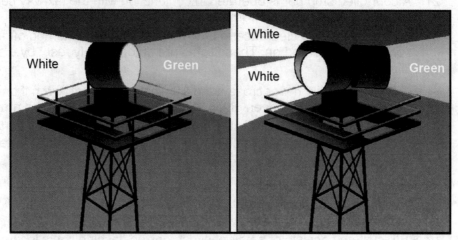

   e.   Operation of the green and white rotating beacon in Class B, C, D, and E surface areas during the day often indicates that the weather is below basic VFR weather minimums.

      1)   Less than 3 SM visibility, and/or
      2)   Ceiling less than 1,000 ft.

      NOTE: However, there is no regulatory requirement for daylight operation of the rotating beacon.

   f.   The beacon for a lighted heliport flashes green, yellow, and white, 30 to 45 times per minute.

8.   **Obstructions** are marked and lighted to warn pilots of their presence during daytime and nighttime conditions. They may be marked/lighted in any of the following combinations:

   a.   Aviation red obstruction lights -- flashing aviation red beacons and steady aviation red lights at night. Aviation orange and white paint is used for daytime marking.

   b.   Medium-intensity flashing white obstruction lights -- flashing medium-intensity white lights during daytime and twilight, with reduced intensity for nighttime operation.

      1)   When this system is used on structures that are 500 ft. AGL or less in height, other methods of marking and lighting the structure may be omitted.

      2)   Aviation orange and white paint is always required for daytime marking on structures exceeding 500 ft. AGL.

   c.   High-intensity white obstruction lights -- flashing high-intensity white lights during daytime with reduced intensity for twilight and nighttime operation. With this type of system, the red obstruction lights and aviation orange and white paint may be omitted.

   d.   Dual lighting -- a combination of flashing aviation red beacons and steady aviation red lights at night and flashing high-intensity white lights in daylight. Aviation orange and white paint may be omitted.

   e.   Catenary lighting -- lighted markers available to increase your ability to locate high-voltage transmission line catenary wires during both day and night.

      1)   A medium-intensity omnidirectional flashing white lighting system provides conspicuity both day and night on catenary support structures. The unique sequential/simultaneous flashing light system alerts you of the associated catenary wires.

3.3 VISUAL GLIDESLOPE INDICATORS

1. Most of the visual glideslope indicators use a system of lights positioned normally on the left side of the runway near the designated touchdown point.

   a. Once you understand the principles and color code of the lighting system, you simply note the colors and adjust your airplane's glide path (i.e., rate of descent) to remain on the visual glideslope.

   b. Visual glideslope indicators are very effective during either daytime or nighttime, especially during approaches over water or featureless terrain where sources of visual references are lacking or misleading.

      1) Visual glideslope indicators provide optimal descent guidance during the approach and minimize the possibility of undershooting or overshooting the designated touchdown area.

   c. When using a visual glideslope indicator, you should not begin your descent until you are aligned with the runway.

      1) Lateral guidance is provided by the runway or runway edge lights.

   d. When you make an approach to land on a runway at a controlled airport that has an operating visual slope indicator, you are required to remain at or above the glideslope until it is necessary to descend for a safe landing.

      1) This requirement does not prohibit you from making normal corrections above or below the glideslope for the purpose of remaining on the glideslope.

2. The **visual approach slope indicator (VASI)** is a system of lights arranged to provide visual descent guidance during an approach.

   a. VASI lights are visible from 3 to 5 miles during the day and sometimes more than 20 miles at night.

      1) The glide path of the VASI provides for safe obstacle clearance to a distance of 4 NM from the runway's threshold within 10° of the extended runway centerline.

   b. Basically, the VASI system uses color differentiation between red and white.

      1) Each light unit projects a beam of light having a white segment in the upper part of the beam and a red segment in the lower part of the beam.

      2) VASI may consist of 2, 4, 6, 12, or 16 light units arranged in bars that are referred to as near, middle, and far bars.

         a) The VASI lights are normally located on the left side of the runway.

         b) VASI systems with 12 or 16 light units have the lights on both sides of the runway.

c.   Most VASI systems consist of two bars (near and far) that provide one visual glide path, which is normally set at 3°.

1)   When on the proper glide path, you will, in effect, overshoot the downwind (near) bars and undershoot the upwind (far) bars. Thus, the downwind bars will be seen as white and the upwind bars as red.

2)   From a position below the glide path, you will see all the light bars as red. From above the glide path, all the light bars will appear white.

3)   Passing through the glide path from a low position, you will see a transition in color from red to white. This transition will occur if you maintain or gain altitude.

4)   Passing through the glide path from a high position, you will see a transition in color from white to red. This transition will occur if you begin above the VASI glide path and your rate of descent is too great (i.e., exceeds the VASI glide path).

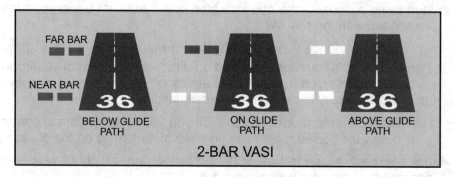

d.   Some VASI systems consist of three bars (near, middle, and far), which provide an additional glide path to accommodate high cockpit aircraft.

1)   The lower glide path is provided by the near and middle bars and is normally set at 3°, while the upper glide path, provided by the middle and far bars, is normally 1/4° higher.

a)   This higher glide path is intended for use only by high cockpit aircraft to provide a sufficient threshold crossing height.

2)   When using a three-bar VASI, it is not necessary to use all three bars. The near and middle bars constitute a two-bar VASI for using the lower glide path. Also, the middle and far bars constitute a two-bar VASI for using the upper glide path.

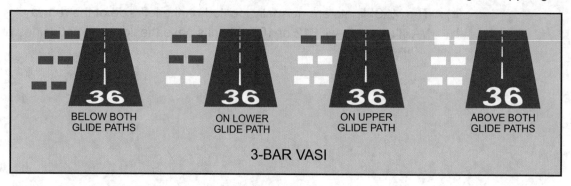

e.   The figure below illustrates some of the VASI variations you may encounter.

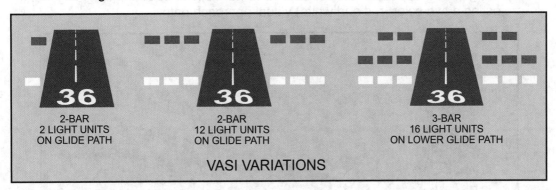

VASI VARIATIONS

3.   The **precision approach path indicator (PAPI)** uses lights similar to the VASI but in a single row of either two or four lights.

a.   The row of light units is normally installed on the left side of the runway.

b.   PAPI systems have an effective visual range of about 5 miles during the day and up to 20 miles at night.

c.   The glide path indications are depicted below.

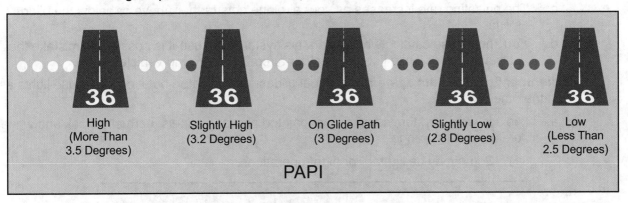

PAPI

4.   The **tri-color approach slope indicator** normally consists of a single light unit projecting a three-color visual approach path into the final approach area of the runway.

a.   The tri-color system has a useful range of approximately 1/2 to 1 mile during the day and up to 5 miles at night, depending on visibility conditions.

b.   The tri-color system uses a red, amber, and green light. You will see

1)   A red light when you are below the glide path
2)   An amber light when you are above the glide path
3)   A green light when you are on the glide path

c.   Caution: You may see a dark amber color during the transition from green to red when you begin to descend below the glide path.

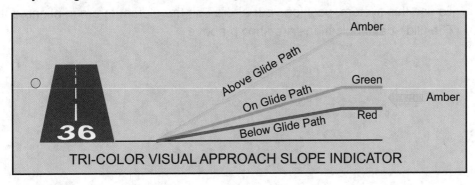

TRI-COLOR VISUAL APPROACH SLOPE INDICATOR

5. **Pulsating visual approach slope indicators** normally consist of a single light unit projecting a two-color (red and white) visual approach path.

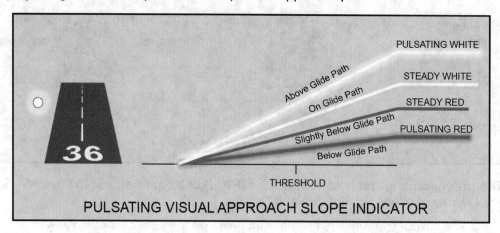

PULSATING VISUAL APPROACH SLOPE INDICATOR

a. The pulsating system has a useful range of about 4 miles during the day and up to 10 miles at night.
b. The glideslope indications are depicted above.
c. The pulsating rate increases as your airplane gets farther above or below the glide slope.
d. You should use caution when using this system because it is possible to mistake the pulsating red or white light for another aircraft or a ground vehicle.

6. **Alignment of elements system** is a visual glideslope indicator, but it does not use lights as in the other systems.

a. It is a low-cost system consisting of painted plywood panels, normally black and white or fluorescent orange.

    1) Some may be lighted for night operations.

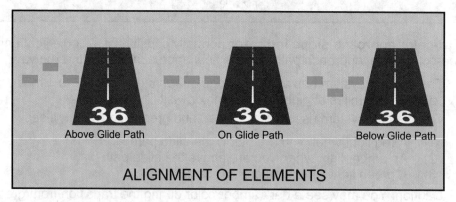

ALIGNMENT OF ELEMENTS

b. The useful range of this system is approximately 3/4 mi.
c. To use this system, position your aircraft so the elements are in alignment.
d. The glide path indications are shown above.

3.4 WIND AND LANDING DIRECTION INDICATORS AND SEGMENTED CIRCLES

1. It is important for you to know the wind direction when landing or taking off at an airport.

    a. At an airport with an operating control tower, ATC provides this information.

        1) At an airport with a Flight Service Station (FSS) and without an operating control tower, the FSS can provide you with the wind information.

    b. At an airport without an operating control tower, you may be able to receive wind information from an FBO at the airport.

    c. You may also be able to obtain wind information from automated weather systems located at some airports.

2. Virtually all airports have a wind indicator of one of the following types:

    a. Wind socks (or cones) are fabric "socks" through which wind blows.

        1) The large end of the wind sock points into the wind; thus, the wind blows through the sock from the large end to the small end.

        2) The vertical angle out from the pole indicates the strength of the wind.

            a) A limp sock means no wind.

            b) A horizontal sock means strong wind.

            c) A sock that is moving back and forth may indicate a variable or a gusty wind.

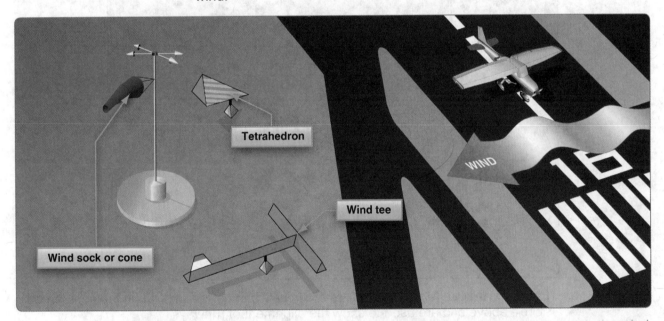

    b. Wind (landing) tees have the stem (bottom) of the "T" pointing in the direction the wind is GOING (indicating that landings should be in the opposite direction). Think of the wind tee as a small airplane (with the wings represented by the crossbar or top of the "T") landing into the wind.

        1) The landing tee indicates the direction of the wind but not the wind velocity.

    c. Tetrahedrons point to the direction from which the wind is COMING (indicating that landings should be in that direction).

        1) A tetrahedron will indicate the direction of the wind but not the wind velocity.

3. Some airports have a landing direction indicator (tetrahedron or landing tee) that is manually set by the airport operator to show the direction of landings and takeoffs.

    a. Think of the tetrahedron as a delta-wing jet fighter landing into the wind.
    b. Pilots are cautioned against using the tetrahedron as a wind indicator.
    c. When making a runway selection by use of a tetrahedron in very light or calm wind conditions, you should use extreme caution when selecting a runway because the tetrahedron may not be aligned with the designated calm-wind runway.

4. Where wind or landing direction indicators do not exist, observe the flow of traffic or use natural indicators.

    a. Smoke from ground fires, power plants, etc., shows wind direction.
    b. The water on the windward side of lakes and ponds tends to be calm, leaving a glassy surface that can be easily identified when airborne.
    c. The term windward refers to the side of the lake or pond that the wind is coming from.

5. The segmented circle system, if installed, provides traffic pattern information at airports without operating control towers. It consists of the following:

    a. The **segmented circle** is located in a position affording maximum visibility to pilots in the air and on the ground. A wind and/or landing direction indicator is usually in the center.

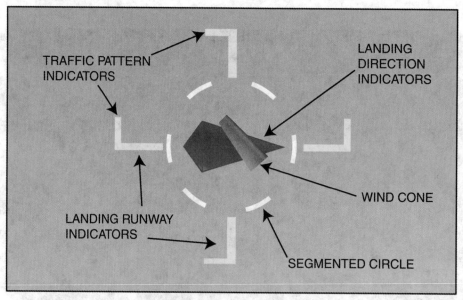

    b. **Landing runway (strip) indicators** are installed in pairs as shown in the segmented circle above and are used to show the alignment of runways.
    c. **Traffic pattern indicators** are arranged in pairs with the landing runway indicators and are used to indicate the direction of turns when there is a variation from the normal left traffic pattern.

        1) If the airport has no segmented circle, traffic pattern indicators may be installed on or near the runway ends.

    d. EXAMPLE: In the figure above, the wind is blowing from the bottom right of the box, and the airport operator has adjusted the tetrahedron to show the horizontal runway to be in use, with landings and departures to the right of the box.

        1) The traffic pattern indicators show the left traffic pattern is to be used on this runway.

3.5 AIRPORT TRAFFIC PATTERNS

1. Established airport traffic patterns ensure that air traffic flows into and out of an airport in an orderly manner. You should use the basic rectangular airport traffic pattern at the recommended altitude unless modified by air traffic control (ATC) or by approved visual markings at the airport.

2. **The Basic Rectangular Airport Traffic Pattern**

    a. The traffic pattern altitude is usually 1,000 ft. above the elevation of the airport, unless otherwise specified in the Chart Supplement. Using a common altitude is the key to minimizing collision risk.

    b. At all airports, the direction of traffic flow is to the left, unless right turns are indicated by

        1) Visual markings (i.e., traffic pattern indicators) on the airport
        2) Control tower instructions

    c. The basic rectangular traffic pattern consists of five "legs" positioned in relation to the runway in use, as illustrated on the next page.

        1) The **departure leg** of the traffic pattern is a straight course aligned with and leading from the takeoff runway.
        2) The **crosswind leg** is horizontally perpendicular to the extended centerline of the takeoff runway. It is entered by making a 90° turn from the upwind leg.
        3) The **downwind leg** is flown parallel to the landing runway but in a direction opposite to the intended landing direction.
        4) The **base leg** is the transitional part of the traffic pattern between the downwind leg and the final approach leg.
        5) The **final approach leg** is a descending flight path starting at the completion of the base-to-final turn and extending to the point of touchdown.

    d. The **upwind leg** is commonly misunderstood to be another name for the departure leg.

        1) It is actually a separate leg of the pattern entirely.
        2) The upwind leg is used to side-step the departure leg. This may be done in the case of a go-around or aborted landing.

e.   The traffic pattern

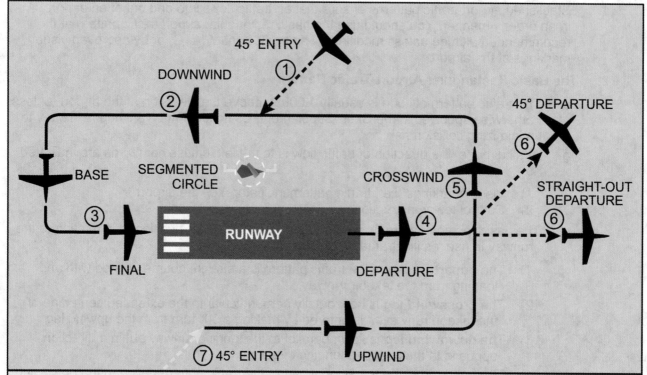

Key:

1. Enter pattern in level flight, abeam the midpoint of the runway, at pattern altitude.
2. Maintain pattern altitude until abeam approach end of the landing runway on the downwind leg.
3. Complete turn to final at least 1/4 mi. from the runway.
4. Continue straight ahead until beyond departure end of runway.
5. If remaining in the traffic pattern, commence turn to crosswind leg beyond the departure end of the runway, within 300 ft. of pattern altitude.
6. If departing the traffic pattern, continue straight out, or exit with a 45° left turn (right turn for right traffic pattern) beyond the departure end of the runway, after reaching pattern altitude.
7. There are a few airports in the U.S. that require a 45° entry to the upwind leg of the traffic pattern.

3. **Entering a Traffic Pattern**

    a.   At an airport with an operating control tower, the controller will direct when and where you should enter the traffic pattern.

        1)   Once you are in the pattern, the controller may request that you perform some maneuvers for better traffic spacing, including

            a)   Shortening or extending the downwind leg; increasing or decreasing your speed; or performing a 360° turn or S-turns to provide spacing ahead of you.

    b.   To enter the traffic pattern at an airport without an operating control tower, inbound pilots are expected to observe other aircraft already in the pattern and to conform to the traffic pattern in use.

        1)   If no other aircraft are in the pattern, traffic and wind indicators on the ground must be checked to determine which runway and traffic pattern direction should be used.

            a)   Overfly the airport at least 500 to 1,000 ft. above the traffic pattern altitude.

            b)   After the proper traffic pattern direction has been determined, you should proceed to a point well clear of the pattern before descending to the pattern altitude.

        2)   When approaching an airport for landing, you should enter the traffic pattern at a 45° angle to the downwind leg at the midpoint of the runway.

            a)   You should always be at the proper traffic pattern altitude before entering the pattern.

        3)   One method to enter the traffic pattern at an airport without an operating control tower is to fly in the landing direction parallel to, and slightly to one side of, the runway.

            a)   Once you are about 15 sec. past the departure end of the runway, turn 45° in the same direction as the traffic pattern direction (i.e., turn left if the runway is using left traffic; turn right if the runway is using right traffic).

            b)   Continue on this heading for approximately 2 NM; then make a descending 180° turn in the same direction as the traffic pattern to traffic pattern altitude, and enter the downwind leg at approximately a 45° angle at midfield.

4. **Departing a Traffic Pattern**

    a.   At airports with an operating control tower, ATC will generally approve the most expedient turnout for the direction of flight.

    b.   At airports without an operating control tower, you should depart straight out or with a 45° turn in the dircction of the traffic pattern after reaching pattern altitude.

3.6 LAND AND HOLD SHORT OPERATIONS (LAHSO)

1. Land and hold short operations (LAHSO) take place at some airports with an operating control tower in order to increase airport capacity and improve the flow of traffic.

    a. LAHSO requires that you land and hold short of an intersecting runway, an intersecting taxiway, or some other designated point on a runway.

2. Before accepting a clearance to land and hold short, you must determine that you can safely land and stop within the available landing distance.

3. Student pilots should not participate in the LAHSO program.

4. The pilot in command has the final authority to accept or decline any land and hold short (LAHSO) clearance.

    a. You are expected to decline a LAHSO clearance if you determine it will compromise safety.

5. You should receive a LAHSO clearance only when there is a minimum ceiling of 1,000 ft. and visibility of 3 SM.

    a. The intent of having basic VFR weather conditions is to allow pilots to maintain visual contact with other aircraft and ground vehicle operations.

3.7 WAKE TURBULENCE

1. Wake turbulence is a phenomenon resulting from the passage of an aircraft through the atmosphere. The term includes thrust stream turbulence, jet blast, jet wash, propeller wash, and rotor wash, both on the ground and in the air, but wake turbulence mostly refers to wingtip vortices.

2. **Wingtip vortices.** Lift is generated by the pressure differential between the upper and lower wing surfaces. The lower pressure occurs over the upper wing surface. The higher pressure occurs under the wing.

    a. This pressure differential triggers a roll-up of the airflow behind the wing. It results in swirling air masses trailing downstream of the wingtips. After the roll-up is completed, the wake consists of two counter-rotating cylindrical vortices.

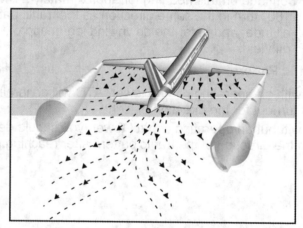

3. The strength of an airplane's wingtip vortices is governed by the weight, speed, and wing shape of the generating aircraft.

    a. The angle of attack of the wing directly affects the strength of its vortex.

        1) To maintain level flight:

            a) As weight increases, angle of attack increases.
            b) A wing in the clean configuration (flaps retracted) has a greater angle of attack than when flaps are extended.
            c) As airspeed decreases, angle of attack increases.

b. Thus, the greatest vortex strength occurs when the generating aircraft is HEAVY, CLEAN, and SLOW, e.g., during landing and especially during takeoff.

c. Wake turbulence presents a hazard to any aircraft that is significantly lighter than the generating aircraft.

   1) An airplane encountering such wake turbulence could incur major structural damage while in flight.

   2) Altitude upset and loss of directional control are also possible outcomes of encountering wake turbulence.

4. Trailing vortices have certain behavioral characteristics that can help you visualize the wake location and avoid it.

a. Vortices are generated from the moment the airplane rotates for takeoff (i.e., nosewheel off the ground) because trailing vortices are a by-product of wing lift.

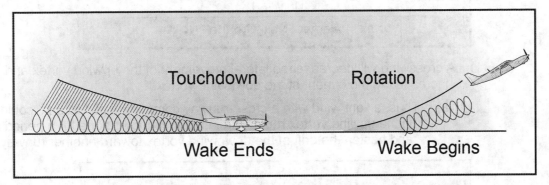

b. The vortex circulation is outward, upward, and around the wingtips.

   1) The vortices remain spaced about a wingspan apart, drifting with the wind, at altitudes greater than a wingspan from the ground.

   2) If you encounter persistent vortex turbulence, a slight change of altitude and lateral position (preferably upwind) will provide a flight path clear of the turbulence.

c. Vortices from larger (transport category) aircraft sink at a rate of several hundred feet per minute, slowing their descent and diminishing in strength with time and distance behind the generating aircraft.

   1) Atmospheric turbulence will hasten the breakup of the vortices.

   2) You should fly at or above the large aircraft's flight path, altering course as necessary to avoid the area behind and below the generating aircraft.

      a) However, vertical separation of 1,000 ft. may be considered safe.

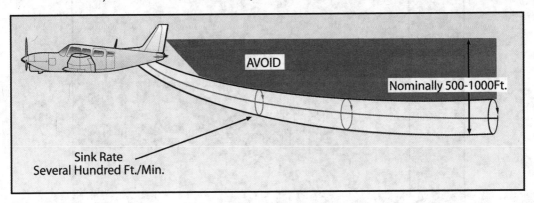

d.   When the vortices of large aircraft sink close to the ground (within 100 to 200 ft.), they tend to move laterally over the ground at a speed of about 2 or 3 kt.

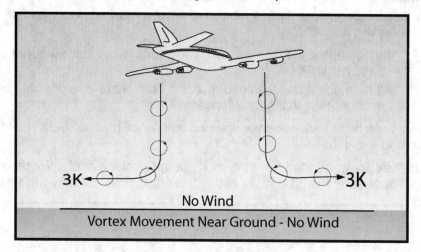

1)   A crosswind will decrease the lateral movement of the upwind vortex and increase the movement of the downwind vortex.

a)   Thus, a light wind with a cross-runway component of 1 to 5 kt. could result in the upwind vortex remaining in the touchdown zone for a period of time and hasten the drift of the downwind vortex toward another runway.

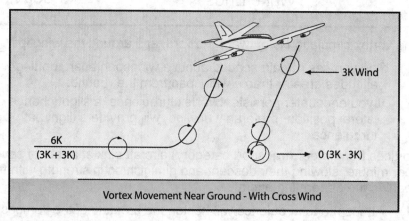

2)   A tailwind condition can move the vortices of the preceding aircraft forward into the touchdown zone.

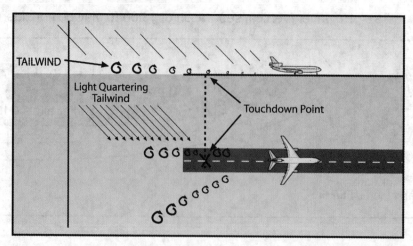

a)   A light quartering tailwind requires the maximum caution.

5. **Operational Problem Areas**

    a.   Although serious, even fatal, accidents can be caused by wake encounters, not all wake encounters are hazardous.

        1)   A wake encounter can be one or more jolts with varying severity depending upon

            a)   The direction of the wake encounter

            b)   The weight of the generating aircraft

            c)   The size of your airplane

            d)   The distance from the generating aircraft

            e)   The point of vortex encounter

        2)   The probability of an induced roll increases when your airplane's heading is generally aligned or parallel with the flight path of the generating aircraft.

    b.   You must avoid the area below and behind the generating aircraft, especially at low altitudes where even a momentary wake encounter could be hazardous.

        1)   Avoiding a wake encounter is not always easy to do. Some accidents have occurred even though the pilot of the trailing aircraft had carefully noted that the aircraft in front was at a considerably lower altitude.

            a)   The flight path of the lead aircraft does not always remain below the flight path of the trailing aircraft.

    c.   You should be particularly alert in calm wind conditions and situations in which the vortices could

        1)   Remain in the touchdown area

        2)   Drift from aircraft operating on a nearby runway

        3)   Sink into the takeoff or landing path from a crossing runway

        4)   Sink into the traffic pattern from other airport operations

6. The following vortex avoidance procedures are recommended:

    a.   Landing behind a larger aircraft that is landing on the same runway -- Stay at or above the larger aircraft's final approach flight path. Note the aircraft's touchdown point and land beyond it.

    b.   Landing behind a larger aircraft that is landing on a parallel runway closer than 2,500 ft. to your runway -- Consider possible vortex drift to your runway. Stay at or above the larger aircraft's final approach path and note its touchdown point.

    c.   Landing behind a larger aircraft that is landing on a crossing runway -- Cross above the larger aircraft's flight path.

    d.   Landing behind a larger aircraft departing on the same runway -- Note the larger aircraft's rotation point. Land well prior to the rotation point.

    e.   Landing behind a larger aircraft departing on a crossing runway -- Note the larger aircraft's rotation point.

        1)   If it rotates past the intersection, continue your approach and land prior to the intersection.

        2)   If the larger aircraft rotates prior to the intersection, avoid flight below the larger aircraft's flight path.

            a)   Abandon the approach unless your landing is ensured well before reaching the intersection.

    f.   Departing behind a larger aircraft taking off -- Note the larger aircraft's rotation point. You should rotate prior to the larger aircraft's rotation point. Continue to climb above and stay upwind of the larger aircraft's climb path until turning clear of its wake.

        1)   Avoid subsequent headings that will cross below and behind a larger aircraft.

        2)   Be alert for any critical takeoff situation that could lead to a vortex encounter.

    g.   Intersection takeoffs on the same runway -- Be alert to adjacent larger aircraft operations, particularly upwind of your runway. If intersection takeoff clearance is received, avoid a subsequent heading that will cross below a larger aircraft's path.

h.   Departing or landing after a larger aircraft has executed a low approach, a missed approach, or a touch-and-go landing -- Vortices settle and move laterally near the ground, so the vortex hazard may exist along the runway and in your flight path.

1)   Ensure that an interval of at least 2 min. has elapsed before your takeoff or landing.

i.   En route VFR -- Avoid flight below and behind a larger aircraft's path. If you observe a larger aircraft above and on the same track as your airplane (meeting or overtaking), adjust your position laterally, preferably upwind.

7.   **Helicopters**

a.   In a slow hover taxi or a stationary hover near the surface, helicopter main rotors generate downwash producing high-velocity outwash vortices to a distance approximately three times the diameter of the rotor.

1)   When rotor downwash hits the surface, the vortex circulation is outward, upward, around, and away from the main rotors in all directions.

2)   You should avoid operating your airplane within three rotor diameters of any helicopter in a slow hover taxi or stationary hover.

b.   In forward flight, departing or landing helicopters produce a pair of strong, high-speed trailing vortices similar to wingtip vortices of larger fixed-wing aircraft.

1)   You should use caution when operating behind or crossing behind landing and departing helicopters.

8.   **Jet Engine Exhaust**

a.   During ground operations, jet engine blast (thrust stream turbulence) can cause damage and upsets if encountered at close range.

1)   Thus, you need to maintain an adequate separation during ground operations.

2)   An illustration of exhaust velocities behind a wide-body jet at takeoff power is below.

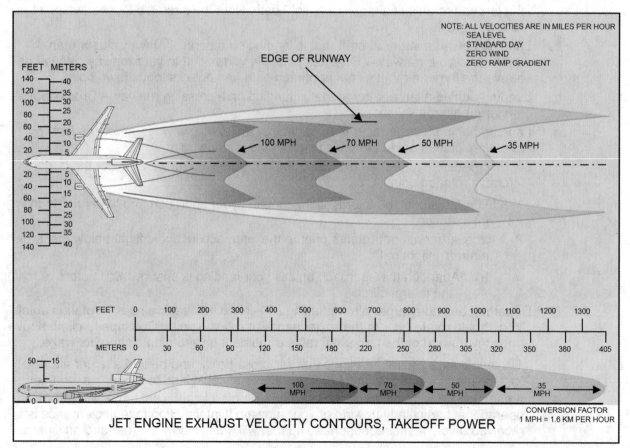

JET ENGINE EXHAUST VELOCITY CONTOURS, TAKEOFF POWER

9.   **Pilot Responsibility**

   a.   The flight disciplines necessary to ensure vortex avoidance during VFR operations must be exercised by you, the pilot.

   1)   You should exercise vortex visualization and avoidance procedures with the degree of concern that you demonstrate when avoiding collisions.

   b.   Wake turbulence may be encountered by aircraft in flight as well as by aircraft operating in the airport movement area.

   c.   Remember that, in operations conducted behind all aircraft, acceptance of instructions from ATC in the following situations is an acknowledgment that you will ensure safe takeoff and landing intervals and that you accept the responsibility for providing wake turbulence separation.

   1)   Traffic information
   2)   Instructions to follow an aircraft
   3)   Acceptance of a visual approach clearance

   d.   Pilots operating lighter aircraft on visual approaches in-trail to aircraft producing strong wake vortices should use the following procedures to assist in avoiding wake turbulence.

NOTE: These procedures do not apply when conducting an instrument approach; ATC will provide separation.

   1)   Fly on or above the glide path, which may be furnished by an ILS, a visual approach slope system, by other ground-based approach slope guidance systems, or by other means.

   a)   In the absence of visible glide path guidance, you may very nearly duplicate a 3° glideslope by adhering to the "3-to-1" principle.

   i)   EXAMPLE: Fly 3,000 ft. AGL at 10 miles from touchdown, 1,500 ft. AGL at 5 miles, 1,200 ft. AGL at 4 miles, and so on to touchdown.

   b)   Aircraft producing strong wake vortices are being asked to remain on, not above, the glide path, or a 3-to-1 glide path.

   2)   If you have visual contact with the preceding heavier aircraft and also with the runway, you may further adjust for possible wake turbulence by the following:

   a)   Pick a point of landing no less than 1,000 ft. from the threshold of the runway.

   b)   Establish a line of sight to that landing point above and in front of the heavier preceding aircraft.

   c)   When possible, note the point of landing of the preceding aircraft and adjust your point of intended landing as necessary.

   i)   EXAMPLE: A puff of smoke may appear at the 1,000-ft. markings of the runway, showing that touchdown was at that point; thus, adjust your point of intended landing to the 1,500-ft. markings.

   d)   Maintain the line of sight to the point of intended landing above and ahead of the heavier aircraft; maintain it to touchdown.

   e)   Land beyond the point of landing of the preceding heavier aircraft.

   3)   During visual approaches, you may ask ATC for updates on separation and groundspeed with respect to heavier preceding aircraft, especially when there is any question of safe separation from wake turbulence.

10. **ATC Wake Turbulence Separations**

a. Because of the possible effects of wake turbulence, ATC is required to apply no less than specified minimum separation for aircraft operating behind a heavy jet (capable of takeoff weights of more than 255,000 lb.) and, in certain instances, behind large nonheavy aircraft, i.e., Boeing 757 (B757).

    1) A large aircraft has a maximum certificated takeoff weight of more than 41,000 lb. up to 255,000 lb.

    2) A small aircraft has a maximum certificated takeoff weight of 41,000 lb. or less.

b. Separation is applied to aircraft operating directly behind a heavy jet or a B757 at the same altitude or less than 1,000 ft. below.

    1) Small aircraft operating behind heavy jet/B757 -- 5 miles

c. Separation, measured at the time the preceding aircraft is over the landing threshold, is provided to small aircraft.

    1) Small aircraft landing behind heavy jet -- 6 miles
    2) Small aircraft landing behind B757 -- 5 miles
    3) Small aircraft landing behind large aircraft -- 4 miles

d. Additionally, appropriate time or distance intervals are provided to departing aircraft.

    1) Two minutes or the appropriate 4- or 5-mile radar separation when takeoff behind a heavy jet/B757 jet will be

        a) From the same threshold

        b) On a crossing runway with projected flight paths crossing

        c) From the threshold of a parallel runway when staggered ahead of that of the adjacent runway by less than 500 ft. and when the runways are separated by less than 2,500 ft.

e. ATC may not reduce or waive the intervals described in items b. through d. above.

f. A 3-min. interval will be provided when a small aircraft will take off

    1) From an intersection on the same runway (same or opposite direction) behind a departing large aircraft

    2) In the opposite direction on the same runway behind a large aircraft takeoff or low/missed approach

NOTE: This 3-min. interval may be waived upon specific pilot request.

g. A 3-min. interval will be provided for all aircraft taking off when the operations are as described in items f.1) and 2) above, the preceding aircraft is a heavy jet/B757 jet, and the operations are on either the same runway or parallel runways separated by less than 2,500 ft.

    1) ATC may not reduce or waive this interval.

h. You may request additional separation, i.e., 2 min. instead of 4 or 5 miles for wake turbulence avoidance.

    1) This request to ground control should be made as soon as practicable and at least before taxiing onto the runway.

i. ATC may anticipate separation and need not withhold a takeoff clearance from an aircraft departing behind a large/heavy aircraft if there is reasonable assurance that the required separation will exist when the departing aircraft starts the takeoff roll.

3.8 COLLISION AVOIDANCE

1. Scanning the sky for other aircraft is a key factor in collision avoidance. You and your copilot (or right-seat passenger), if there is one, should scan continuously to cover all areas of the sky visible from the cockpit.

   a. You must develop an effective scanning technique that maximizes your visual capabilities.

      1) While the eyes can observe an approximate 200° arc of the horizon at one glance, only a very small center area (the fovea) can send clear, sharply focused messages to the brain. All visual information that is not processed directly through the fovea will be less detailed.

      2) An aircraft that is 7 mi. away may appear in sharp focus within the foveal center of vision but must be as close as 7/10 mi. to be recognized by less central vision.

   b. Each of your eyes also has a blind spot. Try this simple demonstration:

      1) Hold this page at arm's length in front of your face and cover your right eye with your hand.

      2) While focusing your left eye on the right X, slowly move the page toward your face.

      3) At a certain distance, the airplane on the left will seem to disappear.

      4) If a real aircraft were in this blind spot and blocked from view of the other eye by a part of your airplane, the other aircraft would essentially be invisible.

   c. Effective scanning is accomplished with a series of short, regularly spaced eye movements that bring successive areas of the sky into the central visual field.

      1) Each eye movement should not exceed 10°.
      2) Each area should be observed for at least 1 sec. to enable detection.

   d. Visual tasks inside the cabin should represent no more than 1/4 to 1/3 of the scan time outside or no more than 4 to 5 sec. on the instrument panel for every 16 sec. outside.

      1) You must realize that your eyes may require several seconds to refocus when switching your view from items in the cockpit to distant objects.

   e. Effective scanning also helps avoid "empty-field myopia."

      1) When flying above the clouds or in a haze layer that provides nothing specific to focus on outside the aircraft, the eyes tend to relax and seek a comfortable focal distance, which may range from 10 to 30 ft.

      2) For you, this means looking without seeing, which is dangerous.

2. **Collision Avoidance**

    a.   Determining relative altitude -- Use the horizon as a reference point. If you see another aircraft above the horizon, it is probably on a higher flight path. If it appears to be below the horizon, it is probably flying at a lower altitude.

    b.   Taking appropriate action -- You must be familiar with the rules of right-of-way so that, if an aircraft is on an obvious collision course, you can take the appropriate evasive action.

    c.   Considering multiple threats -- The decision to climb, descend, or turn is a matter of personal judgment, but you should anticipate that the other pilot may also be making a quick maneuver. Watch the other aircraft during the maneuver, but begin your scanning again immediately. There may be even more aircraft in the area!

    d.   Observing collision course targets -- Any aircraft that appears to have no relative motion and stays in one scan quadrant is likely to be on a collision course. Also, if a target shows no lateral or vertical motion but increases in size, take evasive action.

    e.   Recognizing high hazard areas

        1)   Airways, VORs, and airport traffic areas are places where aircraft tend to cluster.
        2)   Remember that most collisions occur on days when the weather is good.

    f.   Practicing cockpit management -- Study maps, checklists, and manuals BEFORE flight, along with other proper preflight planning (e.g., noting necessary radio frequencies). Also, organizing cockpit materials can reduce the time you need to look at them during flight, permitting more scan time.

    g.   Improving windshield conditions -- Dirty or bug-smeared windshields can greatly reduce your ability to see other aircraft. Keep a clean windshield.

    h.   Considering visibility conditions -- Smoke, haze, dust, rain, and flying toward the sun can also greatly reduce the ability to detect other aircraft.

    i.   Being aware of visual obstructions in the cockpit

        1)   You may need to move your head to see around blind spots caused by fixed aircraft structures, such as door posts, wings, etc. It may even be necessary occasionally to maneuver your airplane (e.g., lift a wing) to facilitate seeing.
        2)   Check that curtains and other cockpit objects (e.g., maps that glare on the windshield) are removed and stowed during flight.

    j.   Using lights

        1)   Day or night, exterior lights can greatly increase the visibility of any aircraft.
        2)   Keep interior lights low at night so that you can see out in the dark.

    k.   Requesting ATC support -- ATC facilities often provide radar traffic advisories (e.g., flight following) on a workload-permitting basis. Use this support whenever possible or when required.

        1)   Nevertheless, being in a radar environment (i.e., where traffic is separated by radar) still requires vigilance to avoid collisions. Radar does not relieve you of the responsibility to see and avoid other aircraft.

3.   **Near Midair Collision (NMAC)**

   a.   Most midair collision accidents and reported NMAC incidents occur during good VFR weather conditions (i.e., clear days) and during daylight when more aircraft are likely to be flying.

   b.   Near Midair Collision Reporting

   1)   Purpose and data uses. The primary purpose of the NMAC Reporting Program is to provide information for use in enhancing the safety and efficiency of the National Airspace System through the development of safety programs and other recommendations.

   2)   Definition. A NMAC is defined as an incident associated with the operation of an aircraft in which a possibility of collision occurs as a result of proximity of less than 500 feet.

   3)   Reporting responsibility. It is the responsibility of the pilot and/or flight crew to determine whether a NMAC did actually occur and, if so, to initiate a NMAC report.

   a)   Be specific because ATC will not interpret a casual remark to mean that a NMAC is being reported.

   b)   The pilot should state "I wish to report a near midair collision."

   4)   Where to file reports. Pilots and/or flight crew members involved in NMAC occurrences are urged to report each incident immediately:

   a)   By radio or telephone to the nearest FAA ATC facility or FSS.

   b)   In writing, in lieu of the above, to the nearest Flight Standards District Office (FSDO).

   5)   Items to be reported.

   a)   Date and time (UTC) of incident.

   b)   Location of incident and altitude.

   c)   Identification and type of reporting aircraft, aircrew destination, name and home base of pilot.

   d)   Identification and type of other aircraft, aircrew destination, name and home base of pilot.

   e)   Type of flight plans; station altimeter setting used.

   f)   Detailed weather conditions at altitude or flight level.

   g)   Approximate courses of both aircraft: indicate if one or both aircraft were climbing or descending.

   h)   Reported separation in distance at first sighting, proximity at closest point horizontally and vertically, and length of time in sight prior to evasive action.

   i)   Degree of evasive action taken, if any (from both aircraft, if possible).

   j)   Injuries, if any.

   6)   Investigation. The FSDO in whose area the incident occurred is responsible.

   a)   An investigation will be conducted, and when possible, interviews will take place.

   i)   Both flight and ATC procedures will be evaluated.

   ii)   Enforcement action will be pursued if the investigation reveals a violation of an FAA regulation has occurred.

4.   **Runway Incursion Avoidance**

a.   The FAA defines **runway incursion** as any occurrence at an aerodrome involving the incorrect presence of an aircraft, vehicle, or person on the protected area of a surface designated for the landing and takeoff of aircraft. Some examples of runway incursions are

   1)   At an airport without an operating control tower, a departing aircraft may taxi into position for takeoff without first checking for landing traffic. If an aircraft is on short final when this happens, a go-around will be necessary, or a collision could result.

   2)   While taxiing at an airport with a complex taxiway layout, a pilot may become confused as to his or her location and inadvertently cross or turn onto a runway that is being used by another aircraft. Depending on the timing of the incursion, the other aircraft may have to abort a takeoff or perform a go-around. A collision may be unavoidable.

   3)   At an airport with an operating control tower, a pilot may misunderstand a clearance (or fail to obtain the correct clearance due to inattention) and cross a runway of which (s)he was instructed to hold short. The pilot could also turn onto the wrong runway when cleared for takeoff. Any aircraft using these runways may have to abort a takeoff or perform a go-around. Again, a collision may be unavoidable.

b.   Runway incursions are a significant safety issue the FAA is dedicated to reducing or eliminating through education and training.

   1)   The FAA created the Office of Runway Safety to assist in pilot training and prevent runway incursions.

      a)   This department holds pilot meetings around the United States through participation with local FSDOs.

      b)   Access the Office of Runway Safety online at www.faa.gov/airports/runway_safety/.

   2)   Pilots must be informed on airport information before beginning a flight.

      a)   Transient pilots should be aware of potential construction issues and proper taxi procedures at destination airports.

      b)   Based pilots should not grow complacent due to familiarity with local airport operations.

         i)   All pilots must listen closely to controller and/or other aircraft transmissions.

c.   Runway incursions most likely to cause accidents are common at high-volume airports with complex taxiway layouts and multiple parallel or intersecting runways.

   1)   The vast majority are caused by general aviation pilots who are confused or disoriented, do not understand a controller's instructions, or are not paying attention to their surroundings.

   2)   The likelihood of an accident increases when the visibility is low.

d.   The potential for runway incidents and accidents can be reduced through adequate planning, coordination, and communication. The following are some practices to help prevent a runway incursion:

1)   Read back all runway/taxiway crossing and/or hold instructions.
2)   Review airport layouts prior to taxi, before landing if able, and while taxiing as needed.
3)   Review NOTAMs for up-to-date information.
4)   Be familiar with airport signs and markings.
5)   Request progressive taxi from ATC when unsure of taxi route.
6)   Check for traffic before crossing any runway or taxiway or entering a runway or taxiway.
7)   Make sure aircraft position and taxi lights are on whenever aircraft is moving.
8)   When landing, clear the active runway in a timely fashion.
9)   Use proper phraseology and good radio discipline at all times.
10) Write down complex taxi instructions.

5.   **Traffic Detection Systems**

a.   Traffic detection systems are becoming affordable enough that more and more general aviation aircraft are equipped with them. There are generally two types of traffic detection systems: active and passive systems.

1)   An **active system** emits interrogation signals and does not rely on ground radar.
2)   A **passive system** relies on transponder replies triggered by ground and airborne components.

a)   Passive systems will display traffic similar to active systems; however, they generally have a range of less than 7 nautical miles.
b)   Because passive systems rely on relayed information, they often display delayed information.

b.   **Traffic Alert and Collision Avoidance System (TCAS)**

1)   TCAS is an active system that can detect aircraft transponder signals. There are three system variations that offer increasing levels of sensitivity and information to the pilot:

a)   TCAS I

i)   Allows the pilot to see the relative position and velocity of other transponder-equipped aircraft within a 10 to 20-mile range
ii)   Provides a warning when an aircraft in the vicinity gets too close
iii) Does NOT provide instructions on how to maneuver in order to avoid the aircraft

b)   TCAS II

i)   Provides pilots with airspace surveillance, intruder tracking, threat detection, and avoidance maneuver instructions
ii)   Provides traffic advisories (TAs) and resolution advisories (RAs)

•   Resolution advisories provide recommended maneuvers in a vertical direction (climb or descend only) to avoid conflicting traffic.

c)   TCAS III

i)   Very similar to TCAS II
ii)   Utilizes interrogation of, and replies from, airborne radar beacon transponders and provides traffic advisories and resolution advisories in the vertical AND horizontal planes to the pilot

2)   A typical TCAS display and resolution advisory are shown in the following figure.

a)   The white arrow shows that the pilot is being told to climb at 1,500-2,000 feet per minute to avoid the conflicting traffic.

c.   **Traffic Information System (TIS)**

1)   TIS is a passive system that provides many of the functions available in TCAS.

a)   Unlike TCAS, TIS is a ground-based service available to all aircraft equipped with Mode S transponders.

2)   TIS takes advantage of the Mode S data link to communicate collision avoidance information to aircraft. This information is presented to the pilot via a cockpit display.

3)   TIS system uses track reports provided by ground-based Mode S surveillance systems to retrieve traffic information.

a)   Because it is available to all Mode S transponders, TIS offers an inexpensive alternative to TCAS.

4)   A typical TIS display is shown below:

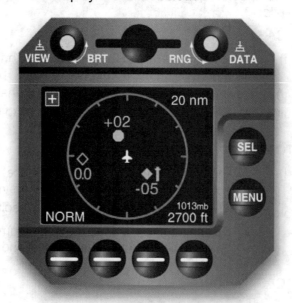

3.9 RADIO COMMUNICATIONS AND PHRASEOLOGY

1. Airplane communication radios greatly facilitate flying. Pilots use radios to

    a. Obtain air traffic control (ATC) clearances

        1) Ground control
        2) Tower control, e.g., takeoffs and landings
        3) Approach and departure control (in the vicinity of the airport)
        4) En route control

    b. Obtain weather briefings, file flight plans, etc., with Flight Service Stations (FSSs)

    c. Communicate with FBOs and each other on CTAF, UNICOM, and MULTICOM frequencies

2. Airplane communication radios operate on the VHF (very high frequency) band between 118.000 MHz and 136.975 MHz.

    a. These radios are classified as 720 or 760, depending on the number of channels they can accommodate.

        1) The 720 and 760 channel radios use 0.025 MHz spacing (118.025, 118.050, etc.), with the 720 having a frequency range up to 135.975 and the 760 going up to 136.975.

    b. VHF radios are limited to line-of-sight transmissions; thus, aircraft at higher altitudes are able to transmit and receive at greater distances.

3. Radio communications are a critical link in the ATC system. The link can be a strong bond between you and the controller, or it can be broken with surprising speed and disastrous results.

    a. The single most important factor in pilot-controller communications is understanding.

        1) Good phraseology enhances safety and is a mark of a professional pilot.
        2) Jargon, chatter, and "CB" slang have no place in ATC communications.

4. **Phonetic Alphabet**

    a. You should use the phonetic alphabet when identifying your airplane during initial contact with air traffic control facilities.

A	.-	Alpha	(AL-FAH)		T	-	Tango	(TANG-GO)
B	-...	Bravo	(BRAH-VOH)		U	..-	Uniform	(YOU-NEE-FORM)
C	-.-.	Charlie	(CHAR-LEE) or (SHAR-LEE)		V	...-	Victor	(VIK-TAH)
D	-..	Delta	(DELL-TAH)		W	.--	Whiskey	(WISS-KEY)
E	.	Echo	(ECK-OH)		X	-..-	Xray	(ECKS-RAY)
F	..-.	Foxtrot	(FOKS-TROT)		Y	-.--	Yankee	(YANG-KEY)
G	--.	Golf	(GOLF)		Z	--..	Zulu	(ZOO-LOO)
H	....	Hotel	(HOH-TEL)					
I	..	India	(IN-DEE-AH)					
J	.---	Juliett	(JEW-LEE-ETT)		1	.----	One	(WUN)
K	-.-	Kilo	(KEY-LOH)		2	..---	Two	(TOO)
L	.-..	Lima	(LEE-MAH)		3	...--	Three	(TREE)
M	--	Mike	(MIKE)		4	....-	Four	(FOW-ER)
N	-.	November	(NO-VEM-BER)		5	.....	Five	(FIFE)
O	---	Oscar	(OSS-CAH)		6	-....	Six	(SIX)
P	.--.	Papa	(PAH-PAH)		7	--...	Seven	(SEV-EN)
Q	--.-	Quebec	(KEH-BECK)		8	---..	Eight	(AIT)
R	.-.	Romeo	(ROW-ME-OH)		9	----.	Nine	(NIN-ER)
S	...	Sierra	(SEE-AIR-RAH)		0	-----	Zero	(ZEE-RO)

    b. Additionally, use the phonetic equivalents for single letters and for spelling out groups of letters or difficult words during adverse communication conditions.

    c. Work through the listing of alphabetic phonetic equivalents, saying each out loud to learn it.

        1) Note that the Morse code is also provided. Although it is not used as frequently as it once was, occasionally you may need it for identification, e.g., at a VOR without voice facilities. You need not learn the Morse code; just keep it handy.

5.   **Figures**

    a.   Figures indicating hundreds and thousands in round numbers, as for ceiling heights and upper wind levels up to 9,900, are spoken in accordance with the following:

        1)   EXAMPLES: 500 is "FIVE HUNDRED"

                              4,500 is "FOUR THOUSAND FIVE HUNDRED"

    b.   Numbers above 9,900 are spoken by separating the digits preceding the word "thousand."

        1)   EXAMPLES: 10,000 is "ONE ZERO THOUSAND"

                              13,500 is "ONE THREE THOUSAND FIVE HUNDRED"

    c.   Airway numbers. Airways are routes between navigational aids, such as VORs (i.e., airways are highways in the sky).

        1)   EXAMPLE: V12 is "VICTOR TWELVE"

    d.   All other numbers are spoken by pronouncing each digit.

        1)   EXAMPLE: 10 is "ONE ZERO"

    e.   When a radio frequency contains a decimal point, the decimal point is spoken as "POINT."

        1)   EXAMPLE: 122.1 is "ONE TWO TWO POINT ONE"

6.   **Altitudes and Flight Levels**

    a.   Up to but not including 18,000 ft. MSL, state the separate digits of the thousands, plus the hundreds, if appropriate.

        1)   EXAMPLES: 12,000 is "ONE TWO THOUSAND"

                              12,500 is "ONE TWO THOUSAND FIVE HUNDRED"

    b.   At and above 18,000 ft. MSL (FL 180), state the words "flight level" followed by the separate digits of the flight level.

        1)   EXAMPLE: FL 190 is "FLIGHT LEVEL ONE NINER ZERO" (19,000 ft. MSL)

7.   **Directions.** The three digits of bearing, course, heading, and wind direction should always be magnetic. The word "TRUE" must be added when it applies.

    a.   EXAMPLES:

        1)   (Magnetic course) 005 is "ZERO ZERO FIVE"
        2)   (True course) 050 is "ZERO FIVE ZERO TRUE"
        3)   (Magnetic bearing) 360 is "THREE SIX ZERO"
        4)   (Magnetic heading) 100 is "ONE ZERO ZERO"
        5)   (Wind direction) 220 is "TWO TWO ZERO"

    b.   Wind velocity (speed) is always included with wind direction, e.g., "THREE FOUR ZERO AT ONE ZERO."

        1)   ATC gives winds in magnetic direction.
        2)   FSS gives winds in true direction from weather reports and forecasts.

8. **Speeds**

    a. Say the separate digits of the speed followed by the word "knots."

        1) EXAMPLES: 250 is "TWO FIVE ZERO KNOTS"
            185 is "ONE EIGHT FIVE KNOTS"

    b. The controller may omit the word "knots" when using speed adjustment procedures, e.g., "INCREASE SPEED TO ONE FIVE ZERO."

9. **Time**

    a. Aviation uses an international standard time with a 24-hour clock system to establish a common time.

    b. The international standard time is called Coordinated Universal Time (UTC). The term "Zulu" (Z) may be used to denote UTC. This used to be referred to as Greenwich Mean Time (GMT).

        1) UTC is actually the time at the 0° meridian, which passes through the Royal Observatory in Greenwich, England.

    c. The FAA uses UTC or Zulu time for all operations. Use the time conversion table below to find UTC. For daylight time, subtract 1 hour.

        1) When converting from UTC or Zulu time to local time, subtract the hours.

Time Zone	UTC
Eastern Standard Time	+5 hr.
Central Standard Time	+6 hr.
Mountain Standard Time	+7 hr.
Pacific Standard Time	+8 hr.
Alaska Standard Time	+9 hr.
Hawaii Standard Time	+10 hr.

    d. The 24-hr. clock system is used in radio transmissions. The hour is indicated by the first two figures and the minutes by the last two figures.

        1) EXAMPLES: 0000 (midnight) is "ZERO ZERO ZERO ZERO"
            0920 (9:20 a.m.) is "ZERO NINER TWO ZERO"
            1850 (6:50 p.m.) is "ONE EIGHT FIVE ZERO"

10. In virtually all situations, your radio broadcasts can be thought of as

    a. To whom you are talking

    b. Who you are

    c. Where you are

    d. What you want to do

    e. To whom you are talking (when making common traffic advisories in uncontrolled airport areas)

3.10 AIRPORTS WITHOUT AN OPERATING CONTROL TOWER

1. At an airport that does not have an operating control tower, there is no air traffic control over movements of aircraft on the ground or around the airport in the air. The term "uncontrolled airport" is also used to mean an airport without an operating control tower.

    a. It is essential that pilots be alert, look for other traffic, and exchange information when approaching or departing an airport without an operating control tower.

        1) This is of particular importance because other aircraft may not have communication capability or pilots may not communicate their presence or intentions.

    b. To achieve the greatest degree of safety, it is essential that all radio-equipped aircraft transmit/receive on a common frequency identified for the purpose of airport advisories.

2. The key to communicating at an airport without an operating control tower is the selection of the correct frequency. The term **common traffic advisory frequency (CTAF)** is synonymous with this program.

    a. CTAF is a frequency designated for the purpose of carrying out airport advisory practices while operating to or from an airport without an operating control tower.

        1) CTAF may be a UNICOM, MULTICOM, FSS, or tower frequency.
        2) The CTAF at an airport is indicated on the sectional chart by a Ⓒ next to the appropriate frequency.

    b. Pilots of inbound aircraft should monitor and communicate as appropriate on the CTAF 10 NM from the airport.

        1) Pilots of departing aircraft should monitor and communicate on the CTAF from start-up, during taxi, and until 10 NM from the airport unless the Federal Aviation Regulations or local procedures require otherwise.

    c. Pilots of aircraft conducting other than arriving or departing operations at altitudes normally used by arriving and departing aircraft should monitor/communicate on the CTAF while within 10 NM of the airport unless the Federal Aviation Regulations or local procedures require otherwise.

    d. There are three ways for you to communicate your intentions and obtain airport/traffic information when operating at an airport without an operating control tower:

        1) Local airport advisory (LAA)
        2) UNICOM (an aeronautical advisory station)
        3) A self-announced broadcast

3. **LAA** is a service provided at selected FSSs physically located at airports that do not have control towers or where the towers are operated on a part-time basis.

    a. The FSS should be contacted on the CTAF for airport advisories, including traffic and weather information.

    b. Recommended LAA phraseologies

        1) Inbound example

            a) Pilot: JONESBORO RADIO, PIPER TOMAHAWK 1617T IS 10 MILES SOUTH, AT (ALTITUDE), LANDING JONESBORO, REQUEST AIRPORT ADVISORY.

        2) Outbound example

            a) Pilot: JONESBORO RADIO, TOMAHAWK 1617T, READY TO TAXI, VFR, DEPARTING TO THE (DIRECTION), REQUEST AIRPORT ADVISORY.

    c. The FSS provides wind direction and speed, favored or designated runway, altimeter setting, known traffic, Notices to Airmen (NOTAMs), airport taxi routes, airport traffic pattern information, and instrument approach procedures.

        1) A pilot should inform the FSS of the runway (s)he intends to use.

4. **UNICOM** is a nongovernment air/ground radio communication station that may provide airport advisories at airports where there is no tower or FSS. UNICOM stations may provide pilots with weather information, wind direction, the recommended runway, or other necessary information.

   a. If the UNICOM frequency is designated as the CTAF, it will be identified on aeronautical charts and the Chart Supplement.

      1) UNICOM frequencies include 122.8, 122.7, 122.725, 122.975, and 123.0 MHz.

   b. When you are communicating with a UNICOM station, the following practices will help reduce frequency congestion, facilitate a better understanding of your intentions, help identify the location of aircraft in the traffic pattern, and enhance safety of flight.

      1) Select the correct UNICOM/CTAF frequency.

      2) State the identification (i.e., airport name) of the UNICOM station you are calling at the beginning and end of each transmission.

      3) Speak slowly and distinctly.

      4) Approximately 10 NM from the airport, report altitude; state your airplane type, airplane identification, location relative to the airport, your decision to land or overfly; and request wind information and runway in use.

      5) Report on downwind, base, and final approach.

      6) Report leaving the runway.

   c. Recommended UNICOM phraseologies

      1) Inbound examples

         a) Pilot: JONESVILLE UNICOM CESSNA ONE ZERO TWO FOXTROT, 10 MILES NORTH DESCENDING THROUGH (ALTITUDE) LANDING JONESVILLE, REQUEST WIND AND RUNWAY INFORMATION JONESVILLE.

            i) Response: CESSNA CALLING JONESVILLE, WIND THREE FOUR ZERO AT SEVEN, RUNWAY THREE SIX IN USE WITH TWO AIRCRAFT IN THE PATTERN.

         b) Pilot: JONESVILLE TRAFFIC CESSNA ONE ZERO TWO FOXTROT ENTERING (DOWNWIND/BASE/FINAL) FOR RUNWAY THREE SIX (FULL STOP/TOUCH-AND-GO) JONESVILLE.

         c) Pilot: JONESVILLE TRAFFIC CESSNA ONE ZERO TWO FOXTROT CLEAR OF RUNWAY THREE SIX JONESVILLE.

      2) Outbound examples

         a) Pilot: JONESVILLE UNICOM CESSNA ONE ZERO TWO FOXTROT (LOCATION ON AIRPORT) TAXIING TO RUNWAY THREE SIX, REQUEST WIND AND TRAFFIC INFORMATION JONESVILLE.

         b) Pilot: JONESVILLE TRAFFIC CESSNA ONE ZERO TWO FOXTROT DEPARTING RUNWAY THREE SIX. REMAINING IN THE PATTERN/ DEPARTING THE PATTERN TO THE (DIRECTION) (AS APPROPRIATE) JONESVILLE.

5. **MULTICOM** is a frequency (122.9 MHz) used for self-announced procedures at airports without operating control towers that are not served by an FSS or a UNICOM.

   a. At such an airport, the MULTICOM frequency will be identified on charts as the CTAF.

   b. Use the same phraseology as explained for UNICOM.

6.   **Summary of Recommended Communication Procedures**

FACILITY AT AIRPORT	FREQUENCY USE	COMMUNICATION/BROADCAST PROCEDURES	
		OUTBOUND	INBOUND
1. UNICOM (no tower or FSS)	Communicate with UNICOM station on published CTAF frequency (122.7, 122.8, 122.725, 122.975, or 123.0). If unable to contact UNICOM station, use self-announced procedures on CTAF.	Before taxiing and before taxiing on the runway for departure.	10 NM out. Entering downwind, base, and final. Leaving the runway.
2. No tower, FSS, or UNICOM	Self-announce on MULTICOM frequency 122.9.	Before taxiing and before taxiing on the runway for departure.	10 NM out. Entering downwind, base, and final. Leaving the runway.
3. No tower in operation, FSS open	Communicate with FSS on CTAF frequency.	Before taxiing and before taxiing on the runway for departure.	10 NM out. Entering downwind, base, and final. Leaving the runway.
4. FSS closed (no tower or tower closed)	Self-announce on CTAF.	Before taxiing and before taxiing on the runway for departure.	10 NM out. Entering downwind, base, and final. Leaving the runway.

7.   Observing and avoiding other aircraft at an airport without an operating control tower is of paramount importance.

   a.   Relatedly, being considerate to the other pilots should have high priority both in the air and on the ground.

   b.   Self-announce position and intentions on the appropriate CTAF frequency.

   c.   Make a 360° turn at the end of the runway before takeoff to scan carefully for local traffic.

   d.   Follow local traffic pattern, noise abatement, and other procedures diligently.

   e.   Final approach should not be made shorter than necessary. A short final may lead to a missed approach because aircraft may taxi to the runway without seeing you.

   f.   Finally, do not assume absence of traffic because few airplanes use an airport.

3.11 AUTOMATED WEATHER REPORTING SYSTEMS

1.   Automated weather reporting systems are increasingly being installed at airports. These systems consist of various sensors, a processor, a computer-generated voice subsystem, and a transmitter to broadcast local, minute-by-minute weather data directly to the pilot.

   a.   Automated surface observation systems can provide pilots with weather information over discrete VHF frequencies or over the voice portion of a local NAVAID.

   b.   These systems provide information that can be used by flight crews to make approach decisions, and by the National Weather Service to generate aviation routine weather reports (METARs).

   c.   Pilots planning approaches to airports where ATIS (refer to Subunit 3.13 for more information on this system) is not available may be able to obtain current airport conditions from an automated weather facility.

2. Two common types of automated systems are used throughout the country:

   a. **Automated Weather Observing System (AWOS)**

      1) Exists on four levels of complexity. Each level is more advanced and provides more information.

         a) **AWOS-A** only reports altimeter setting. Any other information is advisory only.

         b) **AWOS-1** usually reports altimeter setting, wind data, temperature, dew point, and density altitude.

         c) **AWOS-2** provides the information provided by AWOS-1 plus visibility.

         d) **AWOS-3** provides the information provided by AWOS-2 plus cloud/ceiling data.

      2) Transmits on a discrete VHF radio frequency.

      3) Engineered to be receivable to a maximum of 25 NM from the site and a maximum altitude of 10,000 feet above ground level.

         a) At many locations, AWOS signals may be received on the surface of the airport, but local conditions may limit the maximum AWOS reception distance and/or altitude.

      4) Transmits a 20 to 30 second weather message updated each minute.

         a) Pilots monitor the designated frequency for the automated weather broadcast.

         b) There is no two-way communication capability.

   b. **Automated Surface Observing System (ASOS)/Automated Weather Sensor System (AWSS)**

      1) Primary surface weather observing system of the U.S.

         a) AWSS is a follow-on program that provides identical data as ASOS.

         b) ASOS/AWSS is more sensitive and provides more information than AWOS.

      2) Designed to support aviation operations and weather forecast activities

         a) ASOS/AWSS will provide continuous minute-by-minute observations and perform the basic observing functions necessary to generate an aviation routine weather report (METAR) and other aviation weather information.

      3) Transmitted and received by the pilot in exactly the same way as AWOS

3. The table below indicates what information is provided by each automated weather reporting system type.

WEATHER REPORTING SYSTEMS					
Element Reported	AWOS-A	AWOS-1	AWOS-2	AWOS-3	ASOS
Altimeter	X	X	X	X	X
Wind		X	X	X	X
Temperature/ Dew Point		X	X	X	X
Density Altitude		X	X	X	X
Visibility			X	X	X
Clouds/Ceiling				X	X
Precipitation					X
Remarks					X

3.12 AIRPORTS WITH AN OPERATING CONTROL TOWER

1. An airport with an operating control tower normally has both of the following:

    a. Ground control for control of aircraft taxiing on the surface of the airport (except the runway)

    b. Tower control for control of aircraft on the active runway and in the vicinity of the airport

2. Many busy airports also have approach control and departure control.

    a. The approach or departure controller coordinates arriving and departing traffic, usually for a busy airport with a control tower.

3. **Clearance delivery** is a required communication at very busy and medium-density airports. It is used before contacting ground control to obtain departure instructions.

4. **Automatic Terminal Information Service (ATIS)** is a continuous airport advisory service also provided at busy airports.

3.13 AUTOMATIC TERMINAL INFORMATION SERVICE (ATIS)

1. If available, the ATIS frequency is listed on the sectional chart just under the tower control frequency for the airport, e.g., ATIS 125.05. ATIS provides a continuous transmission that provides information for arriving and departing aircraft, including

    a. Time of the latest weather report

    b. Sky conditions, visibility, and obstructions to visibility

        1) The absence of a sky condition or ceiling and/or visibility and obstructions to visibility on ATIS indicates a sky condition of 5,000 ft. or above and visibility of 5 SM or more.

            a) A remark on the broadcast may state, "The weather is better than 5,000 and 5," or the existing weather may be broadcast.

    c. Temperature and dewpoint (degrees Celsius)

    d. Wind direction (magnetic) and velocity

    e. Altimeter

    f. Other pertinent remarks, instrument approach, and runway in use

        1) The departure runway will be given only if it is different from the landing runway, except at locations having a separate ATIS for departure.

2. The purpose of ATIS is to relieve the ground controllers' and approach controllers' workload. They need not repeat the same information.

3. The ATIS broadcast is updated whenever any official weather is received, regardless of content or changes, or when a change is made in other pertinent data, such as a runway change. Each new broadcast is labeled with a letter of the alphabet at the beginning of the broadcast; e.g., "This is information alpha" or "information bravo."

    a. Every aircraft arriving at or departing from an airport with ATIS should monitor ATIS to receive that airport's weather information before contacting approach, tower, clearance delivery, or ground control.

    b.   When you contact approach, tower, clearance delivery, or ground control, you should indicate that you have the ATIS information by stating "with information (the letter code labeling the broadcast)."

        1)   EXAMPLES:

            a)   DAYTONA APPROACH, CESSNA 66421, TWO ZERO MILES NORTH, INBOUND TO DAYTONA REGIONAL WITH INFORMATION ALPHA.

            b)   DAYTONA GROUND, CESSNA 66421, AT DAYTONA BEACH AVIATION, REQUEST TAXI, VFR SOUTHBOUND WITH INFORMATION BRAVO.

        2)   The phrase "have numbers" does not indicate receipt of the ATIS broadcast and should never be used for this purpose.

            a)   "Have numbers" means you have received only the wind, runway, and altimeter information.

3.14 GROUND CONTROL

1.   At an airport with an operating control tower, you will usually talk with ground control before taxiing. The ground controller coordinates the movement of aircraft on the surface of the airport. When you call ground control, you should say five things:

    a.   Address the ground controller, e.g., "Gainesville ground."

    b.   Give the type of airplane and the airplane's number, e.g., "Beech Skipper 66421."

    c.   Identify your location, e.g., "north ramp," and the FBO (if more than one).

    d.   Indicate where you want to go and that you are ready to taxi, e.g., "Taxi VFR southbound."

    e.   Tell the ground controller that you have ATIS (if appropriate), e.g., "with information Golf" if Golf is the current ATIS designation.

2.   The ground controller will respond with four items:

    a.   The airplane identification, e.g., "Skipper 66421."

    b.   Directions to taxi to the active runway, e.g., "Taxi runway 10."

    c.   The wind direction and speed, e.g., "Wind 140 at 7."

    d.   The altimeter setting, e.g., "Altimeter 29.93." After receiving this information, you should check and reset your altimeter if necessary.

    NOTE: Wind and altimeter will not be given if ATIS is available.

3.   You should acknowledge the controller, e.g., "Beech Skipper 66421 taxi runway 10." ATC may use an abbreviated call sign here, e.g., "421." Continue to monitor ground control as you taxi (you will switch to the tower frequency just before you are ready to take off).

    a.   You are required to read back to the controller your runway assignment. A good practice is to read back all clearances.

    b.   Be careful to note if you are given a clearance other than to the active runway; e.g., "Hold short of Runway 24." Do NOT cross Runway 24.

        1)   You are required to read back to the controller all runway hold short instructions.

    c.   Whenever you need directions, ask ground control; e.g., "Ground, Beech Skipper 66421 unfamiliar with airport. Request progressives to active runway."

        1)   Progressives are step-by-step routing directions.

3.15 TOWER CONTROL

1. The tower controller coordinates all aircraft activity on the active runway and in the vicinity of the airport.

2. When you are ready for takeoff, tell the tower three things:

    a. Address the tower, e.g., "Gainesville tower."
    b. Identify your airplane, e.g., "Beech Skipper 66421."
    c. State your intention (request), e.g., "Ready to take off runway 6."

3. The tower controller may then issue a clearance for takeoff if appropriate, e.g., "Beech Skipper 66421 cleared for takeoff Runway 6, left turn northbound approved." However, listen carefully to the response.

    a. The controller may issue certain restrictions on your departure, such as right turn or maintain runway heading, or you may ask for your direction of flight.
    b. The tower may not clear you due to traffic, e.g., "Skipper 66421, hold short of Runway 6, landing traffic."

        1) You must read back all runway hold short instructions, e.g., "Hold short of Runway 6, Skipper 66421."

    c. Once you have received a clearance for takeoff, you should acknowledge, e.g., "Beech 66421 cleared for takeoff Runway 6."
    d. If there is a departure control to contact, the tower will direct you to that frequency when appropriate, e.g., "Beech 66421 contact departure control 125.65, good day."
    e. If you are going to a nearby practice area and it is customary to monitor the tower, you should do so.

        1) Practice areas (for student pilots and instruction) are usually designated by the FAA or local airport authorities to keep instructional activities from interfering with normal traffic.
        2) Ask your flight instructor about this.

4. Tower control is also used for landing. It is good practice to contact tower control 15 NM out so the controller has time to route you to the active runway and coordinate your approach with the other traffic.

    a. Address the tower, stating who you are, where you are, and what you want.
    b. EXAMPLE: "Jacksonville Tower, Beech Skipper 66421, 15 mi. southwest, landing."

3.16 APPROACH CONTROL AND DEPARTURE CONTROL (FOR VFR AIRCRAFT)

1. The approach or departure controller coordinates arriving or departing traffic, usually to a busy airport with a control tower. These controllers coordinate traffic outside the traffic area.

    a. Use of approach and departure control is mandatory in Class B and Class C airspace areas for all aircraft, including VFR traffic.

        1) Class B airspace exists around major airports (e.g., Atlanta, Georgia).
        2) Class C airspace exists around other busy airports (e.g., Jacksonville, Florida).

    b. Use of approach and departure control is highly encouraged in Terminal Radar Service Areas (TRSAs), but it is not mandatory.

2. When approaching an area serviced by approach control, you should contact approach control for traffic advisories, sequencing for landing, and instructions for flying through a busy area.

3. Departure control is used for leaving busy traffic areas and required for use in leaving airports within Class B and Class C airspace areas.

    a. If requested and/or mandatory, tower will switch you over to departure control when appropriate.

    b. If you request departure control from the tower without prior arrangement, you will have to give your type of airplane, call sign, location, altitude, request, etc., to departure control as you did to approach control coming in.

3.17 CLEARANCE DELIVERY

1. A clearance delivery frequency is used at busy airports (usually airports within Class B or Class C airspace areas) to issue clearances to aircraft on the ground prior to taxiing.

    a. Clearance delivery frequency may be found in the Chart Supplement. It is also generally given in the ATIS broadcast.

2. Call clearance delivery before contacting the ground controller, and tell him or her five things:

    a. Give your type of aircraft and identification, e.g., "Cessna 1152L."
    b. State that you are VFR, e.g., "VFR."
    c. Give your destination, e.g., "Jacksonville."
    d. Request the altitude at which you wish to fly, e.g., "At 4,500 ft."
    e. State that you have the current ATIS, e.g., "with information bravo."

3. The controller will respond with a clearance for you consisting of

    a. Direction to fly after departure, e.g., "Fly runway heading."
    b. An altitude to climb to, e.g., "Up to but not above 2,000 ft."
    c. The frequency for departure control, e.g., "Departure frequency will be 125.65."
    d. A transponder code setting, e.g., "Squawk 4645."

4. You should copy the clearance; then read it back to the controller.

3.18 EMERGENCIES

1. If your airplane is experiencing an emergency such as loss of power, if you become doubtful about any condition that could adversely affect flight safety, or if you become apprehensive about your safety for any reason, use the emergency frequency, which is 121.5 MHz.

    a. When you broadcast on the emergency frequency, you will receive immediate attention at the FSSs and towers monitoring 121.5.

    b. All towers, FSSs, and radar facilities monitor the emergency frequency, but normally only one FAA facility at a given location monitors the frequency.

    c. If you are already on an ATC control frequency, e.g., a control tower or approach control, you should declare an emergency with that facility since its controllers are already conversant with your call sign, location, etc.

2. You should immediately state your

    a. Airplane call sign
    b. Location and altitude
    c. Problem
    d. Extent of the distress, e.g., requiring no delay, priority, or emergency handling

3. If equipped with a radar beacon transponder and if unable to establish voice communications with an air traffic control facility, set the transponder to Code 7700.

3.19 RADIO FAILURE PROCEDURES

1. ATC light signals are used to communicate with aircraft that have no radios or have experienced radio communication equipment failure at an airport with an operating control tower.

    a. ATC light signals have the meaning shown in the following table:

LIGHT GUN SIGNALS			
COLOR AND TYPE OF SIGNAL	**MOVEMENT OF VEHICLES, EQUIPMENT, AND PERSONNEL**	**AIRCRAFT ON THE GROUND**	**AIRCRAFT IN FLIGHT**
STEADY GREEN	Cleared to cross, proceed, or go	Cleared for takeoff	Cleared to land
FLASHING GREEN	Not applicable	Cleared for taxi	Return for landing (to be followed by steady green at the proper time)
STEADY RED	STOP	STOP	Give way to other aircraft and continue circling
FLASHING RED	Clear the taxiway/runway	Taxi clear of the runway in use	Airport unsafe, do not land
FLASHING WHITE	Return to starting point on airport	Return to starting point on airport	Not applicable
ALTERNATING RED AND GREEN	Exercise Extreme Caution!!!!	Exercise Extreme Caution!!!!	Exercise Extreme Caution!!!!

2. **Radio Failure Procedures at Airports with Operating Control Towers in Class D, Class E, and Class G Airspace**

    a. Arriving Aircraft

        1) If you receive no response to your transmission inbound, you may have radio failure.

        2) If you are receiving tower transmissions but none are directed toward you, you should suspect a transmitter failure.

            a) Determine the direction and flow of traffic, enter the traffic pattern, and look for light signals. Change your transponder code to 7600.

            b) During daylight, acknowledge tower transmissions or light signals by rocking your wings. At night, acknowledge by blinking the landing or navigation lights.

            c) After landing, telephone the tower to advise them of the situation.

        3) If you are receiving no transmissions on tower or ATIS frequency, suspect a receiver failure.

            a) Transmit to the tower in the blind your position, situation, and intention to land.

            b) Determine the flow of traffic, enter the pattern, and wait for light signals.

            c) Acknowledge signals as described above and by transmitting in the blind.

            d) After landing, telephone the tower to advise them of the situation.

    b.   Departing Aircraft

        1)   If you experience radio failure prior to leaving the parking area, make every effort to have the equipment repaired.

        2)   If you are unable to have the malfunction repaired, call the tower by telephone and request authorization to depart without two-way radio communications.

            a)   If tower authorization is granted, you will be given departure information and requested to monitor the tower frequency or watch for light signals, as appropriate.

            b)   During daylight, acknowledge tower transmissions or light signals by promptly executing action authorized by light signals.

                i)   When in the air, rock your wings.

            c)   At night, acknowledge by blinking the landing or navigation lights.

        3)   If your radio malfunctions after departing the parking area (ramp), watch the tower for light signals or monitor the appropriate (ground or tower) frequency. However, you should return to the ramp.

3.20 EMERGENCY LOCATOR TRANSMITTER (ELT)

1.   Emergency locator transmitters (ELTs) of various types are independently powered and of incalculable value in an emergency. They were developed as a means of locating downed aircraft and their occupants.

    a.   The newest ELTs available transmit on 406 MHz, providing better reliability and reception due to satellite monitoring.

        1)   Older ELTs are designed to emit a distinctive audio tone for homing purposes on the emergency frequencies 121.5 MHz and 243.0 MHz only.

        2)   Satellite monitoring for non-406 MHz ELTs is no longer available. Older ELTs will still transmit on 121.5 MHz and 243.0 MHz as appropriate to the unit's design.

    b.   The power source is designed to be capable of providing power for continuous operation for at least 48 hr. or more at a very wide range of temperatures. The ELT can expedite search and rescue operations as well as facilitate accident investigation.

    c.   The ELT is required for most general aviation and small private aircraft. The pilot and other occupants could survive a crash impact only to die of exposure before they are located.

2.   The ELT is equipped with a gravity switch that, when armed, automatically activates the ELT upon an impact of sufficient force.

    a.   Once the transmitter is activated and the signal detected, search aircraft with homing equipment can locate the scene. Search aircraft use special search patterns to locate the transmitter site.

3.   ELTs generally have three switch positions: "ON," "OFF," and "ARMED."

    a.   "On" provides continuous signal broadcast.

    b.   "Off" means no broadcast is possible and the gravity switch cannot be activated.

    c.   "Armed" means the gravity switch will be activated in a crash situation, which turns on the broadcast.

    d.   Normally, the ELT is in a rear area of the airplane and is always set on "armed." It is affixed as far aft as possible to avoid possible damage from crash impact.

4. Do not inadvertently activate the ELT in the air or on the ground.

    a. Accidental or unauthorized activation will generate an emergency signal that will lead to expensive and wasteful searches.

    b. A false ELT signal could also interfere with genuine emergency transmissions and hinder or prevent the timely location of crash sites.

        1) Frequent false alarms could also result in complacency and decrease the vigorous reaction that must be attached to all ELT signals.

    c. Numerous cases of inadvertent activation have occurred as a result of aerobatics, hard landings, movement by ground crews, and airplane maintenance. These false alarms can be minimized by monitoring 121.5 MHz as follows:

        1) In flight when a receiver is available
        2) Prior to engine shutdown at the end of each flight
        3) When the ELT is handled during installation or maintenance
        4) When maintenance is being performed in the vicinity of the ELT
        5) When the airplane is moved by a ground crew

    d. If an ELT signal is heard, turn off your ELT to determine whether it is transmitting. If it has been activated, maintenance might be required before the unit can be returned to the "armed" position.

5. Pilots are encouraged to monitor 121.5 MHz while in flight to assist in identifying possible emergency ELT transmissions. On receiving a signal, the pilot should report the following information to the nearest ATC facility or FSS:

    a. Position at the time the signal was first heard and last heard
    b. Position at maximum signal strength
    c. Flight altitude and frequency (i.e., 121.5 MHz or 243.0 MHz)
    d. If possible, position relative to a navigation aid

6. ELTs should be tested in accordance with the manufacturer's instructions, preferably in a shielded or screened room to prevent the broadcast of signals that could trigger a false alert.

    a. When this cannot be done, airplane operational testing is authorized on 121.5 MHz and 243.0 MHz as follows:

        1) Tests should be conducted only during the first 5 min. after any hour.

            a) If tests must be made at any other time, they must be coordinated with the nearest FAA control tower or FSS.

        2) Tests should be no longer than three audible sweeps.

        3) If the antenna is removable, a dummy load should be substituted during test procedures.

        4) Airborne tests are not authorized.

7. ELT batteries must be replaced or recharged (if rechargeable) when

    a. The battery has been used for more than 1 cumulative hour.
    b. 50% of the battery's useful life has expired.

3.21 ATC RADAR

1. Radar is a method in which radio waves are transmitted into the air and received when they have been reflected by an object in the path of the beam. This is known as primary radar.

    a. Range is determined by measuring the time it takes (at the speed of light) for the radio wave to go out to the object and return to the receiving antenna.

    b. Direction is determined by the position of the rotating antenna when the reflected portion of the radio wave is received.

2. The characteristics of radio waves are such that they normally travel in a continuous straight line unless they are affected by the following:

    a. The bending of the radio wave caused by abnormal phenomena such as temperature inversions.

        1) This bending may cause extraneous blips to appear on the radarscope if the radio wave has been bent toward the ground or may decrease the detection range if the wave is bent upward.

    b. Radar energy that strikes dense objects (e.g., precipitation, ground obstacles, mountains, etc.) will be reflected and displayed on the radarscope, blocking out aircraft at the same range and greatly weakening or completely eliminating the display of targets at a greater range.

        1) Secondary radar and the electronic elimination of stationary and slow-moving targets by a method called moving target indicator (MTI) are effectively used to combat ground clutter and some weather phenomena.

    c. Relatively low-altitude aircraft will not be seen if they are screened by mountains or are below the radar beam due to the earth's curvature. Remember, radar operates by line of sight.

3. The **Air Traffic Control Radar Beacon System (ATCRBS)**, also known as secondary radar, consists of three major components:

    a. **Interrogator.** This ground-based radar beacon transmitter-receiver scans at the same time as primary radar and transmits discrete radio signals requesting all transponders on the mode being used to reply.

        1) The replies received from the transponders are displayed on the radarscope along with primary radar targets (aircraft with no transponder).

    b. **Transponder.** This airborne (i.e., installed on your airplane) radar beacon transmitter-receiver automatically receives the signals from the interrogator and selectively replies with a specific pulse group (code) only to those interrogations received on the mode to which it is set.

        1) These replies are independent of, and much stronger than, a primary radar return.

    c. **Radarscope.** This component is used to display returns from both the primary and secondary radar systems. These returns, called targets, are what the controller refers to in the control and separation of traffic.

        1) A video mapping unit generates an actual map on the radarscope, depicting data such as airports, navigation aids, obstructions, prominent geographic features, etc.

3.22 TRANSPONDER OPERATION

1. Since most airplanes you will fly will be equipped with a transponder, you should understand the proper operating procedures. The figure below illustrates a typical transponder.

a. The function switch controls the application of power and selects the operating mode. It has five positions:

1) OFF -- turns the transponder off.

2) STY or SBY (standby) -- turns the transponder on for equipment warm-up. The transponder does not reply to interrogations in this position.

3) ON -- turns the transponder on and allows the transponder to reply to Mode A (no altitude reporting) interrogations.

4) ALT -- turns the transponder on and allows the transponder to transmit either Mode A or Mode C (altitude reporting) replies as requested by the interrogating signal.

5) TEST -- checks operation of the transponder.

b. The reply/monitor light flashes to indicate when the transponder is replying to interrogations. This light will glow steadily during initial warm-up, during transmission of the IDENT signal, and during a self-test operation to show proper operation.

c. The IDENT (ID) switch, when depressed, selects a special identifier signal that is sent with the transponder reply to an interrogation signal, thus allowing the controller to confirm an aircraft identity or to identify an aircraft.

1) The IDENT signal should be used only at the request of a controller.

d. The dimmer (DIM) control allows the pilot to control the intensity level of the reply light.

e. The self-test (TST) switch causes the transponder to generate a self-interrogating signal to provide a check of the transponder operation.

f. Code selector knobs (four) allow you to set the proper four-digit transponder code.

g. Code selector windows (four) display the selected code. In each window, any number between zero and seven can be selected, allowing a total of 4,096 possible codes.

2. **Mode C (Automatic Altitude Reporting)**

a. This system converts your airplane's altitude in 100-ft. increments to coded digital information, which is transmitted in the reply to the interrogating radar facility.

b. If your airplane is Mode C-equipped, you must set your transponder to reply Mode C (i.e., set function switch to ALT) unless ATC requests otherwise.

1) If ATC requests that you "STOP ALTITUDE SQUAWK," you should set the function switch from ALT to ON.

    c.   An instruction by ATC, "STOP ALTITUDE SQUAWK, ALTITUDE DIFFERS (number of feet) FEET," may be an indication that your transponder is transmitting incorrect altitude information or that you have an incorrect altimeter setting. Plus or minus 300 ft. is the normal limit of error that ATC will accept.

       1)   The encoding altimeter equipment of the Mode C function is preset to a setting of 29.92. Computers at the radar facility correct for current altimeter settings and display indicated altitudes on the radarscope.

       2)   Although an incorrect altimeter setting has no effect on the Mode C altitude information transmitted by the transponder, it will cause you to fly at a different altitude.

       3)   When a controller indicates that an altitude readout is invalid, you should check to verify that your airplane's altimeter is set correctly.

    d.   Mode C is required when flying

       1)   At or above 10,000 ft. MSL, except in that airspace below 2,500 ft. AGL
       2)   Within 30 NM of a Class B airspace primary airport
       3)   Within and above a Class C airspace area
       4)   Into, within, or across the U.S. ADIZ (Air Defense Identification Zone)

    e.   For IFR operations in controlled airspace, the automatic pressure altitude reporting system (Mode C) must be tested and inspected every 24 calendar months.

3.   All VFR pilots should set their transponders to code 1200 unless otherwise instructed by ATC.

    a.   Transponders should be turned to the ON or ALT (if Mode C-equipped) position as late as practicable prior to takeoff and to the SBY position as soon as practicable after clearing the active runway.

    b.   Transponders are required to be inspected and tested every 24 calendar months.

    c.   Certain special codes have been set aside for emergency use.

       1)   7500 is the code for hijacking.
       2)   7600 is the code for lost radio communications.
       3)   7700 is the code for an emergency.
       4)   7777 is the code used for military interceptor operations.

    d.   When making code changes, you should avoid the selection of codes 7500, 7600, or 7700. These codes will cause alarms to be activated at the radar facility.

       1)   EXAMPLE: When switching from code 2700 to 7200, switch first to 2200 then to 7200, NOT to 7700 and then 7200.

4.   Controllers will use the following phraseology when referring to the operation of the transponder:

    a.   SQUAWK (number) -- Operate transponder on designated code (number).

    b.   IDENT -- Engage the IDENT feature of the transponder.

    c.   SQUAWK (number) and IDENT -- Select the specified code and then engage the IDENT feature of transponder.

    d.   SQUAWK STANDBY -- Switch function switch to SBY.

    e.   SQUAWK ALTITUDE -- Switch function selector to ALT to activate Mode C.

    f.   STOP ALTITUDE SQUAWK -- Switch function selector from ALT to ON.

    g.   STOP SQUAWK -- Turn transponder off (i.e., OFF position).

    h.   SQUAWK MAYDAY -- Select code 7700.

    i.   SQUAWK VFR -- Operate transponder on code 1200.

5.   **Mode S (Selective)**

    a.   Mode S (Selective) transponders are designed to help air traffic control in busy areas and allow automatic collision avoidance.

        1)   Mode S transponders allow TCAS (Traffic Alert and Collision Avoidance System) and TIS (Traffic Information System) to function.

        2)   Refer to Subunit 3.8, item 5., for more information on these systems.

    b.   Mode S transponders broadcast information about the equipped aircraft to the Secondary Surveillance Radar (SSR) system, TCAS receivers on board aircraft, and to the ADS-B system.

        1)   This information includes the call sign of the aircraft and/or the transponder's permanent unit code (i.e., not the four digit user-entered squawk code).

        2)   These transponders also receive ground-based radar information through a datalink and can display that information to pilots to aid in collision avoidance.

3.23   RADAR SERVICES TO VFR AIRCRAFT

1.   ATC radar facilities provide a variety of services to participating VFR aircraft on a workload-permitting basis.

    a.   To participate, you must be able to communicate with ATC, be within radar coverage, and be radar identified by the controller.

    b.   Among the services provided are

        1)   VFR radar traffic advisory service (commonly known as flight following)
        2)   Terminal radar programs
        3)   Radar assistance to lost aircraft

2.   **VFR Flight Following**

    a.   To obtain flight following, you should contact ATC on the appropriate frequency after leaving the traffic area of your departure airport.

        1)   Use the departure frequency listed for the airport in the Chart Supplement.

        2)   Inform ATC that you are requesting VFR flight following, and announce your departure point and destination.

        3)   The controller will assign you a transponder code and ask your aircraft type and cruising altitude.

    b.   When you are using flight following, ATC will advise you of any traffic that may be in a position to warrant your attention.

        1)   Radar traffic information given to you will include the following:

            a)   The traffic's position relative to yours in terms of the 12-hr. clock or distance and direction with respect to a fix

                i)   EXAMPLES:

                    •   "TRAFFIC at 1 O'CLOCK" would be about 30° right of your airplane's nose.

                    •   "TRAFFIC 8 miles (NM) SOUTH OF AIRPORT SOUTHEAST BOUND"

            b)   Distance from you in nautical miles (NM)

            c)   Direction in which the target is heading

            d)   Type of aircraft and altitude, if known

2) The controller can only observe your airplane's track (course) on the radarscope; thus, the traffic advisories are based on this, and you should take into account your wind correction angle to maintain track.

    a) When given a traffic advisory of traffic at 1 o'clock, you should look from the nose of your airplane to the right wing for the traffic.

    b) Once you have the traffic in sight, you should report this to the controller and maintain visual contact until the traffic is no longer a factor in your flight.

        i) If you do not see the traffic, you should report "NEGATIVE TRAFFIC" to the controller.

c. When receiving this service, you must monitor the assigned frequency at all times to preclude the controller's concern for radio failure or emergency assistance to aircraft under his or her control.

    1) This service does not include vectors (i.e., headings provided by ATC) away from conflicting traffic unless requested by the pilot.

    2) You should inform the controller when changing altitude.

    3) When advisory service is no longer desired, advise the controller before changing frequency, and then change your transponder code to 1200.

    4) When you are outside the controller's airspace, the controller will advise you that radar service is terminated and instruct you to squawk VFR.

3. **Terminal Radar Programs**

a. Terminal radar programs for VFR aircraft are classified as basic, TRSA, Class C, and Class B service.

    1) Basic radar service provides safety alerts, traffic advisories, and limiting vectoring on a workload-permitting basis.

    2) TRSA service provides sequencing and separation for all participating VFR aircraft operating within a Terminal Radar Service Area (TRSA).

b. Many larger airports have radar facilities that can provide radar advisories, sequencing, and, in some cases, separation from other participating aircraft.

    1) Many of these airports are identified as TRSAs, Class C airspace areas, and Class B airspace areas on the sectional chart.

        a) Other airports that have radar facilities are indicated in the Chart Supplement.

    2) Pilot participation in this program, although voluntary for VFR traffic, is urged whenever available.

        a) Participation is mandatory when operating in a Class B or Class C airspace area.

c. When arriving, you should contact approach control on the published frequency and state your position, altitude, and destination, and indicate that you have received the ATIS (if available).

    1) The proper frequency may be found on the sectional chart or in the Chart Supplement.

    2) Approach control will specify when to contact the tower.

d. When departing, you should inform ground control or clearance delivery of your destination and/or route of flight and proposed cruising altitude.

    1) ATC will normally advise participating VFR aircraft when leaving the geographical limits of the controller's radar. Radar service is not terminated unless specifically stated by the controller.

e.   While operating in Class B airspace, Class C airspace, or a TRSA, you

1)   Must maintain an altitude when ATC assigns it unless the altitude assignment is to maintain at or below a specified altitude

2)   Should coordinate with ATC prior to any altitude change when not assigned an altitude

4.   **Radar Assistance to Lost Aircraft**

a.   If you become lost, ATC can provide you with radar assistance and vectors to your desired destination.

1)   You must be within radar coverage to use this service.

b.   To find the proper frequency for ATC in your area, you may need to contact the nearest control tower or FSS.

1)   Inform ATC that you are lost, and state your last known position and destination.

2)   By assigning you a transponder code and observing you on radar, the controller will be able to tell you your position and suggest a heading to your destination.

c.   An emergency situation can easily be avoided by asking for help as soon as you are in doubt as to your exact position.

1)   Taking advantage of flight following when available keeps you operating within the ATC system and allows you always to keep a controller "at your fingertips."

5.   You must clearly understand that these programs in no way relieve you of your primary responsibility of flying the airplane legally and safely.

a.   It is still your task to

1)   See and avoid other traffic
2)   Adjust your operations and flight path as necessary to avoid wake turbulence
3)   Maintain appropriate terrain and obstruction clearance
4)   Maintain basic VFR visibility and distance from clouds

b.   If ATC assigns a route, heading, and/or altitude that will make you compromise your responsibilities in the above areas, you must contact the controller to advise him or her and obtain a revised clearance or instructions.

3.24 GENERAL DIMENSIONS OF AIRSPACE

1.   Because of the nature of operations within certain airspace areas, restrictions are required for safety reasons.

a.   The complexity or density of aircraft movements in other airspace areas may result in additional aircraft and pilot requirements for operation within such airspace.

b.   It is important that you be familiar with the operational requirements for the various airspace segments.

2.   The federal airspace system is classified into six class designations.

a.   The objectives of this airspace classification are to

1)   Simplify the airspace designations
2)   Increase standardization of equipment and pilot requirements for operations in various classes of airspace
3)   Promote pilot understanding of ATC services available
4)   Achieve international commonality and satisfy our responsibilities as a member state of ICAO (International Civil Aviation Organization)

b.   The diagram and table on the following page show the airspace classification and summarize the classifications with regard to the requirements and services available in each class of airspace.

c.   Note that the airspace designated as Class F in the ICAO system is not used in the U.S.

d.   This airspace classification conforms with the ICAO airspace system.

3.   Depictions of airspace types can be found in Study Unit 9, Subunit 3, beginning on page 431.

3.25 CONTROLLED AND UNCONTROLLED AIRSPACE

1.   **Controlled airspace** is defined as an area within which ATC service is provided to IFR and VFR flights in accordance with the airspace classification.

a.   Controlled airspace is designated as Class A, Class B, Class C, Class D, and Class E airspace.

b.   Class G airspace is considered to be uncontrolled.

2.   The distinction between **uncontrolled airspace** and the various types of controlled airspace relates to the following factors (refer to the airspace table on the following page).

a.   ATC clearance requirements

b.   Pilot qualification requirements

c.   VFR flight visibility and distance from clouds requirements

   1)   An airplane may be operated clear of clouds in Class G airspace at night below 1,200 ft. AGL when the visibility is less than 3 SM but more than 1 SM in an airport traffic pattern and within 1/2 mi. of the runway.

   2)   Except when operating under a special VFR clearance, you may not operate your airplane beneath the ceiling under VFR within the lateral boundaries of the surface areas of Class B, Class C, Class D, or Class E airspace designated for an airport when the ceiling is less than 1,000 ft.

      a)   You may not take off, land, or enter the traffic pattern of an airport unless ground visibility is at least 3 SM. If ground visibility is not reported, flight visibility must be at least 3 SM.

      b)   Thus, an airport within one of these surface areas is IFR when the ceiling is less than 1,000 ft. **or** the visibility is less than 3 SM.

   3)   Special VFR (SVFR)

      a)   **SVFR conditions** means that the current weather conditions are less than that required for basic VFR flight while operating within the lateral boundaries of the Class B, Class C, Class D, or Class E surface area that has been designated for an airport and in which some aircraft are permitted to operate under VFR.

      b)   SVFR operations may only be conducted

         i)   With an ATC clearance (you must request the clearance)
         ii)   Clear of clouds
         iii) With flight visibility of at least 1 SM

c)   To take off or land under a SVFR clearance, the ground visibility must be at least 1 SM.

     i)   If ground visibility is not reported, then flight visibility must be at least 1 SM.

d)   To request a SVFR clearance at night, you must have an instrument rating and your airplane must be IFR certified.

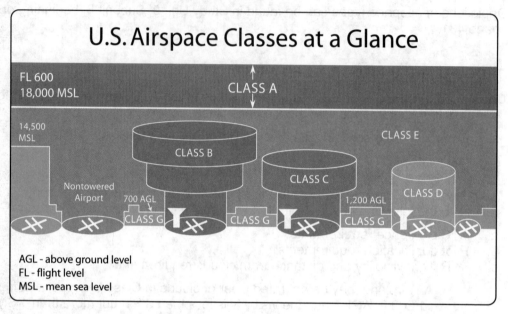

Airspace Features	Class A	Class B	Class C	Class D	Class E	Class G
Operations Permitted	IFR	IFR and VFR	IFR and VFR	IFR and VFR	IFR and VFR	IFR and VFR
Entry Requirements	ATC clearance	ATC clearance	ATC clearance for IFR All require radio contact.	ATC clearance for IFR All require radio contact.	ATC clearance for IFR All IFR require radio contact.	None
Minimum Pilot Qualifications	Instrument rating	Private, Recreational*, Sport*, or student certificate*	Student certificate	Student certificate	Student certificate	Student certificate
Two-way Radio Communications	Yes	Yes	Yes	Yes	Yes for IFR	No
VFR Minimum Visibility	... see chart on the following page ...					
VFR Minimum Distance from Clouds	... see chart on the following page ...					
Aircraft Separation	All	All	IFR, SVFR, and runway operations	IFR, SVFR, and runway operations	IFR and SVFR	None
Conflict Resolution	N/A	N/A	Between IFR and VFR ops	No	No	No
Traffic Advisories	N/A	N/A	Yes	Workload permitting	Workload permitting	Workload permitting
Safety Advisories	Yes	Yes	Yes	Yes	Yes	Yes
Differs from ICAO	No	Yes[1]	Yes[2]	Yes for VFR[2]	No	Yes for VFR[3]

[1] ICAO does not have speed restrictions in this class -- U.S. speed limit is 250 KIAS.
[2] ICAO requires an ATC clearance for VFR.
[3] ICAO requires 3 statute miles visibility.
* Additional training/endorsements required

Cloud Clearance and Visibility Required for VFR

Airspace	Flight Visibility	Distance from Clouds
Class A	Not Applicable	Not applicable
Class B	3 SM	Clear of Clouds
Class C	3 SM	500 ft. below 1,000 ft. above 2,000 ft. horiz.
Class D	3 SM	500 ft. below 1,000 ft. above 2,000 ft. horiz.
Class E:		
Less than 10,000 ft. MSL	3 SM	500 ft. below 1,000 ft. above 2,000 ft. horiz.
At or above 10,000 ft. MSL	5 SM	1,000 ft. below 1,000 ft. above 1 SM horiz.

Airspace	Flight Visibility	Distance from Clouds
Class G:		
1,200 ft. or less above the surface (regardless of MSL altitude)		
Day	1 SM	Clear of clouds
Night, except as provided in 2.c.1 on page 197	3 SM	500 ft. below 1,000 ft. above 2,000 ft. horiz.
More than 1,200 ft. above the surface but less than 10,000 ft. MSL		
Day	1 SM	500 ft. below 1,000 ft. above 2,000 ft. horiz.
Night	3 SM	500 ft. below 1,000 ft. above 2,000 ft. horiz.
More than 1,200 ft. above the surface and at or above 10,000 ft. MSL	5 SM	1,000 ft. below 1,000 ft. above 1 SM horiz.

3.26 CLASS A AIRSPACE

1. **Class A** airspace is generally the airspace from 18,000 ft. MSL up to and including flight level (FL) 600, including the airspace overlying the waters within 12 NM of the coast of the 48 contiguous states and Alaska.

2. **Operating Rules and Pilot/Equipment Requirements**

   a. An IFR clearance to enter and operate within Class A airspace is mandatory. Thus, you must be instrument-rated to act as PIC of an airplane in Class A airspace.

      1) There are specific exceptions to this rule that allow VFR operations in Class A airspace. A written request must be submitted to the FAA 4 days in advance of the flight in order to be considered for this exception.

   b. Two-way radio communication, appropriate navigational capability, and a Mode C transponder are required.

3.27 CLASS B AIRSPACE

1. **Class B** airspace is generally the airspace from the surface to 10,000 ft. MSL surrounding the nation's busiest airports in terms of IFR operations or passenger enplanements (e.g., Atlanta, Chicago).

   a. The configuration of each Class B airspace area is individually tailored and consists of a surface area and two or more layers.

2. **Operating Rules and Pilot/Equipment Requirements for VFR Operations**

   a. An ATC clearance is required prior to operating within Class B airspace.

   b. Two-way radio communication capability is required.

   c. Mode C transponder is required within and above the lateral limits of Class B airspace and within 30 NM of the primary airport.

d.   The PIC must be at least a private pilot, or a student or recreational pilot, who seeks private pilot certification and has met the requirements of 14 CFR 61.95 (see page 241).

1)   Also, the following Class B primary airports require that the pilot in command hold at least a private pilot certificate to take off or land at these airports:

Atlanta Hartsfield Airport, GA	Newark Int'l Airport, NJ
Boston Logan Airport, MA	New York Kennedy Airport, NY
Chicago O'Hare Int'l Airport, IL	New York LaGuardia Airport, NY
Dallas/Ft. Worth Int'l Airport, TX	San Francisco Int'l Airport, CA
Los Angeles Int'l Airport, CA	Washington National Airport, DC
Miami Int'l Airport, FL	Andrews Air Force Base, MD

3.   For IFR operations, an operable VOR is required in addition to a two-way radio and a Mode C transponder.

4.   **Mode C Veil**

a.   The Mode C veil is the airspace within 30 NM of a Class B primary airport, from the surface up to 10,000 ft. MSL.

b.   Unless otherwise authorized by ATC, aircraft (with some exceptions) operating within this airspace must be equipped with a Mode C transponder.

3.28   CLASS C AIRSPACE

1.   **Class C** airspace surrounds those airports that have an operational control tower, are serviced by a radar approach control, and have a certain number of IFR operations or passenger enplanements.

a.   Class C airspace normally consists of

1)   A surface area with a 5-NM radius that extends from the surface to 4,000 ft. AGL
2)   A shelf area with a 10-NM radius that extends from 1,200 ft. to 4,000 ft. AGL

b.   The general dimensions of Class C airspace are as shown in the airspace diagram on page 198.

1)   The outer area, which is the airspace area between 10 NM and 20 NM from the primary Class C airport, is not considered Class C airspace.

a)   Radar services in this area are available but not mandatory.

2.   **Operating Rules and Pilot/Equipment Requirements**

a.   Two-way radio communications must be established and maintained with ATC before entering and while operating in Class C airspace.

b.   Minimum equipment needed to operate in Class C airspace:

1)   4096 code transponder, with
2)   Mode C (altitude encoding) capability when within and above Class C airspace, and
3)   Two-way communication capability.

c.   When departing from a satellite airport without an operating control tower, you must contact ATC as soon as practicable after takeoff.

d.   No specific pilot certification is required.

3.29 CLASS D AIRSPACE

1. **Class D** airspace surrounds those airports that have both an operating control tower and weather services available and that are not associated with Class B or C airspace.

    a. Airspace at an airport with a part-time control tower is classified as Class D airspace only when the control tower is operating.

    b. Class D airspace is depicted by a blue segmented (dashed) circle on a sectional chart.

    c. Class D airspace normally extends from the surface up to and including 2,500 ft. above the airport elevation and is charted in MSL.

    1) The lateral dimensions of Class D airspace are based on the instrument procedures for which the controlled airspace is established.

2. **Operating Rules and Pilot/Equipment Requirements**

    a. Two-way communications must be established and maintained with ATC prior to entering and while operating in Class D airspace.

    b. When departing a non-tower satellite airport within Class D airspace, you must establish and maintain two-way radio communication with the primary airport's control tower.

    1) The primary airport is the airport for which the Class D is designated.
    2) A satellite airport is any other airport within the Class D airspace area.

    c. Two-way radio communication with the control tower is required for landings and takeoffs at all tower-controlled airports regardless of weather conditions.

    d. No specific pilot certification is required.

3.30 CLASS E AIRSPACE

1. **Class E** airspace is any controlled airspace that is not Class A, B, C, or D airspace.

    a. Except for 18,000 ft. MSL (the floor of Class A airspace), Class E airspace has no defined vertical limit, but rather it extends upward from either the surface or a designated altitude to the overlying or adjacent controlled airspace.

2. There are no specific pilot certification or equipment requirements to operate under VFR in Class E airspace.

    a. While generally no equipment is required to operate VFR in Class E airspace, there are some airports with operational control towers within the surface area of Class E airspace. In these circumstances, you must establish and maintain two-way radio communication with the control tower if you plan to operate to, from, or through an area within 4 NM from the airport, from the surface up to and including 2,500 ft. AGL.

3. **Types of Class E Airspace**

    a. **Surface area designated for an airport**

    1) When designated as a surface area for an airport, the Class E airspace will be configured to contain all instrument approach procedures (IAP).

    b. **Extension to a surface area**

    1) Some Class E airspace areas serve as extensions to Class B, Class C, and Class D surface areas designated for an airport.
    2) This Class E airspace provides controlled airspace to contain IAPs without imposing a communication requirement on pilots operating under VFR.

c. **Airspace used for transition**

1) This Class E airspace begins at either 700 ft. or 1,200 ft. AGL and is used to transition aircraft operating under IFR to/from the terminal or en route environment.

d. **En route domestic areas**

1) This Class E airspace extends upward from a specified altitude. En route domestic areas provide controlled airspace in those areas where there is a requirement to provide IFR en route ATC services but where the federal airway system is inadequate.

e. **Federal airways**

1) Federal airways (e.g., VOR or Victor airways) are Class E airspace areas and, unless otherwise specified, extend upward from 1,200 ft. AGL to, but not including, 18,000 ft. MSL.

f. **Offshore airspace areas**

1) This Class E airspace extends upward from a specified altitude to, but not including, 18,000 ft. MSL.

2) Offshore airspace areas provide controlled airspace beyond 12 NM from the coast of the U.S. in those areas where there is a requirement to provide IFR en route ATC services and within which the U.S. is applying domestic ATC procedures.

g. **Unless designated at a lower altitude**, Class E airspace begins at 14,500 ft. MSL or 1,200 ft. AGL, whichever is higher, and extends to, but does not include, 18,000 ft. MSL. It includes the airspace overlying the waters within 12 NM of the coast of the 48 contiguous states and Alaska and that airspace above FL 600, but it excludes

1) The Alaskan peninsula west of 160° W longitude and
2) The airspace below 1,500 ft. AGL unless specifically so designated.

3.31 CLASS G AIRSPACE

1. **Class G** airspace is that airspace that has not been designated as Class A, Class B, Class C, Class D, or Class E airspace (i.e., it is uncontrolled airspace).

a. Class G airspace exists beneath the floor of controlled airspace in areas where the controlled airspace does not extend down to the surface.

b. Class G airspace vertical limit is up to, but not including, 14,500 ft. MSL.

2. No specific pilot certification or airplane equipment is required in Class G airspace.

a. While generally no equipment is required to operate VFR in Class G airspace, there are some airports with operational control towers within the surface area of Class G airspace. In these circumstances, you must establish and maintain two-way radio communication with the control tower if you plan to operate to, from, or through an area within 4 NM from the airport, from the surface up to and including 2,500 ft. AGL.

3.32 SPECIAL-USE AIRSPACE

1. **Prohibited areas** -- airspace within which flight is prohibited. Such areas are established for security or other reasons of national welfare.

   a. Prohibited areas protect government interests as well as ecologically sensitive areas.

   b. Prohibited areas are often surrounded by large temporary flight restrictions (TFRs) when certain situations exist.

      1) Because prohibited areas protect areas the President often visits, pilots must be aware that large TFRs will be implemented around those areas when the President is present.

   c. Prohibited areas have varied ceilings but all begin at the surface. Depending on the area protected, prohibited area ceilings range from 1,000 feet MSL to 18,000 feet MSL.

   d. Notices of new, uncharted prohibited areas are disseminated via the NOTAM system.

2. **Restricted areas** -- airspace within which flight, while not wholly prohibited, is subject to restrictions. Restricted areas denote the existence of unusual, often invisible hazards to aircraft such as artillery firing, aerial gunnery, or guided missiles.

   a. The size and shape of restricted airspace areas vary based on the operation areas they restrict.

   b. Restricted areas are often placed next to, or stacked on top of, each other.

      1) The altitudes of restricted areas vary based on the operations conducted within them.

   c. If a restricted area is active, a pilot must receive prior permission of the controlling agency before attempting to fly through it.

      1) Times and altitudes of operation as well as the name of the controlling agency can be found on the sectional aeronautical chart.

3. **Warning areas** -- airspace of defined dimensions, extending from 3 NM outward from the coast of the U.S., that contains activity that may be hazardous to nonparticipating aircraft. The purpose of a warning area is to warn nonparticipating pilots of the potential danger (such as the hazards in restricted areas).

   a. A warning area may be located over domestic or international waters or both.

   b. Warning areas should be thought of exactly as restricted areas are.

      1) Because they are outside the 3 NM airspace boundary of U.S. airspace, they cannot be regulated as restricted areas are.

   c. Times and altitudes of operation can be found on the sectional aeronautical chart.

4. **Military operations areas (MOA)** -- airspace established to separate certain military training activities from IFR traffic.

   a. Pilots operating under VFR should exercise extreme caution while flying within an MOA when military activity is being conducted.

      1) Before beginning a flight that crosses an MOA, contact any FSS within 100 NM of the area to obtain accurate real-time information concerning the MOA hours of operation.

      2) Prior to entering an active MOA, contact the controlling agency for traffic advisories.

   b. MOAs are often placed next to or stacked on top of each other.

      1) The altitudes of MOAs vary based on the operations conducted within them.

      2) Times and altitudes of operation as well as the name of the controlling agency can be found on the sectional aeronautical chart.

    c.   MOAs are often found in conjunction with restricted areas.

        1)   Pay careful attention to such airspace when planning crossing flights to ensure you do not violate active restricted airspace.

5.   **Alert areas** -- areas depicted on aeronautical charts to inform nonparticipating pilots of areas that may contain a high volume of pilot training or an unusual type of aerial activity.

    a.   All activity within an alert area is conducted in accordance with Federal Aviation Regulations.

        1)   There is no specific controlling agency for an alert area nor is crossing clearance required/given.

    b.   Pilots of participating aircraft as well as pilots transiting the area are equally responsible for collision avoidance.

6.   **Controlled firing areas** -- areas containing activities that, if not conducted in a controlled environment, could be hazardous to nonparticipating aircraft.

    a.   The activities are suspended immediately when spotter aircraft, radar, or ground lookout positions indicate an aircraft might be approaching the area.

    b.   These areas are not depicted on charts because the pilot is not required to take action.

3.33 OTHER AIRSPACE AREAS

1.   **Airport advisory areas** encompass the areas within 10 SM of airports that have no operating control towers but where FSSs are located. At such locations, the FSS provides advisory service to arriving and departing aircraft. Participation in the Local Airport Advisory (LAA) program is recommended but not required.

2.   **Military training routes (MTRs)** are developed for use by the military for the purpose of conducting low-altitude (below 10,000 ft. MSL), high-speed training (more than 250 kt.).

    a.   The routes above 1,500 ft. AGL are flown, to the maximum extent possible, under IFR.

        1)   The routes at 1,500 ft. AGL and below are generally flown under VFR.

    b.   Extreme vigilance should be exercised when flying through or near these routes.

3.   **Temporary flight restrictions (TFRs)** contain airspace where the flight of aircraft is prohibited without advanced permission and/or an FAA waiver. This restriction exists because the area inside the TFR is often of key importance to national security or national welfare. TFRs may also be put into effect in the vicinity of any incident or event that by its nature may generate such a high degree of public interest that hazardous congestion of air traffic is likely.

    a.   TFRs are very different from other forms of airspace because they are often created, canceled, moved, and/or changed.

        1)   The temporary nature of TFRs can make keeping track of their locations and durations challenging.

    b.   TFRs protect government interests as well as the general public.

    c.   TFRs often surround other forms of airspace when extra security is necessary.

        1)   Because TFRs protect the President, pilots must be aware that large TFRs will be implemented around any area where the President is present.

    d.   A Notice to Airmen (NOTAM) implementing temporary flight restrictions will contain a description of the area in which the restrictions apply.

        1)   The size and shape of TFRs vary based on the areas they protect.

            a)   Most TFRs are in the shape of a circle and are designed to protect the center of that circle.

            b)   TFRs always have defined vertical and lateral boundaries as indicated in the NOTAMs.

4. Flight limitations in the proximity of **space flight operations** are designated in a NOTAM.

5. **Flight restrictions in the proximity of Presidential and other parties** are put into effect by a regulatory NOTAM to establish flight restrictions.

    a. Restrictions are required because numerous aircraft and large assemblies of persons may be attracted to areas to be visited or traveled by the President or Vice President, heads of foreign states, and other public figures.

        1) In addition, restrictions are imposed in the interest of providing protection to these public figures.

    b. Presidential TFRs are issued with as much advanced notice as possible, given security concerns.

        1) The President is always surrounded by a 10-nautical mile no-fly zone from the surface to 18,000 feet MSL.

            a) NO aircraft may operate in this area without a waiver or the advanced permission of the FAA.

        2) The President is also surrounded by a 30-nautical mile TFR.

            a) Certain limited operations are allowed in this area.

6. Tabulations of **parachute jump areas** in the U.S. are contained in the Chart Supplement.

7. **VFR corridor** is airspace through Class B airspace, with defined vertical and lateral boundaries, in which aircraft may operate without an ATC clearance or communication with ATC. A VFR corridor is, in effect, a hole through the Class B airspace.

8. **Class B airspace VFR transition route** is a specific flight course depicted on a VFR terminal area chart for transiting a specific Class B airspace.

    a. These routes include specific ATC-assigned altitudes, and you must obtain an ATC clearance prior to entering the Class B airspace.

    b. On initial contact, you should inform ATC of your position, altitude, route name desired, and direction of flight. After a clearance is received, you must fly the route as depicted and, most importantly, follow ATC instructions.

9. **Terminal Radar Service Area (TRSA)**

    a. TRSAs are not controlled airspace from a regulatory standpoint (i.e., they do not fit into any of the airspace classes) because TRSAs were never subject to the rulemaking process.

        1) TRSAs are areas where participating pilots can receive additional radar services, known as TRSA Service. Pilots operating under VFR are encouraged to participate in the TRSA Service. However, participation is voluntary.

    b. The primary airports within the TRSA are Class D airspace.

        1) The remaining portion of the TRSA normally overlies Class E airspace beginning at 700 or 1,200 ft. AGL.

10. **National security areas (NSA)** -- airspace established at locations where there is a requirement for increased security and safety of ground facilities

    a. Pilots are requested to voluntarily avoid flying through the depicted NSA.

    b. When necessary, flight in a NSA may be prohibited, and this prohibition will be disseminated by NOTAM.

3.34 SPECIAL FLIGHT RULES AREAS

1. When necessary for safety or security, special flight rules areas (SFRA) will be established by the FAA to modify the rules for operating within a given airspace area.

    a. These are not actually a type of airspace, but merely modifications to existing airspace.

    b. Communication requirements, transponder usage, routing, speed limitations, and other like factors are all subject to change when special flight rules are in effect.

2. SFRAs are designated on sectional and terminal area charts using a blue line with blue shaded boxes on the inside, or protected side, of the area.

    a. A box can be found near the area identifying it as a SFRA.

    b. A regulatory reference will be provided as well to allow pilots to learn more about the rules in effect.

3. EXAMPLES:

    a. Grand Canyon National Park

        1) Due to the high number of aircraft operating near the Grand Canyon, special flight rules were enacted to prevent near misses and midair collisions.

        2) 14 CFR Part 93, Subpart U, defines the boundaries and operating requirements within the Grand Canyon National Park Special Flight Rules Area.

            a) The rule establishes minimum altitudes, explains the pilot authorization process, and identifies flight free zones where all operations are prohibited.

    b. Los Angeles International Airport

        1) The Class B airspace around the LAX airport handles a very high volume of arriving and departing air traffic as well as flight instruction activities.

            a) To accommodate simplicity in VFR operations, a special flight rules area was created to modify the communication requirements and entry/exit procedures of Class B airspace.

        2) Operations within this area are governed by 14 CFR Part 93, Subpart G.

            a) The regulation defines the affected area and provides conditions for operations within it.

    c. Washington, D.C.

        1) The airspace around the U.S. capital has changed many times since the events of September 11, 2001. In the interests of national security, a special flight rules area was established to permanently modify a specific area within the Tri-Area Class B airspace surrounding Washington, D.C.

            a) Formerly an ADIZ area, the SFRA imposes many of the old ADIZ entry, operation, and exit requirements, such as flight plan filing, discrete transponder codes, and pre-takeoff clearance at affected airports.

        2) The D.C. SFRA is centered on the Reagan National VOR/DME station.

            a) The outer ring has a radius of 30 miles and is active 24 hours a day from the surface to 18,000 feet MSL.

            b) The inner ring is a flight restricted zone (FRZ) that can only be entered by pilots individually screened and approved by the Transportation Security Administration (TSA).

        3) 14 CFR Part 93, Subpart V, defines the boundaries and operating requirements within the Washington, D.C., Special Flight Rules Area.

     d.   Other SFRAs exist as well. The previous examples were used only for illustrative purposes to show the wide range of causes for implementation of a special flight rules area.

4.   Before operating in a special flight rules area, you should become familiar with the regulations associated with it.

     a.   Failure to comply with special flight rules can result in injury and destruction of property.

     b.   Punitive, civil, and criminal charges may be brought against offending pilots, depending on the severity and intent of the infraction.

     c.   Refer to 14 CFR Part 93 to learn more about the various SFRAs in the U.S. and how to comply with each one's operating requirements.

         1)   Bear in mind that all SFRAs differ in size, complexity, and scope of operation.

         2)   You must review each area's regulatory information before attempting to operate within the area.

3.35 NEXT GENERATION AIR TRANSPORTATION SYSTEM (NEXTGEN)

1.   The FAA has already started implementing NextGen.

2.   NextGen is comprised of six programs that are changing the way the National Airspace System (NAS) operates. These six programs are primarily FAA internal system upgrades that are necessary to deploy additional capabilities. They include

     a.   Automatic Dependent Surveillance–Broadcast (ADS-B)
     b.   Data Communications (Data Comm)
     c.   En Route Automation Modernization (ERAM)
     d.   Terminal Automation Modernization and Replacement (TAMR)
     e.   NAS Voice System (NVS)
     f.   System Wide Information Management (SWIM)

3.   Of the six programs above, ADS-B has the largest direct impact for aircraft operations. ADS-B is a precise satellite-based surveillance system. The use of satellites allows ATC to control areas that were not previously covered by line-of-sight radar facilities.

     a.   ADS-B technology will replace air traffic control's dependency on ground-based radar tracking and control systems.

     b.   ADS-B Out uses GPS technology to determine an aircraft's location, airspeed, and other data and broadcasts that information to a network of ground stations. The ground stations then relay the data at least once per second to air traffic control displays and to nearby aircraft equipped to receive the data via ADS-B In.

     c.   ADS-B Out will be required in the following airspace:

         1)   **Class A, B, and C airspace**

         2)   **Class E airspace** areas at or above 10,000 ft. MSL over the 48 states and DC, excluding airspace at and below 2,500 ft. AGL

         3)   Airspace within 30 NM at **certain busy airports** from the surface up to 10,000 ft. MSL; airports listed in Appendix D to Part 91

         4)   Above the ceiling and within the lateral boundaries of a **Class B or Class C airspace** area up to 10,000 ft. MSL

         5)   Class E airspace over the Gulf of Mexico at and above 3,000 ft. MSL within 12 NM of the coastline of the United States

6)   The following figure depicts ADS-B airspace requirements:

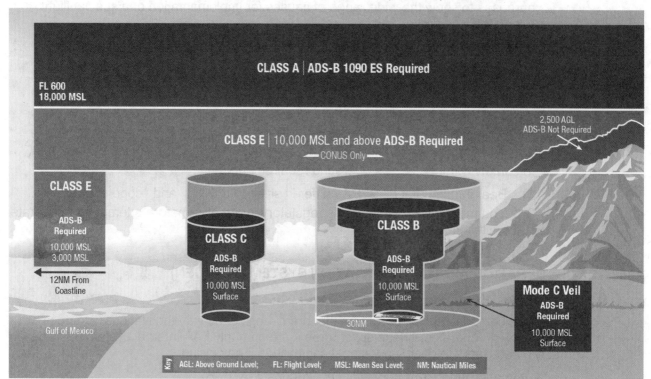

d.   All aircraft (with a few exceptions) have been required to be equipped with a certified ADS-B Out avionics unit since January 1, 2020. For more information, refer to 14 CFR 91.225 and 14 CFR 91.227. ADS-B In is not part of the mandate.

1)   Aircraft operations above 18,000 feet (FL 180) or internationally require a Mode S transponder operating on 1090 MHz with Extended Squitter (1090ES). A 1090 MHz receiver is needed to process Traffic Information Service-Broadcast (TIS-B) information. Flight Information Services Broadcast (FIS-B) is not available with 1090ES.

2)   Aircraft operating within U.S. airspace below FL 180 can use either a 1090ES or a Universal Access Transceiver (UAT) operating on 978 MHz. UAT is the data link that enables ADS-B for general aviation by broadcasting both position and performance information, while also receiving in-flight weather and traffic data.

a)   Operators of aircraft equipped with ADS-B In can receive weather and traffic position information directly to the cockpit via Flight Information Services-Broadcast (FIS-B). On most systems, the traffic is displayed on the GPS moving map or multi-function display (MFD) with altitude and velocity information. In addition to traffic, ADS-B In offers the following services to pilots:

i)   Weather information including radar, METARs, and TAFs can be accessed from the cockpit in flight.

ii)   TFR and NOTAM data can be also be accessed by pilots in flight.

iii)   Terrain awareness information can be displayed on the GPS or MFD.

END OF STUDY UNIT

STUDY UNIT FOUR
FEDERAL AVIATION REGULATIONS

(83 pages of outline)

NOTE: The FAA now refers to the Federal Aviation Regulations as "14 CFR" rather than "FAR." CFR stands for Code of Federal Regulations, and the Federal Aviation Regulations are in Title 14. For example, FAR Part 1 and FAR 61.109 are now referred to as 14 CFR Part 1 and 14 CFR 61.109, respectively.

This study unit contains outlines of relevant sections from 14 CFR Parts 1, 21, 39, 43, 61, 67, and 91 and NTSB Part 830. In the 14 CFR section listing on the previous five pages, we list only the sections outlined in this study unit. At the end of the outline for Parts 61, 67, and 91, we list the sections that are not outlined.

CAUTION: Federal Aviation Regulations are federal law and **must** be complied with. Our outlines provide only an overview. Consult current Federal Aviation Regulations to ensure you have the most up-to-date information.

4.1 FEDERAL AVIATION REGULATIONS

The primary purpose of this study unit is to outline (paraphrase) the Federal Aviation Regulations we feel are particularly relevant to pilots. These include 14 CFR Parts 1, 21, 39, 43, 61, 67, and 91, and NTSB Part 830. Many parts of the regulations are not relevant to the general pilot population (e.g., Part 103, Ultralight Vehicles).

Obtain your copy of Gleim *FAR/AIM*, which contains a reprint of 14 CFR Parts 1, 43, 48, 61, 67, 68, 71, 73, 91, 97, 99, 103, 105, 107, 110, 117, 119, 120, 133, 135, 136, 137, 141, and 142 and NTSB Part 830. Transportation Security Administration (TSA) Parts 1540, 1550, 1552, and 1562 are also reproduced. Additionally, the *Aeronautical Information Manual (AIM)* is reprinted with full-color graphics in the same book. For a digital version, visit www.gleim.com/aviation/faraim.

4.2 PART 1 – DEFINITIONS AND ABBREVIATIONS

This part contains several pages of definitions and abbreviations used throughout the Federal Aviation Regulations. You should use Part 1 any time you do not understand the meaning of a word or an abbreviation.

1.1 General Definitions

Only selected terms relevant to most pilots are included here.

1. **Administrator** means the FAA administrator or any person to whom (s)he has delegated his or her authority in the matter concerned.

2. **Aircraft** means a device that is used or intended to be used for flight in the air.

3. **Airframe** means the fuselage, booms, nacelles, cowlings, fairings, airfoil surfaces (excluding propellers of engines), and landing gear of an aircraft and their accessories and controls.

4. **Airplane** means an engine-driven fixed-wing aircraft heavier than air that is supported in flight by the dynamic reaction of the air against its wings.

5. **Airport** means an area of land or water that is used or intended to be used for the landing and takeoff of aircraft, and includes its buildings and facilities, if any.

6. **Air traffic** means aircraft operating in the air or on an airport surface, exclusive of loading ramps and parking areas.

7. **Air traffic clearance** means an authorization by air traffic control, for the purpose of preventing a collision between known aircraft, for an aircraft to proceed under specified traffic conditions within controlled airspace.

8. **Air traffic control** means a service operated by appropriate authority to promote the safe, orderly, and expeditious flow of air traffic.

9. **Alternate airport** means an airport at which an aircraft may land if a landing at the intended airport becomes inadvisable.

10. **Category**

    a. Category, as used with respect to the certification, ratings, privileges, and limitations of airmen, means a broad classification of aircraft.

        1) EXAMPLES: Airplane, rotorcraft, glider, and lighter-than-air.

    b. Category, as used with respect to the certification of aircraft, means a grouping of aircraft based upon intended use or operating limitations.

        1) EXAMPLES: Transport, normal, utility, acrobatic, limited, restricted, and provisional.

11. **Ceiling** means the height above the Earth's surface of the lowest layer of clouds or obscuring phenomena that is reported as "broken," "overcast," or "obscuration," and not classified as "thin" or "partial."

12. **Civil aircraft** means aircraft other than public aircraft.

13. **Class**

    a. Class, as used with respect to the certification, ratings, privileges, and limitations of airmen, means a classification of aircraft within a category having similar operating characteristics.

        1) EXAMPLES: Single-engine, multi-engine, land, water, gyroplane, helicopter, airship, and free balloon.

    b. Class, as used with respect to certification of aircraft, means a broad grouping of aircraft having similar characteristics of propulsion, flight, or landing.

        1) EXAMPLES: Airplane, rotorcraft, glider, balloon, landplane, and seaplane.

14. **Commercial operator** means a person who uses an aircraft to transport persons or property for compensation or hire.

    a. If it is doubtful that an operation is for compensation or hire, the test applied is whether the operation is merely incidental to the person's other business or is, in itself, a major enterprise for profit.

15. **Controlled airspace** means an airspace of defined dimensions within which air traffic control service is provided to IFR flights and to VFR flights in accordance with the airspace classification.

    a. Note that controlled airspace is a generic term that covers Class A, Class B, Class C, Class D, and Class E airspace.

16. **Crewmember** means a person assigned to perform duty in an aircraft during flight time.

17. **Decision height (DH)** means the height above ground level (AGL) at which a decision must be made during an instrument approach, either to continue the approach or to execute a missed approach. This can also be referred to as **decision altitude (DA)**, which is expressed in feet above mean sea level (MSL).

18. **Flight plan** means specified information relating to the intended flight of an aircraft that is filed orally or in writing with air traffic control.

19. **Flight time** means pilot time that commences when an aircraft moves under its own power for the purpose of flight and ends when the aircraft comes to a rest after landing.

20. **Flight visibility** means the average forward horizontal distance from the cockpit of an aircraft in flight at which prominent unlighted objects may be seen and identified by day and prominent lighted objects may be seen and identified by night.

21. **Ground visibility** means prevailing horizontal visibility near the Earth's surface as reported by the United States National Weather Service or an accredited observer.

22. **IFR conditions** means weather conditions below the minimum for flight under visual flight rules.

23. **IFR over-the-top** means the operation of aircraft over-the-top on an IFR flight plan when cleared by ATC to maintain "VFR conditions" or "VFR conditions on top."

24. **Instrument** means a device using an internal mechanism to indicate visually or aurally the attitude, altitude, or operation of an aircraft or aircraft part. It includes electronic devices for automatically controlling an aircraft in flight.

25. **Large aircraft** means an aircraft having a maximum certificated takeoff weight of more than 12,500 lb.

26. **Light-sport aircraft** means an aircraft, other than a helicopter or powered-lift, that, since its original certification, has continued to meet the following conditions:

    a. A maximum takeoff weight of not more than

        1) 1,320 pounds for aircraft not intended for operation on water.
        2) 1,430 pounds for an aircraft intended for operation on water.

    b. A maximum airspeed in level flight with maximum continuous power (V_H) of not more than 120 knots CAS under standard atmospheric conditions at sea level.

    c. A maximum never-exceed speed (V_{NE}) of not more than 120 knots CAS for a glider.

    d. A maximum stalling speed or minimum steady flight speed without the use of lift-enhancing devices (V_{S1}) of not more than 45 knots CAS at the aircraft's maximum certificated takeoff weight and most critical center of gravity.

    e. A maximum seating capacity of no more than two persons, including the pilot.

    f. A single, reciprocating engine, if powered.

    g. A fixed or ground-adjustable propeller if a powered aircraft other than a powered glider.

    h. A fixed or feathering propeller system if a powered glider.

    i. A fixed-pitch, semi-rigid, teetering, two-blade rotor system, if a gyroplane.

    j. A nonpressurized cabin, if equipped with a cabin.

    k. Fixed landing gear, except for an aircraft intended for operation on water or a glider.

        1) Fixed or retractable landing gear, or a hull, for an aircraft intended for operation on water.
        2) Fixed or retractable landing gear for a glider.

27. **Maintenance** means inspection, overhaul, repair, and preservation of the aircraft and replacement of parts, but excludes preventive maintenance.

28. **Major alteration** means an alteration not listed in the aircraft, aircraft engine, or propeller specifications that

    a. Might appreciably affect weight, balance, structural strength, performance, powerplant operation, flight characteristics, or other qualities affecting airworthiness; or

    b. Is not done according to accepted practices or cannot be done by elementary operations.

29. **Major repair** means a repair that

    a. If improperly done, might appreciably affect weight, balance, structural strength, performance, powerplant operation, flight characteristics, or other qualities affecting airworthiness; or

    b. Is not done according to accepted practices or cannot be done by elementary operations.

30. **Manifold pressure** means absolute pressure as measured at the appropriate point in the induction system and is usually expressed in inches of mercury.

31. **Medical certificate** means an acceptable evidence of physical fitness on a form prescribed by the FAA administrator.

32. **Minimum descent altitude (MDA)** means the lowest altitude, expressed in feet above mean sea level, to which a descent is authorized on final approach or during circle-to-land maneuvering in execution of a standard instrument approach procedure.

33. **Minor alteration** means an alteration other than a major alteration.

34. **Minor repair** means a repair other than a major repair.

35. **Night** means the time between the end of evening civil twilight and the beginning of morning civil twilight, as published in the *American Air Almanac*, converted to local time.

36. **Nonprecision approach procedure** means a standard instrument approach procedure in which no electronic glide slope is provided.

37. **Operate** (with respect to aircraft) means use, cause to use, or authorization to use aircraft for the purpose (except as provided in regulation 91.13, Careless or Reckless Operation) of air navigation including the piloting of aircraft, with or without the right of legal control (as owner, lessee, or otherwise).

38. **Operational control**, with respect to a flight, means the exercise of authority over initiating, conducting, or terminating a flight.

39. **Over-the-top** means above the layer of clouds or other obscuring phenomena forming the ceiling.

40. **Pilotage** means navigation by visual reference to landmarks.

41. **Pilot in command (PIC)** means the person who

    a. Has final authority and responsibility for the operation and safety of the flight;

    b. Has been designated as pilot in command before or during the flight; and

    c. Holds the appropriate category, class, and type rating, if appropriate, for the conduct of the flight.

42. **Positive control** means control of all air traffic, within designated airspace, by air traffic control.

43. **Precision approach procedure** means a standard instrument approach procedure in which an electronic glide slope, such as ILS and PAR, is provided.

44. **Preventive maintenance** means simple or minor preservation operations and the replacement of small standard parts not involving complex assembly operations.

45. **Rating** means a statement that, as part of a certificate, sets forth special conditions, privileges, and limitations.

46. **Small aircraft** means an aircraft having a maximum certificated takeoff weight of 12,500 lb. or less.

47. **Special VFR conditions** mean meteorological conditions that are less than those required for basic VFR flight in controlled airspace and in which some aircraft are permitted flight under VFR.

48. **Special VFR operations** means aircraft operating in accordance with ATC clearances within controlled airspace in meteorological conditions less than the basic VFR weather minimums.

    a. Such operations must be requested by the pilot and approved by ATC.

49. **Stopway** means an area beyond the takeoff runway, no less wide than the runway and centered on the extended centerline of the runway, able to support the airplane during an aborted takeoff without causing structural damage to the airplane. A stopway is also designated by the airport authorities for use in decelerating the airplane during an aborted takeoff.

50. **Synthetic vision** means a computer-generated image of the external scene topography from the perspective of the flight deck that is derived from aircraft attitude, high-precision navigation solution, and database of terrain, obstacles, and relevant cultural features.

51. **Synthetic vision system** means an electronic means to display a synthetic vision image of the external scene topography to the flight crew.

52. **Traffic pattern** means the traffic flow that is prescribed for aircraft landing at, taxiing on, or taking off from an airport.

53. **VFR over-the-top,** with respect to the operation of aircraft, means the operation of an aircraft over-the-top under VFR when it is not being operated on an IFR flight plan.

1.2 Abbreviations and Symbols

1. General

AFM means airplane flight manual.

AGL means above ground level.

ATC means air traffic control.

CAS means calibrated airspeed.

DME means distance-measuring equipment compatible with TACAN.

FAA means Federal Aviation Administration.

FSTD means flight simulation training device.

FTD means flight training device.

HIRL means high-intensity runway light system.

IAS means indicated airspeed.

ICAO means International Civil Aviation Organization.

LSA means light sport aircraft.

MEL means minimum equipment list.

MSL means mean sea level.

NDB (ADF) means nondirectional beacon (automatic direction finder).

NM means nautical mile.

RBN means radio beacon.

REIL means runway end identification lights.

RNAV means area navigation.

TACAN means ultra-high-frequency tactical air navigational aid.

TAS means true airspeed.

TCAS means a traffic alert and collision avoidance system.

TDZL means touchdown zone lights.

V_A means design maneuvering speed.

V_C means design cruising speed.

V_{FE} means maximum flap extended speed.

V_H means maximum speed in level flight with maximum continuous power.

V_{LE} means maximum landing gear extended speed.

V_{LO} means maximum landing gear operating speed.

V_{LOF} means lift-off speed.

V_{MC} means minimum control speed with the critical engine of a multi-engine airplane inoperative.

V_{MO}/M_{MO} means maximum operating limit speed.

V_{NE} means never-exceed speed.

V_{NO} means maximum structural cruising speed.

V_R means rotation speed.

V_S means the stalling speed or the minimum steady flight speed at which the airplane is controllable.

V_{S0} means the stalling speed or the minimum steady flight speed in the landing configuration.

V_{S1} means the stalling speed or the minimum steady flight speed obtained in a specific configuration.

V_X means speed for best angle of climb.

V_Y means speed for best rate of climb.

VFR means visual flight rules.

VHF means very high frequency.

VOR means very-high-frequency omnirange station.

VORTAC means collocated VOR and TACAN.

2. Instrument related

ALS means approach light system.

ASR means airport surveillance radar.

CAT II means Category II.

DA means decision altitude.

DH means decision height.

FM means fan marker.

GS means glide slope.

IFR means instrument flight rules.

ILS means instrument landing system.

IM means ILS inner marker.

INT means intersection.

LDA means localizer-type directional aid.

LMM means compass locator at middle marker.

LOC means ILS localizer.

LOM means compass locator at outer marker.

MAA means maximum authorized IFR altitude.

MALS means medium-intensity approach light system.

MALSR means medium-intensity approach light system with runway alignment indicator lights.

MCA means minimum crossing altitude.

MDA means minimum descent altitude.

MEA means minimum en route IFR altitude.

MM means ILS middle marker.

MOCA means minimum obstruction clearance altitude.

MRA means minimum reception altitude.

NOPT means no procedure turn required.

OM means ILS outer marker.

PAR means precision approach radar.

RAIL means runway alignment indicator light system.

RCLM means runway centerline marking.

RCLS means runway centerline light system.

RVR means runway visual range as measured in the touchdown zone area.

SALS means short approach light system.

SSALS means simplified short approach light system.

SSALSR means simplified short approach light system with runway alignment indicator lights.

4.3 PART 21 – CERTIFICATION PROCEDURES FOR PRODUCTS AND ARTICLES

Subpart H -- Airworthiness Certificates

21.175 Airworthiness Certificates: Classification

1. **Standard airworthiness certificates** are issued for aircraft type certificated in the normal, utility, acrobatic, commuter, or transport category, and for manned free balloons, and for aircraft designated by the Administrator as special classes of aircraft.

2. **Special airworthiness certificates** are primary, restricted, limited, light-sport, and provisional airworthiness certificates, special flight permits, and experimental certificates.

21.181 Duration

1. Airworthiness certificates remain in force as long as maintenance and alteration of the aircraft are performed per Federal Aviation Regulations.

21.197 Special Flight Permits

1. A special flight permit may be issued for an aircraft that may not currently meet applicable airworthiness requirements but is capable of safe flight, for the following purposes:

    a. Flying the aircraft to a base where repairs, alterations, or maintenance are to be performed, or to a point of storage.

    b. Delivering or exporting the aircraft.

    c. Production flight testing new production aircraft.

    d. Evacuating aircraft from areas of impending danger.

    e. Conducting customer demonstration flights in new production aircraft that have satisfactorily completed production flight tests.

2.   A special flight permit may also be issued to authorize the operation of an aircraft at a weight in excess of its maximum certificated takeoff weight for flight beyond the normal range over water, or over land areas where adequate landing facilities or appropriate fuel is not available.

    a.   The excess weight that may be allowed is limited to the additional fuel, fuel-carrying facilities, and navigation equipment necessary for the flight.

3.   The permit issued is an authorization, including conditions and limitations for flight, which is set forth in the certificate holder's operations specifications.

21.199 Issue of Special Flight Permits

1.   An applicant for a special flight permit must submit a statement in a form and manner prescribed by the FAA, indicating

    a.   The purpose of the flight.

    b.   The proposed itinerary.

    c.   The crew required to operate the aircraft and its equipment, e.g., pilot, co-pilot, navigator, etc.

    d.   The ways, if any, in which the aircraft does not comply with the applicable airworthiness requirements.

    e.   Any restriction the applicant considers necessary for safe operation of the aircraft.

    f.   Any other information considered necessary by the FAA for the purpose of prescribing operating limitations.

2.   The FAA may make, or require the applicant to make, appropriate inspections or tests necessary for safety.

4.4   PART 39 – AIRWORTHINESS DIRECTIVES

39.1 Purpose of this Regulation

1.   The regulations in this part provide a legal framework for FAA's system of Airworthiness Directives.

39.3 Definition of Airworthiness Directives

1.   FAA's airworthiness directives are legally enforceable rules that apply to aircraft, aircraft engines, propellers, and appliances (e.g., vacuum pump, alternator, navigation radios, etc.).

39.5 When does FAA issue airworthiness directives?

1.   FAA issues an airworthiness directive addressing a product when it finds that

    a.   An unsafe condition exists in the product and

    b.   The condition is likely to exist or develop in other products of the same type design.

39.7 What is the legal effect of failing to comply with an airworthiness directive?

1.   Anyone who operates a product that does not meet the requirements of an applicable airworthiness directive is in violation of this section.

39.9 What if I operate an aircraft or use a product that does not meet the requirements of an airworthiness directive?

1.   If the requirements of an airworthiness directive have not been met, you violate 39.7 each time you operate the aircraft or use the product.

39.11 What actions do airworthiness directives require?

1. Airworthiness directives specify inspections you must carry out, conditions and limitations you must comply with, and any actions you must take to resolve an unsafe condition.

39.13 Are airworthiness directives part of the Code of Federal Regulations?

1. Yes, airworthiness directives are part of the Code of Federal Regulations, but they are not codified in the annual edition.

2. FAA publishes airworthiness directives in full in the Federal Register as amendments to this regulation.

4.5   PART 43 – MAINTENANCE, PREVENTIVE MAINTENANCE, REBUILDING, AND ALTERATION

43.1 Applicability

1. This part prescribes rules governing the maintenance, preventive maintenance, rebuilding, and alteration of any aircraft having a U.S. airworthiness certificate as well as the airframe, aircraft engine(s), propeller(s), appliances, and component parts of such aircraft.

2. This part does not apply to any aircraft for which the FAA has issued an experimental certificate, unless the FAA has previously issued a different kind of airworthiness certificate for that aircraft.

3. This part applies to certain aircraft issued a special airworthiness certificate in the light-sport category.

43.3 Persons Authorized to Perform Maintenance, Preventive Maintenance, Rebuilding, and Alterations

1. A person who holds a pilot certificate (e.g., private pilot) may perform preventive maintenance on any airplane owned or operated by that pilot which is not used in air carrier services.

43.7 Persons Authorized to Approve Aircraft, Airframes, Aircraft Engines, Propellers, Appliances, or Component Parts for Return to Service after Maintenance, Preventive Maintenance, Rebuilding, or Alteration

1. To approve the airplane for return to service after preventive maintenance was done by a pilot, the pilot must hold at least a private pilot certificate.

2. To approve an aircraft in the light-sport category for return to service after preventative maintenance is done, the pilot must hold at least a sport pilot certificate.

43.9 Maintenance Records

1. After preventive maintenance has been performed, the signature, certificate number, the kind of certificate held by the person approving the work, the date the work was performed, and a description of the work must be entered in the aircraft maintenance records.

Appendix A. Major Alterations, Major Repairs, and Preventive Maintenance

1. Preventive maintenance means simple or minor preservation operations and the replacement of small standard parts not involving complex assembly operations.

2. A complete list of operations that are classified as preventive maintenance is included in the complete regulation. Some common examples include

    a.   Removal, installation, and repair of landing gear tires;
    b.   Replenishing hydraulic fluid;
    c.   Servicing landing gear struts; and
    d.   Replacing landing light bulbs.

4.6 PART 61 – CERTIFICATION: PILOTS, FLIGHT INSTRUCTORS, AND GROUND INSTRUCTORS

Part 61 contains 11 subparts, labeled A through K. Parts G, H, and K are not outlined in this book.

Subpart A – General
Subpart B – Aircraft Ratings and Pilot Authorizations
Subpart C – Student Pilots
Subpart D – Recreational Pilots
Subpart E – Private Pilots
Subpart F – Commercial Pilots

Subpart G – Airline Transport Pilots
Subpart H – Flight Instructors Other than Flight
        Instructors with a Sport Pilot Rating*
Subpart I – Ground Instructors
Subpart J – Sport Pilots
Subpart K – Flight Instructors with a Sport Pilot Rating*

*Covered thoroughly in Gleim *Flight Instructor Flight Maneuvers and Practical Test Prep.*

NOTE: Only selected sections are outlined below through page 252. Page 253 contains the section titles of Part 61 that are not outlined.

Subpart A -- General

61.1 Applicability and Definitions

1. Part 61 prescribes

    a. The requirements for issuing pilot, flight instructor, and ground instructor certificates and ratings; the conditions under which those certificates and ratings are necessary; and the privileges and limitations of those certificates and ratings

    b. The requirements for issuing pilot, flight instructor, and ground instructor authorizations; the conditions under which those authorizations are necessary; and the privileges and limitations of those authorizations

    c. The requirements for issuing pilot, flight instructor, and ground instructor certificates and ratings for persons who have taken courses approved by the FAA under 14 CFR Parts 141 and 142

2. Definitions of terms used in Part 61

    a. **Aeronautical experience** means pilot time obtained in an aircraft, flight simulator, or flight training device for meeting the appropriate training and flight time requirements for a pilot certificate, rating, flight review, or recency of flight experience requirements.

    b. **Authorized instructor** means a person who

        1) Holds a current flight instructor certificate (i.e., a CFI) when conducting ground or flight training in accordance with the privileges of his or her flight instructor certificate

        2) Holds a valid ground instructor certificate when conducting ground training in accordance with the privileges and limitations of his or her ground instructor certificate

        3) Is authorized by the FAA to provide ground or flight training under Part 61, 121, 135, or 142 when conducting ground or flight training under that authority

    c. **Cross-country time** means

        1) Except as provided in 2) or 3) on the next page, time acquired during a flight that

            a) Is conducted by a person who holds a pilot certificate

            b) Is conducted in an aircraft

            c) Includes a landing at a point other than departure

            d) Involves the use of dead reckoning, pilotage, electronic navigation aids, radio aids, or other navigation systems to navigate to the landing point

2) For the purpose of meeting the aeronautical experience requirements for a private pilot certificate, a commercial pilot certificate, or an instrument rating, or for the purpose of exercising recreational pilot privileges, time acquired during a flight that

a) Is conducted in an appropriate aircraft

b) Includes a point of landing that is at least a straight-line distance of more than 50 NM from the original departure point

c) Involves the use of dead reckoning, pilotage, electronic navigation aids, radio aids, or other navigation systems to navigate to the landing point

3) For the purpose of meeting the aeronautical experience requirements for an airline transport pilot (ATP) certificate, time acquired during a flight that

a) Is conducted in an appropriate aircraft

b) Is at least a straight-line distance of more than 50 NM from the original departure point

c) Involves the use of dead reckoning, pilotage, electronic navigation aids, radio aids, or other navigation systems

d. **Examiner or evaluator** means any person who is authorized by the FAA to conduct a pilot proficiency test or a practical test for a pilot certificate or rating, or a person who is authorized to conduct a knowledge test.

e. **Flight time** means pilot time that commences when an aircraft moves under its own power for the purpose of flight and ends when the aircraft comes to rest after landing.

f. **Flight training** means that training, other than ground training, received from an authorized instructor in flight in an aircraft.

g. **Flight training device**, **flight simulation training device (FSTD)**, or **flight simulator** means a device that

1) Is a replica of the instruments, equipment, panels, and controls of an aircraft, or set of aircraft, in an open flight deck or in an enclosed cockpit, including the hardware and software for the systems installed that are necessary to simulate the aircraft in both ground and flight operations

2) Need not have a force (motion) cueing or visual system

3) Has been evaluated, qualified, and approved by the FAA

h. **Full flight simulator (FFS)** means a replica of a specific type; or make, model, and series aircraft cockpit.

1) It includes the assemblage of equipment and computer programs necessary to represent aircraft operations in ground and flight conditions and a visual system providing an out-of-the-cockpit view.

2) It must have a system that provides cues at least equivalent to those of a three-degree-of-freedom motion system and has the full range of capabilities of the systems installed in the device as described in 14 CFR Part 60 and the qualification performance standards (QPS) for a specific FFS qualification level.

3) It has been evaluated, qualified, and approved by the FAA.

i. **Ground training** means that training, other than flight training, received from an authorized instructor.

j. **Instrument training** means that time in which instrument training is received from an authorized instructor under actual or simulated instrument conditions.

k. **Training time** means training received

1) In flight from an authorized instructor

2) On the ground from an authorized instructor

3) In a flight simulator or flight training device from an authorized instructor

61.2 Exercise of Privilege

1.   This section exists to officially define and regulate the use of two words throughout Part 61, currency and validity.

    a.   Currency requires that no person exercise the privileges of an airman certificate, rating, endorsement, or authorization issued under Part 61 unless that person meets the appropriate airman and medical recency requirements specific to the intended activity.

    b.   Validity requires that no person exercise the privileges of an airman certificate, rating, endorsement, authorization, or medical certificate if those privileges are surrendered, suspended, revoked, or expired.

        1)   Government-issued identification cannot be used for any purpose required by Part 61 if that identification is surrendered, suspended, revoked, or expired.

61.3 Requirement for Certificates, Ratings, and Authorizations

1.   An appropriate pilot certificate, a current and appropriate medical certificate, and a current and valid photo identification are required to be in your personal possession or readily accessible in the airplane when acting as pilot in command or as a required pilot flight crewmember.

    a.   A flight instructor is not required to have a current medical certificate, provided (s)he is not acting as pilot in command or as a required pilot flight crewmember.

    b.   A medical certificate is not required when exercising the privileges of a ground instructor certificate.

2.   A person who holds a flight instructor certificate must have that certificate in his or her physical possession or readily accessible in the airplane when exercising the privileges of that flight instructor certificate.

    a.   No person other than the holder of a flight instructor certificate with the appropriate rating(s) may

        1)   Give training required to qualify a person for solo flight and solo cross-country flight

        2)   Endorse a person for a pilot, flight instructor, and/or ground instructor certificate or rating issued under Part 61

        3)   Endorse a pilot logbook to show training given

        4)   Endorse a student pilot certificate and logbook for solo operating privileges

    b.   A flight instructor certificate is not necessary if the training is given

        1)   By a holder of an ATP certificate, provided the training is given in accordance with the privileges of the certificate and conducted under a Part 121 or 135 training program

        2)   By a person who is qualified under Part 142, provided the training is conducted in accordance with an approved Part 142 training program

        3)   By the holder of a ground instructor certificate

        4)   By an authorized flight instructor who is not certificated by the FAA (i.e., a military flight instructor)

3.   You must hold an instrument rating (airplane) to act as PIC of an airplane operating under IFR or in weather conditions less than the minimums prescribed for VFR flight.

4. Each person who holds a ground instructor certificate must have that certificate in his or her physical possession or immediately accessible when exercising the privileges of that certificate.

   a. A ground instructor with the appropriate rating may

      1) Give ground training required to qualify a person for solo flight and solo cross-country flight

      2) Endorse a person for a knowledge test required for a pilot, flight instructor, or ground instructor certificate or rating

      3) Endorse a pilot logbook to show ground training given

   b. A ground instructor certificate is not necessary if the training is given

      1) By the holder of a flight instructor certificate in accordance with the privileges of that certificate

      2) By the holder of an ATP certificate, provided the training is conducted under an approved Part 121 or 135 training program

      3) Under a Part 142 program by a qualified Part 142 instructor

5. You must present your pilot and/or medical certificate for inspection upon a request from the FAA; an authorized representative of the NTSB; or any federal, state, or local law enforcement officer.

61.4 Qualification and Approval of Flight Simulators and Flight Training Devices

1. Each flight simulator and flight training device used for training, and for which an airman is to receive credit to satisfy any training, testing, or checking requirement under this chapter, must be qualified and approved by the Administrator for

   a. The training, testing, and checking for which it is used;

   b. Each particular maneuver, procedure, or crewmember function performed; and

   c. The representation of the specific category and class of aircraft, type of aircraft, particular variation within the type of aircraft, or set of aircraft for certain flight training devices.

2. Any device used for flight training, testing, or checking that has been determined to be acceptable to or approved by the Administrator prior to August 1, 1996, which can be shown to function as originally designed, is considered to be a flight training device, provided it is used for the same purposes for which it was originally accepted or approved and only to the extent of such acceptance or approval.

3. The Administrator may approve a device other than a flight simulator or flight training device for specific purposes.

61.5 Certificates and Ratings Issued under this Part

1. The following certificates are issued to a person who satisfactorily accomplishes the training and certificate requirements:

   a. Pilot certificates

      1) Student pilot
      2) Sport pilot
      3) Recreational pilot
      4) Private pilot
      5) Commercial pilot
      6) Airline transport pilot

   b. Flight instructor certificates

   c. Ground instructor certificates

2.   The following ratings may be placed on a pilot certificate:

    a.   Aircraft category ratings

        1)   Airplane
        2)   Rotorcraft
        3)   Glider
        4)   Lighter-than-air
        5)   Powered-lift

    b.   Airplane class ratings

        1)   Single-engine land
        2)   Multi-engine land
        3)   Single-engine sea
        4)   Multi-engine sea

    c.   Instrument rating

        1)   Private
        2)   Commercial
        3)   Flight instructor

61.7 Obsolete Certificates and Ratings

1.   Holders of certain obsolete free balloon and other certificates with category ratings without class ratings may not exercise those pilot privileges.

61.11 Expired Pilot Certificates and Reissuance

1.   Procedures are given for reissuing certain expired certificates and ratings.

61.13 Issuance of Airman Certificates, Ratings, and Authorizations

1.   If you want to apply for a certificate or rating, or to add a rating to an existing certificate, you must do so in the manner and on the form designated by the FAA.

2.   If you meet all the requirements of Part 61 (i.e., training, knowledge test, and practical test), you are entitled to the certificate or rating sought.

3.   If your medical certificate contains special limitations, but you meet all other requirements for a particular pilot certificate, that pilot certificate will be issued to you containing operating limitations that the FAA has determined to be necessary.

4.   If your pilot, flight instructor, or ground instructor certificate has been suspended, you may not apply for any certificate or rating during the suspension.

5.   If your pilot, flight instructor, or ground instructor certificate has been revoked, you may not apply for any certificate or rating for 1 year after the revocation.

61.15 Offenses Involving Alcohol or Drugs

1.   Conviction for a violation of any law relating to drugs or alcohol is the basis for

    a.   The denial of an application for a certificate or rating for up to 1 year after the final conviction

    b.   The suspension or revocation of any existing certificates or ratings

61.16 Refusal to Submit to an Alcohol Test or to Furnish Test Results

1. If you refuse to submit test results for drugs or alcohol when requested by the FAA, you may not receive a certificate or rating for a period of 1 year.

2. Your refusal is also grounds for suspension or revocation of existing certificates or ratings.

61.17 Temporary Certificate

1. A temporary certificate is issued to you after successful completion of your practical test. It is valid for a maximum of 120 days or until

   a. The expiration date shown on the certificate is reached.
   b. You receive your permanent certificate.
   c. Notice is given that the certificate or rating sought is denied.

61.18 Security Disqualification

1. When the Transportation Security Administration (TSA) has notified the FAA in writing that a person poses a security threat, that person is not eligible to hold any certificate, rating, or authorization under this part.

2. Issuance of an Initial Notification of Threat Assessment by the TSA.

   a. The FAA will hold in abeyance an application for a certificate, rating, or authorization until the TSA's final threat assessment review.
   b. The FAA will suspend any certificate, rating, or authorization held pending the outcome of the TSA's final threat assessment review.

3. Issuance of a Final Notification of Threat Assessment by the TSA.

   a. The FAA will deny an application for a certificate, rating, or authorization.
   b. The FAA will revoke any certificate, rating, or authority held.

61.19 Duration of Pilot and Instructor Certificates and Privileges

1. All pilot and ground instructor certificates issued under Part 61 are issued without an expiration date.

2. Any pilot certificate is no longer valid if it is surrendered, suspended, or revoked.

   a. The FAA may request that a suspended or revoked certificate be returned to them.

3. A flight instructor certificate is valid only while you have a current pilot certificate; the flight instructor certificate expires at the end of 24 calendar months after it was last issued or renewed.

4. Pilots who hold paper pilot certificates may not exercise the privileges of those certificates after March 31, 2010. They must be replaced with plastic certificates.

   a. This excludes temporary pilot certificates, which are still valid in paper form.

61.21 Duration of a Category II and a Category III Pilot Authorization (for other than Part 121 and Part 135 use)

1. A Category II or a Category III pilot authorization expires at the end of the sixth month after it was issued or renewed.

61.23 Medical Certificates: Requirement and Duration

1. A person must hold

   a. A first-class medical certificate when exercising the privileges of an ATP certificate

   b. At least a second-class medical certificate when exercising the privileges of a commercial pilot certificate

   c. At least a third-class medical certificate

      1) When exercising the privileges of a private, recreational, or student pilot certificate

      2) When exercising the privileges of a flight instructor certificate if the CFI is acting as PIC or as a required pilot flight crewmember

      3) Prior to taking a practical test that is performed in an airplane for a certificate or rating at a recreational, private, commercial, or ATP certificate level

2. A person is not required to hold a medical certificate when

   a. Exercising the privileges of a flight instructor certificate if the person is not acting as PIC or serving as a required pilot flight crewmember

   b. Exercising the privileges of a ground instructor certificate

   c. Taking a test or check for a certificate, rating, or authorization conducted in a flight simulator or flight training device

3. Duration of a medical certificate

   a. A first-class medical certificate expires at the end of the last day of

      1) The 12th month after the date of the examination for operations requiring an airline transport certificate if under age 40

      2) The 6th month after the date of examination for operations requiring an airline transport certificate if age 40 or older

      3) The 12th month after the date of examination for operations requiring only a commercial pilot certificate

      4) The period specified in item c. below for operations requiring only a private, recreational, flight instructor (when acting as PIC), or student pilot certificate

   b. A second-class medical certificate expires at the end of the last day of

      1) The 12th month after the date of examination for operations requiring a commercial pilot certificate

      2) The period specified in item c. below, for operations requiring only a private, recreational, flight instructor (when acting as PIC), or student pilot certificate

   c. A third-class medical certificate for operations requiring a private, recreational, flight instructor (when acting as PIC), or student pilot certificate expires at the end of the last day of

      1) The 60th month after the date of examination if the person has not reached his or her 40th birthday on or before the date of the examination.

      2) The 24th month after the date of examination if the person has reached his or her 40th birthday on or before the date of examination.

4. BasicMed allows a pilot to conduct certain operations using a U.S. driver's license instead of a medical certificate as long as the pilot

   a. Has held an FAA medical certificate at any time after July 14, 2006, the most recent of which

      1) May have been a special issuance medical certificate.

         a) A one-time special issuance medical certificate must be obtained for certain cardiovascular, neurological, and mental health conditions.

      2) May be expired.

      3) Cannot have been suspended, revoked, withdrawn, or denied.

   b. Completes an approved medical education course in the preceding 24 calendar months in accordance with 14 CFR Part 68.

   c. Receives a comprehensive medical examination from a state-licensed physician in the previous 48 calendar months in accordance with 14 CFR Part 68.

      1) The exam is not required to be conducted by an aviation medical examiner (AME).

61.25 Change of Name

1. To change your name on your pilot certificate, you must submit your current pilot certificate and a copy of the marriage license, court order, or other document verifying the change.

   a. The documents will be returned after inspection.

61.27 Voluntary Surrender or Exchange of Certificate

1. A holder of a certificate may voluntarily surrender it for cancellation or for the issuance of a certificate at a lower grade or with specific ratings deleted.

2. When doing so, a pilot must state in writing: "This request is made for my own reasons, with full knowledge that my (insert name of certificate or rating as appropriate) may not be reissued to me unless I again pass the tests prescribed for its issuance."

61.29 Replacement of a Lost or Destroyed Airman or Medical Certificate or Knowledge Test Report

1. A request for the replacement of a lost or destroyed pilot certificate or knowledge test report must be made online at www.faa.gov or by a signed letter to the Department of Transportation · FAA · Airmen Certification Branch · PO Box 25082 · Oklahoma City, OK 73125. Letter must be accompanied by a check or money order payable to the FAA.

2. A request for the replacement of a lost or destroyed medical certificate must be made by a signed letter to the Department of Transportation · FAA · Aerospace Medical Certification Division · PO Box 26200 · Oklahoma City, OK 73125. Letter must be accompanied by a check or money order payable to the FAA.

3. The letter requesting replacement of a lost or destroyed pilot certificate, medical certificate, or knowledge test report must include your name; permanent mailing address (including ZIP code; or if the permanent mailing address includes a post office box number, then the person's current residential address); date and place of birth; grade, number, and date of issuance of the certificate and ratings, if applicable; date of medical examination, if applicable; and date of knowledge test, if applicable. Allow 4-6 weeks for processing your request.

4. A fax from the FAA showing that the certificate (pilot and/or medical) or knowledge test report was issued may be used for a period not to exceed 60 days, pending the arrival of the replacement certificate or knowledge test report.

   a. To receive a temporary pilot certificate, medical certificate, or knowledge test report, call (866) 878-2498.

61.31 Type Rating Requirements, Additional Training, and Authorization Requirements

1.   Type ratings are required when operating any turbojet-powered airplane or other aircraft specified by the FAA through aircraft type certificate procedures.

2.   To act as pilot in command of a complex airplane (an airplane that has a retractable landing gear, flaps, and a controllable pitch propeller), you must receive and log ground and flight training from an authorized instructor in a complex airplane and receive a one-time logbook endorsement that you are proficient to operate a complex airplane.

3.   To act as pilot in command of a high-performance airplane (an airplane with an engine of more than 200 horsepower), you must receive and log ground and flight training from an authorized instructor in a high-performance airplane and receive a one-time logbook endorsement that you are proficient to operate a high-performance airplane.

4.   To act as pilot in command of a pressurized airplane that has a service ceiling or maximum operating altitude, whichever is lower, above 25,000 ft. MSL, you must have both ground and flight instruction in such an airplane and obtain a logbook endorsement.

5.   To act as pilot in command of a tailwheel airplane, you must receive flight instruction in such an airplane and obtain a logbook endorsement of competence. Training must include

     a.   Normal and crosswind takeoffs and landings
     b.   Wheel landings, unless the manufacturer does not recommend them
     c.   Go-around procedures

6.   To act as pilot in command of an airplane that the FAA has determined requires airplane type-specific training, you must receive and log type-specific training in the airplane and receive a logbook endorsement from an authorized instructor that you are proficient in the operation of the airplane and its systems.

61.33 Tests: General Procedure

1.   Required tests (i.e., knowledge and practical) are given at times and places and by persons designated by the FAA.

61.35 Knowledge Test: Prerequisites and Passing Grades

1.   To take a pilot knowledge test, you must

     a.   Receive an endorsement (if required) from an authorized instructor certifying that you have accomplished the appropriate ground training or a home-study course required for the certificate or rating sought and that you are prepared for the test.
     b.   Present proper identification that contains your photograph, signature, date of birth (which shows you meet, or will meet, the age requirement for the certificate sought), and the actual residential address, if different from your mailing address.

2.   The FAA will specify the minimum passing grade for the knowledge test (usually 70%).

61.37 Knowledge Tests: Cheating or Other Unauthorized Conduct

1.   You may not

     a.   Copy or intentionally remove a pilot knowledge test from the testing site
     b.   Give to another or receive from another a copy of the test
     c.   Give help to another or receive help from another while taking the test
     d.   Take the test on behalf of another
     e.   Use any material as an aid during the test

          1)   You are permitted to take and use a flight computer, plotter, and calculator (you must erase all memory in the calculator before you start your test).

     f.   Intentionally cause, assist, or participate in any act contrary to this part

2. If caught in any of these acts, you will be ineligible to take a test or receive any certificates or ratings for a period of 1 year. These acts are also grounds to suspend or revoke any certificate or ratings you already possess.

61.39 Prerequisites for Practical Tests

1. To be eligible for a practical test, you must
   a. Have passed any required pilot knowledge tests within the preceding 24 months
   b. Have the required instruction and aeronautical experience as prescribed in Part 61
   c. Have at least a current third-class medical certificate
   d. Meet the minimum age requirements as given in Part 61
   e. Obtain a written statement, if required, from a CFI certifying that (s)he has given you flight instruction in preparation for the practical test within the preceding 2 calendar months and finds you competent to pass the test and that you have satisfactory knowledge of the areas shown to be deficient on your pilot knowledge test
   f. Have a completed and signed application form

61.41 Flight Training Received from Flight Instructors Not Certificated by the FAA

1. Flight instruction may be credited toward the requirements of a pilot certificate or rating issued under Part 61 if it is received from
   a. A U.S. military flight instructor or a foreign military flight instructor of an ICAO-member nation in a program for training military pilots
   b. An authorized flight instructor of a member nation of ICAO and the flight instruction is given outside the U.S.

61.43 Practical Tests: General Procedures

1. Your ability to perform the required tasks on the practical test is based on your ability to safely
   a. Perform the tasks specified in the areas of operation for the certificate or rating sought within the approved standards.
   b. Demonstrate mastery of the airplane with the successful outcome of each task performed never seriously in doubt.
   c. Demonstrate satisfactory proficiency and competency within the approved standards.
   d. Demonstrate sound judgment.
   e. Demonstrate single-pilot competence if the airplane is type certificated for single-pilot operations.

2. If you fail any of the required areas of operation, the entire practical test is failed.

3. Either you or the examiner may discontinue the practical test at any time when the failure of a task has caused the failure of the practical test.

4. If a practical test is discontinued, you are entitled to credit for those areas of operation that were passed, but only if you
   a. Pass the remainder of the practical test within 60 days after the date the practical test was discontinued.
   b. Present to the examiner for the retest the original notice of disapproval form or the letter of discontinuance form, as appropriate.
   c. Satisfactorily accomplish any additional training needed and obtain the appropriate instructor endorsements, if additional training is required.
   d. Present to the examiner for the retest a properly completed and signed application.

61.45 Practical Tests: Required Aircraft and Equipment

1. For your practical test, you must furnish an appropriate U.S.-registered airplane that has a current airworthiness certificate.

2. The airplane furnished for the practical test must have

    a. The equipment for each area of operation required by the practical test
    b. No operating limitations precluding the performance of a required area of operation
    c. Two pilot seats with adequate outside visibility for each pilot to operate the airplane safely
    d. All flight and power controls accessible and easily controlled by both pilots
    e. A satisfactory view-limiting device, e.g., a hood or a pair of goggles, for testing of flight by reference to instruments only

61.47 Status of an Examiner Who Is Authorized by the Administrator to Conduct Practical Tests

1. An examiner represents the FAA for the purpose of conducting practical tests for certificates and ratings issued under Part 61 and observing an applicant's ability to perform the areas of operation on the practical test.

2. The examiner is not the pilot in command unless (s)he acts in that capacity in order to perform the practical test; e.g., your practical test is for a second in command for an airplane that requires more than one pilot. This determination must be made prior to starting the checkride.

    a. For most practical tests (e.g., private, instrument, commercial, etc.), you are the pilot in command.

3. Neither you nor your examiner is considered a passenger of the other, and therefore neither is responsible for the passenger-carrying provisions of the Federal Aviation Regulations.

61.49 Retesting after Failure

1. If you fail a knowledge or practical test, you may reapply for the test after you have received

    a. The necessary training from an authorized instructor who determines that you are ready to pass the test
    b. An endorsement from that instructor

61.51 Pilot Logbooks

1. All the training and aeronautical experience used to meet the requirements for a certificate, rating, or flight review must be shown by a reliable record, e.g., a logbook.

    a. All flight time used to meet the recent flight requirements must also be logged (e.g., three takeoffs and landings within the preceding 90 days).
    b. All other time need only be logged at your discretion.

2. Each logbook entry shall include

    a. General information

        1) Date
        2) Total flight time or lesson time
        3) Location where the aircraft departed and arrived or, for lessons in a flight simulator or a flight training device, location where the lesson occurred
        4) Type and identification of aircraft, flight simulator, or flight training device, as appropriate
        5) Name of the safety pilot, if required by 14 CFR 91.109 (see page 261)

    b.   Type of pilot experience or training

        1) Pilot in command or solo

        2) Second in command

        3) Flight and ground training received from an authorized instructor

        4) Training received in a flight simulator or flight training device from an authorized instructor

    c.   Conditions of flight

        1) Day or night

        2) Actual instrument

        3) Simulated instrument conditions in flight, a flight simulator, or a flight training device

3.   **Solo** time means that a pilot is the sole occupant of the airplane. This time is logged as pilot-in-command time.

4.   **Pilot in Command (PIC)**

    a.   A student pilot may log PIC time only when the student pilot

        1) Is the sole occupant of the airplane (solo)

        2) Has a current solo flight endorsement

        3) Is undergoing training for a pilot certificate or rating

    b.   A sport, recreational, private, commercial, or ATP pilot may log as PIC time only the time during which that person

        1) Is the sole manipulator of the controls of an aircraft for which the pilot is rated

        2) Is the sole occupant of the airplane

        3) Except for a sport or recreational pilot, is acting as PIC of an airplane that requires more than one pilot under the airplane's type certificate or the Federal Aviation Regulations under which the flight is conducted

5.   **Second-in-command (SIC)** time is logged when you are acting as SIC on an aircraft requiring more than one pilot by the type certificate of the airplane or by the Federal Aviation Regulations and you hold the appropriate category, class, and rating for the aircraft being flown.

6.   **Instrument time** is logged when you operate the airplane solely by reference to instruments under actual or simulated conditions.

    a.   Each entry must include the place and type of each instrument approach completed and the name of the safety pilot for each simulated instrument flight.

    b.   An authorized flight instructor may log instrument time when conducting instrument flight instruction in actual instrument flight conditions.

7.   **Training time** is logged when you receive training from an authorized instructor in an airplane, flight simulator, or flight training device.

    a.   Your logbook must be endorsed in a legible manner by the authorized instructor and include a description of the training given, the length of the lesson, and the authorized instructor's signature, certificate number, and certificate expiration date.

8.   You must present your logbook upon reasonable request by the FAA, a member of the NTSB, or a local or state law enforcement officer.

9.   As a student pilot, you must carry your logbook with you on all solo cross-country flights.

61.53 Prohibition on Operations during Medical Deficiency

1.   You may not act as a pilot in command or required pilot flight crewmember while you have a known medical problem that would make you unable to meet the requirements of your current medical certificate (i.e., Class I, II, or III).

61.55 Second-in-Command Qualifications

1. To serve as SIC of an airplane requiring more than one pilot flight crewmember, you must

    a. Hold at least a private pilot certificate with the appropriate category and class ratings
    b. Hold an instrument rating if the flight is conducted under IFR

2. Before you serve as SIC, you must have within the past 12 calendar months

    a. Become familiar with all information and operations of the airplane
    b. Performed and logged the following procedures:

        1) Three takeoffs and landings to a full stop as sole manipulator of the controls
        2) Engine-out procedures while executing the duties of a PIC
        3) Crew resource management training

61.56 Flight Review

1. To act as pilot in command of an aircraft, you must have

    a. Satisfactorily accomplished a flight review or completed a proficiency check or a practical test for a new certificate/rating within the preceding 24 calendar months, or
    b. Satisfactorily completed at least the basic phase of the FAA Pilot Proficiency Program.

        1) This program is commonly known as the "WINGS" program.

            a) The program has three phases: Basic, Advanced, and Master.

                i) Knowledge credits and flight credits are given based on successful completion of phase requirements.

            b) Each pilot is given guidance to create a personalized, custom-tailored curriculum and flight proficiency syllabus suitable to his or her unique flight requirements.

            c) The focus of the program is education, review, and proficiency in the applicable Airman Certification Standards for each individual pilot.

                i) The Areas of Operation emphasized concern the primary causal factors for aviation accidents.

        2) For more information, visit the FAA Safety Team webpage at www.faasafety.gov.

            a) Click the "WINGS – Learn More!" link to learn more about the program and begin participating.

2. A student pilot is not required to accomplish a flight review provided (s)he is undergoing training for a certificate and has a current solo flight endorsement as required under 14 CFR 61.87.

3. A flight review consists of a minimum of 1 hr. of ground instruction and 1 hr. of flight instruction. The review must include

    a. The current general operating and flight rules of Part 91
    b. Those maneuvers and procedures necessary for the pilot to demonstrate the appropriate pilot privileges

61.57 Recent Flight Experience: Pilot in Command

1. You may not act as pilot in command of an airplane carrying passengers or of an airplane certificated for more than one required pilot flight crewmember, unless

    a. You have made three takeoffs and landings within the preceding 90 days in an aircraft of the same category and class of the aircraft to be flown (e.g., airplane single-engine land) and, if a type rating is required, in the same type.

        1) In a tailwheel airplane, the landings must have been made to a full stop.

    b.   To carry passengers at night, you have made three takeoffs and landings to a full stop at night within the preceding 90 days in an aircraft of the same category, class, and type (if required) to be used.

        1)   Here, night refers to the period beginning 1 hr. after sunset to 1 hr. before sunrise.

2.   Instrument rating recent flight experience

    a.   To act as PIC of an airplane under IFR, you must have logged the following flight experience (actual or simulated) within the previous 6 months:

        1)   At least six instrument approaches
        2)   Holding procedures
        3)   Intercepting and tracking courses through the use of navigation systems

    b.   Alternatively, you must pass an instrument proficiency check in an airplane, flight simulator, or flight training device.

    c.   If you do not meet the experience requirements during the prescribed time or 6 months thereafter, then you must pass an instrument proficiency check given by a CFII or an FAA inspector/examiner in an aircraft that is appropriate to the aircraft category.

61.58 Pilot-in-Command Proficiency Check: Operation of an Aircraft that Requires More than One Pilot Flight Crewmember or Is Turbojet-Powered

1.   This section contains the pilot-in-command proficiency check requirements and duration for aircraft certificated for more than one required crewmember.

61.59 Falsification, Reproduction, or Alteration of Applications, Certificates, Logbooks, Reports, or Records

1.   You cannot make or cause to be made

    a.   Any fraudulent or intentionally false statement on any application for a certificate or rating

    b.   Any fraudulent or intentionally false entry in your logbook or record to show compliance with any regulatory requirement

    c.   Any reproduction, for fraudulent purpose, of any certificate or rating

    d.   Any alteration of any certificate or rating

2.   Any commission of one of the above acts is grounds to suspend or revoke any existing certificate or rating and can be used to deny any application for a certificate or rating.

61.60 Change of Address

1.   If you make a change in your permanent address, you may not exercise the privileges of your pilot certificate after 30 days (from the day you move) unless you notify the FAA in writing to the FAA Airmen Certification Branch · PO Box 25082 · Oklahoma City, OK 73125.

2.   While you must notify the FAA if your address changes, you are not required to carry a certificate that shows your current address. The FAA will not issue a new certificate upon receipt of your new address.

    a.   If you would like a new certificate that shows your current address, you can request one online at www.faa.gov or you can send a signed request and a $2 fee (for each certificate, if you have more than one) to the address shown in item 1. above. Your request must include your name, date and place of birth, Social Security and/or certificate number, and the reason you are requesting a new certificate.

Subpart B -- Aircraft Ratings and Pilot Authorizations

61.61 Applicability

1. This subpart prescribes the requirements for the issuance of additional aircraft ratings after a pilot certificate is issued, and the requirements for, and limitations of, pilot authorizations issued by the FAA.

61.63 Additional Aircraft Ratings (Other than on an Airline Transport Pilot Certificate)

1. To be eligible for an aircraft rating after you have been issued a pilot certificate, you must meet the following requirements:

    a. For a category rating, you must meet the requirements of this part for the issue of the certificate appropriate to the privileges for which the category rating is sought. A knowledge test is not required if you already hold a category rating for powered aircraft. A logbook endorsement attesting to your knowledge and proficiency in the areas of operation required.

    b. For a class rating to be added to a pilot certificate, you must present a logbook certified by an authorized flight instructor attesting to the training you received and your competence in the areas of operation required. You must also pass a practical test applicable to the aircraft category and class rating sought. A knowledge test is not required if you already hold a category rating for powered aircraft at your pilot certificate level.

    c. For a type rating, you must hold or concurrently obtain an instrument rating and pass a practical test applicable to the certificate you hold and the type rating you seek. You must also pass a practical test under instrument operations in the aircraft for which the type rating is sought. Aircraft variations and related test requirements are also discussed here.

61.64 Use of a Flight Simulator and Flight Training Device

1. This section explains and regulates the use of flight simulators and flight training devices in flight training and practical tests for the airplane, helicopter, and powered-lift ratings.

    a. Definitions of these two systems can be found in 14 CFR Part 1.

        1) The flight-simulator-specific sections of this regulation define the minimum simulator and pilot applicant requirements to allow for the use of the equipment.

            a) Appropriately qualified equipment and pilots who meet minimum experience requirements are both required before a flight simulator can be used for training or practical test credit.

                i) The flight-training-device-specific section of this regulation only covers minimum equipment qualifications for use.

61.65 Instrument Rating Requirements

1. To be eligible for an instrument rating (airplane), you must

    a. Hold at least a private pilot certificate.

    b. Be able to read, speak, write, and understand the English language.

    c. Pass a knowledge test (covered by Gleim *Instrument Pilot FAA Knowledge Test Prep*).

    d. Pass a practical test (covered by Gleim *Instrument Pilot Flight Maneuvers and Practical Test Prep*).

2. You must have received and logged ground training from an authorized instructor or completed a home-study on the following aeronautical knowledge areas:

   a. Federal Aviation Regulations that apply to flight operations under IFR
   b. Appropriate information that applies to flight operations under IFR in the *Aeronautical Information Manual (AIM)* (the *AIM* is contained in Gleim *FAR/AIM*)
   c. ATC system and procedures for instrument flight operations
   d. IFR navigation and approaches by use of navigation systems
   e. Use of IFR en route and instrument approach procedure charts
   f. Procurement and use of aviation weather reports and forecasts and the elements of forecasting weather trends based on that information and personal observation of weather conditions
   g. Safe and efficient operation of the airplane under instrument flight rules and conditions
   h. Recognition of critical weather situations and wind shear avoidance
   i. Aeronautical decision making and judgment
   j. Crew resource management, including crew communication and coordination

3. You must receive and log training from an authorized instructor (CFII) in an airplane, full flight simulator, or flight training device that includes the following areas of operation:

   a. Preflight preparation
   b. Preflight procedures
   c. ATC clearances and procedures
   d. Flight by reference to instruments
   e. Navigation systems
   f. Instrument approach procedures
   g. Emergency operations
   h. Postflight procedures

4. Aeronautical experience. You must have logged

   a. At least 50 hr. of cross-country time as PIC, of which 10 hr. must be in airplanes

      1) Each flight must have a landing at least 50 NM (straight-line distance) from the original departure point.

   b. A total of 40 hr. of actual or simulated instrument time, to include

      1) At least 15 hr. of instrument flight training from a CFII in an airplane
      2) At least 3 hr. of instrument training from a CFII in preparation for the practical test within 60 days of the test
      3) At least one cross-country flight in an airplane that is performed under IFR with an authorized instructor and consists of

         a) A distance of at least 250 NM along airways or ATC-directed routing
         b) An instrument approach at each airport
         c) Three different kinds of approaches with the use of navigation systems

5. If the instrument training was provided by an authorized instructor in a full flight simulator or flight training device,

   a. A maximum of 20 hr. may be logged if the training was conducted under Part 61.
   b. A maximum of 30 hr. may be logged if the training was conducted under Part 142.

61.67 Category II Pilot Authorization Requirements

1. This section contains the certification, experience, and practical test requirements for a Category II pilot authorization.

61.68 Category III Pilot Authorization Requirements

1. This section contains the certification, experience, and practical test requirements for a Category III pilot authorization.

61.69 Glider and Unpowered Ultralight Vehicle Towing: Experience and Training Requirements

1. This section contains the certificate, logbook endorsement, and experience requirements for acting as a pilot in command of an aircraft towing gliders.

61.71 Graduates of an Approved Training Program Other than under This Part: Special Rules

1. This section prescribes procedures and policies for Part 141 flight school or Part 142 training center graduates to apply for certificates and ratings as a result of the instruction they received.

61.73 Military Pilots or Former Military Pilots: Special Rules

1. This section contains the requirements for military and former military pilots to apply for a private or commercial certificate or an instrument rating.

61.75 Private Pilot Certificate Issued on the Basis of a Foreign Pilot License

1. This section contains the policies, procedures, and requirements concerning the issuance of a U.S. private pilot certificate based on a foreign pilot certificate. It also contains the requirement for an instrument rating to be issued and the medical standards and limitations and operating privileges and limitations for pilots holding a U.S. certificate based on a foreign pilot certificate.

61.77 Special Purpose Pilot Authorization: Operation of a Civil Aircraft of the U.S. and Leased by a non-U.S. Citizen

1. This section contains the policies, procedures, and requirements concerning the issuance of a special purpose pilot authorization to foreign pilots licensed under the Convention on International Civil Aviation.

Subpart C -- Student Pilots

61.81 Applicability

1. This subpart prescribes the requirements for the issuance of student pilot certificates, the conditions under which those certificates are necessary, and the general rules and limitations for holders of those certificates.

61.83 Eligibility Requirements for Student Pilots

1. To be eligible for a student pilot's certificate, you must

    a. Be at least 16 years old.
    b. Be able to read, write, and converse fluently in English, or you will have limitations placed on the certificate as necessary for safety.

61.85 Application

1. An application for a student pilot certificate is made on a form and in a manner approved by the Administrator.

2. The application must be submitted to a Flight Standards District Office, a designated pilot examiner, an airman certification representative associated with a pilot school, a flight instructor, or another person authorized by the Administrator.

61.87 Solo Requirements for Student Pilots

1. You must pass a knowledge test administered by your CFI on 14 CFR Parts 61 and 91, airspace rules and procedures for the airport where the solo flight will be done, and the operational characteristics of the make and model of airplane you will fly solo.

    a. Your CFI will endorse your logbook certifying that you have successfully completed a presolo knowledge test.

2. In a single-engine airplane, you must receive and log flight instruction in the following 15 flight maneuvers:

1. Proper flight preparation procedures, including preflight planning and preparation, powerplant operation, and aircraft systems 2. Taxiing or surface operations, including runups 3. Takeoffs and landings, including normal and cross-wind 4. Straight-and-level flight and turns in both directions 5. Climbs and climbing turns 6. Airport traffic patterns, including entry and departure procedures 7. Collision avoidance, wind shear avoidance, and wake turbulence avoidance 8. Descents, with and without turns, using high and low drag configurations	9. Flight at various airspeeds from cruise to slow flight 10. Stall entries from various flight attitudes and power combinations with recovery initiated at the first indication of a stall, and recovery from a full stall 11. Emergency procedures and equipment malfunctions 12. Ground reference maneuvers 13. Approaches to the landing area with simulated engine malfunctions 14. Slips to a landing 15. Go-arounds

3. Before you can fly solo, your student logbook must be endorsed by your CFI for the specific make and model of airplane you are flying.

4. The logbook endorsement is valid for 90 days after which another endorsement is required. The logbook endorsement by your CFI certifies

    a. Flight instruction in the make and model of airplane to be used for solo flight
    b. Proficiency in the 15 maneuvers listed above
    c. Competency for safe solo flight in that make and model of airplane

61.89 General Limitations

1. As a student pilot, you may **not** act as a pilot in command of an aircraft under the following conditions:

    a. On a flight carrying passengers
    b. On a flight carrying property for compensation or hire
    c. In return for compensation or hire
    d. In furtherance of a business
    e. On an international flight
    f. With visibility below 3 SM during daylight hours or below 5 SM at night
    g. Above an overcast, i.e., without visual reference to the surface
    h. In violation of any CFI-imposed limitations in your logbook

2. You may not act as a crewmember on an aircraft requiring more than one pilot unless you are receiving dual instruction on board the aircraft and no passengers are carried.

61.93 Solo Cross-Country Flight Requirements

1.   You may not operate an aircraft in solo cross-country unless properly authorized by an instructor.

   a.   The term "cross-country flight," as used in this section, means a flight beyond a radius of 25 NM from the point of departure.

2.   You may not make a solo landing (except in an emergency) other than at the airport from which you are authorized to depart.

   a.   Your CFI may, however, authorize you to practice solo takeoffs and landings at an airport within 25 NM of the base airport provided

      1)   Your CFI has given you flight training at the other airport, and the training includes flight in both directions over the route, entering and exiting the traffic pattern, and takeoffs and landings at the other airport.

      2)   Your CFI determines that you are proficient to make the flight and endorses your logbook authorizing the flight.

      3)   The purpose of the flight is to practice takeoffs and landings at the other airport.

3.   In a single-engine airplane, you must receive and log flight training from your CFI in the following areas before being authorized to conduct solo cross-country flights:

   a.   Use of aeronautical charts for VFR navigation using pilotage and dead reckoning with the aid of a magnetic compass

   b.   Use of the airplane's performance charts pertaining to cross-country flight

   c.   Procurement and analysis of aviation weather reports and forecasts, including

      1)   Recognition of critical weather situations
      2)   Estimating visibility while in flight

   d.   Emergency procedures

   e.   Traffic pattern procedures that include

      1)   Area arrival
      2)   Area departure
      3)   Entry into the traffic pattern
      4)   Approach

   f.   Procedures and operating practices for collision avoidance, wake turbulence precautions, and wind shear avoidance

   g.   Recognition, avoidance, and operational restrictions of hazardous terrain features in the geographical area where the cross-country flight will be flown

   h.   Procedures for operating the instruments and equipment installed in the airplane to be flown, including recognition and use of the proper operational procedures and indications

   i.   Use of radios for VFR navigation and two-way communications

   j.   Takeoff, approach, and landing procedures, including short-field, soft-field, and crosswind takeoffs, approaches, and landings

   k.   Climbs at best angle (V_X) and best rate (V_Y)

   l.   Control and maneuvering solely by reference to flight instruments, including straight and level flight, turns, descents, climbs, use of radio aids, and ATC directives

4. Your student logbook must be endorsed by your CFI attesting that you have received the instruction on the previous page and have demonstrated an acceptable level of proficiency.

    a. Student pilots seeking a sport pilot certificate before their first solo cross-country flight must receive training for control and maneuvering solely by reference to flight instruments, including straight-and-level flight, turns, descents, climbs, and the use of radio aids and ATC directives. This only applies when receiving training for cross-country flight in an airplane that has a V_H greater than 87 knots CA.

5. A CFI must also endorse your logbook for each solo cross-country flight after

    a. Reviewing your preflight planning and preparation
    b. Certifying that you are prepared to make a safe flight under the known circumstances and any CFI-imposed limitations listed in the endorsement

6. An endorsement can be made for repeated solo cross-country flight to an airport less than 50 NM after dual cross-country flight in both directions with landings and takeoffs at the airports to be used, with any given conditions set by your CFI.

61.94 Student Pilot Seeking a Sport Pilot Certificate or a Recreational Pilot Certificate: Operations at Airports Within, and in Airspace Located Within, Class B, C, and D Airspace, or at Airports with an Operational Control Tower in Other Airspace

1. A student pilot seeking a sport pilot certificate or a recreational pilot certificate who wishes to fly in Class B, C, and D airspace, or at any airport with an operational control tower, must receive and log ground and flight training from an authorized instructor in specific areas of knowledge and operation, such as

    a. Radio communications, navigation systems and facilities, and radar services.
    b. Controlled airport operations, including three takeoffs and full-stop landings and flight in the traffic pattern.
    c. Applicable flight rules of 14 CFR Part 91 for operations in Class B, C, and D airspace and air traffic control clearances.
    d. Ground and flight training for the specific Class B, C, or D airspace and/or airport for which the solo flight is authorized, if applicable, within the 90-day period preceding the date of the flight in that airspace. The flight training must be received in the specific airspace area and/or airport for which solo flight is authorized.

2. The authorized instructor who provides the training must provide a logbook endorsement that certifies the student has received that training and is proficient to conduct solo flight in that specific airspace and/or and in the required areas of knowledge and operation.

61.95 Operations in Class B Airspace and at Airports Located within Class B Airspace

1. In order for you to solo in Class B airspace or at a specific airport within Class B airspace, you must have

    a. Received both ground and flight training on that Class B airspace area. The flight training must have been given in the specific Class B airspace area or at the specific airport in the Class B airspace area where you will be operating.
    b. Obtained a current 90-day logbook endorsement from the CFI who gave the training which says that you have received the required training and have been found competent to operate in the specific Class B airspace area or at the specific airport within the Class B airspace area.

    NOTE: Solo student operations are not allowed at the primary airports of certain Class B airspace areas.

Subpart D -- Recreational Pilots

61.96 Applicability and Eligibility Requirements: General

1. This subpart prescribes the requirements for the issuance of recreational pilot certificates and ratings, the conditions under which those certificates and ratings are necessary, and the general operating rules for recreational pilots.

2. To be eligible to be a recreational pilot, you must

    a. Be at least 17 years of age.
    b. Be able to read, speak, write, and understand the English language, or limitations will be placed on the certificate as necessary for safety.
    c. Hold at least a valid third-class medical certificate unless operating under the privileges of 14 CFR 61.23(c)(3).
    d. Pass a knowledge test (covered by Gleim *Private Pilot and Recreational Pilot FAA Knowledge Test Prep*).
    e. Pass a practical test.

61.97 Aeronautical Knowledge

1. You must receive and log ground training from an authorized instructor or complete a home-study course on the following aeronautical knowledge areas:

    a. Applicable Federal Aviation Regulations that relate to recreational pilot privileges, limitations, and flight operations
    b. Accident reporting requirements of the NTSB
    c. Use of the applicable portions of the *AIM* and FAA advisory circulars
    d. Use of aeronautical charts for the VFR navigation using pilotage with the aid of a magnetic compass
    e. Recognition of critical weather situations from the ground and in flight, wind shear avoidance, and the procurement and use of aviation weather reports and forecasts
    f. Safe and efficient operation of airplanes, including collision avoidance, and recognition and avoidance of wake turbulence
    g. Effects of density altitude on takeoff and climb performance
    h. Weight and balance computations
    i. Principles of aerodynamics, powerplants, and airplane systems
    j. Stall awareness, spin entry, spins, and spin recovery techniques
    k. Aeronautical decision making and judgment
    l. Preflight action that includes

        1) How to obtain information on runway lengths at airports of intended use, data on takeoff and landing distances, weather reports and forecasts, and fuel requirements
        2) How to plan for alternatives if the planned flight cannot be completed or delays are encountered

61.98 Flight Proficiency

1. You must receive and log ground and flight training from an authorized instructor on the following areas of operation:

    a. Preflight preparation
    b. Preflight procedures
    c. Airport operations
    d. Takeoffs, landings, and go-arounds
    e. Performance maneuvers
    f. Ground reference maneuvers
    g. Navigation
    h. Slow flight and stalls
    i. Emergency operations
    j. Postflight procedures

61.99 Aeronautical Experience

1. You must receive and log at least 30 hr. of flight training time that includes at least

    a. 15 hr. of flight training from an authorized instructor that consists of at least

        1) 2 hr. of flight training en route to an airport that is located more than 25 NM from where you normally train, which includes at least three takeoffs and three landings at the airport located more than 25 NM away

        2) 3 hr. of flight training in preparation for the practical test, within the preceding 2 calendar months from the month of the test

    b. 3 hr. of solo flight in an airplane

61.100 Pilots Based on Small Islands

1. If you are located on an island from which the required flight of 25 NM cannot be accomplished without flying over water more than 10 NM from the nearest shoreline, you are not required to make it.

    a. If airports are available without flying over water more than 10 NM from the nearest shoreline, you must complete a flight with your instructor between those two airports, which must include three landings at the other airport.

    b. A certificate issued under these conditions will contain the following endorsement:

        Passenger carrying prohibited in flights more than 10 NM from (name of island).

2. This limitation will be removed if you present satisfactory evidence of compliance with the requirement of a flight over 25 NM to an FAA inspector or designated pilot examiner.

61.101 Recreational Pilot Privileges and Limitations

1. As a recreational pilot, you may

    a. Carry only one passenger

    b. Not pay less than the equal share of the operating expenses of a flight with a passenger, provided the expenses involve only fuel, oil, airport expenses, or airplane rental fees

2. You may act as PIC on a flight that is within 50 NM from the departure airport, provided that you have

    a. Received ground and flight training for takeoff, departure, arrival, and landing procedures at the departure airport

    b. Received ground and flight training for the area, terrain, and aids to navigation that are in the vicinity of the departure airport

    c. Been found proficient to operate an airplane at that departure airport and in the area within 50 NM from that airport

    d. Received a logbook endorsement from an authorized instructor that permits flight within 50 NM from the departure airport

        1) You are required to carry your logbook with you on the flight.

3. You may act as PIC of an airplane that exceeds 50 NM from the departure airport, provided that you have

    a. Received ground and flight training from an authorized instructor on the cross-country training requirements for a private pilot

    b. Been found proficient in cross-country flying

    c. Received a logbook endorsement from an authorized instructor that you have received and been found proficient in the cross-country training requirements for a private pilot

        1) You are required to carry your logbook with you on the flight.

4. As a recreational pilot, you may NOT act as pilot in command of an aircraft when

   a. It is certificated for more than four occupants, with more than one powerplant, with a powerplant of more than 180 HP, or with retractable landing gear.
   b. It is classified as a multi-engine airplane, powered-lift, glider, airship, or balloon.
   c. It is carrying a passenger or property for compensation or hire.
   d. The flight is for compensation or hire.
   e. The flight is in furtherance of a business.
   f. The flight is between sunset and sunrise.
   g. The flight is in airspace in which communications with air traffic control (ATC) are required.
   h. The flight is at an altitude of more than 10,000 ft. MSL or 2,000 ft. AGL, whichever is higher.
   i. The flight or surface visibility is less than 3 SM.
   j. You are without visual reference to the surface.
   k. You are on a flight outside the United States, unless authorized by the country in which the flight is conducted.
   l. You are demonstrating that aircraft in flight to a prospective buyer.
   m. The aircraft is used in a passenger-carrying airlift and sponsored by a charitable organization.
   n. It is towing any object.

5. As a recreational pilot, you may not act as a required pilot flight crewmember on any aircraft for which more than one pilot is required by the type certificate of the aircraft or the regulations under which flight is conducted.

6. As a recreational pilot, if you have logged fewer than 400 flight hr. and have not logged pilot-in-command time within the preceding 180 days, you may not act as pilot in command of an aircraft until you have received flight training from an authorized flight instructor who certifies in your logbook that you are competent to act as pilot in command of the aircraft.

7. The recreational pilot certificate states, "Holder does not meet ICAO requirements."

8. For the purpose of obtaining additional certificates or ratings while under the supervision of an authorized flight instructor, as a recreational pilot, you may fly as sole occupant of an aircraft

   a. For which you do not hold an appropriate category or class rating
   b. Within airspace that requires communication with ATC
   c. Between sunset and sunrise, provided flight or surface visibility is at least 5 SM

   NOTE: For any of these situations, you must carry your logbook that has been properly endorsed for each flight by an authorized flight instructor.

Subpart E -- Private Pilots

61.102 Applicability

1. This subpart prescribes the requirements for the issuance of private pilot certificates and ratings, the conditions under which those certificates are necessary, and the general rules for holders of those certificates.

61.103 Eligibility Requirements: General

1. To be eligible to be a private pilot, you must

   a. Be at least 17 years of age.

   b. Be able to read, write, and converse fluently in English, or you will have limitations placed on the certificate as necessary for safety.

   c. Pass a knowledge test (covered by Gleim *Private Pilot and Recreational Pilot FAA Knowledge Test Prep*).

   d. Pass a practical test (covered by Gleim *Private Pilot Flight Maneuvers and Practical Test Prep*).

61.105 Aeronautical Knowledge

1. You must receive and log ground training from an authorized instructor or complete a home-study course on the following aeronautical knowledge areas:

   a. Applicable Federal Aviation Regulations that relate to private pilot privileges, limitations, and flight operations

   b. Accident reporting requirements of the NTSB

   c. Use of the applicable portions of the *AIM* and FAA advisory circulars

   d. Use of aeronautical charts for VFR navigation, using pilotage, dead reckoning, and navigation systems

   e. Radio communication procedures

   f. Recognition of critical weather situations from the ground and in flight, wind shear avoidance, and the procurement and use of aviation weather reports and forecasts

   g. Safe and efficient operation of airplanes, including collision avoidance, and recognition and avoidance of wake turbulence

   h. Effects of density altitude on takeoff and climb performance

   i. Weight and balance computations

   j. Principles of aerodynamics, powerplants, and airplane systems

   k. Stall awareness, spin entry, spins, and spin recovery techniques

   l. Aeronautical decision making and judgment

   m. Preflight action that includes

      1) How to obtain information on runway lengths at airports of intended use, takeoff and landing distances, weather reports and forecasts, and fuel requirements

      2) How to plan for alternatives if the planned flight cannot be completed or delays are encountered

61.107 Flight Proficiency

1. For a single-engine airplane, you must receive and log ground and flight training from an authorized instructor on the following areas of operation:

    a. Preflight preparation
    b. Preflight procedures
    c. Airport operations
    d. Takeoffs, landings, and go-arounds
    e. Performance maneuvers
    f. Ground reference maneuvers
    g. Navigation
    h. Slow flight and stalls
    i. Basic instrument maneuvers
    j. Emergency operations
    k. Night operations
    l. Postflight procedures

61.109 Aeronautical Experience

1. For a single-engine airplane, you must log at least 40 hr. of flight time that includes

    a. 20 hr. of flight training from an authorized flight instructor, including at least

        1) 3 hr. of cross-country, i.e., to other airports
        2) 3 hr. at night, including

            a) One cross-country flight of over 100 NM total distance
            b) 10 takeoffs and 10 landings to a full stop at an airport

        3) 3 hr. of instrument flight training in an airplane
        4) 3 hr. in airplanes in preparation for the private pilot practical test within the preceding 2 calendar months from the month of the test

        NOTE: A maximum of 2.5 hr. of instruction may be accomplished in an FAA-approved flight simulator or flight training device representing an airplane.

    b. 10 hr. of solo flight time in an airplane, including at least

        1) 5 hr. of cross-country flights
        2) One solo cross-country flight of at least 150 NM total distance, with full-stop landings at a minimum of three points and with one segment of the flight consisting of a straight-line distance of at least 50 NM between the takeoff and landing locations
        3) Three solo takeoffs and landings to a full stop at an airport with an operating control tower

61.110 Night Flying Exceptions

1. A person who resides and receives flight training in Alaska but does not meet the night flight training requirements

    a. May be issued a pilot certificate with a limitation stating, "Night flying prohibited."
    b. Must comply with the night flight training requirements within 12 calendar months after the pilot certificate was issued

        1) At the end of the 12-month period, the certificate will become invalid for use until the person complies with the night training requirement.

2. The limitation will be removed from the certificate when the person presents to an examiner a logbook endorsement from an authorized instructor that verifies accomplishment of the night flight training requirements.

61.111 Cross-Country Flights: Pilots Based on Small Islands

1. If you are located on an island from which the required cross-country flights cannot be made without flying over water more than 10 NM from the nearest shoreline, you need not comply with the cross-country flight experience requirements.

   a. If airports are available without flying over water more than 10 NM from the nearest shoreline, you must complete two round-trip solo flights between the two airports that are farthest apart.

      1) You must make a landing at each airport on both flights.

   b. A certificate issued under these conditions will contain the following endorsement:

      Passenger carrying prohibited on flights more than 10 NM from (name of island).

2. Upon meeting the cross-country training requirements, the limitation will be removed from your pilot certificate.

61.113 Private Pilot Privileges and Limitations: Pilot in Command

1. As a private pilot, you may not act as pilot in command of an aircraft that is carrying passengers or property for compensation or hire, nor may you be paid to act as pilot in command, **except**

   a. You may act as pilot in command, for compensation or hire, of an aircraft in connection with any business or employment if the flight is only incidental to that business or employment and the aircraft does not carry passengers or property for compensation or hire.

2. You may equally share the operating expenses of a flight with passengers, provided the expenses involve only fuel, oil, airport expenditures, or airplane rental fees.

3. If you are an aircraft salesperson and have at least 200 hr. of logged flight time, you may demonstrate an airplane in flight to a prospective buyer.

4. You may act as pilot in command of a charitable, nonprofit, or community event flight described in 14 CFR 91.146, if the sponsor and pilot comply with the requirements of 14 CFR 91.146.

5. You may be reimbursed for aircraft operating expenses that are directly related to search and location operations, provided the expenses involve only fuel, oil, airport expenditures, or rental fees, and the operation is sanctioned and under the direction and control of a local, state, or federal agency; or an organization that conducts search and location operations.

6. If you meet the requirements of 14 CFR 61.69, you may act as a pilot in command of an aircraft towing a glider or unpowered ultralight vehicle.

7. On May 1, 2017, third-class medical reform, known as BasicMed, became effective.

   a. A private pilot may act as pilot in command of an aircraft without holding a medical certificate issued under Part 67 provided the pilot holds a valid U.S. driver's license, meets the requirements of 14 CFR 61.23(c)(3), and complies with this section and all of the following conditions and limitations:

      1) The aircraft is authorized to carry no more than six occupants, has a maximum takeoff weight of no more than 6,000 lb., and is operated with no more than five passengers on board.

      2) The flight, including each portion of the flight, is not carried out

         a) At an altitude that is more than 18,000 ft. above mean sea level,

         b) Outside the United States unless authorized by the country in which the flight is conducted, or

         c) At an indicated airspeed exceeding 250 kt.

   3)   The pilot has available in his or her logbook

   a)   The completed medical examination checklist required under 14 CFR 68.7
        and

   b)   The certificate of course completion required under 14 CFR 61.23(c)(3).

61.117 Private Pilot Privileges and Limitations: Second in Command of Aircraft Requiring More than One Pilot

1.   You may not be paid to act as second in command (SIC) of an aircraft type certificated for more than one required pilot, except as provided under 14 CFR 61.113.

2.   You may not act as SIC if the aircraft is operated for compensation or hire.

Subpart F -- Commercial Pilots

61.121 Applicability

1.   This subpart prescribes the requirements for the issuance of commercial pilot certificates and ratings, the conditions under which those certificates and ratings are necessary, and the limitations upon those certificates and ratings.

61.123 Eligibility Requirements: General

1.   To be eligible for a commercial pilot certificate, you must

   a.   Be at least 18 years of age.

   b.   Be able to read, speak, write, and understand the English language, or limitations will be placed on your certificate as necessary for safety.

   c.   Pass a knowledge test (covered by Gleim *Commercial Pilot FAA Knowledge Test Prep*).

   d.   Pass a practical test (covered by Gleim *Commercial Pilot Flight Maneuvers and Practical Test Prep*).

61.125 Aeronautical Knowledge

1.   You must receive and log ground training from an authorized instructor or complete a home-study course on the following aeronautical knowledge areas:

   a.   Applicable Federal Aviation Regulations that relate to commercial pilot privileges, limitations, and flight operations

   b.   Accident reporting requirements of the NTSB

   c.   Basic aerodynamics and the principles of flight

   d.   Meteorology to include recognition of critical weather situations, wind shear recognition and avoidance, and the use of aviation weather reports and forecasts

   e.   Safe and efficient operation of airplanes

   f.   Weight and balance computations

   g.   Use of performance charts

   h.   Significance and effects of exceeding airplane performance limitations

   i.   Use of aeronautical charts and a magnetic compass for pilotage and dead reckoning

   j.   Use of air navigation facilities

   k.   Aeronautical decision making and judgment

   l.   Principles and functions of airplane systems

   m.   Maneuvers, procedures, and emergency operations appropriate to the airplane

   n.   Night and high-altitude operations

   o.   Procedures for operating within the National Airspace System

61.127 Flight Proficiency

1. For a single-engine airplane, you must receive and log ground and flight training from an authorized instructor on the following areas of operation:

   a. Preflight preparation
   b. Preflight procedures
   c. Airport operations
   d. Takeoffs, landings, and go-arounds
   e. Performance maneuvers
   f. Ground reference maneuvers
   g. Navigation
   h. Slow flight and stalls
   i. Emergency operations
   j. High-altitude operations
   k. Postflight procedures

61.129 Aeronautical Experience

1. For a single-engine airplane, you must log at least 250 hr. of flight time as a pilot that consists of at least

   a. 100 hr. in powered aircraft, of which 50 hr. must be in airplanes
   b. 100 hr. as pilot in command flight time, which includes at least

      1) 50 hr. in airplanes
      2) 50 hr. in cross-country flight of which at least 10 hr. must be in airplanes

   c. 20 hr. of training in the areas of operation listed in 14 CFR 61.127 that includes at least

      1) 10 hr. of instrument training, of which at least 5 hr. must be in a single-engine airplane
      2) 10 hr. of training in an airplane that has a retractable landing gear, flaps, and controllable pitch propeller, or is turbine-powered
      3) One cross-country flight of at least 2 hr. in a single-engine airplane in day-VFR conditions, consisting of a total straight-line distance of more than 100 NM from the original point of departure
      4) One cross-country flight of at least 2 hr. in a single-engine airplane in night-VFR conditions, consisting of a straight-line distance of more than 100 NM from the original point of departure
      5) 3 hr. in a single-engine airplane in preparation for the practical test within the 60 days preceding the test

   d. 10 hr. of solo flight in a single-engine airplane training in the areas of operation listed in 14 CFR 61.127, which includes at least

      1) One cross-country flight of not less than 300 NM total distance, with landings at a minimum of three points, one of which is a straight-line distance of at least 250 NM from the original departure point

         a) In Hawaii, the longest segment need have only a straight-line distance of at least 150 NM.

      2) 5 hr. in night-VFR conditions with 10 takeoffs and 10 landings (with each landing involving a flight in the traffic pattern) at an airport with an operating control tower

      NOTE: The 250 hr. of flight time as a pilot may include 50 hr. in an approved flight simulator or training device that is representative of a single-engine airplane.

61.131 Exceptions to the Night Flying Requirements

1. A person who receives flight training in, and resides in, Alaska but does not meet the night flight training requirements

   a. May be issued a pilot certificate with a limitation stating, "Night flying prohibited."

   b. Must comply with the night flight training requirements within 12 calendar months after the pilot certificate was issued

      1) At the end of the 12-month period, the certificate will become invalid for use until the person complies with the night training requirement.

2. The limitation will be removed from the certificate when the person presents to an examiner a logbook endorsement from an authorized instructor that verifies accomplishment of the night flight training requirements.

61.133 Commercial Pilot Privileges and Limitations

1. You may act as PIC of an airplane

   a. Carrying persons or property for compensation or hire, provided you are qualified under the Federal Aviation Regulations that govern that operation (i.e., Part 91, 121, or 135)

   b. For compensation or hire, provided you are qualified under the Federal Aviation Regulations that govern that operation (i.e., Part 91, 121, or 135)

2. If you do not have an instrument rating (airplane), your commercial pilot certificate will be issued with a limitation prohibiting the carriage of passengers for hire in airplanes

   a. On cross-country flights of more than 50 NM
   b. At night

Subpart I -- Ground Instructors

61.211 Applicability

1. This subpart prescribes the requirements for the issuance of ground instructor certificates and ratings, the conditions under which those certificates and ratings are necessary, and the limitations upon those certificates and ratings.

61.213 Eligibility Requirements

1. To be eligible for a ground instructor certificate or rating, you must

   a. Be at least 18 years of age.

   b. Be able to read, speak, write, and understand the English language, or limitations will be placed on your certificate as necessary for safety.

   c. Pass a knowledge test on fundamentals of instructing (covered by Gleim *Fundamentals of Instructing FAA Knowledge Test Prep*), unless you

      1) Hold an FAA ground or flight instructor certificate,
      2) Hold a current teacher's certificate authorizing you to teach at an educational level of the 7th grade or higher, or
      3) Are employed as a teacher at an accredited college or university.

   d. Pass a knowledge test for the basic, advanced, or instrument ground instructor rating.

61.215 Ground Instructor Privileges

1. A basic ground instructor (BGI) is authorized to provide

   a. Ground training in the aeronautical knowledge areas required for a sport, recreational, or private pilot certificate

   b. Ground training required for a sport, recreational, or private pilot flight review

   c. A recommendation for the sport, recreational, or private pilot knowledge test

2. An advanced ground instructor (AGI) is authorized to provide

   a. Ground training in the aeronautical knowledge areas required for any certificate or rating except for the areas required for an instrument rating

   b. Ground training required for any flight review except for the training required for an instrument rating

   c. A recommendation for a knowledge test required for any certificate or rating except for an instrument rating

3. An instrument ground instructor (IGI) is authorized to provide

   a. Ground training in the aeronautical knowledge areas required for an instrument rating

   b. Ground training required for an instrument proficiency check

   c. A recommendation for the instrument rating knowledge test

61.217 Recent Experience Requirements

1. You may not perform the duties of a ground instructor unless, within the preceding 12 months,

   a. You have served for at least 3 months as a ground instructor.

   b. You have received an endorsement from an authorized ground or flight instructor certifying that you have demonstrated proficiency in the subject areas appropriate to your ground instructor certificate.

Subpart J -- Sport Pilots

61.301 What is the purpose of this subpart, and to whom does it apply?

1. The sport pilot regulations describe all of the requirements, privileges, and limitations of the sport pilot certificate.

61.303 If I want to operate a light-sport aircraft, what operating limits and endorsement requirements in this subpart must I comply with?

1. Whether you hold a medical certificate, a U.S. driver's license or neither, and what certificate you hold (sport or recreational), will determine the category, class and type of aircraft you are allowed to operate, with associated limitations.

61.305 What are the age and language requirements for a sport pilot certificate?

1. You must be at least 17 years old and be able to read, write, and understand the English language to be eligible to apply for a sport pilot certificate.

61.307 What tests do I have to take to obtain a sport pilot certificate?

1. You must pass knowledge and flight tests in established areas of knowledge and operation, and receive appropriate logbook endorsements from an authorized instructor.

61.309 What aeronautical knowledge must I have to apply for a sport pilot certificate?

1. With the exception of some ultralight pilots, you must receive and log ground training from an authorized instructor or complete a home-study course on specified aeronautical knowledge areas.

61.311 What flight proficiency requirements must I meet to apply for a sport pilot certificate?

1. With the exception of some ultralight pilots (as specified in 14 CFR 61.329), to apply for a sport pilot certificate, you must receive and log ground and flight training from an authorized instructor on the specified areas of operation relevant to your category and class of aircraft.

61.313 What aeronautical experience must I have to apply for a sport pilot certificate?

1. With the exception of some ultralight pilots (as specified in 14 CFR 61.329), the category and class of aircraft for which you are applying for a sport pilot certificate will determine the aeronautical experience requirements you must meet.

61.315 What are the privileges and limits of my sport pilot certificate?

1. If you hold a sport pilot certificate, you may act as pilot in command of a light-sport aircraft with limitations on the operating conditions you are allowed, such as airspace, altitude, airspeed limitations, etc.

61.317 Is my sport pilot certificate issued with aircraft category and class ratings?

1. Your sport pilot certificate will not include any associated category and class ratings. The FAA will provide you with a logbook endorsement for the category, class, and make and model of aircraft in which you are authorized to act as pilot in command.

61.321 How do I obtain privileges to operate an additional category or class of light-sport aircraft?

1. If you hold a sport pilot certificate and seek to operate an additional category or class of light-sport aircraft, you are required to

   a. Receive an appropriate endorsement from the authorized instructor who conducted your previous sport pilot training,

   b. Complete a proficiency check with a different (authorized) instructor and receive an appropriate endorsement from this instructor,

   c. Complete an application form acceptable to the FAA and present this to the authorized instructor who did your proficiency check, and

   d. Receive a logbook endorsement from the instructor who conducted the proficiency check certifying you are proficient in the applicable areas of operation and that you are authorized for the additional category and class light-sport aircraft privilege.

61.325 How do I obtain privileges to operate a light-sport aircraft at an airport within, or in airspace within, Class B, C, and D airspace, or in other airspace with an airport having an operational control tower?

1. A sport pilot who wishes to operate in Class B, C, or D airspace, or at an airport with an operational control tower, must receive and log ground and flight training in specified knowledge areas from an authorized instructor and receive an appropriate endorsement from that same instructor in the following knowledge areas and areas of operation:

   a. The use of radios, communications, navigational systems/facilities, and radar services;

   b. Operations at airports with an operating control tower to include three takeoffs and landings to a full stop, with each landing involving a flight in the traffic pattern at an airport with a control tower; and

   c. Applicable flight rules for operations in Class B, C, and D airspace and ATC clearances.

61.327 Are there specific endorsements to operate a light-sport aircraft based on V_H?

1. A sport pilot who wishes to operate an aircraft with a V_H greater than 87 knots CAS must receive and log appropriate ground and flight training from an authorized instructor and receive an appropriate logbook endorsement from that same instructor.

Part 61 Sections Not Outlined

Subpart G -- Airline Transport Pilots (see Gleim *Airline Transport Pilot FAA Knowledge Test Prep*)

Subpart H -- Flight Instructors Other than Flight Instructors with a Sport Pilot Rating (see Gleim *Flight Instructor Flight Maneuvers and Practical Test Prep*)

Subpart K -- Flight Instructors with a Sport Pilot Rating (see Gleim *Flight Instructor Flight Maneuvers and Practical Test Prep*)

4.7 PART 67 – MEDICAL STANDARDS AND CERTIFICATION

Subpart A -- General

67.1 Applicability

1. This subpart prescribes the medical standards and certification procedures for issuing medical certificates for airmen and for remaining eligible for a medical certificate.

67.3 Issue

1. Persons meeting the prescribed medical standards are entitled to an appropriate medical certificate.

67.4 Application

1. An applicant for a first-, second-, and third-class medical certification must

    a. Apply on a form and in a manner prescribed by the Administrator

    b. Be examined by an aviation medical examiner

        1) An applicant may obtain a list of aviation medical examiners

            a) From the FAA Office of Aerospace Medicine home page on the FAA website

            b) From any FAA Regional Flight Surgeon

            c) By contacting the Manager of the Aerospace Medical Education Division, PO Box 26200, Oklahoma City, Oklahoma 73125

    c. Show proof of age and identity by presenting government-issued photo identification (e.g., a valid U.S. driver's license, identification card issued by a driver's license authority, military identification, or passport)

67.7 Access to the National Driver Register

1. When applying for a medical certificate, you must execute an express consent form authorizing the FAA to obtain your driving record from the National Driver Register.

Subpart D -- Third Class Airman Medical Certificate

67.301 Eligibility

1. To be eligible for a third-class medical certificate or to remain eligible, you must meet the requirements of this subpart.

67.303 Eye

1. You must have distant vision of 20/40 or better in each eye separately, with or without corrective lenses.

    a. If corrective lenses are necessary for 20/40 vision, the medical certificate will have a limitation that corrective lenses must be worn.

2. You must have near vision of 20/40 or better.

3. You must be able to perceive those colors necessary for the safe performance of pilot duties.

4. You must not have a serious pathology of the eye.

67.305 Ear, Nose, Throat, and Equilibrium

1. You must demonstrate acceptable hearing by

    a. The ability to hear an average conversational voice in a quiet room, using both ears, at a distance of 6 ft. from the examiner, with your back to the examiner

    b. The results of a hearing test

2. You must not have a disease or condition of the middle or internal ear, nose, oral cavity, pharynx, or larynx that

    a. Interferes with, or is aggravated by, flying or may reasonably be expected to do so

    b. Interferes with clear and effective speech communication

3. You must not have a disease or condition that is manifested by, or that may reasonably be expected to be manifested by, vertigo or a disturbance of equilibrium.

67.307 Mental

1. You must not have an established medical history or clinical diagnosis of any of the following:

    a. A personality disorder

    b. A psychosis

    c. A bipolar disorder

    d. Substance dependence, except where there is established clinical evidence, satisfactory to the FAA, of recovery, including sustained total abstinence from the substance(s) for not less than the preceding 2 years.

        1) Substance includes alcohol and various drugs.

2. You must not have abused any substance [as described in 1.d.1) above] within the preceding 2 years. Substance abuse is defined as

    a. Use of a substance in a situation in which that use was physically hazardous;

    b. A verified positive drug test result, an alcohol test result of 0.04 or greater alcohol concentration, or a refusal to submit to a drug or alcohol test required by the U.S. Department of Transportation or an agency of the U.S. Department of Transportation; or

    c. Misuse of a substance that the Federal Air Surgeon determines makes the person unable to safely perform the duties or exercise the privileges of the airman certificate applied for or held.

3. You must not have any other personality disorders, neurosis, or other mental condition that the FAA has determined would make you unable to perform the duties of a pilot safely.

67.309 Neurologic

1. You must not have an established medical history or clinical diagnosis of any of the following:

    a. Epilepsy

    b. A disturbance of consciousness without satisfactory medical explanation of the cause

    c. A transient loss of control of nervous system function(s) that cannot be explained

2. You must not have any other neurologic condition that the FAA has determined would make you unable to perform the duties of a pilot safely.

67.311 Cardiovascular

1. You must not have an established medical history or clinical diagnosis of any of the following:

    a. Myocardial infarction
    b. Angina pectoris
    c. Coronary heart disease that has required treatment or, if untreated, has been symptomatic or clinically significant
    d. Cardiac valve replacement
    e. Permanent implantation of a pacemaker
    f. Heart replacement

67.313 General Medical Condition

1. You must not have an established medical history or clinical diagnosis of diabetes mellitus that requires insulin or any other hypoglycemic drug for control.

2. You must not have any other organic, functional, or structural disease, defect, or limitation, or medication or treatment that the FAA has found would cause you to be unable to perform your pilot duties safely.

67.315 Discretionary Issuance

1. If you do not meet the conditions for a medical certificate, you may apply for the discretionary issuance of a certificate under 14 CFR 67.401.

Subpart E -- Certification Procedures

67.401 Special Issuance of Medical Certificates

1. The Federal Air Surgeon may issue a medical certificate to you (if you do not meet the standards) if you show that you can perform the duties authorized by the certificate without endangering public safety during that period (e.g., 2 or 3 years for a third-class medical certificate).

    a. The Federal Air Surgeon may authorize a special medical flight test, practical test, or medical evaluation for this purpose.

2. In issuing a medical certificate under this section, the Federal Air Surgeon may do any or all of the following:

    a. Limit the duration of the certificate
    b. Condition the continued effect of the certificate on the result of subsequent medical tests, examinations, or evaluations
    c. Impose any operational limitation on the certificate needed for safety
    d. Condition the continued effect of a third-class medical certificate on compliance with a statement of functional limitations issued to you in coordination with the Director, Flight Standards Service

67.403 Applications, Certificates, Logbooks, Reports, and Records: Falsification, Reproduction, or Alteration; Incorrect Statements

1. Any fraudulent application, record, report, reproduction, or alteration involving medical certificates is the basis for the FAA's suspending or revoking any airman, ground instructor, or medical certificate or rating held by the person who perpetrated the fraud or alteration.

67.405 Medical Examinations: Who May Perform?

1. Any aviation medical examiner may give the examination for the second- or third-class certificate.

   a. Any aviation medical examiner who is specifically designated for the purpose may perform examinations for the first-class medical certificate.

2. You may obtain a list of aviation medical examiners in your area from your local FSDO.

67.407 Delegation of Authority

1. This section contains legalese concerning the FAA's right to designate authority to aviation medical examiners to issue medical certificates.

67.409 Denial of Medical Certificate

1. A person who has been denied a medical certificate has 30 days to appeal the denial to the Federal Air Surgeon in Oklahoma City.

67.413 Medical Records

1. The FAA may request additional medical information of airmen and applicants for medical certificates if the information is necessary to determine if they meet the medical standards. If individuals refuse to release requested medical information, the FAA has the right to suspend, modify, or revoke any medical certificate held or application made.

67.415 Return of Medical Certificate after Suspension or Revocation

1. Upon the FAA's request, you must return a suspended or revoked medical certificate to the FAA.

Part 67 Sections Not Outlined

Subpart B -- First-Class Airman Medical Certificate

67.101	Eligibility
67.103	Eye
67.105	Ear, nose, throat, and equilibrium
67.107	Mental
67.109	Neurologic
67.111	Cardiovascular
67.113	General medical condition
67.115	Discretionary issuance

Subpart C -- Second-Class Airman Medical Certificate

67.201	Eligibility
67.203	Eye
67.205	Ear, nose, throat, and equilibrium
67.207	Mental
67.209	Neurologic
67.211	Cardiovascular
67.213	General medical condition
67.215	Discretionary issuance

4.8 PART 91 – GENERAL OPERATING AND FLIGHT RULES

Subpart A -- General

91.1 Applicability

1.   This part prescribes rules governing the operation of most aircraft within the U.S., including the waters within 3-12 NM of the U.S. coast.

2.   This part applies to each person on board an aircraft being operated under this part.

3.   This part also establishes requirements to support the continued airworthiness of each airplane.

91.3 Responsibility and Authority of the Pilot in Command

1.   As the pilot in command of your airplane, you are directly responsible for, and are the final authority as to, the operation of that airplane.

2.   Thus, in emergencies, you may deviate from the Federal Aviation Regulations to the extent needed to maintain the safety of the airplane and passengers.

3.   If you do deviate from the Federal Aviation Regulations in such an emergency, you may be required to file a written report with the FAA.

91.5 Pilot in Command of Aircraft Requiring More than One Required Pilot

1.   A pilot may not operate an aircraft that is type certificated for more than one required flight crewmember unless the pilot in command meets the requirements of 14 CFR 61.58.

91.7 Civil Aircraft Airworthiness

1.   You may not operate an aircraft that is not in an airworthy condition.

2.   You, as the pilot in command, are responsible for determining whether the aircraft is fit for safe flight.

   a.   The pilot in command shall discontinue the flight when an unairworthy mechanical, electrical, or structural condition occurs.

91.9 Civil Aircraft Flight Manual, Marking, and Placard Requirements

1.   You may not operate an aircraft that has an approved flight manual unless that manual is aboard the aircraft.

2.   You may not operate contrary to any limitations specified in that manual.

91.11 Prohibition on Interference with Crewmembers

1.   No person may intimidate, assault, threaten, or interfere with a crewmember while (s)he is performing his or her duties aboard an aircraft.

91.13 Careless or Reckless Operation

1.   You may not operate your airplane in a careless or reckless manner so as to endanger the life or property of another.

91.15 Dropping Objects

1.   Dropping objects from an airplane is not prohibited provided you take reasonable precautions to avoid injury or damage to persons or property.

91.17 Alcohol or Drugs

1. You may not act, or attempt to act, as a crewmember of a civil aircraft

   a. While under the influence of drugs or alcohol
   b. Within 8 hr. after the consumption of any alcoholic beverage
   c. While having .04% by weight or more alcohol in your blood
   d. While using any drug that affects your faculties in any way contrary to safety

2. Except in an emergency, no person who appears to be under the influence of drugs or alcohol (except those under medical care) may be carried aboard an aircraft.

3. Upon request of a law enforcement officer or an FAA employee, you must submit to a test to determine alcohol concentration in the blood or breath.

91.19 Carriage of Narcotic Drugs, Marihuana, and Depressant or Stimulant Drugs or Substances

1. You may not operate an aircraft within the United States with knowledge that any of these substances are aboard. This rule does not apply to flights that are authorized by the federal government or a state government or agency.

91.21 Portable Electronic Devices

1. Portable electronic devices other than portable voice recorders, hearing aids, pacemakers, electric shavers, etc., may not be operated on aircraft operated IFR or aircraft operated by holders of an air carrier operating certificate or an operating certificate.

2. The pilot in command or operator of the aircraft can make certain exceptions to this rule so long as the electronic devices will not interfere with the communication or navigation systems of the aircraft.

91.23 Truth-in-Leasing Clause Requirement in Leases and Conditional Sales Contracts

1. This section contains legalese concerning the truth-in-leasing clause that the FAA requires to be in leases and conditional sales contracts of large U.S. aircraft.

91.25 Aviation Safety Reporting Program: Prohibition against Use of Reports for Enforcement Purposes

1. The FAA will not use reports submitted to the National Aeronautics and Space Administration (NASA) under the Aviation Safety Reporting Program (ASRP) in any enforcement action except those concerning criminal offenses and/or accidents.

   a. ASRP is a voluntary program designed to encourage a flow of information concerning deficiencies and discrepancies in the aviation system. It is explained in AC 00-46, *Aviation Safety Reporting Program.*

   b. The primary objective is to obtain information to evaluate and enhance the safety and efficiency of the present system. Operations covered include

      1) Departure, en route, approach, and landing operations and procedures
      2) ATC procedures
      3) Pilot/controller communications
      4) Aircraft movement on the airport
      5) Near midair collisions

c.   NASA acts as an independent third party to receive and analyze these reports.

1)   NASA ensures that no information that might reveal the identity of any party involved in an occurrence or incident reported under the ASRP is released to the FAA, except

a)   Information concerning criminal offenses
b)   Information concerning accidents

NOTE: Reports concerning criminal activities or accidents are not de-identified prior to their referral to the appropriate agency.

2)   Each report has a tear-off portion that contains your name and address. This portion is returned to you with a date indicating NASA's receipt of the report.

d.   The filing of a report concerning an incident or occurrence involving a violation of the Federal Aviation Regulations is considered by the FAA to be an indication of a constructive attitude. Such an attitude will help prevent future violations. Accordingly, although a violation may be found, neither a civil penalty nor certificate suspension will be imposed if

1)   The violation was inadvertent and not deliberate.
2)   The violation did not involve a criminal offense or action which shows a lack of qualification or competency.
3)   The person has not been found in any prior FAA enforcement action to have committed a violation of the Federal Aviation Regulations for a period of 5 years prior to the date of the occurrence.
4)   The person proves (by the returned identification portion) that, within 10 days after the violation, (s)he completed and delivered or mailed a written report of the incident to NASA under the ASRP.

2.   If you believe you have violated a Federal Aviation Regulation and may be subject to an enforcement action, you can complete a NASA ARC Form 277 (available online at http://asrs.arc.nasa.gov) within 10 days and avoid possible enforcement action.

a.   You should also use the form to report any deficiencies and discrepancies in our aviation system.
b.   NASA ARC Form 277 can be submitted electronically or printed and mailed.

Subpart B -- Flight Rules

91.101 Applicability

1.   This subpart prescribes flight rules governing the operation of aircraft within the U.S. and within 12 NM from the coast of the U.S.

91.103 Preflight Action

1.   Prior to every flight, you are required to familiarize yourself with all available information concerning that flight and specifically to determine

a.   Runway lengths at airports of intended use and your airplane's takeoff and landing requirements
b.   On cross-country flights, weather, fuel requirements, alternate airports available, and any known traffic delays

91.105 Flight Crewmembers at Stations

1. Required flight crewmembers' seatbelts must be fastened while the crewmembers are at their stations.

2. Required flight crewmembers' shoulder harnesses, if installed, must be fastened during takeoff and landing unless the crewmember would be unable to perform required duties with the shoulder harness fastened.

91.107 Use of Safety Belts, Shoulder Harnesses, and Child Restraint Systems

1. You may not take off without first briefing your passengers on how to fasten and unfasten their safety belts and shoulder harnesses, if installed.

    a. You must also notify them to fasten their safety belts and shoulder harnesses (if installed) before the airplane can taxi, takeoff, or land.

2. During taxiing, takeoff, or landing, each passenger who is 2 years of age or older must be in a seat with the safety belt and shoulder harness, if installed, fastened.

3. The section also describes the types of child restraint systems that are acceptable.

91.109 Flight Instruction: Simulated Instrument Flight and Certain Flight Tests

1. Dual instruction in civil aircraft (except manned free balloons) must be given in aircraft with dual controls. Dual instrument instruction may be given in a single-engine airplane with a single throwover control wheel when

    a. The person manipulating the controls has at least a private pilot certificate with appropriate category and class ratings, and

    b. The instructor determines that it can be done safely.

2. To conduct simulated instrument flight, you must

    a. Have at least a private pilot with appropriate category and class ratings at the other set of controls, i.e., the safety pilot.

        1) Since the safety pilot is required, (s)he is a required flight crewmember who must also have a valid medical certificate.

    b. Ensure that the safety pilot has adequate sideward and forward flight visibility or that another observer in the aircraft supplements the observer at the controls.

    c. Ensure that either dual controls (except in lighter-than-air aircraft) or a single throwover control that meets the requirements of a. and b. above is present for the observer.

3. Aircraft used for an ATP practical test, a class or type rating, or a Part 121 proficiency flight evaluation must have a pilot at the controls (other than the one being evaluated) who is fully qualified to act as pilot in command of that aircraft.

91.111 Operating near Other Aircraft

1. You may not operate your airplane so close to another aircraft as to create a collision hazard.

2. You may not operate your airplane in formation flight except by arrangement with the pilot in command of each aircraft in the formation.

3. You may not operate an aircraft that is carrying passengers for hire in formation flight.

91.113 Right-of-Way Rules: Except Water Operations

1. Converging. When aircraft of the same category are converging at approximately the same altitude (except head-on), the aircraft to the right has the right-of-way.

    a. Balloons, gliders, and airships have the right-of-way over an airplane.
    b. Aircraft towing or refueling other aircraft have the right-of-way over all other engine-driven aircraft.

2. Approaching head-on. The pilot of each aircraft shall alter course to the right.

3. Overtaking. An aircraft that is being overtaken has the right-of-way.

    a. The overtaking aircraft shall alter course to the right.

4. Landing. Aircraft on final approach to land or while landing have the right-of-way over other aircraft in flight or on the ground.

    a. When two or more aircraft are approaching the airport for landing, the lower aircraft has the right-of-way.

        1) You may not take advantage of this rule to cut in front of another aircraft which is on final approach or to overtake that aircraft.

91.115 Right-of-Way Rules: Water Operations

1. This section contains the right-of-way rules for aircraft operating on water with respect to other aircraft or vessels.

91.117 Aircraft Speed

1. You may not operate an airplane at an indicated airspeed greater than 250 kt. if you are under 10,000 ft. MSL or operating within Class B airspace.

2. You may not operate an aircraft at or below 2,500 ft. above the surface within 4 NM of the primary airport of Class C or Class D airspace at an indicated airspeed of more than 200 kt.

3. You may not operate under Class B airspace or in a VFR corridor through such a Class B airspace area at an indicated airspeed greater than 200 kt.

4. If your minimum safe speed in your airplane is faster than the speed normally allowed, you may operate at that minimum safe speed.

91.119 Minimum Safe Altitudes: General

1. Except for takeoff and landing, the following altitudes are required:

    a. You must have sufficient altitude for an emergency landing without undue hazard to persons or property on the surface if your engine fails.
    b. Over congested areas of a city, town, or settlement, or over an open-air assembly of persons, you must have 1,000 ft. of clearance over the highest obstacle within a 2,000-ft. radius of your airplane.
    c. Over other than congested areas, you must have an altitude of 500 ft. above the surface.
    d. Over open water or sparsely populated areas, you must remain at least 500 ft. from any person, vessel, vehicle, or structure.

91.121 Altimeter Settings

1. Below 18,000 feet MSL, you must maintain an altitude by reference to an altimeter that has been set to

    a. The current reported altimeter setting of a station along your route and within 100 NM of your aircraft,

    b. An appropriate available station, or

    c. The elevation of your departure airport or an appropriate altimeter setting available before departure.

2. At or above 18,000 feet MSL, the pilot must set his or her altimeter to 29.92" Hg.

91.123 Compliance with ATC Clearances and Instructions

1. Once you have been given ATC instructions or a clearance, you may not deviate from it unless you obtain amended instructions or clearance, an emergency exists, or the deviation is in response to a traffic alert and collision avoidance system (TCAS) resolution advisory.

    a. If you deviate from a clearance in an emergency or in response to a TCAS resolution advisory, you must notify ATC as soon as possible.

    b. If you are given priority by ATC in an emergency, you must submit a detailed report of the emergency within 48 hr. to the manager of that ATC facility, if requested.

        1) The report may be requested even if you do not deviate from any rule of Part 91.

2. If you are uncertain about the meaning of an ATC clearance, you should immediately ask for clarification from ATC.

91.125 ATC Light Signals

1. ATC light signals have the meaning shown in the following table:

LIGHT GUN SIGNALS			
COLOR AND TYPE OF SIGNAL	**MOVEMENT OF VEHICLES, EQUIPMENT, AND PERSONNEL**	**AIRCRAFT ON THE GROUND**	**AIRCRAFT IN FLIGHT**
STEADY GREEN	Cleared to cross, proceed, or go	Cleared for takeoff	Cleared to land
FLASHING GREEN	Not applicable	Cleared for taxi	Return for landing (to be followed by steady green at the proper time)
STEADY RED	STOP	STOP	Give way to other aircraft and continue circling
FLASHING RED	Clear the taxiway/runway	Taxi clear of the runway in use	Airport unsafe, do not land
FLASHING WHITE	Return to starting point on airport	Return to starting point on airport	Not applicable
ALTERNATING RED AND GREEN	Exercise Extreme Caution!!!!	Exercise Extreme Caution!!!!	Exercise Extreme Caution!!!!

91.126 Operating on or in the Vicinity of an Airport in Class G Airspace

1.   When approaching to land at an airport without an operating control tower in Class G airspace, you must make all turns in the traffic to the left, unless the airport displays light signals or markings indicating right turns.

2.   Communications with control towers

   a.   You may not operate your airplane to, from, through, or on an airport having an operational control tower unless two-way radio communication is established with the control tower.

   b.   Communications must be established prior to 4 NM from the airport, up to and including 2,500 ft. AGL.

   c.   If your radio fails in flight, you may operate your airplane and land if weather conditions are at or above basic VFR weather minimums, visual contact with the tower is maintained, and a clearance to land is received (e.g., light signal).

   1)   If your radio fails while operating under IFR, you must comply with 14 CFR 91.185.

91.127 Operating on or in the Vicinity of an Airport in Class E Airspace

1.   When operating on or in the vicinity of an airport in a Class E airspace area, you should make all turns in the traffic pattern to the left unless the airport displays light signals or markings indicating right turns.

   a.   When departing, you must comply with the established traffic pattern for that airport.

2.   For a discussion of communications with control towers, see 91.126 above.

91.129 Operations in Class D Airspace

1.   Communications with ATC in Class D airspace

   a.   You must establish two-way radio communication with the ATC facility providing air traffic services prior to entering and while operating within the Class D airspace area.

   b.   When departing from the primary airport or a satellite airport with an operating control tower, you must establish and maintain two-way radio communication with the control tower.

   1)   The primary airport is the airport for which the Class D airspace area is designated.

   2)   A satellite airport is any other airport within the Class D airspace area.

   c.   When departing from a satellite airport without an operating control tower, you must establish and maintain two-way radio communication with the ATC facility providing air traffic services to the Class D airspace area as soon as practicable after departing.

   d.   If your radio fails in flight, you may operate your airplane and land if weather conditions are at or above basic VFR weather minimums, visual contact with the tower is maintained, and a clearance to land is received (e.g., light signal).

   1)   If your radio fails while operating under IFR, you must comply with 14 CFR 91.185.

2.   When you are approaching to land on a runway served by a visual approach slope indicator, you must remain at or above the glide slope until a lower altitude is necessary for a safe landing.

   a.   However, you are not prohibited from making normal bracketing maneuvers above or below the glide slope for the purpose of remaining on the glide slope.

3. When approaching to land, you should make left turns in the traffic pattern unless directed otherwise by the tower.

4. When departing, you must comply with any departure procedures established for that airport by the FAA.

5. You may not, at any airport with an operating control tower, operate your airplane on a runway or taxiway, or take off or land, unless an appropriate clearance is received from ATC.

91.130 Operations in Class C Airspace

1. You must establish two-way radio communication with the appropriate ATC facility before entering Class C airspace and maintain communication while you are within the Class C airspace area.

2. If you depart from the primary airport (the airport for which the Class C airspace area is designated) or a satellite airport (any other airport within the Class C airspace area) with an operating control tower, two-way radio communication must be established and maintained with the tower and as instructed by ATC while in the Class C airspace area.

    a. From a satellite airport without an operating control tower, you must establish two-way radio communication with ATC as soon as practicable after departing.

3. Unless otherwise authorized by the ATC facility having jurisdiction over the Class C airspace area, you must have a transponder with altitude encoding while operating in the Class C airspace area and the airspace above the ceiling and within the lateral boundaries of the Class C airspace area.

91.131 Operations in Class B Airspace

1. You must have an ATC clearance to operate within a Class B airspace area.

2. If it is necessary to conduct training operations within a Class B airspace area, procedures established for these flights within the Class B airspace area must be followed.

3. In order to land at an airport within a Class B airspace area or even operate within the Class B airspace area, you must be one of the following:

    a. A student pilot who has been instructed and authorized to operate in that specific Class B airspace area by a flight instructor (with a specific CFI logbook signoff required)

    b. A sport pilot who has met the requirements of 14 CFR 61.325

    c. A recreational pilot who has met the requirements of 14 CFR 61.101(d)

    d. At least a private pilot

4. However, certain Class B airspace area primary airports require the pilot to hold at least a private pilot certificate to land or take off. These are the busiest airports, such as Atlanta Hartsfield and Chicago O'Hare.

5. The equipment aboard your aircraft must include operative two-way radio communications and a transponder with altitude encoding (Mode C).

91.133 Restricted and Prohibited Areas

1. You may not operate your airplane within a restricted area contrary to the restrictions imposed or within a prohibited area, unless you have the permission of the using or controlling agency, as appropriate.

91.135 Operations in Class A Airspace

1. Operations in Class A airspace must be done under IFR and in accordance with the following:

   a. You must have an ATC clearance prior to entering Class A airspace.
   b. Each aircraft must be equipped with two-way communication radios, and each pilot must maintain contact with ATC while in Class A airspace.
   c. The aircraft must be equipped with an altitude encoding transponder.
   d. ATC may grant exceptions to these requirements. All exceptions must be requested 4 days before the proposed flight except for a transponder malfunction. If your transponder malfunctions, immediate approval can be granted to your ultimate destination, including intermediate stops, or to an appropriate repair facility.

91.137 Temporary Flight Restrictions in the Vicinity of Disaster/Hazard Areas

1. The FAA may issue a Notice to Airmen (NOTAM) to establish temporary flight restrictions

   a. To protect persons and property from a hazard associated with an incident on the surface
   b. To provide a safe environment for the operation of disaster relief aircraft
   c. To be observed in airspace above events generating a high degree of public interest

2. When a NOTAM is issued under 1.a., you may not operate your airplane in the area unless it is directed by an official in charge of on-scene emergency activities.

3. When a NOTAM is issued under 1.b., you may not operate your airplane in that area unless one of the following conditions is met:

   a. Your airplane is involved in relief activity and directed by an official in charge on the scene.
   b. Your airplane is carrying law enforcement officials.
   c. The operation is conducted directly to or from an airport in the area or is necessitated because VFR flight is impracticable, notice is given to the proper authority for receiving disaster relief advisories, relief activities are not hampered, and the flight is not solely for observation of the disaster.
   d. Your airplane is carrying properly accredited news representatives, a proper flight plan is filed, and the flight is above the altitude used by relief aircraft.
   e. Your airplane is operating under an ATC approved IFR flight plan.

4. When a NOTAM is issued under 1.c., you may not operate your airplane in the area unless one of the following conditions is met:

   a. See 3.c., except for the notice requirement.
   b. The airplane is operating under an ATC approved IFR flight plan.
   c. Your airplane is carrying incident or event personnel or law enforcement officials.
   d. See relevant portions of 3.d.

5. Flight plans filed and notice given must include the following:

   a. Aircraft identification, type, and color
   b. Radio frequencies to be used
   c. Times of entry and exit from the area
   d. Name of news organization and purpose of flight
   e. Any other information requested by ATC

91.138 Temporary Flight Restrictions in National Disaster Areas in the State of Hawaii

1. This section contains the procedures for notification and operating within areas designated as national disaster areas in the state of Hawaii to which temporary flight restrictions apply.

91.139 Emergency Air Traffic Rules

1. When the FAA administrator determines that an emergency condition exists, or will exist, relating to the FAA's ability to operate the ATC system and during which normal flight operations conducted under Part 91 cannot be done at the required level of safety and efficiency, the following will be done:

    a. The administrator will immediately issue an air traffic rule or regulation in response to the emergency.

    b. The Administrator or Associate Administrator for Air Traffic may utilize the NOTAM system to provide notification of the issuance of the rule or regulation.

        1) The NOTAMs will have information concerning the rules and regulations that govern flight operations, navigational facilities, and the designation of that airspace in which the rules and regulations apply.

2. When a NOTAM has been issued under this section, you may not operate your airplane within the designated airspace, except in accordance with the authorizations, terms, and conditions prescribed in the regulation covered by the NOTAM.

91.141 Flight Restrictions in the Proximity of the Presidential and Other Parties

1. You may not operate your airplane over or in the vicinity of any area to be visited or traveled by the President, the Vice President, or other public figures contrary to the restrictions established by the FAA in a NOTAM.

91.143 Flight Limitation in the Proximity of Space Flight Operations

1. You may not operate your airplane within the areas designated by NOTAM for space flight operation except when authorized by ATC.

91.144 Temporary Restriction on Flight Operations during Abnormally High Barometric Pressure Conditions

1. When barometric pressure exceeds 31.00 in. of mercury, the FAA will set forth operating requirements via Notices to Airmen.

    a. The FAA may waive the NOTAMed requirements for emergency operations where the operations can be done safely.

91.145 Management of Aircraft Operations in the Vicinity of Aerial Demonstrations and Major Sporting Events

1. The FAA will issue a NOTAM designating an area of airspace in which a temporary flight restriction applies when it determines a restriction is necessary to protect persons or property on the surface or in the air in the vicinity of an aerial demonstration or major sporting event.

    a. The NOTAM will be issued at least 30 days in advance unless the FAA finds good cause for a shorter period and explains this in the NOTAM.

    b. The NOTAM will state the name of the aerial demonstration or sporting event and specify the effective dates and times, the geographic features or coordinates, and any other restrictions or procedures governing flight operations in the designated airspace.

2. When a NOTAM has been issued, no person may operate an aircraft or device, or engage in any activity within the designated airspace area, except in accordance with the NOTAM, unless otherwise authorized.

3. **Flight restricted airspace area for an aerial demonstration**

   a. Normally be limited to

      1) A 5-nautical mile radius from the center of the demonstration
      2) An altitude of 17,000 feet mean sea level (for high performance aircraft) or 13,000 feet above the surface (for certain parachute operations)

4. **Flight restricted area for a major sporting event**

   a. Normally be limited to

      1) A 3-nautical mile radius from the center of the event
      2) An altitude of 2,500 feet above the surface

91.146 Passenger-Carrying Flights for the Benefit of a Charitable, Nonprofit, or Community Event

1. Definitions

   a. **Charitable event** means an event that raises funds for the benefit of a charitable organization recognized by the Department of the Treasury whose donors may deduct contributions under Section 170 of the Internal Revenue Code (26 U.S.C. Section 170).

   b. **Community event** means an event that raises funds for the benefit of any local or community cause that is not a charitable event or nonprofit event.

   c. **Non-profit event** means an event that raises funds for the benefit of a nonprofit organization recognized under State or Federal law as long as one of the organization's purposes is the promotion of aviation safety.

2. Passenger-carrying flights for the benefit of a charitable, nonprofit, or community event are not subject to the certification requirements of Part 119 or the drug and alcohol testing requirements in Part 120 as long as certain requirements are met.

3. Pilots and sponsors of events described in this section are limited to no more than four events per calendar year.

91.147 Passenger-Carrying Flights for Compensation or Hire

1. This section explains how operators can obtain FAA approval to conduct passenger-carrying flights for compensation or hire.

2. This rule only applies if passenger-carrying flights are not conducted under 14 CFR 91.146.

Visual Flight Rules

91.151 Fuel Requirements for Flight in VFR Conditions

1. You may not fly VFR during the day unless there is enough fuel to fly to the destination and at least 30 min. beyond that point.

2. You may not fly VFR at night unless there is enough fuel to fly to the destination and at least 45 min. beyond that point.

91.153 VFR Flight Plan: Information Required

1. Unless otherwise authorized by ATC, when filing a VFR flight plan, you must include the following information:

    a. Aircraft identification number and, if different, radio call sign
    b. Type aircraft
    c. Full name and address of pilot in command
    d. Point and proposed time of departure
    e. Proposed route, cruising altitude, and true airspeed
    f. Point of first intended landing and the estimated time en route
    g. Amount of fuel on board (in hours)
    h. Number of persons in the airplane
    i. Any other information you or ATC believes is necessary

2. If a flight plan has been activated, you should notify the appropriate authority (i.e., FSS) upon canceling or completing the flight.

91.155 Basic VFR Weather Minimums

1. Except as provided in this section and 14 CFR 91.157, you may not operate your airplane under VFR when the flight visibility or the distance from clouds is less than prescribed for the corresponding altitude in the following table:

Cloud Clearance and Visibility Required for VFR

Airspace	Flight Visibility	Distance from Clouds
Class A	Not Applicable	Not applicable
Class B	3 SM	Clear of Clouds
Class C	3 SM	500 ft. below 1,000 ft. above 2,000 ft. horiz.
Class D	3 SM	500 ft. below 1,000 ft. above 2,000 ft. horiz.
Class E:		
Less than 10,000 ft. MSL	3 SM	500 ft. below 1,000 ft. above 2,000 ft. horiz.
At or above 10,000 ft. MSL	5 SM	1,000 ft. below 1,000 ft. above 1 SM horiz.

Airspace	Flight Visibility	Distance from Clouds
Class G:		
1,200 ft. or less above the surface (regardless of MSL altitude)		
Day	1 SM	Clear of clouds
Night, except as provided in 2 below.	3 SM	500 ft. below 1,000 ft. above 2,000 ft. horiz.
More than 1,200 ft. above the surface but less than 10,000 ft. MSL		
Day	1 SM	500 ft. below 1,000 ft. above 2,000 ft. horiz.
Night	3 SM	500 ft. below 1,000 ft. above 2,000 ft. horiz.
More than 1,200 ft. above the surface and at or above 10,000 ft. MSL	5 SM	1,000 ft. below 1,000 ft. above 1 SM horiz.

2. An airplane may be operated clear of clouds in Class G airspace at night below 1,200 ft. AGL when the visibility is less than 3 SM but not less than 1 SM in an airport traffic pattern and within 1/2 mi. of the runway.

3. Except when operating under a special VFR clearance, you may not operate your airplane beneath the ceiling under VFR within the lateral boundaries of the surface areas of Class B, Class C, Class D, or Class E airspace designated for an airport when the ceiling is less than 1,000 ft.

    a. You may not take off, land, or enter the traffic pattern of an airport unless ground visibility is at least 3 SM. If ground visibility is not reported, flight visibility must be at least 3 SM.

91.157 Special VFR Weather Minimums

1. These special minimums apply to VFR traffic operating within the lateral boundaries of the surface areas of Class B, Class C, Class D, or Class E airspace designated for an airport.

2. Special VFR operations may be conducted only

    a. With an ATC clearance
    b. Clear of clouds
    c. With flight visibility of at least 1 SM

3. To take off or land under VFR, ground visibility must be at least 1 SM.

    a. If ground visibility is not reported, then flight visibility must be at least 1 SM.

        1) If the airport at which the airplane is located is a satellite airport that does not have weather reporting capabilities, the term flight visibility includes the visibility from the cockpit of the airplane in the takeoff position.

4. Operation under special VFR at night is prohibited unless both the pilot and the aircraft are IFR rated and equipped.

91.159 VFR Cruising Altitude or Flight Level

1. All VFR aircraft above 3,000 ft. AGL and below 18,000 ft. MSL in level cruising flight must maintain specified altitudes.

2. The altitude prescribed is based upon the magnetic course (not magnetic heading).

3. For magnetic courses of 0° to 179°, use odd thousand foot MSL altitudes plus 500 ft., e.g., 3,500; 5,500; or 7,500.

4. For magnetic courses of 180° to 359°, use even thousand foot MSL altitudes plus 500 ft., e.g., 4,500; 6,500; or 8,500.

5. When operating above 18,000 feet MSL, you must maintain the altitude or flight level assigned by ATC.

91.161 Special Awareness Training Required for Pilots Flying under VFR within a 60-NM Radius of the Washington, DC VOR/DME

1. No person may serve as a PIC or as SIC of an aircraft while flying within a 60-nautical mile radius of the DCA VOR/DME under VFR unless that pilot has completed Special Awareness Training and holds a certificate of training completion.

2. The Special Awareness Training consists of information to educate pilots about the procedures for flying in the Washington, DC area and, more generally, in other types of special use airspace.

    a. This free training is available on the FAA's website.
    b. Upon completion of the training, each person will need to print out a copy of the certificate of training completion.

3. Each person who holds a certificate for completing the Special Awareness Training must present it for inspection upon request from an authorized party.

4. Failure to complete the Special Awareness Training course on flying in and around the Washington, DC Metropolitan Area is not a violation if an emergency is declared by the pilot, as described under 14 CFR 91.3(b), or there was a failure of two-way radio communications when operating under IFR as described under 14 CFR 91.185.

5. The requirements of this section do not apply if the flight is being performed in an aircraft of

    a. An air ambulance operator certificated to conduct Part 135 operations,
    b. The U.S. Armed Forces, or
    c. A law enforcement agency.

Instrument Flight Rules

91.167 Fuel Requirements for Flight in IFR Conditions

1. You may not operate in IFR conditions unless there is enough fuel to fly

    a. To your first airport of intended landing
    b. From there to an alternate airport (if required)
    c. After that, for 45 min. at normal cruise speed

2. An alternate airport is not required if, for 1 hr. before and 1 hr. after the proposed ETA, the ceiling is forecast to be at least 2,000 feet above the airport elevation, and the visibility 3 SM.

91.169 IFR Flight Plan: Information Required

1. An alternate airport is required to be listed on an IFR flight plan except when

    a. The first airport of intended landing has a prescribed instrument approach procedure, and
    b. At least 1 hr. before and 1 hr. after the ETA, the weather reports or forecasts indicate

        1) Ceiling of at least 2,000 ft. above the airport elevation and
        2) Visibility of at least 3 SM.

2. IFR Alternate Airport Weather Minimums

    a. To list an airport as an alternate airport, current weather forecasts must indicate that, at the ETA at the alternate airport, the ceiling and visibility at that airport will be at or above the following, as applicable:

        1) Specified alternate weather minimums in a published instrument approach procedure at that airport
        2) If the alternate airport weather minimums are not specified and

            a) If the airport has a precision approach procedure: ceiling of 600 ft. and visibility of 2 SM
            b) If the airport has a nonprecision approach procedure: ceiling of 800 ft. and visibility of 2 SM
            c) If an instrument approach procedure has not been published: ceiling and visibility minimums allowing descent from the MEA, approach, and landing under basic VFR

3. When a flight plan has been activated, the pilot in command, upon canceling or completing the flight under the flight plan, shall notify an FSS or ATC facility.

91.171 VOR Equipment Check for IFR Operations

1. No person may fly IFR using VOR navigation unless within the last 30 days the on-board VOR equipment has been checked and is within the following tolerances:

    a. For a VOT, ±4°
    b. For a ground checkpoint, ±4°
    c. For an airborne checkpoint, ±6°
    d. For dual systems checked against each other, within 4°

2. Each person making the VOR operational check must enter the date, place, bearing error, and sign the aircraft log or other record.

91.173 ATC Clearance and Flight Plan Required

1. No person may operate an aircraft in controlled airspace under IFR unless that person has

    a. Filed an IFR flight plan and
    b. Received an appropriate clearance.

91.175 Takeoff and Landing under IFR

1. Instrument approaches

    a. All instrument approaches performed while operating under IFR must be per standard instrument approach procedures described in 14 CFR Part 97.
    b. Standard instrument approach procedures are prescribed for each airport and are known as approach charts (or plates).

2. Authorized DA/DH or MDA

    a. The decision altitude/height (DA/DH) is the altitude in a precision IFR approach (ILS or PAR) at which the pilot must decide whether to continue or to execute a missed approach.
    b. The MDA (minimum descent altitude) is the lowest altitude authorized on the final approach during a circle to land or other nonprecision instrument approach procedure.

3. You may not operate below the DH or MDA unless all of the following conditions are met:

    a. The airplane is descending in a position to land at a normal rate of descent using normal maneuvers.
    b. Flight visibility is not less than the prescribed minimum visibility on the approach chart.
    c. Visual reference is possible to one of the following:

        1) Approach light system
        2) Runway threshold
        3) Threshold markings
        4) Threshold lights
        5) Runway end identifier lights
        6) VASI
        7) Touchdown zone markings
        8) Touchdown zone lights
        9) Runway or runway markings
        10) Runway lights

4. A missed approach must be executed when either of the following conditions exist:

    a. The requirements of 3. above are not met either at or below the DH or MDA.
    b. An identifiable part of the airport is not distinctly visible during a circling approach at or above the MDA, unless the inability to see results from a normal bank of the airplane during the approach.

5. You may not land if the flight visibility is less than the minimum prescribed on the chart for your intended approach.

6. Takeoff minimums for flights operating under Parts 121, 125, 129, or 135 require

    a. 1 SM visibility for aircraft having two engines or less and 1/2 SM visibility for those with more than two engines or
    b. The visibility prescribed under Part 97 (i.e., nonstandard takeoff minimums at a specific airport listed in the approach charts).

7. Civil aircraft flying under IFR in or out of military airports must comply with the IFR procedures and the takeoff and landing minimums prescribed by the military authority having jurisdiction of that airport.

8. Comparable Values of RVR (runway visual range) and Ground Visibility

RVR (ft.)	Visibility (SM)
1,600	1/4
2,400	1/2
3,200	5/8
4,000	3/4
4,500	7/8
5,000	1
6,000	1-1/4

9. Operations on Unpublished Routes and Use of Radar in Instrument Approach Procedures

   a. ATC may use radar to change published instrument approach procedures using radar vectors.
   b. When operating on an unpublished route or while being radar-vectored, you must maintain the last assigned altitude until the aircraft is established on a segment of a published route or instrument approach procedures, unless a different altitude is assigned by ATC.
   c. Once you are established on the prescribed routing, published altitudes apply.
   d. Once at the final approach course or fix, you can complete the instrument approach using the published procedure or continue with radar vectoring.

10. Procedure turns are not authorized when the instrument approach chart indicates "No PT," unless you are cleared to make such turns by ATC.

11. ILS components include

   a. A localizer
   b. A glide slope
   c. An outer marker
   d. A middle marker
   e. An inner marker when Categories II or III are available
   f. The approach lighting system (ALS) [not listed in 14 CFR 91.175(k)]

12. Surveillance radar or DME, VOR, ADF fixes, or a suitable RNAV system in conjunction with a fix identified in the standard instrument approach procedure may be substituted for the outer marker.

   a. Only a compass locator or precision radar may be substituted for the middle marker.

91.177 Minimum Altitudes for IFR Operations

1. You may not operate an aircraft IFR below minimum prescribed altitude.

   a. If no prescribed minimum altitudes are published, you must maintain an altitude of 2,000 ft. above the highest obstacle within a horizontal distance of 4 NM from your course in mountainous areas.

      1) If your course is not in mountainous areas, the minimum altitude restriction is only 1,000 ft. above the highest obstacle.

2. When both an MEA (minimum en route altitude) and an MOCA (minimum obstruction clearance altitude) are prescribed, you may operate below the MEA down to, but not below, the MOCA when within 22 NM of the VOR.

3. You must climb to a higher minimum IFR altitude immediately after passing the point beyond which the new minimum altitude applies.

   a. When ground obstructions intervene, the point beyond which a higher minimum altitude applies shall be crossed at or above the applicable MCA (minimum crossing altitude).

91.179 IFR Cruising Altitude or Flight Level

1. In controlled airspace: If you are operating IFR in level cruising flight, you must maintain the altitude or flight level assigned by ATC.

    a. However, if the ATC clearance assigns "VFR conditions on top," you must maintain an altitude or flight level as prescribed by 14 CFR 91.159 (which is even or odd thousand feet MSL plus 500 ft.).

2. In uncontrolled airspace: Operating IFR in level cruising flight

    a. On a magnetic course of 0° through 179°, fly any odd thousand-foot MSL altitude (such as 5,000; 7,000; or 9,000); or

    b. On a magnetic course of 180° through 359°, fly any even thousand-foot MSL altitude (such as 4,000; 6,000; or 8,000).

91.180 Operations within Airspace Designated as Reduced Vertical Separation Minimum (RVSM) Airspace

1. 14 CFR 91.180 and 14 CFR Part 91 appendix G regulate RVSM minimums.

2. RVSM airspace begins at flight level (FL) 290 and extends up to and includes FL 410.

3. ATC separates aircraft by 1,000 feet vertically in RVSM airspace.

4. Operators must be authorized by the administrator prior to operating in RVSM airspace.

    a. Each operator must submit a data packet to the administrator establishing compliance with the applicable RVSM aircraft requirements.

5. The administrator grants authority to operate in RVSM airspace either in the operator's operations specifications or by the issuance of a Letter of Authorization.

6. Each person requesting a clearance to operate within RVSM airspace shall correctly annotate the flight plan filed with air traffic control with the status of the operator and aircraft with regard to RVSM approval.

91.181 Course to Be Flown

1. In controlled airspace under IFR, unless authorized by ATC, you must fly

    a. On the centerline of an Air Traffic Service (ATS) route (e.g., federal airway, RNAV route, etc.) or

    b. Along the direct course between the navigational aids or fixes defining any other route.

2. This regulation does not prohibit maneuvering in VFR conditions to avoid other air traffic.

91.183 IFR Communications

1. While operating IFR in controlled airspace, you must monitor the appropriate ATC frequency and report the following to ATC:

    a. The time and altitude of passing each designated reporting point, or the reporting points specified by ATC

        1) Except that, while under radar control, only the passing of those points specifically requested by ATC needs to be reported.

    b. Any unforecast weather conditions encountered

    c. Any other information relating to the safety of flight

91.185 IFR Operations: Two-Way Radio Communications Failure

1. Unless otherwise authorized by ATC, if you experience two-way radio communications failure when operating under IFR, you shall comply with the following rules:

   a. **VFR conditions.** If the failure occurs in VFR weather conditions or if VFR weather conditions are encountered after the failure, continue the flight under VFR and land as soon as practicable.

   b. **IFR conditions.** If the failure occurs in IFR conditions or if a. above cannot be complied with, continue the flight as follows:

      1) **Route**

         a) By the route assigned in the last ATC clearance received;

         b) If being radar vectored, by the direct route from the point of radio failure to the fix, route, or airway specified in the vector clearance;

         c) In the absence of an assigned route, by the route that ATC has advised may be expected in a further clearance; or

         d) In the absence of an assigned route or a route that ATC has advised may be expected in a further clearance, by the route filed in the flight plan.

      2) **Altitude.** At the highest of the following altitudes for the route segment being flown:

         a) The altitude or flight level assigned in the last ATC clearance received

         b) The minimum altitude for IFR operations

         c) The altitude or flight level ATC has advised may be expected in a further clearance

      3) **Leave clearance limit**

         a) When the clearance limit specified in your last ATC clearance is a fix from which an approach begins, commence descent or descent and approach as close as possible to the expect further clearance (EFC) time if one has been received or, if one has not been received, as close as possible to the ETA as calculated from the filed or amended (with ATC) ETE.

         b) If the clearance limit is not a fix from which an approach begins, leave the clearance limit at the EFC time if one has been received. If no EFC time has been received, continue past the clearance limit, and proceed to a fix from which an approach begins and commence descent or descent and approach as close as possible to the ETA as calculated from the filed or amended (with ATC) ETE.

91.187 Operation under IFR in Controlled Airspace: Malfunction Reports

1. The pilot in command of each aircraft operating in controlled airspace under IFR must report as soon as practicable to ATC any malfunctions of navigational, approach, or communication equipment occurring in flight.

2. Each report must include

   a. Aircraft identification

   b. Equipment affected

   c. Degree to which the capability of the pilot to operate under IFR in the ATC system is impaired

   d. Nature and extent of assistance desired from ATC

91.189 Category II and III Operations: General Operating Rules

1. No person may operate a civil aircraft in a Category II or III operation unless the flight crew of the aircraft consists of a pilot in command and a second in command who both hold the appropriate authorizations and ratings prescribed in 14 CFR 61.3.

2. This section does not apply to operations conducted under 14 CFR Parts 121, 125, 129, or 135.

91.191 Category II and Category III Manual

1. You may not operate a civil aircraft of U.S. registry in a Category II or a Category III operation unless all of the following apply:

    a. There is available in the aircraft a current, approved Category II or Category III manual for that aircraft.

    b. The operation is conducted in accordance with that manual.

    c. The instruments and equipment listed in the manual are inspected and maintained according to the maintenance program contained in that manual.

2. This section does not apply to operations conducted under 14 CFR Parts 121 or 135.

91.193 Certificate of Authorization for Certain Category II Operations

1. The Administrator may issue a certificate of authorization allowing deviations from the requirements of 14 CFR 91.189, 91.191, and 91.205(f) for the operation of small aircraft identified as Category A aircraft in Category II operations.

    a. Category A aircraft are those aircraft that have a speed of 1.3 V_{so} less than 91 kt.

2. This authorization does not permit the carrying of persons or property for compensation or hire.

Subpart C -- Equipment, Instrument, and Certificate Requirements

91.203 Civil Aircraft: Certifications Required

1. You may not operate a civil aircraft unless it has in it both of the following:

    a. An appropriate and current airworthiness certificate which is posted near the aircraft entrance for passengers and crew to see

    b. A registration certificate issued to the aircraft owner

2. You are also required to have

    a. An approved Airplane Flight Manual or Pilot's Operating Handbook accessible to the pilot

    b. The aircraft's weight and balance information

3. An easy way to remember the required documents is by using the memory aid **ARROW**:

   A irworthiness certificate
   R egistration
   R adio station license
   O perating limitations
   W eight and balance

   NOTE: A radio station license is required only if the airplane is flown outside of U.S. airspace (i.e., to another country). Additionally, on these flights you are required to have a restricted radiotelephone operator permit. These are requirements of the Federal Communications Commission (FCC), not FAA requirements.

91.205 Powered Civil Aircraft with Standard Category U.S. Airworthiness Certificates: Instrument and Equipment Requirements

1. You may not operate a powered civil aircraft with a standard category U.S. airworthiness certificate without the specified operable instruments and equipment.

2. Required equipment: VFR - day

    a. Airspeed indicator

    b. Altimeter

    c. Magnetic direction indicator (compass)

    d. Tachometer for each engine

    e. Oil pressure gauge for each engine using a pressure system

    f. Temperature gauge for each liquid-cooled engine

    g. Oil temperature gauge for each air-cooled engine

    h. Manifold pressure gauge for each altitude engine

    i. Fuel gauge indicating the quantity of fuel in each tank

    j. Landing gear position indicator, if the aircraft has a retractable landing gear

    k. For small airplanes certificated after March 11, 1996, an approved anticollision light system

    l. Approved flotation gear for each occupant and one pyrotechnic signaling device if the aircraft is operated for hire over water beyond power-off gliding distance from shore

    m. Approved safety belt with approved metal-to-metal latching device for each occupant who is 2 years of age or older

    n. For small civil airplanes manufactured after July 18, 1978, an approved shoulder harness for each front seat

    o. An emergency locator transmitter (ELT), if required by 14 CFR 91.207

    p. For normal, utility, and acrobatic category airplanes with a seating configuration, excluding pilot seats, of nine or less, manufactured after December 12, 1986, a shoulder harness for each seat in the airplane

3. Required equipment: VFR - night

    a. All equipment listed in 2. above

    b. Approved position (navigation) lights

    c. Approved aviation red or white anticollision light system on all U.S.-registered civil aircraft

    d. If the aircraft is operated for hire, one electric landing light

    e. An adequate source of electricity for all electrical and radio equipment

    f. A set of spare fuses or three spare fuses for each kind required which are accessible to the pilot in flight

4. Required equipment: IFR

    a. All equipment listed in 2. above for operations during the day and all the equipment listed in 3. above for IFR operations at night

    b. Two-way radio communication and navigation equipment suitable for the route to be flown

    c. Gyroscopic rate-of-turn indicator

    d. Slip-skid indicator

    e. Sensitive altimeter adjustable for barometric pressure

    f. A clock displaying hours, minutes, and seconds with a sweep-second pointer or digital presentation

    g. Generator or alternator of adequate capacity

    h. Gyroscopic pitch and bank indicator (artificial horizon)

    i. Gyroscopic direction indicator (directional gyro or equivalent)

91.207 Emergency Locator Transmitters

1. ELT batteries must be replaced after 1 cumulative hr. of use or after 50% of their useful life (or charge, if rechargeable) expires.

2. The expiration date for batteries used in an ELT must be legibly marked on the outside of the transmitter.

3. The ELT must be inspected every 12 calendar months for

    a. Proper installation
    b. Battery corrosion
    c. Operation of the controls and crash sensor
    d. Sufficient signal radiated from its antenna

4. This regulation also lists 11 conditions for which an ELT is not required in aircraft.

91.209 Aircraft Lights

1. During the period from sunset to sunrise, you may not operate an aircraft unless it has lighted position (navigation) lights.

2. You may not park or move an aircraft in, or in dangerous proximity to, a night flight operations area of an airport unless the aircraft

    a. Is clearly illuminated,
    b. Has lighted position lights, or
    c. Is in an area that is marked by obstruction lights.

3. At all times, you must use anticollision lights (i.e., rotating beacon and/or strobe lights) if your airplane is so equipped.

    a. The anticollision light may be turned off if you (the pilot in command) determine that it would be in the interest of safety, given the operating conditions, to turn it off.

91.211 Supplemental Oxygen

1. At cabin pressure altitudes above 12,500 ft. MSL up to and including 14,000 ft. MSL, the required minimum crew must use oxygen after 30 min. at those altitudes.

2. At cabin pressure altitudes above 14,000 ft. MSL, the required minimum flight crew must continuously use oxygen.

3. At cabin pressure altitudes above 15,000 ft. MSL, each passenger must be provided supplemental oxygen.

91.213 Inoperative Instruments and Equipment

1. You may not take off in an aircraft with inoperative instruments or equipment installed unless

    a. An approved minimum equipment list (MEL) exists for that specific aircraft. Note that the MEL is a list of equipment that does NOT have to be operable.

        1) This includes the different flight limitations placed upon the aircraft when that equipment is inoperative; e.g., you cannot fly at night if the landing light is out.

    b. The aircraft has within it a letter of authorization, issued by the FAA FSDO in the area where the operator is based, authorizing operation of the aircraft under the MEL. The MEL and authorization letter constitute an STC (supplemental type certificate) for the aircraft.

    c. The approved MEL must

        1) Be prepared in accordance with specified limitations and
        2) Provide how the aircraft is to be operated with the instruments and equipment in an inoperative condition.

    d.   The aircraft records available to you must include an entry describing the inoperative instruments and equipment.

    e.   The aircraft must be operated under all applicable conditions and limitations contained in the MEL and the letter of authorization.

2.   The following instruments and equipment may NOT be included in an MEL:

    a.   Instruments and equipment that are specifically or otherwise required by the airworthiness requirements under which the aircraft is type-certificated and which are essential to the safe operation of the aircraft

    b.   Instruments and equipment required by an Airworthiness Directive

    c.   Instruments and equipment required for operations by the Federal Aviation Regulations

3.   You may take off in a light, piston-driven airplane with inoperative equipment and no MEL under any of the following conditions:

    a.   An FAA Master MEL (MMEL) has not been developed by the FAA and the inoperative equipment is not required by the aircraft manufacturer's equipment list, any other Federal Aviation Regulations, ADs, etc.

    b.   An FAA MMEL exists, and the inoperative equipment is not required by the MMEL, the aircraft manufacturer's equipment list, any other Federal Aviation Regulation, ADs, etc.

    c.   The inoperative equipment is removed, or deactivated and placarded "inoperative."

    d.   You or an appropriate maintenance person determines that the inoperative equipment does not constitute a hazard.

        1)   The aircraft is deemed to be in a "properly altered condition" by the FAA.

4.   Special flight permits (from the FAA) are possible under 14 CFR Part 21 when the requirements previously noted cannot be met.

NOTE: 14 CFR 91.213 applies the MEL concept to all aircraft but provides an "out" for Part 91 operations if an FAA Master MEL has not been developed for a particular type of aircraft **or** the equipment is not required by the Master MEL, the aircraft manufacturer's equipment list, Federal Aviation Regulations, ADs, etc.

91.215 ATC Transponder and Altitude Reporting Equipment and Use

1.   Mode C transponder equipment is required in all Class A, Class B, and Class C airspace areas.

2.   All aircraft certified with an engine-driven electrical system must have Mode C transponder equipment

    a.   Within 30 NM of the primary airport of a Class B airspace area from the surface up to 10,000 ft. MSL

    b.   Above 10,000 ft. MSL, excluding airspace at or below 2,500 ft. AGL

3.   All aircraft must have Mode C transponder equipment

    a.   Within a Class C airspace area, above the ceiling, and within the lateral limits of the Class C airspace area

    b.   Within 10 NM of certain specified airports (except below 1,200 ft. AGL outside of the lateral boundaries of the surface area designated for that airport)

4.   If the airplane you are flying is equipped with a Mode C transponder and is maintained in accordance with 14 CFR 91.413, you must have it on in all controlled airspace, not just the airspace specified above.

91.217 Data Correspondence between Automatically Reported Pressure Altitude Data and the Pilot's Altitude Reference

1. You may not operate your transponder on Mode C (automatic pressure altitude reporting equipment)

   a. When ATC directs you to turn off Mode C

   b. Unless, as installed, the equipment was tested and calibrated to transmit altitude data within 125 ft. of the altimeter used to maintain flight altitude for altitudes ranging from sea level to maximum operating altitude of the airplane

   c. Unless the altimeters and digitizers in that equipment meet certain specified standards

91.219 Altitude Alerting System or Device: Turbojet-Powered Civil Airplanes

1. This section sets forth the altitude alerting system requirements for turbojet-powered, U.S.-registered civil airplanes.

91.221 Traffic Alert and Collision Avoidance System Equipment and Use

1. All traffic alert and collision avoidance systems and equipment must be approved by the FAA and, if installed, must be on and operating.

91.223 Terrain Awareness and Warning System

1. No person may operate a turbine-powered, U.S.-registered airplane configured with six or more passenger seats, excluding any pilot seat, unless that airplane is equipped with an approved terrain awareness and warning system.

2. The Airplane Flight Manual shall contain appropriate procedures for

   a. The use of the terrain awareness and warning system and

   b. Proper flight crew reaction in response to the terrain awareness and warning system audio and visual warnings.

3. The following operations are excluded from compliance with this rule:

   a. Parachuting operations when conducted entirely within a 50-nautical mile radius of the airport where the flight began

   b. Firefighting operations

   c. Flight operations conducted for the aerial application of chemicals and other substances

91.225 ADS-B Out Equipment and Use

1. After January 1, 2020, unless otherwise authorized by ATC, no person may operate an aircraft in the airspace listed below unless the aircraft has the appropriate ADS-B equipment installed.

   a. Below 18,000 ft. MSL

   b. In Class A, B, or C airspace

   c. Except as provided in item 2. below, within 30 NM of an airport listed in Appendix D, Section 1, of Part 91, from the surface upward to 10,000 ft. MSL

   d. Above the ceiling and within the lateral boundaries of a Class B or Class C airspace area designated for an airport upward to 10,000 ft. MSL

   e. Except as provided in item 2. below, in Class E airspace within the 48 contiguous states and the District of Columbia at and above 10,000 ft. MSL, excluding the airspace at and below 2,500 ft. above the surface

   f. In Class E airspace at and above 3,000 ft. MSL over the Gulf of Mexico from the coastline of the U.S. out to 12 NM

2. The requirements in item 1. above do not apply to any aircraft that was not originally certificated with an electrical system or that has not subsequently been certified with such a system installed, such as balloons and gliders.

3. Each person operating an aircraft equipped with ADS-B Out must operate this equipment in the transmit mode at all times.

4. Requests for ATC-authorized deviations from these requirements must be made to the appropriate ATC facility and within the appropriate time period.

91.227 ADS-B Out Equipment Performance Requirements

1. The following definitions apply for this section:

   a. **ADS-B Out** is a function of an aircraft's onboard avionics that periodically broadcasts the aircraft's state vector (3-dimensional position and 3-dimensional velocity) and other required information.

   b. **Navigation Accuracy Category for Position (NACp)** specifies the accuracy of a reported aircraft's position.

   c. **Navigation Accuracy Category for Velocity (NACv)** specifies the accuracy of a reported aircraft's velocity.

   d. **Navigation Integrity Category (NIC)** specifies an integrity containment radius around an aircraft's reported position.

   e. **Position Source** refers to the equipment installed onboard an aircraft used to process and provide aircraft position (e.g., latitude, longitude, and velocity) information.

   f. **Source Integrity Level (SIL)** indicates the probability of the reported horizontal position exceeding the containment radius defined by the NIC on a per-sample or per-hour basis.

   g. **System Design Assurance (SDA)** indicates the probability of an aircraft malfunction causing false or misleading information to be transmitted.

   h. **Total latency** is the total time between when the position is measured and when the position is transmitted by the aircraft.

   i. **Uncompensated latency** is the time for which the aircraft does not compensate for latency.

2. 1090 MHz ES and UAT Broadcast Links and Power Requirements

   a. Aircraft operating in Class A airspace must have equipment installed that meets the antenna and power output requirements of Class A1, A1S, A2, A3, B1S, or B1 equipment as defined in TSO-C166b, Extended Squitter Automatic Dependent Surveillance-Broadcast (ADS-B) and Traffic Information Service-Broadcast (TIS-B) Equipment Operating on the Radio Frequency of 1090 Megahertz (MHz).

   b. Aircraft operating in airspace designated for ADS-B Out, but outside of Class A airspace, must have equipment installed that meets the antenna and output power requirements of either

      1) Class A1, A1S, A2, A3, B1S, or B1 as defined in TSO-C166b or

      2) Class A1H, A1S, A2, A3, B1S, or B1 equipment as defined in TSO-C154c, Universal Access Transceiver (UAT) Automatic Dependent Surveillance-Broadcast (ADS-B) Equipment Operating on the Frequency of 978 MHz.

Subpart D -- Special Flight Operations

91.303 Aerobatic Flight

1. Aerobatic flight is not permitted

    a. Over any congested area of a city, town, or settlement
    b. Over an open air assembly of persons
    c. Within the lateral boundaries of the surface areas of Class B, Class C, Class D, or Class E airspace designated for an airport
    d. Within 4 NM of the centerline of any federal airway
    e. Below an altitude of 1,500 ft. AGL
    f. With flight visibility at less than 3 SM

2. Aerobatic flight means an intentional maneuver involving an abrupt change in an aircraft's attitude, an abnormal attitude, or an abnormal acceleration not necessary for normal flight.

91.305 Flight Test Areas

1. Flight tests may be conducted only over open water or sparsely populated areas having light air traffic.

91.307 Parachutes and Parachuting

1. Emergency parachutes cannot be carried aboard an airplane unless they meet FAA specifications.

2. Except in emergencies, persons may not make parachute jumps from airplanes unless in accordance with 14 CFR Part 105.

3. Unless each occupant of the aircraft is wearing an approved parachute, no pilot carrying another person may execute any intentional maneuver that exceeds

    a. A bank of 60° relative to the horizon
    b. A nose-up or nose-down attitude of 30° relative to the horizon

4. Item 3. does not apply to flight tests for pilot certifications or ratings or to spins and other flight maneuvers required for any certificate or rating if given by a CFI.

91.309 Towing: Gliders and Unpowered Ultralight Vehicles

1. This section contains equipment requirements and general operating rules when operating an aircraft that is towing a glider.

91.311 Towing: Other than under Sec. 91.309

1. A pilot of an aircraft may not tow anything other than a glider except in accordance with the terms of a certificate of waiver issued by the FAA.

Subpart E -- Maintenance, Preventive Maintenance, and Alterations

91.401 Applicability

1. This subpart gives the rules governing maintenance, preventive maintenance, and alteration of U.S.-registered aircraft.

91.403 General

1. The owner or operator of an aircraft is primarily responsible for maintaining the aircraft in an airworthy condition.

   a. An operator is a person who uses, causes to be used, or authorizes to be used an aircraft for the purpose of air navigation, including the piloting of an aircraft, with or without the right of legal control (i.e., owner, lessee, or otherwise).

      1) Thus, the pilot in command is also responsible for ensuring that the aircraft is maintained in an airworthy condition and that all Airworthiness Directives are complied with.

2. You may not operate an aircraft contrary to any airworthiness limitations specified by the manufacturer. This rule includes following the required replacement time, inspection intervals, and related procedures.

91.405 Maintenance Required

1. Each owner or operator shall have the aircraft inspected as prescribed in 14 CFR 91.409, 91.411, and 91.413.

2. Between inspections, any discrepancies shall be dealt with in accordance with 14 CFR Part 43.

91.407 Operation after Maintenance, Preventive Maintenance, Rebuilding, or Alteration

1. You may not operate an aircraft that has undergone any maintenance, preventive maintenance, rebuilding, or alteration unless

   a. It has been approved for return to service by a person authorized by 14 CFR 43.7.
   b. The logbook entry required by 14 CFR 43.9 and 43.11 has been made.

2. You may not operate an aircraft that has been significantly altered or rebuilt to the extent that it changes its flight characteristics until it has been test-flown by an appropriately rated pilot with at least a private pilot certificate.

91.409 Inspections

1. Annual inspections are good through the last day of the 12th calendar month after the previous annual inspection.

   EXAMPLE: An aircraft has its annual inspection on March 22, 2017. The latest day this inspection is good through is March 31, 2018.

   a. An annual inspection must be performed by a certified mechanic (A&P) who also has an inspection authorization (IA).

2. Airplanes that are used to carry people for hire or to provide flight instruction for hire must undergo an annual or 100-hr. inspection within the preceding 100 hr. of flight time.

   a. The 100 hr. may not be exceeded by more than 10 hr. if necessary to reach a place at which an inspection can be performed.
   b. The next inspection, however, is due 200 hr. from the prior inspection; e.g., if the inspection is done at 105 hr., the next inspection is due in 95 hr.
   c. If you have an inspection done prior to 100 hr., you cannot add the time remaining to 100 hr. to the next inspection.

91.411 Altimeter System and Altitude Reporting Equipment Tests and Inspections

1. This section sets forth the static pressure system, altimeter, and automatic pressure altitude reporting system inspection and maintenance requirements.

91.413 ATC Transponder Tests and Inspections

1. You may not use an ATC transponder unless it has been tested within the last 24 calendar months and found to comply with the required standards.

2. This test must be done by a certified repair shop.

91.415 Changes to Aircraft Inspection Programs

1. Whenever the FAA determines that a change in the approved aircraft inspection program is required to maintain safety, the owner or operator shall, after notification, make the required change.

2. The owner or operator may petition against this change within 30 days of receiving the notice of the change.

91.417 Maintenance Records

1. Each owner or operator shall keep the following records:

   a. Alteration or rebuilding records
   b. 100-hr. inspections
   c. Annual inspections
   d. Progressive and other required inspections

2. The records must be kept for each aircraft (airframe), engine, propeller, and appliance.

3. Each record shall include a description of the work performed, the date of completion, and the signature and certificate number of the person performing the work.

91.419 Transfer of Maintenance Records

1. Any owner or operator who sells a U.S.-registered aircraft must, at the time of the sale, transfer to the new owner the following records:

   a. Records of maintenance, preventive maintenance, and alteration
   b. Records of all 100-hr., annual, progressive, and other required inspections

91.421 Rebuilt Engine Maintenance Records

1. The owner or operator may use a new maintenance record for an aircraft engine rebuilt by the manufacturer or a shop approved by the manufacturer.

2. Each shop that grants zero time to an engine shall enter the following items into the new record:

   a. A signed statement of the date the engine was rebuilt
   b. Each change made as required by an Airworthiness Directive
   c. Each change made in compliance with a Manufacturer's Service Bulletin

3. A rebuilt engine is one that is completely disassembled, inspected, repaired, reassembled, tested, and approved to the same tolerances as new.

Part 91 Sections Not Outlined

Subpart D -- Special Flight Operations

Subpart F -- Large and Turbine-Powered Multiengine Airplanes and Fractional Ownership Program Aircraft

Subpart G -- Additional Equipment and Operating Requirements for Large and Transport Category Aircraft

Program Management

4.9 NTSB PART 830 -- NOTIFICATION AND REPORTING OF AIRCRAFT ACCIDENTS OR INCIDENTS AND OVERDUE AIRCRAFT, AND PRESERVATION OF AIRCRAFT WRECKAGE, MAIL, CARGO, AND RECORDS

Subpart A -- General

830.1 Applicability

1. This part concerns reporting accidents, incidents, and certain other occurrences involving U.S. civil aircraft and preservation of the wreckage, mail, cargo, and records.

830.2 Definitions

1. **Aircraft accident** -- an occurrence that takes place between the time any person boards an aircraft with the intention of flight until such time as all such persons have disembarked, and in which one of the following results:

    a. Any person suffers death or serious injury as a result of being in or upon the aircraft or by direct contact with the aircraft or anything attached thereto.

    b. The aircraft receives substantial damage.

2. **Fatal injury** -- an injury resulting in death within 30 days of the accident

3. **Incident** -- an occurrence other than an accident, associated with the operation of an aircraft, that affects or could affect the safety of operations

4. **Operator** -- any person who causes or authorizes the operation of an aircraft, such as the owner, lessee, or bailee of an aircraft

5. **Serious injury** -- any injury that

    a. Requires hospitalization for more than 48 hr., commencing within 7 days from the date the injury was received

    b. Results in a fracture of any bone (except simple fractures of fingers, toes, or nose)

    c. Causes severe hemorrhages or nerve, muscle, or tendon damage

    d. Involves injury to any internal organ

    e. Involves second- or third-degree burns, or any burns affecting more than 5% of the body surface

6. **Substantial damage** -- damage or failure that adversely affects the structural strength, performance, or flight characteristics of the aircraft and that would normally require major repair or replacement of the affected component

    a. Engine failure; damage limited to an engine; bent fairings or cowling; dented skin; small puncture holes in the skin or fabric; ground damage to rotor or propeller blades; damage to landing gear, wheels, tires, flaps, engine accessories, brakes, or wingtips are not considered "substantial damage."

Subpart B -- Initial Notification of Aircraft Accidents, Incidents, and Overdue Aircraft

830.5 Immediate Notification

1. The nearest NTSB office must be notified immediately when an aircraft is overdue and is believed to be involved in an accident, when an accident occurs, or when any of the following incidents occur:

    a. Flight control system malfunction or failure

    b. Inability of any required flight crewmember to perform normal flight duties as a result of injury or illness

    c. Failure of any internal turbine engine component that results in the escape of debris other than out of the exhaust path

    d. In-flight fire

    e. Aircraft collision in flight

    f. Damage to property, other than the aircraft, estimated to exceed $25,000 for repair (including materials and labor) or fair market value in the event of total loss, whichever is less

    g. Release of all or a portion of a propeller blade from an aircraft, excluding release caused solely by ground contact

    h. A complete loss of information, excluding flickering, from more than 50% of an aircraft's glass cockpit displays, which generally include

        1) Primary flight display (PFD)
        2) Primary navigation display (PND)
        3) Other integrated displays

    i. Airborne Collision and Avoidance System (ACAS) resolution advisories issued either

        1) When an aircraft is being operated on an IFR flight plan and compliance with the advisory is necessary to avert a substantial risk of collision between two or more aircraft

        2) To an aircraft operating in class A airspace

    j. Damage to helicopter tail or main rotor blades, including ground damage, that requires major repair or replacement of the blade(s)

    k. Any event in which an aircraft operated by an air carrier

        1) Lands or departs on a taxiway, incorrect runway, or other area not designed as a runway

        2) Experiences a runway incursion that requires the operator or the crew of another aircraft or vehicle to take immediate corrective action to avoid a collision

830.6 Information to Be Given in Notification

1. The notification required in NTSB Part 830.5 on the previous page must contain the following information, if available:

   a. Type, nationality, and registration marks of the aircraft
   b. Name of owner and operator of the aircraft
   c. Name of the pilot in command
   d. Date and time of the accident
   e. Last point of departure and point of intended landing of the aircraft
   f. Position of the aircraft with reference to some easily defined geographical point
   g. Number of persons aboard, number killed, and number seriously injured
   h. Nature of the accident, the weather, and the extent of damage to the aircraft, so far as is known
   i. A description of any explosives, radioactive materials, or other dangerous articles carried

Subpart C -- Preservation of Aircraft Wreckage, Mail, Cargo, and Records

830.10 Preservation of Aircraft Wreckage, Mail, Cargo, and Records

1. The operator of an aircraft is responsible for preserving any aircraft wreckage, cargo, mail, and all records until the NTSB takes custody.

2. The wreckage may be disturbed only to

   a. Remove persons injured or trapped
   b. Protect the wreckage from further damage
   c. Protect the public from injury

3. When it is necessary for aircraft wreckage, mail, or cargo to be disturbed or moved, sketches, descriptive notes, and photographs shall be made of the accident locale, if possible, including original position and condition of the wreckage and any significant impact marks.

4. The operator of an aircraft involved in an accident or incident shall retain all records and reports, including all internal documents and memoranda dealing with the event, until authorized by the NTSB to the contrary.

Subpart D -- Reporting of Aircraft Accidents, Incidents, and Overdue Aircraft

830.15 Reports and Statements to Be Filed

1. The operator of an aircraft shall file a report on NTSB Form 6120.1 within 10 days after an accident or after 7 days if an overdue aircraft is still missing.

   a. The form can be obtained by contacting the nearest NTSB office or FSDO.

      1) A full listing of NTSB regional offices may be found at www.ntsb.gov/about/Pages/OfficeLocation.aspx.

   b. NTSB Form 6120.1 is a very detailed, 11-page form.
   c. The report shall be filed at the nearest NTSB office.

2. A report on an incident for which notification is required by NTSB Part 830.5 must be filed only as requested by an authorized representative of the Board.

3. Each crewmember shall, as soon as physically able, attach a statement concerning the facts, conditions, and circumstances relating to the accident or incident.

4.10 SUMMARY OF CURRENT 14 CFR PART NUMBERS

The purpose of this section is to provide a brief description of the various "Parts" of the Code of Federal Regulations (CFR) that are commonly called the Federal Aviation Regulations (14 CFR). This section is intended as a reference so that, when a 14 CFR part is mentioned, you will have a general notion of how the Federal Aviation Regulations are organized. Currently, the Federal Aviation Regulations have over 70 parts organized under the following 12 subchapters:

A -- Definitions and General Requirements
B -- Procedural Rules
C -- Aircraft
D -- Airmen
E -- Airspace
F -- Air Traffic and General Operating Rules
G -- Air Carriers and Operators for Compensation or Hire: Certification and Operations
H -- Schools and Other Certificated Agencies
I -- Airports
J -- Navigational Facilities
K -- Administrative Regulations
N -- War Risk Insurance

A -- DEFINITIONS AND GENERAL REQUIREMENTS

1. **Definitions and Abbreviations** -- several pages of definitions of terms and abbreviations used throughout the Federal Aviation Regulations

3. **General Requirements** -- applies to any person who makes a record or entry regarding a type-certificated product, or a product, part, appliance or material that may be used on a type-certificated product

B -- PROCEDURAL RULES

11. **General Rulemaking Procedures** -- applies to the issue, amendment, and repeal of rules and orders for airspace assignment and use, and other substantive rules

13. **Investigation and Enforcement Procedures** -- prescribes the procedures to be used by the FAA in enforcing the Federal Aviation Regulations

14. **Rules Implementing the Equal Access to Justice Act of 1980** -- prescribes the parties eligible for the award of attorney fees and other expenses who are parties to certain administrative proceedings before the FAA, and the proceedings that are covered under the Equal Access to Justice Act. It also explains how to apply for awards, and the procedures and standards used to make them.

15. **Administrative Claims under Federal Tort Claims Act** -- applies to claims asserted under the Federal Tort Claims Act for money damages against the U.S. for injury, for loss of property, or for personal injury or death caused by the negligent or wrongful act or omission of an FAA employee

16. **Rules of Practice for Federally-Assisted Airport Enforcement Proceedings** -- governs the proceedings involving federally-assisted airports, whether the proceedings are instituted by the FAA or by a complaint filed with the FAA

17. **Procedures for Protests and Contract Disputes** -- applies to all protests or contract disputes against the FAA

C -- AIRCRAFT

21. **Certification Procedures for Products and Parts** -- prescribes procedural requirements for the issue of type certificates and changes to those certificates, the issue of production certificates, the issue of airworthiness certificates, and the issue of export airworthiness approvals. It also prescribes the procedure requirements for the approval of certain materials, parts, processes, and appliances.

23. **Airworthiness Standards: Normal, Utility, Acrobatic, and Commuter Category Airplanes** -- prescribes airworthiness standards for the issue of type certificates and changes to those certificates for airplanes in the normal, utility, acrobatic, and commuter categories

25. **Airworthiness Standards: Transport Category Airplanes** -- prescribes airworthiness standards for the issue of type certificates and changes to those certificates for transport category airplanes

26. **Continued Airworthiness and Safety Improvements for Transport Category Airplanes** -- establishes requirements for support of the continued airworthiness of and safety improvements for transport category airplanes. These requirements may include performing assessments, developing design changes, developing revisions to Instructions for Continued Airworthiness (ICA), and making necessary documentation available to affected persons. Requirements of this part that establish standards for design changes and revisions to the ICA are considered airworthiness requirements.

27. **Airworthiness Standards: Normal Category Rotorcraft** -- prescribes airworthiness standards for the issue of type certificates and changes to those certificates for normal category rotorcraft with maximum weights of 7,000 lb. or less

29. **Airworthiness Standards: Transport Category Rotorcraft** -- prescribes airworthiness standards for the issue of type certificates and changes to those certificates for transport category rotorcraft

31. **Airworthiness Standards: Manned Free Balloons** -- prescribes airworthiness standards for the issue of type certificates and changes to those certificates for manned free balloons

33. **Airworthiness Standards: Aircraft Engines** -- prescribes airworthiness standards for the issue of type certificates and changes to those certificates for aircraft engines

34. **Fuel Venting and Exhaust Emission Requirements for Turbine Engine Powered Airplanes** -- prescribes the fuel venting and exhaust emission requirements for turbine engine powered airplanes and the test procedures specified in the Clean Air Act

35. **Airworthiness Standards: Propellers** -- prescribes airworthiness standards for the issue of type certificates and changes to those certificates for propellers

36. **Noise Standards: Aircraft Type and Airworthiness Certification** -- prescribes noise standards for the issue of the following certificates: type certificates, and changes to those certificates, and standard airworthiness certificates for all aircraft

39. **Airworthiness Directives** -- prescribes airworthiness directives that apply to aircraft, aircraft engines, propellers, or appliances (referred to as "products") when an unsafe condition exists in a product and that condition is likely to exist or develop in other products of the same type design. It also prescribes inspections and the conditions and limitations, if any, under which those products may continue to be operated.

43. **Maintenance, Preventive Maintenance, Rebuilding, and Alteration** -- prescribes rules governing the maintenance, preventive maintenance, rebuilding, and alteration of any
    a. Aircraft having a U.S. airworthiness certificate
    b. Airframe, aircraft engine, propeller, or appliance of such an aircraft

45. **Identification and Registration Marking** -- prescribes the requirements for
    a. Identification of aircraft and identification of aircraft engines and propellers that are manufactured under the terms of a type or production certificate
    b. Identification of certain replacement and modified parts produced for installation on type-certificated products
    c. Nationality and registration marking of U.S.-registered aircraft

47. **Aircraft Registration** -- prescribes the requirements for registering aircraft, Certificate of Aircraft Registrations, and Dealers' Aircraft Registration Certificates

49. **Recording of Aircraft Titles and Security Documents** -- applies to the recording of certain conveyances affecting title to, or any interest in, any registered aircraft, any specifically identified aircraft engine of 750 or more rated takeoff horsepower, or any specifically identified aircraft propeller able to absorb 750 or more rated takeoff shaft horsepower

D -- AIRMEN

60. **Flight Simulation Training Device Initial and Continuing Qualification and Use** -- prescribes the rules governing the initial and continuing qualification and use of all aircraft flight simulation training devices (FSTD) used for meeting training, evaluation, or flight experience requirements for flight crewmember certification or qualification

61. **Certification: Pilots, Flight Instructors, and Ground Instructors** -- prescribes the requirements for issuing pilot, flight instructor, and ground instructor certificates and ratings, the conditions under which those certificates and ratings are necessary, and the privileges and limitations of those certificates and ratings

63. **Certification: Flight Crewmembers Other than Pilots** -- prescribes the requirements for issuing flight engineer and flight navigator certificates and the general operating rules for holders of those certificates

65. **Certification: Airmen Other than Flight Crewmembers** -- prescribes the requirements for issuing the following certificates and associated ratings and the general operating rules for the holders of those certificates and ratings:

   a. Air traffic control tower operators
   b. Aircraft dispatchers
   c. Mechanics
   d. Repairmen
   e. Parachute riggers

67. **Medical Standards and Certification** -- prescribes the medical standards for issuing medical certificates for airmen

   a. It sets forth the medical standards and certification procedures for 1st-class, 2nd-class, and 3rd-class medical certificates and indicates who may administer these exams.

E -- AIRSPACE

71. **Designation of Class A, B, C, D, and E Airspace Areas; Air Traffic Service Routes; and Reporting Points** -- defines Class A, Class B, Class C, Class D, and Class E airspace areas; air traffic service routes; and reporting points

73. **Special Use Airspace** -- prescribes the requirements for airspace designated as special use airspace such as restricted and prohibited areas

77. **Safe, Efficient Use, and Preservation of the Navigable Airspace**

   a. Establishes standards for determining obstructions in navigable airspace
   b. Sets forth the requirements for notice to the FAA of certain proposed construction or alteration
   c. Provides for aeronautical studies of obstructions to air navigation to determine their effect on the safe and efficient use of airspace
   d. Provides for public hearings on the hazardous effect of proposed construction or alteration on air navigation
   e. Provides for establishing antenna farm areas

F -- AIR TRAFFIC AND GENERAL OPERATING RULES

91. **General Operating and Flight Rules** -- prescribes rules governing the operation of aircraft (other than moored balloons, kites, unmanned rockets, and unmanned free balloons) within the United States

93. **Special Air Traffic Rules** -- prescribes special air traffic rules for operating aircraft in certain areas identified in this part.

95. **IFR Altitudes** -- prescribes altitudes governing the operation of aircraft under IFR on federal airways, jet routes, area navigation low or high routes, or other direct routes for which an MEA (minimum en route altitude) is designated in this part. In addition, it designates mountainous areas and changeover points.

97. **Standard Instrument Procedures** -- prescribes standard instrument approach procedures for instrument letdown to airports in the United States and the weather minimums that apply to takeoffs and landings under IFR at those airports

99. **Security Control of Air Traffic** -- prescribes rules for operating civil aircraft in a defense area, or into, within, or out of the United States through an Air Defense Identification Zone (ADIZ). ADIZs are areas of airspace over land or water in which the ready identification, location, and control of civil aircraft are required in the interest of national security.

101. **Moored Balloons, Kites, Amateur Rockets and Unmanned Free Balloons** -- prescribes the operation of moored balloons, kites, unmanned rockets, and unmanned free balloons

103. **Ultralight Vehicles** -- prescribes rules governing the operation of ultralight vehicles in the United States

105. **Parachute Operations** -- prescribes rules governing parachute jumps made in the United States except parachute jumps necessary because of an in-flight emergency

G -- AIR CARRIERS AND OPERATORS FOR COMPENSATION OR HIRE: CERTIFICATION AND OPERATIONS

110. **General Requirements** -- lists several important definitions used throughout subchapter G

117. **Flight and Duty Limitations and Rest Requirements: Flightcrew Members** -- prescribes duty and rest requirements relating to commercial operations and operators governed by subchapter G

119. **Certification: Air Carriers and Commercial Operators** -- prescribes the certification requirements to obtain a certificate authorizing operations under Part 121, 125, or 135

120. **Drug and Alcohol Testing Program** -- prescribes rules and procedures for testing airmen for use of drugs and alcohol

121. **Operating Requirements: Domestic, Flag, and Supplemental Operations** -- prescribes rules governing the domestic, flag, and supplemental operations of each person who holds or is required to hold an air carrier certificate or operating certificate under Part 119

125. **Certification and Operations: Airplanes Having a Seating Capacity of 20 or More Passengers or a Maximum Payload Capacity of 6,000 Pounds or More; and Rules Governing Persons on Board Such Aircraft** -- prescribes rules governing the operations of U.S.-registered civil airplanes that have a seating configuration of 20 or more passengers or a maximum payload capacity of 6,000 lb. or more when common carriage is not involved

129. **Operations: Foreign Air Carriers and Foreign Operators of U.S.-Registered Aircraft Engaged in Common Carriage** -- prescribes the rules governing the operation within the United States of each foreign air carrier holding a permit issued by the U.S. Department of Transportation

    a.   It also applies to U.S.-registered aircraft operated in common carriage by a foreign person or foreign air carrier solely outside the U.S.

133. **Rotorcraft External-Load Operations** -- prescribes airworthiness certification rules and operating and certification rules for civil rotorcraft conducting external-load operations

135. **Operating Requirements: Commuter and On Demand Operations and Rules Governing Persons on Board Such Aircraft** -- prescribes the rules governing the commuter or on-demand operations of each person who holds or is required to hold an air carrier certificate or operating certificate under Part 119

136. **Commercial Air Tours and National Parks Air Tour Management** -- applies to each person operating or intending to operate a commercial air tour in an airplane or helicopter. The rules also apply to all occupants of the airplane or helicopter engaged in a commercial air tour.

137. **Agricultural Aircraft Operations** -- prescribes rules governing agricultural aircraft operations within the United States and the issue of commercial and private agricultural aircraft operator certificates for those operations

139. **Certification of Airports** -- prescribes rules governing the certification and operation of land airports that serve any scheduled or unscheduled passenger operation of an air carrier that is conducted with an aircraft having a seating capacity of more than 30 passengers

H -- SCHOOLS AND OTHER CERTIFICATED AGENCIES

141. **Pilot Schools** -- prescribes the requirements for issuing pilot school certificates, provisional pilot school certificates, and associated ratings and the general operating rules for the holders of those certificates and ratings

142. **Training Centers** -- prescribes the requirements governing the certification and operation of aviation training centers. With some exceptions, this part provides an alternative means to accomplish training required by Part 61, 63, 121, 125, 127, 135, or 137.

145. **Repair Stations** -- prescribes the requirements for issuing repair station certificates and associated ratings to facilities for the maintenance and alteration of airframes, powerplants, propellers, or appliances. It also prescribes the general operating rules for the holders of those certificates and ratings.

147. **Aviation Maintenance Technician Schools** -- prescribes the requirements for issuing aviation maintenance technician school certificates and associated ratings, and the general operating rules for the holders of those certificates and ratings

I -- AIRPORTS

150. **Airport Noise Compatibility Planning** -- prescribes the procedures, standards, and methodology governing the development, submission, and review of airport noise exposure maps and airport noise compatibility programs by operators of public use airports (including heliports), including the process for evaluating and approving or disapproving those programs

151. **Federal Aid to Airports** -- prescribes the policies and procedures for administering the Federal-aid Airport Program under the Federal Airport Act, as amended

152. **Airport Aid Program** -- prescribes the policies and procedures for administering the Airport Aid Program for airport development and planning grant projects under the Airport and Airway Development Act of 1970, as amended

153. **Airport Operations** -- prescribes requirements governing Aviation Safety Inspector access to public-use airports and facilities to perform official duties

155. **Release of Airport Property from Surplus Property Disposal Restrictions** -- applies to releases from terms, conditions, etc., in any deed, surrender of leasehold, or other instrument of transfer or conveyance by which some right, title, or interest of the United States in real or personal property was conveyed to a non-federal public agency to be used by that agency in developing, improving, operating, or maintaining a public airport or to provide a source of revenue from non-aviation business at a public airport

156. **State Block Grant Pilot Program** -- applies to grant applicants for the state block grant pilot program and to those states receiving block grants available under the Airport and Airway Improvement Act of 1982, as amended. This part prescribes the procedures by which a state may apply to participate and describes the administration, responsibilities, and enforcement of the program by the participating state.

157. **Notice of Construction, Alteration, Activation, and Deactivation of Airports** -- applies to persons proposing to construct, alter, activate, or deactivate a civil or joint-use (civil/military) airport, and sets forth requirements for notice to the FAA administrator

158. **Passenger Facility Charges (PFCs)** -- applies to PFCs as may be approved by the FAA and imposed by a public agency that controls a commercial service airport. This part also describes the procedures for reducing funds apportioned under Section 507(a) of the Airport and Airway Improvement Act of 1982 (as amended) to a large or medium hub airport that imposes a PFC.

161. **Notice and Approval of Airport Noise and Access Restrictions** -- implements the Airport Noise and Capacity Act of 1990 and applies to airports imposing restrictions on Stage 2 and Stage 3 aircraft (as defined in Part 36) operations and the FAA procedures of evaluating these restrictions imposed by airport operators

169. **Expenditures of Federal Funds for Nonmilitary Airports or Air Navigation Facilities Thereon** -- prescribes the requirements for issuing a written recommendation and certification that a proposed project is reasonably necessary for use in air commerce or in the interests of national defense

J -- NAVIGATIONAL FACILITIES

170. **Establishment and Discontinuance Criteria for Air Traffic Control Services and Navigational Facilities** -- sets forth establishment and discontinuance criteria for navigation aids and air traffic control towers

171. **Non-Federal Navigation Facilities** -- sets forth minimum requirements for the approval and operation of non-federal VOR, NDB, ILS, and other navigational facilities that are to be involved in the approval of instrument flight rules and air traffic control procedures related to those facilities

K -- ADMINISTRATIVE REGULATIONS

183. **Representatives of the Administrator** -- describes the requirements for designating private persons to act as representatives of the Administrator (FAA) in examining, inspecting, and testing persons and aircraft for the purpose of issuing airman and aircraft certificates

185. **Testimony by Employees and Production of Records in Legal Proceedings, and Service of Legal Process and Pleadings** -- names the FAA officials upon whom legal process or pleadings may be served in any legal proceeding concerning the FAA and who otherwise perform the functions in legal proceedings concerning the FAA with respect to testimony by FAA employees and production of FAA records in legal proceedings

187. **Fees** -- prescribes fees only for FAA services for which fees are not prescribed in other parts of the Federal Aviation Regulations

189. **Use of Federal Aviation Administration Communications System** -- describes the kinds of messages that may be transmitted by FAA communications stations and prescribes the charges therefor

193. **Protection of Voluntarily Submitted Information** -- describes when and how the FAA protects from disclosure safety and security information that you submit voluntarily to the FAA

N -- WAR RISK INSURANCE

198. **Aviation Insurance** -- prescribes the eligibility, types of insurance, and amount of insurance coverage available for aircraft operating outside the U.S. and under the direction of the U.S. government that are necessary to carry out the foreign policy of the U.S.

END OF STUDY UNIT

STUDY UNIT FIVE
AIRPLANE PERFORMANCE AND WEIGHT AND BALANCE

(30 pages of outline)

Performance means the ability of an airplane to accomplish certain things that make it useful for certain purposes. For example, the ability of the airplane to land and take off in a very short distance is important to the pilot who operates in and out of confined fields. The ability to carry heavy loads, fly at high altitudes at fast speeds, or travel long distances is essential performance for operators of airlines and executive-type airplanes. The charts and tables used to determine an airplane's performance are found in Section 5, Performance, of that airplane's FAA-approved Airplane Flight Manual (AFM) and/or Pilot's Operating Handbook (POH).

The weight and balance of the airplane will also affect airplane performance and must be reviewed prior to each flight, particularly cross-country flights. The information and charts used to determine an airplane's weight and balance are found in Section 6, Weight and Balance/Equipment List, of that airplane's AFM/POH. You should never attempt a flight until you are satisfied with the weight and balance condition.

5.1 DETERMINANTS OF AIRPLANE PERFORMANCE

1. **Air density** is perhaps the single most important factor affecting airplane performance. The general rule is that, as air density decreases, airplane performance decreases.

   a. Temperature, altitude, barometric pressure, and humidity all affect air density. The density of the air DECREASES as

      1) Air temperature INCREASES
      2) Altitude INCREASES
      3) Barometric pressure DECREASES
      4) Humidity INCREASES

   b. The engine produces power in proportion to the density of the air.

      1) As air density decreases, the power output of the engine decreases.

         a) This decrease in power is true of all engines not equipped with a supercharger or turbocharger.

    c.   The propeller produces thrust in proportion to the mass of air being accelerated through the rotating blades.

        1)   As air density decreases, propeller efficiency decreases.

    d.   The wings produce lift as a result of the air passing over and under them.

        1)   As air density decreases, the lift efficiency of the wing decreases.

2.   **Effect of Air Density on Lift and Drag**

    a.   Lift and drag vary directly with the density of the air.

        1)   As air density increases, lift and drag increase.
        2)   As air density decreases, lift and drag decrease.

    b.   Air density is affected by pressure, temperature, and humidity.

        1)   At an altitude of 18,000 ft., the density of the air is one-half the density at sea level (given standard conditions). If an airplane is to maintain the same lift at high altitudes, the amount of air flowing over the wing must be the same as at lower altitudes. Thus, the speed of the air over the wings (airspeed) must be increased at high altitudes.

            a)   This is why an airplane requires a longer takeoff distance to become airborne at higher altitudes than with similar conditions at lower altitudes.

        2)   Because air expands when heated, warm air is less dense than cool air.

            a)   When other conditions remain the same, an airplane will require a longer takeoff run on a hot day than on a cool day.

        3)   Because water vapor weighs less than an equal amount of dry air, moist air (high relative humidity) is less dense than dry air (low relative humidity).

            a)   Therefore, when other conditions remain the same, the airplane will require a longer takeoff run on a humid day than on a dry day.

            b)   The condition is compounded on a hot, humid day because the expanded air can hold much more water vapor than on a cool day. The more moisture in the air, the less dense the air.

    c.   Less dense air also causes other performance losses besides the loss of lift. Engine horsepower and propeller efficiency decrease because not as many air molecules are available for combustion, resulting in a loss of power, and because propeller blades (which are airfoils) are less effective when air is less dense.

        1)   Since the propeller is not pulling with the same force and efficiency as when the air is dense, it takes longer to obtain the necessary forward speed to produce the lift required for takeoff.

            a)   Thus, the airplane requires a longer takeoff run.
            b)   The rate of climb will also be lower for the same reasons.

    d.   From the above discussion, it is obvious that a pilot should beware of high, hot, and humid conditions, i.e., high altitudes, hot temperatures, and high moisture content (high relative humidity).

3.   **Conditions that Affect an Airplane's Takeoff Performance**

    a.   As air density decreases, the takeoff run increases.

        1)   If an airplane of a given weight and configuration is operated at a higher density altitude, the airplane will still require the same amount of dynamic pressure to produce the lift required to become airborne.

            a)   Thus, the airplane will take off at the same indicated airspeed at all density altitudes because the airspeed indicator measures the dynamic pressure, as explained in Study Unit 2, Subunit 4.

            b)   Due to the reduced air density, the true airspeed will be greater.

b. A headwind will shorten the takeoff run and increase the angle of climb relative to the ground.

c. A tailwind will increase the takeoff run and decrease the angle of climb relative to the ground.

    1) Taking off with a tailwind decreases performance significantly.

d. A runway that is muddy, wet, soft, rough, or covered with snow or tall grass has a retarding force and increases the takeoff distance.

e. On takeoff, an upslope runway provides a retarding force that impedes acceleration, resulting in a longer ground run.

    1) Downhill operations will usually shorten the distance.

4. **Conditions that Affect an Airplane's Cruise Performance**

a. As air density decreases (e.g., an increase in altitude), available engine power decreases.

    1) However, because drag also decreases, less thrust is required to maintain a given airspeed.

    2) Thus, fuel consumption decreases as altitude increases.

b. A headwind will decrease groundspeed and consequently increase the total amount of fuel consumed for that flight.

    1) A tailwind will increase the groundspeed and conserve fuel.

5. **Conditions that Affect an Airplane's Landing Performance**

a. As air density decreases, required landing distance increases.

    1) However, indicated airspeed for landing is the same for an airplane at all altitudes.

b. A headwind will require a steeper approach angle and shorten the landing roll.

c. A tailwind will require a shallower approach angle and increase the landing roll.

    1) Landing with a tailwind decreases performance significantly.

d. A runway that is muddy, wet, soft, rough, or covered with snow or tall grass may decrease the landing roll.

    1) However, ice or snow covering the surface (except for deep snow or slush) will affect braking action and increase the landing roll considerably.

e. Landing uphill usually results in a shorter landing roll.

    1) Downhill operations will usually increase the landing roll.

5.2 STANDARD ATMOSPHERE

1. The **international standard atmosphere (ISA)** is a hypothetical atmosphere based on certain average conditions worldwide. These include

a. A sea-level surface temperature of 15°C (59°F)

b. A sea-level surface pressure of 29.92 in. Hg (1013.2 hPa)

    1) Hg is the abbreviation for mercury.

    2) hPa is the abbreviation for hectoPascal, which is the unit of pressure measurement in the metric system.

c. Relative humidity of 0%

d. A standard temperature lapse rate (i.e., a decrease in temperature as altitude increases) of approximately 2°C per 1,000 ft.

e. A standard pressure lapse rate (i.e., a decrease in pressure as altitude increases) of approximately 1 in. Hg per 1,000 ft.

f. A standard decrease in density as altitude increases

2.   The ISA provides a basis from which to determine air density and thus to evaluate airplane performance in actual atmospheric conditions.

   a.   The performance charts prepared by airplane manufacturers are based on the ISA and analytically expanded for various parameters (e.g., weight, altitude, temperature, etc.). They appear in the airplane's AFM/POH.

3.   The following table shows the standard atmospheric conditions in 1,000 ft. increments up to 20,000 ft.

   a.   Note the rate of decrease in atmospheric pressure and temperature as altitude increases in light of the statements made in 1.d. and 1.e. previously.

Standard Atmosphere			
Altitude (ft)	Pressure (in. Hg)	Temp. (°C)	Temp. (°F)
0	29.92	15.0	59.0
1,000	28.86	13.0	55.4
2,000	27.82	11.0	51.9
3,000	26.82	9.1	48.3
4,000	25.84	7.1	44.7
5,000	24.89	5.1	41.2
6,000	23.98	3.1	37.6
7,000	23.09	1.1	34.0
8,000	22.22	-0.9	30.5
9,000	21.38	-2.8	26.9
10,000	20.57	-4.8	23.3
11,000	19.79	-6.8	19.8
12,000	19.02	-8.8	16.2
13,000	18.29	-10.8	12.6
14,000	17.57	-12.7	9.1
15,000	16.88	-14.7	5.5
16,000	16.21	-16.7	1.9
17,000	15.56	-18.7	-1.6
18,000	14.94	-20.7	-5.2
19,000	14.33	-22.6	-8.8
20,000	13.74	-24.6	-12.3

5.3 PRESSURE ALTITUDE

1.   In the ISA, sea-level surface pressure is 29.92 in. Hg (1013.2 hPa).

   a.   In this hypothetical atmosphere, pressure falls at a fixed rate as altitude increases.
   b.   Thus, in the standard atmosphere, any given pressure can be found at only one specific altitude.

2.   Pressure altitude is a theoretical altitude, based on your physical altitude when adjusted for nonstandard pressure.

   a.   High barometric pressure decreases pressure altitude; low barometric pressure increases pressure altitude.

3.   Pressure altitude can be determined by either of two methods:

   a.   By setting the barometric scale of the altimeter to 29.92 and reading the indicated altitude, or
   b.   By applying a conversion factor to the elevation according to the reported altimeter setting, as shown on the right side of the chart on page 302.

5.4 DENSITY ALTITUDE

1. Density altitude is a measurement of the density of the air.

   a. Density altitude is also a theoretical altitude. It is pressure altitude adjusted for nonstandard temperature.

      1) As air density decreases, density altitude is said to increase.

   b. Density altitude is used in determining an airplane's performance capabilities.

2. Because of the inescapable influence density altitude has on an airplane and engine performance, every pilot should understand its effects. Air density is affected by pressure, temperature, and humidity.

   a. The density of air is directly proportional to pressure.

      1) Since air is a gas, it can be compressed or expanded.

         a) When air is compressed (resulting in increased pressure), a greater amount of air occupies a given volume; thus, the density of air is increased.

         b) When pressure is decreased on a given volume of air, the air expands and occupies a greater space; thus, the density of air is decreased.

   b. The density of air varies inversely with temperature.

      1) As the temperature of the air increases, the air expands, occupying more volume.

         a) Thus, a given volume holds less air, and air density is decreased.

      2) As air temperature decreases, the air contracts and density is increased.

   c. Humidity is the amount of water vapor in the air and is not generally considered a major factor in density altitude computation because the effect of humidity is related more to engine power than to aerodynamic efficiency.

      1) Because water vapor weighs less than dry air, any given volume of moist air weighs less (i.e., is less dense) than an equal volume of dry air.

         a) Warm, moist air is less dense (i.e., has a higher density altitude) than cold, dry air.

      2) Humidity affects engine power because the water vapor uses airspace that is available for vaporized fuel.

         a) As humidity increases, less air enters the cylinders, causing a slight increase in density altitude.

      3) Aircraft performance charts do not account for variations in humidity.

         a) If high humidity does exist, it is wise to add 10% to your computed takeoff distance and anticipate a reduced climb rate.

   d. In the atmosphere, both temperature and pressure decrease with altitude and have conflicting effects on density. However, the fairly rapid drop in pressure as altitude is increased usually has a dominating effect over the decrease in temperature.

      1) Thus, we can expect the air density to decrease with altitude.

3. At power settings of less than 75% or density altitudes above 5,000 ft., it is essential that a normally aspirated engine be leaned for maximum power on takeoff unless the engine is equipped with an automatic altitude mixture control.

   a. The excessively rich mixture adds another detriment to overall performance.

   b. Turbocharged engines need not be leaned for takeoff in high density altitude conditions because they are capable of producing manifold pressure equal to or higher than sea level pressure.

    c.   At airports of higher elevations, such as those in the western U.S., high temperatures sometimes have such an effect on density altitude that safe operations may be impossible.

        1)   Even at lower elevations with excessively high temperature or humidity, airplane performance can become marginal, and it may be necessary to reduce the airplane's weight for safe operations.

4.   Density altitude is determined by finding the pressure altitude (indicated altitude when the airplane's altimeter is set to 29.92) and adjusting for the temperature.

    a.   This adjustment is made using a density altitude chart or a flight computer.

5.   **Density Altitude Chart**

    a.   Adjust the airport elevation to pressure altitude based upon the actual altimeter setting in relation to the standard altimeter setting of 29.92.

        1)   On the chart below, the conversion in feet is provided for different altimeter settings.

    b.   Plot the intersection of the actual air temperature (listed on the horizontal axis of the chart) with the pressure altitude (indicated by the diagonal lines).

    c.   Move straight across to the vertical column. This is the density altitude.

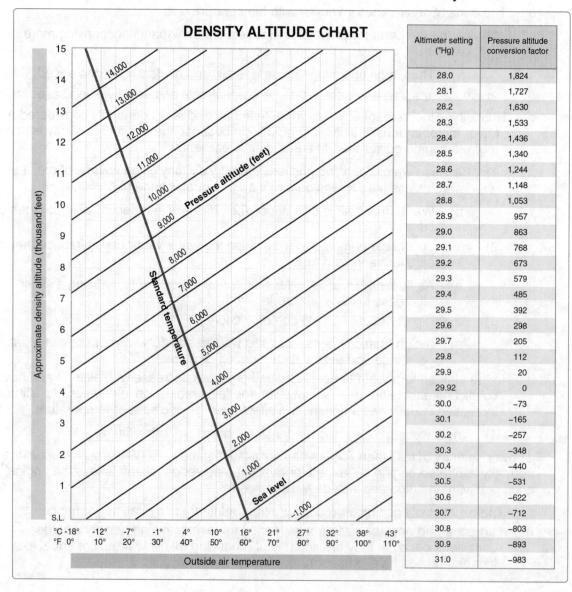

DENSITY ALTITUDE CHART

Altimeter setting ("Hg)	Pressure altitude conversion factor
28.0	1,824
28.1	1,727
28.2	1,630
28.3	1,533
28.4	1,436
28.5	1,340
28.6	1,244
28.7	1,148
28.8	1,053
28.9	957
29.0	863
29.1	768
29.2	673
29.3	579
29.4	485
29.5	392
29.6	298
29.7	205
29.8	112
29.9	20
29.92	0
30.0	−73
30.1	−165
30.2	−257
30.3	−348
30.4	−440
30.5	−531
30.6	−622
30.7	−712
30.8	−803
30.9	−893
31.0	−983

d. EXAMPLE: Outside air temperature 90°F
Altimeter setting 30.20" Hg
Airport elevation 4,725 ft.

1) Note that the altimeter setting of 30.20" Hg requires a –257-ft. correction factor.

2) Subtract 257 ft. from field elevation of 4,725 ft. to obtain pressure altitude of 4,468 ft.

3) Locate 90°F on the bottom axis of the chart, and move up vertically to intersect the diagonal pressure altitude line of 4,468 ft.

4) Move horizontally to the left axis of the chart to obtain the density altitude of 7,400 ft.

e. Some performance charts may require only pressure altitude and temperature; thus, you will not use a density altitude chart.

5.5 TAKEOFF PERFORMANCE

1. The minimum takeoff distance is of primary interest in the operation of any airplane because it defines the runway requirements.

   a. The minimum takeoff distance is determined by using the minimum safe speed that allows for a sufficient safety margin above stall speed, provides satisfactory control, and an initial rate of climb.

2. To obtain minimum takeoff distance, the forces that act on the airplane must provide the maximum acceleration during the takeoff roll. Any item that alters the takeoff speed or acceleration rate during the takeoff roll will affect the takeoff distance.

   a. The effect of gross weight on takeoff distance is significant, and proper consideration of this item must be made.

      1) Increased gross weight produces a threefold effect on takeoff performance.

         a) A higher takeoff speed is necessary to produce the greater lift required to get the airplane airborne.

         b) There is a greater mass to accelerate; thus, the rate of acceleration is reduced.

         c) Retarding force (drag and ground friction) is increased; thus, the takeoff distance is increased.

   b. Wind direction and velocity will have a significant effect on the takeoff roll.

      1) A headwind will reduce the overall takeoff distance because the airplane will reach its takeoff airspeed at a lower groundspeed, thus becoming airborne sooner than in calm wind.

      2) A tailwind will increase the takeoff distance because the airplane must achieve a greater groundspeed to attain the takeoff speed, thus becoming airborne later than in calm wind.

      3) The effects of a crosswind on takeoff performance will vary, depending on the wind direction. A 90° crosswind will have very little effect on takeoff distance.

      4) A gusting wind situation will require that the airplane's takeoff speed be increased slightly, thus keeping the airplane on the ground longer and increasing the overall takeoff roll.

   c. Takeoff distances in an airplane's AFM/POH are based on paved, dry, level runway conditions.

      1) A rough, dirt, or grass landing strip will retard acceleration and will considerably lengthen the takeoff distance.

      2) Standing water, snow, or slush on a paved runway or an uphill-sloping runway will also increase the takeoff distance.

d. The effect of proper takeoff speed is especially important when runway lengths and takeoff distances are critical.

   1) The takeoff speed specified in the airplane's AFM/POH is generally the minimum safe speed at which the airplane can become airborne.

   2) Attempting to take off below the recommended airspeed could mean that the airplane may stall, be difficult to control, or have a very low initial rate of climb.

      a) In some cases, an excessive angle of attack may not allow the airplane to climb out of ground effect.

   3) An excessive airspeed may improve the initial rate of climb and feel of the airplane, but it will produce an undesirable increase in takeoff distance.

e. An increase in density altitude has the following effects on takeoff performance:

   1) Decreased thrust and thus reduced accelerating force.

      a) Non-turbocharged engines have less available power.
      b) Propeller efficiency is decreased.

   2) Greater takeoff speed.

      a) A higher true airspeed is required to provide sufficient lift for takeoff.
      b) However, indicated airspeed will remain the same regardless of density altitude.

   3) Accurate determination of pressure altitude (not field elevation) and temperature is essential for predicting takeoff performance.

f. The most critical conditions of takeoff performance are the result of some combination of high gross weight, high airport elevation, high temperature, and unfavorable wind.

3. Takeoff performance data can normally be found in Section 5, Performance, in the airplane's AFM/POH. These data may be presented in either a graph or a chart.

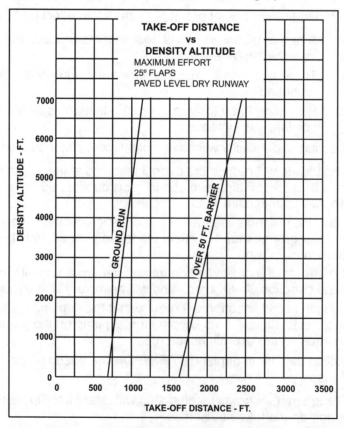

a. Takeoff performance graphs are presented either in terms of density altitude (as in the above example) or in terms of pressure altitude and temperature.

1) First, compute the density altitude using a chart (see page 302).

2) Second, find the density altitude on the left-hand side of the graph. Move horizontally to the right until you intersect the ground run line or the 50-ft. barrier line as appropriate.

3) From either point of intersection, drop vertically to the bottom of the graph to determine the takeoff distance in feet for your airplane.

4) EXAMPLE: At a density altitude of 1,000-ft., the ground run would be 750 ft., and it would require approximately 1,750 ft. to clear a 50-ft. obstacle with flaps at 25° and a paved, level, and dry runway.

b. Takeoff performance charts can often incorporate more variables, including headwind, gross weight, altitude, and temperature.

1) Takeoff performance is affected by the airplane's gross weight. The chart below gives the data for gross weight of 1,700, 2,000, and 2,300 lb. If you are carrying a gross weight between these figures, you must interpolate.

2) Headwind alternatives are 0, 10, and 20 kt. If actual headwind is between these figures, you must interpolate.

3) The altitudes given are sea level, 2,500, 5,000, and 7,500 ft. MSL. You must interpolate for altitudes between these numbers.

4) Separate distances are given for the ground run and for clearing a 50-ft. obstacle.

5) The notes to the chart indicate that you must

a) Increase the distance 10% for each 25°F above standard temperature at any altitude. Temperatures given on the chart are standard.

b) Increase distance (either for a ground run or for clearing an obstacle) by 7% of the "50-ft. obstacle" distance if using a dry grass runway rather than a paved runway.

6) EXAMPLE: If your gross weight is 2,150 lb. with no headwind at 5,000 ft. and 41°F, your ground run on a paved runway with no flaps would be 1,080 ft. This is halfway between the 905 ft. at 2,000 lb. and 1,255 ft. at 2,300 lb.

a) If the temperature were 66°F, you would have to add 10%, or 108 ft. Thus, your total ground run would be 1,188 ft.

TAKE-OFF DATA
TAKE-OFF DISTANCE FROM HARD SURFACE RUNWAY WITH FLAPS UP

GROSS WEIGHT POUNDS	IAS AT 50 MPH	HEADWIND KNOTS	AT SEA LEVEL & 59°F		AT 2500 FT. & 50°F		AT 5000 FT. & 41°F		AT 7500 FT. & 32°F	
			GROUND RUN	TOTAL TO CLEAR 50 FT. OBS	GROUND RUN	TOTAL TO CLEAR 50 FT. OBS	GROUND RUN	TOTAL TO CLEAR 50 FT. OBS	GROUND RUN	TOTAL TO CLEAR 50 FT. OBS
2300	68	0	865	1525	1040	1910	1255	2480	1565	3855
		10	615	1170	750	1485	920	1955	1160	3110
		20	405	850	505	1100	630	1480	810	2425
2000	63	0	630	1095	755	1325	905	1625	1120	2155
		10	435	820	530	1005	645	1250	810	1685
		20	275	580	340	720	425	910	595	1255
1700	58	0	435	780	520	920	625	1095	765	1370
		10	290	570	335	680	430	820	535	1040
		20	175	385	215	470	270	575	345	745

NOTES: 1. Increase distance 10% for each 25°F above standard temperature for particular altitude.

2. For operation on a dry, grass runway, increase distances (both "ground run" and "total to clear 50 ft. obstacle") by 7% of the "total to clear 50 ft. obstacle" figure.

5.6 CLIMB PERFORMANCE

1. Climb performance depends upon the airplane's reserve thrust (affects climb angle) and reserve power (affects climb rate). Reserve thrust/power is the available thrust/power over and above that required to maintain level flight at a given airspeed.

   a. EXAMPLE: If an airplane has an engine that produces 200 total available horsepower (HP) and the airplane requires only 130 HP at a certain level flight airspeed, the power available for climb is 70 HP.

2. Two airspeeds important to climb performance are the best angle-of-climb speed (V_X) and the best rate-of-climb speed (V_Y).

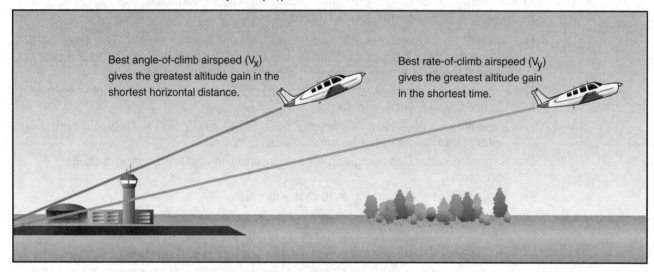

Best angle-of-climb airspeed (V_x) gives the greatest altitude gain in the shortest horizontal distance.

Best rate-of-climb airspeed (V_y) gives the greatest altitude gain in the shortest time.

   a. V_X provides the greatest gain in altitude for distance traveled over the ground and is used to clear obstacles immediately after takeoff on short-length runways.

      1) V_X occurs at the speed where the most reserve thrust is available. This speed is rather slow, probably very near the recommended takeoff speed of the airplane.

   b. V_Y provides the greatest gain in altitude over a period of time and is used during a normal takeoff or after clearing all obstacles during departure when V_X was used.

      1) V_Y occurs at the speed where the most reserve power is available. This speed is always faster than V_X (up to the absolute ceiling) due to the decreased drag encountered at a shallower climb angle.

   c. These airspeeds are found in the airplane's AFM/POH.

3. The climb performance of an airplane is affected by certain variables. Climb performance is most critical with high gross weight, at high altitude, in obstructed takeoff areas, or during malfunction of an engine in a multi-engine airplane.

   a. The conditions of the airplane's maximum climb angle or maximum climb rate occur at specific speeds, and variations in speed will produce variations in climb performance.

   b. Weight has a very pronounced effect on airplane performance.

      1) If weight is added to the airplane, it must fly at a higher angle of attack to maintain a given altitude and speed.

         a) A higher angle of attack increases induced drag (due to the additional lift being produced) as well as parasite drag (due to the additional fuselage area exposed to the relative wind).

            i) Additional power is needed to overcome increased drag, which means that less reserve power is available for climbing.

      2) Generally, an increase in weight will reduce the maximum rate of climb and require a higher climb speed.

c. An increase in altitude will also increase the power required and decrease the power available. Thus, altitude greatly affects climb performance.

    1) The speeds for maximum rate of climb and maximum angle of climb vary with altitude.

        a) As altitude increases, V_X increases.

        b) As altitude increases, V_Y decreases.

        c) As altitude increases, these various speeds finally converge at the absolute ceiling of the airplane.

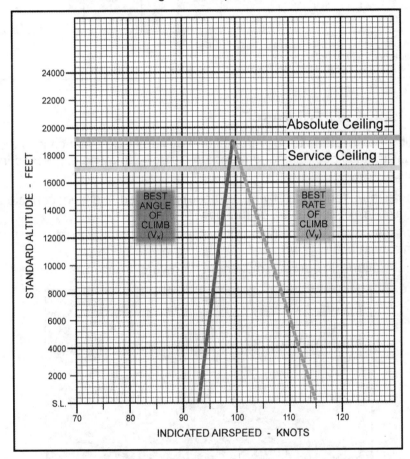

    2) At the **absolute ceiling**, there is no excess of power, and only one speed will allow steady level flight. Thus, the rate of climb is zero.

    3) The **service ceiling** is the altitude at which the airplane is limited to a climb rate of 100 feet per minute (fpm).

4. Climb performance charts are found in the airplane's AFM/POH.

    a. A climb performance chart provides information at various gross weights, altitudes, and temperatures. It states the indicated airspeed, the rate of climb (fpm), and gallons of fuel used.

    b. In the example chart on the next page, the gross weights of 1,700, 2,000, or 2,300 lb. are given on the left. Interpolate as necessary.

    c. Altitudes of sea level, 5,000, 10,000, or 15,000 ft. are given. Interpolate as necessary.

    d. The notes give important information. In the example chart, Note 3 says to decrease rate of climb by 20 fpm for each 10°F above the standard temperatures.

    e. EXAMPLE: With a gross weight of 2,000 lb. and pressure altitude of 5,000 ft. with a temperature of 61°F, the rate of climb is 570 fpm. Note that the 610-fpm rate of climb must be reduced by 40 fpm, since the temperature of 61°F is 20°F above the standard temperature of 41°F.

MAXIMUM RATE-OF-CLIMB DATA

GROSS WEIGHT POUNDS	AT SEA LEVEL & 59°F			AT 5,000 FT. & 41°F			AT 10,000 FT. & 23°F			AT 15,000 FT. & 5°F		
	IAS MPH	RATE OF CLIMB FT/MIN	GAL. OF FUEL USED	IAS MPH	RATE OF CLIMB FT/MIN	FROM S.L. FUEL USED	IAS MPH	RATE OF CLIMB FT/MIN	FROM S.L. FUEL USED	IAS MPH	RATE OF CLIMB FT/MIN	FROM S.L. FUEL USED
2300	82	645	1.0	81	435	2.6	79	230	4.8	78	22	11.5
2000	79	840	1.0	79	610	2.2	76	380	3.6	75	155	6.3
1700	77	1085	1.0	76	825	1.9	73	570	2.9	72	315	4.4

NOTES: 1. Flaps up, full throttle, mixture leaned for smooth operation above 3,000 ft.
2. Fuel used includes warm up and takeoff allowance.
3. For hot weather, decrease rate of climb 20 ft./min. for each 10°F above standard day temperature for particular altitude.

5.7 CRUISE AND RANGE PERFORMANCE

1. The ability of an airplane to convert fuel energy into flying distance is one of the most important items of airplane performance. This ability may be expressed in either range or endurance.

    a. If maximum range (i.e., flying distance) is desired, the flight condition must provide a maximum of speed versus fuel flow.

    b. If maximum endurance (i.e., flying time) is desired, the flight condition must provide a minimum of fuel flow.

    c. The relationship between maximum range/endurance is shown in the following image:

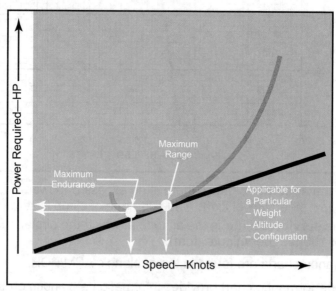

2. Cruise and range performance charts are found in the airplane's AFM/POH. These charts are normally based upon density altitude, the engine RPM setting, and fuel capacity.

    a. Charts in the AFM/POH will usually provide the following information:

        1) The percentage of brake horsepower (% of power)
        2) True airspeed
        3) Range in miles
        4) Endurance in time (hours)

b.   An example of one type of cruise performance chart appears below.

1)   Given the first two columns (altitude and RPM), the last five columns are the result.

2)   EXAMPLE: Given an altitude of 6,500 ft. and 2,500 RPM, you are using 66% power and will achieve a true airspeed of 126 mph, use 7.5 GPH, have an endurance of 4.7 hr., and have a range of 587 SM assuming no wind, standard conditions, etc.

a)   As in all performance charts, you must read the conditions and notes that apply (e.g., Note 4 refers to nonstandard temperature conditions).

CRUISE & RANGE PERFORMANCE				GROSS WEIGHT - 2,200 LBS. STANDARD CONDITIONS ZERO WIND LEAN MIXTURE		
ALTITUDE -- FT.	RPM	PERCENT POWER	TRUE AIR SPEED -- MPH	GALLONS/ HOUR	ENDURANCE HOURS	RANGE MILES
2500	2600	81	136	9.3	3.9	524
	2500	73	129	8.3	4.3	555
	2400	65	122	7.5	4.8	586
	2300	58	115	6.6	5.4	617
	2200	52	108	6.0	6.0	645
4500	2600	77	135	8.8	4.0	539
	2500	69	129	7.9	4.5	572
	2400	62	121	7.1	5.0	601
	2300	56	113	6.4	5.5	628
	2200	51	106	5.7	6.1	646
6500	2700	81	140	9.3	3.8	530
	2600	73	134	8.3	4.2	559
	2500	66	126	7.5	4.7	587
	2400	60	119	6.8	5.2	611
	2300	54	112	6.1	5.7	632
8500	2700	77	139	8.8	4.0	547
	2600	70	132	7.9	4.4	575
	2500	63	125	7.2	4.9	598
	2400	57	118	6.5	5.3	620
	2300	52	109	5.9	5.8	635
10500	2700	73	138	8.3	4.2	569
	2600	66	130	7.6	4.6	590
	2500	60	122	6.9	5.0	610
	2400	55	115	6.3	5.4	625
	2300	50	106	5.7	5.9	631

NOTES: 1. Range and endurance data include allowance for takeoff and climb.
2. Fuel consumption is for level flight with mixture leaned. See Section 4 for proper leaning technique. Continuous operations at powers above 75% should be with full rich mixture.
3. Speed performance is without wheel fairings. Add 2 MPH for wheel fairings.
4. For temperatures other than standard, add or subtract 1% power for each 10°F below or above standard temperature, respectively.

5.8 GLIDE PERFORMANCE

1.   Glide performance is the distance that an airplane will travel with the engine inoperative.

a.   The best glide distance is obtained by gliding at the angle of attack that provides the maximum lift-drag ratio (L/D_{MAX}). This optimal condition is determined for each airplane, and the speed at which it occurs at a given gross weight is used as the recommended best glide airspeed for the airplane.

2.   The effect of wind is to decrease range when gliding with a headwind component and to increase it when gliding with a tailwind component.

a.   The endurance (time) of the glide is unaffected by wind.

3. Variations in gross weight do not affect the gliding angle, provided the proper airspeed is used for each gross weight. Airplane manufacturers generally use a representative operational condition to determine the best glide airspeed.

   a. The fully loaded airplane will sink faster but at a greater forward speed. Although it will reach the ground much more quickly, it will have traveled exactly the same distance as the lighter airplane.

      1) The endurance of the glide is less for a heavier airplane than a lighter one.

4. Glide performance charts can be found in some AFMs/POHs. Note the stated conditions under which the chart values are determined and the manner in which various conditions can change these values.

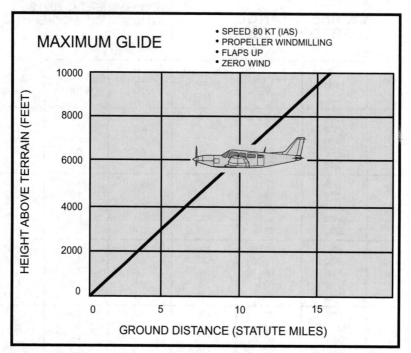

   a. The chart above illustrates a glide ratio of 52,800/6,000 = 8.8 to 1.0 because the airplane will glide 10 SM from 6,000 ft. (in no wind, flaps up, etc.). In other words, when the airplane is at 6,000 ft., the airplane can glide for 10 SM (5,280 ft. in a SM times 10 SM is 52,800 ft.).

5.9 CROSSWIND PERFORMANCE

1. Takeoffs and landings in certain crosswind conditions are inadvisable or even dangerous. If the crosswind is strong enough that the airplane is incapable of preventing a sideways drift, a hazardous landing condition may result.

   a. Always consider the takeoff or landing capabilities with respect to the reported surface wind conditions and the available landing directions.

   b. The airplane's AFM/POH indicates the maximum crosswind component capability of the airplane.

   c. Some AFMs/POHs have a chart so the pilot can determine the crosswind component.

2. Many airplanes have an upper limit to the amount of direct crosswind in which they can land (usually about 20% of stall speed). Crosswinds of less than 90° are converted into a 90° component on graphs. Variables on crosswind component graphs are

    a. Angle between wind and runway
    b. Knots of total wind velocity

3. Refer to the example crosswind component graph below.

    a. Note the example on the graph of a 40-kt. wind at a 30° angle.
    b. Find the 30° wind angle line (A). This is the angle between the wind direction and runway direction, e.g., runway 16 and wind from 190°.
    c. Find the 40-kt. wind velocity arc. Note the intersection of the wind arc and the 30° angle line (B).

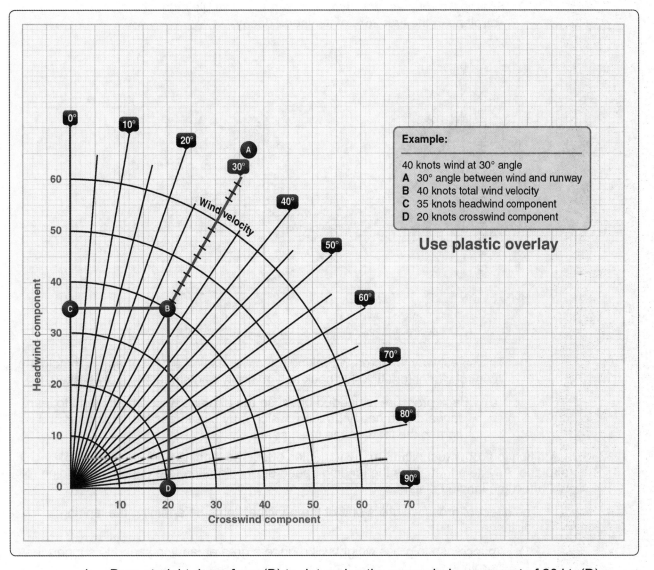

d. Drop straight down from (B) to determine the crosswind component of 20 kt. (D). Landing in this situation is like having a direct crosswind of 20 kt.
e. Back at (B), move horizontally to the left to determine the headwind component of 35 kt. (C). Landing in this situation is like having a headwind of 35 kt.

5.10 LANDING PERFORMANCE

1.   The minimum landing distance is obtained by landing at the minimum safe speed that allows sufficient margin above the stall speed and provides satisfactory control and capability for a go-around.

   a.   Generally, the landing speed is some fixed percentage of the stall speed or minimum control speed for the airplane in the landing configuration. This airspeed is found in the airplane's AFM/POH.

   b.   Minimum landing distance at the specified landing speed is obtained by the forces that act on the airplane, providing maximum deceleration during the landing roll.

   1)   At touchdown, the airplane is still producing lift, so the application of brakes is not effective.

   2)   For most airplanes, aerodynamic drag is the single biggest factor in slowing the airplane in the first 25% of its speed decay.

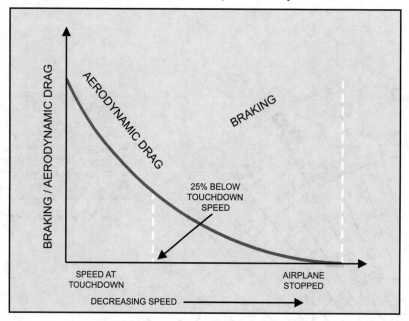

   3)   The safest way to increase braking effectiveness on a dry surface is to hold the control wheel (or stick) full back as you firmly and smoothly apply brakes.

   a)   Back pressure is needed because the airplane will normally tend to lean forward with heavy braking, which may overstress the nose gear and lighten the load on the main gear.

2.   In addition to proper technique, many variables affect the landing performance of an airplane. Any item that alters the landing speed or deceleration rate during the landing roll will affect the landing distance.

   a.   The effect of gross weight is one of the principal items determining the landing distance.

   1)   An increase in gross weight will require a greater landing speed to support the airplane.

   2)   The brakes are required to absorb more energy to stop the airplane, which will increase the landing distance.

b.   The effect of wind must be considered in predicting landing performance. Since the airplane will land at a particular airspeed independent of the wind, the principal effect of wind on landing distance is due to the change in groundspeed at which the airplane touches down.

   1)   A headwind will reduce the landing distance because the groundspeed at touchdown is reduced.

   2)   A tailwind will increase the landing distance because the groundspeed at touchdown is increased.

c.   Density altitude will affect the landing performance. An increase in density altitude will increase the touchdown groundspeed but will not alter the net retarding force.

   1)   The airplane at altitude will land at the same indicated airspeed but, because of the reduced density, the true airspeed (TAS) will be greater.

      a)   Thus, the higher TAS increases the touchdown groundspeed, which increases the landing distance.

   2)   As a general rule, the increase in landing distance is approximately 3.5% for each 1,000 ft. of altitude.

d.   The effect of proper landing speed is important when runway lengths and landing distances are critical.

   1)   The approach speeds specified in the airplane's AFM/POH are normally the minimum safe speeds at which the airplane can be flown.

      a)   Any attempt to approach the runway below the specified speed may mean that the airplane will stall, be difficult to control, or develop high rates of descent.

   2)   A higher-than-recommended speed at landing will improve the controllability somewhat (especially in crosswinds) but will cause an increase in landing distance.

      a)   The airplane may touch down farther down the runway and require more distance to stop.

e.   The runway condition and slope will also affect the landing distance.

   1)   A wet, icy, or snow-covered runway (concrete or grass) will not allow good braking and therefore will increase the landing distance.

      a)   All braking effectiveness may be lost if the airplane's tires are hydroplaning, which is caused by a thin layer of water that separates the tires from the runway.

         i)   Hydroplaning speed (in knots) is about nine times the square root of the tire pressure.

         ii)   Typically, the nosewheel tire will continue to hydroplane after the main wheels have stopped, which leads to steering difficulties.

   2)   A downsloping runway will increase the landing distance because the touchdown may be a little farther down the runway and the braking is not as effective going downhill as on a level or upsloping runway.

f.   The most critical conditions of landing performance are the result of some combination of high gross weight, high density altitude, and unfavorable wind.

   1)   These conditions produce the greatest landing distance and provide critical levels of energy dissipation required of the brakes.

   2)   In all cases, it is necessary to make an accurate prediction of minimum landing distance to compare with the available runway.

3.   Landing distance graphs or tables are found in the airplane's AFM/POH. Most assume a dry, paved, level runway surface. If these surface conditions do not exist, some charts will have correction factors. For those that do not, note that the actual landing performance will not match the values listed in the performance chart.

    a.   The data on the chart is based on the listed associated conditions, i.e., power, flaps, gear, runway, weight, and approach speed.

    b.   You need to distinguish between distances for clearing a 50-ft. obstacle and distances for ground roll.

        1)   Ground roll is the distance from touchdown until the airplane comes to a stop by using the recommended braking technique.

    c.   Example landing distances chart

        1)   Headwind alternatives are 0, 15, and 30 kt. If the actual headwind is between these figures, you must interpolate.

        2)   The altitudes given are sea level, 2,000, 4,000, 6,000, and 8,000 ft. MSL. If your altitude is between these figures, you must interpolate.

        3)   For each headwind and altitude, five outside air temperatures are given. You must interpolate if the current temperature is between two of these figures.

        4)   Ground roll is approximately 45% of the total distance over a 50-ft. obstacle (Note 1 on the Normal Landing Distances chart below).

NORMAL LANDING DISTANCES

ASSOCIATED CONDITIONS

POWER	OFF
FLAPS	35°
GEAR	DOWN
RUNWAY	PAVED, LEVEL, DRY SURFACE
WEIGHT	2750 POUNDS
APPROACH SPEED	85 MPH/74 KTS IAS

NOTES:
1. GROUND ROLL IS APPROXIMATELY 45% OF TOTAL DISTANCE OVER 50-FT. OBSTACLE
2. FOR EACH 100 LBS. BELOW 2750 LBS., REDUCE TABULATED DISTANCE BY 3% AND APPROACH SPEED BY 1 MPH.

WIND COMPONENT DOWN RUNWAY KNOTS	SEA LEVEL		2000 FT		4000 FT		6000 FT		8000 FT	
	OAT °F	TOTAL OVER 50-FT OBSTACLE FEET	OAT °F	TOTAL OVER 50-FT OBSTACLE FEET	OAT °F	TOTAL OVER 50-FT OBSTACLE FEET	OAT °F	TOTAL OVER 50-FT OBSTACLE FEET	OAT °F	TOTAL OVER 50-FT OBSTACLE FEET
0	23	1578	16	1651	9	1732	2	1820	6	1916
	41	1624	34	1701	27	1787	20	1880	13	1983
	59	1670	52	1752	45	1842	38	1942	31	2050
	77	1717	70	1804	63	1899	56	2004	49	2118
	95	1764	88	1856	81	1956	74	2066	66	2187
15	23	1329	16	1397	9	1472	2	1555	6	1644
	41	1372	34	1444	27	1524	20	1611	13	1707
	59	1414	52	1491	45	1575	38	1668	31	1770
	77	1458	70	1540	63	1626	56	1727	49	1833
	95	1502	88	1588	81	1682	74	1784	66	1898
30	23	1079	16	1142	9	1212	2	1289	6	1372
	41	1119	34	1186	27	1260	20	1341	13	1430
	59	1158	52	1230	45	1308	38	1395	31	1489
	77	1199	70	1275	63	1357	56	1449	49	1548
	95	1240	88	1320	81	1407	74	1502	66	1608

        5)   EXAMPLE: Given a weight of 2,750 lb., a 15-kt. headwind at 2,000 ft., and 52°F, the landing distance over a 50-ft. obstacle would be 1,491 ft. Ground roll would be 671 ft. (45% × 1,491 ft.).

5.11 STALL SPEED PERFORMANCE

1. Stall speed performance charts are designed to give an understanding of the speed at which the aircraft stalls in a given configuration (i.e., gear down, flaps retracted).

    a. This type of chart typically takes into account the angle of bank, the position of the gear and flaps, and the throttle position.

2. Use the figure below to find the speed at which the airplane stalls under the following conditions:

    a. Power..Off
    b. Flaps.. Down
    c. Gear.. Down
    d. Angle of bank...............................45°

Gross weight 2,750 lb			Angle of bank			
			Level	30°	45°	60°
			Gear and flaps up			
Power	On	MPH	62	67	74	88
		knots	54	58	64	76
	Off	MPH	75	81	89	106
		knots	65	70	77	92
			Gear and flaps down			
Power	On	MPH	54	58	64	76
		knots	47	50	56	66
	Off	MPH	66	71	78	93
		knots	57	62	68	81

    e. First, locate the correct flap and gear configuration. The bottom half of the chart should be used since the gear and flaps are down. Next, choose the row corresponding to a power-off situation. Now, find the correct angle of bank column, which is 45°. The stall speed is 78 mph, and the stall speed in knots would be 68 kt.

3. This table or a graph representing stall speed performance information may be found in your AFM/POH if it is provided by the manufacturer of your aircraft.

5.12 WEIGHT AND BALANCE OVERVIEW

1. **Effects of Weight on Flight Performance**

    a. Increased weight reduces the flight performance of your airplane in almost every respect. The most important performance deficiencies of the overloaded airplane are

        1) Higher takeoff speed required
        2) Longer takeoff run required
        3) Reduced rate and angle of climb
        4) Shorter range
        5) Reduced cruising speed
        6) Reduced maneuverability
        7) Higher stalling speed
        8) Higher landing speed required
        9) Longer landing roll required
        10) Lower maximum altitude
        11) Excessive weight on the nosewheel

2. **Effects of Weight on Airplane Structure**

    a. An airplane is certified to be able to withstand certain loads placed on its structure.

        1) As long as gross weight and load factor limits are observed, the total load on the airplane will remain within limits.

        2) If the maximum gross weight is exceeded, load factors well within the load factor limits can cause structural damage.

    b. Structural failures from overloading may be dramatic and catastrophic, but more often they affect structural components gradually in a way that is difficult to detect.

        1) The results of habitual overloading tend to be cumulative and may result in structural failure later during completely normal operations.

        2) Overloading can also accelerate metal fatigue.

3. **Effects of Balance on Flight Performance**

    a. The CG location affects the total load placed on the wings in flight.

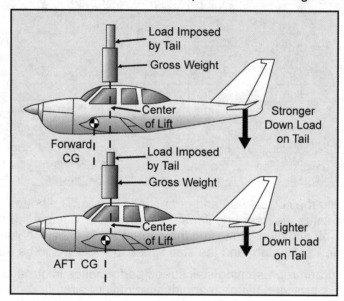

    b. With a forward CG, a greater downward force on the tail is required to maintain level cruising flight.

        1) The total lift required from the wing is increased.

        2) Thus, the wing flies at a higher angle of attack, which results in more drag and a higher indicated stall speed.

    c. With an aft CG, less downward force on the tail is required, resulting in less lift required by the wing.

        1) Thus, the wing flies at a lower angle of attack with less drag and a higher cruise speed.

4. **Effects of Balance on Stability**

    a. In general, an airplane becomes less stable and controllable as the CG moves aft.

        1) The elevator has a shorter arm (i.e., distance) from the CG and requires greater deflection to produce the same result.

        2) Recovery from a stall is more difficult because the airplane's tendency to pitch down is reduced.

        3) If the CG is moved beyond the aft limit, stall and spin recovery may become impossible.

    b.   As the CG moves forward, the airplane becomes more nose-heavy.

        1)   If the CG is moved beyond the forward limit, the elevator may no longer be able to hold the nose up, particularly at low airspeeds, e.g., takeoff, landing, and power-off glides.

5.13 WEIGHT AND BALANCE MANAGEMENT

1.   While there are no specified requirements for a pilot operating under 14 CFR Part 91 to conduct weight and balance calculations prior to each flight, 14 CFR 91.9 requires the pilot in command (PIC) to comply with the operating limits in the approved AFM/POH.

    a.   These limits include the weight and balance of the aircraft.

    b.   To enable pilots to make weight and balance computations, charts and graphs are provided in the approved AFM/POH.

2.   Weight and balance control should be a matter of concern to all pilots. The pilot controls loading and fuel management (the two variable factors that can change both total weight and CG location) of a particular aircraft.

3.   The aircraft owner or operator should ensure that up-to-date information is available for pilot use and that appropriate entries are made in the records when repairs or modifications have been accomplished.

    a.   The removal or addition of equipment results in changes to the CG.

        1)   Weight changes must be accounted for and the proper notations made in weight and balance records.

        2)   The equipment list must be updated, if appropriate.

        3)   Without such information, the pilot has no basis for the necessary calculations and decisions.

4.   Before any flight, the pilot should determine the weight and balance condition of the aircraft. Simple and orderly procedures based on sound principles have been devised by the manufacturer for the determination of loading conditions.

    a.   The pilot uses these procedures and exercises good judgment when determining weight and balance.

        1)   In many modern aircraft, it is not possible to fill all seats, baggage compartments, and fuel tanks, and still remain within the approved weight and balance limits.

        2)   If the maximum passenger load is carried, the pilot must often reduce the fuel load or reduce the amount of baggage.

5.14 WEIGHT AND BALANCE TERMS

1.   **Arm** -- the horizontal distance, usually measured in inches, from the reference datum to the center of gravity (CG) of an item.

    a.   Arms ahead of the reference datum are negative (–), and those behind the reference datum are positive (+).

    b.   When the reference datum is ahead of the airplane, all of the arms are positive and computational errors are minimized.

2.   **Basic empty weight** -- the standard empty weight plus any optional equipment that has been installed.

3.   **Center of gravity (CG)** -- the point at which an airplane would balance if it were possible to suspend it at that point. The distance of the CG from the reference datum is determined by dividing the total moment by the total weight of the airplane.

4. **CG limits** -- the extreme (forward and aft) center of gravity locations within which the airplane must be operated at a given weight.

5. **Maximum landing weight** -- the maximum weight approved for the landing touchdown.

6. **Maximum ramp weight** -- the maximum weight approved for ground maneuvers. It includes the weight of start, taxi, and runup fuel.

7. **Maximum takeoff weight** -- the maximum weight approved for the start of the takeoff run.

8. **Maximum zero fuel weight** -- the maximum weight exclusive of usable fuel.

9. **Moment** -- a force that causes or tries to cause an object to rotate. Moment is the product of the weight (in pounds) of an item multiplied by its arm (in inches). Moments are generally expressed in pound-inches (lb.-in.).

10. **Moment index** -- the moment divided by a reduction number, such as 100 or 1,000, to make the moment value smaller and reduce the chance of mathematical errors in computing the center of gravity.

11. **Payload** -- the weight of occupants, cargo, and baggage.

12. **Reference datum** -- an imaginary vertical plane (or line) from which all horizontal distances are measured for balance purposes. The reference datum may be located anywhere the airplane manufacturer chooses.

    a. One popular location for the reference datum is a specified distance forward of the airplane, measured in inches from some point, such as the leading edge of the wing or the engine firewall.

13. **Standard empty weight** -- the weight of the airframe, engines, and all items that have fixed locations and are permanently installed in the airplane. Standard empty weight includes unusable fuel, full operating fluids, and full oil.

14. **Standard weights** -- established for numerous items involved in weight and balance computations.

    a. Gasoline is 6 lb./U.S. gal.
    b. Oil is 7.5 lb./U.S. gal.
    c. Water is 8.35 lb./U.S. gal.

15. **Station** -- a location along the airplane fuselage usually given in terms of distance from the reference datum.

16. **Unusable fuel** -- the fuel remaining in the airplane's fuel system after a runout test has been completed in accordance with the Federal Aviation Regulations.

17. **Usable fuel** -- the fuel available for flight planning.

18. **Useful load** -- the difference between takeoff weight (or ramp weight if applicable) and basic empty weight.

5.15 BASIC PRINCIPLES OF WEIGHT AND BALANCE

1. **Total weight** is the airplane's basic empty weight plus the weight of everything loaded on it.

    a. The point at which the airplane will balance is the center of gravity (CG). It is the imaginary point at which all the weight is concentrated.
    b. To provide the necessary balance between longitudinal stability and elevator control, the CG is usually located slightly forward of the center of lift.

2. The safe zone within which the CG must fall is called the **CG range**.

    a. The extremities of the range are called the forward and aft CG limits.
    b. These limits are usually specified in inches along the longitudinal axis of the airplane, measured from the datum.

    c.   The **datum** is an arbitrary point established by airplane designers. Its location may vary among different airplanes.

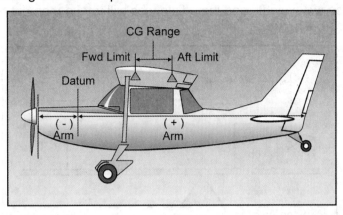

3.   The distance from the datum line to any component part of the airplane or any object loaded on the airplane is called an **arm**.

    a.   If the object or component is located aft of the datum, it is measured in positive (+) inches. If located forward of the datum, it is measured in negative (–) inches.

    b.   Recall that the moment is the weight of an object multiplied by its arm (distance from the datum). The moment is a measurement of the force which causes a tendency of the weight to rotate about a point or axis. It is expressed in lb.-in. or in.-lb.

4.   EXAMPLE: In the diagram below, a weight of 50 lb. is placed at a point 100 in. from the datum (fulcrum). The downward force of the weight at that spot can be determined by multiplying 50 lb. by 100 in., which produces a moment of 5,000 lb.-in. (50 × 100).

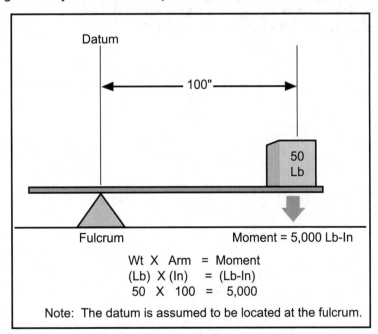

    a.   To establish a balance, a total of 5,000 lb.-in. must be applied to the other end of the board. Any combination of weight and distance which, when multiplied, produces 5,000 lb.-in. moment to the left of the datum will balance the board.

b. If a 100-lb. weight is placed at a point 25 in. to the left of the datum and a second 50-lb. weight is placed at a point 50 in. to the left of the datum, the sum of the product of these two weights and their distances will total a moment of 5,000 lb.-in., which will balance the board.

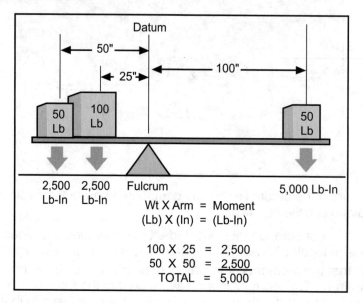

5.16 METHODS OF DETERMINING WEIGHT AND BALANCE

1. By Center of Gravity Calculations (page 321)
2. By Center of Gravity Charts (pages 321 through 323)
3. By Center of Gravity Tables (pages 324 and 325)

5.17 CENTER OF GRAVITY CALCULATIONS

1. The center of gravity (CG) is determined by dividing the total moments by the total weight.
2. Determine the CG location of the airplane shown below.

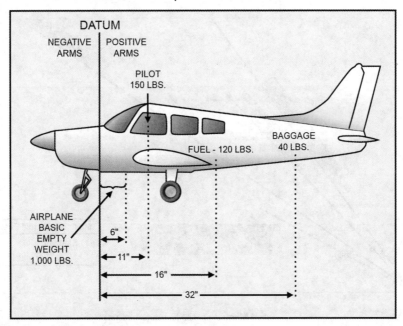

a. First, find the total weight of the airplane.

Item	Weight (lb.) ×	Arm (in.) =	Moment (lb. - in.)
Airplane basic empty weight	1,000	6	6,000
Pilot	150	11	1,650
Baggage	40	32	1,280
Fuel -- 20 gal. (6 lb./gal.)	120	16	1,920
TOTAL	1,310		10,850

1) Presumably, the total weight of 1,310 lb. is within the maximum weight limit. However, even if an airplane is certified for a specified maximum takeoff weight, it will not necessarily take off safely with this load under all conditions.

   a) Conditions that affect takeoff and climb performance are high elevations, high temperatures, and high humidity (high density altitudes).

   b) Other factors to consider prior to takeoff are runway length, surface, and slope; surface wind; and obstacles.

   c) These factors may require a reduction in weight prior to flight.

b. Second, compute the total moments (see the computations above).

c. Last, compute the CG and check to see that it is within the limitations contained in the airplane operating manual.

$$CG = \frac{\text{Total moments (lb.-in.)}}{\text{Total weight (lb.)}} = \frac{10,850}{1,310} = 8.28 \text{ in. aft of datum}$$

5.18 CENTER OF GRAVITY CHARTS

1. Graphs are frequently used to compute center of gravity.

   a. Loading graph -- used to compute the moment of individual items

   b. Center of gravity moment envelope graph -- used to determine whether the airplane's moment is within the acceptable CG moment, given the gross weight of the airplane

2. The **loading graph** may be used to determine the load moment.

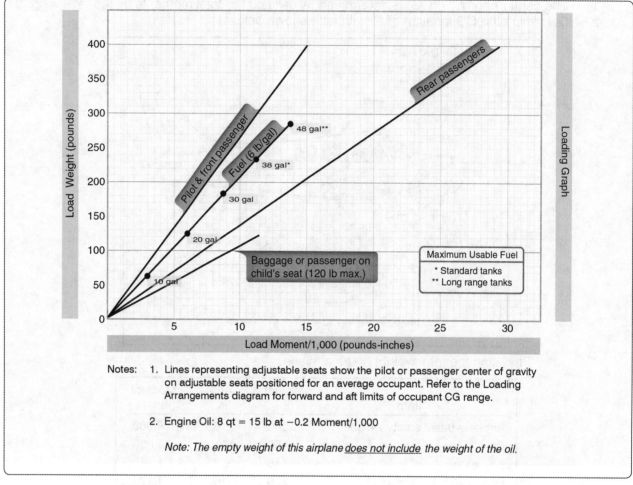

Notes: 1. Lines representing adjustable seats show the pilot or passenger center of gravity on adjustable seats positioned for an average occupant. Refer to the Loading Arrangements diagram for forward and aft limits of occupant CG range.

2. Engine Oil: 8 qt = 15 lb at –0.2 Moment/1,000

Note: The empty weight of this airplane does not include the weight of the oil.

a. On most graphs, the load weight in pounds is listed on the vertical axis. Diagonal lines represent various items such as fuel, baggage, pilot and front seat passengers, and back seat passengers.

   1) Find the appropriate weight in the left-hand column, then travel horizontally to intersect with the diagonal line representing the weight's category.
   2) From the intersection, travel vertically down the chart to read the load moment.

b. Then total the weights and moments for all items being loaded.

c. Note that each moment shown on the graph is actually a moment index, or moment/1,000. The index reduces the moments to smaller, more manageable numbers.

d. EXAMPLE: Determine the load (total) moment/1,000 in the following situation:

	Weight (lb.)	Moment/1,000 (lb.-in.)
Basic empty weight	1,364	51.7
Pilot & front seat passenger	400	?
Baggage	120	?
Usable fuel (38 gal.)	228	?

   1) Compute the moment of the pilot and front seat passenger by referring to the loading graph. Locate 400 on the weight scale, then move horizontally across the graph to intersect the diagonal line representing the pilot and front passenger. Move vertically to the bottom of the scale, which indicates a moment of approximately 15.0.

2) Locate 120 on the weight scale for the baggage. Move horizontally across the graph to intersect the diagonal line representing baggage. Then, move vertically to the bottom of the graph, which indicates a moment of approximately 11.5.

3) Locate 228 on the weight scale for the usable fuel. Move horizontally across the graph to intersect the diagonal line representing fuel. Then, move vertically to the bottom of the graph, which indicates a moment of 11.0.

4) Now add all the weights to determine that the airplane's maximum gross weight is not exceeded. Then add the moments.

	Weight (lb.)	Moment/1,000 (lb.-in.)
Empty weight	1,364	51.7
Pilot & passenger	400	15.0
Baggage	120	11.5
Fuel	228	11.0
	2,112	89.2

3. The **Center of Gravity Moment Envelope chart** is a graph showing CG moment limits for various gross weights. Acceptable limits are established as an area on the graph. This area is called the envelope. Weight is on the vertical axis and moments on the horizontal axis.

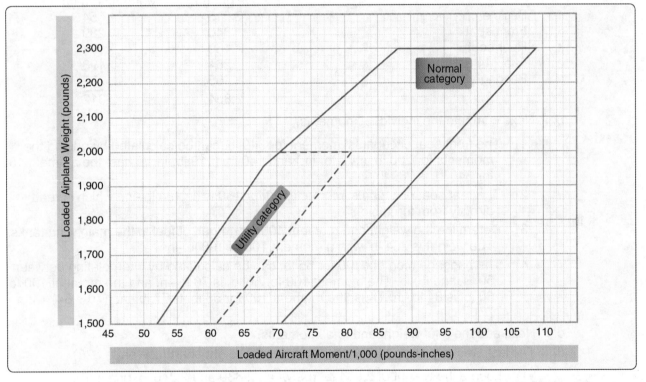

a. Draw a line upward from the loaded aircraft moment on the horizontal axis at the bottom of the chart.

b. Draw a line horizontally from the loaded aircraft weight on the vertical axis at the left-hand side of the chart.

c. The intersection will be within the CG moment envelope if the airplane has been loaded within limits.

d. EXAMPLE: Using the data above, draw a vertical line from 89.2 on the loaded aircraft moment at the bottom of the chart and a horizontal line from 2,112 lb. on the loaded aircraft weight on the left-hand side of the chart. The point of intersection will indicate that the aircraft is within both CG (i.e., normal category) and gross weight (i.e., less than 2,300 lb.) limits.

5.19 CENTER OF GRAVITY TABLES

1. Another approach to determining weight and CG limits is to use

   a. Tables of moments (see the following page)
   b. Tables of moment limits at various weights (see the following page)

2. First, determine total moment from the moment tables. Then check to see if the total moment is within maximum and minimum limits on the moment limit table.

3. EXAMPLE: Determine whether the airplane's weight and balance are within limits given the following data and using the tables on page 325.

Front seat occupants	340 lb.
Rear seat occupants	160 lb.
Fuel (main tanks)	44 gal.
Baggage	55 lb.

   a. As in most weight and balance problems, you should begin by setting up a schedule as below. Note that the empty weight (page 325) is given as 2,015 lb. with a moment/100 of 1,554 lb.-in.

	Weight (lb.)	Moment/100 (lb.-in.)
Basic empty weight	2,015	1,554
Front seat	340	289
Rear seat	160	194
Fuel (44 gal.)	264	198
Baggage	55	77
	2,834	2,312

   b. Next, compute the individual moments.

      1) The front seat occupants' moment for 340 lb. can be calculated by adding the moments for 200 lb. (170 lb.-in.) and 140 lb. (119 lb.-in.). Thus, the moment/100 for 340 lb. is 289 lb.-in.

      2) The rear seat occupants' moment/100 for 160 lb. is 194 lb.-in., which is read directly from the table.

      3) Determine the weight and moment/100 for 44 gal. of fuel in the main wing tanks. The weight is 264 lb. with a moment/100 of 198 lb.-in.

      4) The baggage moment/100 for 55 lb. can be calculated by interpolating between 50 lb. and 60 lb. The moment/100 for 50 lb. is 70 lb.-in. and the moment/100 for 60 lb. is 84 lb.-in. Thus, the moment/100 for 55 lb. is 77 lb.-in. [(70 + 84) ÷ 2 = 77].

   c. Next, add the total weight and total moments.

   d. The last step is to go to the Moment Limits vs. Weight chart (see page 325).

      1) Locate the weight of 2,834 lb. (between 2,830 and 2,840 lb. on chart).

      2) Note the moment/100 of 2,312 lb-in. is within the limits of 2,287 and 2,405 at 2,830 lb.

Useful load weights and moments

Baggage or 5th seat occupant

ARM 140

Weight	Moment 100
10	14
20	28
30	42
40	56
50	70
60	84
70	98
80	112
90	126
100	140
110	154
120	168
130	182
140	196
150	210
160	224
170	238
180	252
190	266
200	280
210	294
220	308
230	322
240	336
250	350
260	364
270	378

Occupants

Front seats ARM 85		Rear seats ARM 121	
Weight	Moment 100	Weight	Moment 100
120	102	120	145
130	110	130	157
140	119	140	169
150	128	150	182
160	136	160	194
170	144	170	206
180	153	180	218
190	162	190	230
200	170	200	242

Usable fuel

Main wing tanks ARM 75

Gallons	Weight	Moment 100
5	30	22
10	60	45
15	90	68
20	120	90
25	150	112
30	180	135
35	210	158
40	240	180
44	264	198

Auxiliary wing tanks ARM 94

Gallons	Weight	Moment 100
5	30	28
10	60	56
15	90	85
19	114	107

*Oil

Quarts	Weight	Moment 100
10	19	5

*Included in basic empty weight.

Empty weight~2,015
MOM/100~1,554
Moment limits vs weight
Moment limits are based on the following weight and center of gravity limit data (landing gear down).

Weight condition	Forward CG limit	AFT CG limit
2,950 lb (takeoff or landing)	82.1	84.7
2,525 lb	77.5	85.7
2,475 lb or less	77.0	85.7

Moment limits vs weight (continued)

Weight	Minimum Moment 100	Maximum Moment 100	Weight	Minimum Moment 100	Maximum Moment 100
2,100	1,617	1,800	2,500	1,932	2,143
2,110	1,625	1,808	2,510	1,942	2,151
2,120	1,632	1,817	2,520	1,953	2,160
2,130	1,640	1,825	2,530	1,963	2,168
2,140	1,648	1,834	2,540	1,974	2,176
2,150	1,656	1,843	2,550	1,984	2,184
2,160	1,663	1,851	2,560	1,995	2,192
2,170	1,671	1,860	2,570	2,005	2,200
2,180	1,679	1,868	2,580	2,016	2,208
2,190	1,686	1,877	2,590	2,026	2,216
2,200	1,694	1,885	2,600	2,037	2,224
2,210	1,702	1,894	2,610	2,048	2,232
2,220	1,709	1,903	2,620	2,058	2,239
2,230	1,717	1,911	2,630	2,069	2,247
2,240	1,725	1,920	2,640	2,080	2,255
2,250	1,733	1,928	2,650	2,090	2,263
2,260	1,740	1,937	2,660	2,101	2,271
2,270	1,748	1,945	2,670	2,112	2,279
2,280	1,756	1,954	2,680	2,123	2,287
2,290	1,763	1,963	2,690	2,133	2,295
2,300	1,771	1,971	2,700	2,144	2,303
2,310	1,779	1,980	2,710	2,155	2,311
2,320	1,786	1,988	2,720	2,166	2,319
2,330	1,794	1,997	2,730	2,177	2,326
2,340	1,802	2,005	2,740	2,188	2,334
2,350	1,810	2,014	2,750	2,199	2,342
2,360	1,817	2,023	2,760	2,210	2,350
2,370	1,825	2,031	2,770	2,221	2,358
2,380	1,833	2,040	2,780	2,232	2,366
2,390	1,840	2,048	2,790	2,243	2,374
2,400	1,848	2,057	2,800	2,254	2,381
2,410	1,856	2,065	2,810	2,265	2,389
2,420	1,863	2,074	2,820	2,276	2,397
2,430	1,871	2,083	2,830	2,287	2,405
2,440	1,879	2,091	2,840	2,298	2,413
2,450	1,887	2,100	2,850	2,309	2,421
2,460	1,894	2,108	2,860	2,320	2,428
2,470	1,902	2,117	2,870	2,332	2,436
2,480	1,911	2,125	2,880	2,343	2,444
2,490	1,921	2,134	2,890	2,354	2,452
			2,900	2,365	2,460
			2,910	2,377	2,468
			2,920	2,388	2,475
			2,930	2,399	2,483
			2,940	2,411	2,491
			2,950	2,422	2,499

5.20 WEIGHT CHANGE AND WEIGHT SHIFT COMPUTATIONS

1.   The FAA provides two formulas for weight change and one formula for weight shift. They are not reproduced here because the following weight change and weight shift formula is much simpler and intuitively appealing. It is adapted from a class handout developed by Dr. Melville R. Byington at Embry-Riddle Aeronautical University (used with permission).

2.   **Basic Theory.** At issue is the question: **If the CG started out there and certain changes occurred, where is it now?** It can be answered directly using a SINGLE, UNIVERSAL, UNCOMPLICATED FORMULA.

   a.   At any time, the CG is simply the sum of all moments divided by the sum of all weights.

$$CG = \frac{\Sigma M}{\Sigma W}$$

   b.   Since CG was known at some previous (#1) loading condition (with moment = M_1 and weight = W_1), it is logical that the previous CG becomes the point of departure. Due to weight addition, removal, or shift, the moment has changed by some amount, ΔM. The total weight has also changed if, and only if, weight has been added or removed. Therefore, the current CG is merely the current total moment divided by the current total weight. In equation format,

$$CG = \text{Current moment/Current weight}$$

$$CG = \frac{M_1 \pm \Delta M}{W_1 \pm \Delta W}$$

   c.   This UNIVERSAL FORMULA will accommodate any weight change and/or CG shift problem. Before proceeding, certain conventions deserve review:

   1)   Any weight added causes a + moment change (weight removed is −).
   2)   Weight **shifted** rearward causes a + moment change (forward is −).
   3)   A weight **shift** changes only the moment ($\Delta W = 0$).

3.   EXAMPLES:

   a.   An airplane takes off at 6,230 lb. with a CG location at station 79.0. What is the location of the CG after 50 gal. (300 lb.) of fuel has been consumed from station 87.0?

$$CG = \frac{M_1 \pm \Delta M}{W_1 \pm \Delta W} = \frac{6{,}230\,(79) - 300\,(87)}{6{,}230 - 300} = 78.6 \text{ in.}$$

   b.   An airplane takes off at 3,000 lb. with CG at station 60. Since takeoff, 25 gal. (150 lb.) of fuel has been consumed. Fuel cell CG is station 65. After takeoff, a 200-lb. passenger moved from station 50 to station 90. Find the resulting CG.

$$CG = \frac{M_1 \pm \Delta M}{W_1 \pm \Delta W} = \frac{3{,}000\,(60) - 150\,(65) + 200\,(90 - 50)}{3{,}000 - 150} = 62.54 \text{ in.}$$

   c.   Gross weight of an airplane is 10,000 lb.; 500 lb. of cargo is shifted 50 in. How far does the CG shift? (Note original CG and direction of shift are unspecified. Since datum is undefined, temporarily define it as the initial CG location, even though it is unknown. This causes M_1 to become zero. Incidentally, the direction of CG shift corresponds precisely to the direction of the weight shift.)

$$CG = \frac{M_1 \pm \Delta M}{W_1 \pm \Delta W} = \frac{500 \times 50}{10{,}000} = 2.5 \text{ in.}$$

END OF STUDY UNIT

STUDY UNIT SIX
AEROMEDICAL FACTORS AND
AERONAUTICAL DECISION MAKING (ADM)

(34 pages of outline)

6.1 FITNESS FOR FLIGHT

1. **Medical Certification**

   a. All airplane pilots must possess valid and appropriate medical certificates to exercise the privileges of their pilot certificates.

      1) The periodic medical examinations required for the medical certificate are conducted by FAA-designated aviation medical examiners (AMEs).

   b. Although a history of certain medical conditions may disqualify a pilot from flying, most pilots who do not meet medical standards may still be qualified under certain conditions.

      1) Conditional qualification may require that either additional medical information be provided or practical flight tests be conducted.

   c. Remember that the Federal Aviation Regulations prohibit you from performing crewmember duties while you have a known medical condition or an aggravation of a known medical condition that would make you unable to meet the standards for your medical certificate.

2. **Pilot Personal Checklist**

   a. Aircraft accident statistics show that pilots should conduct preflight checklists on themselves as well as their aircraft.

      1) Pilot impairment contributes to many more accidents than do failures of aircraft systems.

   b. **I'M SAFE** -- I am NOT impaired by

      I llness
      M edication

      S tress
      A lcohol
      F atigue
      E motion or eating

3. **Illness**

    a.   Even a minor illness can seriously impair your performance as a pilot.

        1)   Fever and other distracting symptoms can impair judgment, memory, alertness, and the ability to make calculations.

        2)   Also, any medication you are taking to combat these symptoms may itself decrease your performance as a pilot.

    b.   The safest rule is not to fly while suffering from any illness.

4. **Medication**

    a.   Pilot performance can be seriously impaired by both prescribed and over-the-counter medications.

        1)   Many medications, such as tranquilizers, sedatives, strong pain relievers, and cough-suppressant preparations, have primary effects that may impair judgment, memory, alertness, coordination, vision, and the ability to make calculations.

            a)   Others, such as antihistamines, blood pressure drugs, muscle relaxants, and agents to control diarrhea and motion sickness, have side effects that may impair the same critical functions.

        2)   Any medication that depresses the nervous system, such as sedatives, tranquilizers, or antihistamines, can make you more susceptible to hypoxia.

MOST COMMONLY EXPERIENCED SIDE EFFECTS AND INTERACTIONS OF OTC MEDICATIONS			
	MEDICATIONS	**SIDE EFFECTS**	**INTERACTIONS**
PAIN RELIEF/FEVER	**ASPIRIN** Alka-Seltzer Bayer Aspirin Bufferin	Ringing in ears, nausea, stomach ulceration, hyperventilation	Increase effect of blood thinners
	ACETAMINOPHEN Tylenol	Liver toxicity (in large doses)	
	IBUPROFEN Advil Motrin Nuprin	Upset stomach, dizziness, rash, itching	Increase effect of blood thinners
COLDS/FLU	**ANTIHISTAMINES** Actifed Dristan Benadryl Drixoral Cheracol-Plus Nyquil Chlortrimeton Sinarest Contac Sinutab Dimetapp	Sedation, dizziness, rash, impairment of coordination, upset stomach, thickening of bronchial secretions, blurring of vision	Increase sedative effects of other medications
	DECONGESTANTS Afrin Nasal Spray Sine-Aid Sudafed	Excessive stimulation, dizziness, difficulty with urination, palpitations	Aggravate high blood pressure, heart disease, and prostate problems
	COUGH SUPPRESSANTS Benylin Robitussin CF/DM Vicks Formula #44	Drowsiness, blurred vision, difficulty with urination, upset stomach	Increase sedative effects of other medications
BOWEL PREPARATIONS	**LAXATIVES** Correctol Ex-Lax	Unexpected bowel activity at altitude, rectal itching	
	ANTI-DIARRHEALS Imodium A-D Pepto-Bismol	Drowsiness, depression, blurred vision (see Aspirin)	
APPETITE SUPPRESSANTS	Acutrim Dexatrim	Excessive stimulation, dizziness, palpitations, headaches	Increase stimulatory effects of decongestants, interfere with high blood pressure medications
SLEEPING AIDS	Nytol Sominex	(Contain antihistamine) Prolonged drowsiness, blurred vision	Cause excessive drowsiness when used with alcohol
STIMULANTS	**CAFFEINE** Coffee, tea, cola, chocolate	Excessive stimulation, tremors, palpitations, headache	Interfere with high blood pressure medications

b. The safest rule is not to fly while taking any medication, unless approved by the FAA.

c. The table on the previous page lists the common over-the-counter medications and outlines some of their possible side effects that could affect your flying abilities. As with all drugs, side effects may vary with the individual and with changes in altitude and other flight conditions.

d. FAA advice on over-the-counter medications:

   1) Read and follow label directions for use of medication.

   2) If the label warns of side effects, do not fly until twice the recommended dosing interval has passed.

      a) EXAMPLE: If the label says "take every 4-6 hours," you should wait at least 12 hr. before you fly.

   3) Remember, the condition you are treating may be as disqualifying as the medication.

   4) When in doubt, ask your AME for advice.

   5) As a pilot, you are responsible for your own personal preflight. Be wary of any illness that requires medicine to make you feel better.

   6) If an illness is serious enough to require medication, it is also serious enough to prevent you from flying.

   7) Do not fly if you have a cold.

      a) Changes in atmospheric pressures with changes in altitude could cause serious ear and sinus problems.

   8) Avoid mixing decongestants and caffeine (contained in coffee, tea, cola, chocolate).

   9) Beware of medications that use alcohol as a base for the ingredients.

5. **Stress**

   a. Stress from the pressures of everyday living can impair pilot performance, often in very subtle ways.

      1) Difficulties can occupy thought processes so as to decrease alertness.
      2) Distraction can so interfere with judgment that unwarranted risks are taken.
      3) Stress and fatigue can be a deadly combination.

   b. When you are under more stress than usual, you should consider delaying flight until your difficulties have been resolved.

6. **Alcohol**

   a. As little as 1 oz. of liquor, 1 bottle of beer, or 4 oz. of wine can impair flying skills.

      1) Even after your body has completely destroyed a moderate amount of alcohol, you can still be severely impaired for many hours by hangover.

      2) Alcohol also renders you much more susceptible to disorientation and hypoxia.

   b. The Federal Aviation Regulations prohibit pilots from performing cockpit duties within 8 hr. after drinking any alcoholic beverage or while under the influence of alcohol.

      1) An excellent rule is to allow at least 12 to 24 hr. "from bottle to throttle," depending on how much you drank and the severity of the residual effects.

7. **Fatigue**

   a. Fatigue can be treacherous because it may not be apparent to you until serious errors are made.

      1) It is best described as either acute (short-term) or chronic (long-term).

    b.   Acute fatigue is the everyday tiredness felt after long periods of physical or mental strain.

        1)   Consequently, coordination and alertness can be reduced.

        2)   Acute fatigue is prevented by adequate rest and sleep, as well as regular exercise and proper nutrition.

    c.   Chronic fatigue occurs when there is not enough time for full recovery between episodes of acute fatigue.

        1)   Performance continues to fall off, and judgment becomes impaired.

        2)   Recovery from chronic fatigue requires a prolonged period of rest.

8.   **Emotion**

    a.   Consider whether you are emotionally upset about anything that may affect you personally.

        1)   Upsetting events, such as serious arguments, death of a family member, separation or divorce, loss of a job, and financial catastrophe, can render a pilot unable to fly an aircraft safely.

        2)   The emotions of anger, depression, and anxiety from such events not only decrease alertness, but also may lead to taking risks that border on self-destruction.

        3)   Any pilot who experiences an emotionally upsetting event should not fly until satisfactorily recovered from it.

9.   **Eating**

    a.   Proper nutrition is important for everyone, but even more so for pilots, who add the physical and mental demands of flying to their daily lives.

        1)   While simply eating the correct food is vital to health and wellbeing, it is also important to eat on a regular schedule and to eat proper portions based on the time of day.

    b.   Besides the benefits of safety in the cockpit, eating right poses obvious general health benefits, such as blood pressure and cholesterol stabilization, heart disease prevention, weight management, and diabetes prevention or control, among other benefits.

        1)   All of these benefits also keep you in compliance with and eligible for medical certification.

    c.   Malnourishment weakens the body and the mind, slowing reaction time to sudden changes and reducing critical thinking skills.

        1)   Eating regularly and correctly will provide you with mental and physical support in the cockpit.

6.2 HYPOXIA

1.   **Hypoxia** is a state of oxygen deficiency in the body sufficient to impair functions of the brain and other organs.

    a.   Although a deterioration in night vision occurs at a cabin pressure altitude as low as 5,000 ft. MSL, other significant effects of altitude hypoxia usually do not occur in the normal, healthy pilot below 12,000 ft. MSL.

    b.   From 12,000 to 15,000 ft. MSL (without supplemental oxygen), judgment, memory, alertness, coordination, and ability to make calculations are impaired.

    c.   Headache, drowsiness, dizziness, and either a sense of well-being (euphoria) or belligerence may occur.

2. **Types of Hypoxia**

     a.   **Hypoxic hypoxia** is a result of insufficient oxygen available to the body as a whole.

          1)   A blocked airway and drowning are obvious examples of how the lungs can be deprived of oxygen, but the reduction in partial pressure of oxygen at high altitude is an appropriate example for pilots.

          2)   The percentage of oxygen in the atmosphere is constant, but its partial pressure decreases proportionately as atmospheric pressure decreases.

              a)   There are fewer oxygen molecules available at the pressure required for them to pass between the membranes in the respiratory system.

                  i)   This decrease in number of oxygen molecules at sufficient pressure can lead to hypoxic hypoxia.

     b.   **Hypemic hypoxia** occurs when the blood is not able to take up and transport a sufficient amount of oxygen to the cells in the body.

          1)   This type of hypoxia is a result of oxygen deficiency in the blood, rather than a lack of inhaled oxygen, and can be caused by a variety of factors, such as

              a)   Reduced blood volume (due to severe bleeding)

              b)   Certain blood diseases (e.g., anemia)

              c)   Hemoglobin, which transports oxygen, is chemically unable to bind oxygen molecules

          2)   The most common form of hypemic hypoxia is carbon monoxide (CO) poisoning. This is explained in greater detail in Subunit 6.5.

          3)   Hypemic hypoxia can also be caused by the loss of blood due to blood donation. Blood can require several weeks to return to normal following a donation.

              a)   Although the effects of the blood loss are slight at ground level, there are risks when flying during this time.

     c.   **Stagnant hypoxia**, or ischemia, results when the oxygen-rich blood in the lungs is not moving, for one reason or another, to the tissues that need it.

          1)   An arm or leg "going to sleep" because the blood flow has accidentally been shut off is one form of stagnant hypoxia.

          2)   This kind of hypoxia can also result from shock, the heart failing to pump blood effectively, or a constricted artery.

          3)   During flight, stagnant hypoxia can occur with excessive acceleration of gravity (Gs).

          4)   Cold temperatures also can reduce circulation and decrease the blood supplied to extremities.

     d.   **Histotoxic hypoxia** is the inability of the cells to effectively use oxygen.

          1)   In this case, enough oxygen is being transported to the cells that need it, but they are unable to make use of it.

          2)   This impairment of cellular respiration can be caused by alcohol and other drugs, such as narcotics and poisons.

              a)   Research has shown that drinking one ounce of alcohol can equate to about an additional 2,000 feet of physiological altitude.

3.   The effects of hypoxia appear after increasingly shorter periods of exposure to increasing altitude.

   a.   Pilot performance can seriously deteriorate within 15 min. at 15,000 ft. MSL.

   b.   At altitudes above 15,000 ft. MSL, the periphery of the visual field turns gray. Only central vision remains (tunnel vision).

   c.   A blue color (cyanosis) develops in the fingernails and lips.

   d.   The ability to take corrective and protective action is lost in 20 to 30 min. at 18,000 ft. MSL.

      1)   This happens in 5 to 12 min. at 20,000 ft. MSL, followed soon by unconsciousness.

4.   Significant effects of hypoxia can occur at even lower altitudes given one or more of the following factors:

   a.   Carbon monoxide inhaled in smoking or from exhaust fumes

   b.   Small amounts of alcohol and low doses of certain drugs (e.g., antihistamines, tranquilizers, sedatives, and analgesics)

   c.   Extreme heat or cold, fever, and/or anxiety

5.   Hypoxia is prevented by understanding the factors that reduce your tolerance to altitude and by using supplemental oxygen above 10,000 ft. during the day and above 5,000 ft. at night.

   a.   Corrective action if hypoxia is suspected or recognized includes

      1)   Use of supplemental oxygen
      2)   An emergency descent to a lower altitude

6.3 DEHYDRATION

1.   **Dehydration** is the excessive loss of water from the body, as from illness or fluid deprivation.

   a.   This fluid loss can occur in any environment. Causes include hot cockpits and flight lines, high humidity, diuretic drinks (i.e., coffee, tea, cola), as well as improper attire.

2.   Some common signs and symptoms of dehydration include headache, fatigue, cramps, sleepiness, dizziness, and with severe dehydration, lethargy and coma.

   a.   Heat exhaustion often accompanies dehydration. Below are the three stages of heat exhaustion, along with accompanying signs and symptoms.

      1)   Heat stress (body temp., 99.5°-100° F) – reduces performance, decision-making ability, alertness, and visual capabilities.

      2)   Heat exhaustion (body temp., 101°-105° F) – fatigue, nausea/vomiting, cramps, rapid breathing, and fainting.

      3)   Heat stroke (body temp., >105° F) – body's heat control mechanism stops working, mental confusion, disorientation, and coma.

3.   To help prevent dehydration and heat exhaustion, you should drink two to four quarts of water every 24 hours. Or, follow the generally prescribed eight-glasses-a-day rule.

   a.   Because each individual is physiologically different, this is only to be used as a guide. Your daily fluid intake should be varied to meet your individual needs depending on work conditions, environment, and individual physiology.

   b.   Other useful tips on avoiding heat exhaustion are limiting your daily intake of caffeine and alcohol (both are diuretics), properly acclimating to major weather and/or climate changes, and planning ahead by carrying sufficient fluids and choosing appropriate attire for the forecast conditions.

6.4 HYPERVENTILATION

1. **Hyperventilation**, which is an abnormal increase in the volume of air breathed in and out of the lungs, can occur subconsciously when you encounter a stressful situation in flight.

    a. This abnormal breathing flushes from your lungs and blood much of the carbon dioxide your system needs to maintain the proper degree of blood acidity.

        1) The resulting chemical imbalance in the body produces dizziness, tingling of the fingers and toes, hot and cold sensations, drowsiness, nausea, and a feeling of suffocation. Often you may react to these symptoms with even greater hyperventilation.

    b. Incapacitation can eventually result from incoordination, disorientation, and painful muscle spasms. Finally, unconsciousness can occur.

2. The symptoms of hyperventilation subside within a few minutes after the rate and depth of breathing are consciously brought back under control.

    a. The buildup of the appropriate balance of carbon dioxide in your body can be hastened by controlled breathing in and out of a paper bag held over your nose and mouth. Also, talking, singing, or counting aloud often helps.

3. It is important to recognize that early symptoms of hyperventilation and hypoxia are similar.

    a. Also, hyperventilation and hypoxia can occur at the same time.

    b. If you are using an oxygen system when symptoms are experienced, set the oxygen regulator immediately to deliver 100% oxygen. This is to make sure you are not experiencing hypoxia.

    c. If it is not hypoxia, give attention to rate and depth of breathing.

6.5 CARBON MONOXIDE POISONING

1. Carbon monoxide is the product of incomplete combustion of material containing carbon. It is found in exhaust fumes and tobacco smoke.

    a. Carbon monoxide itself is a colorless, odorless, and tasteless gas, but it is usually mixed with other gases and fumes that can be detected by sight or smell.

2. When carbon monoxide is taken into the lungs, it combines with hemoglobin, the oxygen-carrying agent in the blood. The affinity of the hemoglobin for carbon monoxide is greater than for oxygen; consequently, hypemic (anemic) hypoxia occurs.

    a. Exposure to even small amounts of carbon monoxide over a period of several hours can reduce your ability to operate an airplane safely.

        1) Long exposure to low carbon monoxide levels is as hazardous as short exposure to relatively high concentrations.

    b. Susceptibility to carbon monoxide poisoning increases with altitude.

        1) The decreasing air pressure deprives your body of oxygen.
        2) When carbon monoxide is added, your body is further deprived of oxygen.

3. Most heaters in light aircraft work by air flowing over the exhaust manifold.

    a. Using these heaters when exhaust fumes are escaping through manifold cracks and seals is responsible for both fatal and nonfatal aircraft accidents from carbon monoxide poisoning.

    b. The danger is greatest during the winter months and at any time when the use of the cabin heating system becomes necessary and outside air vents are closed.

        1) The danger also exists at other times because carbon monoxide may enter the cabin through openings in the firewall and around fairings in the area of the exhaust system.

4. **Symptoms**

   a. Early symptoms of carbon monoxide poisoning are feelings of sluggishness, being too warm, and tightness across the forehead.

   b. These early symptoms may be followed by more intense feelings, such as headache, throbbing or pressure in the temples, and ringing in the ears.

   c. These symptoms may be followed by severe headache, general weakness, dizziness, and gradual dimming of vision.

   d. Large accumulations of carbon monoxide in the body result in loss of muscle power, vomiting, convulsions, coma, and finally death.

5. If you smell exhaust odors or begin to feel any of the symptoms, you should immediately assume carbon monoxide is present and take the following precautions:

   a. Immediately shut off the cabin air heater and close any other openings that might allow air from the engine compartment into the cockpit.

   b. Open outside air vents immediately.

   c. Avoid smoking.

   d. Use supplemental oxygen set to deliver 100% oxygen, if available.

   e. If you are flying, land at the first opportunity, and ensure that any effects from carbon monoxide are gone before further flight.

      1) If symptoms are severe or continue after landing, medical treatment should be sought.

   f. Determine that carbon monoxide is not being allowed to enter the cabin because of a defective exhaust, an unsealed opening between engine compartment and cabin, or any other factor.

6. Tobacco does more than deprive the body of oxygen because of the carbon monoxide content in smoke.

   a. Tobacco smoke lowers the sensitivity of the eye and cuts night vision by approximately 20%.

      1) Nicotine increases the body's heat production 10% to 15% above normal, creating added oxygen demands.

      2) Ironically, the same cigarette that increases the demand for oxygen also reduces the supply.

   b. Careful tests have shown that the carbon monoxide in tobacco smoke can lower the pilot's tolerance to altitude by as much as 5,000 to 6,000 ft. because the blood is saturated with carbon monoxide.

      1) Thus, pilots who smoke are already at altitude before they ever leave the ground and may need supplemental oxygen at a lower altitude than nonsmokers.

7. **Prevention**

   a. Although carbon monoxide is colorless and odorless, it can be detected by commonly available means.

   b. Inexpensive, disposable carbon monoxide detectors can be installed to provide a visual warning of the presence of this deadly gas leaking into the crew compartment.

   c. Electrically powered sensors can be installed remotely or in your aircraft panel to monitor for carbon monoxide. Audible and visual alarms signal the presence of the gas in concentrations as low as 1 ppm (part per million).

6.6 DECOMPRESSION SICKNESS AFTER SCUBA DIVING

1. If you or one of your passengers intends to fly after scuba diving, you should allow the body sufficient time to rid itself of excess nitrogen absorbed during diving.

   a. If this is not done, decompression sickness due to evolved gas (i.e., the nitrogen comes out of solution and forms bubbles in the bloodstream, an effect similar to opening a can of soda) can occur at low altitudes and create a serious in-flight emergency.

2. The recommended waiting time before flight to flight altitudes of up to 8,000 ft. is at least 12 hr. after a dive that has not required controlled ascent (nondecompression diving).

   a. You should allow at least 24 hr. after diving that has required controlled ascent (decompression diving) before flying at any altitude.

   b. The wait time before flight to flight altitudes above 8,000 ft. should be at least 24 hr. after any scuba diving.

3. These recommended altitudes are actual flight altitudes above mean sea level (MSL), not pressurized cabin altitudes. Using actual flight altitudes takes into consideration the risk of decompression of aircraft during flight.

6.7 MOTION SICKNESS

1. Motion sickness is caused by continued stimulation of the tiny portion of the inner ear that controls your sense of balance. The symptoms are progressive.

   a. First, the desire for food is lost.
   b. Then saliva collects in your mouth, and you begin to perspire freely.
   c. Eventually, you become nauseated and disoriented.
   d. The head aches, and there may be a tendency to vomit.

2. If suffering from airsickness, you should

   a. Open the air vents.
   b. Loosen clothing.
   c. Use supplemental oxygen, if available.
   d. Keep the eyes on a point outside the airplane.
   e. Avoid unnecessary head movements.
   f. Cancel the flight and land as soon as possible.

3. Although motion sickness is uncommon among experienced pilots, it does occur occasionally.

   a. Most importantly, it jeopardizes your flying efficiency, particularly in turbulent weather.

   b. Student pilots are frequently surprised by an uneasiness usually described as motion sickness.

      1) This sickness probably results from combining anxiety, unfamiliarity, and the vibration or shaking received from the airplane. These sensations are usually overcome with experience.

   c. Pilots who are susceptible to airsickness should NOT take the preventive drugs that are available over the counter or by prescription.

      1) Research has shown that most motion sickness drugs cause a temporary deterioration of navigational skills or ability to perform other tasks demanding keen judgment.

6.8 SINUS AND EAR BLOCK

1. During ascent and descent, air pressure in the sinuses equalizes with aircraft cabin pressure through small openings that connect the sinuses to the nasal passages.

    a. An upper respiratory infection (e.g., a cold or sinusitis) or nasal allergies can produce enough congestion around one or more of these small openings to slow equalization.

    b. As the difference in pressure between the sinus and the cabin mounts, the opening may become plugged, resulting in **sinus block**. A sinus block, experienced most frequently during descent, can occur in the frontal sinuses, located above each eyebrow, or in the maxillary sinuses, located in each upper cheek.

        1) It usually produces excruciating pain over the sinus area.
        2) A maxillary sinus block can also make the upper teeth ache.
        3) Bloody mucus may discharge from the nasal passages.

2. As the cabin pressure decreases during ascent, the expanding air in the middle ear pushes the eustachian tube open and escapes down it to the nasal passages, thus equalizing ear pressure with the cabin pressure, as shown below.

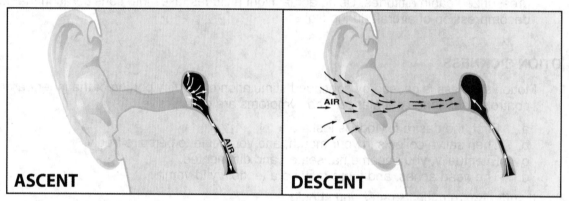

    a. During descent, the pilot must periodically reopen the eustachian tube to equalize pressure.

        1) This can be accomplished by swallowing, yawning, or tensing muscles in the throat.
        2) If these methods do not work, use the Valsalva maneuver. This is the combination of pinching the nostrils shut, closing the mouth and lips, and blowing slowly and gently into the mouth and nose.

    b. Either an upper respiratory infection (e.g., a cold or sore throat) or nasal allergies can produce enough congestion around the eustachian tube to make equalization difficult, if not impossible.

    c. The difference in pressure between the middle ear and the airplane's cabin can build to a level that will hold the eustachian tube closed. This problem, commonly referred to as **ear block**, produces severe ear pain and loss of hearing that can last from several hours to several days.

        1) Rupture of the eardrum can occur in flight or after landing.
        2) Fluid can accumulate in the middle ear and become infected.

3. Sinus and middle ear problems are prevented by not flying with an upper respiratory infection or nasal allergic condition.

    a. Adequate protection is not provided by decongestant spray or drops to reduce congestion around the sinus openings or the eustachian tubes.

        1) Oral decongestants have side effects that can significantly impair pilot performance.

    b. If a sinus block or an ear block does not clear shortly after landing, a physician should be consulted.

6.9 SPATIAL DISORIENTATION

1. Spatial disorientation is a state of temporary confusion resulting from misleading information being sent to the brain by various sensory organs.

2. If you lose outside visual references and become disoriented, you are experiencing spatial disorientation. This occurs when you rely on the sensations of muscles, joints, tissues, and the inner ear to tell you what the airplane's attitude is.

   a. This might occur during a night flight, in clouds, or in dust.

3. The best way to overcome the effects of spatial disorientation is to rely on the airplane flight instruments.

6.10 ILLUSIONS IN FLIGHT

1. Many different illusions can be experienced in flight.

   a. Some can lead to spatial disorientation.
   b. Others can lead to landing errors.
   c. Illusions frequently contribute to fatal aircraft accidents.

2. **Illusions leading to spatial disorientation.** Various complex motions, forces, and certain visual scenes encountered in flight can create illusions of motion and position. Spatial disorientation from these illusions can be prevented only by visual reference to reliable, fixed points on the ground or to flight instruments. Study and be aware of the following illusions. As a pilot, you need a general understanding of the nature and cause of each.

   a. **The leans.** After inadvertently entering a bank attitude too slowly for the motion-sensing system of the inner ear to detect it, an abrupt correction can create the illusion of a bank in the opposite direction. The disoriented pilot may roll the aircraft back into the original, dangerous bank if (s)he relies on his or her own senses, rather than the airplane's instrumentation, to orient the aircraft.

   b. **Coriolis illusion.** Making an abrupt head movement while in a prolonged, constant-rate turn can disturb the motion-sensing system of the inner ear and lead the pilot to believe the aircraft has begun to roll or pitch in another direction. The unwary pilot may put the airplane into a dangerous attitude while attempting to correct the perceived but erroneous change in flight path.

   c. **Graveyard spin.** A proper recovery from a spin that has ceased stimulating the motion-sensing system of the inner ear can create the illusion of spinning in the opposite direction. This illusion is similar to the one described as "the leans." While disoriented, the pilot may inadvertently induce a spin in the opposite direction in an effort to correct for the errant sensation.

   d. **Graveyard spiral.** An observed loss of altitude during a coordinated constant-rate turn that has ceased stimulating the motion-sensing system can create the illusion of being in a descent with the wings level. The disoriented pilot will pull back on the controls, tightening the spiral and increasing the loss of altitude.

   e. **Somatogravic illusion.** A rapid acceleration during takeoff can create the illusion of being in a nose-up attitude. The disoriented pilot will push the aircraft into a nose-low, or dive, attitude. A rapid deceleration by a quick reduction of the throttles can have the opposite effect, with the disoriented pilot pulling the aircraft into a nose-up, or stall, attitude.

   f. **Inversion illusion.** An abrupt change from climb to straight-and-level flight can create the illusion of tumbling backwards. The disoriented pilot will push the aircraft abruptly into a nose-low attitude, possibly intensifying this illusion.

g. **Elevator illusion.** An abrupt upward vertical acceleration, usually caused by an updraft, can create the illusion of being in a climb. The disoriented pilot will push the aircraft into a nose-low attitude. An abrupt downward vertical acceleration, usually caused by a downdraft, has the opposite effect, with the disoriented pilot pulling the aircraft into a nose-up attitude.

h. **False horizon.** Sloping cloud formations, an obscured horizon, a dark and mostly empty vista populated with a combination of terrestrial lights and stars, as well as certain geometric patterns of ground lights, can create the illusion of not being correctly aligned with the true horizon. Without reference to instruments, a pilot may place the airplane in a dangerous attitude based on incorrect visual cues.

i. **Autokinesis.** In the dark, a static light will appear to move about when stared at for several seconds. The disoriented pilot will lose control of the aircraft in attempting to align it with the light.

j. **Size-distance illusion.** When one stares at a point of light, it may appear to approach or recede rapidly. This illusion can be caused by a change in the intensity of the light. When a light gets suddenly brighter, it may appear to be much closer.

k. **Reversible perspective.** At night, an aircraft may appear to be going away from you when it is actually approaching. This illusion is easy to eliminate. Simply use the position lights and their relative arrangements to determine the aircraft's orientation and motion.

l. **Flicker vertigo.** A flickering light or shadow at a constant frequency of four to twenty times a second may cause dizziness, nausea, and, in extreme cases, convulsions and unconsciousness. When flying toward the sun, the propeller can cause a flickering effect, especially when the engine power is reduced for a landing approach. A slight change in power will usually provide the pilot relief from the flicker effect.

3. **Illusions leading to landing errors.** Various surface features and atmospheric conditions encountered while landing can create illusions of incorrect height above and distance from the runway threshold. Landing errors caused by these illusions can be prevented by anticipating them during approaches, visually inspecting unfamiliar airports from the air before landing, using VASI systems when available, and maintaining optimal proficiency in landing procedures. Study the following five illusions to anticipate and cope with them when and if they occur.

a. **Runway width illusion.** A narrower-than-usual runway can create the illusion that the aircraft is at a higher altitude than it actually is. The pilot who does not recognize this illusion will fly a lower approach, with the risk of striking objects along the approach path or landing short. A wider-than-usual runway can have the opposite effect, with the risk of leveling out too high and landing hard or overshooting the runway.

b. **Runway and terrain slopes illusion.** An upsloping runway, an upsloping terrain, or both can create the illusion that the aircraft is at a higher altitude than it actually is. The pilot who does not recognize this illusion will fly a lower approach. A downsloping runway, a downsloping approach terrain, or both can have the opposite effect.

c. **Featureless terrain illusion.** An absence of ground features, as when landing over water, darkened areas, and terrain made featureless by snow, can create the illusion that the aircraft is at a higher altitude than it actually is. The pilot who does not recognize this illusion will fly a lower approach.

d. **Atmospheric illusions.** Rain on the windscreen can create the illusion of greater height, and atmospheric haze the illusion of being at a greater distance from the runway. The pilot who does not recognize these illusions will fly a lower approach. Penetration of fog can create the illusion of pitching up. The pilot who does not recognize this illusion will steepen the approach, often quite abruptly.

e. **Ground lighting illusions.** Lights along a straight path, such as a road, and even lights on moving trains can be mistaken for runway and approach lights. Bright runway and approach lighting systems, especially where few lights illuminate the surrounding terrain, may create the illusion of less distance to the runway. The pilot who does not recognize this illusion will fly a higher approach. Conversely, the pilot overflying terrain that has few lights to provide height cues may make a lower than normal approach.

6.11 VISION

1. Of the body senses, vision is the most important for safe flight. It is important for you to understand your eye's construction and the effect of darkness on the eye.

   a. Two types of light-sensitive nerve endings called **cones** and **rods** are located at the back of the eye, or retina. They transmit messages to the brain via the optic nerve.

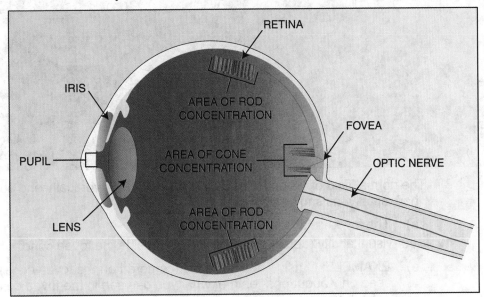

   1) The cones are concentrated around the center of the retina and decrease in number as the distance from the center increases.

      a) Their function is to detect color, details, and distant objects.
      b) They function both in daylight and in moonlight.

   2) The rods are concentrated around the cones and increase in number as the distance from the center increases.

      a) Their function in daylight is to detect objects, particularly those in motion, out of the corner of the eye (i.e., peripheral vision), but they do not give detail or color, only shades of gray.
      b) They function in daylight, in moonlight, and in darkness.

   b. The **fovea** is a small, notched area that is located directly behind the lens on the retina. This area contains cones only.

   1) The fovea is where your vision is the sharpest. Thus, when you look directly at an object, the image is focused mainly on the fovea.

2)   The fovea field of vision is a conical field of only about 1°.

    a)   To demonstrate how small a 1° field is, take a quarter and tape it to a flat piece of glass, such as a window. Now stand 4 1/2 ft. from the mounted quarter and close one eye. The area of your field of view covered by the quarter is a 1° field, similar to your fovea vision.

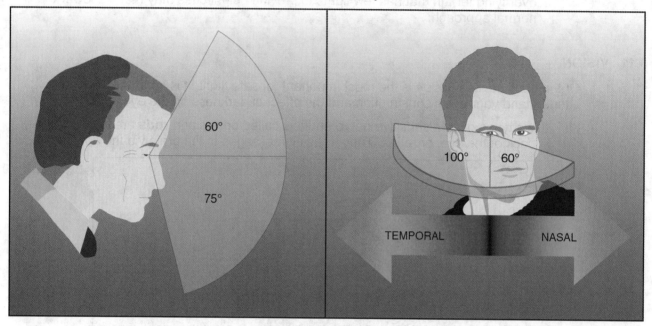

3)   The normal field of vision for each eye is about 135° vertically and about 160° horizontally, as shown above.

    a)   The fovea field is the central 1° field.

4)   Your visual acuity (detail) drops off rapidly outside the fovea cone.

    a)   EXAMPLE: Outside of a 10° cone (centered on the fovea cone), you will see only about one-tenth of what you can see in the fovea cone. In terms of collision avoidance, an aircraft that you are capable of seeing in your fovea cone at 5,000 ft. away must be as close as 500 ft. to detect it with peripheral vision.

c.   The fact that the rods are distributed around the cones and do not lie directly behind the pupils makes **off-center viewing** (i.e., looking to one side of an object) important during night flight.

    1)   During daylight, an object can be seen best by looking directly at it.

        a)   As the cones become less effective as the level of light decreases, you may not be able to see an object if you look directly at it.

            i)   Because the cones are at the center of vision, when they stop working in the dark, a night blind spot develops at your center of vision.

    2)   After some practice, you will find that you can see things more clearly at night by looking to one side of them rather than directly at them.

        a)   Remember that rods do not detect objects while your eyes are moving, only during the pauses.

2.   Adapting your eyes to darkness is an important aspect of night vision.

   a.   When entering a dark area, the pupils of the eyes enlarge to receive as much of the available light as possible.

   b.   It will take approximately 5 to 10 min. (with enough available light) for the cones to become moderately adjusted. After the adjustment, your eyes become 100 times more sensitive than they were before you entered the dark area.

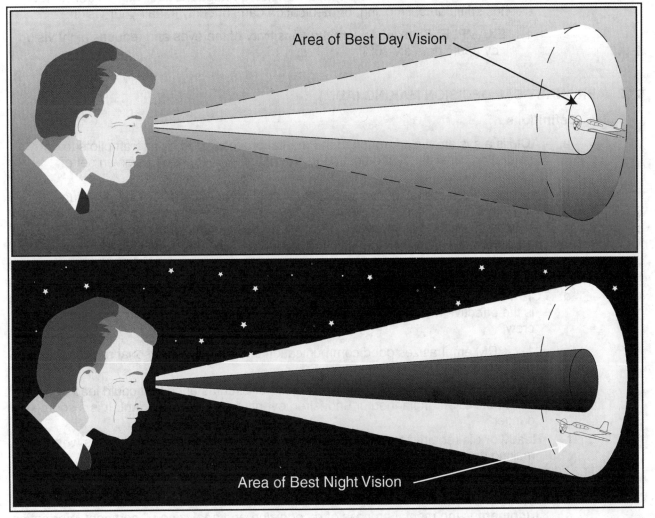

Area of Best Day Vision

Area of Best Night Vision

   c.   After about 30 min., the rods will be fully adjusted to darkness and become about 100,000 times more sensitive to light than they were in the lighted area.

      1)   Because the rods can still function in light of 1/5,000 the intensity at which the cones cease to function, they are used for night vision.

   d.   The rods need more time to adjust to darkness than the cones do to bright light. Your eyes become adapted to sunlight in 10 sec., whereas they need 30 min. to adjust fully to a dark night.

   e.   You must consider the adaptation process before and during night flight.

      1)   First, your eyes should be allowed to adapt to the low level of light, and then they must be kept adapted.

      2)   Next, you must avoid exposing your eyes to any bright light which may cause temporary blindness, possibly resulting in serious consequences.

         a)   Temporary blindness may result in illusions or "after images" during the time your eyes are recovering from the bright light.

3.   The eyes are the first part of your body to suffer from low oxygen at altitude because the capillaries are very small and have a limited capacity to carry oxygen.

   a.   Night vision may be adversely affected above 5,000 ft. MSL.

      1)   Fly at lower altitudes and/or use oxygen when flying at night to maximize your visual acuity.

   b.   Good vision depends on your physical condition. Fatigue, colds, vitamin deficiency, alcohol, stimulants, smoking, or medication can seriously impair your vision.

      1)   EXAMPLE: Smoking lowers the sensitivity of the eyes and reduces night vision by approximately 20%.

6.12 AERONAUTICAL DECISION MAKING (ADM)

1.   **Definitions**

   a.   **ADM** is a systematic approach to the mental process used by aircraft pilots to determine consistently the best course of action in response to a given set of circumstances.

   b.   **Attitude** is a personal motivational predisposition to respond to persons, situations, or events in a given manner that can, nevertheless, be changed or modified through training. This is a sort of "mental shortcut" to decision making.

   c.   **Attitude management** is the ability to recognize hazardous attitudes in oneself and the willingness to modify them as necessary through the application of an appropriate antidote thought.

   d.   **Crew resource management (CRM)** in single-pilot or multiperson crew configurations is the effective use of all personnel and material assets available to a pilot or a flight crew.

      1)   CRM emphasizes good communication and other interpersonal relationship skills.

   e.   **Hazard** is a present condition, event, object, or circumstance that could lead to or contribute to an unplanned or undesired event, such as an accident. It is a source of danger.

   f.   **Headwork** is required to accomplish a conscious, rational thought process when making decisions.

      1)   Good decision making involves risk identification and assessment, information processing, and problem solving.

   g.   **Judgment** is the mental process of recognizing and analyzing all pertinent information in a particular situation, rationally evaluating alternative actions in response to it, and making a timely decision on which action to take.

   h.   **Personality** is the embodiment of personal traits and characteristics of an individual that are set at a very early age and are extremely resistant to change.

   i.   **Poor judgment (PJ) chain** is a series of mistakes that may lead to an accident or incident.

      1)   Two basic principles generally associated with the creation of a PJ chain are

         a)   One bad decision often leads to another.

         b)   As a string of bad decisions grows, it reduces the number of subsequent alternatives for continued safe flight.

      2)   ADM is intended to break the PJ chain before it can cause an accident or incident.

j. **Risk** is the future impact of a hazard that is not controlled or eliminated. It can be viewed as future uncertainty created by the hazard.

k. **Risk management** is the part of the decision-making process which relies on situational awareness, problem recognition, and good judgment to reduce risks associated with flight.

l. **Risk elements** in ADM take into consideration the four fundamental risk elements:

1) The pilot
2) The aircraft
3) The environment
4) The external pressures in any given aviation situation

m. **Single-pilot resource management (SRM)** is the ability for a pilot to manage all resources effectively to ensure the outcome of the flight is successful.

n. **Situational awareness** is pilot knowledge of where the aircraft is in regard to location, air traffic control, weather, regulations, aircraft status, and other factors that may affect flight.

o. **Skills and procedures** are the procedural, psychomotor, and perceptual skills used to control a specific aircraft or its systems.

1) They are "stick and rudder" or airmanship abilities that are gained through conventional training, are perfected, and become almost automatic through experience.

p. **Stress management** is the personal analysis of the kinds of stress experienced while flying and the application of appropriate stress assessment tools and coping mechanisms.

2. **The Decision-Making Process**

a. It is important to understand the decision-making process in order to develop ADM skills. While pilots are well trained to react to emergencies, ADM focuses on decisions requiring a more reflective response.

b. Typically during a flight, some basic steps are followed to make a decision: Examine any changes that occur, gather information, assess risk, and make a decision. These steps are discussed in more detail below.

c. Decision-Making Steps

1) **Defining the problem.** A problem is perceived and, through objective analysis of available information, the nature and severity of the problem is determined. It is critical to ensure that the problem is correctly identified.

2) **Choosing a course of action.** Assess potential actions that may be taken to resolve the situation and what the implications of possible actions may be, then decide on an appropriate response.

3) **Implementing the decision and evaluating the outcome.** Upon selection and implementation of the action, it is important to continue to evaluate the impact of the action. Think ahead and determine how the decision could affect other phases of the flight.

d.   The DECIDE Model is a good tool to use to help remember the elements of the decision-making process.

   1)   **D** etect. The decision maker detects the fact that change has occurred.

   2)   **E** stimate. The decision maker estimates the need to counter or react to the change.

   3)   **C** hoose. The decision maker chooses a desirable outcome (in terms of success) for the flight.

   4)   **I** dentify. The decision maker identifies actions which could successfully control the change.

   5)   **D** o. The decision maker takes the necessary action.

   6)   **E** valuate. The decision maker evaluates the effect(s) of his action countering the change.

e.   The six elements of the DECIDE Model should be treated as a continuous loop. If a pilot practices the DECIDE Model in all decision making, its use can become very natural and result in better decisions being made under all types of situations.

3.   **Risk Management**

a.   The goal of risk management is to proactively identify safety-related hazards and mitigate the associated risks.

   1)   Risk management is an important component of ADM. When a pilot follows good decision-making practices, the inherent risk in a flight is reduced or even eliminated.

   2)   The ability to make good decisions is based on direct or indirect experience and education. The formal risk management decision-making process involves six steps as shown in the figure below.

    b.   It is important to remember the four fundamental principles of risk management.

        1)   **Accept no unnecessary risk.** Unnecessary risk comes without a corresponding return. If you are flying a new airplane for the first time, you might determine that the risk of making that flight in low visibility conditions is unnecessary.

        2)   **Make risk decisions at the appropriate level.** Risk decisions should be made by the person who can develop and implement risk controls. Remember that you are pilot in command, so never let anyone else–not ATC and not your passengers–make risk decisions for you.

        3)   **Accept risk when benefits outweigh dangers (costs).** In any flying activity, it is necessary to accept some degree of risk. A day with good weather, for example, is a much better time to fly an unfamiliar airplane for the first time than a day with low IFR conditions.

        4)   **Integrate risk management into planning at all levels.** Because risk is an unavoidable part of every flight, safety requires the use of appropriate and effective risk management, not just in the preflight planning stage, but in all stages of the flight.

    c.   There are four risk elements involved in decisions made during a flight: the **P**ilot in command, the **A**irplane, the en**V**ironment, and the **E**xternal pressures of the operation. You can remember these items using the PAVE checklist. In decision making, each risk element is evaluated to obtain an accurate perception of circumstances.

        1)   **Pilot.** Consider such factors as competency, condition of health, mental and emotional state, level of fatigue, and many other variables.

        2)   **Airplane.** Assess performance, equipment, or airworthiness.

        3)   **enVironment.** Consider a range of factors not related to pilot or airplane: weather, air traffic control, NAVAIDs, terrain, takeoff and landing areas, and surrounding obstacles.

        4)   **External pressures.** Assessing factors relating to pilot, airplane, and environment is largely influenced by the purpose of the operation. Decisions should be made in the context of why the flight is being made, how critical it is to maintain the schedule, and whether the trip is worth the risks.

    d.   You must carefully process each risk you perceive when analyzing the four risk elements to determine the likelihood of it occurring and the severity of the results of such an occurrence. Use the simple table below to quantify the impact of risks encountered during risk management.

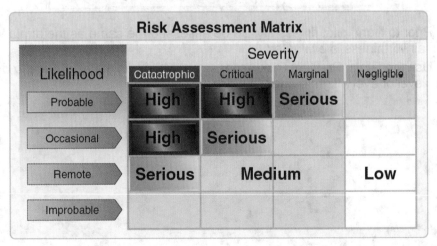

Risk Assessment Matrix				
	Severity			
Likelihood	Catastrophic	Critical	Marginal	Negligible
Probable	High	High	Serious	
Occasional	High	Serious		
Remote	Serious	Medium		Low
Improbable				

    e.   The final step in risk management is reducing, eliminating, or accepting the risks associated with a flight or decision. The goal is obviously to choose the best, safest course of action for a given situation.

        1)   Experience, training, and personal minimum standards will aid you in determining alternative courses of action to reduce and/or eliminate risks.

4.   **Factors Affecting Decision Making**

    a.   Awareness of the decision-making process alone does not ensure the ability to make effective decisions as pilot in command. While some factors during flight may be out of the pilot's control, the pilot can learn to recognize factors that can be managed and learn skills to improve decision making and judgment.

    b.   To make effective decisions regarding the outcome of a flight, a pilot should be aware of personal limitations, such as health, recency of experience, skill level, and attitude. A personal checklist can help determine if a pilot is prepared for a particular flight.

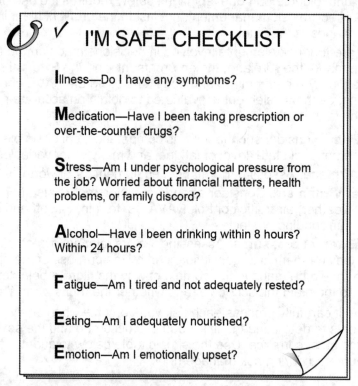

I'M SAFE CHECKLIST

Illness—Do I have any symptoms?

Medication—Have I been taking prescription or over-the-counter drugs?

Stress—Am I under psychological pressure from the job? Worried about financial matters, health problems, or family discord?

Alcohol—Have I been drinking within 8 hours? Within 24 hours?

Fatigue—Am I tired and not adequately rested?

Eating—Am I adequately nourished?

Emotion—Am I emotionally upset?

    c.   Prior to flight, pilot fitness should be assessed the same as the airplane's airworthiness is evaluated.

    d.   Use the Gleim Preflight Risk Assessment Matrix on the next page to determine the risk level of every flight before it begins.

Gleim Preflight Risk Assessment Matrix

During each preflight planning session, use this form to gauge your overall risk. This form is based on the PAVE checklist and will help you determine if your intended flight is riskier than normal based on the factors listed. Making good decisions in the airplane starts on the ground. Grade yourself in each of these categories in an honest, self-evaluative manner. Further note that this list is not exhaustive. If any other factors will affect your flight, you must consider those factors. The go/no-go decision could be entirely based on factors not listed here. **Remember, as the pilot in command, you have the ultimate responsibility for the safety of your flight.**

Before each flight, fill in the appropriate element score in the Rating column and total these numbers to assess your overall flight risk.

	1	2	3	4	5	Rating
Pilot						
Experience	>1500 hours	500-1500 hours	300-500 hours	100-300 hours	<100 hours	
Recency (last 90 days)	>20 hours	15-20 hours	10-14 hours	5-9 hours	<5 hours	
Currency	VFR and IFR		VFR not IFR		Not VFR or IFR	
Emotional Condition	Excellent	Good	Average	Poor	Unacceptable	
Aircraft						
Fuel Reserves	Exceeds requirement		Meets requirement		None	
Time in Type	>400 hours	300-400 hours	200-300 hours	100-200 hours	<100 hours	
Performance	Well within limits		At limits		Outside limits	
Equipment	GPS, weather display	Hand-held GPS	VOR, NDB	Minimum required	Does not meet 14 CFR 91.205	
enVironment						
Airport	Adequate, familiar		Barely adequate		Unfamiliar, inadequate	
Weather (IFR/VFR)	VFR		MVFR	IFR	LIFR	
Runways	Dry, hard, long	Dry, hard, short	Dry, soft, short	Wet, hard, short	Wet, soft, short	
Lighting (Day VFR=1)	Runway, taxiway		Runway only		None	
Terrain	Flat, populated		Flat, unpopulated		Mountainous	
External pressures						
Delays/Diversions	No pressure exists		Inconvenient		Not possible	
Alternate Plans	No pressure exists		Inconvenient		Not possible	
Personal Equipment	Emergency kit		Cell phone only		None available	
Additional Factors						
					Total Risk Rating →	

Risk within normal parameters. Flying is inherently risky. Do not take any unnecessary risks and examine your personal minimums to ensure compliance.	16-33
Elevated risk. Plan for extra time for flight planning. Review your personal minimums to ensure that all your self-determined standards are being met. Carefully analyze any risks near or on the boundaries of your personal minimums. Delay any flight that exceeds your personal minimums until conditions improve.	34-55 Or a 5 in any row
High risk. Plan for extra time for flight planning and consider requesting assistance from a more experienced pilot, if one is available. Carefully examine your personal minimums to ensure none are being violated. Examine methods of reducing the risk to the extent possible. Consider delaying or canceling the flight if risks cannot be reduced to an acceptable level.	56-80 Or a 5 in any two rows

5.   **Operational Pitfalls**

a.   Pilots, particularly those with considerable experience, as a rule always try to complete a flight as planned, please passengers, meet schedules, and generally demonstrate that they have the "right stuff."

   1)   The basic drive to demonstrate the "right stuff" can have an adverse effect on safety and can impose an unrealistic assessment of piloting skills under stressful conditions.

   2)   These tendencies ultimately may lead to practices that are dangerous and often illegal and may lead to a mishap.

b.   All experienced pilots have fallen prey to or have been tempted by one or more of these tendencies in their flying careers. These dangerous tendencies or behavior patterns, which must be identified and eliminated, include

   1)   **Peer pressure.** Poor decision making may be based upon an emotional response to peers rather than an objective evaluation of a situation.

   2)   **Mind set** may produce an inability to recognize and cope with changes in the situation different from those anticipated or planned.

   3)   **Get-there-itis.** This tendency, common among pilots, clouds the vision and impairs judgment by causing a fixation on the original goal or destination, combined with a total disregard for any alternative course of action.

   4)   **Duck-under syndrome** is the tendency to sneak a peek by descending below minimums during an approach, based on a belief that there is always a built-in "fudge" factor that can be used or an unwillingness to admit defeat and shoot a missed approach.

   5)   **Scud running** refers to pushing the capabilities of the pilot and the aircraft to the limits by trying to maintain visual contact with the terrain while trying to avoid physical contact with it.

      a)   This attitude is characterized by the old pilot's joke: "If it's too bad to go IFR, we'll go VFR."

   6)   **Continuing VFR** into instrument conditions often leads to spatial disorientation or collision with ground/obstacles.

      a)   It is even more dangerous if the pilot is not instrument-qualified or current.

   7)   **Getting behind the aircraft** means allowing events or the situation to control your actions rather than the other way around. This dangerous tendency is characterized by a constant state of surprise at what happens next.

   8)   **Loss of positional or situation awareness** is another case of getting behind the aircraft, which results in not knowing your location, being unable to recognize deteriorating circumstances, and/or misjudging the rate of deterioration.

   9)   **Operating without adequate fuel reserves.** Ignoring minimum fuel reserve requirements while either VFR or IFR is generally the result of overconfidence, lack of flight planning, or ignoring the regulations.

   10)   **Descent below the minimum en route altitude** is the duck-under syndrome (previously mentioned) manifesting itself during the en route portion of an IFR flight.

   11)   **Flying outside the envelope** results from an unjustified reliance on the belief (usually mistaken) that the aircraft's high-performance capability meets the demands imposed by the pilot's flying skills (usually overestimated).

   12)   **Neglect of flight planning, preflight inspections, checklists, etc.,** indicates a pilot's unjustified reliance on his or her short- and long-term memory, regular flying skills, repetitive and familiar routes, etc.

6. **Hazardous Attitudes**

   a. **Antiauthority (*Don't tell me!*).** This attitude is found in people who do not like anyone telling them what to do. In a sense, they are saying, "No one can tell me what to do." They may be resentful of having someone tell them what to do or may regard rules, regulations, and procedures as silly or unnecessary. Of course, it is always your prerogative to question authority if you feel it is in error.

   b. **Impulsivity (*Do something quickly!*)** is the attitude of people who frequently feel the need to do something -- anything -- immediately. They do not stop to think about what they are about to do, they do not determine the best alternative, and they do the first thing that comes to mind.

   c. **Invulnerability (*It won't happen to me.*).** Many people feel that accidents happen to others but never to them. They know accidents can happen, and they know that anyone can be affected. However, they never really feel or believe that they will be personally involved. Pilots who think this way are more likely to take chances and increase risk.

   d. **Macho (*I can do it.*).** Pilots who are always trying to prove that they are better than anyone else are thinking *I can do it -- I'll show them*. Pilots with this type of attitude will try to prove themselves by taking risks in order to impress others. While this pattern is thought to be a male characteristic, women are equally susceptible.

   e. **Resignation (*What's the use?*).** Pilots who think *What's the use?* do not see themselves as being able to make a great deal of difference in what happens to them. The pilot is apt to think that things go well due to good luck. When things go badly, the pilot may feel that someone is out to get him or her or may attribute the situation to bad luck. The pilot will leave the action to others, for better or worse. Sometimes, such pilots will even go along with unreasonable requests just to be nice.

7. **Antidotes for Hazardous Attitudes**

   a. Hazardous attitudes, which contribute to poor pilot judgment, can be effectively counteracted by redirecting each hazardous attitude so that appropriate action can be taken.

      1) Recognition of hazardous thoughts is the first step in neutralizing them in the ADM process.

   b. After recognizing and labeling a thought as hazardous, the pilot should correct the hazardous thought by stating the corresponding antidote.

      1) Antidotes should be memorized for each of the hazardous attitudes so that they automatically come to mind when needed.

   c. The hazardous attitude antidotes shown below should be learned thoroughly and practiced.

Hazardous Attitude	Antidote
Antiauthority: *Don't tell me!*	Follow the rules. They are usually right.
Impulsivity: *Do something quickly!*	Not so fast. Think first.
Invulnerability: *It won't happen to me.*	It could happen to me.
Macho: *I can do it.*	Taking chances is foolish.
Resignation: *What's the use?*	I'm not helpless. I can make a difference.

6.13 WEATHER-RELATED DECISION MAKING

1. Making a well educated go/no-go decision as it relates to weather is an important factor in the process of planning and executing a safe flight.

    a. You will have to determine your own personal weather minimums or do so with the guidance of a flight instructor/mentor.

    b. Consider such elements as experience, currency, the aircraft being flown, and any other appropriate factors.

    c. An example of a personal minimums checklist is available on the next page.

        1) Remember that this is just an example. You should create your own personal minimums worksheet to reflect the minimum conditions you feel comfortable operating in.

        2) Bear in mind that over time, as your experience grows, your personal minimums will change.

        3) Plan to review and revise these minimums at least twice a year.

2. When making weather-related decisions, remember to include not only the current weather conditions in your planning, but also the forecast conditions for the estimated time of your arrival. This is true of both cross-country and local flights.

    a. When flying cross-country, always get a complete weather briefing that includes conditions and forecasts for your departure airport, your route of flight, and your destination airport.

3. General rules for making safe weather-related decisions include

    a. Do NOT fly in or near thunderstorms for any reason.

        1) You can safely fly around scattered thunderstorms if you provide sufficient spacing between your aircraft and the storm.

        2) Never attempt to fly through or underneath a thunderstorm.

    b. Do NOT continue VFR flight into IFR conditions, even if you are instrument rated.

        1) If you are on the ground, wait out the weather or file an IFR flight plan.

        2) If you are in the air, turn around. Remain in VFR conditions and file an IFR flight plan, navigate around the weather if possible, or terminate the flight.

    c. Do NOT proceed "on top" of a ceiling, hoping to find a hole on the other end or expecting ATC to "talk you down" if you get caught on top.

    d. Allow more margin for weather at night. It is harder to see the weather getting worse, especially on a dark, moonless night.

4. Refer to Study Unit 7, "Aviation Weather," and Study Unit 8, "Aviation Weather Services," to learn more about weather as it applies to pilots.

    a. You will also learn about the tools available to help you make responsible weather-related decisions.

Baseline Personal Minimums

Weather Condition	VFR	MVFR	IFR	LIFR
Ceiling				
Day				
Night				
Visibility				
Day				
Night				

Turbulence	SE	ME	Make/Model	
Surface Wind Speed				
Surface Wind Gust				
Crosswind Component				

Performance	SE	ME	Make/Model	
Shortest runway				
Highest terrain				
Highest density altitude				

	If you are facing:	Adjust baseline personal minimums to:	
Pilot	Illness, medication, stress, or fatigue; lack of currency (e.g., haven't flown for several weeks)	**A d d**	*At least* 500 feet to ceiling
			At least ½ mi. to visibility
Aircraft	An unfamiliar airplane, or an aircraft with unfamiliar avionics/ equipment		*At least* 500 ft. to runway length
enVironment	Airports and airspace with different terrain or unfamiliar characteristics	**S u b t r a c t**	*At least* 5 kt. from winds
External Pressures	"Must meet" deadlines, passenger pressures, etc.		

6.14 STRESS AND FLYING

1. **What Is Stress?**

   a. Stress is a term used to describe the body's nonspecific response to demands placed on it, whether pleasant or unpleasant, by physical, physiological, or psychological factors known as stressors.

      1) Physical stressors include conditions associated with the environment, such as temperature and humidity extremes, noise, vibration, and lack of oxygen.

      2) Physiological stressors include fatigue, lack of physical fitness, sleep loss, missed meals (leading to low blood sugar levels), and illness.

      3) Psychological stressors are related to social or emotional factors, such as a death in the family, the birth of a baby, a divorce, etc.

         a) Also, they may be related to mental workload, such as analyzing a problem, navigating an aircraft, or making decisions.

   b. Stress is a response to a set of circumstances that induces a change in a pilot's current physiological and/or psychological patterns of functioning, forcing the pilot to adapt to these circumstances.

      1) Stress is an inevitable and necessary part of life that adds motivation to life and heightens a pilot's response to meet any challenge.

      2) Additionally, stress effects are cumulative, eventually adding up to an intolerable burden unless coped with adequately.

   c. Even those things in life you find pleasurable can be stressors, since they represent changes in your environment with which you must deal.

      1) Everyone is stressed to some degree all the time, and a certain amount of stress is good for you.

         a) It keeps you alert and prevents complacency, which helps prevent accidents.

2. **Handling Stress in Flying**

   a. Although some amount of stress is desirable, higher stress levels, particularly over long periods of time, can adversely affect performance.

      1) Thus, performance will generally increase with the onset of stress but will peak and then begin to fall off rapidly as stress levels exceed a pilot's adaptive abilities to handle the situation.

   b. Boredom is seen at the lower stress levels, followed by optimal performance at the moderate stress levels, followed by overload and panic at the highest stress levels, as shown below.

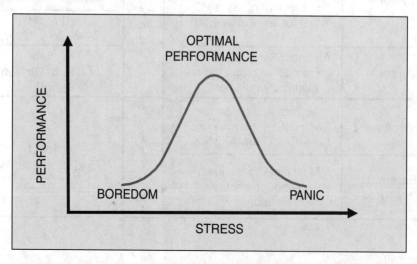

1) Complex or unfamiliar tasks require higher levels of performance than do simple or overlearned tasks.

   a) Thus, complex or unfamiliar tasks are also more subject to the adverse effects of increasing stress than are tasks which are simple or familiar.

c. Accidents often occur when flying task requirements exceed pilot capability.

   1) The difference between pilot capabilities and task requirements is the margin of safety.

   2) In the example below, the margin of safety is minimal during the approach under ideal conditions.

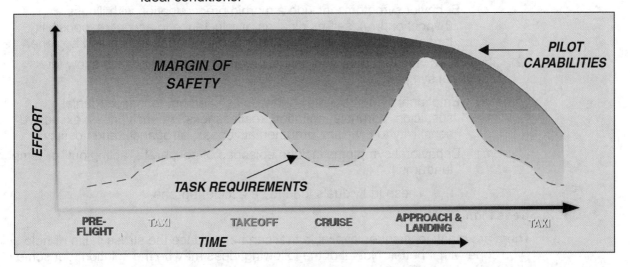

   a) Had an emergency, distraction, or anything else further degraded pilot capabilities (e.g., fatigue, illness, etc.), an accident may have occurred.

d. Stress has a gradual and cumulative effect that develops so slowly that stress can be well established before becoming apparent. There is a limit to a pilot's adaptive nature.

   1) This limit, the stress tolerance level, is based on a pilot's ability to cope with the situation.

   2) If the number or intensity of the stressors becomes too great, the pilot is susceptible to an environmental overload.

      a) At this point, a pilot's performance begins to decline and judgment deteriorates.

3. **Signs of Inadequate Coping**

   a. Individuals who are overstressed (not coping adequately) often show symptoms in three ways:

      1) Emotional
      2) Physical
      3) Behavioral

    b.   These symptoms differ depending on whether the aggression is focused inward or outward.

        1)   Individuals who turn their aggression inward demonstrate the following characteristics:

            a)   Emotional symptoms include depression, preoccupation, sadness, and withdrawal.

            b)   Physical symptoms include headaches, insomnia, appetite changes, weight gain or loss, indigestion, nausea, vomiting, diarrhea, and constipation.

            c)   Behavior symptoms include a morbid preoccupation with illness (hypochondria), self-medication, a reluctance to accept responsibility, tardiness, absenteeism, and poor personal appearance and hygiene.

        2)   Individuals who turn their aggression on other people or objects show few physical symptoms.

            a)   Emotional symptoms may show up as overcompensation, denial, suspicion, paranoia, agitation, restlessness, defensiveness, excessive sensitivity to criticism, argumentativeness, arrogance, and hostility.

            b)   Behavioral symptoms include episodes of desperate "acting out" or temper tantrums.

                i)   These individuals tend to be accident-prone.

4. Life Stress Management

    a.   There are many techniques available that can help reduce the stress in life or help you cope with it better. Not all of the following ideas may be the solution, but some of them should be effective for you.

        1)   Become knowledgeable about stress.
        2)   Take a realistic assessment of yourself.
        3)   Take a systematic approach to problem-solving.
        4)   Develop a lifestyle that will buffer against the effects of stress.
        5)   Practice behavioral management techniques.
        6)   Establish and maintain a strong support network.

5. Cockpit Stress Management

    a.   Good cockpit stress management begins with good life stress management.

        1)   Because many of the stress-coping techniques practiced for life-stress management are not usually practical in flight, you must condition yourself to relax and think rationally when stress appears.

    b.   The following list outlines some thoughts on cockpit stress management:

        1)   Avoid situations that distract you from flying the aircraft.

        2)   Reduce your workload to reduce stress levels. A manageable workload will create a proper environment in which to make good decisions.

        3)   If an emergency does occur, be calm. Think for a moment, weigh the alternatives, and then act.

        4)   Maintain proficiency in your aircraft; proficiency builds confidence. Familiarize yourself thoroughly with your aircraft, its systems, and emergency procedures.

        5)   Know and respect your own personal limits.

        6)   Do not let little mistakes bother you until they build into a big thing. Wait until after you land; then "debrief" and analyze past actions.

        7)   If flying is adding to your stress, either stop flying or seek professional help to manage your stress within acceptable limits.

6.15 IDENTIFYING THE ENEMY

1. Most preventable accidents have one common factor -- **human error** -- rather than a mechanical malfunction.

   a. Very often, the pilot was aware of the possible hazards when the decision (s)he made led to the wrong course of action.

      1) In the interest of expediency, cost savings, self-gratification, or other often irrelevant factors, the incorrect course of action was chosen.

   b. This cycle of decisions began at the flight planning desk with decisions made on how much fuel to carry, the route, the alternate route, and adequate weather conditions.

      1) This cycle continued throughout the flight with decisions made on speed, altitude, and time of descent.

      2) Each flight is a sequence of choices with certain milestones in the sequence that require particular determination and discretion.

   c. While it is true that simple errors of equipment operation are seldom serious, mistakes in judgment can be fatal.

2. **Personal Checklist**

   a. One essential decision point before a flight is the checklist of basic principles that cannot be compromised.

      1) This personal checklist should include the fundamental tenets applicable to every flight.

      2) Once a pilot decides what not to do, the decision on what needs to be done becomes clear.

   b. Consider the following factors that contribute significantly to unsafe flight:

      1) Flight while under the influence of alcohol or drugs, including applicable prescription drugs, is never acceptable.

      2) Flight with a known medical deficiency is never expedient or legal.

      3) Flight outside the certified flight envelope is never safe.

         a) Weight, balance, speed, maneuvers, G-loading, and flight in known icing should be limited to flight manual parameters.

         b) Beyond that, you are in the wilderness, and all discoveries could be unhappy experiences.

      4) Flight with less than the required minimum fuel is never reasonable.

      5) VFR flight into IMC is never justified.

      6) Descent below the applicable minimum en route altitude anywhere is never justified.

      7) Casual neglect of any applicable checklist is never justified.

         a) A checklist may be larger or smaller; however, certain standards should be established for all flights so that the first decision point is whether or not to begin the flight. This decision can be the toughest.

3. **How to Be a Safe Pilot**

   a. A pilot does not have to be a genius to be a safe pilot.

      1) However, a pilot should accept the fact that (s)he is not in possession of all facts or skills for all situations and be willing to accept the recommendations of those who specialize in evaluating, assessing, and administering aviation procedures.

b. Reaching a consensus on all matters within the aviation community can prove difficult, if not impossible.

   1) Even though the rules and procedures are designed to serve most of the people most of the time, a pilot can always argue for different ways of doing things.

   2) An experienced, mature pilot will accept and follow the rules and procedures, which will benefit the aviation community.

      a) The immature, emotionally unbalanced pilot has strong tendencies to satisfy a personal need regardless of the consequences.

c. When a pilot exhibits one or more of the five hazardous attitudes or irrational behavior, that pilot may also be exposing an emotional weakness in his or her personality.

4. **Development of Good Decision-Making Skills**

a. The development of good decision-making skills is far more difficult than developing good flying skills.

   1) Good judgment may mean not flying while under the influence of any medication or when it is too windy, or refusing a revenue flight when it would require flying in marginal weather.

b. Many pilots fail to make proper decisions, sometimes due to a lack of knowledge, but too often as the result of a human tendency to rationalize a situation until it appears justifiable.

   1) When a pilot really wants to do something (i.e., loading that one last passenger when close to maximum gross weight), the pilot can generally make himself or herself believe that it is all right to do it.

      a) A pilot can be his or her own worst enemy.

c. The most important decision a pilot will make is to learn and adhere to published rules, procedures, and recommendations.

   1) Pilots, by learning and adhering to these published rules and procedures, can take most hazards out of flying.

   2) When a pilot operates an aircraft, human lives are held in the balance. Thus, a pilot has a moral responsibility to operate in the safest possible manner.

d. Successful decision making is measured by a pilot's consistent ability to keep himself or herself, any passengers, and the aircraft in good condition regardless of the conditions of any given flight.

6.16 SINGLE-PILOT RESOURCE MANAGEMENT (SRM)

1. SRM is the effective use of all resources (people and materials) to achieve safe and efficient flight operations.

a. Learning to recognize and determine effective and timely **use of resources available** is an essential part of ADM. A pilot must be aware of resources available both inside and outside the cockpit.

   1) **Internal Resources**

      a) Pilot's skill and knowledge developed through training and experience

      b) Aircraft equipment and systems and a thorough understanding of their uses and limitations

      c) Checklists (normal, abnormal, and emergency) essential for verifying that airplane instruments and systems are checked

      d) Aircraft Flight Manual and/or Pilot's Operating Handbook essential for resolving in-flight equipment malfunctions

      e) Aeronautical Charts, Approach Plates, and Chart Supplement for information essential to pilot awareness

      f) Co-pilot and passengers to assist the pilot during high workload and emergency situations

2) **External Resources**

      a) Air Traffic Control and Flight Service Stations provide traffic advisories, airport advisories, radar vectors, weather advisories, direction finding, and assistance in emergency situations.

      b) ATIS, UNICOM, MULTICOM, and other aircraft (pilots) can provide essential information and assistance and relay messages.

      c) Airport signs and markings assist in aircraft ground movement and help to prevent incidents and accidents.

b. **Workload management** is the effective use of planning, prioritizing, and sequencing of tasks to achieve desired results and avoid work overload.

1) With experience, a pilot learns to recognize future workload requirements and to prepare for high workload periods during times of low workload.

2) Use resources, such as ATIS and UNICOM, to know what to expect and be better prepared.

3) Review charts, plates, and performance checklists in advance whenever possible to allow time to focus on other tasks during high workload periods.

4) Recognize work overload situations, then slow down, think, and prioritize. "Aviate, navigate, communicate."

c. **Situational awareness** is the accurate perception of operational and environmental factors that affect the airplane, pilot, and passengers during a specific period of time.

1) When situationally aware, the pilot has an overview of the total operation and is not fixed on one perceived significant factor.

2) A pilot should maintain an awareness of the environmental conditions of the flight, such as spatial orientation of the airplane, and its relationship to terrain, traffic, weather, and airspace.

3) To maintain situational awareness, all of the skills of aeronautical decision making should be used.

d. **Obstacles to Maintaining Situational Awareness**

1) Fatigue, stress, and work overload can cause a pilot to lose overall awareness of the flight situation.

2) Complacency can be an obstacle to situational awareness by reducing a pilot's effectiveness in the cockpit.

2. SRM is about how to gather information, analyze it, and make decisions.

a. Learning how to identify problems, analyze the information, and make informed and timely decisions is not as straightforward as the training involved in learning specific maneuvers.

b. Learning how to judge a situation and "how to think" in the endless variety of situations encountered while flying out in the "real world" is obviously more difficult than maintaining your altitude during a steep turn, or any other flight maneuver.

c. There is no one right answer in ADM; rather, each pilot is expected to analyze each situation in light of experience level, personal minimums, and current physical and mental readiness level and to make his or her own decision.

3. To aid pilots in understanding SRM, the **5P checklist** was created. This checklist looks at five key elements in the SRM process – the Plan, Plane, Pilot, Passengers, and Programming.

    a. Each of these areas consists of a set of challenges and opportunities that face a single pilot.

    b. Each can substantially increase or decrease the risk of successfully completing the flight based on the pilot's ability to make informed and timely decisions.

    c. The 5 Ps are used to evaluate the pilot's current situation at key decision points during the flight or when an emergency arises. These decision points include

        1) Preflight
        2) Pretakeoff
        3) Hourly or at the midpoint of the flight
        4) Predescent
        5) Just prior to the final approach fix (for IFR operations) or just prior to entering the traffic pattern (for VFR operations)

    d. Each of the 5 Ps should be considered at each decision point during a flight.

4. The discussion that follows is an in-depth look at each of the 5 Ps, along with considerations on how to effectively use them in your everyday piloting.

    a. **The 5 Ps: Plan**

        1) The plan can also be called the mission or the task. It contains the basic elements of cross-country planning: weather, route, fuel, current publications, etc.

        2) The plan should be reviewed and updated several times during the course of the flight.

            a) A delayed takeoff due to maintenance, fast-moving weather, and a short-notice temporary flight restriction (TFR) may all radically alter the plan.

            b) The plan is always being updated and modified and is especially responsive to changes in the other four remaining Ps.

        3) Obviously, weather is a huge part of any plan.

            a) The addition of real-time data link weather information provided by advanced avionics gives the pilot a real advantage in inclement weather, but only if the pilot is trained to retrieve and evaluate the weather in real time without sacrificing situational awareness.

            b) Pilots of aircraft without datalink weather or without the ability to effectively interpret it should get updated weather in flight through an FSS.

    b. **The 5 Ps: Plane**

        1) The plane consists of the usual array of mechanical and cosmetic issues that every aircraft pilot, owner, or operator can identify.

        2) With the advent of advanced avionics, the plane has expanded to include database currency, automation status, and emergency backup systems that were unknown a few years ago.

        3) Pilots must regularly review airplane system operations to ensure all systems are within operating limits and to spot potential risk factors while they are more easily manageable.

    c. **The 5 Ps: Pilot**

        1) Flying, especially when used for business transportation, can expose the pilot to high-altitude flying, long distance and endurance, and more challenging weather.

            a) An advanced avionics aircraft, simply due to its advanced capabilities, can expose a pilot to even more of these stresses.

    2) The traditional "I'M SAFE" checklist (covered previously) is a good start for pilot risk assessment.

        a) The combination of late night, pilot fatigue, and the effects of sustained flight at high altitudes may cause pilots to become less discerning, less critical of information, less decisive, and more compliant and accepting.

        b) Just as the most critical portion of the flight arises (e.g., a night instrument approach in inclement weather after a 4-hour flight), the pilot's guard is down the most.

    3) The 5P process helps a pilot to recognize before takeoff the physiological situation that may exist at the end of the flight and to continue updating personal conditions as the flight progresses.

        a) Once risks are identified, the pilot is better equipped to make alternate plans that lessen the effects of these factors and provide a safer solution.

d. **The 5 Ps: Passengers**

    1) Passengers present a unique situation because, depending on the circumstances of the flight, these individuals can be co-pilots.

        a) Passengers can re-read and help you verify checklist items, keep your navigation materials organized and accessible, and assist with many other tasks.

        b) Obviously, in some circumstances, it would not be appropriate to utilize passengers in such a manner.

        c) Be careful to consider what roles your passengers could play in reducing your workload.

    2) Passengers can also create additional pressures on the pilot to complete a flight as planned or take unnecessary risks.

        a) You should plan for passenger pressures any time they will be on board. Planning for this in advance allows you to be ready to handle these situations with a programmed response.

e. **The 5 Ps: Programming**

    1) The advanced avionics in modern aircraft adds an entirely new dimension to the way GA aircraft are flown.

        a) The electronic instrument displays, GPS, and autopilot reduce pilot workload and increase pilot situational awareness.

        b) The pilot must be trained to properly use these avionics for them to be effective.

    2) Although the programming and operation of these devices are fairly simple and straightforward (unlike the analog instruments they replace), they tend to capture the pilot's attention and hold it for long periods of time.

        a) To avoid this phenomenon, the pilot should plan in advance when and where the programming for approaches, route changes, and airport information gathering should be accomplished, as well as times it should not.

        b) Pilot familiarity with the equipment, the route, the local air traffic control environment, and personal capabilities in using the automation should dictate when, where, and how the automation is programmed and used.

5. The SRM process is simple.

    a. At least five times before and during the flight, the pilot should review and consider the plan, plane, pilot, passengers, and programming and make the appropriate decision required by the current situation.

    b. It is often said that failure to make a decision is a decision. Under SRM and the 5 Ps, even the decision to make no changes to the current plan is made through a careful consideration of all the risk factors present.

6.17 AUTOMATION MANAGEMENT

1. In order to avoid potentially dangerous distractions when flying with advanced avionics, the pilot must know, at a minimum, how to manage the

    a. Course deviation indicator (CDI),
    b. Navigation source, and
    c. Autopilot.

2. It is important for a pilot to know the peculiarities of the particular automated system being used. This ensures the pilot knows what to expect, how to monitor for proper operation, and to promptly take appropriate action if the system does not perform as expected.

3. Managing the autopilot means knowing at all times which modes are engaged and which modes are armed to engage.

    a. The pilot needs to verify that armed functions (e.g., navigation tracking or altitude capture) engage at the appropriate time.

    b. In advanced avionics aircraft, proper automation management also requires a thorough understanding of how the autopilot interacts with other systems.

        1) EXAMPLE: With some autopilots, changing the navigation source on the e-HSI from GPS to LOC or VOR while the autopilot is engaged in NAV (course tracking mode) causes the autopilot's NAV mode to disengage.

            a) The autopilot's lateral control will default to ROL (wing level) until the pilot takes action to reengage the NAV mode to track the desired navigation source.

4. Humans are characteristically poor monitors of automated systems.

    a. When passively monitoring an automated system for faults, abnormalities, or other infrequent events, humans tend to perform poorly. The more reliable the system is, the worse the human performance becomes.

        1) For example, the pilot monitors only a backup alert system, rather than the situation that the alert system is designed to safeguard.

        2) It is a paradox of automation that technically advanced avionics can both increase and decrease pilot awareness.

5. Transitioning to Automated Systems

    a. For the GA pilot transitioning to automated systems, it is helpful to note that all human activity involving technical devices entails some element of risk.

        1) Knowledge, experience, and flight requirements increase the odds of safe and successful flights.

        2) The advanced avionics aircraft offers many new capabilities and simplifies the basic flying tasks, but only if the pilot is properly trained and all the equipment is working properly.

END OF STUDY UNIT

STUDY UNIT SEVEN
AVIATION WEATHER

(23 pages of outline)

Despite all of the technological advances in aviation, safety in flight is still subject to weather conditions, such as cloud height, visibility, turbulence, and icing.

Meteorological forecasts are based upon movements of large air masses and upon local conditions at points where weather stations are located. Air masses at times are unpredictable, and weather stations in some areas are spaced widely apart. Thus, you must understand the conditions that could cause unfavorable weather to occur between the stations, as well as the conditions that may be different from those indicated by weather reports and forecasts. Additionally, you must decide whether a particular flight may be hazardous, considering the type of aircraft being flown, the equipment used, flying ability, experience, and physical limitations.

This study unit is designed to help you acquire a general background of aviation weather knowledge and principles by which good judgment can be gained as you acquire more flight experience and undertake further study. For a complete aviation weather reference, obtain a copy of the Gleim *Aviation Weather and Weather Services* book.

7.1 THE EARTH'S ATMOSPHERE

1. Because the sun heats the atmosphere unequally, differences in atmospheric pressure result. This covers a complex ongoing series of air movements around the globe.

    a. These air movements set up chain reactions that culminate in a continuing variety of weather.

2. **Composition.** Air is a mixture of several gases.

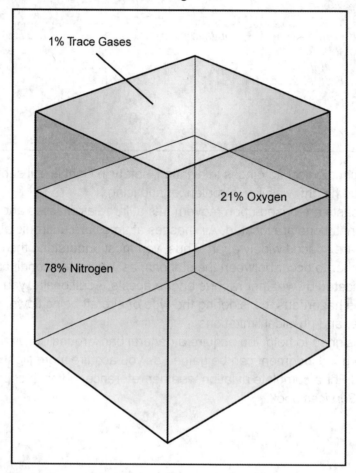

    a. Dry air is about 78% nitrogen and 21% oxygen. The remaining 1% is other gases, such as argon, carbon dioxide, neon, helium, and others.

    b. However, air is never completely dry. It always contains some water vapor in amounts varying from almost zero to about 5% by volume. Although a small value, this water vapor is responsible for major changes in the weather.

3. **Vertical structure.** The atmosphere is classified into layers, or spheres, by the characteristics exhibited in these layers.

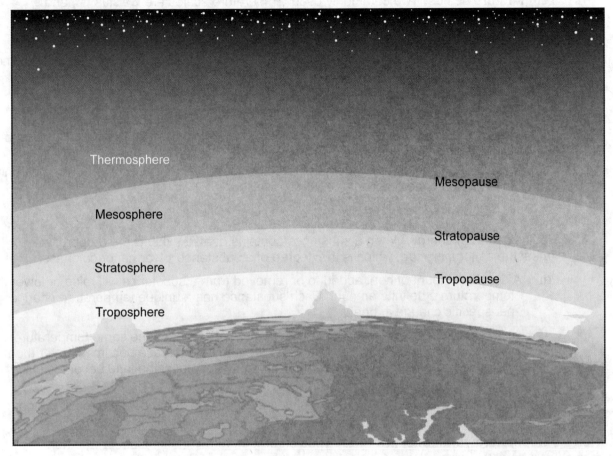

a. The **troposphere** is the layer from the surface to an average altitude of about 7 mi.

    1) The troposphere is characterized by an overall decrease of temperature with increasing altitude.

    2) The height of the troposphere slopes from about 20,000 ft. over the poles to about 65,000 ft. over the Equator (4-12 mi.) and is higher in summer than in winter.

b. At the top of the troposphere is the **tropopause**, a transition zone marking the boundary between the troposphere and the layer above, the stratosphere.

    1) The tropopause is characterized by decreasing winds and constant temperatures with increases in altitude.

c. Above the tropopause is the **stratosphere**, a layer beginning at 4-12 mi.

    1) It is characterized by relatively small changes in temperature with height except for a warming trend near the top (26-29 mi.) and a near absence of water vapor.

d. The upper two layers, the **mesosphere** and the **thermosphere**, are separated by the **mesopause**.

    1) These layers are out of the reach of most pilots (from about 140,000 feet and higher) and are characterized by a sharp drop in temperature through the mesosphere and then a sharp increase in temperature through the thermosphere.

e. From the surface of the Earth to the outer area of the atmosphere, a distance of about 350 miles is covered.

    1) This is roughly the distance between Los Angeles, CA, and Phoenix, AZ.

7.2 TEMPERATURE

1. **Temperature scales.** Two commonly used temperature scales are Celsius (C) and Fahrenheit (F).

   a. The Celsius scale is used in most aviation weather reports, forecasts, and charts.

   b. Two common temperature references are the melting point of pure ice and the boiling point of pure water at sea level.

      1) The boiling point of water is 100°C or 212°F.
      2) The melting point of ice is 0°C or 32°F.

   c. Most flight computers provide for direct conversion of temperature from one scale to the other.

   d. The simple formulas below demonstrate how to mathematically convert from one unit of measure to the other.

   $$°C = \frac{5}{9}(F - 32) \quad \text{or} \quad °F = \frac{9}{5}C + 32$$

2. Heat is a form of energy. When a substance contains heat, it exhibits the property we measure as temperature, which is the degree of a substance's warmth or coldness.

   a. A specific amount of heat added to or removed from a substance will raise or lower its temperature a definite amount. Each substance has a unique temperature change per specific change in heat.

      1) EXAMPLE: If a land surface and a water surface have the same temperature and an equal amount of heat is added, the land surface becomes hotter than the water surface. Conversely, with equal heat loss, the land becomes colder than the water.

   b. Every physical process of weather either is accompanied by or is the result of heat exchanges.

3. **Temperature variations.** Five main types of temperature variations affect weather:

   a. **Diurnal variation.** This change in temperature from day to night and night to day is brought about by the rotation of the Earth.

   b. **Seasonal variation.** Since the Earth's axis is tilted with respect to its orbit, the angle at which a particular spot or region receives solar radiation varies throughout the year. This phenomenon accounts for the temperature variations of the four seasons.

   c. **Variation with latitude.** The sun is nearly overhead in the equatorial regions. Since the Earth is spherical, the sun's rays reach the higher latitudes at an angle. For this reason, the equatorial regions receive the most radiant energy and are the warmest.

   d. **Variations with topography.** Since land heats and cools at a faster rate than water, air temperatures over land vary more widely than those over large bodies of water, which tend to have more minimal temperature changes. Wet soil, swamps, and thick vegetation also help to control temperature fluctuations.

   e. **Temperature variation with altitude.** The amount of temperature decrease with increases in altitude is defined as the **lapse rate**.

      1) Standard sea level temperature is 15°C.
      2) The average standard lapse rate in the troposphere is 2°C per 1,000 ft.
      3) An increase in temperature with an increase in altitude is called an **inversion** because the lapse rate is inverted.

         a) An inversion may occur when the ground cools faster than the air over it. Air in contact with the ground becomes cold, while only a few hundred feet higher, the temperature has changed very little. Thus, the temperature increases with altitude.

         b) Inversions may occur at any altitude.

7.3 ATMOSPHERIC PRESSURE

1. Atmospheric pressure is the force per unit area exerted by the weight of the atmosphere. It is measured per unit area, e.g., pounds per square inch (psi).

    a. The instrument designed for measuring atmospheric pressure is the barometer, with the aneroid barometer being the most common.

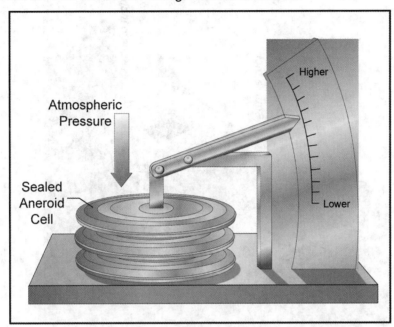

        1) The aneroid barometer consists of a partially evacuated flexible metal cell connected to a registering mechanism. As the atmospheric pressure changes, the metal cell expands or contracts, which drives a needle along a scale calibrated in pressure units.

    b. The commonly used pressure units are inches of mercury (in. Hg.), millibars (mb), and hectoPascal (hPa).

        1) Inches of mercury notation is used in automated weather report broadcasts, and millibar notation is commonly used (interchangeably with hectoPascal notation) on weather charts.

    c. The pressure measured at a station is called the **station pressure**.

    d. Standard atmospheric pressure at sea level is 29.92 in. Hg.

2. **Pressure Variation**

    a. Pressure varies with changes in altitude and temperature of the air. Other factors also affect pressure, but their effects are negligible.

        1) **Altitude.** At higher altitudes, the weight of the air above decreases.

            a) This decrease in pressure from air above results in a lower atmospheric pressure.

                i) The amount of air remains constant as altitude increases, but the pressure exerted on it is less.

ii)   A volume of air at 18,000 ft. above the surface weighs only half of the same volume at sea level.

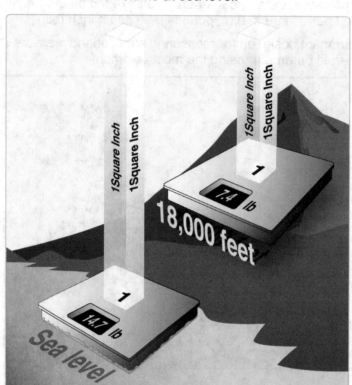

b)   Within the lower few thousand feet of the troposphere (i.e., near the Earth's surface), pressure decreases at a rate of roughly 1 in. Hg per 1,000 ft. of altitude. As one goes higher, this rate of decrease slows.

2)   **Temperature.** Like most substances, air expands as it becomes warmer and shrinks as it cools.

a)   When air is warm and expands, pressure decreases because the same amount of air exists in a larger area.

b)   When air is cooled, it contracts. The pressure is greater than that of the warm air because the same amount of air takes up a smaller area.

b.   **Sea-level pressure.** Since pressure varies with altitude, you cannot accurately compare pressures between airports or weather stations at different altitudes unless you adjust those pressures to a common reference point. The standardized measurement used in aviation is mean sea level (MSL).

1)   EXAMPLE:

a)   Denver, CO, is approximately 5,000 ft. above sea level. If the station pressure in Denver is 24.92 in. Hg, you can determine the sea level pressure with a simple calculation.

b)   The standard pressure lapse rate is 1 in. Hg per 1,000 ft. of altitude. Denver is approximately 5,000 ft. above sea level, which equates to a correction factor of 5 in. Hg.

c)   Add 5 in. Hg to the Denver station pressure to determine the approximate sea-level pressure is 29.92 in. Hg.

d)   The weather observer takes temperature and other factors into account, but this simplified example explains the basic principle of sea-level pressure.

e) The following image graphically explains the previous example as well as shows you that a "standard atmosphere" day in Denver occurs when the pressure is 24.92 in. Hg. (Bear in mind that the temperature would be 5°C on a standard day in Denver due to a corresponding temperature lapse rate with altitude in the troposphere.)

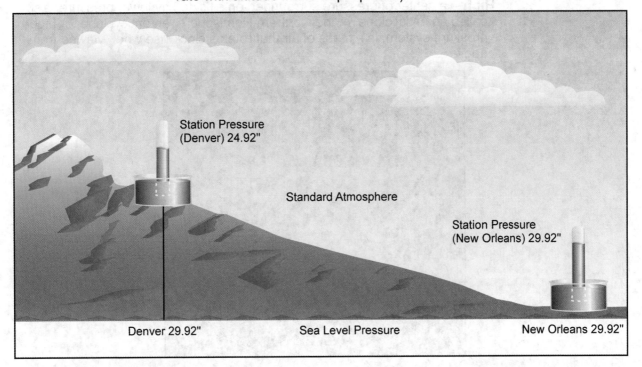

3. **Pressure analyses.** Various weather charts depict lines that connect points of equal pressure. These lines are called **isobars**.

a. Weather charts depicting isobars allow you to see identifiable, organized pressure patterns.

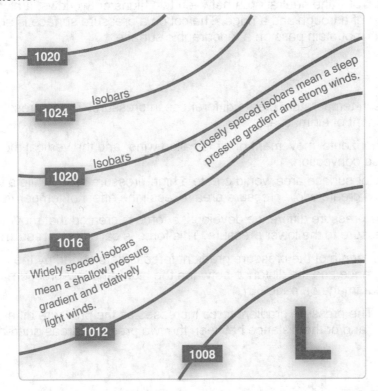

b.   The five pressure systems shown on these charts are defined as follows:

1)   **Low** -- an area of pressure surrounded on all sides by higher pressure, also called a cyclone. In the Northern Hemisphere, a cyclone, or low pressure system, is a mass of air that rotates counterclockwise when viewed from above.

2)   **High** -- a center of pressure surrounded on all sides by lower pressure, also called an anticyclone. In the Northern Hemisphere, an anticyclone, or high-pressure system, is a mass of air that rotates clockwise when viewed from above.

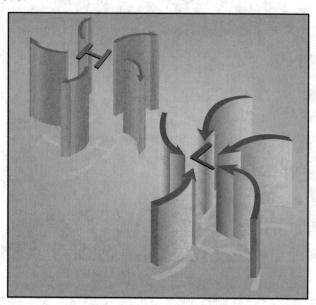

3)   **Trough** -- an elongated area of low pressure, with the lowest pressure along a line marking maximum cyclonic curvature.

4)   **Ridge** -- an elongated area of high pressure, with the highest pressure along a line marking maximum anticyclonic curvature.

5)   **Col** -- the neutral area between two highs or two lows. It also is the intersection of a trough and a ridge. The col on a pressure surface is analogous to a mountain pass on a topographic surface.

7.4 WIND

1.   Differences in temperature create differences in pressure. These pressure differences cause the movement of air masses.

a.   The horizontal movement of air is called wind, and the vertical movement of air is called convection.

b.   A cooler surface area would create a high-pressure area, while a warmer surface area would create a low-pressure area. (Recall the effect of temperature on air pressure.)

2.   Whenever a pressure difference develops, a force is created that moves the air from the higher pressure to the lower pressure. This force is called the **pressure gradient force**.

a.   The strength of the pressure gradient force is determined by the amount of pressure difference and the distance between the high- and low-pressure areas. (See the isobar image on page 367.)

1)   The pressure gradient force increases as the pressure difference increases and/or the distance between the two pressure areas decreases.

3.   Since the Earth rotates, the air does not flow directly from high- to low-pressure areas. In the Northern Hemisphere, it is deflected to the right by what is called the **Coriolis Force**.

   a.   In the Northern Hemisphere, the wind blows clockwise around a high and counterclockwise around a low due to the Coriolis Force.

   b.   The strength of the Coriolis Force is directly proportional to wind speed. The faster the wind, the stronger the Coriolis Force.

4.   At approximately 3,000 ft. AGL and below, friction between the wind and the Earth's surface slows the wind. This reduces the Coriolis Force but does not affect the pressure gradient force.

5.   Since friction does not affect upper-level winds, the pressure gradient force and the Coriolis Force are equal, which causes the wind to flow around, but not into, the low-pressure area.

   a.   Near the surface, friction slows the wind speed, reducing the Coriolis Force but not the pressure gradient force. Thus, the wind flows into the low-pressure area.

      1)   Surface winds are slower and from a different direction than upper-level winds.

6.   When air converges into a low at the surface, it cannot go outward against the pressure gradient nor can it go downward into the ground. It must go upward. Therefore, a low or a trough is an area of rising air.

   a.   Rising air is conducive to cloud development and precipitation. Thus, low-pressure areas are generally associated with bad weather.

   b.   Conversely, air moving out from a high or a ridge depletes the quantity of air and is an area of descending air.

      1)   Descending air tends to dissipate clouds, so highs are usually associated with good weather.

7.   **Types of Wind**

   a.   A **jet stream** is a narrow band of strong winds (50 kt. or more) moving generally from west to east at a level near the tropopause.

   b.   A **valley wind** occurs when colder, denser air in the surroundings settles downward and forces the warmer air near the ground up the mountain slope.

   c.   A **mountain wind** occurs at night when the air near the mountain slope is cooled by terrestrial radiation, becomes heavier than the surrounding air, and sinks along the slope.

   d.   A **katabatic wind** is a wind blowing down an incline, where the incline itself has been a factor in causing the wind. A mountain wind is a good example of a katabatic wind.

   e.   **Sea and land breezes**

      1)   During the day, the land is warmer than the sea.

         a)   Sea breezes are caused by cooler and denser air moving inland off the water.

         b)   Once over the warmer land, the air heats up and rises.

         c)   Currents push the air out over the water where it cools and descends, starting the process over again.

      2)   At night, the wind reverses from the cool land to the warmer water.

         a)   This is called a land breeze.

3)   These breezes occur only when the overall pressure gradient is weak.

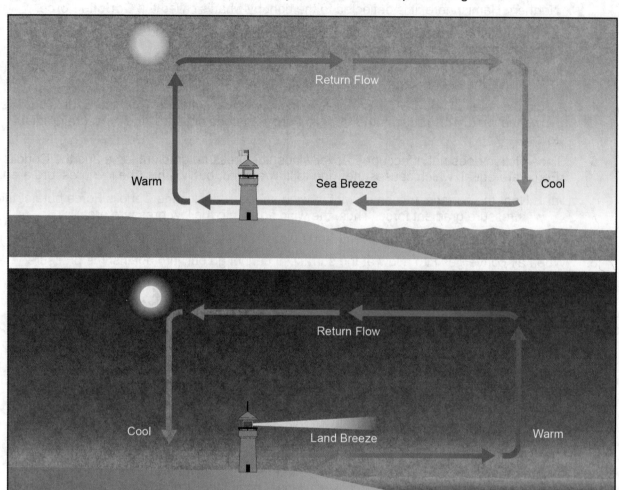

7.5 MOISTURE, CLOUD FORMATION, AND PRECIPITATION

1.   Water vapor is invisible, like the other atmospheric gases, but its quantity in the air can still be measured. It is generally expressed as

a.   Relative humidity -- a ratio of how much actual water vapor is present to the amount that could be present. At 100% relative humidity, the air is saturated.

b.   Dew point -- the temperature to which air must be cooled to become saturated by the water vapor that is already present in that air.

1)   Dew point is compared to air temperature to determine how close the air is to saturation. This difference is referred to as the temperature-dew point spread.

2)   As the temperature and dew point converge, fog, clouds, or rain should be anticipated.

c.   The following image explains relative humidity and dew point:

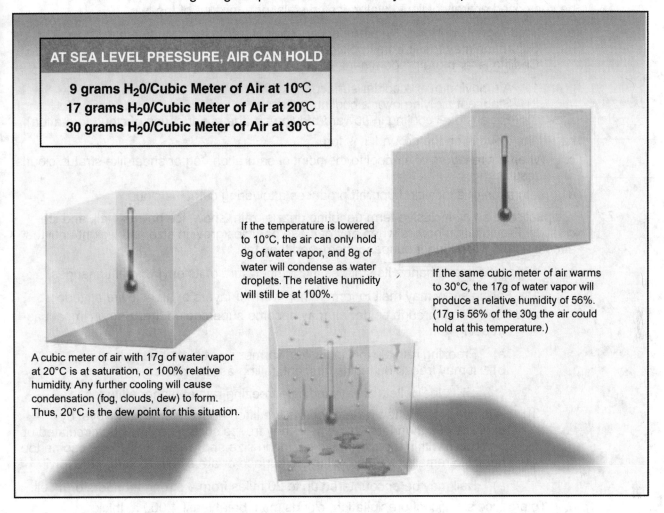

AT SEA LEVEL PRESSURE, AIR CAN HOLD

9 grams H_2O/Cubic Meter of Air at 10°C
17 grams H_2O/Cubic Meter of Air at 20°C
30 grams H_2O/Cubic Meter of Air at 30°C

If the temperature is lowered to 10°C, the air can only hold 9g of water vapor, and 8g of water will condense as water droplets. The relative humidity will still be at 100%.

If the same cubic meter of air warms to 30°C, the 17g of water vapor will produce a relative humidity of 56%. (17g is 56% of the 30g the air could hold at this temperature.)

A cubic meter of air with 17g of water vapor at 20°C is at saturation, or 100% relative humidity. Any further cooling will cause condensation (fog, clouds, dew) to form. Thus, 20°C is the dew point for this situation.

2.   The six possible transformations of water are designated by the following terms:

    a.   **Condensation** -- the change of water vapor to liquid water
    b.   **Evaporation** -- the change of liquid water to water vapor
    c.   **Freezing** -- the change of liquid water to ice
    d.   **Melting** -- the change of ice to liquid water
    e.   **Sublimation** -- the change of ice to water vapor
    f.   **Deposition** -- the change of water vapor to ice

3.   Supercooled water consists of water droplets existing at temperatures below freezing.

    a.   Supercooled water is dangerous because it immediately forms into heavy, clear ice when it strikes an airplane's surface.

4.   Dew forms when the Earth's surface cools to below the dew point of adjacent air as a result of heat radiation. Moisture forms (condenses) on leaves, grass, and exposed objects. This is the same process that causes a cold glass of water to "sweat" in warm, humid weather.

5.   Frost forms in much the same way as dew. The difference is that the dew point of surrounding air must be colder than freezing. Water vapor changes directly to ice crystals or frost (deposition) rather than condensing as dew.

6. Clouds are a visible collection of minute water or ice particles suspended in air. A cloud may be composed entirely of liquid water, ice crystals, or a mixture of the two.

    a. Cloud formation. Normally, air must become saturated for condensation to occur. Saturation may result from cooling the temperature, increasing the dew point, or both. Cooling is far more predominant. There are three ways to cool air to saturation:

        1) Air moving over a colder surface
        2) Stagnant air lying over a cooling surface
        3) Expansional cooling in upward-moving air (the major cause of cloud formation)

    b. If the cloud is on the ground, it is fog.

    c. When entire layers of air cool to the point of saturation, fog or sheet-like stratus clouds result.

    d. Saturation of a localized updraft produces a towering cumulus cloud.

7. Precipitation is an all-inclusive term denoting drizzle, rain, snow, ice pellets, hail, and ice crystals. Precipitation occurs when any of these particles grow in size and weight until the atmosphere can no longer suspend them, and they fall.

    a. Precipitation can change its state as the temperature of its environment changes.

        1) Falling snow may melt to form rain in warmer layers of air at lower altitudes.
        2) Rain falling through colder air may become supercooled, freezing on impact as freezing rain.

            a) Freezing rain always indicates warmer air at higher altitudes.
            b) It may freeze during its descent, falling as ice pellets.

                i) Ice pellets always indicate freezing rain at higher altitudes.

        3) Hailstones form when water droplets are lifted above the freezing level by updrafts of a thunderstorm, where they freeze solid. They may be circulated up and down within the storm, increasing in size and weight until they become too heavy to remain aloft and fall to the surface or are ejected through the anvil.

            a) Hail may be encountered up to 20 miles from a strong thunderstorm cell.

    b. To produce significant precipitation, clouds must be at least 4,000 ft. thick.

7.6 STABLE AND UNSTABLE AIR

1. A stable atmosphere resists any upward or downward displacement. An unstable atmosphere allows upward and downward disturbances to grow into vertical (convective) currents.

    a. Anytime air moves upward, it expands because of decreasing atmospheric pressure. Conversely, downward-moving air is compressed by increasing pressure.

        1) When air expands, it cools, and when compressed, it warms.
        2) These changes are **adiabatic**, meaning that no heat is removed from, or added to, the air.
        3) The terms expansional, or adiabatic, cooling and compressional, or adiabatic, heating are commonly used.

    b. Unsaturated air moving upward and downward cools and warms at about 3.0°C (5.4°F) per 1,000 feet.

        1) This rate is the **dry adiabatic lapse rate** of temperature change and is independent of the temperature of the mass of air through which the vertical movements occur.

   c.   Saturated air moving upward and downward cools and warms at a rate varying between 1.1°C and 2.8°C (2°F and 5°F) per 1,000 feet.

      1) The rate is the **moist adiabatic lapse rate**. Like the dry rate, it is independent of the temperature of the surrounding air mass.

      2) Recall that the standard temperature lapse rate of 2°C per 1,000 feet of altitude gained or lost is only an average lapse rate.

   d.   If air is forced upward, there are two possibilities:

      1) The air may become colder than the surrounding air because its adiabatic rate of cooling is greater than the existing lapse rate of the surrounding air.

         a) The air begins to sink and eventually settles into a stable condition because there is no tendency for any displacement to continue.

      2) The air may remain warmer than the surrounding air despite its cooling because its adiabatic rate of cooling is less than the existing lapse rate.

         a) The air continues to rise and is considered to be in an unstable condition.
         b) This instability could grow into a larger weather system.

   e.   Thus, the difference between the existing lapse rate of a given air mass and the adiabatic rate of cooling in upward-moving air determines whether the air is stable or unstable.

2. **Stability and Instability**

   a.   The stability of the atmosphere varies with location, altitude, and time.

      1) Certain air masses will be more stable or unstable than others.
      2) Often, air stability will be layered.

         a) A layer of stable air may overlie an unstable layer, or vice versa.

   b.   The stability of an air mass determines its typical weather characteristics. When one air mass overlies another, conditions change with height. The following are typical characteristics of stable and unstable air:

      1) Stable air -- stratiform clouds and fog, continuous precipitation, smooth air, and fair-to-poor visibility in haze and smoke.

      2) Unstable air -- cumuliform clouds, showery precipitation, turbulence, and good visibility, except in blowing obstructions, e.g., dust, sand, snow, etc.

3. **Estimating Bases of Cumulus Clouds**

   a.   When air rises in a convective current, it cools at the rate of 3°C (5.4°F) per 1,000 ft. The dew point decreases 0.5°C (1°F) per 1,000 ft.

      1) The standard lapse rate assumes the temperature and dew point then are converging at 2.5°C (4.4°F) per 1,000 ft.
      2) The point at which they converge is the altitude of the base of the clouds.

   b.   The simple formula below will allow you to estimate the altitude of a cloud base.

$$\text{Cloud base (in feet above the ground)} = \frac{\text{Surface temperature} - \text{Dew point spread}}{2.5°C\ (4.4°F)} \times 1{,}000$$

   c.   EXAMPLE:

$$\frac{\text{Surface temperature}}{20°C} \qquad \frac{\text{Surface dew point}}{13°C}$$

$$\text{Cloud base (in feet above the ground)} = \frac{\text{Surface temperature} - \text{Dew point spread}}{2.5°C\ (4.4°F)} \times 1{,}000$$

$$\text{Cloud base (in feet above the ground)} = \frac{7°C}{2.5°C} \times 1{,}000$$

$$\text{Cloud base (in feet above the ground)} = 2.8 \times 1{,}000 = 2{,}800\ \text{feet}$$

7.7 CLOUDS

1. There are four major classifications or families of clouds:

    a. High clouds -- composed almost entirely of ice crystals. The height of the bases of these clouds usually range from about 16,500 ft. to 45,000 ft. in middle latitudes. The high cloud family is cirriform.

    b. Middle clouds -- composed primarily of water, much of which may be supercooled. Cloud bases range from 6,500 ft. to 23,000 ft. in middle latitudes.

    c. Low clouds -- composed almost entirely of water, but at times the water may be supercooled. They can also contain snow and ice particles if temperatures are below freezing. Cloud bases range from the surface to about 6,500 ft. in middle latitudes.

    d. Clouds with extensive vertical development -- usually composed of supercooled water above the freezing level. Bases range from 1,000 ft. or less to above 10,000 ft.

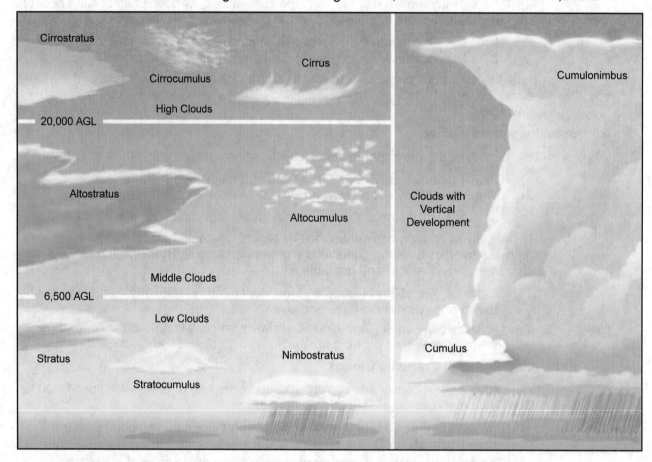

2. The first three families are further classified according to the way they are formed.

    a. Clouds formed by vertical currents in unstable air are cumulus and have a lumpy, billowy appearance.

    b. Clouds formed by the cooling of a stable layer are stratus and have a uniform, sheet-like appearance.

    c. In addition, the prefix "nimbo" or the suffix "nimbus" means raincloud.

        1) For example, a cumulus cloud that produces precipitation is a cumulonimbus.

7.8 AIR MASSES AND FRONTS

1. **Air masses.** When a body of air comes to rest or moves slowly over an extensive area having uniform properties of temperature and moisture, the body of air takes on the same properties.

    a. The area over which the air mass acquires its properties of temperature and moisture is its **source region**. There are many source regions, the best examples being large polar regions, cold northern and warm tropical oceans, and large desert areas.

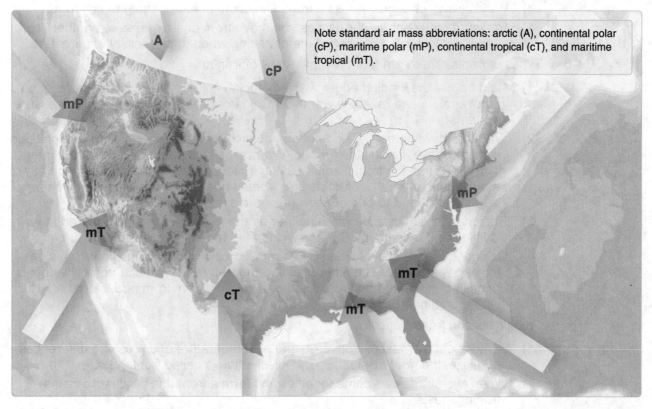

Note standard air mass abbreviations: arctic (A), continental polar (cP), maritime polar (mP), continental tropical (cT), and maritime tropical (mT).

    b. An air mass tends to take on properties of the underlying surface when it moves away from its source region, thus becoming modified. Some ways in which air masses are modified include the following:

        1) Cool air moving over a warm surface is heated from below, generating instability and increasing the possibility of showers.

        2) Warm air moving over a cool surface is cooled from below, increasing stability. If air is cooled to its dew point, stratus clouds and/or fog forms.

        3) Evaporation from water surfaces and falling precipitation adds water vapor to the air. When the water is warmer than the air, evaporation can raise the dew point sufficiently to saturate the air and form stratus clouds or fog.

        4) Water vapor is removed by condensation and precipitation.

2. **Fronts.** The zone between two different air masses is a frontal zone or front. Across this zone, temperature, humidity, and wind often change rapidly over short distances.

    a.   Discontinuities. When you pass through a frontal zone, these changes may be abrupt, indicating a narrow front. A more subtle change indicates a broad and diffused front.

        1)   The most easily recognizable indication that you are passing through a front will be a temperature change.

        2)   Temperature-dew point spread usually differs across a front.

        3)   Wind always changes across a front. Direction, speed, or both will change.

        4)   Pressure may change abruptly as you move from one air mass to another. It is important to keep a current altimeter setting when in the vicinity of a front.

    b.   Types of fronts. There are four principal types of fronts:

        1)   Cold front -- the leading edge of an advancing cold air mass. At the surface, cold air overtakes and replaces warm air. Cold fronts tend to precede high pressure systems.

        2)   Warm front -- the leading edge of an advancing mass of warm air. Since cold air is more dense, it hugs the ground. Warm air slides up and over the cold mass. This elongates the frontal zone making it more diffuse. Warm fronts generally move about one-half as fast as cold fronts under the same wind conditions. Warm fronts tend to precede low pressure systems.

        3)   Stationary front -- occurs when neither air mass is replacing the other and there is little or no movement. Surface winds tend to blow parallel to the front.

        4)   Occluded front -- occurs when a fast-moving cold front catches up with a slow-moving warm front. The difference in temperature within each frontal system is a major factor in determining whether a cold or warm front occlusion (i.e., which will be dominant) occurs.

    c.   Frontolysis and frontogenesis.

        1)   As adjacent air masses converge and as temperature and pressure differences equalize, the front dissipates. This dissipation is called frontolysis.

        2)   When two air masses come together and form a front, the process is called frontogenesis.

    d.   Weather occurring with a front depends on the

        1)   Amount of moisture available
        2)   Degree of stability of the air that is forced upward
        3)   Slope of the front
        4)   Speed of the frontal movement
        5)   Upper wind flow

7.9 TURBULENCE

1.   A turbulent atmosphere is one in which air currents vary greatly over short distances.

    a.   As an airplane moves through these currents, it undergoes changing accelerations that jostle it from its smooth flight path. This jostling is called turbulence.

        1)   An airplane's reaction to turbulence varies with the difference in wind speed in adjacent currents, the size of the airplane, wing loading, airspeed, and altitude.

    b.   The main causes of turbulence are

        1)   Convective currents
        2)   Obstructions to wind flow
        3)   Wind shear

2. **Convective Currents**

  a. Convective currents are localized vertical (both up and down) air movements. For every rising current, there is a compensating downward current.

    1) These currents are a common cause of turbulence, especially at low altitudes.

    2) Convective currents are most active on warm summer afternoons when winds are light.

    3) Because different surfaces absorb and radiate heat differently, care must be taken to anticipate changes in flight path when flying near the ground.

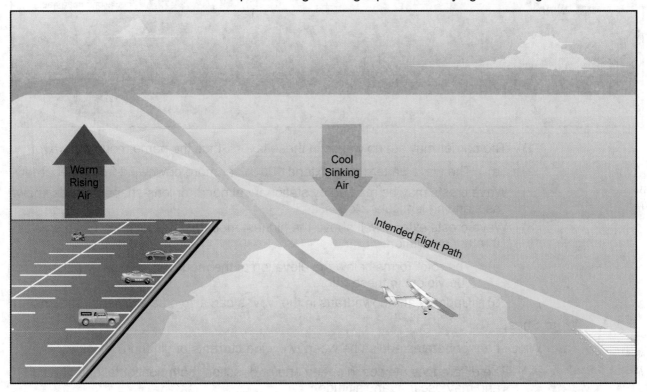

  b. Cumulus clouds indicate convective turbulence.

    1) The cloud top marks the approximate upper limit of the convective current.

    2) Even when the air is too dry for clouds to form, convective currents can still be active.

3. **Obstructions to Wind Flow**

  a. Obstructions, such as buildings, trees, and rough terrain, disrupt smooth wind flow, causing turbulence.

    1) The degree of turbulence depends on the wind speed and roughness of the obstructions. The higher the speed and/or the rougher the surface, the greater the turbulence.

    2) Flying over rugged hills or mountains may present some turbulence problems.

      a) When wind speed across the mountain exceeds about 40 kt., anticipate turbulence.

      b) If the air is unstable, turbulence on the windward side is almost certain. As the air crosses the mountain, it spills down the leeward slope as a violent downdraft.

        i) Hazardous turbulence in unstable air generally does not extend a great distance downwind.

b.   Mountain wave. When stable air crosses a mountain barrier, air flowing up the windward side is relatively smooth, and the wind across the barrier tends to flow in layers.

Standing Lenticular Cloud
Denotes area of intense circulation underneath.

WIND

1)   The barrier may set up waves in these layers, thus the name mountain wave.

   a)   The wave pattern may extend 100 mi. or more downwind from the barrier.

2)   Wave crests may be marked by stationary almond- or lens-shaped clouds known as standing lenticular clouds.

3)   Wave crests extend well above the highest mountain. Under each wave crest is a rotary circulation.

   a)   The rotor forms below the elevation of the mountain peaks. Turbulence can be violent in these rotors.

   b)   Updrafts and downdrafts in the waves can also create violent turbulence.

4.   **Wind Shear**

a.   Wind shear generates eddies between two wind currents of differing velocities.

   1)   The differences may be in speed and/or direction (both horizontal and vertical) and may occur at any altitude.

b.   Wind shear with a low-level temperature inversion.

   1)   A temperature inversion forms near the surface on a clear night with calm or light surface wind. Wind above the inversion may be relatively strong.

      a)   A wind shear zone develops between the calm winds and the stronger winds above.

   2)   When taking off or landing in calm wind under clear skies within a few hours before or after sunrise, be prepared for a temperature inversion.

      a)   A shear zone in the inversion is relatively certain if the wind at 2,000 to 4,000 ft. is 25 kt. or greater.

c.   Wind shear in a frontal zone.

   1)   Wind changes abruptly in the frontal zone and can induce wind shear turbulence.

   2)   The degree of turbulence depends on the magnitude of the wind shear.

d.   Microburst.

   1)   A microburst is a strong downdraft of up to 6,000 feet per minute with horizontal winds near the surface as strong as 45 knots (resulting in a 90-knot shear headwind to tailwind change for a traversing aircraft).

      a)   Microbursts normally occur over horizontal distances of 1 NM and vertical distances of less than 1,000 feet.

2)   If encountered close to the ground, a microburst can make aircraft control difficult.

a)   The figure below shows the effect on an airplane of a microburst encounter on takeoff.

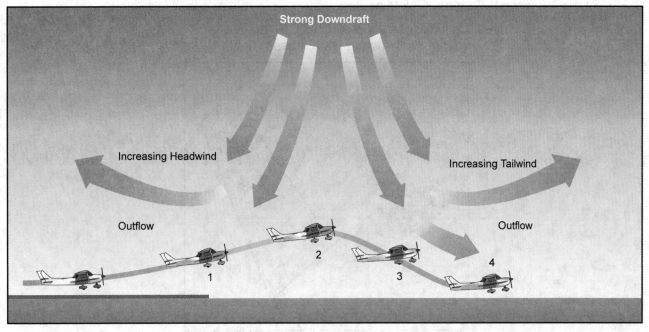

b)   There is an initial headwind (#1) followed by downdrafts (#2), then the wind rapidly shears to a tailwind (#3) and can result in terrain impact or flight dangerously close to the ground (#4).

7.10   ICING

1.   Icing is a cumulative hazard to airplanes. When ice builds up on the surface of an airplane, it increases weight and drag while reducing lift and thrust. These factors tend to slow the airplane and/or force it to descend. Icing can also seriously impair engine performance and flight instruments.

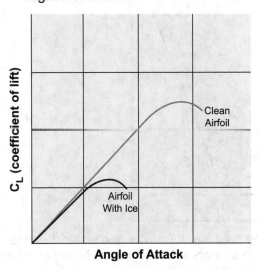
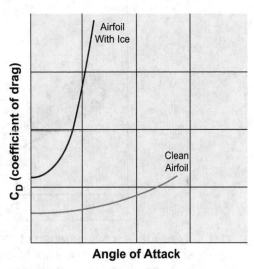

2.   Structural icing will occur if two conditions are met:

a.   The airplane is flying through visible moisture, such as rain or cloud droplets.

b.   The air temperature where the moisture strikes the aircraft is 0°C or cooler.

1)   Aerodynamic cooling can lower the temperature of an airfoil to 0°C even though ambient temperature is slightly higher.

3.   Three types of ice can form on an airplane:

a.   **Clear ice** forms when water droplets that touch the airplane flow across the surface before freezing. Clear ice will accumulate as a smooth sheet. This type of ice forms when the water droplets are large, such as in rain or cumuliform clouds.

1)   Clear ice is very heavy and difficult to remove.
2)   It can substantially increase the gross weight of an airplane.

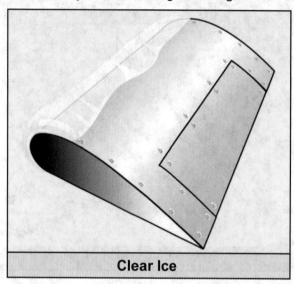

Clear Ice

b.   **Rime ice** forms when water droplets are small, such as those in stratiform clouds or light drizzle, and freeze on impact without spreading. Rime ice is rough and opaque, similar to frost in your home freezer.

1)   Its irregular shape and rough surface greatly decrease the aerodynamic efficiency of an airplane's wings, thus reducing lift and increasing drag.

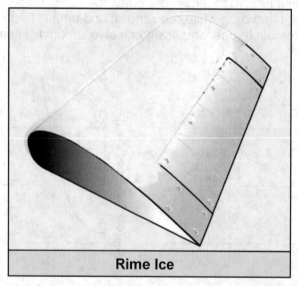

Rime Ice

c.   **Mixed ice** is a combination of clear and rime ice. It forms when water droplets vary in size. Some freeze on impact and some spread before freezing. Mixed ice is opaque and has a very rough surface.

4.   Frost, ice, and/or snow may accumulate on parked airplanes. All frost, ice, and/or snow should be removed before takeoff.

   a.   For a review of frost's effect on an aircraft's aerodynamic performance, refer to page 42 of Study Unit 1.

7.11 THUNDERSTORMS

1.   For a thunderstorm to form, the air must have

   a.   Sufficient water vapor
   b.   An unstable lapse rate
   c.   An initial upward boost (lifting) to start the storm process in motion

      1)   Surface heating, converging winds, sloping terrain, a frontal surface, or any combination of these can provide the necessary lifting.

2.   A thunderstorm cell progresses through three stages during its life cycle:

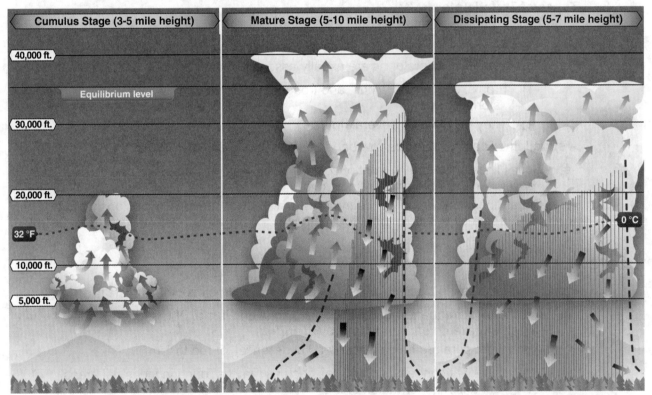

   a   The **cumulus stage**. Although most cumulus clouds do not grow into thunderstorms, every thunderstorm begins as a cumulus. The key feature in the cumulus stage is the updraft.

      1)   Early during the cumulus stage, water droplets are quite small but grow to raindrop size as the cloud grows.

         a)   As the raindrops grow still heavier, they fall. This cold rain drags air with it, creating a cold downdraft coexisting with the updraft.

b. The **mature stage**. Precipitation beginning to fall from the cloud base is the sign that a downdraft has developed and a cell has entered the mature stage.

  1) Cold rain in the downdraft retards compressional (adiabatic) heating, and the downdraft remains cooler than the surrounding air. Thus, its downward speed is accelerated.

  2) The downrushing air spreads outward at the surface, producing strong gusty surface winds, a sharp temperature drop, and a rapid rise in pressure.

  3) Updrafts and downdrafts in close proximity create strong vertical shear and a very turbulent environment.

  4) All thunderstorm hazards reach their greatest intensity during the mature stage.

    a) Hazards include tornadoes, turbulence, icing, hail, lightning, low visibility and ceiling, and effects on an airplane's altimeter.

c. The **dissipating stage**. Downdrafts characterize the dissipating stage of the thunderstorm cell, and the storm dies.

3. **Types of Thunderstorms**

a. Air mass thunderstorms most often result from surface heating and last only about 20 to 90 min.

b. Steady state thunderstorms are usually associated with weather systems.

  1) Fronts, converging winds, and troughs aloft force air upwards to initiate the storms.

  2) They may last for several hours.

4. A **squall line** is a nonfrontal narrow band of steady state thunderstorms.

a. Squall lines often form in front of cold fronts in moist unstable air, but they may also develop in unstable air far removed from any fronts.

b. Squall lines generally produce the most severe thunderstorm conditions (e.g., heavy hail, destructive winds, tornadoes, etc.).

7.12 FOG

1. Fog is a surface-based cloud composed of either water droplets or ice crystals.

a. It is the most frequent cause of IFR conditions and is one of the most persistent weather hazards encountered in aviation.

b. A small temperature-dew point spread is essential for fog to form.

  1) Abundant condensation nuclei, such as may be found in industrial areas, enhance the formation of fog.

c. Fog is classified by the way it forms.

2. **Radiation fog**, or ground fog, is relatively shallow. It forms almost exclusively at night or near daybreak under a clear sky, with little or no wind, and with a small temperature-dew point spread.

a. Terrestrial radiation cools the ground, which cools the air in contact with it.

  1) When the air is cooled to its dew point, fog forms.

b. Radiation fog is restricted to land because water cools little at night.

  1) It is shallow when the wind is calm.
  2) It deepens in wind up to 5 kt.
  3) Stronger winds disperse the fog.

3. **Advection fog** forms when moist air moves over colder ground or water. At sea, it is called sea fog.

   a. Advection fog deepens in wind speeds up to 15 kt.

   b. Wind much stronger than 15 kt. lifts the fog into a layer of low clouds.

   c. Advection fog is more persistent and extensive than radiation fog and can appear during day or night.

4. **Upslope fog** forms as a result of moist, stable air being cooled adiabatically as it moves up sloping terrain.

   a. Once the upslope wind ceases, the fog dissipates.

   b. Upslope fog is often quite dense and extends to high altitudes.

5. **Frontal fog** forms when relatively warm rain falls through cool air; evaporation from the precipitation saturates the cool air and forms fog.

   a. Frontal fog can become quite dense and continue for a long time.

   b. It is most commonly associated with warm fronts.

   c. It occurs near other possible hazards, such as icing, turbulence, and thunderstorms.

6. **Steam fog** forms in winter when cold, dry air passes from land areas over comparatively warm ocean waters.

   a. It is composed entirely of water droplets that often freeze quickly.

   b. Low-level turbulence and hazardous icing can occur.

7. Be especially alert for development of fog when

   a. The temperature-dew point is 10°C (15°F) or less at dusk, and the following morning the skies are clear and winds are light

   b. Moist air is flowing from a relatively warm surface to a colder surface

   c. The temperature-dew point spread is 3°C (5°F) or less and decreasing

   d. A moderate or stronger moist wind is blowing over an extended upslope

      1) Temperature and dew point converge at about 2°C (4°F) for every 1,000 ft. the air is lifted.

   e. Air is blowing from a cold surface (either land or water) over warmer water

      1) This would produce steam fog.

   f. Rain or drizzle falls through cool air

      1) This is especially prevalent during winter ahead of a warm front and behind a stationary front or stagnating cold front.

END OF STUDY UNIT

STUDY UNIT EIGHT
AVIATION WEATHER SERVICES

(37 pages of outline)

Aviation weather services are a combined effort of the National Weather Service (NWS), the FAA, the Department of Defense (DOD), and other aviation groups and individuals. Because of the increasing need for worldwide weather services, foreign weather services also have a vital input into the U.S. weather service.

This study unit contains a brief explanation of the most commonly used weather reports, forecasts, and charts. For a complete and detailed explanation of the topics in this study unit and additional aviation weather reports, forecasts, etc., see the Gleim *Aviation Weather and Weather Services* book.

8.1 FLIGHT SERVICE STATION (FSS)

1. Flight Service Stations (FSSs) are FAA facilities that provide a variety of services to pilots, including pilot weather briefings.

   a. An FSS provides preflight and in-flight briefings, transcribed weather briefings, scheduled and unscheduled weather broadcasts, and it furnishes weather support to flights in its area.

   b. Flight service specialists are certificated pilot weather briefers and, as such, are not authorized to make original forecasts.

      1) They are trained to translate and interpret available forecasts and reports directly into terms of the weather conditions you may expect along your route of flight and at your destination.

2. To contact an FSS by telephone, dial 1-800-WX-BRIEF (1-800-992-7433).

   a. You will talk to a specialist to obtain the latest information.

      1) Press 1 or say "briefer" to speak to a briefer when prompted.

      2) You may say the name of the state for which you are seeking a weather briefing, or you may say "any" to get the first available briefer.

         a) Using the "any" service will help you avoid long hold times during peak operation times.

3) When requesting a briefing, identify yourself as a pilot and provide the following:
   a) Type of flight, VFR or IFR
   b) Aircraft number or your name
   c) Aircraft type
   d) Departure point
   e) Proposed time of departure
   f) Flight altitude(s)
   g) Route of flight
   h) Destination
   i) Estimated time en route (ETE) or estimated time of arrival (ETA)

4) With this background, the briefer can proceed directly with the briefing and concentrate on weather relevant to your flight.

5) The briefing you receive depends on the type requested.

   a) A **standard briefing** should be obtained before every flight because it provides all the necessary information.

   b) An **abbreviated briefing** should be requested when you need information to supplement mass disseminated information or update a previous briefing, or when you need only one or two specific items.

      i) Inform the briefer of the time and source of the previously received information so that necessary information will not be omitted inadvertently.

   c) An **outlook briefing** should be requested whenever your proposed departure time is 6 or more hours from the time of your briefing.

   d) An **in-flight briefing** provides updates on weather conditions affecting your flight.

6) Request a standard briefing any time you are planning a flight and have not received a previous briefing. The briefer will provide the following information in sequence:

   a) Adverse conditions -- significant weather and aeronautical information that might influence you to alter the proposed flight, e.g., hazardous weather conditions, runway closures, NAVAID outages, etc.

   b) VFR flight not recommended (VNR) -- an announcement made by the briefer when conditions are present or forecast, surface or aloft, that in the briefer's judgment would make proposed VFR flight doubtful. The briefer will describe the conditions and affected locations and will announce, "VFR flight is not recommended."

      i) This announcement is advisory in nature. You are responsible for making a final decision as to whether the flight can be conducted safely.

   c) Synopsis -- a brief statement describing the types, locations, and movement of weather systems and/or air masses that may affect the proposed flight.

   d) Current conditions -- reported weather conditions applicable to the flight summarized from all available sources.

      i) This report is omitted if the proposed time of departure is more than 2 hr. away, unless it is requested by you.

   e) En route forecast -- conditions for the proposed route summarized in logical order, i.e., departure/climbout, en route, and descent.

   f) Destination forecast -- at the planned ETA, any significant changes within 1 hr. before and after the planned arrival.

g) Winds aloft -- forecast winds aloft summarized for the proposed route and altitude.

h) NOTAMs -- information from any NOTAM pertinent to the proposed flight.

i) ATC delays -- any known ATC delays and flow control advisories that might affect the proposed flight.

j) Request for PIREPs, if appropriate.

k) The following may be obtained on your request:

   i) Information on military training routes (MTR) and military operations area (MOA) activity within the flight plan area and a 100-NM extension around the flight plan area

   ii) Approximate density altitude data

   iii) Information regarding such items as air traffic services and rules, customs/immigration procedures, ADIZ rules, etc.

   iv) GPS NOTAMs

   v) Other assistance as required

7) Save your questions until the briefing is completed. Ensure that you have all the information you need and that you understand what the briefer told you.

b. The FSSs are here to serve you. You should not hesitate to discuss factors that you do not fully understand.

1) You have a complete briefing only when you have a clear picture of the weather to expect.

2) It is to your advantage to make a final weather check immediately before departure if at all possible.

3. Have an alternate plan of action.

a. When weather is questionable, get a picture of expected weather over a broader area.

1) Preplan a route to take you rapidly away from the weather if it goes sour.

b. When you fly into weather through which you cannot safely continue, you must act quickly.

1) Without preplanning, you may not know the best direction in which to turn; a wrong turn could lead to disaster.

c. A preplanned diversion beats panic. It is better to be safe than sorry.

4. If you are already in flight and you need weather information and assistance, the following services are provided by FSSs:

a. Hazardous Inflight Weather Advisory Service (HIWAS). This is a continuous broadcast service over selected VORs of in-flight aviation weather advisories, i.e., AIRMETs, SIGMETs, convective SIGMETs, severe weather forecast alerts (AWWs), center weather advisories (CWAs), and urgent pilot reports (PIREPs).

b. In-flight weather briefings. A Flight Service Station (FSS) may be contacted in flight using the universal frequency of 122.2 MHz or the frequencies listed on aeronautical charts and the Chart Supplement for the purposes listed below. To use these services, call the local FSS by its locality name and "radio." For example, "(Gainesville) Radio, this is . . . "

1) Receiving timely and meaningful weather information tailored to the type of flight intended, route of flight, and altitude

2) Opening and closing flight plans, position reporting, and disseminating pilot reports

3) Receiving updates on NOTAMs and temporary flight restrictions (TFRs)

8.2 AVIATION ROUTINE WEATHER REPORT (METAR)

1. **Elements.** A METAR report contains the following elements in the following order:

    a. Type of report
    b. ICAO station identifier
    c. Date and time of report
    d. Modifier (as required)
    e. Wind
    f. Visibility
    g. Runway visual range (RVR)
    h. Weather
    i. Sky condition
    j. Temperature/dew point
    k. Altimeter
    l. Remarks (RMK)

> NOTE: The elements in the body of a METAR report are separated by a space, except temperature and dew point, which are separated by a solidus (/). When an element does not occur or cannot be observed, that element is omitted from that particular report.

2. **Example of a METAR Report**

METAR KGNV 201953Z 24015KT 3/4SM R28/2400FT + TSRA BKN008 OVC015CB 26/25 A2985 RMK TSB32RAB32

To aid in the discussion, we have divided the report into the 12 elements:

METAR	KGNV	201953Z	___	24015KT	3/4SM	R28/2400FT	+TSRA
1.	2.	3.	4.	5.	6.	7.	8.

BKN008 OVC015CB	26/25	A2985	RMK TSB32RAB32
9.	10.	11.	12.

1. Aviation routine weather report
2. Gainesville, FL
3. Observation taken on the 20th day at 1953 UTC (or Zulu)
4. Modifier omitted; i.e., not required for this report
5. Wind 240° true at 15 kt.
6. Visibility 3/4 statute miles
7. Runway 28, runway visual range 2,400 ft.
8. Thunderstorm with heavy rain
9. Ceiling 800 ft. broken, 1,500 ft. overcast, cumulonimbus clouds
10. Temperature 26°C, dew point 25°C
11. Altimeter 29.85
12. Remarks: Thunderstorm began at 32 min. past the hour; rain began at 32 min. past the hour.

---

3. **Type of Report** (element 1). The type of report will always appear as the lead element of the report. There are two types of reports:

    a. **METAR** -- an aviation routine weather report
    b. **SPECI** -- a nonroutine aviation weather report

4. **ICAO Station Identifier** (element 2). The METAR uses the ICAO four-letter station identifier.

    a. In the contiguous 48 states, the three-letter domestic location identifier is prefixed with a "K."

        1) EXAMPLE: The identifier for San Francisco, CA, is KSFO.

5. **Date and Time of Report** (element 3). The date and time the observation is taken are transmitted as a six-digit date/time group appended with the letter **Z** to denote Coordinated Universal Time (UTC).

    a. The first two digits are the date followed with two digits for the hour and two digits for minutes.

6. **Modifier** (element 4). There are two modifiers:

   a. **AUTO** -- identifies the report as an automated report with no human intervention

      1) The type of sensor equipment used at the automated station will be encoded in the remarks section of the report.

   b. **COR** -- identifies the report as a corrected report to replace an earlier report with an error

7. **Wind** (element 5). Wind follows the date/time or modifier element.

   a. The average 2-minute direction and speed are reported in a five- or six-digit format.

      1) The first three digits are the direction FROM which the wind is blowing. The direction is to the nearest 10-degree increment referenced to TRUE north.

      2) The last two or three digits are the wind speed in knots -- two digits for speeds less than 100 kt., three digits for speeds greater than 100 kt.

      3) The abbreviation **KT** is appended to denote the use of knots for wind speed.

   b. EXAMPLES:

      1) 24015KT means the wind is from 240° true at 15 kt.
      2) VRB04KT means the wind is variable in direction at 4 kt.
      3) 210103G130KT means the wind is from 210° true at 103 kt. with gusts to 130 kt.
      4) 00000KT means the wind is calm (i.e., less than 1 kt.).

8. **Visibility** (element 6)

   a. The visibility reported is called the prevailing visibility. **Prevailing visibility** is considered representative of the visibility conditions at the observing site. This representative visibility is the greatest distance at which objects can be seen and identified through at least 180° of the horizon circle, which need not be continuous.

   b. Visibility is reported in statute miles with a space and then fractions of statute miles, as needed, with **SM** appended to it.

      1) EXAMPLE: **1 1/2SM** means visibility is one and one-half statute miles.

   c. Automated reporting stations will show visibility less than 1/4 SM as **M1/4SM** and visibility of 10 SM and greater as **10SM**.

9. **Runway Visual Range (RVR)** (element 7)

   a. Runway visual range (RVR) is based on the measurement of a transmissometer made near the touchdown point of an instrument runway, which represents the horizontal distance a pilot will see down the runway from the approach end.

   b. RVR is reported whenever the prevailing visibility is 1 SM or less and/or the RVR for the designated instrument runway is 6,000 ft. or less.

      1) RVR is available only at airports equipped with a transmissometer.

   c. RVR is reported in the following format: **R** identifies the group, followed by the runway heading and parallel designator if needed, a solidus (*I*), and the visual range in feet (meters in other countries) followed with **FT**.

      1) EXAMPLE: **R28/1200FT** means runway 28; visual range is 1,200 ft.

10. **Weather** (element 8). The weather groups are constructed by considering, in sequence, the intensity or proximity, followed by the descriptor and the weather phenomenon; e.g., heavy rain shower is coded as +SHRA. The weather phenomenon represented by UP means unknown precipitation (automated stations only).

a. **Intensity or Proximity**

1) Intensity may be shown with most precipitation types, including those of a showery nature.

a) Intensity levels may be shown with obscurations, such as blowing dust, sand, or snow.

Symbol	Meaning
+	Heavy
(no symbol)	Moderate
–	Light

b) When more than one type of precipitation is present, the intensity refers to the first precipitation type (most predominant).

2) Proximity is applied to and reported only for weather occurring in the vicinity of the airport (between 5 and 10 SM of the usual point of observation) and is denoted by **VC**.

a) VC will replace the intensity symbol; i.e., intensity and VC will never be shown in the same group.

b. **Descriptor.** The following eight descriptors further identify weather phenomena and are used with certain types of precipitation and obscurations.

Coded	Meaning	Coded	Meaning
TS	Thunderstorm	DR	Low drifting
SH	Showers	MI	Shallow
FZ	Freezing	BC	Patchy
BL	Blowing	PR	Partial

1) Although **TS** and **SH** are used with precipitation and may be preceded with an intensity symbol, the intensity applies to the precipitation and not the descriptor.

a) EXAMPLE: **+SHRA** means heavy rain showers.

c. **Precipitation.** Precipitation is any form of water particles, whether solid or liquid, that fall from the atmosphere and reach the ground.

Coded	Meaning	Coded	Meaning
RA	Rain	GR	Hail (1/4 in. or greater)
DZ	Drizzle	GS	Small Hail/Snow Pellets
SN	Snow	PL	Ice Pellets
SG	Snow Grains	IC	Ice Crystals
UP	Unknown Precipitation		

1) **UP** will be used only by automated weather reporting systems to indicate that the system cannot identify the precipitation with any degree of proficiency.

2) **GS** is used to indicate hail less than 1/4 in. in diameter.

3) For **IC** to be reported, the visibility must be reduced by ice crystals to 6 SM or less.

d. **Obscurations to visibility.** Obscurations are any phenomena in the atmosphere, other than precipitation, that reduce horizontal visibility.

Coded	Meaning	Coded	Meaning
FG	Fog (visibility less than 5/8 SM)	PY	Spray
BR	Mist (visibility 5/8 to 6 SM)	SA	Sand
FU	Smoke	DU	Dust
HZ	Haze	VA	Volcanic Ash

1) **FG** is used to indicate fog restricting visibility to less than 5/8 SM.

2) **BR** is used to indicate mist restricting visibility from 5/8 to 6 SM and is never coded with a descriptor.

3) **BCFG** and **PRFG** are used to indicate patchy fog or partial fog only if the prevailing visibility is 7 SM or greater.

e. **Other.** Six other weather phenomena are reported when they occur.

Coded	Meaning	Coded	Meaning
SQ	Squall	SS	Sandstorm
DS	Duststorm	PO	Well-Developed Dust/Sand Whirls
FC	Funnel Cloud	+FC	Tornado or Waterspout

1) A **squall** (**SQ**) is a sudden increase in wind speed of at least 16 kt., with the speed rising to 22 kt. or more and lasting at least 1 minute.

2) **+FC** is used to denote a tornado, waterspout, or well-developed funnel cloud.

   a) The type will be indicated in the remarks.

f. **Examples of Reported Weather Phenomena**

1) **TSRA** means thunderstorm with moderate rain.
2) **+SN** means heavy snow.
3) **–RA FG** means light rain and fog.
4) **VCSH** means showers in the vicinity.

11. **Sky Condition** (element 9). The sky condition is reported in the following format:

a. **Amount.** The amount of sky cover is reported in eighths of sky cover, using the contractions shown below.

Contraction	Meaning	Summation Amount
SKC or CLR*	Clear	0 or 0 below 12,000 ft.
FEW	Few	>0 to 2/8
SCT	Scattered	3/8 to 4/8
BKN	Broken	5/8 to 7/8
OVC	Overcast	8/8
VV	Vertical Visibility (indefinite ceiling)	8/8
CB	Cumulonimbus	When present
TCU	Towering Cumulus	When present

* **SKC** will be reported at manual stations. **CLR** will be used at automated stations when no clouds below 12,000 ft. are reported.

1) A **ceiling** is defined as the lowest broken or overcast layer aloft or vertical visibility into a surface-based obstruction.

   a) The METAR code does not contain a provision for reporting a thin layer (i.e., a layer through which blue sky or higher sky cover is visible). A thin layer will be reported the same as if it were opaque.

b.   **Height.** Cloud bases are reported with three digits in hundreds of feet above ground level (AGL).

1)   When more than one layer is reported, layers are given in ascending order of height. For each layer above a lower layer(s), the sky cover contraction for that layer will be the **total sky cover**, which includes that layer and all lower layers.

a)   EXAMPLE: **SCT010 BKN025 OVC080** reports three layers:

i)   A scattered layer at 1,000 ft.

ii)   A broken layer (ceiling) at 2,500 ft.

iii) A top layer at 8,000 ft. In this case, it is assumed that the total sky covered by all the layers is 8/8. Thus, the upper layer is reported as overcast.

c.   **Type or Vertical Visibility**

1)   If **towering cumulus clouds (TCU)** or cumulonimbus clouds **(CB)** are present, they are reported after the height that represents their base.

a)   EXAMPLES:

i)   **SCT025TCU BKN080 BKN250** means 2,500 ft. scattered towering cumulus, ceiling 8,000 ft. broken, 25,000 ft. broken.

ii)   **SCT008 OVC012CB** means 800 ft. scattered, ceiling 1,200 ft. overcast cumulonimbus clouds.

2)   Height into an indefinite ceiling is preceded with **VV** (vertical visibility) followed by three digits indicating the vertical visibility in hundreds of feet.

a)   The layer is spoken of as an "indefinite ceiling" and indicates total obscuration.

b)   EXAMPLE: **1/8SM FG VV006** means visibility 1/8 SM, fog, indefinite ceiling 600 ft.

12. **Temperature/Dew Point Group** (element 10)

a.   Temperature and dew point are reported in a two-digit form in whole degrees Celsius (C) separated by a solidus (/).

1)   Temperatures below zero are prefixed with **M**.

b.   EXAMPLES:

1)   **15/08** means temperature is 15°C and dew point is 8°C.

2)   **00/M02** means temperature is 0°C and dew point is –2°C.

3)   **M05/** means temperature is –5°C and dew point is missing.

c.   An air mass with a 3°C or less temperature/dew point spread is considered saturated.

13. **Altimeter** (element 11)

a.   The altimeter is reported in a four-digit format representing tens, units, tenths, and hundredths of inches of mercury prefixed with **A**. The decimal point is not reported.

1)   EXAMPLE: **A2995** means the altimeter setting is 29.95 inches of mercury.

14. **Remarks** (element 12)

a.   Remarks will be included in all observations, when appropriate, and are preceded by the contraction **RMK**.

1)   Time entries are shown as minutes past the hour if the time reported occurs during the same hour the observation is taken.

2)   Location of phenomena within 5 SM of the station will be reported as at the station.

a)   Phenomena between 5 and 10 SM will be reported in the vicinity, **VC**.

b)   Phenomena beyond 10 SM will be reported as distant, **DSNT**.

b. There are two categories of remarks:

1) **Automated, manual, and plain language remarks category.** This category of remarks may be generated from either manual or automated weather reporting stations, and they generally elaborate on parameters reported in the body of the report. Some of these remarks include

a) **Station type.** This remark is shown only if the **AUTO** modifier was used.

i) **AO1** means the automated weather station is without a precipitation discriminator.

ii) **AO2** means the automated weather station has a precipitation discriminator.

iii) A precipitation discriminator can determine the difference between liquid and frozen/freezing precipitation.

b) **Beginning and/or Ending Times for Precipitation and Thunderstorms**

i) When precipitation begins or ends, remarks will show the type of precipitation as well as the beginning and/or ending time(s) of occurrence.

- Types of precipitation may be combined if beginning or ending at the same time.
- EXAMPLE: **RAB05E30SNB20E55** means that rain began at 5 min. past the hour and ended at 30 min. past the hour, and snow began at 20 min. past the hour and ended at 55 min. past the hour.

ii) When thunderstorms begin or end, remarks will show the thunderstorm as well as the beginning and/or ending time(s) of occurrence.

- EXAMPLE: **TSB05E40** means the thunderstorm began at 5 min. past the hour and ended at 40 min. past the hour.

2) **Additive and maintenance data remarks category.** Additive data groups are reported only at designated stations, and the maintenance data groups are reported only from automated weather reporting stations. Some of these remarks include

a) **Sensor Status Indicators**

i) If an automated weather reporting station is equipped with the following sensors and they are not working, the following remarks will appear:

- **PWINO** -- present weather identifier not available
- **PNO** -- precipitation amount not available
- **FZRANO** -- freezing rain information indicator not available
- **TSNO** -- lightning information not available
- **VISNO** -- visibility sensor information not available
- **CHINO** -- cloud height indicator information not available

b) **Maintenance indicator.** A maintenance indicator (dollar) sign, **$**, is included when an automated weather reporting system detects that maintenance is needed on the system.

8.3 PILOT WEATHER REPORT (PIREP)

1.   No more timely or helpful weather observations fill the gaps between reporting stations than those observations and reports made by fellow pilots during flight. Aircraft in flight are the only source of direct observations of cloud tops, icing, and turbulence.

   a.   Pilots are also urged to volunteer reports when encountering any unforecasted condition.

2.   A PIREP is transmitted in the format as shown below. Items 1 through 6 are included in all transmitted PIREPs along with one or more of items 7 through 13.

   a.   All altitude references are MSL unless otherwise noted.
   b.   Distances are in nautical miles (NM), and time is in UTC (or Z).

PIREP ELEMENT CODE CHART		
PIREP Element	PIREP Code	Contents
1. Station identifier	XXX	Nearest weather reporting location to the reported phenomenon
2. Report type	UA or UUA	Routine or Urgent PIREP
3. Location	/OV	In relation to a VOR
4. Time	/TM	Coordinated Universal Time
5. Altitude	/FL	Essential for turbulence and icing reports
6. Type aircraft	/TP	Essential for turbulence and icing reports
7. Sky cover	/SK	Cloud height and coverage (sky clear, few, scattered, broken, or overcast)
8. Weather	/WX	Flight visibility, precipitation, restrictions to visibility, etc.
9. Temperature	/TA	Degrees Celsius
10. Wind	/WV	Direction in degrees true north and speed in knots
11. Turbulence	/TB	Intensity
12. Icing	/IC	Type and Intensity
13. Remarks	/RM	For reporting elements not included or to clarify previously reported items

3.   EXAMPLE: OKC UA /OV OKC 063064/TM 1522/FL080/TP C172/TA M04/WV 245040 /TB LGT/RM IN CLR

   a.   The PIREP decodes as follows: Pilot report, 64 NM on the 063-degree radial from the Oklahoma City VOR at 1522 UTC. Flight level is 8,000 ft. Type of aircraft is a Cessna 172. Outside air temperature is –4° C, wind is 245° true at 40 kt., light turbulence, and the aircraft is in clear skies.

8.4 TERMINAL AERODROME FORECAST (TAF)

1.   The terminal aerodrome forecast (TAF) is a concise statement of the expected weather at a specific airport during a 24- or 30-hour period.

   a.   The TAF covers an area within a 5-SM radius of the center of the airport and is prepared four times daily at 0000Z, 0600Z, 1200Z, and 1800Z.

   b.   Many of the weather codes used in the METAR are also used in the TAF.

   c.   The 32 largest airports in the U.S. offer 30-hour forecasts. Every other site provides a 24-hour forecast.

2.   **Elements.** A TAF contains the following elements in the following order (items a-i). Forecast change indicators (items j-l) and probability forecast (item m) are used as appropriate.

<table>
<tr><td></td><td>Forecast of</td><td></td></tr>
<tr><td>Communications Header</td><td>Meteorological Conditions</td><td>Time Elements</td></tr>
<tr><td>a. Type of report</td><td>e. Wind</td><td>j. Temporary (TEMPO)</td></tr>
<tr><td>b. ICAO station identifier</td><td>f. Visibility</td><td>k. From (FM)</td></tr>
<tr><td>c. Date and time of origin</td><td>g. Weather</td><td>l. Becoming (BECMG)</td></tr>
<tr><td>d. Valid period date and time</td><td>h. Sky condition</td><td>m. Probability (PROB)</td></tr>
<tr><td></td><td>i. Wind shear (optional)</td><td></td></tr>
</table>

3.   Example:

```
TAF
KOKC 051130Z 0512/0612 14008KT 5SM BR BKN030 WS018/32030KT
   TEMPO 0513/0516 1SM BR
FM051600 16010KT P6SM SKC
BECMG 0522/0624 20013G20KT 4SM SHRA OVC020
PROB40 0600/0606 2SM TSRA OVC008CB=
```

To aid in the discussion, we have divided the TAF above into elements 1. – 13. as follows:

TAF   KOKC   051130Z   0512/0612   14008KT   5SM   BR   BKN030
1.   2.   3.   4.   5.   6.   7.   8.

WS018/32030KT   TEMPO 0513/0516 1SM BR   FM051600 16010KT P6SM SKC
9.   10.   11.

BECMG 0522/0624 20013G20KT 4SM SHRA OVC020
12.

PROB40 0600/0606 2SM TSRA OVC008CB=
13.

1.   Routine terminal aerodrome forecast

2.   Oklahoma City, OK

3.   Forecast prepared on the 5th day at 1130 UTC (or Z)

4.   Forecast valid from the 5th day at 1200 UTC until 1200 UTC on the 6th day

5.   Wind 140° true at 8 kt.

6.   Visibility 5 SM

7.   Visibility obscured by mist

8.   Ceiling 3,000 ft. broken

   a)   A vertical visibility (VV) may also be forecast as a sky condition when the sky is expected to be obscured by a surface-based phenomena.

9.   Low-level wind shear at 1,800 ft., wind 320° true at 30 kt.

10.   Temporary (spoken as occasional) visibility 1 SM in mist between 1300 UTC and 1600 UTC of the 5th day

11.   From (or after) 1600 UTC on the 5th day, wind 160° true at 10 kt., visibility more than 6SM, sky clear

12.   Becoming (gradual change) wind 200° true at 13 kt., gusts to 20 kt., visibility 4 SM in moderate rain showers, ceiling 2,000 ft. overcast between 2200 UTC and 2400 UTC on the 5th and beginning the 6th day

   a)   BECMG is only used at military airfields.

13.   Probability (40% chance) between 0000 UTC and 0600 UTC of the 6th day of visibility 2 SM, thunderstorm, moderate rain, ceiling 800 ft. overcast, cumulonimbus clouds (The = sign indicates end of forecast.)

4. **Type of Report** (element 1). There are two types of TAF issuances:

    a.   **TAF** means a routine forecast.

    b.   **TAF AMD** means an amended forecast.

5. **ICAO Station Identifier** (element 2). The TAF uses the ICAO four-letter station identifier.

6. **Date and Time of Origin** (element 3). This element is the date and time (UTC) that the forecast is actually prepared. The format is a two-digit date and a four-digit time followed by the letter **Z.**

7. **Valid Period Date and Time** (element 4). The UTC valid period of the forecast is a two-digit date followed by the two-digit beginning hour, a solidus, and the two-digit date and two-digit ending hour.

    a.   Valid periods beginning at 0000 UTC will be indicated as **00**, and valid periods ending at 0000 UTC will be indicated as **24**.

8. **Forecast Meteorological Conditions.** This element is the body of the TAF.

    a.   The wind, visibility, and sky condition elements are always included in the initial date/time group of the forecast.

        1)   Weather is included only if it is significant to aviation.

    b.   If a significant, lasting change in any of the elements is expected during the valid period, a new date/time period with the changes is included.

        1)   Note that, with the exception of a From (FM) group, the new date/time period will include only those elements expected to change; i.e., if a lowering of the visibility is expected but the wind is expected to remain the same, the new period reflecting the lower visibility would not include a forecast wind.

            a)   The forecast wind would remain the same as in the previous period.

    c.   Any temporary conditions expected during a specific date/time period are included with that period.

9. **Wind** (element 5). The wind element is a five- or six-digit group with the forecast surface wind direction (first three digits) referenced to true north and the speed (last two digits or three digits if 100 kt. or greater).

    a.   The abbreviation **KT** is appended to denote the use of knots for wind speed.

    b.   A calm wind (0 kt.) is forecast as **00000KT**.

10. **Visibility** (element 6). The expected prevailing visibility is forecast in statute miles with a space and then fractions of statute miles, as needed, with **SM** appended to it.

    a.   Forecast visibility greater than 6 SM is coded **P6SM**.

11. **Weather** (element 7). The expected weather phenomenon or phenomena are coded in TAF reports using the same format, qualifiers, and phenomena contractions as METAR reports, except **UP** (unknown precipitation).

    a.   Obscurations to vision will be forecast whenever the prevailing visibility is forecast to be 6 SM or less.

    b.   If no significant weather is expected to occur during a specific time period in the forecast, the weather group is omitted for that time period.

        1)   If, after a time period in which significant weather has been forecast, a change to a forecast of no significant weather occurs, the contraction **NSW** (No Significant Weather) will appear as the weather included in becoming (BECMG) or temporary (TEMPO) groups.

            a)   NSW will not be used in the initial time period of a TAF or in from (FM groups).

12. **Sky Conditions** (element 8). TAF sky conditions use the METAR format, except that cumulonimbus clouds (CB) are the only cloud type forecast in TAFs.

13. **Wind Shear** (element 9) (optional data). Wind shear is the forecast of nonconvective low-level winds (up to 2,000 ft. AGL) and is entered after the sky conditions when wind shear is expected. The wind shear element is omitted if not expected to occur.

   a. The forecast includes the height of the wind shear followed by the wind direction and wind speed at the indicated height.

   b. Wind shear is encoded with the contraction **WS**, followed by a three-digit height and winds at the height indicated in the same format as surface winds.

      1) Height is given in hundreds of feet AGL up to and including 2,000 ft.

14. There are three forecast change indicators used when either a rapid, a gradual, or a temporary change is expected in some or all of the forecast meteorological conditions.

   a. The change indicators are

      1) From (FM)
      2) Becoming (BECMG)
      3) Temporary (TEMPO)

   b. Each change indicator marks a time group within the TAF.

   c. The probability (PROB) forecast also indicates a time of forecast weather events.

15. **Temporary (TEMPO) Group** (element 10). The **TEMPO** group is used for any conditions in wind, visibility, weather, or sky condition expected to last for generally less than an hour at a time (occasional) and to occur during less than half the time period.

   a. The **TEMPO** indicator is followed by a four-digit group, a solidus, and another four-digit group giving the beginning day/hour and the ending day/hour of the time period during which the temporary conditions are expected.

   b. Only the changing forecast meteorological conditions are included in **TEMPO** groups.

      1) The omitted conditions are carried over from the previous time group.

16. **From (FM) Group** (element 11). The **FM** group is used when a rapid change, usually occurring in less than 1 hour, is expected.

   a. Typically, a rapid change of prevailing conditions to more or less a completely new set of conditions is associated with a synoptic feature (i.e., cold or warm front) passing through the terminal area.

   b. Appended to the **FM** indicator is the two-digit date and the four-digit hour and minute when the change is expected to begin and continue until the next change group or until the end of the current forecast.

   c. A **FM** group will always mark the beginning of a new line in a TAF report.

   d. Each **FM** group contains all the required elements, i.e., wind, visibility, weather, and sky condition.

      1) Weather and wind shear will be omitted in **FM** groups when it is not significant to aviation.

      2) **FM** groups will not include the contraction **NSW**.

17. **Becoming (BECMG) Group** (element 12). The **BECMG** group is used when a gradual change in conditions is expected over a longer time period, but no longer than 2 hours.

   a. Appended to the **BECMG** indicator is a four-digit group, a solidus, and another four-digit group with the beginning day/hour and the ending day/hour of the change period.

      1) The gradual change will occur within this time period.

   b. Only the changing forecast meteorological conditions are included in **BECMG** groups.

      1) The omitted conditions are carried over from the previous time group.

18. **Probability (PROB) Forecast** (element 13). The **PROB** indicates the chance of thunderstorms or other precipitation events occurring, along with associated weather conditions (wind, visibility, and sky conditions).

    a.   A probability forecast will not be used during the first 6 hr. of a TAF.

    b.   Appended to the **PROB** contraction is the probability value.

        1)   EXAMPLES:

            a)   **PROB40** means there is a 40-49% probability.
            b)   **PROB30** means there is a 30-39% probability.

    c.   Appended to the **PROB** indicator is a four-digit group giving the beginning day/hour and another four-digit group giving the ending day/hour of the time period during which the precipitation or thunderstorms are expected.

8.5 GRAPHICAL AIRMAN'S METEOROLOGICAL ADVISORY (G-AIRMET)

1. The G-AIRMET is a graphical advisory of potentially hazardous weather conditions for aircraft. These conditions are less severe than those reported in SIGMETs, and they are only valid at specific time "snapshots."

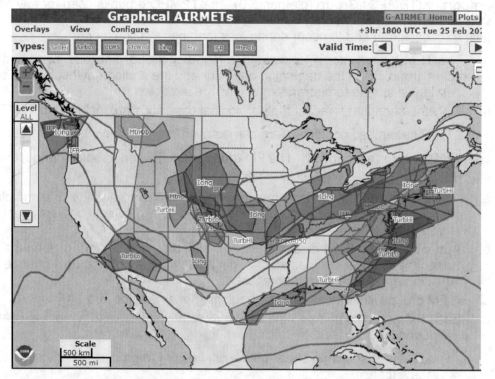

    a.   For G-AIRMETs, forecasters create graphical objects depicting the areas and attributes of AIRMET hazards.

2. G-AIRMETs are issued at discrete times no more than 3 hr. apart for a period of up to 12 hr. into the future (00, 03, 06, 09, and 12 hr.). They are issued at 03:00, 09:00, 15:00, and 21:00 UTC (with updates issued as necessary). AIRMETs are issued by the Aviation Weather Center (AWC) for the contiguous United States and adjacent coastal waters.

3. Graphical snapshots and interactive displays, which help define possible impact upon en route navigation, can be accessed at www.aviationweather.gov/gairmet.

4. G-AIRMET users must keep in mind that if a 00-hr. forecast shows no significant weather and a 03-hr. forecast shows hazardous weather, the change is occurring during the period between the two forecasts.

8.6 GRAPHICAL FORECASTS FOR AVIATION (GFA)

1. An FAA-NWS joint-agency working group recently recommended that the area forecast (FA) be transitioned to more modern digital and graphical forecasts, observations, and communications capabilities that provide improved weather information to decision-makers.

    a. The result of this effort is the Graphical Forecasts for Aviation (GFA).

2. GFA are intended to provide the necessary aviation weather information to give users a complete picture of the weather that may impact flight in the continental U.S. (CONUS).

    a. The GFA web page includes observational data, forecasts, and warnings that can be viewed from 14 hr. in the past to 15 hr. in the future, including thunderstorms, clouds, flight category, precipitation, icing, turbulence, and wind.

    b. Hourly model data and forecasts, including information on clouds, flight category, precipitation, icing, turbulence, wind, and graphical output from the National Weather Service's National Digital Forecast Data (NDFD), are available.

    c. Wind, icing, and turbulence forecasts are available in 3,000-ft. increments from the surface up to 30,000 ft. MSL, and in 6,000-ft. increments from 30,000 ft. MSL to FL480 (48,000 ft. MSL). Turbulence forecasts are also broken into LO (below 18,000 ft. MSL) and HI (at or above 18,000 ft. MSL) graphics.

    d. A maximum icing graphic and maximum wind velocity graphic (regardless of altitude) are also available.

    e. Built with modern geospatial information tools, users can pan and zoom to focus on areas of greatest interest.

    f. GFA can be accessed at www.aviationweather.gov/gfa.

3. A GFA forecast for turbulence intensity at the 9,000-ft. level at 2100Z is shown below.

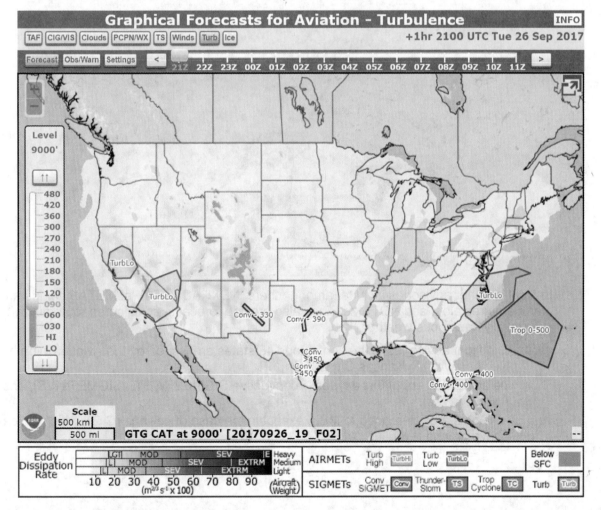

8.7 IN-FLIGHT AVIATION WEATHER ADVISORIES

1.   Flight Service Stations (FSSs) specifically provide en route aircraft with current weather along their route of flight.

   a.   Flight Service is available throughout the country on 122.2 MHz or the frequencies listed on aeronautical charts and the Chart Supplement.

      1)   On a sectional chart, the name of the nearest FSS facility is sometimes indicated in communications boxes.

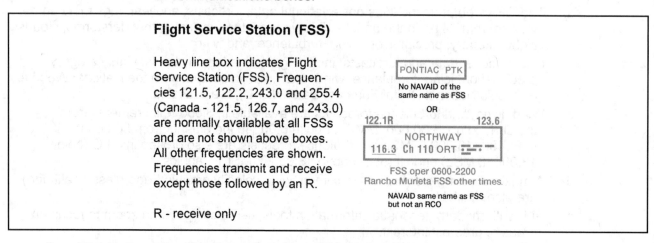

2.   Flight Information Service – Broadcast (FIS-B) is available to aircraft receiving data over 978 MHz (UAT) and provides current weather and aeronautical information in the cockpit.

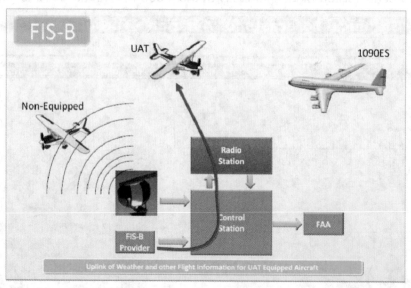

3.   In-flight weather advisories include, among others, NEXRAD, PIREPs, METAR, winds and temperatures aloft, and NOTAMs. They also provide forecasts advising en route aircraft of potentially hazardous weather.

   a.   All in-flight advisories in the contiguous 48 states are issued by the Aviation Weather Center (AWC) in Kansas City, MO.

   b.   The advisories are of three types -- convective SIGMET (WST), SIGMET (WS), and AIRMET (WA).

   c.   All heights are referenced to MSL, except in the case of ceilings (CIG), which indicate above ground level.

4. **Convective SIGMET (WST)**

    a.   Convective SIGMETs are issued in the contiguous 48 states (i.e., none for Alaska and Hawaii) for any of the following:

        1)   Severe thunderstorm due to

            a)   Surface winds greater than or equal to 50 kt.
            b)   Hail at the surface greater than or equal to 3/4 in. in diameter
            c)   Tornadoes

        2)   Embedded thunderstorms

        3)   A line of thunderstorms

        4)   Thunderstorms producing precipitation greater than or equal to heavy precipitation affecting 40% or more of an area of at least 3,000 square miles.

    b.   Any convective SIGMET implies severe or greater turbulence, severe icing, and low-level wind shear. A convective SIGMET may be issued for any convective situation that the forecaster feels is hazardous to all categories of aircraft.

    c.   Three convective SIGMET bulletins, each covering a specified geographic area, are issued. These areas are the Eastern (E), Central (C), and Western (W) U.S.

        1)   These bulletins are issued on a scheduled basis, hourly at 55 min. past the hour (H+55) and as special bulletins on an unscheduled basis.

        2)   Each convective SIGMET bulletin will

            a)   Be made up of one or more individually numbered convective SIGMETs
            b)   Be valid for 2 hr. or until superseded by the next hourly issue
            c)   Consist of either an observation and a forecast or just a forecast

    d.   An outlook, which is a forecast of thunderstorm systems that are expected to require a convective SIGMET issuance during the next 2 to 6 hr., is provided on each hourly bulletin.

    e.   EXAMPLE:

```
CONVECTIVE SIGMET 6E
VALID UNTIL 2255Z
FL
40SE CTY
ISOL SEV TS D20 MOV LTL. TOPS ABV FL450. HAIL TO 1 IN...WIND GUSTS TO
    50 KT POSS.

OUTLOOK VALID 222255-230255
FROM MGM-SAV-70E MIA-FMY-CTY-120SW MSY-BRO-ACT-MGM STNR
    FRONT EXTDS FM CNTRL FL PEN W ACRS NRN GULFMEX. CLUSTERS OF
    SLOW MVG TS WL CONT TO DVLP AS WK TROF MOVES E ACRS CNTRL TX.
    OTR TS ARE DVLPG OVR FL AS NW UPR LVL FLOW CROSSES FRONT.
RFM
```

5. **SIGMET (WS)**

    a.   A SIGMET advises of nonconvective weather that is potentially hazardous to all aircraft.

        1)   In the conterminous U.S., SIGMETs are issued when the following phenomena occur or are expected to occur:

            a)   Severe icing not associated with thunderstorms

            b)   Severe or extreme turbulence or clear air turbulence (CAT) not associated with thunderstorms

            c)   Duststorms, sandstorms, or volcanic ash lowering surface or in-flight visibilities to below 3 SM

            d)   Volcanic eruption

    b.   SIGMETs are identified by alphabetic designators that include NOVEMBER through YANKEE but exclude SIERRA and TANGO.

        1)   The first issuance of a SIGMET is labeled UWS (urgent weather SIGMET), and subsequent issuances are at the forecaster's discretion.

        2)   Issuances for the same phenomenon are sequentially numbered using the original designator until the phenomenon ends.

            a)   Note that no two different phenomena across the country can have the same alphabetic designator at the same time.

    c.   EXAMPLE:

```
DFWW UWS 131740
SIGMET WHISKEY 1 VALID UNTIL 132140
TN AL MS
FROM 40E TRI – 40E CHA – CHA – 60E MGM – MGM – GTR – BNA – 40E TRI
OCNL SVR TURBC BLW 120 AND LLWS DUE TO STG LOW LEVEL SRN FLOW.
   ALSO RPTD BY LRG ACFT. CONDS CONTG BYD 2140Z.
```

6. **AIRMET (WA)**

    a.   AIRMETs are advisories of significant weather phenomena but describe conditions at intensities lower than those that trigger SIGMETs. AIRMETs are intended to be disseminated to all pilots in the preflight and en route phase of flight to enhance safety.

        1)   AIRMET bulletins are issued on a scheduled basis every 6 hours.

            a)   Unscheduled updates and corrections are issued as necessary.

        2)   Each AIRMET bulletin contains

            a)   Any current AIRMETs in effect
            b)   An outlook for conditions expected after the AIRMET valid period

        3)   AIRMETs within each bulletin are valid for 6 hr. and contain details on one or more of the following phenomena when they occur or are forecast to occur:

            a)   Moderate icing

            b)   Moderate turbulence

             c)   Sustained surface winds of 30 kt. or more

            d)   Ceiling less than 1,000 ft. and/or visibility less than 3 SM affecting over 50% of the area at one time

            e)   Extensive mountain obscurement

            f)   Low-level wind shear

            g)   Freezing-level heights

b.   AIRMETs have fixed alphanumeric designators of ZULU for icing and freezing level; TANGO for turbulence, strong surface winds, and low-level wind shear; and SIERRA for instrument flight rules (IFR) and mountain obscuration.

c.   EXAMPLE:

```
MIAT WA 131445
AIRMET TANGO UPDT 2 FOR TURB VALID UNTIL 132100

AIRMET TURB...NC SC GA FL AND CSTL WTRS
FROM TRI – ECG – JAX – TLH – 40W CEW – 50SW ABY – CHA – TRI
OCNL MOD TURB BLW 140 WITH TURB LCL SEV FOR LGT ACFT BLW 080.
   CONDS CONTG BYD ENDG 00Z.
```

7.   **Center Weather Advisory (CWA)** is an unscheduled in-flight air crew, flow control, and air traffic advisory for use in anticipating and avoiding adverse weather conditions in the en route and terminal areas.

a.   A CWA is issued by the Center Weather Service Unit meteorologist located in the Air Route Traffic Control Center (ARTCC), not by the AWC, which issues WSTs, WSs, and WAs.

b.   The CWA is **not** a flight planning forecast but a **nowcast** for conditions beginning within the next 2 hours.

1)   Maximum valid time of a CWA is 2 hr. from the time of issuance.

2)   If conditions are expected to continue beyond the valid period, a statement will be included in the advisory.

c.   A CWA may be issued for the following three situations:

1)   A supplement to an existing in-flight advisory is needed for the purpose of improving or updating the definition of the phenomenon in terms of location, movement, extent, or intensity relevant to the ARTCC area of responsibility.

2)   An in-flight advisory has not yet been issued, but conditions meet in-flight advisory criteria based on current pilot reports, and the information must be disseminated sooner than the AWC can issue the in-flight advisory.

3)   In-flight advisory criteria are not met, but conditions are or will shortly be adversely affecting the safe flow of air traffic within the ARTCC area of responsibility.

d.   EXAMPLE:

```
ZAB1 CWA 222010
ZAB CWA 102 VALID UNTIL 222210
FROM TBE TO AMA TO 40S ROW TO 50SW TCS TO 50WNW INW TO TBE
AREA OF WDLY SCT TS MOV FROM 27015KT. TOPS TO FL400. TS OCNLY IN
   LNS AND CLUSTERS. SMALL HAIL G45 KTS POSS.
```

8.8 WINDS AND TEMPERATURES ALOFT FORECAST (FB)

1. Winds and temperatures aloft are forecast for specific locations in the contiguous U.S.

    a. Forecasts are made four times daily based on 0000Z, 0600Z, 1200Z, and 1800Z data for use during specific time intervals.

2. Below is a sample FB message containing a heading and six FB locations. The heading always includes the time during which the FB may be used (1700-2100Z in the example) and a notation "TEMPS NEG ABV 24000," which means that, since temperatures above 24,000 ft. are always negative, the minus sign is omitted.

FB KWBC 151640

BASED ON 151200Z DATA

VALID 151800Z FOR USE 1700-2100Z TEMPS NEG ABV 24000

FT	3000	6000	9000	12000	18000	24000	30000	34000	39000
ALA			2420	2635–08	2535–18	2444–30	245945	246755	246862
AMA		2714	2725+00	2625–04	2531–15	2542–27	265842	256352	256762
DEN			2321–04	2532–08	2434–19	2441–31	235347	236056	236262
HLC		1707–01	2113–03	2219–07	2330–17	2435–30	244145	244854	245561
MKC	0507	2006+03	2215–01	2322–06	2338–17	2348–29	236143	237252	238160
STL	2113	2325+07	2332+02	2339–04	2356–16	2373–27	239440	730649	731960

---

    a. The line labeled "FT" (forecast levels) shows 9 to 11 standard FB levels.

        1) Through 12,000 ft., the levels are true altitude, and from 18,000 ft. and above, the levels are pressure altitude.

        2) The FB locations are transmitted in alphabetical order.

    b. Note that some lower-level wind groups are omitted.

        1) No winds are forecast within 1,500 ft. of station elevation.

        2) Also, no temperatures are forecast for the 3,000-ft. level or for any level within 2,500 ft. of station elevation.

3. **Decoding**

    a. A four-digit group shows wind direction, in reference to true north, and wind speed.

        1) The first two digits give direction in tens of degrees, and the second two digits are the wind speed in knots.

        2) Look at the St. Louis (STL) forecast for 3,000 ft. The group **2113** means the wind is from 210° at 13 knots.

    b. A six-digit group includes forecast temperatures.

        1) In the STL forecast, the coded group for 9,000 ft. is **2332+02**. The wind is from 230° at 32 kt., and the temperature is plus 2°C.

    c. If the wind speed is forecast to be from 100 to 199 kt., the forecaster will add 50 to the wind direction and subtract 100 from the wind speed. To decode, you must subtract 50 from the wind direction and add 100 to the wind speed.

        1) In the STL forecast, the coded group at 39,000 ft. is 731960. The wind is from 230° (73 – 50 = 23) at 119 kt. (100 + 19 = 119), and the temperature is –60°C.

    d. When the forecast speed is less than 5 kt., the coded group is 9900 and is read LIGHT AND VARIABLE.

8.9 SURFACE ANALYSIS CHART

1. The surface analysis chart is a computer-prepared report showing areas of high and low pressure, fronts, temperatures, dew points, wind directions and speeds, local weather, and visual obstructions.

   a. This chart is transmitted every 3 hours and covers the contiguous 48 states and adjacent areas.

2. Surface weather observations for reporting points are also depicted on this chart.

   a. Each reporting point is illustrated by a station model, which includes the following: Type of Observation; Sky Cover; Clouds; Sea Level Pressure; Pressure Change/ Tendency; Precipitation; Dew Point; Present Weather; Temperature; Wind.

   b. The figures below and on the next page show weather chart symbols for a sample station model.

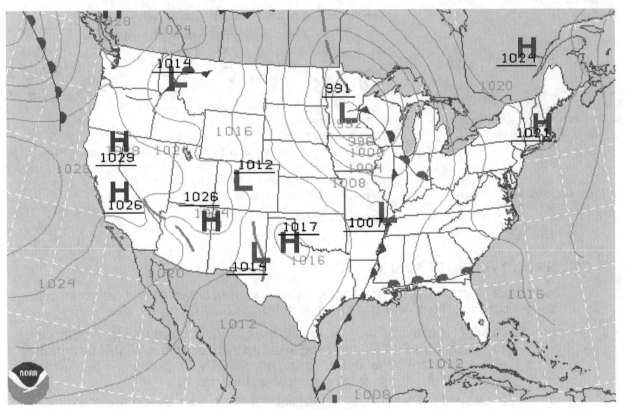

Surface analysis chart.

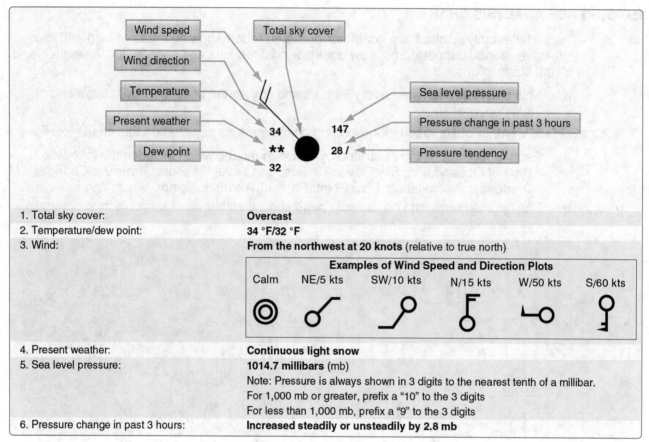

1. Total sky cover:	**Overcast**
2. Temperature/dew point:	**34 °F/32 °F**
3. Wind:	**From the northwest at 20 knots** (relative to true north)

Examples of Wind Speed and Direction Plots					
Calm	NE/5 kts	SW/10 kts	N/15 kts	W/50 kts	S/60 kts

4. Present weather:	**Continuous light snow**
5. Sea level pressure:	**1014.7 millibars** (mb)
	Note: Pressure is always shown in 3 digits to the nearest tenth of a millibar.
	For 1,000 mb or greater, prefix a "10" to the 3 digits
	For less than 1,000 mb, prefix a "9" to the 3 digits
6. Pressure change in past 3 hours:	**Increased steadily or unsteadily by 2.8 mb**

Sample station model and weather chart symbols.

8.10 CEILING AND VISIBILITY ANALYSIS (CVA)

1. The CVA product provides a real-time analysis of current observed and estimated ceiling and visibility conditions across the continental U.S. (CONUS).

   a. The product is primarily intended to help the general aviation pilot [particularly the Visual Flight Rules (VFR)-only pilot] avoid instrument flight rules (IFR) conditions. However, the CVA's overview of ceiling and visibility conditions can be useful to others involved in flight planning or weather briefing.

   b. CVA is issued every 5 min. and is available through www.aviationweather.gov.

2. CVA presents information via a full-CONUS graphic and 18 regional graphics.

   a. Each graphic is rendered on a horizontal grid of 5-km. resolution and shows viewer-selectable representations of ceiling height (AGL), surface visibility in statute miles (SM), and flight category designation.

   b. Each regional display includes an overlay of station plots showing the current ceiling and visibility observations reported at selected METAR stations.

3. The image below shows the flight category (VFR, MVFR, IFR, LIFR) and areas with possible terrain obscurations.

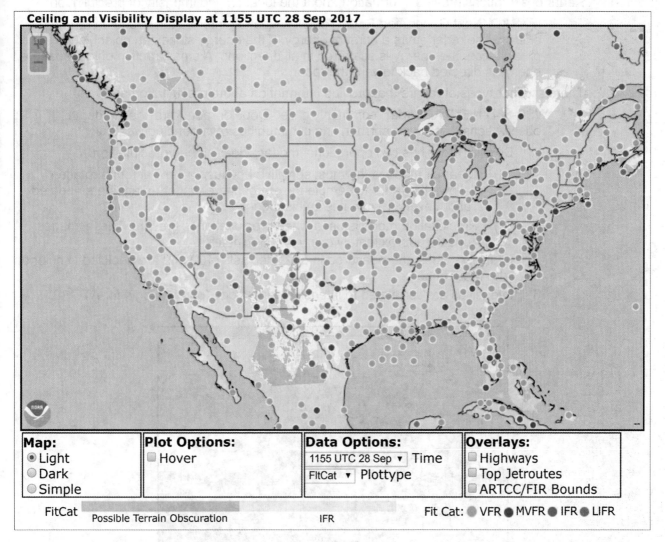

4. The CVA is an analysis of estimated real-time conditions only. It is not a forecast and cannot be used in place of a forecast.

    a. Impacted ceiling and visibility conditions can be highly localized and smaller in scale than the 5-km. grid used to convey CVA information. Thus, small-scale variations in ceiling and visibility conditions may not be represented by CVA, even in regions close to observing stations.

    b. You can zoom in from a high-level national display to regional and local areas.

5. General aviation pilots, weather briefers, and others involved in flight planning can use CVA as a companion to METARs, TAFs, and AIRMETs to help them recognize and avoid IFR conditions.

    a. Along with the foregoing weather information sources, the CVA can aid IFR avoidance and escape for an en route pilot who inadvertently encounters IFR conditions.

    b. Pilots and flight planners must exercise judgment when using CVA information because it is based on recent weather information and calculated estimations. Degrading conditions are more likely as the distance and time increase from the station's reported weather.

8.11 RADAR OBSERVATIONS

1. Radar observations provide information about the location and intensity of precipitation.

    a. NEXRAD (**Nex**t Generation **Rad**ar) obtains weather information based on returned energy. The radar emits a burst of energy. If the energy strikes an object, such as precipitation, the energy is scattered in all directions. A small fraction of that scattered energy is directed back toward the radar.

2. There are four types of radars that provide information about precipitation and wind:

    a. **WSR-88D NEXRAD radar**, commonly called Doppler radar, provides in-depth observations that inform surrounding communities of impending weather.

        1) Doppler radar has two operational modes: clear air and precipitation.

            a) Clear air mode is the most sensitive because a slow antenna rotation allows the radar to sample the atmosphere longer. Images are updated about every 10 minutes in this mode.

            b) Precipitation mode is used when precipitation is present. These images update approximately every 4 to 6 minutes.

        2) Intensity values are measured in dBZ (decibels of Z) and are depicted in color on the radar image.

        3) Intensities are correlated to intensity terminology (phraseology) for ATC purposes.

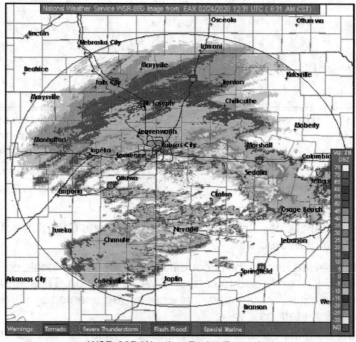

WSR-88D Weather Radar Example.

Reflectivity (dBZ) Ranges	Weather Radar Echo Intensity
<30 dBZ	Light
30–40 dBZ	Moderate
>40–50	Heavy
50+ dBZ	Extreme

WSR-88D Weather Radar Example.

    b. **FAA terminal Doppler weather radar**, installed at some major airports around the country, also aids in providing severe weather alerts and warnings to ATC. Terminal radar ensures pilots are aware of wind shear, gust fronts, and heavy precipitation, all of which are dangerous to arriving and departing aircraft.

    c.   **Airport surveillance radar** is used primarily to detect aircraft, but it also detects the location and intensity of precipitation, which is used to route aircraft traffic around severe weather in an airport environment.

    d.   **Airborne radar** is equipment carried by aircraft to locate weather disturbances. It permits both penetration of heavy precipitation, required for determining the extent of thunderstorms, and sufficient reflection from less intense precipitation.

8.12 SHORT-RANGE SURFACE PROGNOSTIC (PROG) CHART

1. Short-Range Surface Prognostic (PROG) Charts provide a forecast of surface pressure systems, fronts, and precipitation for a 2-day period.

    a.   The forecast area covers the 48 contiguous states, the coastal waters, and portions of Canada and Mexico.

    b.   The forecasted conditions are divided into four forecast periods: 12, 24, 36, and 48 hr.

        1)   Each chart depicts a "snapshot" of weather elements expected at the specified valid time.

2. PROGs (example below) are very similar to surface analysis charts.

    a.   All of the symbols depicted on both charts are the same.

    b.   The primary difference between the two charts is that PROGs are forecast charts, whereas the surface analysis chart is a "current conditions" chart.

        1)   Additionally, PROG charts do not feature station model plots.

    c.   Think of the PROG as a "future" version of the surface analysis chart.

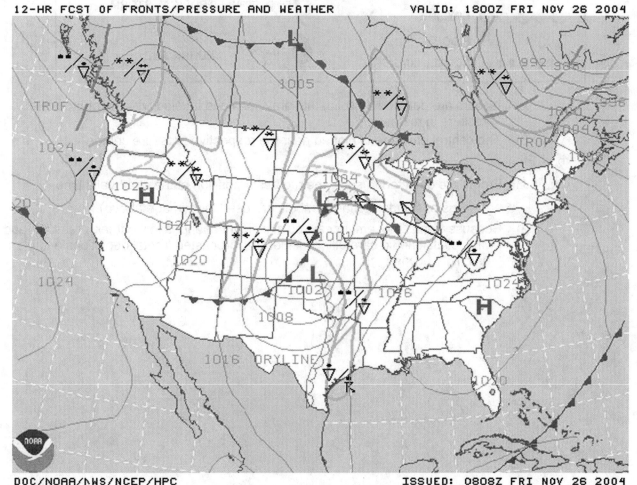

3.   Issuance

a.   The 12- and 24-hr. charts are issued four times a day and are termed "Day 1" PROGs.

b.   The 36- and 48-hr. charts are issued twice daily and are termed "Day 2" PROGs.

4.   Plotted Data

a.   Pressure Systems

1)   Pressure systems are depicted by pressure centers, troughs, isobars, drylines, tropical waves, tropical storms, and hurricanes using standard symbols.

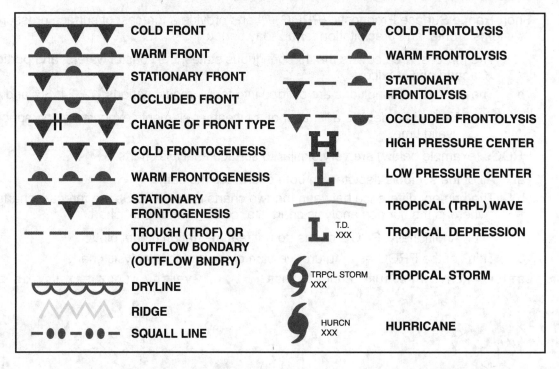

2)   Isobars are denoted by solid, thin gray lines and labeled with the appropriate pressure in millibars.

3)   The central pressure is plotted near the respective pressure center.

b.   Fronts

1)   Fronts are depicted to show their forecast position at the chart valid time.

a)   Again, standard chart symbols are used (see image above).

2)   Because frontal movement causes significant changes in weather, pressure, and wind, pilots should carefully consider the forecasted frontal depictions and plan their flight accordingly.

c.   Precipitation

   1)   Precipitation areas are enclosed by thick, solid green lines.

   2)   Standard precipitation symbols are used to identify precipitation types.

      a)   These symbols are positioned within or adjacent to the associated area of precipitation.

      b)   If adjacent to the area, an arrow will point to the area with which they are associated.

   3)   A mix of precipitation is indicated by the use of two pertinent symbols separated by a slash.

   4)   A bold, dashed gray line is used to separate precipitation within an outlined area with contrasting characteristics.

      a)   EXAMPLE: A dashed line would be used to separate an area of snow from an area of rain.

   5)   Precipitation characteristics are further described by the use of shading.

      a)   Shading or lack of shading indicates the expected coverage of the precipitation.

         i)   Shaded areas indicate the precipitation is expected to have more than 50% (broken) coverage.

         ii)   Unshaded areas indicate 30-50% (scattered) coverage.

Symbol	Meaning	Symbol	Meaning
⌂	Moderate Turbulence	● (over ▽)	Rain Shower
⌂	Severe Turbulence		
⋃	Moderate Icing	✳ (over ▽)	Snow Shower
⋃	Severe Icing	⌐	Thunderstorm
● ●	Rain	∽	Freezing Rain
✕ ✕	Snow	6	Tropical Storm
● ●	Drizzle	6	Hurricane (typhoon)

Depiction	Meaning
	Showery precipitation (thunderstorms/rain showers) covering more than half of the area.
	Continuous stable air precipitation (rain).
	Showery precipitation (snow showers) covering one-half or less of the area.
	Intermittent stable air precipitation (drizzle).
	Showery precipitation (rain showers) embedded in an area of continuous rain covering more than half of the area.

8.13 LOW-LEVEL SIGNIFICANT WEATHER (SIGWX) CHART

1.   The Low-Level Significant Weather (SIGWX) Chart provides a forecast of aviation weather hazards.

   a.   The charts are primarily intended to be used as guidance products for preflight briefings.

   b.   Each chart depicts a "snapshot" of weather expected at the specified valid time.

2.   The forecast domain covers the 48 contiguous states and the coastal waters for altitudes 24,000 ft. MSL (FL240 or 400 millibars) and below.

3.   The figure below is an example of this product.

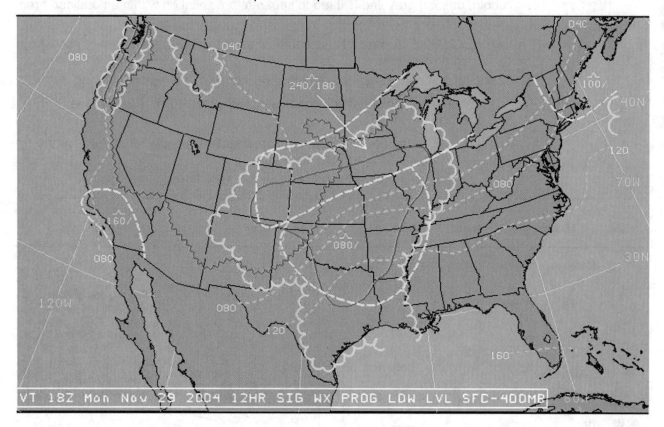

4.   SIGWX charts are issued four times per day by the Aviation Weather Center (AWC).

   a.   Two charts are issued: a 12-hour and a 24-hour chart.

5.   Low-Level SIGWX Charts depict weather flying categories (VFR, IFR, etc.), turbulence, and freezing levels. Icing is not specifically forecast.

a.   See the chart symbol legend below.

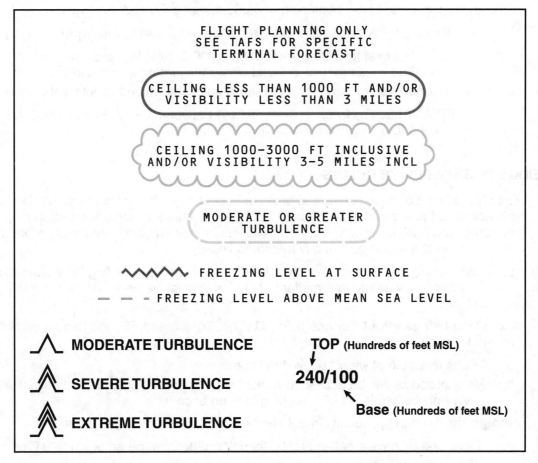

6.   **Flying Categories**

a.   Instrument Flight Rules (IFR) areas are outlined with a solid red line.
b.   Marginal Visual Flight Rules (MVFR) areas are outlined with a scalloped blue line.
c.   Visual Flight Rules (VFR) areas are implied and therefore not depicted.

7.   **Turbulence**

a.   Areas of moderate or greater turbulence are enclosed by bold, dashed yellow lines.
b.   Turbulence intensities are identified by standard symbols, as shown in the figure above.
c.   Turbulence height is depicted by two numbers separated by a solidus (/).

1)   EXAMPLE: An area on the chart with turbulence indicated as **240/100** indicates the turbulence can be expected from the top at FL240 to the base at 10,000 ft. MSL.

2)   When the base height is omitted, the turbulence is forecast to reach the surface.

a)   EXAMPLE: An indication of **080/** identifies a turbulence layer from the surface to 8,000 ft. MSL.

3)   Turbulence associated with thunderstorms is not depicted on the chart.

d.   The intensity symbols and height information may be located within or adjacent to the forecast areas of turbulence.

1)   If located adjacent to an area, an arrow will point to the associated area.

8. **Freezing Levels**

    a. If the freezing level is at the surface, it is depicted by a blue saw-toothed symbol.

    b. Freezing levels above the surface are depicted by fine, green dashed lines labeled in hundreds of feet MSL beginning at 4,000 ft. using 4,000-ft. intervals.

        1) If multiple freezing levels exist, the lines are drawn to the highest freezing level.

            a) For example, **80** identifies the 8,000-ft. freezing level contour.
            b) The lines are discontinued where they intersect the surface.

    c. The freezing level for locations between lines is determined by interpolation.

        1) EXAMPLE: The freezing level midway between the 4,000 and 8,000-ft. lines is 6,000 ft.

8.14 LEIDOS FLIGHT SERVICE ONLINE

1. The official Flight Service contracted provider is Leidos (formerly Lockheed Martin). This service includes answering all types of flight service contacts, including telephone, airborne, and online. According to their website, Leidos provides services to more than 80,000 general aviation community members weekly.

    a. The online Flight Service system offers many functions including flight planning, airport information, weather information, NOTAMs, official weather briefings, and flight plan filing.

2. **Accessing Leidos Flight Service (LFS) Online.** To access LFS, you need a computer and Internet access.

    a. LFS is available at www.1800wxbrief.com.

    b. Many products can be accessed without signing up or logging in, but official briefings may only be accessed after logging in to an account.

3. **Signing Up.** To sign up, select Create New Account under the login menu.

    a. If you already have a call-in profile, the information can be automatically filled in during the sign-up process.

    b. There is no charge to create an account.

4. **Navigating LFS Online.** The main menu provides access to several drop-down menus, including pilot dashboard, weather, flight planning and briefing, airports, UAS (drones), account, links, and help.

    a. You are able to customize your **pilot dashboard** to display frequently accessed weather charts and local weather information to provide convenient weather data at a quick glance immediately when you log in.

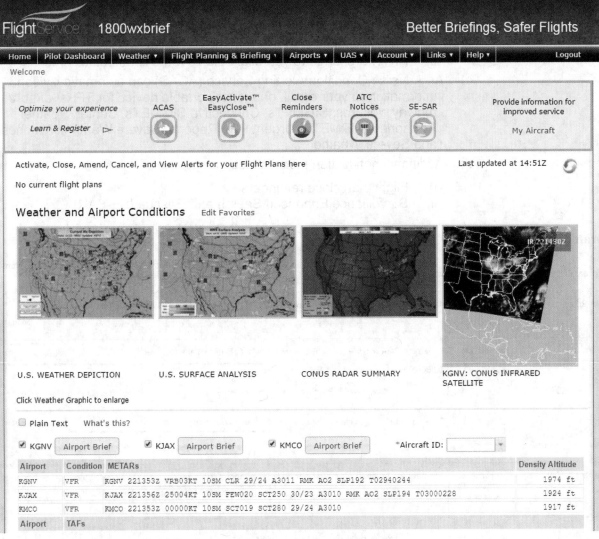

    b. **Weather maps** and digital charts are available with numerous options for selecting various time frames or altitudes, if applicable, for the following:

        1) Current Weather
        2) Adverse Weather Conditions
        3) General Forecasts (Prog Charts)
        4) Winds
        5) Barotropic Level Products (MB Charts)
        6) Thunderstorm & Severe Weather Forecast
        7) Temperature
        8) Radar Summary Charts
        9) Radar
        10) Satellite
        11) Sectionals
        12) UAS Operating Areas

c.   The **Flight Planning and Briefing** section allows access to official weather briefings, flight planning tools, flight plan filing, NavLogs, and a 15-day briefing history.

1) Domestic flight plans should be filed under the ICAO format as shown below.

   a) A specific aircraft profile should be set up in the Pilot Dashboard to receive the most accurate NavLog results, customized to the aircraft intended for the trip.

   b) ATC notices may be set up to automatically email the following information to you:

      i)   Your filed flight plan has been accepted by ATC.
      ii) An ATC change to your flight plan's route is detected.

   c) An Adverse Condition Alerting Service (ACAS) can automatically send information to your email, phone, or portable device for TFRs, airport/runway closures, SIGMETs, Convective SIGMETs, Center Weather Advisories, AIRMETS, Urgent Pilot Reports, Severe Weather Watches, and Severe Weather.

   d) Additional notification tools include

      i)   Flight plan close reminders
      ii) Surveillance Enhanced Search and Rescue (SE-SAR)

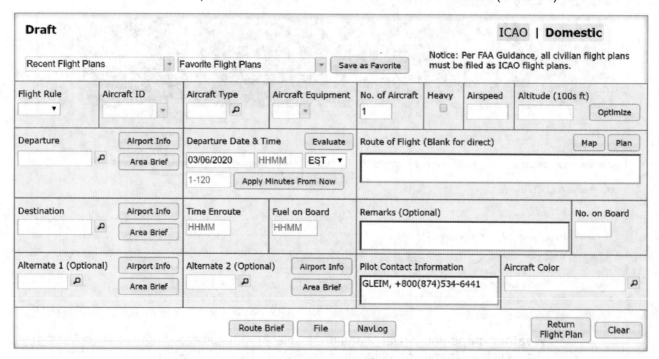

d. The **Airports** section provides detailed airport information including

1) Communications frequencies
2) Geographical information
3) Services available
4) Operations
5) NAVAIDs (Weather services and station type if available)
6) Runways
7) Airport remarks
8) Airport satellite view
9) Airport charts

    a) Airport diagram
    b) IFR approach plates
    c) Chart legends

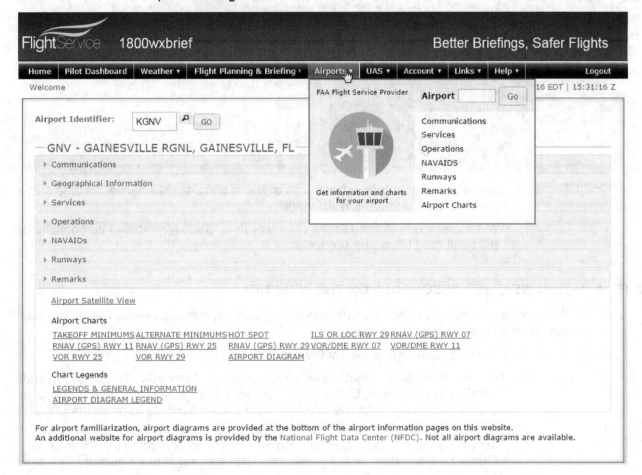

e. **UAS (Drones)** provide several tools for UAS operators to issue NOTAMs and for pilots to view UAS operating areas under the **UAS** drop-down menu.

    1) The operating areas can be viewed for the CONUS, Hawaii, Alaska, Guam, and the Caribbean.

    2) The map can be zoomed in to view a local area. Selecting an operating area highlighted on the map will display additional information, including operating location and times.

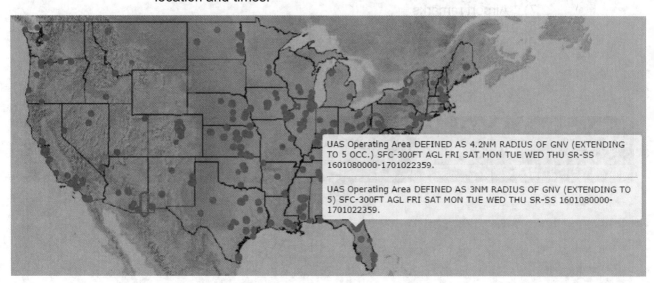

UAS Operating Area DEFINED AS 4.2NM RADIUS OF GNV (EXTENDING TO 5 OCC.) SFC-300FT AGL FRI SAT MON TUE WED THU SR-SS 1601080000-1701022359.

UAS Operating Area DEFINED AS 3NM RADIUS OF GNV (EXTENDING TO 5) SFC-300FT AGL FRI SAT MON TUE WED THU SR-SS 1601080000-1701022359.

f. Extensive help documentation, frequently asked questions, helpful videos, and a user guide are available under the **Help** menu.

    1) We recommend referring to the videos or user guide for detailed instructions on using all the LFS online products.

8.15 AVIATION WEATHER RESOURCES ON THE INTERNET

1. Gleim recommends using official aviation weather sources, such as Leidos Flight Service, to obtain your aviation weather information.

a. **Flight Service (Online): www.1800wxbrief.com**

    1) Leidos is the official Flight Service FAA contracted provider. Its services include answering all types of flight service contacts through telephone, airborne, and online. According to its website, Leidos provides services to more than 80,000 general aviation community members weekly.

    2) Many products can be accessed without signing up or logging in; however, official briefings may be accessed only after logging in to an account.

    3) The main menu provides access to a pilot dashboard, weather, flight planning and briefing, airport information, account, links, and help information.

    4) A user guide and helpful videos with extensive instructions are available under the Help menu.

2.   There are numerous sites on the Internet that distribute syndicated weather information or repackaged weather information derived from official sources.

    a.   Although other sources may not be official, they are a convenient way to access a wide range of weather products quickly.

    b.   Remember to always use official sources for navigation and flight planning. Most sites do not provide an official weather briefing and cannot be used to prove that you obtained sufficient weather information and NOTAMs pertinent to your flight.

    c.   The following sites are popular weather resources for pilots.

        1)   Gleim Aviation Weather: www.GleimAviation.com/resources/weather

           a)   Links to National Weather Service radar images as well as METAR/TAF reports by airport, winds aloft, and area forecast reports. An easy one-stop aviation weather information resource.

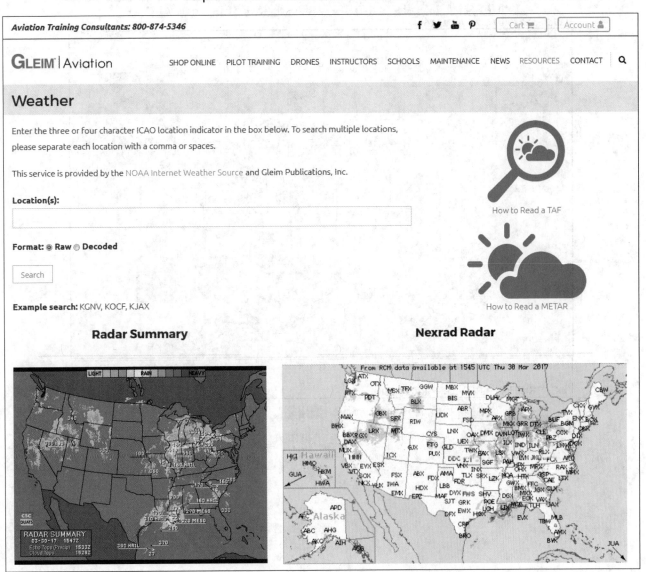

2)   Aviation Weather Center: www.aviationweather.gov

a)   Official products, such as SIGMETs, AIRMETs, weather depiction, surface analysis, PROG Charts, METARs, TAFs, winds aloft forecasts, area forecasts, PIREPs, and excellent National Radar with tops and satellite imagery, etc., are available on this official government website.

NOTE: Accessing this information does NOT constitute an official weather briefing.

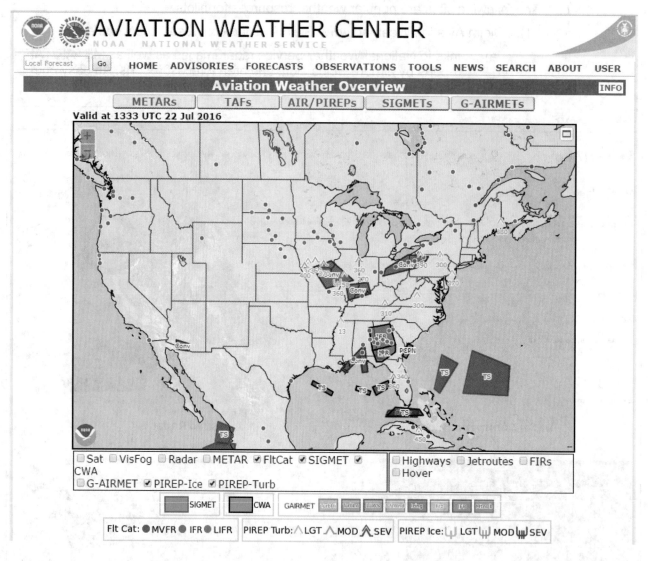

3) National Weather Service: www.weather.gov

    a) The official site of the National Weather Service contains local and national forecast products and full color maps.

        i) Many products are interactive, allowing the user to quickly zoom to specific regions and display a wide range of user-selected weather products including hazards, temperature, winds, sky cover, precipitation, etc.

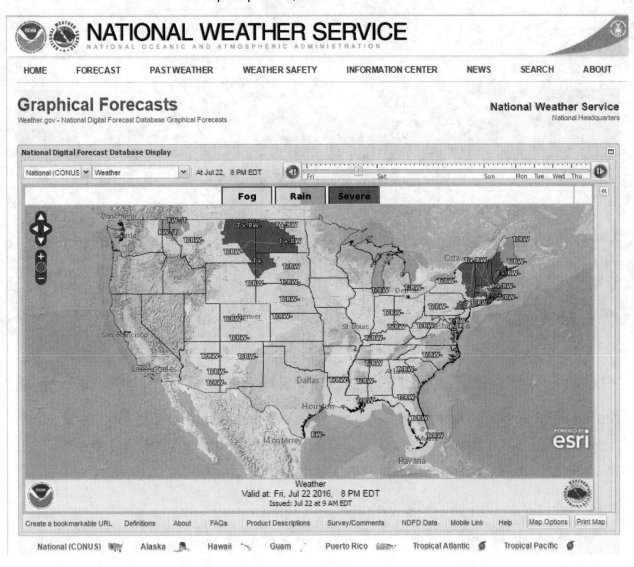

END OF STUDY UNIT

STUDY UNIT NINE
NAVIGATION: CHARTS, PUBLICATIONS, FLIGHT COMPUTERS

(48 pages of outline)

9.1 VFR NAVIGATION CHARTS

1. FAA-Approved Print Providers publish and distribute aeronautical charts of the United States and foreign areas. Digital versions of VFR charts are provided by the FAA at www.faa.gov/air_traffic/flight_info/aeronav/digital_products/vfr. The types of charts most commonly used by pilots flying VFR include

    a. Sectional charts. The scale is 1:500,000 (1 in. = 6.86 NM).

        1) This chart is normally used for VFR navigation.

    b. VFR terminal area charts. The scale is 1:250,000 (1 in. = 3.43 NM).

        1) VFR terminal area charts depict Class B airspace and adjacent areas around very busy airports. Class B airspace, with its many irregular sectors and various altitude floors, is somewhat complex. The pilot can see these details much more easily on a terminal area chart than on a sectional chart because of the difference in scale.

        2) Most of the sectional and VFR terminal area charts are revised semiannually.

2.   The sectional and VFR terminal area charts are designed for visual navigation by slow- and medium-speed aircraft.

   a.   The topographical information featured on these charts portrays surface elevation levels and a great number of visual checkpoints used for VFR flight.

   1)   Checkpoints include populated places, drainage, roads, railroads, and other distinctive landmarks.

   b.   Aeronautical information on sectional charts includes visual and radio aids to navigation, airports, controlled airspace, restricted areas, obstructions, and related data.

3.   Each rectangle on the U.S. maps (shown below) is an area covered by one sectional chart. VFR terminal area charts are also shown.

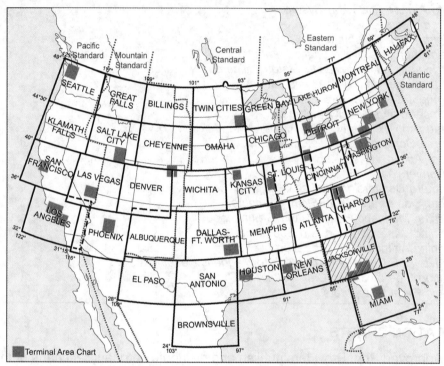

Sectional and VFR Terminal Area Charts for the Conterminous United States

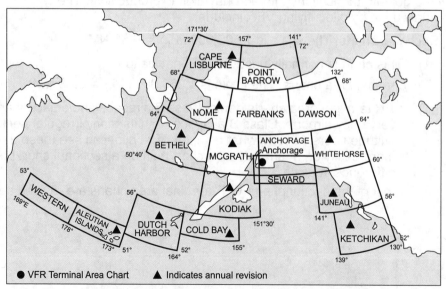

Sectional and VFR Terminal Area Charts for Alaska

4. Obsolete charts must be discarded and replaced by current editions. This is important because revisions to aeronautical information occur constantly.

    a. These revisions include changes in radio frequencies, new obstructions, temporary or permanent closing of certain runways and airports, and other temporary or permanent hazards to flight.

5. VFR aeronautical charts are available in print from most FBOs and pilot supply stores, including online retailers.

9.2 LONGITUDE AND LATITUDE

1. Lines of longitude and latitude provide a common grid system that is the key to navigation. The location of any point on the Earth can be determined by the intersection of the lines of longitude and latitude.

    a. **Lines of latitude**, or **parallels**, are imaginary circles parallel to the Equator. They are drawn as lines on charts running east and west around the world.

        1) They are used to measure degrees of latitude north (N) or south (S) of the Equator.

        2) Angular distance from the Equator to the pole is one-fourth of a circle, or 90°.

        3) The 48 conterminous states of the United States are located between 24° and 49°N latitude.

    b. **Lines of longitude**, or **meridians**, are drawn from the North Pole to the South Pole and are at right angles to the Equator and the parallels.

        1) The **Prime Meridian**, which passes through Greenwich, England, is used as the zero line from which measurements are made in degrees east (E) and west (W) to 180°.

        2) The 48 conterminous states of the United States are located between 67° and 125°W longitude.

        3) Because lines of longitude connect the poles, they mark the direction of true north and south.

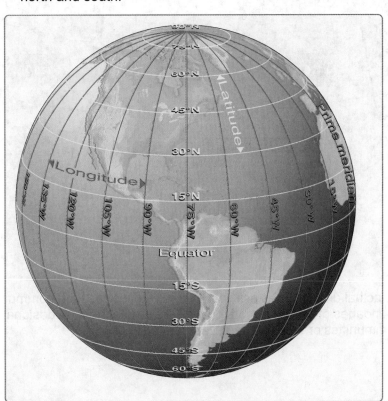

2.   Any specific geographical point on Earth can thus be located by reference to its latitude and longitude.

   a.   EXAMPLES: Washington, D.C., is approximately 39°N latitude, 77°W longitude, and Chicago is approximately 42°N latitude, 88°W longitude.

   b.   The lines of longitude and latitude are printed on aeronautical (e.g., sectional) charts with each degree subdivided into 60 equal segments called minutes; i.e., 1/2° is equal to 30' (the ' is the symbol for min.).

      1)   Each minute shown on lines of longitude equals one nautical mile, and this scale may be used to measure distances on aeronautical charts.

3.   The meridians are also useful for designating time zones.

   a.   A day is defined as the time required for the Earth to make one complete revolution of 360°. Since the day is divided into 24 hr., the Earth revolves at the rate of 15° an hour.

      1)   When the sun is directly above a meridian

         a)   It is noon at that meridian.
         b)   To the west of that meridian, it is forenoon.
         c)   To the east of that meridian, it is afternoon.

   b.   The standard practice is to establish a time belt for each 15° of longitude. This makes a difference of exactly 1 hr. between each belt.

      1)   The Continental United States has four time belts: Eastern (75°), Central (90°), Mountain (105°), and Pacific (120°).

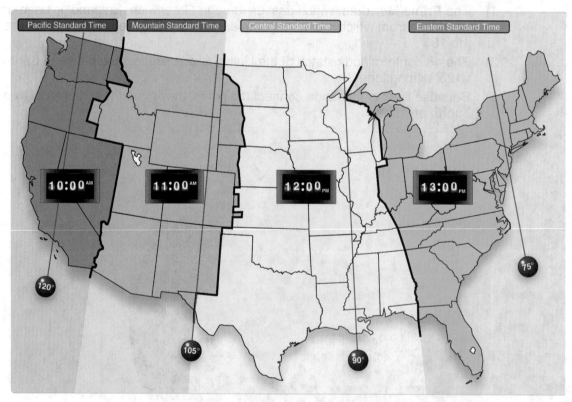

   c.   The actual dividing lines are somewhat irregular because communities near the boundaries often find it more convenient to use the time designations of neighboring communities or trade centers.

4. **Measurement of direction.** By using meridians as a reference, a direction from one point to another can be measured in degrees from true north.

    a. To indicate a course to be followed in flight, draw a line on the chart from the point of departure to the destination, and measure the angle that this line forms with a meridian.

        1) Direction is expressed in degrees.
        2) Course measurement should be taken at a meridian near the midpoint of the course.

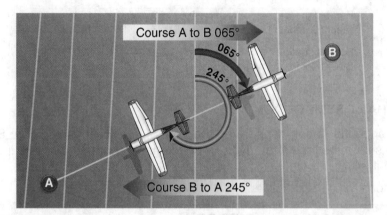

Course A to B 065°
065°
245°
B
Course B to A 245°
A

    b. The course you measure on your sectional chart is known as the **true course**. It is the direction measured by reference to a meridian or to true north. Put another way, it is the direction of intended flight as measured in degrees relative to true north.

5. **Variation**

    a. Variation is the angle between true north and magnetic north.

        1) It is expressed as east variation or west variation, depending upon whether magnetic north is to the east or west of true north.
        2) Variation, when added to or subtracted from true course, results in magnetic course.

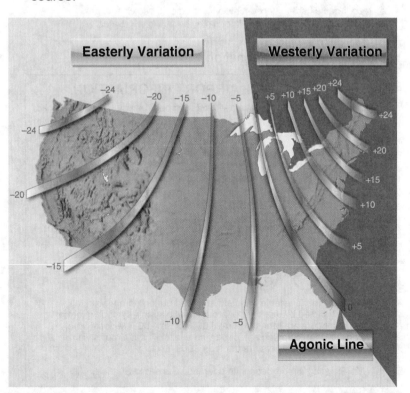

Easterly Variation   Westerly Variation
Agonic Line

6. **Deviation**

   a. Deviation occurs when the compass needle deflects from its proper reading due to interference from aircraft systems, such as electrical circuits, radio, lights, tools, and engine and magnetized metal parts.

   b. Compass deviation is corrected by pilots using a compass deviation card, usually mounted near the compass.

      1) The figure below illustrates a compass deviation card, showing corrections at 30° intervals. Intermediate corrections can be determined by interpolation.

For (Magnetic)	N	30	60	E	120	150
Steer (Compass)	0	28	57	86	117	148

For (Magnetic)	S	210	240	W	300	330
Steer (Compass)	180	212	243	274	303	332

9.3 SECTIONAL CHART SYMBOLOGY

1. The following information appears on the front of every sectional chart. Study it carefully! Few pilots take the time to study the whole legend because they are in a hurry to look at the chart itself.

   a. Airports

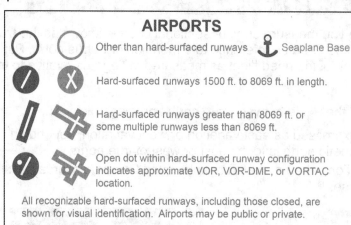

NOTE: On sectional charts, airports having control towers are illustrated in blue; all others are illustrated in magenta.

      1) Additional airport information

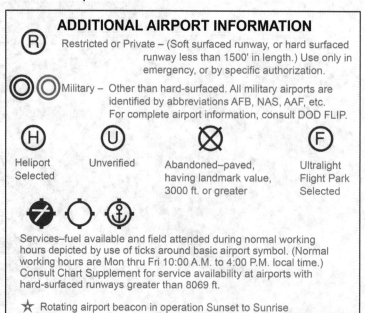

b. Airport data

AIRPORT DATA

Box indicates FAR 93 Special Air Traffic Rules & Airport Traffic Patterns.

FSS

NO SVFR — FAR 91

— Location Identifier

NAME (NAM) (PNAM) ← — ICAO Location Indicator shown outside contiguous U.S.

Runways with Right Traffic Patterns (public use) →

CT - 118.3 ★ **ⓒ ATIS 123.8**

285 **L** 72 *122.95*

→ RP 23, 34 ←

RP ★ Special conditions exist - see Supplement.

VFR Advsy **125.0**   UNICOM

WX CAM ← Weather Camera (AK)

FSS - Flight Service Station   **AOE** ← Airport of Entry

NO SVFR - Fixed-wing special VFR flight is prohibited.

CT - 118.3 - Control Tower (CT) - primary frequency

★ - Star indicates operation part-time. See tower frequencies tabulation for hours of operation.

ⓒ - Follows the Common Traffic Advisory Frequency (CTAF)

ATIS 123.8 - Automatic Terminal Information Service

AFIS 135.2 - Automatic Flight Information Service (AK)

ASOS/AWOS 135.42 - Automated Surface Weather Observing Systems (shown where full-time ATIS not available). Some ASOS/AWOS facilities may not be located at airports.

UNICOM - Aeronautical advisory station

VFR Advsy - VFR Advisory Service shown where full-time ATIS not available and frequency is other than primary CT frequency.

285 - Elevation in feet

L - Lighting in operation Sunset to Sunrise

*L - Lighting limitations exist; refer to Supplement.

72 - Length of longest runway in hundreds of feet; usable length may be less.

When information is lacking, the respective character is replaced by a dash. Lighting codes refer to runway edge lights and may not represent the longest runway or full length lighting.

c. Communication boxes and radio aids to navigation

Frequencies above thin line box are remoted to NAVAID site. Other frequencies at FSS providing voice communication may be available determined by altitude and terrain. Consult Chart Supplement for complete information.

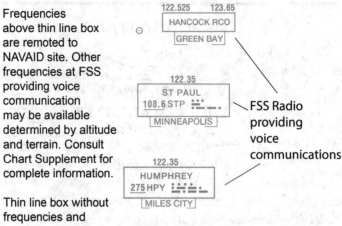

FSS Radio providing voice communications

Thin line box without frequencies and controlling FSS name indicates no FSS frequency available.

VOR

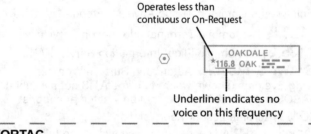

VORTAC

When an NDB NAVAID shares the same name and Morse Code as the VOR NAVAID the frequency can be collocated inside the same box to conserve space.

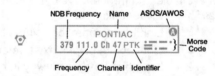

VOR-DME

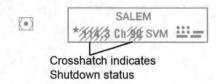

Crosshatch indicates Shutdown status

DME

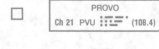

DME co-located at an airport
Note: DMEs are shown without the compass rose.

d.   Airport traffic service and airspace information

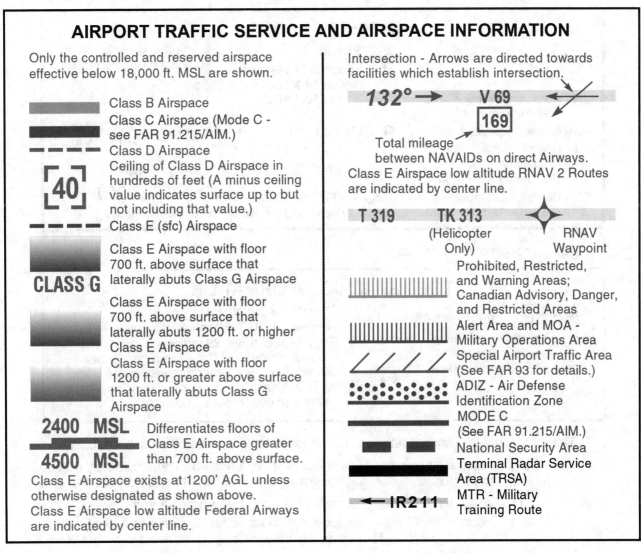

e.   Obstructions

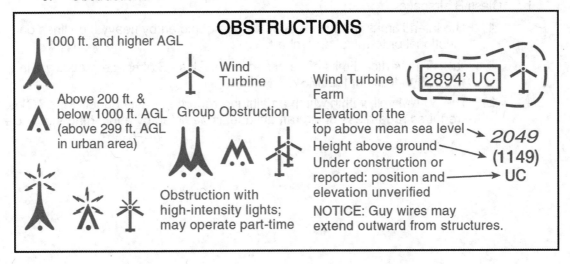

f.   Miscellaneous

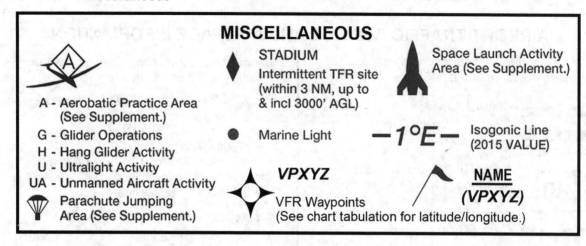

g.   Topographic information

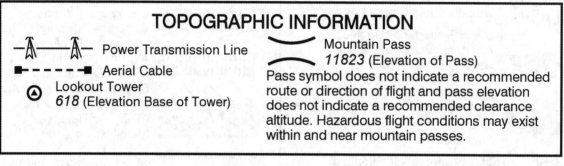

2.   The following information illustrates how airspace is depicted on the sectional chart:

a.   Class A airspace begins at 18,000 feet MSL, extends up to approximately 60,000 feet MSL, and includes the airspace overlying the continental United States and Alaska.

1)   Class A airspace is the domain of jet- and turbo-prop aircraft.

2)   To operate in Class A airspace, you must be an instrument-rated pilot and be on an IFR flight plan. Therefore, it is very unlikely as a private pilot that you will find yourself there.

b.   Class B airspace

1)   The lateral limits of Class B airspace are depicted by heavy blue lines on a sectional or terminal area chart.

a)   The vertical limits of each section of Class B airspace are shown in hundreds of feet MSL.

2)   The 30-NM veil, within which an altitude-reporting transponder (Mode C) is required regardless of aircraft altitude, is depicted by a thin magenta circle.

3) Class B airspace is shown on the sectional chart (below left) and on the diagram (below right).

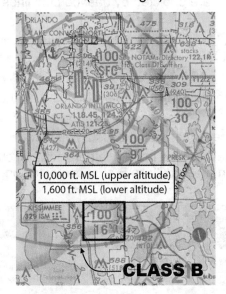

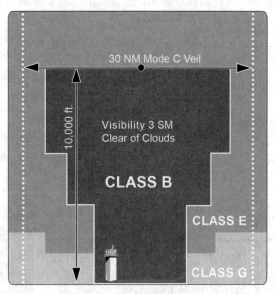

c. Class C airspace

1) The lateral limits of Class C airspace are depicted by solid magenta lines on sectional and some terminal area charts.

a) The vertical limits of each circle are shown in hundreds of feet MSL.

b) The inner surface area extends from the surface upward to the indicated altitude (usually 4,000 ft. above the airport elevation). It extends outward 5 NM from the primary airport.

c) The shelf area extends from the indicated altitude (usually 1,200 ft. above the airport elevation) to the same upper altitude limit as the surface area.

2) Class C airspace is shown on the sectional chart (below left) and on the diagram (below right).

a) Class C airspace vertical limits in the example extend

i) From the surface (SFC) to 4,000 ft. MSL (40) in the surface area

ii) From 1,200 ft. MSL (12) to 4,000 ft. MSL in the shelf area

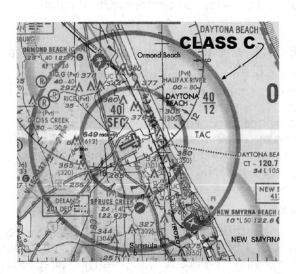

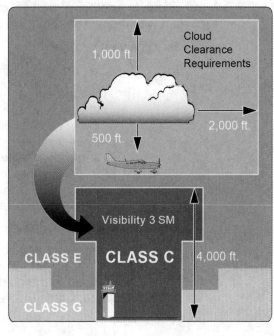

d.   Class D airspace

1)   The lateral limits of Class D airspace are depicted by dashed blue lines on a sectional or terminal area chart.

a)   The ceiling (usually 2,500 ft. above the airport elevation) is shown within the circle in hundreds of feet MSL.

b)   The radius of airspace area is 5 NM.

2)   Class D airspace is shown on the sectional chart (below left) and on the diagram (below right).

a)   The ceiling of Class D airspace in the examples is 2,700 ft. MSL.

b)   If depicted, a dashed magenta line (see bottom left of sectional chart in the example below) illustrates an area of Class E airspace extending upward from the surface.

 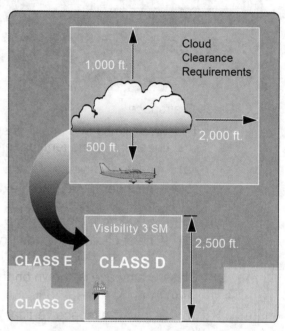

e.   Class E airspace has been created to provide separation services for IFR traffic operating within the airspace. As IFR traffic leaves the airport environment and transitions to another airport or up to Class A airspace, air traffic controllers remain in contact with them. The depiction of Class E airspace on aeronautical charts

1)   Is somewhat complex

a)   The size and shape of Class E airspace is dependent on radar coverage.

i)   In some areas, terrain features such as mountains create radar shadows wherein radar is blocked and airplanes cannot be seen by ATC controllers. These areas are referred to as Class G, or uncontrolled, airspace because ATC cannot administer the separation between aircraft in these shadows. It is important for VFR pilots to have an understanding of Class E airspace, particularly when it comes to the required visibility and cloud separation requirements.

2)   Defines the lateral boundaries and the floor of the airspace

a)   If not depicted on the aeronautical charts, Class E airspace is assumed to begin at 14,500 ft. MSL or 1,500 ft. AGL, whichever is higher. Class E extends up to the next overlying airspace. Where overlying airspace is not depicted, Class E extends upwards to Class A airspace.

3)   Is defined as follows:

Class E airspace beginning at the surface.	
Class E airspace beginning 700 feet AGL.	
Class E airspace beginning 1,200 feet AGL.	
Class E airspace begins at the altitude defined by the zipper line.	**8000 AGL**
Federal Airways, Class E airspace begins at 1,200 feet AGL.	V2N ← 270°

a.   Pilots operating on the eastern half of the United States will very rarely see the shaded blue depiction of Class E. The lack of mountainous terrain east of the Mississippi River provides for improved radar coverage. Most pilots in the east are operating inside a shaded blue line depicted on a sectional chart far to their west; therefore, everything east of this point is inside a shaded blue area. If not depicted, pilots in the east often can assume Class E begins at 1,200 ft. AGL.

f.   Class G airspace is not shown. It is implied to exist everywhere controlled airspace does not exist.

   1)   Class G airspace extends upward from the surface to the floor of overlying controlled airspace.

9.4 FAA ADVISORY CIRCULARS (ACs)

1.   The FAA issues advisory circulars (ACs) to provide a systematic means for issuing nonregulatory material of interest to the aviation public.

   a.   Unless incorporated into a regulation by reference, the contents of an AC are not binding (i.e., they are only advisory in nature).

   b.   An AC is issued to provide guidance and information in its designated subject area or to show a method acceptable to the FAA for complying with a related Federal Aviation Regulation.

2.   ACs are issued in a numbered system of general subject matter areas that correspond with the subject areas in the Federal Aviation Regulations.

   a.   The general subject number and the subject areas are as follows:

      00 -- General
      20 -- Aircraft
      60 -- Airmen
      70 -- Airspace
      90 -- Air Traffic and General Operating Rules
      120 -- Air Carriers, Air Travel Clubs, and Operators for Compensation or Hire: Certification and Operations
      140 -- Schools and Other Certificated Agencies
      150 -- Airport Series
      170 -- Navigational Facilities
      210 -- Flight Information (NOTE: This series is about aeronautical charts and does not relate to a 14 CFR part.)

3.   Access current ACs online at www.faa.gov/regulations_policies/advisory_circulars.

4.   You may view current ACs as PDF documents and print them or save them to your computer for offline viewing.

   a.   Be aware, however, that ACs are regularly updated by the FAA. Always be sure you are using the most current document versions available.

9.5 AERONAUTICAL INFORMATION MANUAL (AIM)

1. The *Aeronautical Information Manual (AIM)* provides pilots with a vast amount of basic flight information and Air Traffic Control (ATC) procedures in the United States. Page changes are published twice a year by the FAA.

   a. This information is vital to you as a pilot so that you may understand the structure and operation of the ATC system and your part in it. Each issue of the *AIM* has a comprehensive and useful index to help you find topics of interest.

   b. Gleim reprints the Federal Aviation Regulations (FARs) and *AIM* as a single book annually. Updates can be obtained by visiting www.GleimAviation.com/updates or emailing update@gleim.com with FAR/AIM and the edition and printing number in the subject line or body of the email.

   c. The *AIM* is also available for free from the FAA at www.faa.gov/air_traffic/publications.

2. **Chapters and Section Titles**

   CHAPTER 1. AIR NAVIGATION
   Section 1. Navigation Aids
   Section 2. Performance-Based Navigation (PBN) and Area Navigation (RNAV)
   CHAPTER 2. AERONAUTICAL LIGHTING AND OTHER AIRPORT VISUAL AIDS
   Section 1. Airport Lighting Aids
   Section 2. Air Navigation and Obstruction Lighting
   Section 3. Airport Marking Aids and Signs
   CHAPTER 3. AIRSPACE
   Section 1. General
   Section 2. Controlled Airspace
   Section 3. Class G Airspace
   Section 4. Special Use Airspace
   Section 5. Other Airspace Areas
   CHAPTER 4. AIR TRAFFIC CONTROL
   Section 1. Services Available to Pilots
   Section 2. Radio Communications Phraseology and Techniques
   Section 3. Airport Operations
   Section 4. ATC Clearances and Aircraft Separation
   Section 5. Surveillance Systems
   Section 6. Operational Policy/Procedures for Reduced Vertical Separation Minimum (RVSM) in the
         Domestic U.S., Alaska, Offshore Airspace and the San Juan FIR
   Section 7. Operational Policy/Procedures for the Gulf of Mexico 50 NM Lateral Separation Initiative
   CHAPTER 5. AIR TRAFFIC PROCEDURES
   Section 1. Preflight
   Section 2. Departure Procedures
   Section 3. En Route Procedures
   Section 4. Arrival Procedures
   Section 5. Pilot/Controller Roles and Responsibilities
   Section 6. National Security and Interception Procedures
   CHAPTER 6. EMERGENCY PROCEDURES
   Section 1. General
   Section 2. Emergency Services Available to Pilots
   Section 3. Distress and Urgency Procedures
   Section 4. Two-way Radio Communications Failure
   Section 5. Aircraft Rescue and Fire Fighting Communications
   CHAPTER 7. SAFETY OF FLIGHT
   Section 1. Meteorology
   Section 2. Altimeter Setting Procedures
   Section 3. Wake Turbulence
   Section 4. Bird Hazards and Flight over National Refuges, Parks, and Forests
   Section 5. Potential Flight Hazards
   Section 6. Safety, Accident, and Hazard Reports
   CHAPTER 8. MEDICAL FACTS FOR PILOTS
   Section 1. Fitness for Flight
   CHAPTER 9. AERONAUTICAL CHARTS AND RELATED PUBLICATIONS
   Section 1. Types of Charts Available
   CHAPTER 10. HELICOPTER OPERATIONS
   Section 1. Helicopter IFR Operations
   Section 2. Special Operations
   APPENDICES
   Appendix 1. Bird/Other Wildlife Strike Report
   Appendix 2. Volcanic Activity Reporting Form (VAR)
   Appendix 3. Abbreviations/Acronyms
   PILOT/CONTROLLER GLOSSARY
   INDEX

9.6 CHART SUPPLEMENT U.S.

1. The Chart Supplement U.S. is published and distributed every 56 days by FAA-Approved Print Providers.

    a. It is a directory of all airports, seaplane bases, and heliports open to the public, including communications data, navigational facilities, and certain special notices and procedures.

    b. Printed Chart Supplements may be purchased from most FBOs or online aviation retailers.

    c. A digital Chart Supplement can be accessed at www.faa.gov/air_traffic/flight_info/ aeronav/digital_products/dafd.

    d. One of these directories is published for each of seven geographic districts:

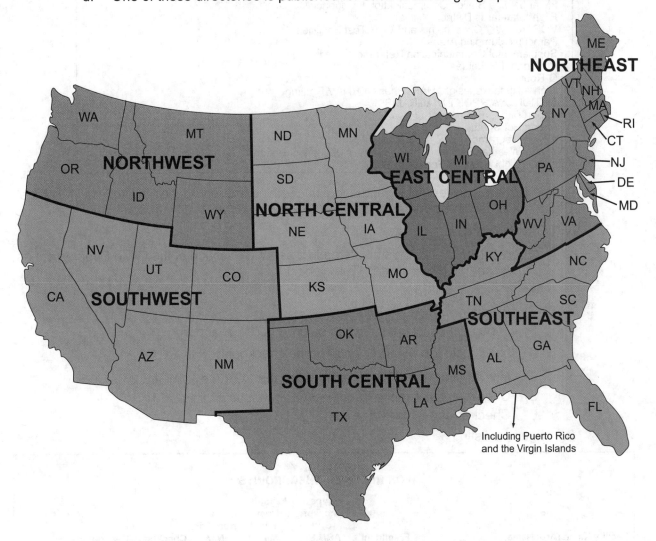

Including Puerto Rico and the Virgin Islands

2. Use of the Chart Supplement is a vital part of your cross-country flight planning.

    a. All pertinent information regarding airports, FSS contact information, etc., is contained in this volume.

    b. The Chart Supplement also contains National Weather Service telephone numbers listed alphabetically by state.

3. **Table of Contents of Each Issue**

GENERAL INFORMATION
   City/Military Airport Cross Reference
   Seaplane Landing Areas
   Abbreviations
SECTION 1: AIRPORT/FACILITY DIRECTORY LEGEND
SECTION 2: AIRPORT/FACILITY DIRECTORY
SECTION 3: NOTICES
   Aeronautical Chart Bulletins
   Special Notices
   Regulatory Notices

SECTION 4: ASSOCIATED DATA
   FAA Telephone Numbers and National Weather Service
   Air Route Traffic Control Centers
   Flight Service Station Communication Frequencies
   Flight Standards District Offices
   VOR Receiver Checkpoints and VOR Test Facilities
   Parachute Jumping Areas
   Supplemental Communication Reference
   Preferred IFR Routes
   Q-Routes
   High Altitude Redesign (HAR) Phase 1 RNAV Routing
SECTION 5: AIRPORT DIAGRAMS
   Airport Diagrams Legend
   Airport Hot Spots
   Airport Diagrams
National Weather Service (NWS) Upper Air Observing Stations
Enroute Flight Advisory Service (EFAS)

4. A sample Chart Supplement legend and explanations are reproduced in Study Unit 9 of the Gleim *Private Pilot and Recreational Pilot FAA Knowledge Test Prep* book.

5. **VOR Checkpoints**

    a. VOR receiver checkpoints are listed in a separate section of the Chart Supplement as the excerpt below illustrates. They include

        1) Facility (airport) name
        2) Frequency and identification
        3) Type of checkpoint: identified as ground (G) or airborne (A)

            a) Includes altitude if an airborne checkpoint

        4) Checkpoint's magnetic direction from the VOR (i.e., radial)
        5) Checkpoint's distance from the VOR in nautical miles (NM)
        6) Checkpoint description

    b. Example listing

KENTUCKY
VOR RECEIVER CHECKPOINTS

Facility Name (Arpt Name)	Freq/Ident	Type Checkpt. Gnd. AB/ALT	Azimuth from Fac. Mag	Dist. from Fac. N.M.	Checkpoint Description
Bowling Green-Warren Co.	117.9/BWG	G	023	2.2	On twy in front of Admin Bldg.
Central City (Muhlenberg Co)	109.8/CCT	A/2500	149	11.0	Over intersection of rwy 23 and central taxiway
Cincinnati (Greater Cincinnati)	117.3/CVG	G	045	2.5	On twy m E of twy B
Clarksville (Campbell AAF)	110.6/CKV	G	298	5	On end of old twy 36 near Maltese Cross
Clarksville (Hopkinsville-Christian Co)	110.6/CKV	A/2000	345	13.5	Over hangar
Cunningham (Barkley)	113.6/CKV	G	043	4.6	Intersection of taxiways and west corner of ramp
London (London-Corbin Arpt-Magee Fld)	116.1/LOZ	G	034	3.8	On parking ramp taxiway entry

9.7 NOTICE TO AIRMEN (NOTAM) SYSTEM

1.   The National Notice to Airmen (NOTAM) System disseminates time-critical aeronautical information that is either of a temporary nature or is not sufficiently known in advance to permit publication on aeronautical charts or in other operational publications.

    a.   NOTAMs contain aeronautical information that could affect the decision to make a flight.

2.   NOTAM information is classified into the following categories:

    a.   **NOTAM (D)** includes such information as airport or primary runway closures, changes in the status of navigational aids, ILSs, radar service availability, and other information essential to planned en route, terminal, or landing operations. Also included is information on airport taxiways, aprons, ramp areas, and associated lighting.

        1)   This type of NOTAM includes (U) NOTAMs and (O) NOTAMs.

            a)   (U) NOTAMs are unverified NOTAMs, which are those that are received from a source other than airport management and have not yet been confirmed by management personnel. This is allowed only at airports where airport management has authorized it by Letter of Agreement.

            b)   (O) NOTAMs are other aeronautical information that does not meet NOTAM criteria but may be beneficial to aircraft operations.

        2)   This information is disseminated for all navigational facilities that are part of the National Airspace System (NAS), all public use airports, seaplane bases, and heliports listed in the Chart Supplement.

        3)   NOTAM (D) information is distributed to air traffic facilities, primarily Flight Service Stations (FSSs), automatically.

            a)   NOTAM (D) information is obtained from a standard pilot briefing. These NOTAMs are available to the briefer along the proposed route of flight.

            b)   You can request specific NOTAMs using an airport or NAVAID identifier.

            c)   Leidos Flight Service Online also provides NOTAM (D) information.

        4)   EXAMPLE: **!MIV MIV RWY 10/28 CLSD WEF 1202011200-1202021600**

            a)   This NOTAM is broken down into its core elements below. Every NOTAM (D) now follows this format.

HEADER			BODY		FOOTER
(!)	Accountable Location	Affected Location	Keyword	Surface Identification	Condition	Effective Times
!	MIV	MIV	RWY	10/28	CLSD	WEF 1202011200-1202021600

            b)   This NOTAM indicates that Runway 10/28 at the Millville Municipal Airport in Millville, New Jersey will be closed from 02/01/12 at 1200Z to 02/02/12 at 1600Z.

    b.   A **Flight Data Center (FDC) NOTAM** is regulatory in nature and includes such information as amendments to published IAPs and other current aeronautical charts. It also advertises temporary flight restrictions caused by such things as natural disasters or large-scale public events that may generate a congestion of air traffic over a site.

        1)   FSSs are responsible for maintaining a file of current, unpublished FDC NOTAMs concerning conditions within 400 NM of their facilities.

        2)   FDC information that concerns conditions beyond 400 NM from the FSS or that is already published is given to you only when you request it.

c. **Pointer NOTAMs**

1) Pointer NOTAMs are issued by a Flight Service Station to highlight or point out another NOTAM, such as an FDC NOTAM or a NOTAM (D).

2) The purpose of a pointer NOTAM is to make pilots aware of the existence of a condition or event that might require a lengthy description, and "point" to the location of more detailed information.

a) This practice is intended to help reduce the volume of NOTAM information provided in a standard briefing.

3) Pilots, who will be operating in this airspace during the effective time, will know where to go to get detailed information, while pilots who are not affected can move on.

4) The keyword used in the pointer NOTAM always refers to the event referenced.

5) EXAMPLE: **!CPR CPR AIRSPACE SEE DDY 12/045 PJE WEF 0802141400-0802141830**

a) In this example, the pointer NOTAM is referencing published NOTAM 12/045 for the Natrona County Airport in Casper, Wyoming.

b) Pointer NOTAMs related to Temporary Flight Restrictions (TFRs) must use the keyword, "AIRSPACE."

d. **Military NOTAMs**

1) Military NOTAMs pertain to U.S. Air Force, Army, Marine, and Navy navigation aids and/or airports that are part of the national airspace system.

e. **FICON NOTAMs** provide notices regarding field condition and information about landing runways, taxiways, and aprons.

f. **TFR NOTAMs** distribute general warnings for the entire FAA airspace and define areas of restricted air travel related to special events or hazardous conditions.

1) Current TFRs are available online at https://tfr.faa.gov/tfr2/list.html.

g. **International NOTAMs** are received from other countries and also generated by the U.S. NOTAM Office.

h. **GPS NOTAMs** are issued in response to testing or interference missions meeting national security requirements.

1) GPS NOTAMs are available online at www.faasafety.gov/SPANS/notices_public.aspx.

3. **Dissemination of NOTAMs**

a. NOTAMs can be obtained from a standard weather briefing by calling 1-800-WX-BRIEF (1-800-992-7433) or online at www.1800wxbrief.com.

b. The FAA NOTAM search page provides information critical to safe aircraft operation and can be accessed at https://notams.aim.faa.gov/notamSearch/nsapp.html#/.

4. NOTAM Contractions

    a.   Contractions are used extensively in NOTAMs. Most are known from common usage or can be deciphered phonetically.

    b.   The list of NOTAM contractions below and on the next page is provided to assist you.

ABN	airport beacon	CDSA	Class D surface area	GC	ground control
ABV	above	CEAS	Class E airspace	GCA	ground control approach
ACC	area control center (ARTCC)	CESA	Class E surface area	GOVT	government
ACCUM	accumulate	CFR	Code of Federal Regulations	GP	glide path
ACFT	aircraft	CGAS	Class G airspace	GPS	Global Positioning System
ACR	air carrier	CHG	change	GRVL	gravel
ACT	active	CIG	ceiling	HAA	height above airport
ADJ	adjacent	CK	check	HAT	height above touchdown
ADZD	advised	CL	center line	HDG	heading
A/FD	Airport/Facility Directory	CLKWS	clockwise	HEL	helicopter
AGL	above ground level	CLR	clearance, clear(s), cleared to	HELI	heliport
ALS	approach light system	CLSD	closed	HIRL	high-intensity runway lights
ALT	altitude	CMB	climb	HIWAS	Hazardous Inflight Weather
ALTM	altimeter	CMSND	commissioned		Advisory Service
ALTN	alternate	CNL	cancel	HLDG	holding
ALTNLY	alternately	COM	communications	HOL	holiday
ALSTG	altimeter setting	CONC	concrete	HP	holding pattern
AMDT	amendment	CPD	coupled	HR	hour
AMGR	airport manager	CRS	course		
AMOS	Automatic Meteorological	CS	Chart Supplement	IAF	initial approach fix
	Observing System	CTC	contact	IAP	instrument approach procedure
AP	airport	CTL	control	INBD	inbound
APCH	approach			ID	identification
AP LGT	airport lights	DALGT	daylight	IDENT	identity/identifier/identification
APP	approach control	DCMSND	decommissioned	IF	intermediate fix
ARFF	aircraft rescue and fire fighting	DCT	direct	ILS	Instrument Landing System
ARR	arrive, arrival	DEGS	degrees	IM	inner marker
ASOS	Automated Surface Observation	DEP	depart/departure	IMC	instrument meteorological
	System	DEPPROC	departure procedures		conditions
ASPH	asphalt	DH	decision height	IN	inch/inches
ATC	Air Traffic Control	DISABLD	disabled	INDEFLY	indefinitely
ATCSCC	Air Traffic Control System	DIST	distance	INFO	information
	Command Center	DLA	delay or delayed	INOP	inoperative
ATIS	Automatic Terminal Information	DLT	delete	ISTR	instrument
	Service	DLY	daily	INT	intersection
AUTH	authority	DME	distance-measuring equipment	INTL	international
AUTOB	Automatic Weather	DMSTN	demonstration	INTST	intensity
	Reporting System	DP	dew point temperature	IR	ice on runway/s
AVBL	available	DRFT	snowbank/s caused by wind		
AWOS	Automatic Weather Observing/		action	KT	knots
	Reporting System	DSPLCD	displaced		
AWY	airway			L	left
AZM	azimuth	E	east	LAA	local airport advisory
		EB	eastbound	LAT	latitude
BA FAIR	braking action fair	ELEV	elevation	LAWRS	Limited Aviation Weather
BA NIL	braking action nil	ENG	engine		Reporting Station
BA POOR	braking action poor	ENRT	en route	LB	pound/pounds
BC	back course	ENTR	entire	LC	local control
BCN	beacon	EXC	except	LOC	local/locally/location
BERM	snowbank/s containing			LCTD	located
	earth/gravel	FAC	facility or facilities	LDA	localizer type directional aid
BLW	below	FAF	final approach fix	LGT	light or lighting
BND	bound	FAN MKR	fan marker	LGTD	lighted
BRG	bearing	FDC	Flight Data Center	LIRL	low-intensity runway lights
BYD	beyond	FI/T	flight inspection temporary	LLWAS	low level wind shear alert system
		FI/P	flight inspection permanent	LM	compass locator at ILS middle
CAAS	Class A airspace	FM	from		marker
CAT	category	FNA	final approach	LDG	landing
CBAS	Class B airspace	FPM	feet per minute	LLZ	localizer
CBSA	Class B surface area	FREQ	frequency	LO	compass locator at ILS outer
CCAS	Class C airspace	FRH	fly runway heading		marker
CCLKWS	counterclockwise	FRI	Friday	LONG	longitude
CCSA	Class C surface area	FRZN	frozen	LRN	LORAN
CD	clearance delivery	FSS	automated/Flight Service Station	LSR	loose snow on runway/s
CDAS	Class D airspace	FT	foot, feet	LT	left turn

MAG	magnetic	PRN	pseudo random noise	T	temperature
MAINT	maintain, maintenance	PROC	procedure	TAA	terminal arrival area
MALS	medium-intensity approach light system	PROP	propeller	TACAN	Tactical Air Navigational Aid
		PSR	packed snow on runway/s	TAR	terminal area surveillance radar
MALSF	medium-intensity approach light system with sequenced flashers	PTCHY	patchy	TDZ	touchdown zone
		PTN	procedure turn	TDZ LG	touchdown zone lights
MALSR	medium-intensity approach light system with runway alignment indicator lights	PVT	private	TEMPO	temporary
				TFC	traffic
		RAIL	runway alignment indicator lights	TFR	temporary flight restriction
MAPT	missed approach point	RAMOS	remote automatic meteorological observing system	TGL	touch and go landings
MCA	minimum crossing altitude			THN	thin
MDA	minimum descent altitude	RCAG	remote communicaton air/ground facility	THR	threshold
MEA	minimum en-route altitude			THRU	through
MED	medium	RCL	runway centerline	THU	Thursday
MIN	minute	RCLL	runway centerline light system	TIL	until
MIRL	medium-intensity runway lights	RCO	remote communication outlet	TKOF	takeoff
MLS	microwave landing system	REC	receive/receiver	TM	traffic management
MM	middle marker	RELCTD	relocated	TMPA	traffic management program alert
MNM	minimum	REIL	runway end identifier lights	TRML	terminal
MNT	monitor/monitoring/monitored	REP	report	TRNG	training
MOC	minimum obstruction clearance	RLLS	runway lead-in lights system	TRSN	transition
MON	Monday	RMNDR	remainder	TSNT	transient
MRA	minimum reception altitude	RNAV	area navigation	TUE	Tuesday
MSA	minimum safe altitude/minimum sector altitude	RPLC	replace	TWR	tower
		RQRD	required	TWY	taxiway
MSAW	minimum safe altitude warning	RRL	runway remaining lights		
MSG	message	RSR	en route surveillance radar	UFN	until further notice
MSL	mean sea level	RSVN	reservation	UNAVBL	unavailable
MU	designate a friction value representing runway surface conditions (Greek letter)	RT	right turn	UNLGTD	unlighted
		RTE	route	UNMKD	unmarked
		RTR	remote transmitter/receiver	UNMNT	unmonitored
MUD	mud	RTS	return to service	UNREL	unreliable
MUNI	municipal	RUF	rough	UNUSBL	unusable
		RVR	runway visual range		
N	north	RVRM	runway visual range midpoint	VASI	visual approach slope indicator
NA	not authorized	RVRR	runway visual range rollout	VDP	visual descent point
NAV	navigation	RVRT	runway visual range touchdown	VGSI	visual glide slope indicator
NB	northbound	RWY	runway	VIA	by way of
NDB	nondirectional radio beacon			VICE	instead/versus
NE	northeast	S	south	VIS	visibility
NGT	night	SA	sand, sanded	VMC	visual meteorological conditions
NM	nautical mile/s	SAT	Saturday	VOL	volume
NMR	nautical mile radius	SAWR	supplementary aviation weather reporting station	VOR	VHF omnidirectional radio range
NONSTD	nonstandard			VORTAC	VOR and TACAN (colocated)
NOPT	no procedure turn required	SB	southbound		
NR	number	SDF	simplified directional facility	W	west
NW	northwest	SE	southeast	WB	westbound
		SFL	sequence flashing lights	WED	Wednesday
OBSC	obscured	SID	standard instrument departure	WEF	with effect from or effective from
OBST	obstruction	SIMUL	simultaneous	WI	within
OM	outer marker	SIR	packed or compacted snow and ice on runway/s	WIE	with immediate effect or effective immediately
OPR	operate				
OPS	operation	SKED	scheduled	WKDAYS	Monday through Friday
ORIG	original	SLR	slush on runway/s	WKEND	Saturday and Sunday
OTS	out of service	SN	snow	WND	wind
OVR	over	SNBNK	snowbank/s caused by plowing	WPT	waypoint
		SNGL	single	WSR	wet snow on runway/s
PAEW	personnel and equipment working	SPD	speed	WTR	water on runway/s
		SSALF	simplified short approach lighting system with sequenced flashers	WX	weather
PAPI	precision approach path indicator				
PAR	precision approach radar	SSALR	simplified short approach lighting system with runway alignment indicator lights		
PARL	parallel				
PAT	pattern				
PAX	passenger	SSALS	simplified short approach lighting system		
PCL	pilot controlled lighting				
PERM	permanent/permanently	SSR	secondary surveillance radar		
PJE	parachute jumping exercise	STA	straight-in approach		
PLA	practice low approach	STAR	standard terminal arrival		
PLW	plow/plowed	SUN	Sunday		
PN	prior notice required	SVC	service		
PPR	prior permission required	SW	southwest		
PREV	previous	SWEPT	swept or broom/broomed		

9.8 FLIGHT COMPUTERS

1. The following subunits explain how to use the Gleim manual flight computer and introduce you to electronic flight computers.

2. For student pilots, we suggest that you first learn how to use a manual flight computer, rather than an electronic one.

   a. When you are first learning how to do your cross-country flight planning and doing computations while flying, the manual flight computer is as fast as the electronic flight computer.

   b. Additionally, the manual flight computer is included in your "pilot kit," it costs less, and it never needs batteries.

   c. As your abilities and needs progress, you can always upgrade to an electronic computer as your budget allows.

3. If you are working toward your instrument rating or commercial pilot certificate, you should use the type of flight computer with which you are most familiar.

9.9 THE GLEIM FLIGHT COMPUTER

1. The flight computer is used to solve navigational problems and compute some aircraft performance. Some of the possible calculations are

   a. Time, speed, or distance to reach a destination
   b. Fuel required to reach a destination
   c. True airspeed
   d. True altitude
   e. Effect of wind on heading and groundspeed
   f. Conversion of nautical miles into statute miles and vice versa
   g. Conversion of Fahrenheit into Celsius and vice versa

2.   A flight computer has two sides: a calculator side and a wind side, as shown in the figure below.

   a.   Note that the calculator side has many more features than you really need for the computations covered in this book. You should focus on the speed index, nautical index, statute index, the miles (outer) scale, and the minutes (inner) scale. These will be explained in the next several subunits.

   b.   Note that the wind side of the computer has a sliding card with a slow-speed scale (30 to 260 kts.) used by most pilots for small airplanes. The opposite side of the sliding card has other useful information, which is discussed later in Subunit 9.25. The Gleim computer does not have a high-speed scale.

   c.   Since the sliding card can be easily removed from the computer for use in measuring distances, determining crosswind components, or filing flight plans, be careful to replace it with the instructions end of the card "up" (i.e., the instructions have the same orientation as the True Index triangle).

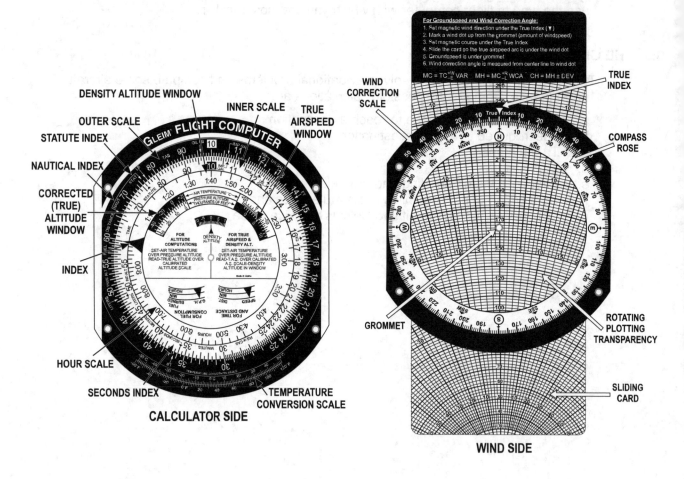

CALCULATOR SIDE

WIND SIDE

9.10 THE CALCULATOR SIDE OF THE FLIGHT COMPUTER

1.   The calculator side consists of a stationary portion with a flat circular portion attached. The circular portion can be turned.

     a.   The numbers along the outside of the stationary portion are referred to as the OUTER SCALE in this study unit, as shown in the figure on the previous page.

         1)   The outer scale is used to represent distance, fuel, groundspeed, true airspeed, or corrected (true) altitude, depending on the calculation being performed.

     b.   The numbers on the edge of the rotating portion are referred to as the INNER SCALE in this study unit, as shown in the figure on the previous page.

         1)   The inner scale is used to represent time, calibrated or indicated airspeed, and calibrated or indicated altitude, depending on the calculation being performed.

         2)   The number "60" on the inner scale has been replaced with a triangular-shaped arrow, referred to as the Index (▲).

            a)   This arrow is used as a reference to a rate, such as knots (nautical miles per hour) or gallons per hour.

     c.   In the center of the rotating portion are three "arcs" (windows) used to compute corrected (true) altitude, density altitude, and true airspeed.

2.   **Scale Values**

     a.   The numbers on the outer and inner scales represent multiples of 10 of the values shown.

         1)   EXAMPLE: The number "20" on either scale may represent 0.2, 2.0, 20, 200, or 2,000.

     b.   On both the outer and inner scales you will notice that the number of tick marks, or graduations, vary between numbers.

         1)   EXAMPLES:

            a)   The first tick mark to the right of "10" may represent 10.1, 101, 1,010, etc.

            b)   The first tick mark to the right of "17" may represent 1.72, 17.2, 172, etc.

            c)   The first tick mark to the right of "35" may represent 3.55, 35.5, etc. The second tick mark to the right of "35" may represent 3.6, 36, 360, etc.

     c.   On the inner scale, minutes may be translated to hours and minutes by reference to the hour scale, which is below and inside the inner scale.

         1)   EXAMPLE: 120 min., or "12" on the inner scale is also 2 hr. as indicated by "2:00" below the "12."

     d.   On the hour scale, the tick marks represent either 5 min. or 10 min.

         1)   EXAMPLE: Between "1:50" and "2:00" the tick mark represents 5 min. Between "4:00" and "4:30" each tick mark represents 10 min.

         2)   The tick marks on the inner scale can be used to supplement the hour scale.

3.   The calculator side of the flight computer is constructed so that any relationship, or ratio, between a number on the outer scale and a number on the inner scale will remain constant for all other numbers on both scales.

     a.   Rotate the inner circle so the "10" is opposite the "10" on the outer scale, and note that all the numbers around both circles are identical.

     b.   Next, rotate "20" under "10" on the outer scale; now all numbers on the inner scale are double those on the outer scale.

9.11 CONVERSION OF NAUTICAL MILES TO STATUTE MILES AND VICE VERSA

1. You can use the calculator side of your flight computer to convert nautical miles (NM) to statute miles (SM) or knots (kt.) to miles per hour (mph).

    a. Remember, the units you use must be equivalent, i.e., nautical miles and knots or statute miles and miles per hour.

2. On the outer scale at "66" there is an arrow labeled "NAUT" (nautical miles), and at "76" there is an arrow labeled "STAT" (statute miles).

3. EXAMPLE: Convert 100 mph to knots.

    a. Rotate the inner scale so that 100, or "10," on the inner scale is under the "STAT" index arrow, as shown in the figure below.

    b. Look at the "NAUT" index arrow on the outer scale to determine 87 kt. on the inner scale.

4. You can also convert nautical or statute miles to kilometers.

    a. The kilometer index is labeled "KM" on the outer scale two tick marks to the right of "12."

5. EXAMPLE: Convert 100 SM to nautical miles and kilometers.

    a. Set "100" under the "STAT" arrow and find 87 NM under the "NAUT" arrow and 161 KM under the "KM" arrow.

6. Use your flight computer to solve these practice problems (answers are located below).

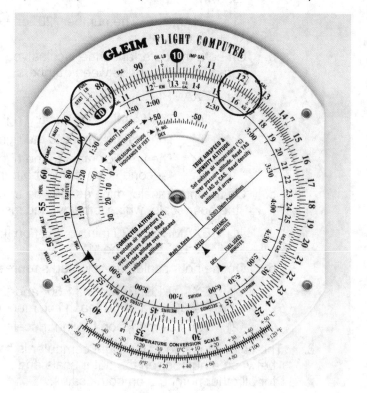

	NM	SM
a.	107	___
b.	139	___
c.	___	181
d.	___	78
e.	320	___

7. Answers to practice problems

    a. 123 SM
    b. 160 SM
    c. 157 NM
    d. 68 NM
    e. 368 SM

9.12 SPEED, DISTANCE, AND TIME COMPUTATIONS

1.   Speed, distance, and time are three interrelated elements. With any two of these elements, you can compute the third (missing) element.

   a.   The computations are

      1)   **Speed = Distance ÷ Time**
      2)   **Distance = Speed × Time**
      3)   **Time = Distance ÷ Speed**

   b.   You can use your flight computer to make the above computations.

      1)   In any problem, both the speed and distance must be in either SM or NM.
      2)   You can convert SM to NM or vice versa easily, as explained in the preceding subunit.

2.   **Determining Time Required**

   a.   If you know the groundspeed and the distance, you can calculate the time.

      1)   **Time = Distance ÷ Speed**

   b.   EXAMPLE: How much time will it take to fly 120 NM at a groundspeed of 100 kt.?

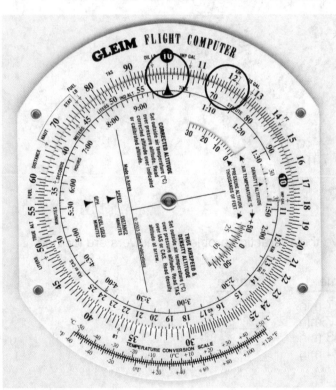

   1)   Rotate the inner scale so the Index is opposite 100 kt., or "10," on the outer scale, as shown in the figure to the left.
   2)   Locate 120 NM, or "12," on the outer scale.
   3)   Under 120 on the outer scale read 72 min. on the inner scale or 1:12 on the hour scale.

   c.   Use your flight computer to solve these practice problems (answers are located below).

	Groundspeed	Distance	Time
1)	80 kt.	300 NM	_____
2)	95 kt.	19 NM	_____
3)	105 kt.	62 NM	_____
4)	120 mph	142 SM	_____

   d.   Answers to practice problems

      1)   225 min., or 3 hr. 45 min.
      2)   12 min.
      3)   35.5 min.
      4)   71 min., or 1 hr. 11 min.

3.   **Determining Distance**

a.   If you know groundspeed and time, you can determine the distance.

1)   **Distance = Speed × Time**

b.   EXAMPLE: How far will the airplane fly in 8 min. at a groundspeed of 90 kt.?

1)   Rotate the inner scale so the Index is opposite 90, as shown in the figure below.
2)   Locate 8 on the inner scale.
3)   Opposite 8 on the inner scale is 12 NM on the outer scale.

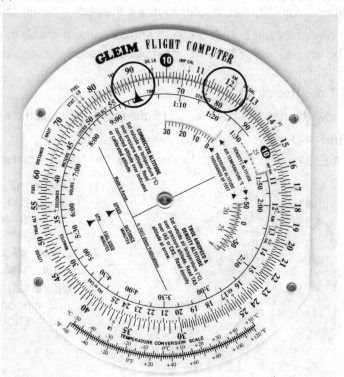

c.   Use your flight computer to solve these practice problems (answers are located below).

	Groundspeed	Time	Distance
1)	107 kt.	3 hr. 27 min.	_____
2)	96 kt.	17 min.	_____
3)	126 kt.	43 min.	_____
4)	72 mph	1 hr. 24 min.	_____

d.   Answers to practice problems

1)   369 NM
2)   27.2 NM
3)   90 NM
4)   101 SM

4. **Determining Groundspeed**

    a.   If you know the time and distance, you can determine the groundspeed.

        1)   **Speed = Distance ÷ Time**

    b.   EXAMPLE: What is the groundspeed if the airplane takes 7 min. to go 10.5 NM?

        1)   Rotate the inner scale so that 10.5 on the outer scale is opposite 7 on the inner scale, as shown in the figure below.

        2)   Locate the Index on the inner scale and read a groundspeed of 90 kt. on the outer scale.

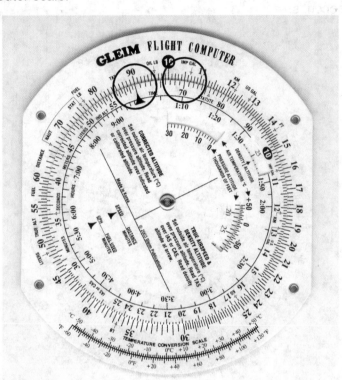

    c.   Use your flight computer to solve these practice problems (answers are located below).

	Distance	Time	Groundspeed
1)	5.5 NM	3 min.	_____
2)	10 NM	6.5 min.	_____
3)	15 NM	9 min.	_____
4)	5 SM	4 min.	_____

    d.   Answers to practice problems

        1)   110 kt.

        2)   92 kt.

        3)   100 kt.

        4)   75 mph

5. **Use of the Seconds Index**

    a. The seconds index is located on the inner circle at "36." There is an arrow labeled "seconds."

        1) The "36" represents 3,600 seconds, which is the number of seconds in 1 hr.

    b. This procedure is used to solve time, distance, and speed problems involving short distances and times in minutes and seconds rather than hours and minutes.

        1) When using the seconds index, the inner scale will now represent seconds, and the hour scale (below and inside the minutes scale) represents minutes and seconds.

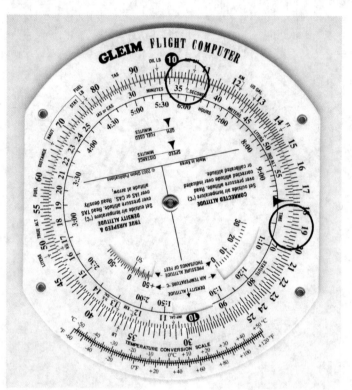

    c. EXAMPLE: How long will it take an airplane to fly 1.9 NM at a groundspeed of 105 kt.?

        1) Rotate the inner scale so that the seconds index (36) is opposite 105 kt., or "10.5," on the outer scale, as shown in the figure above.

        2) Locate 1.9 NM, or "19," on the outer scale.

        3) Opposite 1.9 on the inner scale is the time of 65 seconds.

    d. Use your flight computer to solve these practice problems (answers are below).

	Groundspeed	Time	Distance
1)	96 kt.	2 min.	
2)	100 kt.		0.5 NM
3)	_____	45 sec.	1.7 NM
4)	_____	68 sec.	1.5 NM

    e. Answers to practice problems

        1) 3.2 NM
        2) 18 sec.
        3) 136 kt.
        4) 79 kt.

9.13 FUEL COMPUTATIONS

1.   You may compute either fuel used, fuel consumption rate, or time remaining using computations similar to those for speed, distance, and time.

   a.   The computations are

   1)   **Fuel burned = Fuel consumption rate × Time**
   2)   **Time (available) = Fuel to burn ÷ Fuel consumption rate**
   3)   **Fuel consumption rate = Fuel burned ÷ Time**

   b.   These computations are made on the flight computer in the same way as time and distance computations, except that gallons are used in place of miles.

2.   **Determining Amount of Fuel Used**

   a.   If you know the fuel consumption rate and the time, you can determine the fuel used. Fuel used equals fuel consumption rate multiplied by time.

   b.   EXAMPLE: How much fuel will be used during a flight of 2 hr. and 30 min. if the fuel consumption rate is 8.2 gallons per hour (GPH)?

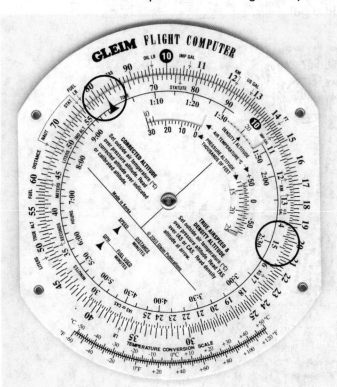

   1)   Rotate the inner scale so the Index is opposite 8.2, or "82," on the outer scale, as shown in the figure to the left.
   2)   Locate 2:30 on the hour scale or 150 min. on the inner scale.
   3)   Opposite 150 is 20.5 gallons on the outer scale.

   c.   Use your flight computer to solve these practice problems (answers are below).

	Consumption Rate	Time	Fuel Used
1)	17.0 GPH	1 hr. 10 min.	_____
2)	7.0 GPH	30 min.	_____
3)	10.2 GPH	2 hr. 5 min.	_____
4)	9.4 GPH	90 min.	_____

   d.   Answers to practice problems

   1)   19.8 gal.
   2)   3.5 gal.
   3)   21.2 gal.
   4)   14.1 gal.

3.   **Determining Endurance**

a.   If you know the fuel consumption rate and usable fuel on board the airplane, you can determine the endurance, or time, the airplane can fly.

1)   **Endurance = Amount of fuel ÷ Fuel consumption rate**

b.   EXAMPLE: If the fuel consumption rate is 10.3 GPH and there are 48 gallons of usable fuel, how long can the airplane fly?

1)   Rotate the inner scale so the Index is opposite 10.3, as shown below.
2)   Locate 48 on the outer scale.
3)   Opposite 48 on the inner scale is 280 min. or 4 hr. 40 min.

c.   Use your flight computer to solve these practice problems (answers below).

	Consumption Rate	Usable Fuel	Endurance (Time)
1)	16.3 GPH	62.0 gal.	_____
2)	8.2 GPH	24.5 gal.	_____
3)	10.6 GPH	50.0 gal.	_____
4)	9.0 GPH	38.0 gal.	_____

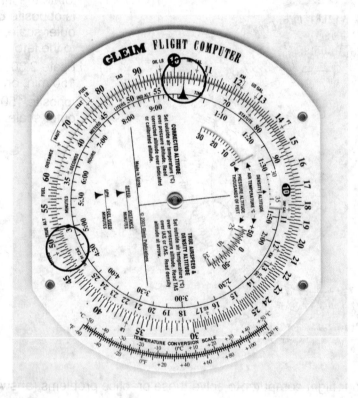

d.   Answers to practice problems

1)   3 hr. 48 min., or 228 min.
2)   2 hr. 59 min., or 179 min.
3)   4 hr. 43 min., or 283 min.
4)   4 hr. 13 min., or 253 min.

4. **Determining Fuel Consumption Rate**

   a. If you know the amount of fuel used and the time, you can determine the fuel consumption rate.

      1) **Fuel consumption rate = Fuel burned ÷ Time**

   b. EXAMPLE: If an airplane used 15.4 gal. on a 1 hr. 25 min. flight, what was the fuel consumption rate in gallons per hour (GPH)?

      1) Rotate the inner scale so that 1:25 on the hour scale, or 85 on the inner scale, is opposite 15.4 on the outer scale, as shown in the figure below.

      2) The fuel consumption rate is on the outer scale opposite the Index, which is 10.9 GPH.

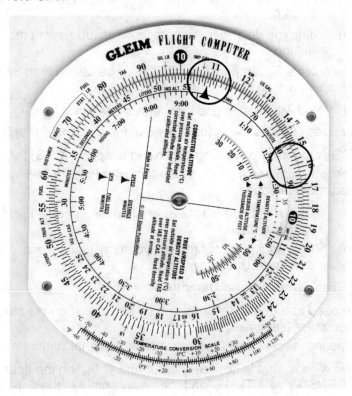

   c. Use your flight computer to solve these practice problems (answers are located below).

	Time	Fuel Used	Consumption Rate
1)	145 min.	16 gal.	_____
2)	54 mln.	17 gal.	_____
3)	1 hr. 15 min.	10.4 gal.	_____
4)	3 hr. 40 min.	36 gal.	_____

   d. Answers to practice problems

      1) 6.6 GPH
      2) 18.9 GPH
      3) 8.3 GPH
      4) 9.8 GPH

9.14 TRUE AIRSPEED AND DENSITY ALTITUDE

1.   Air density affects the indications of the airspeed indicator and the performance of the airplane.

  a.   Density altitude is the theoretical altitude in the standard atmosphere where the density is the same as the actual density you are experiencing in flight.

   1)   Density altitude is found by correcting pressure altitude for nonstandard temperature.

   2)   Pressure altitude can be determined by setting the airplane's altimeter to 29.92 and then reading the altitude.

    a)   If this is done in flight, make a note of the altimeter setting before turning it to 29.92.

    b)   After you determine the pressure altitude, reset the altimeter to the current setting.

   3)   The outside air temperature (OAT) can be determined by reading the current temperature on the airplane's OAT gauge.

    a)   You will need to use the Celsius scale.

  b.   True airspeed (TAS) is the actual speed of the airplane through the air.

   1)   TAS is found by correcting calibrated airspeed (CAS) for density altitude.

   2)   See your airplane's Pilot's Operating Handbook to determine CAS based on indicated airspeed.

    a)   Generally, there is little error at cruise speeds; i.e., CAS equals indicated airspeed (IAS).

    b)   Thus, as a practical matter, you may usually use IAS rather than CAS to determine true airspeed.

2.   **Determining True Airspeed and Density Altitude**

  a.   True airspeed and density altitude can be calculated on the calculator side of your flight computer (see next page).

  b.   Rotate the inner scale until the numbers on the inner and outer scales match.

   1)   The window that is between "1:30" and "1:50" on the hour scale is labeled "DENSITY ALTITUDE" and the arrow points to the density altitude.

    a)   The numbers that rotate through this window are in thousands of feet and range from –10 (or –10,000 ft.) to 45 (or +45,000 ft.).

   2)   The window on the right side below "2:00" and "2:30" on the hour scale is used to set the OAT (above the window) over the pressure altitude (numbers in the window).

    a)   The OAT is in 5°C increments from +50°C on the left side to –70°C on the right side.

    b)   The numbers in the window are in thousands of feet and range from –2 (or –2,000 ft.) to 50 (or +50,000 ft.).

c.   EXAMPLE: What is the TAS and density altitude if the IAS is 130 kt., OAT is –15°C, and the pressure altitude is 5,000 ft.?

   1)   Using the inner window on the right side, locate the OAT of –15°C and rotate the disk so the pressure altitude of 5,000 ft. (which is labeled "5" on the scale) is under –15°C, as shown in the figure below.

   2)   In the window labeled "DENSITY ALTITUDE," read the density altitude of approximately 2,500 ft.

   3)   Locate the IAS of 130 kt., or "13," on the inner scale. Without moving the disk, read the TAS on the outer scale opposite the IAS, which is 135 kt.

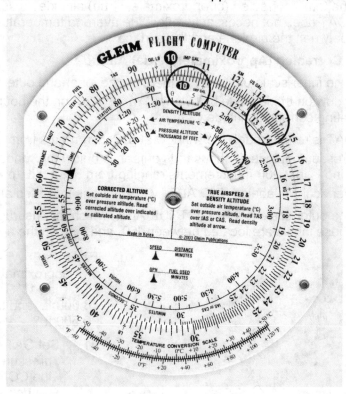

d.   Use your flight computer to solve these practice problems (answers are located below).

	OAT	Pressure Altitude	IAS/CAS	TAS	Density Altitude
1)	+10°C	4,500	95 kt.	_____	_____
2)	0°C	7,000	130 kt.	_____	_____
3)	–20°C	10,000	150 kt.	_____	_____
4)	–10°C	9,500	115 kt.	_____	_____

e.   Answers to practice problems

   1)   102 kt., 4,900 ft.
   2)   144 kt., 7,000 ft.
   3)   169 kt., 8,100 ft.
   4)   131 kt., 8,800 ft.

9.15 CORRECTED (APPROXIMATELY TRUE) ALTITUDE

1. Because temperature affects air density, variations in temperature will affect the indications of the altimeter.

   a. True altitude is the actual altitude of the airplane above mean sea level (MSL).

   b. Indicated altitude is the altitude read directly from the altimeter after it is set to the current altimeter setting.

   c. Corrected (approximately true) altitude is found by correcting indicated altitude for nonstandard temperature and pressure.

      1) The term "corrected (or approximately true) altitude" is used since the indicated OAT does not necessarily reflect the average temperature of the column of air between the airplane and the surface.

2. **Determining Corrected (Approximately True) Altitude**

   a. Rotate the inner scale until the numbers on the inner and outer scale match.

   b. The window on the left side below "1:10" and "1:20" on the hour scale is used for calculating corrected altitude.

      1) OAT is read through the window at 5°C increments from –60°C to +50°C.

      2) Pressure altitude, in thousands of feet, is below the window on the movable disk and is in 2,000-ft. increments ranging from 30,000 ft. to –1,000 ft.

   c. The inner scale is labeled "IND ALT," which means indicated altitude.

      1) The outer scale is labeled "TRUE ALT," which means true (corrected) altitude.

      2) These labels are located between "50" and "55" on the appropriate scale.

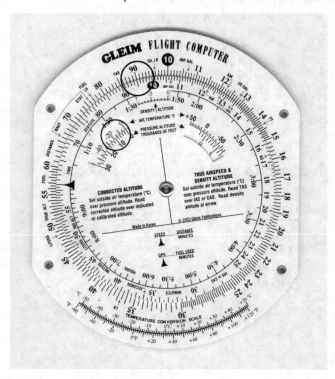

   d. EXAMPLE: What is the "corrected (or approximately true) altitude" if the OAT is –15°C, pressure altitude is 8,000 ft., and the indicated altitude is 9,500 ft.?

      1) Set OAT of –15°C opposite pressure altitude of 8,000 ft. in the CORRECTED ALTITUDE window, as shown in the figure to the left.

      2) Locate the indicated altitude of 9,500 ft., or "95," on the inner scale; over this value on the outer scale is the corrected (or approximately true) altitude of 9,000 ft.

3. Find corrected (approximately true) altitude.

   a. Use your flight computer to solve these practice problems (answers on next page).

	OAT	Pressure Altitude	Indicated Altitude	Corrected Altitude
1)	–15°C	9,000 ft.	9,500 ft.	_____
2)	+10°C	3,500 ft.	3,000 ft.	_____
3)	+20°C	9,000 ft.	10,500 ft.	_____
4)	0°C	2,000 ft.	2,500 ft.	_____

b. Answers to practice problems

    1) 9,100 ft.
    2) 3,000 ft.
    3) 11,400 ft.
    4) 2,400 ft.

9.16 OFF-COURSE CORRECTION

1. When your airplane drifts off course due to a wind shift, an inaccurate winds aloft forecast, or a navigation error on your part, your flight computer can be used to determine how many degrees you must turn to parallel your intended course and how many degrees you must turn to converge on your intended course. To calculate this, you must know your present position and

    a. Distance you have flown from your departure
    b. Distance off course
    c. Distance to your destination

2. EXAMPLE: You determine you are 11 NM off course when 141 NM from your departure point. If 71 NM remains to be flown, what heading correction is needed to converge on your destination?

    a. First, set the distance off course, 11, on the outer scale opposite the distance you have flown from your departure, 141, on the inner scale.

        1) Above the Index, read 4.7°. This is the correction needed to parallel your intended course.

    b. Next, set the distance off course, 11, on the outer scale opposite the distance to your destination, 71, on the inner scale.

        1) Above the Index, read 9.3° to converge.

    c. Finally, add the 4.7° to parallel your intended course and the additional 9.3° to converge for a total of 14°.

        1) Thus, if you are 11 NM off course and have 71 NM to your destination, you must turn 14° toward your intended course to rejoin your intended course at your destination.

3. Find off-course correction.

    a. Use your flight computer to solve these practice problems (answers are located below).

	Distance from Departure	Distance Off Course	Distance to Destination	Total Correction to Converge
1)	150 NM	8 NM	160 NM	_____
2)	240 NM	25 NM	100 NM	_____
3)	60 NM	10 NM	40 NM	_____
4)	100 NM	15 NM	150 NM	_____

    b. Answers to practice problems

        1) 6.2°
        2) 21.3°
        3) 25.0°
        4) 15.0°

9.17 RADIUS OF ACTION

1. Radius of action is the maximum time or distance that an airplane may be flown on a specific course and be able to return to the starting point within a given time.

    a. The amount of fuel available, not including reserve fuel, is the determining factor.

2. EXAMPLE: You have determined that the groundspeed for the outbound leg is 150 kt. and that the groundspeed for the inbound leg is 120 kt. Fuel available, not including reserve, is 4 hr. What is your radius of action?

    a. First, add the groundspeeds together for a sum of 270 (150 + 120).

    b. Rotate the inner scale so that the total time of 4 hr., or 240 min., is opposite the sum of the groundspeeds, 270, on the outer scale.

    c. Without rotating the disk, locate the groundspeed for the inbound leg of 120 kt. on the outer scale. Look directly under 120 to determine a time of 107 min., or 1 hr. 47 min.

        1) You may fly outbound for this amount of time before you must turn to return to the departure point.

    d. Without rotating the disk, locate the outbound groundspeed of 150 kt. to determine a time of 133 min., or 2 hr. 13 min.

        1) The outbound time of 107 min. plus the inbound time of 133 min. equals 240 min., or 4 hr. (107 + 133).

        2) This is equal to the 4 hr. of fuel available.

    e. Place the Index opposite the outbound groundspeed of 150 kt. Locate 107 min. on the inner scale; directly above on the outer scale, read 268 NM.

        1) The radius of action is 268 NM.

9.18 OTHER CONVERSIONS

(Skim this subunit and use only as needed.)

1. **Converting U.S. Gallons to Imperial Gallons**

    a. Near "11" on each scale is an arrow labeled "IMP GAL" (imperial gallon), and near "13" is an arrow labeled "US GAL."

    b. The imperial gallon is used in Canada and is equivalent to about 1.2 U.S. gallons.

    c. To convert U.S. to imperial gallons or vice-versa, place the arrow labeled "IMP GAL" on one scale opposite "US GAL" on the other scale.

        1) Imperial gallons are read on the same scale as the "IMP GAL" arrow, and U.S. gallons are read on the same scale as "US GAL."

    d. EXAMPLE: 35 imperial gallons is equivalent to how many U.S. gallons?

        1) Rotate the inner scale so the arrow labeled "US GAL" on the inner scale is opposite "IMP GAL" on the outer scale.

    e. Locate 35 imperial gallons on the outer scale. Opposite 35 is 42 on the inner scale.

    f. 35 imperial gallons is equivalent to 42 U.S. gallons.

2. **Converting Fuel and Oil Weight**

    a.   Aviation gas (fuel) weighs 6 lb./U.S. gal., and oil weighs 7.5 lb./U.S. gal. (or 4 qt.).

    b.   At "76.8" on the outer scale is an arrow labeled "FUEL LB," and at "96" on the outer scale is an arrow labeled "OIL LB."

        1)   Use these arrows in conjunction with the appropriate "IMP GAL" or "US GAL" arrow on the inner scale.

    c.   EXAMPLE: Determine the weight of 35 U.S. gal. of fuel.

        1)   Rotate the inner scale so the arrow labeled "US GAL" on the inner scale is opposite the arrow labeled "FUEL LB" on the outer scale.

        2)   Locate 35 on the inner scale and directly above read 210 on the outer scale.

        3)   35 U.S. gal. weigh 210 lb.

    d.   EXAMPLE: Determine the weight of 8 qt. (2 U.S. gal.) of oil.

        1)   Rotate the inner scale so that the arrow labeled "US GAL" on the inner scale is opposite the arrow labeled "OIL LB" on the outer scale.

        2)   Locate 2 on the inner scale and directly above read 15 on the outer scale.

        3)   8 qt. (or 2 U.S. gal.) of oil weigh 15 lb.

3. **Converting Feet to Meters, Pounds to Kilograms, and Gallons to Liters**

    a.   A similar process, as previously discussed, can be used to convert feet to meters, pounds to kilograms, gallons to liters, or vice versa.

        1)   Set the appropriately labeled arrows opposite each other on the outer and inner scales.

        2)   Read the value on the scale containing the arrow for the corresponding unit of measure.

    b.   EXAMPLE: Convert 2,300 ft. to meters.

        1)   Rotate the inner scale so that the arrow labeled "METERS" (located at 43.5) on the inner scale is opposite the arrow labeled "FT" (located at 14.3) on the outer scale.

        2)   Locate 2,300 on the outer scale and directly below read 700 on the inner scale.

        3)   2,300 ft. is approximately 700 meters.

4. **Converting Minutes to Seconds**

    a.   To convert minutes to seconds, place the Index opposite the number of minutes on the outer scale.

        1)   Locate the arrow labeled "SECONDS" (located at 36) on the inner scale. Directly above the arrow on the outer scale is the number of seconds.

    b.   EXAMPLE: Convert 1.5 min. to seconds.

        1)   Rotate the inner scale so that the Index is directly under 1.5 on the outer scale.

        2)   Locate the arrow labeled "SECONDS"; directly above the arrow is 90 on the outer scale.

        3)   1.5 min. is equal to 90 sec.

5. **Converting Feet per Nautical Mile to Feet per Minute**

   a. Some IFR departure procedures require a minimum climb rate. Due to the widely varying performance characteristics of various aircraft, the FAA states the required climb performance in feet to be gained per nautical mile covered on the ground.

      1) Since the vertical speed indicator (VSI) in your airplane is calibrated in feet per minute, you must be able to convert to determine whether your airplane can meet the minimum climb performance.

   b. At some airports with noise abatement procedures, the minimum climb rate may be expressed as feet per nautical mile.

   c. To convert, set the Index opposite the groundspeed on the outer scale.

      1) The inner scale will represent the climb rate expressed as feet per nautical mile.
      2) The outer scale will represent the climb rate expressed in feet per minute.

   d. EXAMPLE: With a groundspeed of 90 kt. and a minimum climb requirement of 300 ft. per nautical mile, what is the rate of climb in feet per minute?

      1) Rotate the inner scale so that the Index is directly under the groundspeed of 90 on the outer scale.
      2) Locate 300 on the inner scale and directly above 300 is 450 on the outer scale.
      3) A climb rate of 300 feet per nautical mile with a 90-kt. groundspeed is equivalent to a climb rate of 450 feet per minute.

6. **Converting Mach Number to True Airspeed**

   a. Use the following procedure to convert a Mach number to the true airspeed.

      1) Rotate the inner scale so that "MACH NO. INDEX" appears in the right window. Align the arrow with the known outside air temperature.
      2) On the inner scale, locate the Mach number.
      3) Directly above the Mach number, read the true airspeed on the outer scale.

   b. EXAMPLE: With an outside air temperature of +10°C, what is the true airspeed at Mach 0.9?

      1) Rotate the inner scale so that the arrow labeled "MACH NO. INDEX" is opposite the OAT of +10°C in the right window.
      2) Locate Mach 0.9 on the inner scale.
      3) Directly above 0.9 is the true airspeed of 590 kt. on the outer scale.

9.19 TEMPERATURE CONVERSIONS

1. A temperature conversion scale is provided for your use at the bottom of the calculator side of the flight computer.

   a. The top scale is degrees Celsius, and the bottom scale is degrees Fahrenheit.

2. EXAMPLE: Convert 70°F to Celsius.

   a. Locate 70°F on the bottom scale.
   b. Directly above read 21°C.

9.20 THE WIND SIDE OF THE GLEIM FLIGHT COMPUTER

1.   The wind side of the flight computer allows you to determine the effect of wind on the airplane in terms of heading and groundspeed. Refer to the figure on page 444.

    a.   The wind side consists of a rotating plotting transparency attached to a frame and a sliding card.

        1)   A compass rose is printed on the outside of the plotting transparency.

           a)   The transparency allows you to mark on it with a pencil and to see the grid on the sliding card.

           b)   A small metal rivet called a grommet is located at the center of the plotting transparency.

        2)   At the top of the frame is a large triangle ($\triangledown$) in the center called the True Index.

           a)   A correction scale is shown in degrees left and right of the True Index. This scale can be used when applying the wind correction angle (WCA).

           b)   NOTE: The instructions regarding how to use the wind side of the Gleim flight computer (found on pages 461 through 466 in this book and at the top of the sliding card on the computer itself) require you to set **magnetic values** (i.e., wind direction and course) under the True Index. We have retained the name "True Index" (vs. "Magnetic Index") because this term is the industry standard for flight computers. Do not be concerned about this minor semantic inconsistency.

               i)   We promote the use of magnetic wind direction and course values because many courses are flown directly to or from VORs. VOR compass roses are oriented to magnetic north; thus, it is possible to obtain the magnetic course to or from a VOR directly from the chart, without using a plotter.

    b.   The grid on the sliding card is a section of a large circle.

        1)   The vertical converging lines, called wind correction lines, represent degrees left or right of the center line.

           a)   The wind correction lines are spaced at 2° intervals between the horizontal arcs labeled "30" to "150," and at 1° intervals above the "150" arc.

        2)   The horizontal arcs, called speed arcs, are concentric circles around the center of the circle and represent a distance from the center.

           a)   These arcs are used for speed and are spaced two units (usually knots or miles per hour) apart.

        3)   At the top of the sliding card are directions on how to use the wind side of the flight computer to determine groundspeed and wind correction angle (WCA).

        4)   The reverse (or information) side of the sliding card is discussed on pages 467 and 468.

9.21 DETERMINING MAGNETIC HEADING AND GROUNDSPEED

1. To determine the magnetic heading and groundspeed, you need to know

   a. The magnetic course of your planned flight, as plotted on your sectional chart

      1) Magnetic course (MC) is the true course (TC) corrected for magnetic variation.

$$\text{MC} = \text{TC} \frac{+W}{-E} \text{ Variation}$$

      2) If the flight is to or from a VOR station, magnetic course is determined from the compass rose surrounding the VOR station on the sectional chart.

   b. True airspeed (TAS), as determined from the performance chart(s) in your airplane's FAA-approved Airplane Flight Manual (AFM) and/or Pilot's Operating Handbook (POH)

      1) If the AFM/POH provides TAS in mph, convert mph to knots.

   c. Wind direction and speed, as obtained from the winds aloft forecast

      1) Wind direction is based on **true north**, so you must convert to **magnetic direction** by correcting for magnetic variation.

      2) Refer to a sectional aeronautical chart to determine magnetic variation at the winds aloft reporting site.

      3) Magnetic wind (MW) is the true wind (TW) corrected for magnetic variation.

$$\text{MW} = \text{TW} \frac{+W}{-E} \text{ Variation}$$

2. Be sure that you are using the same units of direction and speed throughout your computations.

   a. Since winds aloft are forecast in knots, you must convert your TAS if it is in mph.

   b. If your course has been determined in magnetic direction (e.g., you are using a VOR radial), you must convert the wind direction to magnetic.

3. As illustrated on the next page, find magnetic heading and groundspeed given the following conditions:

Magnetic course	095°
True airspeed	98 kt.
Magnetic wind	150° at 20 kt.

   a. Rotate the plotting transparency so the magnetic wind direction of 150° is opposite the True Index.

   b. Move the sliding card so the grommet is over a convenient speed arc, such as 100.

   c. Using the speed arcs, place a dot 20 kt. up from the grommet. This represents the wind speed, also called a wind dot. If the grommet is on the 100-kt. speed arc, the dot should be placed on the centerline at the 120-kt. speed arc.

   d. Rotate the plotting transparency so the magnetic course of 095° is opposite the True Index.

   e. Move the sliding card so the wind dot is on the 98-kt. speed arc, which is the TAS.

   f. The WCA is determined by the wind dot and the wind correction lines. In this example, the wind dot is 10° to the right of the center.

$$\text{Magnetic heading (MH)} = \text{MC} \frac{+R}{-L} \text{ WCA}$$

      1) In this problem, MH = 105° (95 + 10).

   g. Groundspeed is read under the grommet; it is 85 kt. in this example.

h. Under the given conditions, the magnetic heading is 105° and the groundspeed is 85 kt.

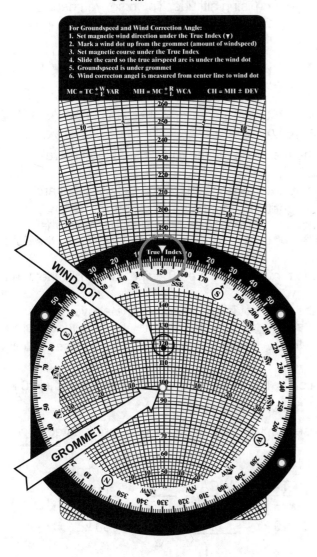

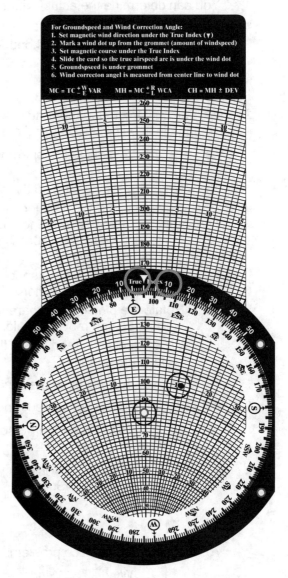

4. Find wind correction angle, magnetic heading, and groundspeed.

a. Use your flight computer to solve these practice problems (answers are located below).

	Wind Direction	Wind Speed	MC	TAS	WCA	MH	Groundspeed
1)	215°	15 kt.	260°	113 kt.	_____	_____	_____ kt.
2)	050°	20 kt.	350°	105 kt.	_____	_____	_____ kt.

b. Answers to practice problems

	WCA	MH	Groundspeed
1)	5°L	255°	102 kt.
2)	10°R	360°	94 kt.

9.22 DETERMINING WIND DIRECTION AND SPEED

1. You can determine the actual winds aloft at your cruising altitude. To do so, you need to know the following:

   a. Magnetic course (actual path of travel)
   b. Magnetic heading
   c. Groundspeed
   d. TAS

2. EXAMPLE: Determine the winds aloft given a TAS of 98 kt., a magnetic course of 095°, a magnetic heading of 105°, and a groundspeed of 85 kt.

   a. Rotate the plotting transparency so the magnetic course (095°) is under the True Index.
   b. Move the sliding card so the grommet is over the groundspeed (85 kt.) speed arc.
   c. Determine the WCA by locating the magnetic heading on the compass rose and, directly above, determine the WCA on the correction scale. In this example, the magnetic heading of 105° is opposite 10° on the correction scale, and it is to the right of the True Index.
   d. Locate the TAS (98 kt.) speed arc, and move right to the 10° wind correction line; mark a wind dot at that location.
   e. Rotate the plotting transparency so the wind dot is on the center line above the grommet, and move the sliding card so the grommet is over the 100-kt. speed arc.
   f. Wind direction is read under the True Index, and the wind speed is the number of units above the grommet.

      1) In this example, the wind direction is 150° magnetic, and the wind speed is 20 kt.

3. Find wind direction, wind speed, and wind correction angle (WCA).

   a. Use your flight computer to solve these practice problems (answers are located below).

	Wind Direction	Wind Speed	MC	TAS	WCA	MH	Ground-speed
1)	___°	___ kt.	130°	150 kt.	_____	142°	147 kt.
2)	___°	___ kt.	100°	110 kt.	_____	085°	80 kt.

   b. Answers to practice problems

	Wind Direction	Wind Speed	WCA
1)	220°	31 kt.	12°R
2)	53°	39 kt.	15°L

9.23 DETERMINING ALTITUDE FOR MOST FAVORABLE WINDS

1. The most-favorable-winds altitude provides you with the highest groundspeed. This altitude is determined by comparing winds aloft at different altitudes, e.g., 3,000 ft., 6,000 ft., and 9,000 ft.

2. The most favorable winds are determined by

   a. Plotting the wind dot for each altitude on the plotting transparency in the same manner as the magnetic heading and groundspeed problems

      1) Label each wind dot so you know what altitude they represent.

   b. Rotating the plotting transparency so the magnetic course is opposite the True Index

   c. For each wind dot, sliding the card so the wind dot is over the speed arc that represents the TAS

      1) Read the groundspeed under the grommet for each wind dot to determine the highest groundspeed.

3. Determine the best altitude and groundspeed for the following conditions:

   a. Use your flight computer to solve this problem (answers are located below).

      1) Winds aloft

         a) 3,000 ft. -- 120° at 15 kt.
         b) 6,000 ft. -- 140° at 10 kt.
         c) 9,000 ft. -- 160° at 25 kt.

      2) Magnetic course is 035° and the TAS is 105 kt.

   b. Answer to practice problem

      1) Groundspeed

         a) 3,000 ft. is 103 kt.
         b) 6,000 ft. is 107 kt.
         c) 9,000 ft. is 117 kt.

      2) The most favorable winds are at 9,000 ft.

9.24 ALTERNATIVE: E6B COMPUTER APPROACH TO MAGNETIC HEADING

1. **Alternative: E6B Computer Approach to Magnetic Heading**

   a. In Subunit 9.21, before computing the WCA and groundspeed (GS) on the wind side of the E6B computer, we converted

      1) TC to MC
      2) Winds (true) to winds (magnetic)

   b. The ALTERNATIVE METHOD suggested on your E6B is to use TC and winds (true) on the wind side of your E6B to compute your true heading (TH) and then convert TH to MH. The advantages of this method are

      1) You convert only one true direction to magnetic, not two.
      2) This is the way it has always been taught.

   c. We suggest converting TC and wind (true) to magnetic because pilot activities are in terms of magnetic headings, courses, runways, radials, bearings, and final approach courses. **When flying, you should always think magnetic, not true.**

      1) While doing magnetic heading problems, you should visualize yourself flying each problem, e.g., a 270° course with a 300° wind will require a right (270°+) heading and have a headwind component.

2. On your E6B, you will find directions such as

   a. Set Wind Direction opposite True Index.
   b. Mark Wind Dot up from Grommet.
   c. Place TC under True Index.
   d. Slide TAS under Wind Dot.
   e. Read GS under Grommet.
   f. Read WCA under Wind Dot.
   g. Complete the problem by use of the formulas.

3. The formulas given are

   TH = TC ± WCA (wind correction angle)
   MH = TH ± magnetic variation (E–, W+)
   CH = MH ± compass deviation

4. We understand this ALTERNATIVE approach is widely used. It was developed prior to the VOR system, compass roses, airways, etc., which are all identified in magnetic direction, **not** true direction. Thus you may use it for textbook exercises, but when flying, think magnetic.

9.25 INFORMATION SIDE OF SLIDING CARD (GLEIM E6B)

1. Three boxes provide information.

    a. The first, or top, box includes common ICAO flight plan equipment codes and surveillance codes.

ICAO Flight Plan Common Equipment
B: LPV
D: DME
F: ADF
G: GNSS
L: ILS
O: VOR
S: VOR, VHF Comm, & ILS
W: RVSM
Y: VHF 8.33 kHz

ICAO Surveillance Codes
A: Mode A
C: Modes A and C
E: Mode S, ID, Alt, ADS-B Squitter
S: Mode S, Alt, & ID
See AIM for enhanced surveillance suffixes

    b. The middle box shows the standard holding pattern entries.

STANDARD HOLDING PATTERN

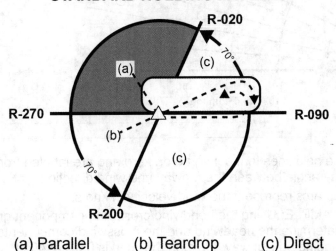

(a) Parallel   (b) Teardrop   (c) Direct

c. The bottom box contains a headwind/crosswind component graph, which is used to determine the headwind and crosswind components of a crosswind on a runway.

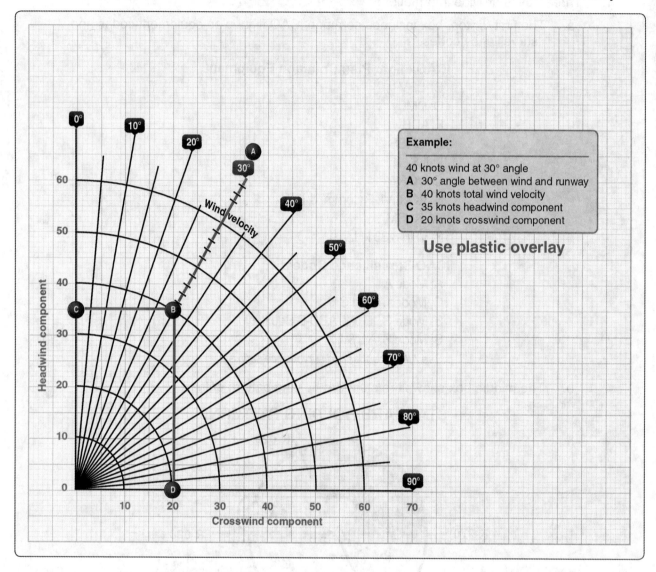

1) The bold lines that converge on zero and are labeled from 0° to 90° represent the angle between the runway and wind direction.
2) The arcs represent the wind velocity in knots.
3) EXAMPLE: Using the headwind/crosswind component graph depicted above, determine the headwind and the crosswind components of the wind for a landing on Runway 36 when the wind is 030° at 40 kt.

   a) The angle between the runway (360° or 0°) and the wind (030°) is 30° (A).
   b) Enter the graph at the 30° line and move down to the wind speed arc of 40 kt. (B).
   c) From this point, move horizontally to the left margin to determine a headwind component of 35 kt. (C).
   d) Return to the point of the 30° angle and 40 kt. speed arc. Now, move vertically down to determine a crosswind component of 20 kt. (D).
   e) Landing in this situation is like having a 20 kt. direct crosswind.

2. On the side margins of the card are mileage scales for sectional charts.

   a. One side is in nautical miles, and the other side is in statute miles.

9.26 ELECTRONIC FLIGHT COMPUTERS

1. Electronic flight computers perform the functions of manual flight computers in a fashion similar to the way pocket calculators perform the functions of slide rules.

    a. They perform all the functions of both sides of the manual computer through prompted entries of required variables on a keypad.

        1) The results of the desired computations are then shown on an electronic display.

    b. Electronic flight computers are also capable of weight and balance calculations.

2. Electronic computers have certain advantages over the manual flight computers.

    a. Greater precision of computations
    b. Automatic placement of decimal points
    c. Greater ease of performing multi-part problems
    d. Much faster on wind correction problems
    e. Capable of weight and balance calculations

3. Some disadvantages of the electronic flight computers are that

    a. The cost can be 10 or more times that of a manual flight computer.
    b. The greater precision of the electronic computers can be misleading because values such as fuel consumption or winds aloft are usually imprecise.

4. As a student pilot, you should first learn how to use the manual flight computer (explained and illustrated on pages 443 through 468). After learning to use a manual flight computer, you will be in a better position to use and appreciate an electronic flight computer. In addition, you will learn more about navigation.

5. These computers may be used on the FAA knowledge tests at PSI computer testing centers during practical tests.

    a. However, no instructional material (e.g., operating or instruction manuals for the computers) may be taken to the test site or used during the test.
    b. If you plan to use an electronic flight computer during your FAA knowledge test, practice with it on all of the practice problems in this study unit.

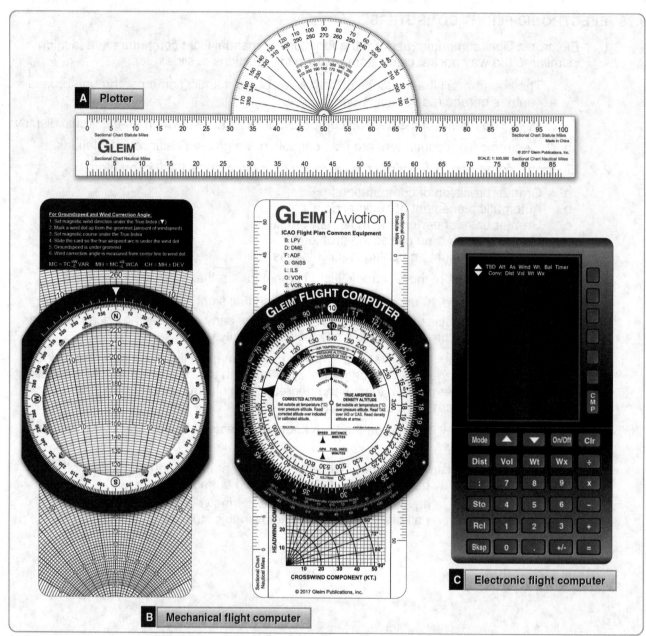

A plotter (A), the computational and wind side of a mechanical flight computer (E6B) (B), and an electronic flight computer (C).

END OF STUDY UNIT

STUDY UNIT TEN
NAVIGATION SYSTEMS

(30 pages of outline)

General aviation airplanes make use of a variety of navigation systems. The use of these systems is sometimes referred to as radio navigation. These systems utilize radio waves in order to provide guidance. Pilots use these systems to plan and fly a precise course to their destination, increasing both the safety and efficiency of flight.

These navigation systems use ground-based and space-based (satellite) stations to transmit signals to navigation radio receivers installed in the airplane. The pilot can manipulate the individual instruments to make the best use of them for each flight by selecting the course (s)he wishes to fly.

Before learning the operational procedures, you should obtain at least a basic knowledge of the characteristics and limitations of various radio navigation systems.

10.1 CHARACTERISTICS OF RADIO WAVES

1. Radio waves dissipate as they encounter resistance from the environment.

   a. Mountain ranges, trees, water, and land all dissipate the energy of radio signals, reducing their strength.

   b. Radio waves that travel into the upper atmosphere are also affected as energy is absorbed by molecules of air, water, and dust.

2. A radio wave normally radiates from an antenna in all directions.

   a. Part of the energy travels along the ground (ground wave) until its energy is dissipated.

   b. The remainder of the transmitted energy travels upward into space (sky wave).

3. The characteristics of radio waves vary according to their frequency, as do the behaviors of their ground and sky waves.

   a. These characteristics determine the design, use, and limitations of both ground and airborne equipment.

4. Low frequency (LF) radio waves.

    a. At frequencies below 300 kHz, there is substantial energy in the ground and sky waves.

    b. The sky wave is reflected by the ionosphere by highly charged particles (ions) caused by the Sun's radiation.

        1) This reflection of the radio wave permits reception of the signals at varying distances from the antenna.

        2) The transmission distance is determined by factors such as the height and density of the ionosphere (which varies with the time of day, seasons, and latitude due to the Sun's radiation) and the angle at which the radio wave strikes the ionosphere.

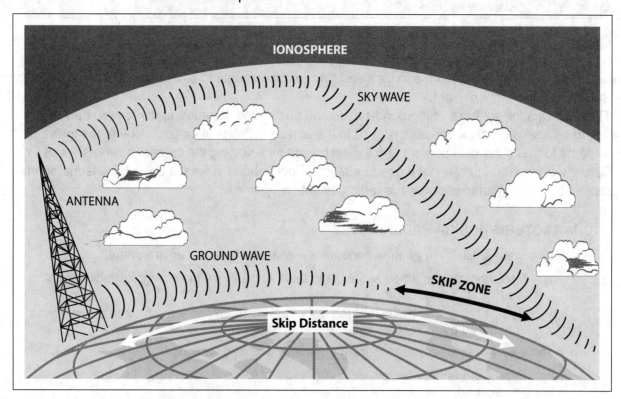

    c. The distance between the transmitting antenna and the point where the sky wave first returns to the ground is called the **skip distance**.

        1) The distance between the point where the ground wave can no longer be received and the sky wave returns is the **skip zone**.

    d. Since solar radiation varies the height and density of the ionosphere, great changes in skip distances occur at dawn and dusk when fading of signals is more prevalent.

5. Very high frequency (VHF) and ultra high frequency (UHF) radio waves.

    a. At frequencies above 30 MHz, there is practically no ground wave and ordinarily no reflection of the sky wave by the ionosphere.

    b. Use of VHF/UHF signals is possible only if the transmitting and/or receiving antennas are raised sufficiently above the surface of the Earth to allow the use of a direct wave.

        1) This is known as **line-of-sight transmission**.

    c. Since most of your airplane's radio navigation and all the communication radios operate in the VHF/UHF band, it is vital that you understand the importance of this limitation.

    d. The use of VHF/UHF radio waves is limited by the position of the receiver in relation to the transmitter, as shown below.

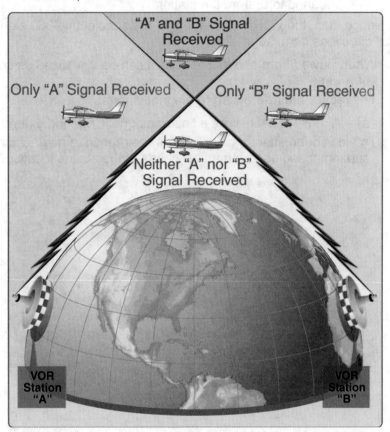

        1) Thus, the range of VHF/UHF transmission increases with altitude.

10.2 VHF OMNIDIRECTIONAL RANGE (VOR)

1.   The VOR is a very high frequency (VHF) radio transmitting ground station.

   a.   The VOR transmits two signals -- an omnidirectional signal and a rotating signal.

   1)   The omnidirectional signal pulsates 30 times per second, and the rotating signal rotates 30 revolutions per second.

   2)   The omnidirectional signal is timed so that it pulsates at the same instant that the rotating signal passes through magnetic north.

   3)   The VOR receiver in your airplane times the interval between reception of the omnidirectional pulse and the rotating signal.

   a)   The receiver converts this time interval into degrees as your magnetic bearing to or from the station.

   b.   In essence then, the VOR can be thought of as projecting 360 signals (or **radials**) out in all directions from the station.

   1)   When viewed from above, the radials can be visualized as spokes from the hub of a wheel.

   2)   The radials are referenced to magnetic north.

   a)   A radial is defined as a line of magnetic bearing extending FROM the VOR.

   3)   To aid in orientation, a compass rose reference to magnetic north is superimposed on aeronautical charts at the station location.

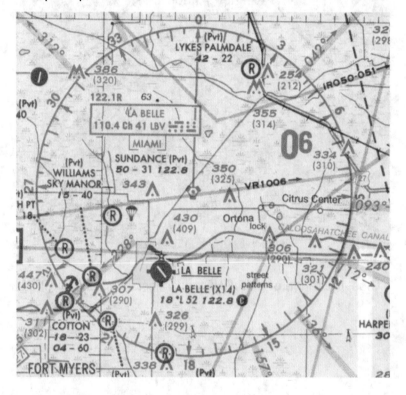

c.   The VOR ground station is a small, low building topped with a flat white disk upon which are located the antennas and a fiberglass antenna shelter. It has the appearance of an inverted ice cream cone about 30 ft. in height.

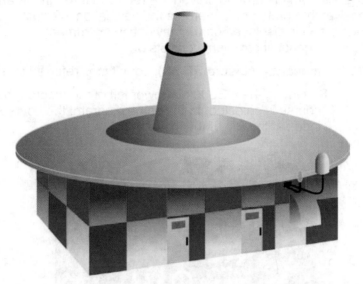

1)   VOR ground stations transmit within a VHF band of 108.00 to 117.95 MHz.

a)   Since VHF signals are subject to line-of-sight restrictions, the reception range varies proportionally to the altitude of the receiving equipment.

d.   For the purpose of this discussion, the term VOR will be used to include the following types of ground stations:

1)   **VOR** provides azimuth (i.e., magnetic course) information.

2)   **VORTAC** (VOR/tactical air navigation) provides azimuth in addition to range information from the tactical air navigation (TACAN) component.

a)   If your airplane is equipped with distance-measuring equipment (DME), your distance from the station in nautical miles (NM) will be displayed on the instrument.

b)   TACAN is used by some military aircraft.

3)   **VOR/DME** provides azimuth and range information similar to the VORTAC, but does not have the TACAN component.

e.   VOR locations are indicated on aeronautical charts.

1)   A compass rose surrounding each VOR indicates magnetic bearings or courses.

2)   Some radials that lead from one VOR to another are marked in blue on sectional charts and in black on IFR low-altitude en route charts. These are called Victor airways.

3)   A radio communication box indicating the VOR name, frequency, and other information is located near each VOR depicted on aeronautical charts.

2.   The VOR equipment in your airplane includes an antenna, a receiver with a tuning device, and a VOR navigation instrument.

   a.   VOR signals from the ground station are received through the antenna.

   b.   The receiver interprets and separates the navigation information.

   c.   The information is displayed on the navigation instrument.

   d.   The VOR navigation instrument consists of

      1)   An **omnibearing selector (OBS)**, sometimes referred to as the course selector

         a)   By turning the OBS knob (lower left of the diagram below), the desired course is selected. In the same diagram, the course is shown under the index at the top of the instrument, i.e., 360°.

      2)   A **course deviation indicator (CDI)**, referred to as the needle

         a)   The CDI needle is hinged to move laterally across the face of the instrument.

         b)   It indicates the position of the selected course relative to your airplane.

         c)   The CDI needle centers when your airplane is on the selected radial, as shown in the diagram above.

      3)   A **TO/FROM indicator**, also called a sense indicator or ambiguity indicator

         a)   The TO/FROM indicator shows whether the selected course will take your airplane TO or FROM the station.

            i)   It does not indicate the airplane's heading.

            ii)   In the diagram above, the selected course of 360° will take the airplane TO the station.

3.   The **horizontal situation indicator (HSI)** is a more advanced VOR navigation device, but one that offers increased situation awareness to the pilot.

   a.   The HSI is a direction indicator that uses the output from a flux valve to drive the compass card.

      1)   It combines the magnetic compass with navigation signals and a glideslope, and it gives the pilot an indication of the location of the aircraft with relationship to the chosen course or radial.

2) In the figure below, the aircraft magnetic heading displayed on the compass card under the lubber line is 184°.

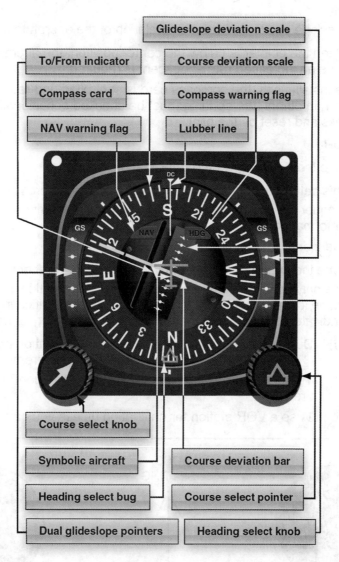

3) The course select pointer shown is set to 295°; the tail of the pointer indicates the reciprocal, 115°. The course deviation bar operates with a VOR/Localizer (VOR/LOC) or GPS navigation receiver to indicate left or right deviations from the course selected with the course select pointer; operating in the same manner, the angular movement of a conventional VOR/LOC needle indicates deviation from course.

b. The desired course is selected by rotating the course select pointer, in relation to the compass card, by means of the course select knob.

1) The HSI has a fixed aircraft symbol and the course deviation bar displays the aircraft's position relative to the selected course.

c. The TO/FROM indicator is a triangular pointer.

1) When the indicator points to the head of the course select pointer, the arrow shows the course selected. If properly intercepted and flown, the course will take the aircraft to the chosen facility.

2) When the indicator points to the tail of the course, the arrow shows that the course selected, if properly intercepted and flown, will take the aircraft directly away from the chosen facility.

d. When the NAV warning flag appears, it indicates no reliable signal is being received.

e. The appearance of the HDG flag indicates the compass card is not functioning properly.

f. The glideslope pointer indicates the relation of the aircraft to the glideslope.

   1) When the pointer is below the center position, the aircraft is above the glideslope and an increased rate of descent is required.

g. In some installations, the compass card is controlled and realigned automatically; however, in others, the heading must be checked occasionally against the magnetic compass and reset by the pilot.

4. **Using the VOR**

a. Determine the frequency of the VOR station.

   1) This determination is normally made during your cross-country planning.

   2) Frequencies can be found in the Chart Supplement or in the appropriate information box on your aeronautical chart.

b. Tune and identify the station.

   1) Tune the appropriate frequency in on your VOR receiver.

   2) The only positive method of identifying a VOR station is by its three-letter Morse code identification or by the recorded voice identification, which is always indicated by the use of the word "V-O-R" following its name.

   a) During periods of maintenance, the VOR station may transmit the word "T-E-S-T" (– . ... –), or the identifier may be removed.

   b) To monitor the station identifier, select the "ident" feature on the VOR receiver.

   3) Do not use a VOR station for navigation unless you can positively identify it.

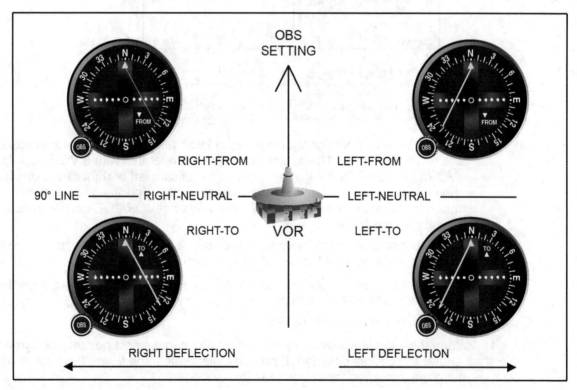

c. Interpret VOR indications (see the diagram on the previous page).

1) When you select a course in the OBS, imagine that you have drawn a line through the VOR station in the direction of the course.

a) The line should extend outward from the VOR in both the direction of the selected course and the direction of its reciprocal.

b) Imagine an arrowhead at the end of the line in the direction of the desired course, as in the diagram.

c) Now look at the diagram and imagine the VOR in the center.

i) Rotate the diagram until the arrowhead points in the direction of your OBS setting.

ii) Note that, when you are facing in the direction of the OBS setting, the CDI needle points to the right if you are left of the course and points to the left if you are right of the course.

iii) If you are directly on the course line, the CDI needle will be centered.

2) Imagine also a line drawn through the VOR perpendicular to the selected course, as shown on the previous page.

a) Again, rotate the diagram until the arrowhead points in the direction of the OBS setting, and imagine that you are facing in that same direction.

i) If you are below the 90° line, the TO/FROM indicator will read TO.

ii) If you are above the 90° line, it will read FROM.

iii) If you are anywhere on the 90° line, you will see a neutral (i.e., a blank TO/FROM window, NAV, OFF, or red flag) indication.

- You will also see a neutral indication if the VOR signal is too weak for reliable navigation.

3) The diagram should be used to understand how to interpret VOR indications in flight. Remember that you must rotate the diagram so the omnibearing direction is pointed in the direction in which your OBS is set (i.e., the selected course).

a) When flying, interpret the needle by envisioning your airplane being on a heading indicated by the OBS.

i) You can immediately tell which quadrant you are in -- TO or FROM, left or right.

4) Note that the airplane's heading does not affect the VOR navigation instrument.

    a) The airplane's position (not heading) relative to the VOR determines the CDI and TO/FROM indications.

        i) The following diagram illustrates this point:

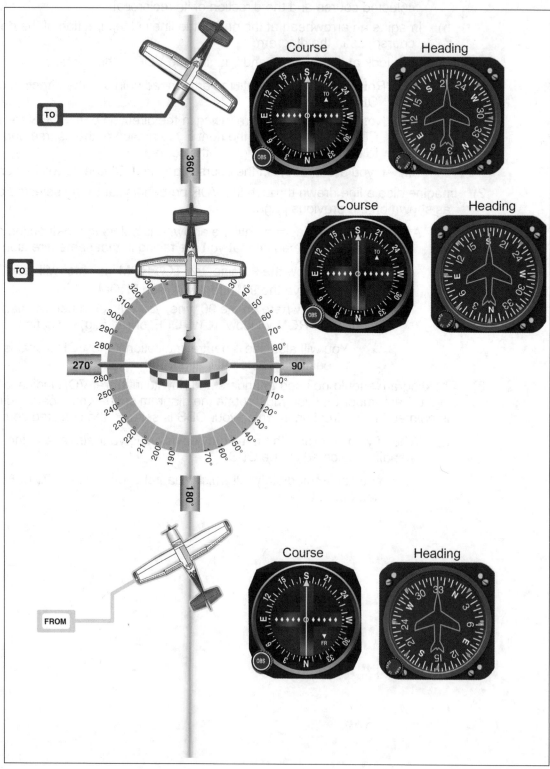

b) Thus, to obtain a useful indication, your airplane must be heading in the same general direction as your OBS setting.

   i) A right CDI deflection will indicate that the desired course is to your right, and a left deflection will indicate that it is to your left.

   ii) A TO indication will show that your present course will move you closer to the station, and a FROM indication means that it will take you farther from the station.

c) Always be sure that your OBS setting agrees with the direction in which you intend to fly.

5. **VOR Navigation**

   a. Using the VOR for navigation will generally require some combination of the following procedures:

      1) Flying directly to a VOR station
      2) Intercepting a desired VOR radial, either inbound or outbound
      3) Tracking a VOR radial
      4) Determining your position using two VOR stations

   b. Flying directly to a VOR station

      1) Tune and identify the station.
      2) Turn the OBS until a TO indication is shown and the CDI needle is centered. Then turn the airplane to the heading indicated by the OBS setting.

         a) If necessary, adjust the OBS once more to center the needle.

      3) Once you are on the desired radial, you must track that course (i.e., keep the CDI needle centered) by using crosswind corrections.

      4) Track the course you are on inbound to the station as outlined in d., beginning on page 483.

   c. Intercepting a desired VOR radial, either inbound or outbound

      1) Tune and identify the station.
      2) Turn to a heading that roughly parallels the course you wish to fly (i.e., if you wish to fly TO the station on the 180° radial, turn the airplane to the reciprocal heading of the radial, 360°, as illustrated on the next page).
      3) Rotate the OBS until the CDI needle centers with a TO indication. Then determine the difference between the radial you are on and the radial you wish to intercept.

         a) If the CDI centers on 340° TO the station, it indicates you are on the 160° radial FROM the station, 20° to the east of the radial you are planning to intercept.

         b) Double the difference (i.e., 40°) and use that figure as your intercept angle. Do not use intercept angles of less than 20° or more than 90°.

      4) Rotate the OBS to the desired course (360° TO the station).
      5) The CDI will indicate the course is to your left. Your intercept angle suggests a 40° turn to the left, or 320°.
      6) Hold this magnetic heading constant until the CDI begins to center, indicating that you are on the desired radial or course.
      7) Turn to the magnetic heading corresponding to the selected course, and track that radial.

         a) With practice, you will learn to lead the turn to prevent overshooting the course as you intercept it.

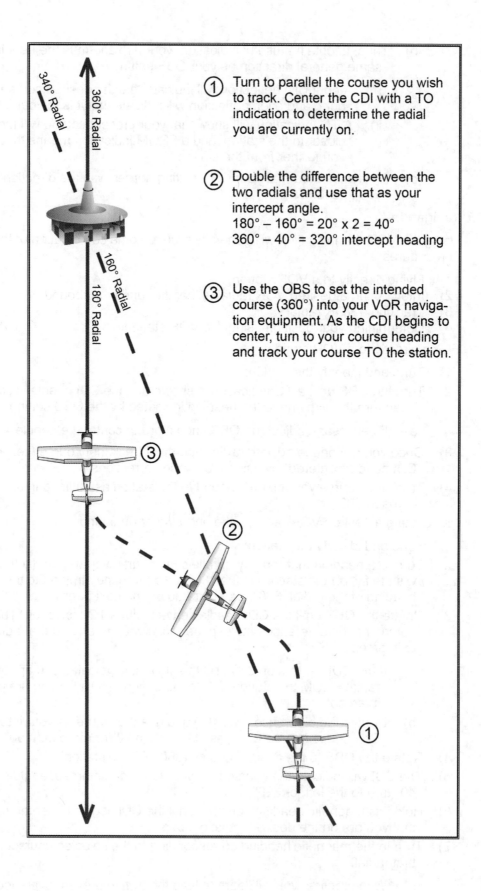

① Turn to parallel the course you wish to track. Center the CDI with a TO indication to determine the radial you are currently on.

② Double the difference between the two radials and use that as your intercept angle.
180° − 160° = 20° x 2 = 40°
360° − 40° = 320° intercept heading

③ Use the OBS to set the intended course (360°) into your VOR navigation equipment. As the CDI begins to center, turn to your course heading and track your course TO the station.

340° Radial

360° Radial

160° Radial

180° Radial

d. Tracking a VOR radial

1) In the diagram below, you are tracking inbound on the 170° radial on a magnetic course of 350° to the station (Point 1).

2) If a heading of 350° is maintained with a wind from the right, as shown in the diagram, the airplane will drift to the left of the intended track (Point 2).

   a) As the airplane drifts off course, the CDI needle will gradually move to the right of center and indicate the direction of the desired radial.

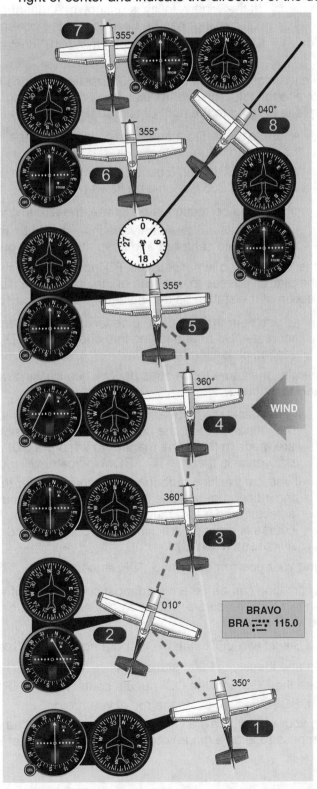

3) To return to the desired radial, the airplane heading must be altered 20° to the right. As the airplane returns to the desired track, the CDI needle will slowly return to center (Point 3).

    a) When the CDI is centered, the airplane will be on the desired radial again, and a left turn must be made toward, but not to, the original heading of 350° in order to establish a wind-drift correction.

        i) The amount of correction depends upon the strength of the wind. If the wind velocity is unknown, a trial-and-error method (i.e., bracketing) can be used to find the correct heading.

        ii) Assume, for this example, that a 10° correction, or a heading of 360°, is maintained.

4) While maintaining a heading of 360°, assume that the CDI needle begins to move to the left. This means that the wind correction of 10° is too great, and the airplane is flying to the right of course (Point 4).

    a) A turn to the left to a heading of 350° should be made to permit the airplane to return to the desired radial.

    b) When the CDI needle centers, a smaller wind-drift correction of 5°, or a heading of 355°, should be flown (Point 5).

        i) If this correction is adequate, the airplane will remain on the radial.

        ii) If not, small heading variations should be made to keep the CDI needle centered and keep the airplane on the radial.

5) As the VOR station is passed, the TO indication will change to FROM (Point 6). If the aircraft passes to one side of the station, the CDI needle will deflect in the direction of the station as the indicator changes to FROM.

    a) As you near the station, the sensitivity of your equipment will appear to increase. Do not be fooled into chasing the CDI with large corrections as station passage nears.

6) Generally, the same techniques apply when tracking outbound as those used for tracking inbound.

    a) If the intent is to fly over the station and track outbound on the reciprocal of the inbound radial, the course selector need not be changed. Corrections are made in the same manner to keep the CDI needle centered. The only difference is that the TO/FROM indicator will indicate FROM (Point 7).

    b) If you are tracking outbound on a course other than the reciprocal of the inbound radial, this new course or radial must be set in the course selector, and a turn must be made to intercept this course. After this course is reached, tracking procedures are the same as previously discussed (Point 8).

e. Determining your position using two VOR stations

1) Your position can be determined most conveniently if your airplane is equipped with two VOR receivers, but your position can also be determined using only one VOR receiver.

    a) Select two VOR stations that are not in line with each other.

2) Tune and identify the first station.

3) Rotate the OBS until the CDI needle centers with a FROM indication.

4) The OBS setting indicates the radial you are on.

5) With your plotter, draw a line on your aeronautical chart from the VOR (using the compass rose as a guide) out along the radial you are on.

         6)   If you have only one VOR receiver, repeat these steps using the second VOR station.

             a)   If you have two VOR receivers, use one VOR receiver for each VOR station.

         7)   The intersection of these radials on your chart is your approximate location.

             a)   By using your map and ground references, you should be able to establish your location precisely.

         8)   The radials should be as close as possible to 90° to each other for the most accurate location.

6.   The accuracy of course alignment when using the VOR is excellent, generally within 1°. However, components of the VOR receiver in your airplane will deteriorate over time and will adversely affect the receiver's accuracy. The best assurance of maintaining an accurate VOR receiver is to have periodic checks and calibrations performed.

    a.   The FAA has provided pilots with the following means of checking VOR receiver accuracy:

         1)   FAA VOR test facilities
         2)   Certified airborne checkpoints
         3)   Certified checkpoints on the airport surface

    b.   VOR test facilities (VOTs) are available on a specific frequency at certain airports. The facility permits you to check the accuracy of your VOR receiver while you are on the ground.

         1)   Tune and identify the VOT on your VOR receiver.

             a)   The frequency is found in the Chart Supplement.
             b)   Two means of identification are used:

                 i)   A series of dots
                ii)   A continuous tone

         2)   Turn the OBS until the CDI needle centers.

             a)   The indicated course should be either 0° or 180°, regardless of your position on the airport.
             b)   If 0°, the TO/FROM indicator should indicate FROM.
             c)   If 180°, the TO/FROM indicator should indicate TO.

         3)   Accuracy of the VOR receiver should be ±4°.

    c.   Certified airborne and ground checkpoints consist of certified radials that should be received (i.e., CDI needle centered with a FROM indication) over specific points or landmarks while airborne in the immediate vicinity of the airport or at a specific point on the airport surface.

         1)   Accuracy of the VOR receiver should be

             a)   ±6° for airborne checks
             b)   ±4° for ground checks

    d.   If your airplane is equipped with two separate VOR receivers, you may check one system against the other.

         1)   Tune, identify, and center the CDI needle of each VOR receiver to the same VOR station. Ensure that each has the same TO/FROM indication.
         2)   The maximum variation between the two indicated bearings should be 4°.

e. Locations of VOTs and airborne and ground checkpoints are published in the Chart Supplement.

f. It is possible for the VOR receiver to display acceptable accuracy close to the VOR or VOT and display out-of-tolerance readings when located at greater distances where the signal weakens.

1) A certified repair facility should recalibrate the VOR receiver on a yearly basis.

g. While VOR receiver accuracy checks are not required for VFR flight, it is a good practice to follow the IFR guidelines.

7. **Tips on Using the VOR**

a. Positively identify the station by its code or voice identification.

b. Keep in mind that VOR signals are line-of-sight. A weak signal or no signal at all will be received if the airplane is too low or too far from the station.

c. When navigating TO a station, determine the inbound radial and use it. If the airplane drifts, do not reset the OBS, but correct for drift and fly a heading that will compensate for wind drift.

d. If minor needle fluctuations occur, avoid changing headings immediately. Wait momentarily to see if the needle recenters. If it does not, then correct.

e. When flying TO a station, always fly the selected course with a TO indication. When flying FROM a station, always fly the selected course with a FROM indication.

1) If this is not done, the action of the CDI needle will be reversed (i.e., reverse sensing).

a) If the airplane is flown toward a station with a FROM indication or away from a station with a TO indication, the CDI needle will indicate corrections in the opposite direction to that which it should.

b) EXAMPLE: If the airplane drifts to the right of a radial being flown, the needle will move to the right or point away from the radial. If the airplane drifts to the left of the radial being flown, the needle will move left or in the opposite direction of the radial.

f. When flying from one VOR to another, fly FROM the first VOR until about the halfway point. Then tune in the next VOR and fly TO it.

1) Changing to the next VOR may require a slight adjustment to your OBS to center the CDI needle.

2) Relying on a VOR for only one-half the distance will help prevent weak signals.

g. Be certain that the heading indicator agrees with an accurate magnetic compass.

10.3 DISTANCE-MEASURING EQUIPMENT (DME)

1. VORTAC and VOR/DME ground stations provide distance information to those airplanes equipped with distance-measuring equipment (DME).

a. DME operates on a UHF band of 962 to 1213 MHz, and, like the VOR signal, it is subject to line-of-sight restrictions.

b. To use DME, select the VORTAC or VOR/DME frequency band as you do with the VOR. The DME will then be tuned to the correct UHF band. This is called a **paired frequency**.

     c.   When using both VOR and DME, you must ensure that each is operating properly by listening for the identifiers.

        1)   The DME identifier is transmitted one time for each three or four times the VOR identifier is transmitted.

        2)   A single coded identification transmitted every 30 sec. indicates that the DME is operative but the VOR is inoperative.

           a)   The absence of the single coded identification every 30 sec. indicates the DME is inoperative.

2.   The DME in the airplane includes a transceiver and a small shark fin-type antenna. The DME display is on the face of the transceiver and may be part of the VOR receiver or a separate unit, as shown below.

     a.   The DME shown above has a mode selector. In the FREQ mode, distance and frequency are displayed, while distance, groundspeed, and time-to-station are displayed in the GS/T mode.

3.   In the operation of DME, your airplane first transmits a signal (interrogation) to the ground station. The ground station (transponder) then transmits a signal back to your airplane.

     a.   The DME in your airplane records the round-trip time of this signal exchange. From this it can compute

        1)   Distance (NM) to the station
        2)   Groundspeed (kt.) relative to the station
        3)   Time (min.) to the station at the current groundspeed

     b.   The mileage readout is the direct distance from the airplane to the DME ground facility. This is commonly referred to as **slant-range** distance.

        1)   The difference between a measured distance on the surface and the DME slant-range distance is known as slant-range error.

           a)   Slant-range error is smallest at low altitude and long range.

           b)   This error is greatest when the airplane is at a high altitude close to or over the ground station, at which time the DME receiver will display altitude in NM above the station.

           c)   Slant-range error is negligible if the airplane is 1 NM or more from the ground facility for each 1,000 ft. of altitude above the elevation of the facility.

     c.   To use the groundspeed and/or time-to-station function of the DME, you must be flying directly to or from the station.

        1)   Flying in any other direction will provide you with false groundspeed and time-to-station information.

10.4 AUTOMATIC DIRECTION FINDER (ADF)

1. Some airplanes are equipped with an ADF radio, which receives radio signals in the low-to-medium frequency bands of 190 kHz to 1750 kHz.

    a. Two types of ground stations may be used with the ADF:

        1) Nondirectional radio beacons (NDB), which operate in the frequency band of 190 to 535 kHz

        2) Commercial broadcast (AM) radio stations, which operate in the frequency band of 540 to 1620 kHz

2. The equipment in the airplane includes two antennas, a receiver with a tuning device, and a navigational display.

    a. The two antennas are the **loop antenna** and the **sense antenna**.

        1) A loop antenna is used as the directional antenna.

            a) The loop antenna determines the direction in which the signal is the strongest, but it cannot determine whether the station is in front of or behind the airplane (known as loop ambiguity).

        2) The sense antenna is nondirectional and allows the ADF to determine the direction the signal originates from.

    b. The receiver allows you to tune the correct frequency and function selectors, as shown below.

    c. The navigational display consists of a dial upon which the azimuth (0° to 360°) is printed and a needle that rotates to point to the station the receiver has tuned in.

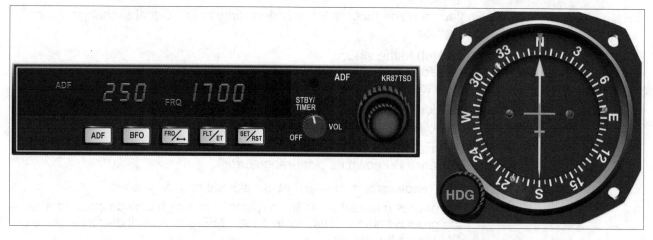

        1) Some ADF dials can be rotated to align the azimuth with the airplane heading (as shown above). This is called a **movable card indicator**.

        2) Other ADF dials are fixed, with the 0° - 180° points on the azimuth aligned with the longitudinal axis of the airplane. On these dials, the 0° position on the azimuth represents the nose of the airplane. This is called a **fixed-card indicator**.

            a) Our discussion will be based on the fixed-card indicator.

3. **Using the ADF**

    a. Tune and identify the station.

    b. ADF orientation (See diagram below.)

        1) **Relative bearing** is the value to which the indicator (needle) points on the azimuth dial. This value is the angle measured clockwise from the nose of the airplane to a line drawn from the airplane to the station.

            a) In other words, it is the number of degrees the airplane would have to turn to the right to be pointed at the station.

        2) **Magnetic bearing to the station** is the angle formed by a line drawn from the airplane to the station and a line drawn from the airplane to magnetic north.

            a) In other words, it is the magnetic heading the airplane would be on if it were pointed at the station.

            b) The magnetic bearing (MB) to the station can be determined by adding the relative bearing (RB) to the magnetic heading (MH) of the airplane, or MB (to) = RB + MH.

                i) EXAMPLE: If the relative bearing is 190° and the magnetic heading is 30°, the magnetic bearing to the station is 220° (190° + 30°). This means that, in still air, a magnetic heading of approximately 220° would be flown to the station.

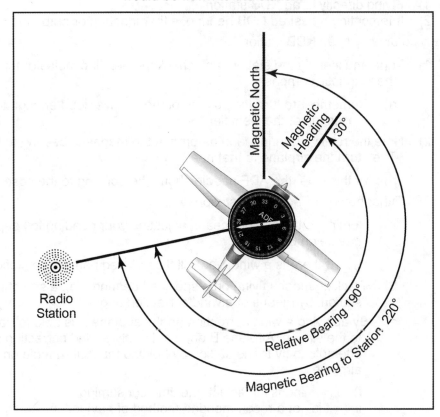

            c) If the total is greater than 360°, subtract 360° from the total to obtain the correct magnetic bearing to the station.

                i) EXAMPLE: If the relative bearing is 270° and magnetic heading is 300°, 360° is subtracted from the total, or 570° − 360° = 210°, which is the magnetic bearing to the station.

3) To determine the magnetic bearing from the station, 180° is added to or subtracted from the magnetic bearing to the station. You would use this reciprocal bearing when plotting your position.

4) You will orient yourself more readily if you think in terms of nose/tail and left/right needle indications, visualizing the ADF dial in terms of the longitudinal axis of the airplane.

    a) When the needle points to 0°, the nose of the airplane points directly to the station.

    b) With the needle on 210°, the station is 30° to the left of the tail.

    c) With the needle on 090°, the station is off the right wingtip.

5) The movable-card ADF can be manually rotated to indicate the airplane's heading at the top of the instrument.

    a) If you rotate the ADF manually, the needle will then indicate the magnetic bearing to the station; thus, you will not be required to use the ADF formula.

4. **ADF Navigation**

  a. Using the ADF for navigation will generally require some combination of the following procedures:

    1) Flying directly to an NDB station
    2) Intercepting a desired NDB bearing, either inbound or outbound

  b. Flying directly to an NDB station

    1) Tune and identify the station, and check the heading indicator for agreement with the magnetic compass.

      a) Remember to turn the volume of the receiver loud enough to monitor reception of the identifier.

    2) Note the relative bearing, and determine the magnetic bearing to the station. Then turn the airplane to that heading.

      a) At this time, the ADF needle should be pointing to the nose, or 0°.

    3) Either home or track to the station.

      a) Homing to the station means adjusting your heading to keep the ADF needle on 0°.

        i) If there is a wind, you will fly a curved path to the station.

      b) Tracking means flying on a specified bearing, i.e., a straight path to the station, by means of a wind correction angle.

      c) By applying a wind correction angle, airplane A is able to track directly to the station. Airplane B does not apply a wind correction angle, and attempts to fly to the station by holding the ADF needle on the nose of the airplane.

        i) Homing is inefficient and time consuming.

        ii) It is not a recommended method of navigation.

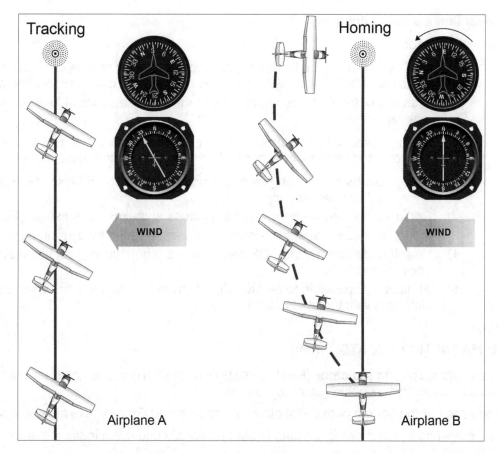

Tracking

Homing

WIND

WIND

Airplane A

Airplane B

c. Intercepting a desired NDB bearing, either inbound or outbound

1) Tune and identify the station.

2) Turn to a heading to parallel your desired bearing in the same direction as the course to be flown.

3) Note whether the station is to the right or left of the nose to track inbound. Determine the number of degrees of needle deflection from the 0° position, and double this amount for the interception angle, but do not use less than 20° or more than 90°.

a) Interception of an outbound bearing is accomplished in the same manner, except to substitute the 180° position for the 0° position on the ADF dial.

4) Turn your airplane toward the desired magnetic heading the number of degrees determined for the interception angle.

5) Maintain the interception heading until the needle is deflected the same number of degrees from the zero position as the angle of interception (minus lead appropriate to the rate of bearing change).

6) Turn to the magnetic heading corresponding to the desired bearing, and track that bearing either to or from the station.

a) Note that there is approximately a one-to-one relationship between heading change and ADF needle movement, unless close to the NDB.

5. **Advantages and Limitations**

    a. Advantages

        1) ADF does not rely on line-of-sight, which may allow reliable navigational signals at lower altitudes than VOR and may also provide greater reception range.

    b. The limitations of the ADF are mainly due to the characteristics of low- or medium-frequency radio waves.

        1) During the period just before and after sunrise or sunset, the radio waves may be reflected by the ionosphere, which causes erratic needle movements.

            a) Stations transmitting on frequencies lower than 350 kHz are least affected by this phenomenon.

        2) Radio waves may be bent when they cross shorelines at small angles.

        3) In mountainous areas, the radio waves can be reflected by mountains.

        4) Near thunderstorms, the ADF needle has a tendency to point toward lightning discharges.

        5) At night, it is possible to receive signals from a distant station which could interfere with the station being used.

10.5 RADIO MAGNETIC INDICATOR (RMI)

1. The **radio magnetic indicator (RMI)** consists of a rotating compass card and one or more navigation indicators, which point to stations.

2. The knobs at the bottom of the RMI allow you to select ADFs or VORs as stations.

3. The magnetic heading of the airplane is always directly under the index at the top of the instrument.

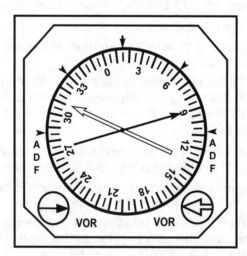

4. The bearing pointer displays magnetic bearings to selected navigation stations.

    a. The tail of the indicator tells you which radial you are on or the magnetic bearing FROM the station.

10.6 AREA NAVIGATION (RNAV)

1. Area navigation (RNAV) allows a pilot to fly a selected course to a predetermined point without the need to overfly ground-based navigation facilities. The most common types of RNAV equipment used by small general aviation aircraft are

   a. VORTAC-based
   b. GPS (Global Positioning System)

2. RNAV allows you to fly directly from your departure airport to your destination airport, or from waypoint to waypoint.

   a. A **waypoint** is a geographical position that is determined by a radial and distance from a VORTAC station or by using latitude/longitude coordinates.
   b. Flying direct saves time and fuel and lowers operating expenses.

10.7 VORTAC-BASED RNAV

1. VORTAC-based RNAV is based on azimuth (i.e., a VOR radial) and distance information (DME) generated by VORTAC ground stations.

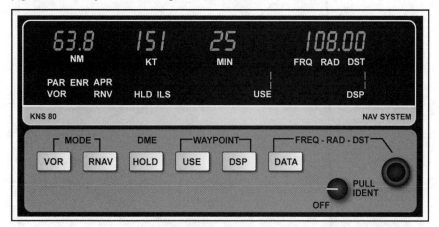

   a. A waypoint is defined by a radial and distance from the VORTAC.
   b. Navigation is to these waypoints rather than the VORTAC stations.

2. VORTAC RNAV is a method of "moving" VORs. That is, when the position of a waypoint is entered into the RNAV, the display unit (which resembles a VOR receiver) allows the pilot to navigate to the waypoint using the RNAV unit as if it were a VOR.

   a. This is known as the **course line computer (CLC)**.

3. For example, as shown in the figure below, the value of side (A) is the measured DME distance to the VORTAC from the airplane.

    a. The following information should be set into the RNAV unit:

        1) The radial (1) and the distance (B) from the VORTAC to the waypoint

    b. The bearing from the VORTAC to the airplane, angle (2), is measured by the VOR receiver.

    c. The CLC in the VORTAC RNAV unit compares angles (1) and (2) and determines angle (3).

    d. With this information, the CLC, by means of trigonometric functions, continuously solves, for side (C), the distance in NM and the magnetic course from the airplane to the waypoint. The result is presented on the cockpit display (i.e., VOR indicator) of the RNAV unit.

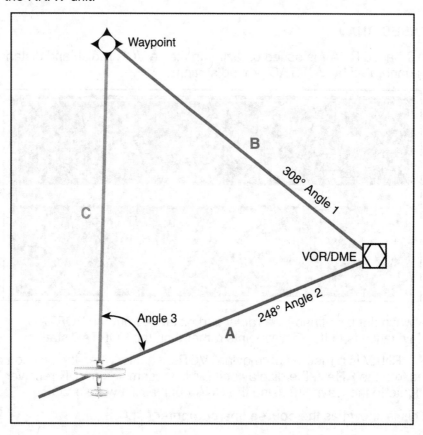

4. The advantages of the VORTAC RNAV system stem from the ability of the airborne computer to locate the waypoint whenever the airplane is within reception range of the VORTAC.

10.8 GLOBAL POSITIONING SYSTEM (GPS)

1. GPS is a satellite-based radio navigational, positioning, and time transfer system operated by the Department of Defense (DOD).

    a. GPS provides highly accurate position and velocity information and precise time on a continuous global basis to an unlimited number of users.

    b. GPS is unaffected by weather and provides a worldwide common grid reference based on latitude and longitude.

2.   A GPS receiver measures distance from a satellite using the travel time of a radio signal.

a.   Each satellite transmits a specific code, called a **coarse/acquisition (CA) code**, which contains information on the satellite's position, the GPS system time, and the health and accuracy of the transmitted data.

1)   Knowing the speed at which the CA code travels (approximately 186,000 miles per second) and the exact broadcast time, the distance traveled by the signal can be computed from the arrival time.

a)   GPS satellites utilize very accurate atomic clocks in order to calculate signal travel time.

i)   The GPS receiver's clock is continuously updated with the GPS system time by the CA codes.

b.   The GPS receiver matches each satellite's CA code with an identical copy of the code contained in the receiver's database.

1)   By shifting its copy of the satellite's code in a matching process and by comparing this shift with its internal clock, the receiver can calculate how long it took the signal to travel from the satellite to the receiver.

a)   The distance derived from this method of computing distance is called a **pseudo-range** (or an apparent range) because it is not a direct measurement of distance but a measurement based on time.

2)   Pseudo-range is subject to several error sources, such as ionospheric and tropospheric delays and mulitpath.

c.   In addition to knowing the distance to a satellite, a GPS receiver needs to know the satellite's exact position in space, which is known as its ephemeris.

1)   Each satellite transmits information about its exact orbital location.
2)   The GPS receiver uses the information to establish the location of the satellite.

d.   Using the calculated pseudo-range and position information supplied by the satellite, the GPS receiver mathematically determines its position by triangulation.

1)   The GPS receiver needs at least four satellites to yield a three-dimensional position (latitude, longitude, and altitude) and time solution.

a)   If the four calculated lines of position do not pass through the same point in space, the receiver will assume the error is caused by its internal clock and will adjust until all lines of position agree.

b)   A GPS receiver can calculate position with only three satellites, but the pilot has to provide the receiver with one of the lines of position in the form of altitude.

2)   The GPS receiver computes navigational values, such as distance and bearing to a waypoint, groundspeed, etc., by using the airplane's known position and referencing that to the receiver's database.

e.   The GPS constellation of satellites is designed so that a minimum of five are always observable by a user anywhere on earth.

f.   The GPS receiver verifies the usability of the signals received from the satellites through **receiver autonomous integrity monitoring (RAIM)** to determine if a satellite is providing corrupted information.

1)   At least one satellite, in addition to those required for navigation, must be in view for the receiver to perform the RAIM function.

a)   Thus, RAIM needs a minimum of five satellites in view, or four satellites and a barometric altimeter setting (baro-aiding), to detect a problem.

i)   To ensure baro-aiding is available, the current altimeter setting must be entered into the receiver as described in the operating manual.

2)   For receivers capable of doing so, RAIM needs six satellites in view (or five satellites with baro-aiding) to isolate the corrupt satellite signal and remove it from the navigation solution.

g.   RAIM messages vary somewhat between receivers; however, generally there are two types:

1)   One type indicates that not enough satellites are available to provide RAIM.

2)   The second type indicates that the RAIM has detected a potential error that exceeds the limit for the current phase of flight.

NOTE: Without RAIM capability, you have no assurance of the accuracy of the GPS position.

h.   GPS receivers can be used for VFR navigation, and some properly certified GPS receivers can be used for IFR navigation.

3.   **GPS NOTAMs/Aeronautical Information**

a.   GPS satellite outages are issued as GPS NOTAMs, both domestically and internationally.

1)   However, the effect of an outage on the intended flight cannot be determined unless the pilot has a RAIM availability prediction program that allows the exclusion of a satellite predicted to be out of service based on the NOTAM information.

b. You may obtain GPS RAIM availability information by specifically requesting GPS aeronautical information from an FSS specialist.

    1) GPS RAIM information can be obtained for a period of 1 hr. before to 1 hr. after your ETA (3 hr.) or during a 24-hr. period at a particular airport.

        a) FSS specialists will provide the information for the 3-hr. period unless you specifically ask otherwise.

    2) GPS RAIM information is necessary for IFR pilots using GPS for instrument approaches and/or instrument departures.

4. **Conventional vs. GPS Navigation Data**

a. There may be slight differences between the heading information portrayed on navigation charts and the GPS navigation display when flying along an airway.

b. All magnetic courses defined by a VOR radial are determined by the application of magnetic variation at the VOR.

    1) However, GPS operations may use an algorithm to apply the magnetic variation at the current position, which may produce small differences in the displayed course.

    2) Both operations should produce the same desired ground track.

5. **Wide Area Augmentation System (WAAS)**

a. WAAS is designed to improve the accuracy, integrity, and availability of GPS signals.

    1) WAAS allows GPS to be used as the aviation navigation system from takeoff through Category I precision approaches.

    2) Unlike traditional ground-based navigation aids, WAAS covers a more extensive service area.

        a) System Operation

            i) Wide area ground reference stations are linked to the WAAS network. Signals from the GPS satellites are monitored by these stations to determine satellite clock and ephemeris corrections.

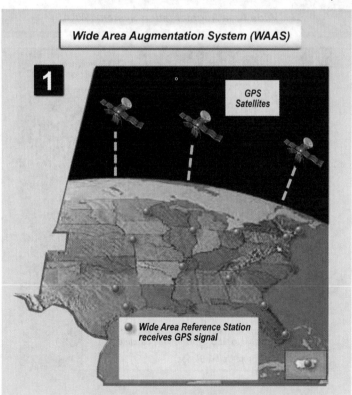

Wide Area Augmentation System (WAAS)

GPS Satellites

Wide Area Reference Station receives GPS signal

ii)   Each station in the network relays the data to a wide area master station where the correction information is computed.

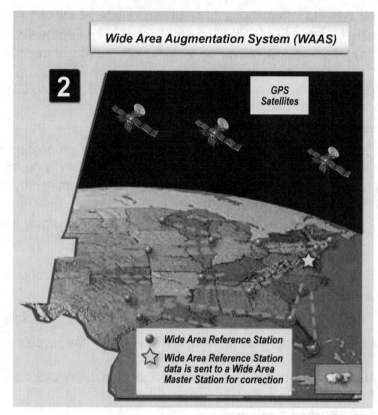

iii)   A correction message is prepared and uplinked to a geostationary satellite (GEO) via a ground uplink station.

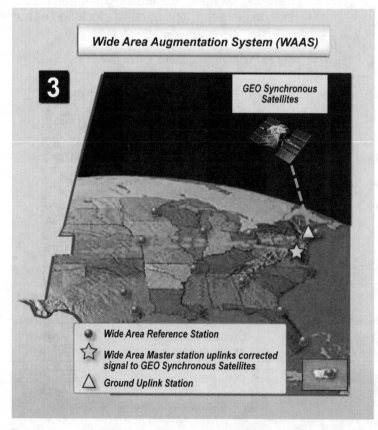

iv) The GEO satellite broadcasts the WAAS-corrected signal on the same frequency as GPS to WAAS receivers within the broadcast coverage area.

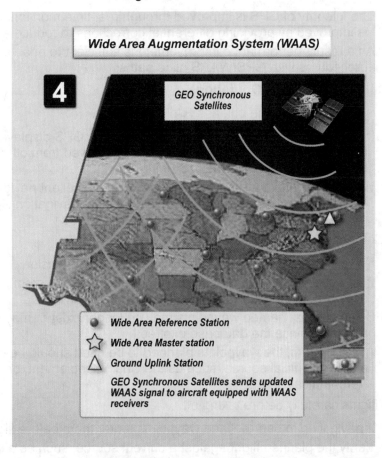

v) WAAS receivers display a vastly more accurate positional representation to the user.

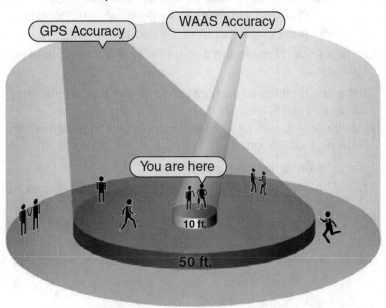

b.   In addition to providing the correction signal, WAAS provides an additional measurement to the aircraft receiver, improving the availability of GPS by providing, in effect, an additional GPS satellite in view.

1)   The integrity of GPS is improved through real-time monitoring, and the accuracy is improved by providing differential corrections to reduce errors.

2)   As a result, performance improvement is sufficient to enable approach procedures with GPS/WAAS glide paths.

6.   **Tips for Using GPS for VFR Operations**

a.   Always check to see if the unit has RAIM capability.

1)   If no RAIM capability exists, be suspicious of a GPS displayed position when any disagreement exists with the position derived from other radio navigation systems, pilotage, or dead reckoning.

2)   While a hand-held GPS receiver can provide excellent navigation capability to VFR pilots, be prepared for intermittent loss of navigation signal, possibly with no RAIM warning to the pilot.

b.   Check the currency of the database, if any.

1)   If expired, update the database using the current revision.

2)   If an update of an expired database is not possible, disregard any moving map display of airspace for critical navigation decisions.

3)   Be aware that named waypoints may no longer exist or may have been relocated since the database expired.

4)   At a minimum, the waypoints planned to be used should be checked against a current official source, such as the Chart Supplement, or a Sectional Aeronautical Chart.

c.   Plan flights carefully before taking off.

1)   If navigating to user-defined waypoints, enter them before flight, not on the fly.

2)   Verify the planned flight against a current source, such as a current sectional chart.

a)   There have been cases in which one pilot used waypoints created by another pilot that were not where the pilot flying was expecting.

b)   This generally resulted in a navigation error.

d.   Minimize head-down time in the aircraft and keep a sharp lookout for traffic, terrain, and obstacles.

1)   Just a few minutes of preparation and planning on the ground make a great difference in the air.

2)   Another way to minimize head-down time is to become very familiar with the receiver's operation.

a)   Most receivers are not intuitive.

b)   The pilot must take the time to learn the various keystrokes, knob functions, and displays that are used in the operation of the receiver.

c)   Some manufacturers provide computer-based tutorials or simulations of their receivers.

d)   Take the time to learn about the particular unit before using it in flight.

END OF STUDY UNIT

STUDY UNIT ELEVEN
CROSS-COUNTRY FLIGHT PLANNING

(22 pages of outline)

Cross-country flight means flying the airplane from one airport to another, often over considerable distances. Most pilots take pride in their ability to navigate with precision. To execute a flight that follows a predetermined plan directly to the destination and arrive safely with no loss of time because of poor navigation is a source of real satisfaction. Lack of navigational skill could lead to unpleasant and sometimes dangerous situations in which adverse weather, approaching darkness, or fuel shortage may force a pilot to attempt a landing under hazardous conditions.

Air navigation is not limited, however, to the actual guiding of an airplane from one place to another. Navigation begins and ends on the ground. The major planning concerns of cross-country flight are preflight preparation, including the procurement and analysis of weather information, and the creation of a navigation log.

11.1 PREFLIGHT PREPARATION

1. Normally, you will have at least 1 day to plan a cross-country flight. Once you know where you are going, you can start your initial planning.

   a. You should follow the weather so that you have a general understanding of the location and movement of pressure systems and fronts.

      1) Weather information is normally gathered by watching various weather programs on television, checking weather resources on the Internet, or contacting a Flight Service Station (FSS).

      2) This background knowledge will help you understand the weather briefing you will receive on the day of your flight.

   b. Obtain the appropriate charts and other navigation publications (e.g., Chart Supplement) that you will need for your cross-country flight.

      1) You can obtain all required NOTAMs from https://notams.aim.faa.gov/ notamSearch/nsapp.html#/ or by specifically requesting any "published NOTAMs" from an FSS specialist during your weather briefing.

      2) Be sure that you use only current charts and publications. Revisions to aeronautical information occur constantly.

         a) These revisions may include changes in radio frequencies, new obstructions, temporary or permanent closing of runways and airports, and other temporary or permanent hazards to flight.

c.   Draw a course line on your sectional chart from the center of your departure airport to the center of your destination airport.

1)   If your route is direct, it will consist of a single straight line between the airports.

2)   If your route is not direct, it will consist of two or more straight line segments.

a)   EXAMPLE: A VOR station that is off the direct route but will make navigating easier may be chosen.

b)   EXAMPLE: An active restricted or prohibited area along your proposed route may force you to navigate around it, preventing a straight-line flight.

3)   Make sure the course line is dark enough to read easily but light enough not to obscure any chart information.

4)   If a fuel stop is required, show the airport as an intermediate stop or as the first leg of your flight.

d.   Once you have your course line(s) drawn, survey where your flight will be taking you.

1)   Look for available alternate airports en route.

2)   Look at the type of terrain and obstructions, e.g., mountains, swamps, large bodies of water, that could be a factor if an off-airport landing became necessary.

a)   Mentally prepare for any type of emergency situation and the action to be taken during your flight.

3)   By knowing the highest terrain and obstructions, you will know the minimum safe altitude to meet the requirements of 14 CFR Part 91.

4)   You should check the course and areas on either side of your planned route to determine if any type of airspace along your route should concern you (e.g., restricted, prohibited, etc.) or if any airspace has special operational requirements (e.g., Class B, C, or D airspace).

5)   After you have looked at all of these aspects, you may choose an alternate route that offers fewer hazards and more safety options than your initial choice.

e.   Establish visual checkpoints for your flight.

1)   There is no set rule for selecting a landmark as a checkpoint. Every locality has its own peculiarities.

2)   As a general rule, do not place complete reliance on any single landmark.

3)   You should have a checkpoint within 5 NM of your departure airport that you can fly over to establish you on your desired course.

a)   If you depart from an airport where ATC provides radar vectors for traffic reasons, be sure to keep track of your position since ATC may inform you to "resume own navigation" at a point that is not on your course line.

4)   Subsequent checkpoints should be easy to see and identify and should be spaced roughly 10 NM apart along your proposed route of flight.

f.   Use your plotter to determine the true course (TC), the total distance of your flight, and the distance between each checkpoint.

1)   Place the small hole in the center of the protractor section over a meridian (line of longitude), and then align either the bottom or upper edge of the plotter with your course line, as shown on the next page.

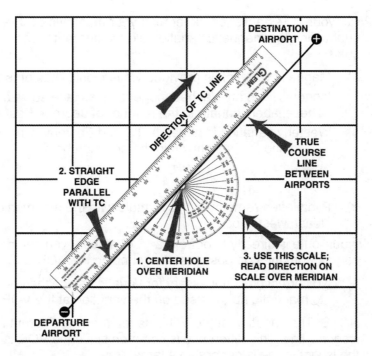

a)   In the illustration above, the TC, which is read on the scale over the meridian, is 043°. Ensure that you use the proper scale for your direction of flight.

b)   Meridians are not parallel lines. They converge at the poles. Therefore, course measurements should be made near the midpoint of each segment.

2)   If your course is nearly north or south and does not cross a meridian, place the hole of your plotter over a parallel (line of latitude), and use the inner scale as shown below.

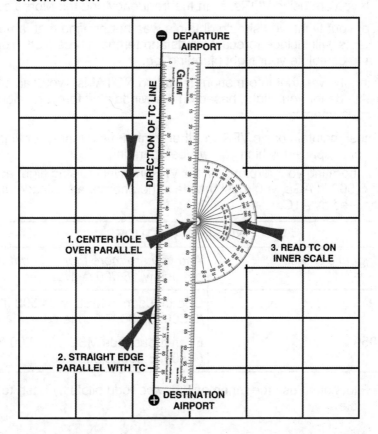

3) With your TC established, determine your magnetic course (MC) by adding or subtracting the magnetic variation along your route, shown on the sectional chart.

　　a) Magnetic variation is provided via isogonic lines on sectional charts.

　　b) Isogonic lines are dashed magenta lines labeled with a number and letter. These labels equate to the number of degrees East or West to correct for.

　　c) Westerly variation is added to TC and Easterly variation is subtracted from TC to find MC, as shown in the equation below.

$$\text{MC} \ = \ \text{TC} \ {}^{+W}_{-E} \text{ Var.}$$

　　d) Pilots often remember this formula with the mnemonic device, "east is least, west is best."

4) If your route is directly to or from a VOR station, you can determine the magnetic course from the compass rose surrounding the VOR.

　　a) No correction is necessary for variation since the compass rose is oriented to magnetic north based on the variation at the VOR station.

　　NOTE: The variation at the VOR station may be different from the nearest isogonic line. This difference is common since the VOR is site specific while the isogonic line is general to a large area.

g. Next, measure the total distance of the course, as well as the distance between checkpoints.

1) Use the nautical mile scale at the bottom of the plotter.

h. Complete as much as you can of your navigation log. Sample navigation logs are presented on pages 521 and 522. (Feel free to photocopy them to use on your cross-country flights.)

1) Fill in the checkpoints you have selected.
2) If you are using VORs, fill in the frequency and the Morse code identifier.

2. On the day of your flight, you should obtain a weather briefing that, among many other important items, will include forecast winds and temperatures aloft. You will use this information to complete your flight planning log.

3. After obtaining the weather information (including NOTAMs), you can select the most favorable altitude for your flight, based on the winds aloft forecast, cloud heights, and the following requirements:

a. You must maintain basic VFR weather minimums during your flight, depending on the class of airspace in which you will be operating.

b. When operating your airplane under VFR in level cruising flight at an altitude of more than 3,000 ft. AGL, you must maintain the appropriate altitude unless otherwise authorized by ATC.

VFR CRUISING ALTITUDES	
If your magnetic course is:	*And you are more than 3,000 ft. AGL but below 18,000 ft. MSL, fly:*
0° to 179°....................	Odd thousands MSL, plus 500 ft. (3,500, 5,500, 7,500, etc.)
180° to 359°..................	Even thousands MSL, plus 500 ft. (4,500, 6,500, 8,500, etc.)

1) Pilots often use the mnemonic device "odd pilots fly east" to help remember this rule.

c.   Ensure that you maintain an altitude appropriate for obstacle and/or terrain clearance as defined in the Federal Aviation Regulations.

1)   Within each quadrangle bounded by lines of longitude and latitude on the sectional chart are large, bold numbers that represent the maximum elevation figure (MEF).

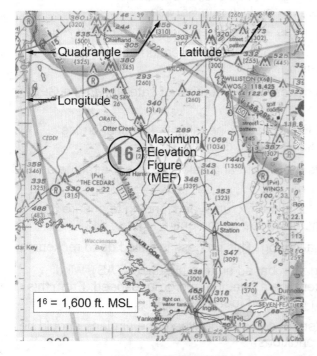

$1^6 = 1,600$ ft. MSL

a)   The MEF on the left is given in thousands and hundreds of feet MSL.

b)   The MEF is based on information available concerning the highest known feature in each quadrangle, including terrain and obstructions (trees, towers, antennas, etc.).

c)   Since the sectional chart is published once every 6 months, you must also check the Aeronautical Chart Bulletin in the Chart Supplement for major changes to the sectional chart (e.g., new obstructions).

2)   14 CFR 91.119 requires the following minimum altitudes except during takeoffs and landings:

a)   If an engine fails, an altitude allowing an emergency landing without undue hazards to persons or property on the ground

b)   Over any congested area of a city, town, or settlement, or over any open air assembly of persons, an altitude 1,000 ft. above the highest obstacle within a horizontal radius of 2,000 ft. of the airplane

c)   Over other than congested areas, an altitude of 500 ft. AGL except

i)   No closer than 500 ft. to any person, vessel, vehicle, or structure when over open water or sparsely populated areas

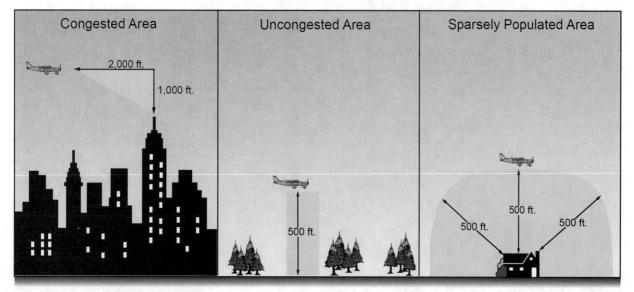

3) You are requested to maintain a minimum altitude of 2,000 ft. AGL over the following:

   a) National parks, monuments, seashores, lakeshores, recreation areas, and scenic riverways administered by the National Park Service

   b) National wildlife refuges, big game refuges, and wildlife ranges administered by the U.S. Fish and Wildlife Service

   c) Wilderness and primitive areas administered by the U.S. Forest Service

d. Ensure that you maintain an altitude that allows for the reception of any radio navigation facilities that you will be using.

   1) EXAMPLE: Flying in a valley may restrict the number of satellites that a GPS receiver can "see" or acquire.

4. Use the performance charts in your AFM/POH to determine takeoff distance, cruise performance (i.e., TAS and fuel consumption), and landing distance.

   a. As with all flights, be sure to calculate the weight and balance of your airplane as it will be when loaded for the flight.

      1) Check the weight and balance for takeoff, cruise, and landing to ensure the airplane's CG will remain in the envelope for the entire flight.

5. You are now ready to complete your navigation log. This process is called dead reckoning.

   a. **Dead reckoning** is a means of navigation based on true airspeed (TAS), wind direction and speed, and MC to determine a heading and groundspeed. From this process, you can determine time en route and fuel consumption.

      1) Thus, dead reckoning is a system of determining where the airplane should be based on certain theoretical conditions.

         a) Literally, the term is derived from deduced reckoning, i.e., ded., or "dead" reckoning.

         b) As such, dead reckoning navigation is always in need of review and revision due to unexpected or changing conditions.

   b. Use your flight computer to determine the wind correction angle (WCA) and estimated groundspeed based on the forecast winds (convert wind direction from true to magnetic) at your cruising altitude, MC, and TAS.

      1) Refer to Study Unit 9 for detailed instructions on how to complete this step.

   c. MC is TC corrected for magnetic variation (+W or –E).

    d.   Magnetic heading (MH) is MC adjusted for WCA (+R or –L).

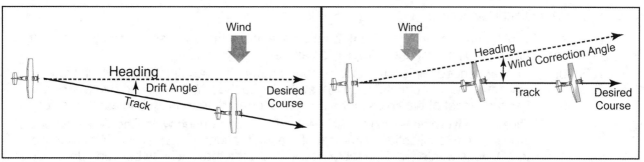

Flight Without Wind Correction   Flight With Wind Correction

    e.   Compass heading (CH) is MH corrected for compass deviation.

        1)   See the compass deviation card in your airplane to determine the deviation value for the cardinal heading closest to your MH.

        2)   If necessary, interpolate between deviation values to determine an accurate deviation correction.

    f.   Estimated time en route (ETE) is computed based on groundspeed and distance.

    g.   Estimated fuel consumption is computed based on fuel flow and ETE.

        1)   **VFR fuel requirements.** Federal Aviation Regulations require that there be sufficient fuel (based on forecast wind and weather conditions) to fly to the intended destination at normal cruise speed AND be able to continue on for

            a)   30 min. in daytime AND
            b)   45 min. at night.

6.   On the day of your flight, you should

    a.   Obtain a complete weather briefing. Based on the information you receive, you may

        1)   Be able to proceed with the flight as planned;

        2)   Need to adjust your route of flight, plan different alternate airports, or plan extra fuel stops; or

        3)   Cancel the flight altogether.

    b.   Complete a navigation log with current winds aloft information.

    c.   Be sure to have your pilot and medical certificates in your possession.

        1)   A student pilot is also required to carry his or her logbook.

    d.   Thoroughly preflight your airplane, and make sure that it is appropriately fueled and that all equipment is operational.

    e.   Complete a weight-and-balance computation.

11.2 FLIGHT PLAN (ICAO)

1.   ICAO Flight Plan

   a.   Flight plans contain specific information relating to the proposed flight of an aircraft, and controllers use them to provide air traffic services.

   b.   For experienced pilots who have used the domestic FAA flight plan (which was discontinued on August 27, 2019), switching to the ICAO format is relatively simple because most of the fields in the domestic form are found in the international form.

   c.   While some wording is slightly different, pilots experienced with filing domestic plans will see close similarities with most of the international fields, allowing them to file ICAO plans with ease. The table below illustrates the similarity between domestic and ICAO fields.

Domestic Fields	ICAO Field Equivalents
Aircraft Identification	Aircraft Identification
Type (of Flight)	Flight Rules
Aircraft Type	Type of Aircraft
Special Equipment*	Equipment (COM/NAV)*
Departure Point	Departure Aerodrome**
Departure Time	Time
True Airspeed	Cruising Speed
Cruising Altitude	Level
Route of Flight	Route**
Destination	Destination Aerodrome**
Est Time Enroute	Total EET
Remarks	Other Information/Remarks
Fuel on Board	Endurance
Number Aboard	Persons on Board
Color of Aircraft	Aircraft Color and Markings
Pilot's Name & Other Information	Pilot in Command

   *This field is optional
   **ICAO IFR Flight Plans require 4 character location identifiers

   d.   For additional guidance, refer to the *Aeronautical Information Manual (AIM)* paragraph 5-1-9.

Approved OMB No. 2120-0026
Exp. 7/31/2020

U S Department of Transportation
Federal Aviation Administration

International Flight Plan

PRIORITY   ADDRESSEE(S)

<=FF

<=

FILING TIME   ORIGINATOR   <=

SPECIFIC IDENTIFICATION OF ADDRESSEE(S) AND / OR ORIGINATOR

3 MESSAGE TYPE   7 AIRCRAFT IDENTIFICATION   8 FLIGHT RULES   TYPE OF FLIGHT

<=(FPL   <=

9 NUMBER   TYPE OF AIRCRAFT   WAKE TURBULENCE CAT.   10 EQUIPMENT

/   /   <=

13 DEPARTURE AERODROME   TIME

<=

15 CRUISING SPEED   LEVEL   ROUTE

<=

TOTAL EET

16 DESTINATION AERODROME   HR   MIN   ALTN AERODROME   2ND ALTN AERODROME

<=

18 OTHER INFORMATION

<=

SUPPLEMENTARY INFORMATION (NOT TO BE TRANSMITTED IN FPL MESSAGES)

19   ENDURANCE   EMERGENCY RADIO
        HR   MIN   UHF   VHF   ELT
— E/   PERSONS ON BOARD   R/   U   V   E
                  P/

SURVIVAL EQUIPMENT   JACKETS
        POLAR DESERT MARITIME JUNGLE   LIGHT FLUORES UHF   VHF
        / P   D   M   J   / L   F   U   V

DINGHIES
NUMBER CAPACITY COVER   COLOR
D /   C   <=

AIRCRAFT COLOR AND MARKINGS
A/

REMARKS
N /   <=

PILOT-IN-COMMAND
C/   )<=

FILED BY   ACCEPTED BY   ADDITIONAL INFORMATION

FAA Form 7233-4 (7/15)

2. The ICAO flight plan form is shown on the previous page. Items preceding Item 7 are completed by ATC and COM services. Items that the pilot is required to complete are listed and described as follows:

    a. **Item 7: Aircraft Identification**

        1) Aircraft identification must not exceed seven alphanumeric characters and must be either

            a) An approved FAA/ICAO company or organizational designator, followed by the flight number, or

            b) An aircraft registration mark without any hyphens or blanks.

    b. **Item 8a/8b: Flight Rules and Type of Flight**

        1) Flight Rules

            a) One of the following may be selected:

                i)   I -- IFR
                ii) V -- VFR

            b) If the flight requires both IFR and VFR flight rules in different phases of the flight, separate flight plans should be filed for each portion of the flight. Composite flight plans must not be filed because an IFR flight plan must be routed to ATC and a VFR flight plan must be routed to a Flight Service Station for search and rescue services.

        2) Type of Flight

            a) G -- General Aviation
            b) S -- Scheduled Air Service
            c) N -- Non-Scheduled Air Transport Operation
            d) M -- Military
            e) D -- DVFR
            f) X -- Other than any of the defined categories above

    c. **Item 9: Number of Aircraft, Type of Aircraft, and Wake Turbulence Category**

        1) Number of Aircraft

            a) This field is required when there is more than one aircraft in flight (up to 99).

        2) Type of Aircraft

            a) Provide the appropriate 2-4 character aircraft type designator listed in FAA Order 7360.1, *Aircraft Type Designators*.

            b) When there is no designator for the aircraft type, use "ZZZZ" and provide a description in Item 18, preceded with "TYP/."

        3) Wake Turbulence Category

            a) H -- HEAVY, maximum certificated takeoff mass of 300,000 lb. or more.

            b) M -- MEDIUM, maximum certificated takeoff mass between 15,500 lb. and 300,000 lb.

            c) L -- LIGHT, maximum certificated takeoff mass of 15,500 lb. or less.

d. **Item 10a/10b: Equipment and Capabilities**

1) Navigation, Communication, and Approach Aid Capabilities

a) A list of codes appears in the table below.

Navigation, Communication, and Approach Aid Capabilities

A	GBAS Landing System	J7	CPDLC FANS 1/A SATCOM (Iridium)
B	LPV (APV with SBAS)	K	MLS
C	LORAN C	L	ILS
D	DME	M1	ATC SATVOICE (INMARSAT)
E1	FMC WPR ACARS	M2	ATC SATVOICE (MTSAT)
E2	D-FIS ACARS	M3	ATC SATVOICE (Iridium)
E3	PDC ACARS	O	VOR
F	ADF	P1	CPDLC RCP 400
G	GNSS – If any portion of the flight is planned to be conducted under IFR, it refers to GNSS receivers that comply with requirements of Annex 10, Volume I	P2	CPDLC RCP 240
		P3	SATVOICE RCP 400
		P4-P9	Reserved for RCP
		R	PBN Approved
H	HF RTF	T	TACAN
I	Inertial Navigation	U	UHF RTF
J1	CPDLC ATN VDL	V	VHF RTF
J2	CPDLC FANS 1/A HFDL	W	RVSM Approved
J3	CPDLC FANS 1/A VDL Mode A	X	MNPS Approved
J4	CPDLC FANS 1/A Mode 2	Y	VHF with 8.33 kHz Channel Spacing Capability
J5	CPDLC FANS 1/A SATCOM (INMARSAT)	Z	Other equipment carried or other capabilities
J6	CPDLC FANS 1/A SATCOM (MTSAT)		

b) For example, filing "O" in Item 10 means the aircraft is VOR capable. However, if your aircraft is equipped with VHF, VOR, and ILS, simply file "S." If you also have an IFR-approved GPS, the letter "G" should be added to the box, along with the letter "R" if the aircraft is able to accept Performance-Based Navigation (PBN) routes and procedures.

i) PBN is the term now used to describe all services and routing that utilize RNAV or RNP technology. Therefore, code "R" is required in your flight plan if you are utilizing RNAV or RNP in any phase of your flight. If you do list "R" in Item 10, that only informs ATC that your onboard equipment is PBN-approved, but it does not describe its capabilities. You must then fill in the type of PBN equipment available onboard the aircraft in Item 18, Other Information.

2)   Surveillance Capabilities

a)   A list of codes appears in the table below.

Surveillance Capabilities

Insert "N" if no surveillance equipment for the route to be flown is carried, or the equipment is unserviceable, or

Insert one or more of the following descriptors, to a maximum of 20 characters, to describe the serviceable surveillance equipment and/or capabilities on board:

SSR Modes A and C

A	Transponder	Mode A (4 digits – 4096 codes)
C	Transponder	Mode A (4 digits – 4096 codes)

SSR Mode S

E	Transponder	Mode S, including aircraft identification, pressure-altitude, and extended squitter (ADS-B) capability
H	Transponder capability	Mode S, including aircraft identification, pressure-altitude, and enhanced surveillance
I	Transponder	Mode S, including aircraft identification, but no pressure-altitude capability
L	Transponder	Mode S, including aircraft identification, pressure-altitude, extended squitter (ADS-B), and enhanced surveillance capability
P	Transponder	Mode S, including pressure-altitude, but no aircraft identification capability
S	Transponder	Mode S, including both pressure-altitude and aircraft identification capability
X	Transponder	Mode S, with neither aircraft identification nor pressure-altitude

NOTE: Enhanced surveillance capability is the ability of the aircraft to downlink aircraft-derived data via Mode S transponder.

ADS-B

B1 ADS-B with dedicated 1 090 MHz ADS-B "out" capability
B2 ADS-B with dedicated 1 090 MHz ADS-B "out" and "in" capability
U1 ADS-B with "out" capability using UAT
U2 ADS-B with "out" and "in" capability using UAT
V1 ADS-B with "out" capability using VDL Mode 4
V2 ADS-B with "out" and "in" capability using VDL Mode 4

ADS-C

D1 ADS-C with FANS 1/A capabilities
G1 ADS-C with ATN capabilities

Alphanumeric characters not included above are reserved.

NOTE:

1. The RSP specification(s) if applicable, will be listed in Item 18 following the indicator SUR/, using the characters 'RSP' followed by the specifications value. Currently RSP180 and RSP400 are in use.

2. Additional surveillance equipment or capabilities will be listed in Item 18 following the indicator SUR/, as required by the appropriate authority.

b)   If your aircraft is Mode A or C capable, fill Item 10b with "A" or "C," respectively. If your aircraft is Mode S capable, there are seven options to choose from: E, H, I, L, P, S, or X.

e. **Item 13: Departure Airport**

   1) The airport should be identified using the four-letter location identifier.

   2) FSS- and FAA-contracted flight plan filing services will allow up to 11 characters in the departure field. This will permit entry of non-ICAO identifier airports and other fixes, such as an intersection, fix/radial/distance, and latitude/longitude coordinates. Other electronic filing services may require a different format.

f. **Item 15: Cruising Speed, Cruising Altitude/Flight Level, and Route**

   1) Cruising Speed

      a) Enter "N" followed by the requested cruising speed as true airspeed in knots in 4 digits. If in Mach, use "M" followed by 3 digits.

   2) Cruising Altitude/Flight Level

      a) Enter "F" followed by the requested flight level in 3 digits. If requesting a lower altitude, enter "A" followed by the altitude in 3 digits.

   3) Route

      a) Provide the requested route of flight using a combination of published routes, latitude/longitude, and/or fixes.

g. **Item 16: Destination Airport, Total Estimated Elapsed Time, and Alternate Airport**

   1) Destination Airport

      a) The airport should be identified using the four-letter location identifier.

      b) FSS- and FAA-contracted flight plan filing services will allow up to 11 characters in the departure field. This will permit entry of non-ICAO identifier airports and other fixes, such as an intersection, fix/radial/distance, and latitude/longitude coordinates. Other electronic filing services may require a different format.

   2) Total Estimated Elapsed Time

      a) All flight plans must include the total estimated elapsed time (EET) from departure to destination in hours (H) and minutes (M), in the format HHMM.

   3) Alternate Airport

      a) When necessary, specify an alternate airport in Item 16 using the 4-letter location identifier. When the airport does not have a 4-letter location identifier, include "ZZZZ" in Item 16c and file the non-standard identifier in Item 18, preceded with "ALTN/."

h. **Item 18: Other Information**

   1) Include all other necessary information relevant to your flight in this section in the approved format.

i. **Item 19: Flight-Specific Supplemental Information**

   1) Supplemental information should not be transmitted as part of an IFR flight plan to ATC. The ATC system will reject an FPL message that contains Item 19.

   2) The minimum required entries for Item 19 for a domestic flight are Endurance, Persons on Board, Pilot Name and Contact Information, and Color of Aircraft. Additional entries may be required by foreign air traffic services or at the pilot's discretion.

3. For a more in-depth description of each item, FAA guidance is available in the *AIM* as "Appendix A: FAA Form 7233-4 – International Flight Plan."

4. VFR flight plans are not mandatory, but they are highly recommended as a safety precaution. In the event that you do not reach your destination as planned, the FAA will institute a search for you. This process will begin 30 min. after you were scheduled to reach your destination.

5. Flight plans can be filed in the air by radio, but it is best to file a flight plan prior to departing either by phone or online.

   a. After takeoff, contact the FSS by radio on the appropriate frequency and report your takeoff time so your flight plan can be activated, or opened.

6. When a VFR flight plan is filed, it will be held by the FSS until 1 hour after the proposed departure time and then canceled unless

   a. The actual departure time is received.

   b. A revised proposed departure time is received.

   c. At the time of filing, the FSS is informed that the proposed departure time will be met, but the actual time cannot be given because of inadequate communication.

      1) This procedure must be initiated by the pilot.

7. Your FSS specialist will be glad to assist you and answer any questions. Occasionally, you may have to file a flight plan without an ICAO form in front of you. Ask the specialist to prompt you for the required information.

8. ALWAYS CLOSE YOUR FLIGHT PLAN!

   a. Add "Close your flight plan" to your after-landing checklist.

   b. If you do not close your flight plan, the FAA will have to devote its limited and valuable resources attempting to determine if you did in fact arrive safely.

      1) If the FAA cannot locate you or your airplane, it will contact the appropriate Rescue Coordination Center, which will institute a search and rescue mission, the cost of which may be your responsibility.

   c. It is particularly important to notify an FAA (FSS or ATC) facility when you are late (over 30 min.) or have diverted to an alternate route or destination.

   d. While en route, you can identify yourself and your location to FSSs along your route (especially convenient if you are obtaining weather information), which will assist the FAA personnel if they have to look for you.

   e. If you cannot reach the FSS to close your flight plan, call FSS at 800-992-7433 or any ATC facility, which will relay the message.

   f. VFR flight plans require the pilot to call FSS or ATC to close them. When flying on an IFR flight plan to an airport with a control tower, ATC at the destination airport will automatically close the flight plan; no action by the pilot is required.

11.3 WEIGHT AND BALANCE

1. Weight-and-balance calculations must be reviewed prior to each flight. On local training flights without baggage and with full fuel, weight and balance should not be a problem. On cross-country flights, weight and balance data warrant more attention.

2. Weight-and-balance calculations involve the following factors:

   a. Limitations and data

      1) The maximum weight
      2) The empty weight and center of gravity (CG) location
      3) The useful load
      4) The composition of the useful load, including the total weight of oil and fuel with full tanks

   b. Load distribution

3. Operation in excess of the maximum weight or outside CG limits is prohibited and extremely dangerous.

4. Use the airplane's certified weight and balance information (normally located in the AFM/POH) to calculate the weight and balance.

   a. Make sure you are within maximum weight and CG limits.
   b. Weight-and-balance calculations are covered in Study Unit 5.

11.4 NAVIGATION

1. Three major types of navigation are in use today:

   a. **Pilotage** is the navigation of your airplane using your sectional chart to fly from one visible landmark to another.

      1) Pilotage becomes difficult in areas without prominent landmarks or under conditions of low visibility.
      2) During your flight, you will use pilotage in conjunction with dead reckoning to verify your calculations and keep track of your position.
      3) You will be tested on your pilotage skills in both the commercial and private practical tests.

   b. **Dead reckoning** is the navigation of your airplane by means of computations based on true airspeed, course, heading, wind direction and speed, groundspeed, and elapsed time.

      1) During your flight, you will keep track of your actual compass heading and the time.

         a) Mark down the time over every checkpoint. This will allow you to compare your estimated groundspeed to your actual groundspeed and revise fuel estimates as necessary.
         b) From this, you can determine the actual wind conditions, groundspeed, time en route, and fuel consumption.
         c) Thus, you can deduce your time of arrival at your next checkpoint and the amount of fuel that will be used.

    2)   A thorough understanding of dead reckoning will enable you to lessen the likelihood of becoming disoriented or confused about your location.

        a)   Should you get lost, your dead reckoning skills can help reorient you and get you back on your planned flight path.

        b)   By using information from the portion of the flight already completed, it is possible to use dead reckoning to narrow down the search for identifiable landmarks. Once you have determined your position, you can correct for any navigation errors or unforeseen changes in wind speed or direction.

  c. **Navigation systems**

    1)   Navigation systems are covered in Study Unit 10.

    2)   The most important thing to remember when using navigation systems in flight is to not overly rely on them. Even if your airplane is equipped with GPS navigation capabilities, you should not skip your responsibility to plan for the flight in advance.

        a)   ALWAYS have a backup plan, especially when flying cross-country.

11.5 DIVERSION TO AN ALTERNATE AIRPORT

1.   Among the aeronautical skills that you must develop is the ability to plot courses in flight to alternate destinations when continuation of the flight to the original destination is impracticable.

  a. Reasons include

    1)   Low fuel
    2)   Bad weather
    3)   Pilot or passenger fatigue, illness, etc.
    4)   Airplane system or equipment malfunction
    5)   Any other reason that causes you to decide to divert to an alternate airport

  b. The diversion may be accomplished by means of pilotage, dead reckoning, and/or navigation systems.

2.   Most diversions to alternates are weather related because VFR cross-country flight is so susceptible to weather changes. Learn to recognize adverse weather conditions.

  a. Adverse weather conditions are those that decrease visibility and/or cloud ceiling height.

    1)   Understanding your preflight weather forecasts will enable you to look for signs of adverse weather (e.g., clouds, wind changes, precipitation).

    2)   Contact the nearest FSS for updated weather information.

  b. At the first sign of deteriorating weather, you should divert to an alternate. Attempting to remain VFR while the ceiling and visibility are getting below VFR minimums is a dangerous practice.

  c. In order to remain VFR, you may be forced to lower altitudes and possibly marginal visibility. Under these conditions, visibility relates to time as much as distance.

    1)   At 100 kt., your airplane is traveling at approximately 170 ft./sec.; thus, related to 3 SM of visibility, you can see approximately 90 sec. ahead of your airplane.

        a)   This time decreases as your airspeed increases and/or visibility decreases.

    2)   Flying in marginal visibility conditions decreases your reaction time for collision avoidance, since another airplane will be closer to you before you will see and react.

3. Diversion is easiest when you know your present location and are aware of alternate airports.

    a. You should continually monitor your position on your sectional chart and the proximity of useful alternate airports.

    b. Check the maximum elevation figure (MEF) in each latitude-longitude quadrant of your route to determine the minimum safe altitude.

        1) Remember, MEF is expressed in feet above MSL, which will enable you to make a quick determination by checking your altimeter.

    c. Determine that your alternate airport will meet the needs of the situation.

        1) If the diversion is due to weather, ensure that your alternate is in an area of good weather; otherwise, you may be forced into the same situation again.

        2) Ensure that the alternate airport has a runway long enough for your arrival and future departure.

        3) If the diversion was due to low fuel, ensure that the alternate has fuel available. The availability of fuel can be determined by looking at the airport symbol on the sectional chart (tick marks around the airport symbol) or by looking in the Chart Supplement.

    d. Determine that your intended route does not penetrate adverse weather or special-use airspace.

4. Divert on a TIMELY basis. The longer you wait, the fewer advantages or benefits there are to making the diversion.

    a. If your diversion results from an emergency, it is vital to divert to the new course as soon as possible.

        1) Consider the relative distance to all suitable alternates.

        2) Select the alternative most appropriate to the emergency at hand.

        3) Change your heading to establish the approximate course immediately.

        4) Later, compute wind correction, actual distance, and estimated time and fuel required.

    b. Courses to alternates can be estimated with reasonable accuracy by using a straightedge and the compass roses shown surrounding VOR stations on the sectional chart or by using your plotter.

        1) VOR radials and airway courses printed on the chart are already oriented to magnetic direction. These can be used to approximate a new magnetic course during VFR diversions.

        2) If a VOR is not available for planning purposes, use your plotter as you would for planning a cross-country flight to determine a true course. Apply magnetic variation to determine a new magnetic course.

        3) Distances can be determined by

            a) Using the measurement scale on your plotter

            b) Marking the appropriate place on a piece of paper with a finger or pencil and then using

                i) The mileage scale at the bottom of the chart

                ii) A line of longitude, with 1 min. of latitude (marked north and south on a line of longitude) equal to 1 NM

    c. If navigation systems are used to divert to an alternate, you should

        1) Select the appropriate facility.
        2) Tune and identify the appropriate facility.
        3) Determine the course or radial to intercept or follow.
        4) Set heading indicator to agree with the magnetic compass.

    d.   Once established on your new course, use the known (or forecast) wind conditions to determine an estimated groundspeed, ETA, and fuel consumption to your alternate airport.

        1)   Update as you pass over your newly selected checkpoints.

11.6 LOST PROCEDURES

1. Nobody plans to get lost, especially in an airplane, but almost all pilots eventually find themselves disoriented. It is critically important that you learn to recognize disorientation quickly and train yourself to methodically implement corrective action to become reoriented.

2. **Steps to Avoid Becoming Lost**

    a.   Always use a properly prepared navigation log on cross-country flights.

    b.   Plan ahead, know what your next landmark will be, and look for it.

        1)   Anticipate the indication of your radio navigation systems.

        2)   If you know what you expect to see, you will more quickly recognize an error caused by poor reception or improper tuning.

    c.   If your radio navigation systems or your visual observations of landmarks do not confirm your expectations, become attentive to the situation and take action.

3. The greatest hazard to a pilot who fails to arrive at a given checkpoint at a particular time is panic.

    a.   The natural reaction is to fly to where it is assumed the checkpoint is located.

        1)   On arriving at that point and not finding the checkpoint, the pilot usually assumes a second position, and then, panicked, will fly in another direction for some time.

        2)   As a result of this wandering, the pilot may have no idea where the airplane is located.

    b.   Generally, if planning is correct and the pilot uses basic dead reckoning until the ETA, the airplane is going to be within a reasonable distance of the planned checkpoint.

    c.   When you become lost, you should

        1)   Maintain your original heading and watch for landmarks.

        2)   Identify the nearest concentration of prominent landmarks.

            a)   If you see an unmistakable landmark, fly to it, positively identify it on your sectional chart, and proceed from there.

        3)   Use all available radio navigation systems/facilities and/or ask for help from any ATC facility.

        4)   Plan a precautionary landing if weather conditions get worse and/or your airplane is about to run out of fuel.

4. As soon as you begin to wonder where you are, remember the point at which you last were confident of your location and select the best course of action.

    a. Watch your heading. Know what it is and keep it constant.

        1) Do not panic. You are not "lost" yet.

    b. Recompute your expected radio navigation indications and visual landmarks.

        1) Reconfirm your heading (compass and heading indicator should agree).
        2) Confirm correct radio frequencies and settings.
        3) Review your sectional chart, noting last confirmed landmark.

    c. Attempt to reconfirm present position.

    d. Use all available means to determine your present location, including asking for assistance.

    e. The best course of action will depend on factors such as ceiling, visibility, hours of daylight remaining, fuel remaining, etc.

        1) Given the current circumstances, you will have to decide the best course of action.

        2) Understand and respect your own and your airplane's limitations.

5. When unsure of your position, you should continue to fly the original heading and watch for recognizable landmarks while rechecking the calculated position.

    a. A climb to a higher altitude may assist you in locating more landmarks.

    b. By plotting the estimated distance and compass direction flown from your last noted checkpoint as though there was no wind, you can determine a point that will be the center of a circle. Your airplane's position should be found within that circle.

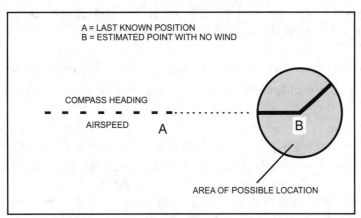

        1) If you are certain the wind is no more than 30 kt. and it has been less than 30 min. since the last known checkpoint was crossed, the radius of the circle should be approximately 15 NM.

        2) Continue straight ahead and check the landmarks within this circle.

            a) The most likely position will be downwind from your desired course.

6. If the above procedure fails to identify your position, you should change course toward the nearest prominent landmark or concentration of prominent landmarks shown on your chart.

    a. If you have a prominent landmark in sight, such as a coastline, interstate highway, or a major river, proceed toward it.

    b. When a landmark is recognized or a probable fix obtained, you should at first use the information both cautiously and profitably.

        1) No abrupt change in course should be made until a second or third landmark is positively identified to corroborate the first.

7. Use all available navigation systems (VOR, ADF, GPS) to locate your position.

    a. Use at least two VOR/NDB facilities to find the radial or bearing from the station that you are located on. Plot these lines on your chart. The point where they intersect is your position.

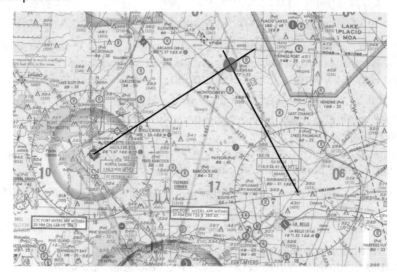

    b. Most GPS units have a function that will display the nearest airport and give its bearing and distance.

8. You can obtain assistance by contacting an ATC or FSS facility or using the emergency frequency of 121.5 MHz if you encounter a distress or urgent condition.

    a. An **urgent condition** is one in which you are concerned about safety and require timely but not immediate assistance. An urgent condition is a potential distress condition.

        1) Begin your transmission by announcing "PAN-PAN" three times.

    b. A **distress condition** is one in which you feel threatened by serious and/or imminent danger and require immediate assistance.

        1) Begin your transmission by announcing "MAYDAY" three times.
        2) If you have a transponder, squawk 7700 (general emergency).

    c. After establishing contact, work with the person to whom you are talking. Remain calm, cooperate, and remain in VFR conditions.

    d. ATC and FSS personnel are ready and willing to help, and there is no penalty for using them. Delay in asking for help has often caused accidents.

9. Plan a precautionary landing if deteriorating weather and/or fuel exhaustion is imminent.

    a. If these conditions and others (e.g., darkness approaching) threaten, it is recommended that you make a precautionary landing while adequate visibility, fuel, and daylight are still available.

    b. It is most desirable to land at an airport, but if one cannot be found, a suitable field may be used.

        1) Prior to an off-airport landing, you should first survey the area for obstructions or other hazards.

11.7 IFR CROSS-COUNTRY PROCEDURES

1.   The initial planning of IFR cross-country flights is similar to VFR flight planning. Some of the differences are

    a.   Your route will be based on airways or direct routes if your airplane is RNAV equipped.

        1)   Remember that you must know where you are at all times, so on direct routes, determine the MH.

    b.   Some pilots use an abbreviated navigation log, as shown on page 522.

    c.   You are required to file an IFR flight plan.

2.   During the conduct of the cross-country flight, you need to keep track of ETEs, groundspeed, and position.

    a.   You never know when there may be a radar outage or when radar contact may be lost, and ATC may request a position report.

Flight Planner

PIC:				Date:					Aircraft:		Pax:		Route:	
CURRENT WEATHER CONDITIONS									WX		Runway Diagram		WX	Runway Diagram
STATION	CEILING	WIND DIR	WIND SPEED	VIS	TEMP	DEW	ALT		GND				GND	
									TWR/ CTAF				TWR/ CTAF	
									APPR				APPR	

FROM	TO	TAS	ALT	TC	WIND Dir/Sp	WCA +R -L	TH	VAR +W -E	MH	DEV	CH	DIS	GS	ETE	ETA	ATA	FUEL	NOTES
TOTALS																		

NOTAMS	Departure Forecast	Arrival Forecast	Notes

WINDS ALOFT:	DEPARTURE TIME:	FUEL DEPARTURE:	*Did you close your flight plan?*
	ARRIVAL TIME:	FUEL ARRIVAL:	

ABBREVIATED NAVIGATION LOG

FLIGHT LOG

DEPARTURE POINT	VOR	RADIAL	DISTANCE	TIME		TAKEOFF	GROUND SPEED
	IDENT.	TO	LEG	POINT-POINT			
	FREQ.	FROM	REMAINING	CUMULATIVE			
CHECK POINT					ETA		
					ATA		
DESTINATION							
		TOTAL					
			DATE				

PREFLIGHT CHECK LIST

EN ROUTE WEATHER/WEATHER ADVISORIES

DESTINATION WEATHER

WINDS ALOFT

ALTERNATE WEATHER

FORECASTS

NOTAMS/AIRSPACE RESTRICTIONS

END OF STUDY UNIT

APPENDIX A
YOUR FLIGHT REVIEW

The purpose of this appendix is to guide you through the steps you must take to remain current once you have received your pilot certificate. As a student pilot, you were probably flying fairly often, practicing precision maneuvers, and receiving regular critiques from your CFI. Now that you are on your own as a certified pilot, you may be flying less often and flying more for pleasure and less to practice precision maneuvers. You must make a conscious effort not only to maintain the basic proficiency you gained during your initial training but also to perform beyond the minimum standards required of you as a student pilot.

14 CFR 61.56 requires every pilot to successfully complete a flight review every 2 years. This flight review must consist of a minimum of 1 hr. of ground training, including a review of the current operating and flight rules of 14 CFR Part 91, and 1 hr. of flight training on any maneuvers and procedures that the CFI giving the review feels are necessary for you to demonstrate that you can safely act as a certified pilot. The flight review may be given by any appropriately rated CFI. In addition, the FAA (and your authors) recommends that you maintain some sort of personal currency program.

PERSONAL CURRENCY PROGRAM

1. You should consider designing a currency program tailored to the specific needs of the type of flying you will be doing.

    a. You might take an hour or so of instruction every few months from a local CFI.

        1) Each periodic lesson might cover a different set of maneuvers, such as stalls, pattern work, hoodwork, etc.

    b. You might be able to integrate practice with normal flights.

        1) For example, you might make a few short- or soft-field takeoffs and landings at the end of a cross-country flight.

2. You may elect to participate in the FAA's Pilot Proficiency Program (commonly referred to as the WINGS program).

    a. The program is web-based, and all pilot progress is tracked online at www.faasafety.gov.

        1) Registration and participation in the program is voluntary and completely free of charge.

        2) Information on use of the program can be found in the FAA's WINGS Pilot Proficiency Program User's Guide at www.faasafety.gov/documents/wings_manual.pdf.

    b. The program consists of three phases: Basic, Advanced, and Master.

        1) Completion of at least the Basic phase satisfies the flight review requirement.

        2) Maintaining the requirements of the Basic phase every 12 months will make it possible for you to forgo ever having to take another flight review with a CFI.

c. Following are the program training requirements:

1) Basic Phase

    a) 2 required knowledge credits
    b) 1 elective knowledge credit
    c) 2 required flight credits
    d) 1 elective flight credit

2) Advanced Phase

    a) 1 required knowledge credit
    b) 2 elective knowledge credits
    c) 1 required flight credit
    d) 2 elective knowledge credits

3) Master Phase

    a) 1 required knowledge credit
    b) 2 elective knowledge credits
    c) 1 required flight credit
    d) 2 elective knowledge credits

4) The requirement to perform certain credits is based on the FAA determination of knowledge and/or skills critical to flight safety.

    a) The subjects required to be covered have been identified by the FAA as major accident causal factors.

    b) Because the WINGS program is web-based, as accident trends change, so will the content of the program.

5) Elective credits may be selected from a list automatically generated for you by the system when you register online. Alternatively, you may request that any aviation safety-related courses you have recently completed be accepted as credit.

d. Ground and flight training conducted by an authorized instructor can be used to meet the requirements of the WINGS program if it meets the training requirements of a WINGS credit element.

1) If your instructor is registered with FAA Safety, simply log in to your account and request credit for training received.

2) If your instructor is not registered with FAA Safety, that instructor should give you a logbook endorsement to indicate what WINGS requirements you have met. A sample endorsement for flight and ground training is included in section 9.4 of the WINGS Pilot Proficiency User's Guide link on the previous page.

    a) Show either of these endorsements to a FAA Safety Representative or Program Manager to have credit added to your WINGS account.

    b) To find your local FAA Safety Representative or Program Manager, search online at www.faasafety.gov/FAASTApp/directory.

e. Gleim offers many online courses that qualify for WINGS credit. Visit www.GleimAviation.com/shop to learn more about these course options.

3. Explore the wide range of publications and other commercially developed materials available for use in personal currency programs.

    a. Sources for these materials include

        1) Pilot examiners
        2) Flight schools
        3) Individual CFIs
        4) Accident prevention program managers
        5) Accident prevention counselors
        6) The Internet
        7) The Aircraft Owners and Pilots Association (AOPA)

    b. For information regarding the sources, contact the accident prevention program manager at the nearest FSDO.

    c. To ensure staying up-to-date in regulatory changes and flying techniques, you should also regularly read aviation periodicals of your choice.

4. Consider adding a new rating onto your pilot certificate.

    a. An instrument rating is an obvious choice for a private pilot.

        1) The training will greatly improve your technical skill in flying.
        2) More importantly, your cross-country navigation skills will be greatly enhanced.
        3) You will become a safer pilot all around.

    b. Earning a new rating (or certificate) satisfies the flight review requirement.

STRUCTURE AND INTENT OF THE FLIGHT REVIEW

1. To act as pilot in command, you must successfully complete a flight review within 2 years after your last flight review or checkride for a rating or certificate.

    a. A flight review can be conducted by any appropriately rated CFI.

2. The basic purpose of the flight review is to provide a periodic check and assessment of your aviation knowledge and flying skills.

    a. Hopefully, the flight review will bring to light any weaknesses that might adversely affect your flying safely.

    b. The flight review should encompass and meet the following factors and goals:

        1) Provide an evaluation of your flying ability and of you as an overall pilot
        2) Provide a learning experience rather than a pressure "test" atmosphere

3. The flight review should be tailored to meet your needs, based on the types of flying you generally do.

    a. The primary purpose is to assess your knowledge and ability to fly safely. Thus, the FAA does not have standard guidelines or a list of maneuvers.

    b. You should be assessed on your broad awareness of regulations, procedures, and good practices.

4.   Consider many factors in selecting a CFI.

  a.   Presumably, you are in regular contact with a CFI for advanced training, checkouts at a local FBO for rentals, or a similar reason.

   1)   The CFI with whom you have regular contact will probably be the one you use for your flight review.

  b.   You may, however, wish to use another CFI for your flight review to

   1)   Benefit from the experience of another CFI
   2)   Avoid waiting for your CFI
   3)   Gain rental privileges at another FBO, etc.

  c.   The CFI (and you) must be rated in the category and class of aircraft you wish to use.

   1)   If you want to take your flight review in a multi-engine airplane, the CFI must hold a multi-engine rating on his or her pilot and flight instructor certificates.
   2)   If you complete a flight review in one category and class of aircraft, you are considered proficient in all categories and classes in which you are rated. You do not have to take a flight review in each one.

  d.   Consider your compatibility with the CFI in terms of personality and experience.

   1)   You and the CFI should take a similar approach to the flight review.
   2)   Taking a flight review with a CFI who has much more experience than you can be a tremendous learning experience.

5.   A flight review is valid for 24 calendar months.

  a.   If you complete a flight review on October 15, 2019, another flight review will be due by October 31, 2021.

  b.   If you do not accomplish your flight review in 24 calendar months, it does not mean your certificate is invalid.

   1)   A pilot certificate is valid until it is suspended, revoked, or surrendered.

  c.   If you do not accomplish the flight review, you are not allowed to act as pilot in command until you have done so.

   1)   Solo flight is not allowed because, even though you are not carrying passengers, you are acting as the pilot in command.

THE PREFLIGHT REVIEW INTERVIEW

1.   Before undertaking the flight review, the CFI you have chosen should interview you to determine the nature of your flying and operating requirements.

  a.   This discussion will provide you both with an opportunity to assess each other and determine what each expects to encounter and gain during the flight review.

  b.   In addition, you and your CFI should review all the necessary paperwork, including all required aircraft documents.

2.   During the interview, your CFI will consider the following elements in formulating a plan for your flight review:

  a.   The type of aircraft you fly

   1)   A flight review in a twin-engine airplane should be different from one conducted in a small, two-seat tailwheel airplane with no radios.
   2)   Your CFI may recommend that you take the flight review in the airplane you usually fly, in the most complex airplane you fly, or perhaps in more than one category/class of airplane.

b.	The type of flying you do

1)	If you usually conduct long-distance flights into large airports, you may need a review on classes of airspace, navigation systems, and high-density airport operations, rather than soft-field landing techniques.

2)	Conversely, if you only fly locally out of a grass field, you should have a review of procedures at airports without operating control towers and short- and soft-field techniques, rather than clearance delivery procedures.

3)	If you are anticipating making a flight that is significantly different from the type of flying you usually do, you might ask for some review on that different type of flying.

c.	The amount and recency of your flight experience

1)	If you have not flown in several years, you may require an extensive review of basic maneuvers and Federal Aviation Regulations, including recent changes in airspace and other requirements.

a)	Your CFI may even recommend that you undertake a complete refresher course.

2)	If you are upgrading to a newer or faster airplane, your CFI might emphasize knowledge of aircraft systems and performance or cross-country procedures appropriate to a faster airplane.

3)	In any case, your CFI will ensure that you review all the areas in which (s)he determines that you should receive training in order to operate safely.

3.	At the end of the interview, you and your CFI should reach an understanding based on the previous considerations regarding how the flight review will be conducted.

a.	Your CFI may provide you with reading materials or recommend publications for study before actually undertaking the flight review.

b.	(S)he should also review with you the criteria for satisfactory completion of your flight review.

c.	A suggested flight review plan and checklist form is presented on page 530.

1)	While the Federal Aviation Regulations do not require that this form be completed, you may want your CFI to complete it so that you have a record of the scope and content of the review.

2)	This form is good for CFIs to keep in their records also.

THE GROUND PORTION OF THE FLIGHT REVIEW

1.	Your CFI should tailor the review of general operating and flight rules to your needs.

a.	The objective is to ensure that you are aware of the applicable regulations and procedures to operate safely in various classes of airspace under an appropriate range of weather conditions.

b.	The review should be broad enough to meet this objective, yet provide you with a more comprehensive review in those areas in which your knowledge is weaker.

2.	Although the Federal Aviation Regulations specify a review of 14 CFR Part 91 only, your CFI may wish to review other topics, such as those listed below and on the next page. (Refer to the appropriate study units in this book.)

a.	Regulations

1)	Pilot certificates and other 14 CFR Part 61 requirements
2)	Airplane documents and records
3)	Air traffic control and airspace

    b.   FAA-approved Airplane Flight Manual (AFM) and/or Pilot's Operating Handbook (POH)

        1)   Airplane performance and limitations
        2)   Weight and balance
        3)   Airplane systems and operating procedures
        4)   Emergency procedures
        5)   Preflight inspection

    c.   Cross-country flying

        1)   Flight planning and obtaining weather information
        2)   Avoidance of hazardous weather (including wake turbulence)
        3)   The interpretation of aeronautical charts

THE FLIGHT PORTION OF THE FLIGHT REVIEW

1.   The maneuvers and procedures covered during the flight review will be those which, in the opinion of your CFI, are necessary for you to perform in order to demonstrate that you can safely exercise the privileges of your pilot certificate.

    a.   The flight review may include a flight to the practice area or to another airport with maneuvers accomplished while en route.

    b.   It could also include simulated instrument flight.

    c.   Regardless of your experience, your CFI may wish to review at least those maneuvers considered critical to safe flight, such as stalls, slow flight, and takeoffs and landings.

2.   Your CFI will construct a review sequence which closely resembles your typical flight, including maneuvers and procedures such as those listed below.

    a.   Airport operations

        1)   Preflight inspection
        2)   Use of checklist and cockpit resource management
        3)   Radio communication
        4)   Collision avoidance
        5)   Ground and traffic pattern operations
        6)   Takeoffs and landings (normal, crosswind, short- and soft-field)
        7)   Go-arounds

    b.   Maneuvers

        1)   Stalls
        2)   Maneuvering during slow flight
        3)   Steep turns

    c.   Emergency procedures

        1)   Simulated forced landings and other emergency operations
        2)   Flight by reference to instruments
        3)   Systems failure

    d.   Cross-country flying

        1)   Navigation systems (if airplane equipped)
        2)   Navigation by pilotage and dead reckoning

3.   The flight review need not be limited to evaluation purposes.

    a.   Your CFI may provide additional instruction in weak areas or, if you wish, defer this instruction to a follow-up flight.

COMPLETING THE FLIGHT REVIEW

1. A flight review should always be concluded with a helpful, positive discussion and suggestions for improvement.

    a. In order for the flight review to be of any real value, you must receive this appraisal with an open mind.

    b. You should receive an objective picture of your current ability to fly safely, as demonstrated during the flight review.

    c. Your CFI should complete the flight review plan and checklist.

2. Your CFI will not endorse your logbook indicating an unsatisfactory flight review, but (s)he may, if you wish, sign your logbook to record instruction given.

    a. (S)he will then recommend additional training or practice in the areas of the flight review that were unsatisfactory.

    b. If 24 months have not yet elapsed since your last flight review, you may continue to fly and practice on your own.

        1) If your 24 months have expired, you must take instruction or be accompanied by a current pilot in order to practice.

    c. If you feel your CFI has unfairly judged you, you do have the option of completing the flight review with another CFI.

        1) However, a different CFI will not be familiar with your strengths and weaknesses and will probably wish to conduct another complete review.

3. When you successfully complete a flight review, your logbook must be endorsed, as shown below, by the CFI who gave the review.

I certify that (First name, MI, Last name), (pilot certificate), (certificate number), has satisfactorily completed a flight review of Sec. 61.56(a) on (date).		
Date *Signature*	*CFI No.*	*Expiration Date*

    a. The logbook endorsement is the only record you have of the flight review.

4. Most flight reviews are logged as dual, i.e., flight training.

FLIGHT REVIEW PLAN AND CHECKLIST

Name _____ Date _____

Grade of Certificate _____ Certificate No. _____

Ratings and Limitations _____

Class of Medical _____ Date of Medical _____

Total Flight Time _____ Time in Type _____

Aircraft to Be Used: Make and Model _____ N# _____

Location of Review _____

I. REVIEW OF 14 CFR PART 61

Ground Training Hours: _____ (minimum 1 hr.)

Remarks: _____

II. REVIEW OF MANEUVERS AND PROCEDURES (List in order of anticipated performance.)

A. _____

B. _____

C. _____

D. _____

E. _____

F. _____

G. _____

H. _____

I. _____

J. _____

Flight Training Hours: _____ (minimum 1 hr.)

Remarks: _____

III. OVERALL COMPLETION OF REVIEW

Remarks: _____

Signature of CFI _____ Date _____

Certificate No. _____ Expiration Date _____

I have received a flight review that consisted of the ground training and flight maneuvers and procedures noted above.

Signature of the Pilot _____ Date _____

APPENDIX B
INSTRUMENT PROFICIENCY CHECK

1. **Recent IFR Experience**

    a. You may not act as pilot in command under IFR or in IMC unless you have performed and logged under simulated or actual instrument conditions within the past 6 calendar months in either an airplane, an airplane flight simulator, or an airplane flight training device,

       1) At least six instrument approaches
       2) Holding procedures
       3) Intercepting and tracking courses through the use of navigation systems

2. **Instrument Proficiency Check**

    a. If you did not meet the recent IFR experience requirement within the past 12 calendar months, you must pass an instrument proficiency check in an airplane, given by an FAA inspector, a designated pilot examiner, an approved (FAA or military) check pilot, or a CFII consisting of at least the tasks required by the Instrument Rating Airman Certification Standards.

       1) The FAA may authorize the use of a flight simulator or flight training device for the instrument proficiency check.

    b. Most pilots will seek a CFII to conduct the instrument proficiency check.

       1) Use the same selection and interview process as explained for the flight review.
       2) A suggested instrument proficiency check plan and checklist form is presented on pages 532 and 533.

          a) This suggested plan and checklist should not be considered all-inclusive and is not intended to limit either you or your CFII from selecting appropriate maneuvers and procedures above those required in the standards.

          b) You should have your CFII complete this instrument proficiency plan and checklist so that you have a record of the scope and content of the instrument proficiency check. This form is also good for CFIIs to keep in their records.

    c. For an instrument review, see the Gleim *Instrument Pilot Flight Maneuvers and Practical Test Prep* book.

3. Logbook endorsement for a satisfactory completion of an instrument proficiency check:

I certify that (First name, MI, Last name), (pilot certificate), (certificate number), has satisfactorily completed the instrument proficiency check of Sec. 61.57(d) in a (list make and model of aircraft) on (date).

Date	Signature	CFI No.	Expiration Date

INSTRUMENT PROFICIENCY CHECK PLAN AND CHECKLIST

Name _____ Pilot Certificate No. _____

Certificate and Ratings _____

Date of Last Check _____

Class of Medical _____   Date of Medical _____

Total Time _____   Time in Type Aircraft _____

Total Instrument Time: _____ Simulated _____ Actual _____ Flight Simulator/Training Device _____

In Last 180 Days: Simulated _____ Actual _____ Flight Simulator/Training Device _____

Approaches/Last 180 Days: Precision _____ Nonprecision _____

Aircraft to Be Used _____ N# _____

Location of Check _____

I. **KNOWLEDGE PORTION OF PROFICIENCY CHECK**

    A.   14 CFR Part 91 Review

        1.   Subpart B (Instrument Flight Rules)

        2.   Subpart C (Equipment, Instrument, and Certificate Requirements)

        3.   Subpart E (Maintenance)

    B.   Instrument en route and approach charts, including DPs and STARs

    C.   Weather analysis and knowledge

    D.   Preflight planning, including performance data, fuel, alternate, NOTAMs, and appropriate FAA publications

    E.   Aircraft systems related to IFR operations*

    F.   Aircraft flight instruments and navigation equipment*

    G.   Airworthiness status of aircraft and avionics for IFR flight

    H.   Other areas:

        _____

        _____

        _____

*Required by the Instrument Rating Airman Certification Standards

INSTRUMENT PROFICIENCY CHECK PLAN AND CHECKLIST (CONTINUED)

II. REQUIRED SKILL PORTION OF PROFICIENCY CHECK** (Include location.)

    A.   Instrument flight deck check _____

    B.   ATC clearances _____

    C.   Compliance with departure, en route, and arrival procedures and clearances _____

    D.   Holding procedures _____

    E.   Straight-and-level flight _____

    F.   Change of airspeed _____

    G.   Constant airspeed climbs and descents _____

    H.   Rate climbs and descents _____

    I.   Recovery from unusual flight attitudes _____

    J.   Intercepting and tracking navigational systems and arcs _____

    K.   Nonprecision instrument approach (type) _____

    L.   Nonprecision approach (type) _____

    M.   ILS instrument approach _____

    N.   Missed approach procedures _____

    O.   Circling approach procedures _____

    P.   Landing from a straight-in or circling approach _____

    Q.   Loss of communications _____

    R.   One engine inoperative during straight-and-level flight and
         turns (multi-engine only) _____

    S.   One engine inoperative -- instrument approach (multi-engine only) _____

    T.   Loss of gyro attitude and/or heading indicators _____

    U.   Checking instruments and equipment _____

III. OVERALL COMPLETION OF PROFICIENCY CHECK

Remarks: _____

_____

_____   _____

Signature of CFII   Date

_____   _____

Certificate No.   Expiration Date

I have received an instrument proficiency check that consisted of the knowledge review and skill demonstration of the procedures noted.

_____   _____

Signature of the Pilot   Date

**Required by the Instrument Rating Airman Certification Standards

APPENDIX C
SPORT PILOT ADDENDUM

The purpose of this appendix is to provide information about Light Sport Aircraft (LSA) and sport pilot certification.

INTRODUCTION AND DEFINITIONS

1. **Introduction**

    a. On July 20, 2004, the FAA unveiled the long-awaited sport pilot rule, which includes a major rewrite of 14 CFR Parts 43 and 61 and introduces the new sport pilot certificate and a new category of aircraft – light-sport aircraft (LSA). In addition, the rule

        1) Allows a person to earn a pilot certificate for sport flying in only 20 hours.
        2) Reduces the cost of flying through a consensus standard that was developed to oversee design and production of light-sport aircraft.
        3) Adds new repairman certificates.

2. **Definitions**

    a. **Consensus standard** means, for the purpose of certificating light-sport aircraft, an industry-developed consensus standard that applies to aircraft design, production, and airworthiness, including

        1) Standards for aircraft design and performance,
        2) Required equipment,
        3) Manufacturer quality assurance systems,
        4) Production acceptance test procedures,
        5) Operating instructions,
        6) Maintenance and inspection procedures,
        7) Identification and recording of major repairs and major alterations, and
        8) Continued airworthiness.

    b. **Light-sport aircraft (LSA).** Basically, an LSA is a small, simple-to-operate, low-performance airplane that, since its original certification, meets the following criteria:

        1) A maximum takeoff weight of 1,320 lb. or less (1,430 lb. for aircraft intended to operate off the water)
        2) A maximum airspeed in level flight with maximum continuous power (V_H) of not more than 120 knots CAS
        3) A maximum stalling speed or minimum steady flight speed of not more than 45 knots CAS at maximum certificated takeoff weight
        4) A seating capacity of no more than two persons
        5) A single reciprocating engine with a fixed or ground-adjustable propeller
        6) Has a non-pressurized cabin
        7) Has fixed landing gear

   c.   **Special light-sport aircraft (SLSA)** are aircraft that comply with industry-developed standards.

   d.   **Experimental light-sport aircraft (ELSA)** are aircraft that do not meet the definition of an ultralight and are assembled from a kit. ELSA do not have to comply with the operating limitations of an SLSA. An ELSA is basically a manufactured kit version of an SLSA and can be built without the restriction of the 51% rule.

   e.   Light-sport aircraft do not include helicopters or powered-lift. LSA can include lighter-than-air aircraft (600 lb. maximum takeoff weight), gliders, most gyroplanes, powered parachutes, and weight-shift-control aircraft.

       1)   **Powered parachute** means a powered aircraft comprised of a flexible or semi-rigid wing connected to a fuselage so that the wing is not in position for flight until the aircraft is in motion.

       2)   **Weight-shift-control aircraft** means a powered aircraft with a framed pivoting wing and fuselage controllable only in pitch and roll by the pilot's ability to change the aircraft's center of gravity with respect to the wing.

CERTIFICATION PROCEDURES FOR PRODUCTS

1.   **Types of Airworthiness Certificates**

   a.   The FAA issues standard airworthiness certificates for aircraft type certificated in the normal, utility, acrobatic, or transport category.

   b.   Special airworthiness certificates are

       1)   **Primary.** These are for simple-design aircraft that are manufactured under a production certificate, but can be assembled as a kit by the owner. For example, a company such as RANS, Inc., may offer a kit version of one of their production aircraft.

       2)   **Restricted.** These are for aircraft that are limited to special purposes such as crop dusting, aerial surveying, cloud seeding, and pipeline patrol.

       3)   **Limited.** These are for surplus military aircraft converted to civilian use.

       4)   **Light-sport.** These are for small, simple-to-operate, low performance airplanes (LSA).

       5)   **Provisional airworthiness.** These certificates are issued for special purpose flight operations and are limited in duration, usually to 12 or 24 months.

       6)   **Special flight permits.** These are usually referred to as ferry permits. They are generally used to fly an unairworthy aircraft to a place where repairs can be made.

       7)   **Experimental.** These certificates are issued for kit planes, built from plans, or amateur-built aircraft that do not have type certificates or for some reason do not conform to their type certificates. They are commonly referred to as homebuilts.

2.   **Special Airworthiness Certificates**

a.   A special airworthiness certificate in the light-sport category is effective as long as the aircraft meets the definition of a light-sport aircraft, the aircraft is kept original except for approved alterations, and the aircraft remains in a safe and flyable condition. The special airworthiness certificate for light-sport aircraft includes five classes:

1)   Airplane
2)   Glider
3)   Lighter-than-air
4)   Powered parachute
5)   Weight-shift

b.   To be eligible for a special airworthiness certificate in the light-sport category,

1)   An applicant (aircraft owner or person purchasing the aircraft) must provide the FAA with

a)   The aircraft's operating instructions,
b)   The aircraft's maintenance and inspection procedures,
c)   The manufacturer's statement of compliance, and
d)   The aircraft's flight training supplement.

2)   The aircraft must not have been previously issued a standard, primary, restricted, limited, or provisional airworthiness certificate or an equivalent airworthiness certificate issued by a foreign civil aviation authority.

3)   The aircraft must be inspected by the FAA and found to be in a condition for safe operation.

c.   Manufacturer's statement of compliance for light-sport aircraft.

1)   A manufacturer's statement of compliance must

a)   Identify the aircraft, year built, and consensus standard used;
b)   State that it meets all requirements of the consensus standard;
c)   State that the aircraft conforms to the manufacturer's design data;
d)   Show that the manufacturer will make available the following documents:

i)   The aircraft's operating instructions
ii)   The aircraft's maintenance and inspection procedures
iii)   The aircraft's flight training supplement

e)   State that the manufacturer will monitor and correct any safety issues;
f)   State that, if the FAA requests, the manufacturer will provide access to its facilities; and
g)   State that the manufacturer has

i)   Ground and flight-tested the aircraft;
ii)   Found the aircraft performance acceptable; and
iii)   Determined that the aircraft is in a condition for safe operation.

2)   For light-sport aircraft manufactured outside the United States to be eligible for a special airworthiness certificate in the light-sport category,

a)   The aircraft must meet the requirements listed in b. above and
b)   The FAA must be provided with evidence that

i)   The aircraft was manufactured in a country with which the United States has a Bilateral Airworthiness Agreement; and
ii)   The aircraft is eligible for an airworthiness certificate, flight authorization, or other similar certification in its country of manufacture.

3. **Experimental Certificates**

   a.   An experimental certificate is issued for operating amateur-built aircraft, exhibition, air-racing, operating primary kit-built aircraft, or operating light-sport aircraft, and the duration of the certificate is unlimited unless the FAA establishes an expiration date.

   b.   A person who builds an aircraft from a kit and wants to be issued an experimental certificate (thus certifying the aircraft as an ELSA) must provide the following:

      1)   Evidence that an aircraft of the same make and model was manufactured and assembled by the aircraft kit manufacturer and issued a special airworthiness certificate in the light-sport category.

      2)   The aircraft's operating instructions.

      3)   The aircraft's maintenance and inspection procedures.

      4)   The manufacturer's statement of compliance for the aircraft kit and assembly instructions that meet the consensus standard.

      5)   The aircraft's flight training supplement.

      6)   For an aircraft kit manufactured outside of the United States, evidence that the aircraft kit was manufactured in a country with which the United States has some type of an Airworthiness Agreement.

   (All of the items in b. are supplied by the kit manufacturer.)

LSA MAINTENANCE, PREVENTIVE MAINTENANCE, REBUILDING, AND ALTERATION

1. **General**

   a.   This section explains who can perform maintenance, preventive maintenance, rebuilding, and alterations on a light-sport aircraft.

      1)   A sport pilot may perform preventive maintenance on an aircraft owned or operated by that pilot if the aircraft has been issued a special airworthiness certificate in the light-sport category (excluding some previously certificated aircraft with a standard category airworthiness certificate that meet the LSA definition, e.g., Piper, Aeronca, Luscombe, Taylorcraft, Ercoupe, etc.).

      2)   A sport pilot who wants to do maintenance, preventive maintenance, and alterations on his or her aircraft can get a light sport aircraft repairman certificate. The repairman (light-sport aircraft) certificate is eligible for two ratings: inspection and maintenance.

         a)   An inspection rating is for the owner of an ELSA who wants to perform his or her own "annual condition" inspection.

            i)   To earn an inspection rating, the owner must attend and pass a 16-hour FAA-approved training course on inspecting the particular class of aircraft they own.

         b)   The maintenance rating allows the holder to perform "maintenance for hire" on the class of SLSA (s)he is trained on and to perform the "annual condition" inspection on both ELSA and SLSA.

            i)   A holder of a maintenance rating can also perform mandatory service bulletins.

            ii)   To earn a maintenance rating, an individual must attend and pass a 120-hour FAA-approved training course for maintenance privileges on airplane class aircraft.

      3)   The annual condition inspection required on a SLSA can be completed by an A&P rated mechanic or an appropriately rated repair station, in addition to being completed by a light-sport repairman with a maintenance rating.

4) The annual condition inspection required on an ELSA can be completed by an A&P rated mechanic or an appropriately rated repair station, in addition to being completed by a light-sport repairman with an inspection rating (only on an aircraft owned by that person).

5) An inspection authorization (IA) is not required for signoff of the annual condition inspections.

b. This section explains who can approve aircraft airframes, aircraft engines, propellers, appliances, or component parts for return to service after maintenance, preventive maintenance, rebuilding, and alteration.

1) A person who holds a repairman certificate (light-sport aircraft) with a maintenance rating may approve an SLSA for return to service.

2) A person who holds at least a sport pilot certificate may approve an aircraft (issued a special airworthiness certificate in the light-sport category) owned or operated by that pilot for return to service after performing **preventive maintenance** allowed under 14 CFR Part 43.

2. **Repairman Certificates**

a. **Inspection rating.** A person who holds an inspection rating on a repairman certificate can conduct an annual inspection on the make, model, and N number of the ELSA on that person's repairman certificate. Basically, this applies only to a person who built his or her own LSA from a kit supplied by a manufacturer.

b. **Maintenance rating.** A person who holds a maintenance rating on a repairman certificate can conduct the annual condition inspections on both the ELSA and SLSA as designated on their repairman certificate by class (weight shift control, powered parachute, airplane, gyroplane).

SPORT PILOT CERTIFICATES

1. **General**

a. A sport pilot certificate is issued without a category or class rating. Any additional category and class privileges are endorsed in the pilot's logbook.

1) A sport pilot must carry his or her logbook or other evidence of required authorized instructor endorsements on all flights.

b. No medical certificate is required. A student sport pilot or the holder of a sport pilot certificate with glider or balloon privileges is not required to hold a medical certificate. In addition, a person who holds a flight instructor certificate with a sport pilot rating in a glider or balloon does not need to hold a medical certificate.

c. Holders of sport pilot certificates can use a current and valid U.S. driver's license in lieu of a medical certificate when exercising the privileges of

1) A sport pilot certificate (in an LSA) and a student pilot certificate while seeking sport pilot privileges in a light-sport aircraft other than a glider or balloon;

2) A flight instructor certificate with a sport pilot rating while acting as pilot in command or serving as a required flight crewmember of a light-sport aircraft other than a glider or balloon.

d. A person using a current and valid U.S. driver's license to meet the requirements of a medical certificate must

1) Comply with each restriction and limitation imposed by that person's U.S. driver's license and any judicial or administrative order applying to the operation of a motor vehicle;

2) Have been found eligible for at least a third-class medical certificate at the time of his or her most recent application (if the person has applied for a medical certificate);

3) Not have had his or her most recently issued medical certificate (if the person has held a medical certificate) suspended or revoked or most recent Authorization for a Special Issuance of a Medical Certificate withdrawn; and

4) Not know or have reason to know of any medical condition that would make that person unable to operate a light-sport aircraft in a safe manner.

2. **Student Pilots**

   a. Age and language requirements for a sport pilot certificate.

      1) To be eligible for a sport pilot certificate, you must

         a) Be at least 17 years old (or 16 years old if you are applying to operate a glider or balloon).

         b) Be able to read, speak, write, and understand English. If you cannot read, speak, write, and understand English because of medical reasons, the FAA may place limits on your certificate as necessary for the safe operation of light-sport aircraft.

   b. To obtain a sport pilot certificate, you must pass the following tests:

      1) **Knowledge test.** You must pass a knowledge test on the applicable aeronautical knowledge areas listed in 14 CFR 61.309.

         a) Before you may take the knowledge test for a sport pilot certificate, you must receive a logbook endorsement from the authorized instructor who trained you or reviewed and evaluated your home-study course on the aeronautical knowledge areas listed in 14 CFR 61.309 certifying you are prepared for the test.

      2) **Practical test.** You must pass a practical test on the applicable areas of operation listed in 14 CFR 61.309 and 14 CFR 61.311.

         a) Before you may take the practical test for a sport pilot certificate, you must receive a logbook endorsement from the authorized instructor who provided you with flight training on the areas of operation specified in 14 CFR 61.309 and 14 CFR 61.311 in preparation for the practical test.

         b) The endorsement certifies that you meet applicable aeronautical knowledge and experience requirements and are prepared for the practical test.

   c. Aeronautical knowledge required to apply for a sport pilot certificate.

      1) Sport pilot applicants must receive and log ground training from an instructor or complete a home-study course on the following aeronautical knowledge areas:

         a) Applicable regulations that relate to sport pilot privileges, limits, and flight operations.

         b) Accident reporting requirements of the National Transportation Safety Board.

         c) Use of the applicable portions of the *AIM* and FAA advisory circulars.

         d) Use of aeronautical charts for VFR navigation using pilotage, dead reckoning, and navigation systems, as appropriate.

         e) Recognition of critical weather situations from the ground and in flight, wind shear avoidance, and the procurement and use of aeronautical weather reports and forecasts.

         f) Safe and efficient operation of aircraft, including collision avoidance, and recognition and avoidance of wake turbulence.

         g) Effects of density altitude on takeoff and climb performance.

         h) Weight and balance computations.

         i) Principles of aerodynamics, powerplants, and aircraft systems.

         j) Stall awareness, spin entry, spins, and spin recovery techniques, as applicable.

         k) Aeronautical decision making and risk management.

2)   Preflight actions that include

    a)   How to get information on runway lengths at airports of intended use, data on takeoff and landing distances, weather reports and forecasts, and fuel requirements; and

    b)   How to plan for alternatives if the planned flight cannot be completed or if you encounter delays.

d.   Flight proficiency requirements for a sport pilot certificate.

1)   To apply for a sport pilot certificate, you must receive and log ground and flight training from an instructor on the following areas of operation, as appropriate, for airplane single-engine land or sea, glider, gyroplane, airship, balloon, powered parachute land or sea, and weight-shift-control aircraft land or sea privileges:

    a)   Preflight preparation

    b)   Preflight procedures

    c)   Airport, seaplane base, and gliderport operations, as applicable

    d)   Takeoffs (or launches), landings, and go-arounds

    e)   Performance maneuvers and, for gliders, performance speeds

    f)   Ground reference maneuvers (not applicable to gliders and balloons)

    g)   Soaring techniques (applicable only to gliders)

    h)   Navigation

    i)   Slow flight (not applicable to lighter-than-air aircraft and powered parachutes)

    j)   Stalls (not applicable to lighter-than-air aircraft, gyroplanes, and powered parachutes)

    k)   Emergency operations

    l)   Post-flight procedures

e.   Aeronautical experience required to apply for a sport pilot certificate.

1)   An applicant for a sport pilot certificate (airplane category) must have the following aeronautical experience:

If you are applying for a sport pilot certificate with . . .	Then you must log at least . . .	Which must include at least . . .
(a) Airplane category and single-engine land or sea class privileges,	(1) 20 hours of flight time, including at least 15 hours of flight training from an authorized instructor in a single-engine airplane and at least 5 hours of solo flight training in the areas of operation listed in Sec. 61.311, and basic instrument maneuvers under simulated instrument conditions as indicated in Sec. 61.93(e)(12),	(i) 2 hours of cross-country flight training, (ii) 10 takeoffs and landings to a full stop (with each landing involving a flight in the traffic pattern) at an airport, (iii) One solo cross-country flight of at least 75 nautical miles total distance, with a full-stop landing at a minimum of two points and one segment of the flight consisting of a straight-line distance of at least 25 nautical miles between the takeoff and landing locations, and (iv) 2 hours of flight training with an authorized instructor on those areas of operation specified in Sec. 61.311 in preparation for the practical test within the preceding 2 calendar months from the month of the test.

f. As a sport pilot student, you may not act as pilot in command

   1) Of an aircraft other than a light-sport aircraft

   2) At night

   3) At an altitude of more than 10,000 feet MSL, or 2,000 feet AGL, whichever is higher

   4) In Class B, C, and D airspace, or from an airport having an operational control tower without having received the required ground and flight training and an endorsement from an authorized instructor

g. Seeking additional privileges.

   1) A student sport pilot who wants to operate in Class B, C, and D airspace, or at an airport having an operational control tower, must receive and log ground and flight training from an authorized instructor in the following aeronautical knowledge areas and areas of operation:

      a) The use of radios, communications, navigation systems and facilities, and radar services.

      b) Operations at airports with an operating control tower, to include three takeoffs and landings to a full stop, with each landing involving a flight in the traffic pattern at an airport with an operating control tower.

      c) Applicable flight rules of Part 91 for operations in Class B, C, and D airspace and air traffic control clearances.

      d) Ground and flight training for the specific Class B, C, or D airspace for which the solo flight is authorized, if applicable, within the 90-day period preceding the date of the flight in that airspace. The flight training must be received in the specific airspace area for which solo flight is authorized.

      e) Ground and flight training for the specific airport located in Class B, C, or D airspace for which the solo flight is authorized, if applicable, within the 90-day period preceding the date of the flight at that airport. The flight and ground training must be received at the specific airport for which solo flight is authorized.

         i) The instructor who provides the training must provide a logbook endorsement that certifies the student has received that training and is proficient to conduct solo flight in that specific airspace or at that specific airport and in the aeronautical knowledge areas required.

h. Cross-country time.

   1) In order to meet the aeronautical experience requirements for a sport pilot certificate (except for powered parachute privileges), cross country flight time

      a) Is defined as a straight line distance of more than 25 nautical miles from the original point of departure; and

      b) Involves, as applicable, the use of dead reckoning; pilotage; electronic navigation aids; radio aids; or other navigation systems to navigate to the landing point.

i. Practical test.

   1) A practical test for a sport pilot certificate may be conducted in a single seat light-sport aircraft provided that the

      a) Examiner agrees to conduct the test;

      b) Examiner is in a position to observe the operation of the aircraft and evaluate the proficiency of the applicant; and

      c) Pilot certificate of an applicant successfully passing the test is issued a pilot certificate with the limitation, "No passenger carriage and flight in a single-seat light-sport aircraft only."

3. **Sport Pilots**

    a.   General Limitations and Endorsement Requirements

        1)   Use the following table to determine what operating limits and endorsement requirements apply to pilots operating light-sport aircraft. The medical certificate specified in this table must be valid.

If you hold . . .	And you hold . . .	Then you may operate . . .	And . . .
(1) A medical certificate,	(i) A sport pilot certificate,	(A) Any light-sport aircraft for which you hold the endorsements required for its category and class,	(1) You must hold any other endorsements required by this subpart, and comply with the limitations in Sec. 61.315.
	(ii) At least a recreational pilot certificate with a category and class rating,	(A) Any light-sport aircraft in that category and class,	(1) You do not have to hold any of the endorsements required by this subpart, nor do you have to comply with the limitations in Sec. 61.315.
	(iii) At least a recreational pilot certificate but not a rating for the category and class of light-sport aircraft you operate,	(A) That light-sport aircraft, only if you hold the endorsements required in Sec. 61.321 for its category and class,	(1) You must comply with the limitations in Sec. 61.315, except Sec. 61.315(c)(14) and, if a private pilot or higher, Sec. 61.315(c)(7).
(2) Only a U.S. driver's license	(i) A sport pilot certificate,	(A) Any light-sport aircraft for which you hold the endorsements required for its category and class,	(1) You must hold any other endorsements required by this subpart, and comply with the limitations in Sec. 61.315.
	(ii) At least a recreational pilot certificate with a category and class rating,	(A) Any light-sport aircraft in that category and class,	(1) You do not have to hold any of the endorsements required by this subpart, but you must comply with the limitations in Sec. 61.315.
	(iii) At least a recreational pilot certificate but not a rating for the category and class of light-sport aircraft you operate,	(A) That light-sport aircraft, only if you hold the endorsements required in Sec. 61.321 for its category and class,	(1) You must comply with the limitations in Sec. 61.315, except Sec. 61.315(c)(14) and, if a private pilot or higher, Sec. 61.315(c)(7).

FLIGHT INSTRUCTOR CERTIFICATES WITH A SPORT PILOT RATING

1. **Logbooks**

    a.   A flight instructor with a sport pilot rating must carry his or her logbook or other evidence of required authorized instructor endorsements on all flights when providing flight training.

2. **Ground Instructors**

    a.   A person who holds a basic ground instructor rating is authorized to provide

        1)   Ground training in the aeronautical knowledge areas required for the issuance of a sport pilot certificate, recreational pilot certificate, private pilot certificate, or associated ratings under Part 61;

        2)   Ground training required for a sport pilot, recreational pilot, and private pilot flight review; and

        3)   A recommendation for a knowledge test required for the issuance of a sport pilot certificate, recreational pilot certificate, or private pilot certificate under Part 61.

3. **Flight Instructor Privileges**

    a.   A flight instructor (including flight instructors not holding just a sport pilot rating) conducting sport pilot instruction are recommended to have 5 hours in the aircraft type before giving instruction in that aircraft toward a sport pilot certificate.

        1)   The 5-hour rule is a recommendation; it is not mandatory.

ABBREVIATIONS AND ACRONYMS

14 CFR	Title 14 of the Code of Federal Regulations
ADF	automatic direction finder
ADIZ	Air Defense Identification Zone
ADM	aeronautical decision making
ADS-B	Automatic Dependent Surveillance-Broadcast
AFM	Airplane Flight Manual
AGL	above ground level
AI	attitude indicator
ALS	approach light system
ALT	altimeter
AME	aviation medical examiner
ASI	airspeed indicator
ATC	air traffic control
ATIS	Automatic Terminal Information Service
ATS	Air Traffic Service
CAS	calibrated airspeed
CDI	course deviation indicator
CFI	certificated flight instructor
CFII	certificated flight instructor -- instrument
CG	center of gravity
CH	compass heading
CHT	cylinder head temperature
CL	center of lift
CP	center of pressure
CRM	crew resource management
CTAF	Common Traffic Advisory Frequency
DA	decision altitude
DH	decision height
DME	distance measuring equipment
DVFR	defense VFR
EFC	expect further clearance
EFD	electronic flight display
EGT	exhaust gas temperature
ELT	emergency locator transmitter
ETA	estimated time of arrival
ETE	estimated time en route
FAA	Federal Aviation Administration
FBO	fixed-base operator
FDC	Flight Data Center
FFS	full flight simulator
FL	flight level
fpm	feet per minute
FSDO	Flight Standards District Office
FSS	Flight Service Station
FSTD	flight simulation training device
GPH	gallons per hour
GPS	global positioning system
GPU	ground power unit
HI	heading indicator
HIRL	high-intensity runway lights
IAS	indicated airspeed
ICAO	International Civil Aviation Organization
IFR	instrument flight rules
ILS	instrument landing system
IMC	instrument meteorological conditions
ISA	International Standard Atmosphere
kt.	knots (nautical miles per hour)
L/D_{MAX}	maximum lift-to-drag ratio
LAA	local airport advisory
LF	low frequency
LIRL	low-intensity runway lights
MC	magnetic course
MCA	minimum crossing altitude
MDA	minimum descent altitude
MEF	maximum elevation figure
MEL	minimum equipment list
MF	medium frequency

MFD	multi-function display
MH	magnetic heading
MIRL	medium-intensity runway lights
MMEL	master minimum equipment list
MOA	military operations area
MOCA	minimum obstruction clearance altitude
MP	manifold pressure
mph	miles (statute) per hour
MSL	mean sea level
MTR	military training route
NAS	national airspace system
NAVAID	navigation aid
NDB	nondirectional radio beacon
NM	nautical mile
NTSB	National Transportation Safety Board
OAT	outside air temperature
OBS	omnibearing selector
PAPI	precision approach path indicator
PAR	precision approach radar
PCL	pilot control of lighting
PFD	primary flight display
PIC	pilot in command
POH	Pilot's Operating Handbook
RAIL	runway alignment indicator lights
RCLS	runway centerline lighting system
RNAV	area navigation
RPM	revolutions per minute
SFRA	Special Flight Rules Area
SM	statute mile
STC	supplemental type certificate
SUA	special-use airspace
SVFR	special visual flight rules (VFR)
T&SI	turn-and-slip indicator
TACAN	tactical air navigation
TAS	true airspeed
TC	true course (navigation)
TC	turn coordinator (flight instrument)
TCAS	traffic alert and collision avoidance system
TDZL	touchdown zone lighting
TH	true heading
TRSA	Terminal Radar Service Area
TSA	Transportation Security Administration
UHF	ultra high frequency
UTC	Coordinated Universal Time
V_A	design maneuvering speed
VASI	visual approach slope indicator
V_{FE}	maximum flap extended speed
VFR	visual flight rules
VHF	very high frequency
VLF	very low frequency
V_{LO}	landing gear operating speed
V_{NE}	never-exceed speed
V_{NO}	maximum structural cruising speed
VNR	VFR flight not recommended
VOR	VHF omnidirectional range
VORTAC	collocated VOR and TACAN
VOT	VOR test facility
V_R	rotation speed
V_{S1}	stalling speed or the minimum steady flight speed obtained in a specific configuration
VSI	vertical speed indicator
V_{SO}	stalling speed or the minimum steady flight speed in the landing configuration
V_X	best angle of climb speed
V_Y	best rate of climb speed
WCA	wind correction angle

AUTHORS' RECOMMENDATIONS

Gleim cooperates with and supports all aspects of the flight training industry, particularly organizations that focus on aviation recruitment and flight training. Below are some of the top organizations for anyone interested in aviation.

EXPERIMENTAL AIRCRAFT ASSOCIATION: YOUNG EAGLES PROGRAM

The Experimental Aircraft Association's (EAA) Young Eagles Program has provided free introductory flights to over 1 million young people ages 8 to 17. This program helps young people understand the important role aviation plays in our daily lives and provides insight into how an airplane flies, what it takes to become a pilot, and the high standards flying demands in terms of safety and quality.

NOTE: The Gleim *Learn to Fly* booklet (available for free at www.GleimAviation.com/learn-to-fly) is used as "ground school" training for Young Eagles programs. For more information about the Young Eagles Program, visit www.youngeagles.org or call 1-877-806-8902.

AIRCRAFT OWNERS AND PILOTS ASSOCIATION

The Aircraft Owners and Pilots Association (AOPA) hosts an informational web page on getting started in aviation for those still dreaming about flying, those who are ready to begin, and those who are already making the journey. Interested individuals can order a FREE subscription to Flight Training Magazine, which explains how amazing it is to be a pilot. Other resources are available, such as a flight school finder, a guide on what to expect throughout training, an explanation of pilot certification options, a FREE flight training newsletter, and much more. To learn more, visit www.aopa.org.

CIVIL AIR PATROL: CADET ORIENTATION FLIGHT PROGRAM

The Civil Air Patrol (CAP) Cadet Orientation Flight Program is designed to introduce CAP cadets to flying. The program is voluntary and primarily motivational, and it is designed to stimulate cadets' interest in and knowledge of aviation.

Each orientation flight is approximately 1 hour, follows a prescribed syllabus, and is usually in the local area of the airport. Except for takeoff, landing, and a few other portions of the flight, cadets are encouraged to handle the controls. For information about the CAP cadet program nearest you, visit www.gocivilairpatrol.com.

WOMEN IN AVIATION INTERNATIONAL

Women in Aviation International (WAI) is a nonprofit organization dedicated to the encouragement and advancement of women in all aviation career fields and interests. Its diverse membership includes astronauts, corporate pilots, maintenance technicians, air traffic controllers, business owners, educators and students, journalists, flight attendants, air show performers, airport managers, and many others.

WAI provides year-round resources to assist women in aviation and encourage young women to consider aviation as a career. WAI also offers educational outreach programs to educators, aviation industry members, and young people nationally and internationally. An annual Girls in Aviation Day was recently initiated for girls ages 8 to 17. Learn more at www.wai.org.

NINETY-NINES

The Ninety-Nines (99s) is an international organization of women pilots with thousands of members from over 40 countries. Its goal is to promote advancement of aviation through education, scholarships, and mutual support. The 99s have co-sponsored over 75% of FAA pilot safety programs in the U.S. and annually sponsor hundreds of educational programs, such as aerospace workshops for teachers, airport tours for school children, fear-of-flying clinics for airline passengers, and flight instructor revalidation seminars. Learn more at www.ninety-nines.org.

INDEX